LATE ROMAN ITALY

In memory of Mike Clover and Wolf Liebeschuetz

Late Roman Italy

Imperium to Regnum

Edited by
Jeroen W. P. Wijnendaele

EDINBURGH
University Press

Edinburgh University Press is one of the leading university presses in the UK. We publish academic books and journals in our selected subject areas across the humanities and social sciences, combining cutting-edge scholarship with high editorial and production values to produce academic works of lasting importance. For more information visit our website: edinburghuniversitypress.com

© editorial matter and organisation Jeroen W. P. Wijnendaele, 2023, 2024
© the chapters their several authors, 2023, 2024

Edinburgh University Press Ltd
13 Infirmary Street, Edinburgh, EH1 1LT

First published in hardback by Edinburgh University Press 2023

Typeset in 10 / 12 Bembo by
IDSUK (DataConnection) Ltd

A CIP record for this book is available from the British Library

ISBN 978 1 3995 1802 4 (hardback)
ISBN 978 1 3995 1803 1 (paperback)
ISBN 978 1 3995 1804 8 (webready PDF)
ISBN 978 1 3995 1805 5 (epub)

The right of Jeroen W. P. Wijnendaele to be identified as the editor of this work has been asserted in accordance with the Copyright, Designs and Patents Act 1988, and the Copyright and Related Rights Regulations 2003 (SI No. 2498).

Contents

List of Illustrations vii
Acknowledgements ix
List of Contributors x

Introduction: Italy and Its Place in the Roman Empire of Late Antiquity 1
Jeroen W. P. Wijnendaele

Part I: Political Developments

1. Italy from the Crisis of the Third Century to the Tetrarchy 15
   Umberto Roberto

2. New Paths to Power: The Bipartite Division of Italy and Its Realignment of Society and Economy in the Fourth Century 35
   Noel Lenski

3. Court, Crisis and Response: Italy from Gratian to Valentinian III 67
   Mark Humphries

4. The Final Western Emperors, Odoacer and Late Roman Italy's Resilience 86
   Jeroen W. P. Wijnendaele

Part II: Institutions

5. Administering Late Roman Italy: Geographical Changes and the Appearance of Governors 111
   Daniëlle Slootjes

6. How the West Was Run: Local Government in Late Roman Italy 130
   Stuart McCunn

7. Armed Forces in Late Roman Italy 153
   Philip Rance

Part III: Society, Economy and Environment

8. Elite Women and Gender-Based Violence in Late Roman Italy 201
   Ulriika Vihervalli and Victoria Leonard

9. Land of the Free? Considering Smallholders and Economic Agency in Late Antique Italy 223
   Niels P. Arends

10. The Human Landscape and Palaeoecology of Late Roman Italy 287
    Edward M. Schoolman

11. Cities and Urban Life in Late Roman Italy: Transformations of the Old, Impositions of the New 304
    Neil Christie

Part IV: Religion

12. From Local Authority to Episcopal Power: The Changing Roles of Roman and Italian Bishops 339
    Bronwen Neil

13. Violence and Episcopal Elections in Late Antique Rome, AD 300–500 356
    Samuel Cohen

14. Religious Minorities in Late Roman Italy: Jewish City-Dwellers and Their Non-Jewish Neighbours 384
    Jessica van 't Westeinde

Part V: Culture

15. Christian Sarcophagi in Late Roman Italy: Culture and Connection 411
    Miriam A. Hay

16. Late Roman Italy in Latin Panegyric: From the *Panegyrici Latini* to Ennodius 454
    Adrastos Omissi

17. Stepping Out of the Shadows: Italy in Late Antique Historiography 475
    Peter Van Nuffelen

    Epilogue: Late Roman Italy – Paths Explored and Paths to Explore 490
    Giusto Traina

Index 495

ILLUSTRATIONS

Figures

Figure I.1	Map of Late Roman Italy.	xiv–xv
Figure 2.1	Schematic diagram of the *dioecesis Italiciana* in the early fifth century.	41
Figure 2.2	Total number of months when an emperor is present in Italy.	43
Figure 2.3	Total number of months when an emperor is present in Italy by year.	44
Figure 10.1	Summary pollen diagram and selected non-pollen palynomorphs (NPP) from Lago Lungo, Rieti basin.	293
Figure 11.1	Grumentum: view of forum showing the location of the late Roman metal-workshop.	307
Figure 11.2	Luni statue base (reused).	308
Figure 11.3	Brescia: collection of gilded bronze later imperial busts.	309
Figure 11.4	Aerial view of the 'lost' Roman city of Potentia.	311
Figure 11.5	Rome's Amphitheatrum Castrense and associated line of the Aurelianic Walls.	313
Figure 11.6	Location and site plan for the excavated *domus* complexes at the Palazzo Valentini, Rome.	317
Figure 11.7	Late Roman *domus*, Palazzo Valentini.	318
Figure 11.8	Palazzo Valentini: view of the Domus A triclinium with its geometric mosaic floor.	318
Figure 11.9	Aquileia: reconstruction of the early fourth-century episcopal complex.	319
Figure 11.10	Exterior view of Aquileia's cathedral church and baptistery of the later fourth century.	320
Figure 11.11	The Porta Pinciana on the north-western flank of the Aurelianic Walls of Rome.	323
Figure 11.12	Colosseum, Rome: inscription recording repairs to the monumental complex at the end of the fifth century following earthquake damage.	325

Figure 15.1	Frieze sarcophagus with Meleager and the Calydonian boar hunt. c. AD 190, Rome.	417
Figure 15.2	Left short end with men carrying nets in preparation for the hunt.	417
Figure 15.3	Right short end with Atalanta and Meleager.	418
Figure 15.4	Frieze sarcophagus with hunting scenes, and biblical scenes on the lid. c. AD 320, made in Rome.	421
Figure 15.5	Double-register frieze sarcophagus 'of Adelphia' with biblical scenes. Mid-fourth century AD, made in Rome.	426
Figure 15.6	Sarcophagus with latticework front, and lid with biblical scenes. Mid-fourth century AD, excavated in Sasso.	431
Figure 15.7	Front of a frieze sarcophagus (or loculus plaque) with biblical scenes. c. AD 300.	434
Figure 15.8	Frieze sarcophagus with biblical scenes. Early fourth century AD. Capua.	436
Figure 15.9	City-gate sarcophagus with biblical scenes. Late fourth century AD, made in Rome.	440
Figure 15.10	Left short end, with Cain and Abel.	441
Figure 15.11	Right short end, with Adam and Eve.	441

Tables

Table 2.1	Restoration of *Laterculus Veronensis* 10.	37
Table 2.2	First known or only known governorships of those who held an Italian governorship and at least one subsequent office (284–395).	58
Table 2.3	Geographical distribution of governorships for individuals with known geographic origin who held at least one Italian governorship.	59
Table 2.4	Higher imperial offices known to have been held by individuals who held at least one Italian governorship.	60
Table 5.1	Provinces and governors of the diocese of Italy at the end of the fourth century.	116

Acknowledgements

This volume grew out of a conference I organized at Ghent University on 10–12 January 2019, generously sponsored by the Research Foundation – Flanders ('FWO Vlaanderen'), the Roman Society Research Center, the Faculty of Arts and Philosophy, and the History Department of Ghent University. The idea to tackle a multifaceted history of late Roman Italy c. AD 250–500 grew out of my then-project on 'The Origins of European Kingship', of which Italy was a fundamental part. I quickly realized that despite the many advances in regional studies of the late Roman and late antique world, we were still lacking a dedicated study on this key region during this pivotal era. There is no question that here we have the most richly documented western region of the second quarter millennium, going through a rollercoaster of transformations. The time was right to give it the proper due that it merits. The original conference generated stimulating discussions, not only because of the present contributors' presentations, but also thanks to interventions from Sarah Bühler, Jan Willem Drijvers, Immacolata Eramo, Michael Hanaghan and Daniel Knox. My Ghent colleagues Danny Praet, Lieve Van Hoof, Koen Verboven and Kristof Vermote helped out on various occasions, as did our students Leonard Adriaen and Sébastien De Kimpe (who, we must say, produced an outstanding poster for the occasion). Looking back, it seems almost inconceivable that this volume came to life during the first two years of the COVID-19 pandemic, with virtually every contributor experiencing all the trials and tribulations that came along with it. It is a testament to their endurance, erudition and expertise, combined with the meticulous feedback of the peer reviewers, that we have the present work. I owe a great debt to Gavin Kelly for introducing me to the wonderful staff at Edinburgh University Press. It was a pleasure to work with Rachel Bridgewater, Isobel Birks, Jane Burkowski and their colleagues, who did an excellent job in producing this tome. Last but not least, I still had the chance to discuss the genesis of this project with Mike Clover and Wolf Liebeschuetz. Both remained as sharp, witty and encouraging as ever, and are dearly missed now in our community. It is with great affection that I dedicate this volume to their memory.

Jeroen W. P. Wijnendaele
Ghent, August 2022

Contributors

Niels P. Arends studied Ancient History at Leiden University and History at King's College London, before starting his PhD at the University of St Andrews in 2020. He is interested in the social and economic history of late antique Italy, more specifically its countryside. He is also active as a compliance officer for the Dutch Compliance Institute, contributing to financial expertise with the humanities in mind.

Neil Christie is Professor of Archaeology at the University of Leicester. He has widely published on the archaeology of late antique and early medieval Italy, exploring particularly themes of urban and rural change. A key synthesis was his *From Constantine to Charlemagne: an Archaeology of Italy, AD 300–800* (2006). Urban themes are also debated in collections such as *Vrbes extinctae: Archaeologies of Abandoned Classical Cities*, eds N. Christie and A. Augenti (2012) and *Urban Transformations in the Late Antique West: Materials, Agents, and Models*, eds A. Carneiro, N. Christie and P. Diarte-Blasco (2020).

Samuel Cohen is an Associate Professor in the Department of History, California State University, Sonoma. His research focuses on social and religious conflict and its relationship to community formation and the construction of authority in late antique Italy and the Mediterranean more broadly. He is particularly interested in how rhetoric was mobilised to construct and contest meaning in polemical texts. Dr Cohen has published numerous book chapters and articles on these and related subjects.

Miriam A. Hay is an Early Career Research Associate at the Institute of Classical Studies, School of Advanced Study, University of London. She is currently working on a monograph on late Roman sarcophagi based on her PhD thesis ('Classical Remains and Christian Remembrance: Reviewing Late Roman Sarcophagi'), completed in the Department of Classics and Ancient History at the University of Warwick in 2019 as a Wolfson scholar, as well as other projects relating to early Christian visual and material culture.

CONTRIBUTORS

Mark Humphries is Professor of Ancient History at Swansea University. He is the author of numerous studies of Italy, Rome and imperial politics in Late Antiquity, including *Communities of the Blessed: Social Environment and Religious Change in Northern Italy AD 200–400* (1999) and *Cities and the Meanings of Late Antiquity* (2019). He is currently completing a study of the reign of Valentinian I. He is one of the general editors of the Translated Texts for Historians series.

Noel Lenski is Dunham Professor of Classics and History at Yale University and author of the monographs *Failure of Empire: Valens and the Roman State in the Fourth Century A.D.* (2002) and *Constantine and the Cities: Imperial Authority and Civic Politics* (2016) as well as numerous articles and volumes on Roman state and society in Late Antiquity. His co-authored translation of and commentary on the *Liber iudiciorum – Leges Visigothorum* is forthcoming.

Victoria Leonard is a Fellow of the Royal Historical Society and a Research Fellow at the Centre for Arts, Memory and Communities, Coventry University. She is also a Research Fellow at the Institute of Classical Studies, University of London. Victoria's research focuses on the late antique and early medieval western Mediterranean, with a special interest in social network analysis, historiography, and gender, violence and theories of the body. She published her monograph, *In Defiance of History: Orosius and the Unimproved Past* (2022), and edited with Laurence Totelin and Mark Bradley the volume *Bodily Fluids in Antiquity* (2021).

Stuart McCunn is an Adjunct Professor of History at Southern Connecticut State University and the University of New Haven. He has published several book reviews on a variety of late antique topics and is the author of "What's in a Name? The Evolving Role of Frumentarii" for *Classical Quarterly*. He is currently preparing a monograph on late Roman army supply for publication and working on a chapter on logistics for an edited volume on the *limitanei*.

Bronwen Neil is Professor of Ancient History in the Department of History and Archaeology at Macquarie University, Sydney. She is the author of several books on bishops of Rome and their letters in Late Antiquity, including *Leo the Great* (2009) and, with Pauline Allen, *The Letters of Gelasius I (492–96): Pastor and Micro-Manager of the Church of Rome* (2014), and co-editor with Matthew dal Santo of *A Companion to Gregory the Great* (2013). Her most recent book is *Dreams and Divination from Byzantium to Baghdad (400–1000 CE)* (2021).

Adrastos Omissi is the Lecturer in Latin Literature in Classics at the University of Glasgow. He is the author of *Emperors and Usurpers in the Later Roman Empire: Civil War, Panegyric, and the Construction of Legitimacy in the Later Roman Empire* (2018) and the co-editor of *Imperial Panegyric from Diocletian to Honorius* (2020). He writes on power, civil war, panegyric and the court culture of the later Roman Empire.

Philip Rance is a Senior Research Fellow at the Centre for Advanced Study, Sofia, has taught ancient and medieval history and Greek language and literature at universities in Germany and the United Kingdom, and held senior research fellowships at Berlin, Munich, Istanbul and Wolfenbüttel. He has published extensively on late antique historiography, warfare and martial culture, Late/Vulgar Latin, and Greek, Roman and Byzantine technical-scientific writing, its manuscript tradition and reception. He is preparing a translation of and commentary on Maurice's *Strategikon* and editing a *Companion to Military Culture in Late Antiquity* and a *Companion to Greek and Roman Military Literature*.

Umberto Roberto is Full Professor of Roman History at Università degli Studi di Napoli 'Federico II'. He has published in the field of Roman imperial history and Late Antiquity, including two critical editions: *Ioannis Antiocheni fragmenta ex Historia chronica* (2005); *Iulius Africanus, Chronographiae*, ed. with M. Wallraff, with a translation by W. Adler (2007); and the following books: *Le Chronographiae di Sesto Giulio Africano* (2011); *Roma capta: il sacco della città dai Galli ai Lanzichenecchi* (2012); *Diocleziano* (2014); *Il nemico indomabile: Roma contro i Germani* (2018); *Il secolo dei Vandali* (2020).

Edward M. Schoolman teaches ancient and medieval history at the University of Nevada, Reno, and is the author of *Rediscovering Sainthood in Italy: Hagiography and the Late Antique Past in Medieval Ravenna* (2016) and co-editor, with Marianne Sághy, of *Pagans and Christians in the Late Roman Empire: New Evidence, New Approaches* (2017). He has published on the history of late antique and early medieval Ravenna and Antioch, and currently works on the economic and political drivers of landscape change and the intersections of palaeoecology and environmental history in the pre-modern Mediterranean.

Daniëlle Slootjes holds the Chair of Ancient History at the University of Amsterdam, Netherlands. She has published extensively on late antique Roman administration, geography, the history of early Christianity and crowd behaviour in the period of Late Antiquity and the Byzantine Empire.

Giusto Traina is Full Professor of Roman History at Université Paris-Sorbonne, France. Among his latest books, he is most noted in the anglophone world for his *428 AD: an Ordinary Year at the End of the Roman Empire* (2009; updated French edition: 2020), in which he gives a panoramic view across the geographical extent of the later Roman Empire in a single year. He recently published *Histoire incorrecte de Rome* (2021) and edited *Mondes en guerre*, volume 1: *De la préhistoire au Moyen Âge* (2019).

Peter Van Nuffelen is Professor of Ancient History at Ghent University, Belgium. His research interests are ancient religion and philosophy, and the history of Late Antiquity. His recent publications include *Penser la tolérance dans l'Antiquité tardive* (2018) and, with L. Van Hoof, *The Fragmentary Latin Histories of Late Antiquity (AD 300–620): Edition,*

Translation and Commentary (2020) and *Jordanes: Romana and Getica* (Translated Texts for Historians 75, 2020). An edition of fragmentary Greek chronicles is in preparation.

Jessica van 't Westeinde is Researcher at the Department of Ancient History, Eberhard-Karls University of Tübingen. Her first book, *Roman Nobilitas in Jerome's Letters*, appeared with Mohr Siebeck in 2021. She has published several studies that consider Jewish and Christian subjects in the wider sociocultural and political context of the Roman Empire. At Tübingen, she is working on a new monograph, *Jews and the City: a History of Jewish Urban Life in Ancient Cityscapes (2nd–7th Centuries CE)*.

Ulriika Vihervalli is Lecturer in Late Antique History at the University of Liverpool. She researches and publishes on sex, violence and gender in the late antique and early medieval worlds. She is currently preparing a monograph entitled *The Self-Inspecting Mirror: Negotiating Sexual Norms in the Late Antique West*.

Jeroen W. P. Wijnendaele is a Senior Fellow of the Bonn Center for Dependency and Slavery Studies. He is the author of *The Last of the Romans: Bonifatius, Warlord and comes Africae* (2015), and has published various articles and book chapters on the political and military history of the late Roman Empire. Dr Wijnendaele was guest editor of the *Journal of Late Antiquity*'s 2019 theme issue on *Warfare and Food-Supply in the Late Roman Empire*. At the moment, he is preparing a new monograph on *Rome's Disintegration: Violence, War, and the End of Empire in the West*.

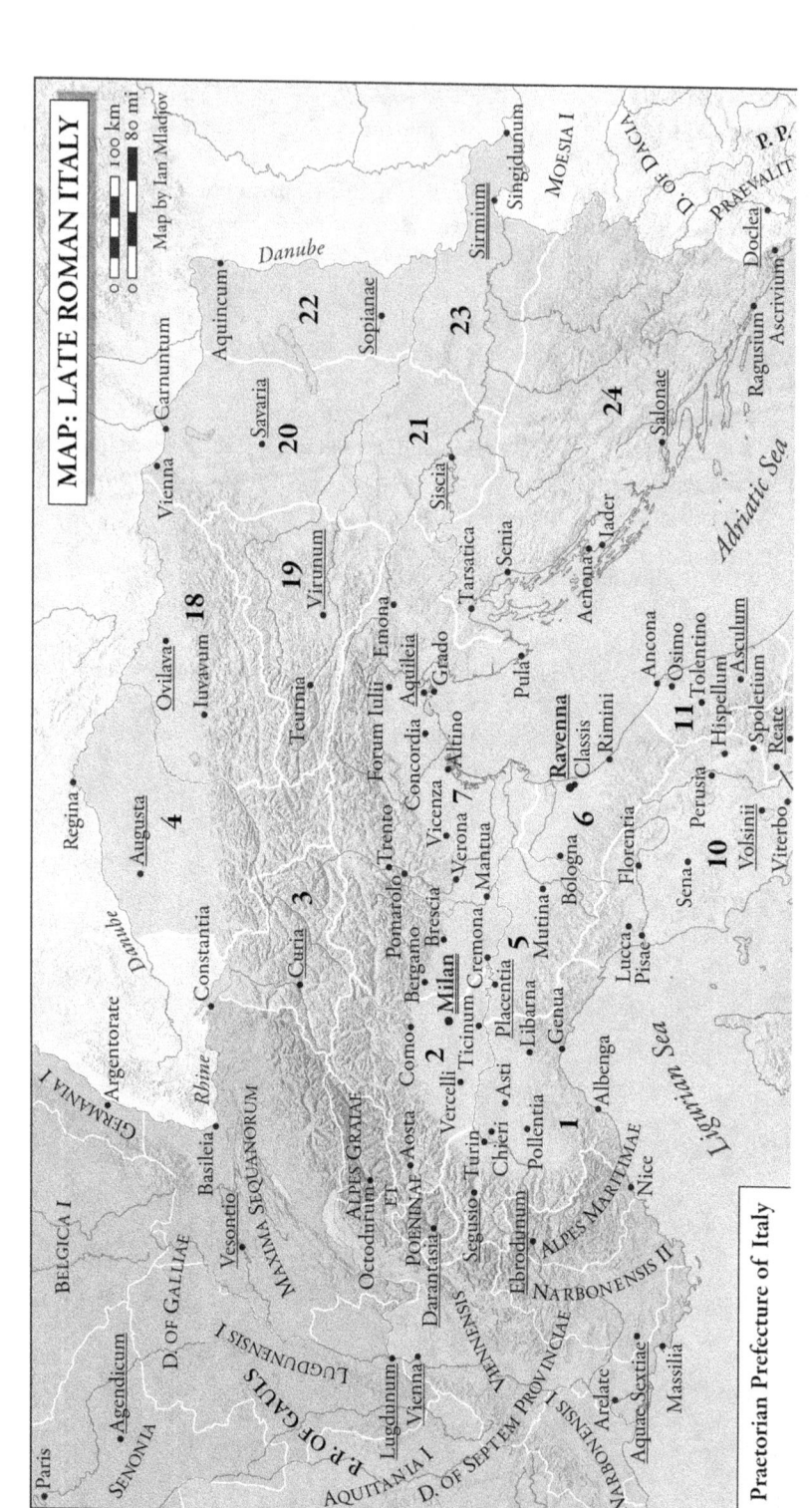

Diocese of Italia Annonaria
1 Alpes Cottiae
2 Liguria
3 Raetia I
4 Raetia II
5 Aemilia
6 Flaminia et Picenum Annon.
7 Venetia et Histria

Diocese of Italia Suburbicaria
8 Sardinia
9 Corsica
10 Tuscia et Umbria
11 Picenum Suburbicarium
12 Valeria
13 Campania
14 Samnium
15 Sicilia
16 Lucania et Brutii
17 Apulia et Calabria

Diocese of Illyricum
18 Noricum Ripense
19 Noricum Mediterr.
20 Pannonia I
21 Savia
22 Valeria Ripensis
23 Pannonia II
24 Dalmatia

Diocese of Africa
25 Africa Zeugitana
26 Byzacena
27 Numidia
28 Mauretania Sitifensis

Introduction: Italy and Its Place in the Roman Empire of Late Antiquity

Jeroen W. P. Wijnendaele

A Tale of Two Triumphs and Two Tragedies

Sixty tame lions, forty wild horses, thirty-two elephants, thirty tame leopards, twenty wild asses, ten elk, ten giraffes, ten hyenas, ten tigers, ten wild lions, six hippopotami and one very lonely rhinoceros. This entire veritable zoo that had previously belonged to Gordian III was just one selection of animals put on display at the Colosseum, and brutally slaughtered with countless other animals in April of the year 1000.[1] That is the Roman year 1000 or our year AD 248. For three days and three nights, the city populace celebrated their *ludi saeculares*, and this millennial edition was one to remember indeed. The games were orchestrated by the emperor Marcus Julius Philippus (colloquially known as Philip 'the Arab'). The production of this feature is reported by that most wonderful pastiche of late antique literature, the *Historia Augusta*.[2] While many of the Lives/*Vitae* of third-century emperors in this collection are outlandish fabrications, positive evidence that this exotic carnage was not a figment of literary imagination can be found in the coin series Philip had struck for the occasion. These *ludi saeculares* were probably a creative recycling of arcane rites initiated by Augustus a quarter-millennium earlier. While Augustus himself would have raised an eyebrow to see a Levantine assuming the very same powers he had crafted out of the Republic's deathbed, he would have still recognised Philip's Rome and Italy as in the excellent condition he had bequeathed to it. On its supposed thousand-year anniversary, Rome was unquestionably the *caput mundi* of an *imperium*, and if not *sine fine*, then still encompassing the entire Mediterranean world and its European hinterland. Philip's *ludi saeculares* are one terminus for Italy at the threshold of the second quarter of the first millennium. Our second triumph takes us to its *terminus ante quem*.

In the year 500, we find ourselves back in the city of Rome for another round of ceremony and celebrations. The emperor celebrated his *tricennalia*, or thirty years in power, and first entered in triumphal procession before hosting races in the Circus Maximus. The imperial palace and the city wall had been in dire need of restoration, and thus Italy's Prince showered his munificence by earmarking two hundred pounds of

---

[1] *Hist. Aug., Gordiani tres* 33.
[2] On the *Historia Augusta*, see now Cameron 2011; Stover and Woudhuysen 2022.

gold from the annual wine tax. He also ensured that the impoverished masses received 120,000 modii of grain each year. In proper imperial fashion, he listened to petitions of the people and had his grants to them inscribed on bronze tablets and set up in the public spaces. Meanwhile he rounded off his visit to the *urbs* by settling a dispute between the high priests, marrying off one of his sisters to a fellow aristocrat, and having one of his commanders beheaded.[3] The idea of continuity with Augustus is even more stressed by the then-current monarch's reluctance to fully embrace in public the powers at his disposal. Some senators had the temerity to acclaim him Augustus in public inscriptions, but his favourite title always remained merely *princeps*.[4] Neither Philip's *ludi saeculares* nor Theoderic's *adventus* were triumphs in the traditional Roman sense, but they were certainly grand ceremonial occasions of ostentatious display and conspicuous consumption. Italy's rulers put the best possible face on their regime in order to awe their subjects into believing that they were experiencing the full might of their governments. Yet scratch away the veneer, and one cannot help but notice cracks in the foundations on both occasions. Kyle Harper recently noted that with the benefit of hindsight, Philip's celebrations look like 'the inhabitants of Rome enjoying the ancient equivalent of cocktails on the deck of the Titanic'.[5] One could create a dissonant parallel by offering a tale of two bishops in the years prior to Theoderic's *adventus* and after Philip's *ludi*, respectively.

Only two years after the *ludi saeculares*, to quote the *Vita* of Carthage's bishop Cyprian,

> there broke out a dreadful plague, and excessive destruction of a hateful disease invaded every house in succession of the trembling populace, carrying off day by day with abrupt attack numberless people, everyone from his own house. All were shuddering, fleeing, shunning the contagion, impiously exposing their own friends, as if with the exclusion of the person who was sure to die of the plague, one could exclude death itself also. There lay about the meanwhile, over the whole city, no longer bodies, but the carcasses of many, and, by the contemplation of a lot which in their turn would be theirs, demanded the pity of the passers-by for themselves. (*Vita Cypriani* 9)

This plague, which Harper argues could have been similar to modern Ebola, was soon followed by the breakdown of frontiers, the rise of rival regimes in Gaul and the Levant, and the collapse of the imperial currency.[6] Rome eventually weathered the storm, but the transformed empire that emerged in the final quarter of that century was one that bore little resemblance to the Augustan settlement.

Two things stand out regarding Italy: on the orders of Aurelian (270–5) Rome was invested with a massive fortified city wall.[7] A few decades later, as Umberto Roberto

---

[3] *Anon. Vales.* 2.67–9.
[4] *CIL* 10.6850–2.
[5] Harper 2017, 119.
[6] That is not to say that one has to subscribe entirely to Harper's fundamentally negative trajectory. Yet it is to his credit to have revived the debate on *Romania*'s environmental history, which is now one of the most lively domains in our field. For further discussion, see especially Erdkamp 2019; Sessa 2019; and Chapter 10 in this volume.
[7] Dey 2011.

(Chapter 1) and Daniëlle Slootjes (Chapter 5) lay out, Italy finally underwent a process of 'provincialisation' to the extent it even had to pay taxes for the first time since the Republican conquest of Macedon in 167 BC. Similarly, Theoderic's *adventus* arrived only several years after the most dire war, of a scale in geographical reach, duration and intensity which Italy had probably not experienced since the nadir of the second triumvirate. Ennodius describes how

> the venerable bishop Epiphanius turned his attention to the restoration of [Pavia] and considered how he could fill it as soon as possible with worthy inhabitants. And although, thanks to his prayers, no tempest of those turbulent times had brought complete desolation to the city, yet it did not suffice for him that, after the destruction of all the cities of Liguria, Pavia should rejoice and content herself in the possession of only her own citizens. So as a diligent cultivator he began to gather certain flowers from the number of the citizens of the neighbouring cities and to transplant in his own garden plants whose productivity he had already tested and from which a cautious and expert owner would gather fruit in a season.[8]

Just to be clear: this is not Epiphanius setting up a botanical shop, but deporting Roman citizens from other cities to restock Pavia's depleted population.[9]

While it has been recently argued that Theoderic was a western Roman emperor in everything but name,[10] it is hard not to see the sharp contrast between Italy in his day and that of Philip, not to mention that of Augustus. Though the empire continued to thrive in the East, in the West it had become at best a mere 'commonwealth' in which Italy was one – albeit not just any one – polity among others. Official western emperors had gone the way of the dodo. Theoderic's Roman attire, his invincible mustachios and fabulous helmet hair, as displayed on the Senigallia Medallion, had not dazzled everyone into forgetting that he had begun his thirty-year reign as the leader of a Danubian army crawling out of the wreck of Attila's disintegrated realm. In 250 years, many other things had drastically changed. To point out just two of the other most profound features, we might highlight the Christianisation of the peninsula, with Theoderic previously having to settle a dispute over the choice of Rome's bishop, and the altered physical and demographic landscape; the 120,000 modii of grain which Theoderic allocated to the poor in Rome pale in comparison with the nearly 4 million the city had received annually a century earlier.[11] Between Philip the Arab's celebrations and those of Theoderic, late Roman Italy has an important story to tell.

Italy in the Wider Late Roman World

Italy cannot be studied in isolation from the wider late Roman Imperial world, and it is here that we will briefly sketch the interregional context of its history during

---

[8] *Vit. Epiph.* 120–1.
[9] I owe this observation to Tina Sessa.
[10] Arnold 2014.
[11] For a summary of the debate and further references to the Late Roman *annona*, see Wijnendaele 2019, 299–301.

the second quarter of the first millennium. At the full-blown height of the crisis of the third century, during Gallienus' sole reign (c.260–8), Italy formed the core of an empire on the verge of disintegration. Gallic emperors had established a regime over the western transalpine provinces, while the local dynasty of Palmyra took control over the Levantine provinces.[12] Meanwhile, with Gothic tribes raiding Asia Minor's coasts and the Balkans as far as Greece, the effective reach of Gallienus' government at times barely stretched further than Africa, Dalmatia and Italy. Gallienus was also the last traditional senatorial emperor to reign from Rome. The following century would see a reinvigorated Roman Empire, yet one where Rome – and most of Italy – lost its spot in the limelight. Gallienus' successors, who had nearly all risen through the ranks as soldiers from humble origins, fought hard to reintegrate the various provinces under control of rival emperors: a process which was only completed with Constantius I's reconquest of Britain in 296. At this point, we enter a Roman world that could be described as 'an empire turned inside-out' (to borrow Bryan Ward-Perkins' dictum) with political power shifting to the frontiers.

The price of reincorporating these provinces – and above all their armies and aristocracies – was an acceptance by Diocletian and his co-rulers that Gaul, Illyricum and the Levant had emerged as new powerblocks that required their own governments within a larger imperial framework. With the exception of Maxentius (306–12), emperors no longer resided in Rome during the fourth century. The Roman Empire from the Tetrarchy to the Valentinianic dynasty was essentially one without a capital. Instead, the capital was simply where the emperors resided with their court, whether it be Antioch, Milan or Trier.[13] Even Constantinople did not emerge as a permanent seat of eastern imperial governance until the reign of Theodosius I.[14] However, the absence of emperors did not mean that Italy suddenly became a backwater, as Noel Lenski makes clear (Chapter 2). Fourth-century Italy still sheltered the wealthiest nobility of the Roman world, as can still be seen today in the stupendous mosaics in the villa of Piazza Armerina in Sicily. Land was the basis of this wealth, and the new imperial order granted the Roman and Italian senatorial aristocracy even more opportunities for exploitation (though as Niels P. Arends argues in great detail, this did not turn common farmers into helpless bystanders (Chapter 9)). Constantine I's reforms granted the senatorial aristocracy new prospects to become partners in imperial governments. One of the most enduring legacies of these reforms is the 'bipartite' (after Lenski) division into Annonaria and Suburbicaria, which set north and south on a diverging 'bipolar' (after Roberto) path in terms of administration, power, wealth and cultural complexion which resonates even into present-day Italy. Constantine I's choice of Christianity as the favourite religion of his dynasty was equally monumental, yet Bronwen Neil observes that even for the rest of the fourth and fifth centuries it did not turn Italian bishops – even Rome's – into the powerful actors that posterity remembered them as (Chapter 12). Likewise, Samuel Cohen observes that imperial

---

[12] This period has long suffered from neglect, but De Blois 2018 is destined to become the seminal survey.
[13] Maier 2019.
[14] Croke 2010.

authorities often looked askance at the violence triggered by certain episcopal elections (Chapter 13).

These various new dynamics intensified with the re-establishment of western emperors in Italy, starting with Gratian's move to Milan in the early 380s. Yet this came with significant repercussions for the other western provinces. Chief among these was Gaul, which had been the *Hausmacht* of the Constantinian dynasty, and had experienced an almost continuous imperial presence at Trier for roughly a century from Maximian to Magnus Maximus (285–387).[15] The usurpation of the latter, and to a certain extent that of Eugenius (392–4), should be seen as attempts to forcefully realign Gallic and Italian interests. Yet Theodosius I's civil wars with these western rivals not only inflicted heavy losses on the western field army, but also resulted in the permanent establishment of western emperors in Italy. By extension, this also meant the dissolution of an imperial court west of the Alps.[16] These factors contributed greatly to the chain reaction of crises that were to bedevil the Imperial West throughout the fifth century. This period is mostly known for the establishment of various non-Roman armed groups in Africa, Britain, Gaul and Spain.[17] Yet many of these, especially Alaric's Goths in the 400s, could only succeed the way they did because of the institutionalisation of child-emperorship in East and West following Theodosius I's death in 395. This fuelled internecine rivalries among those who wished to become power brokers at the court. While the Eastern court managed to stamp out the worst of these tendencies, the infighting in western Roman high command became one of the most corrosive elements enabling the transformation of what began as the settlement of non-Roman military auxiliaries into autonomous *regna* ('kingdoms').

As Philip Rance outlines, with emperors residing permanently in Italy again, the defence of the peninsula was prioritised at the expense of all other western provinces (Chapter 7). Already in the early 400s, troops were recalled from Britain and Gaul to ward off Alaric. Meanwhile, senatorial aristocrats who dominated the imperial government were eager to help in reconstruction efforts if the city of Rome was affected, yet resisted attempts to contribute decisively through taxation. With Geiseric's conquests of the richest African provinces in the 430s, this dynamic became unsustainable in the long run. Mark Humphries points out that eastern Roman emperors such as Theodosius II and Leo I, following precedents set by Theodosius I in 388 and 394, undertook several attempts to shore up their imperial twin between 410 and 468, to the point that Italy at times effectively fell under a Constantinopolitan hegemony (Chapter 3). By the later fifth century, the Imperial West became effectively reduced

---

[15] This is reflected in the *Expositio totius mundi*, composed at some point in the later 350s, whose author asserts that Gaul needed its own *imperator* (15).

[16] This was not lost on contemporaries; see Sid. Apoll. *Carm.* 5.356–60.

[17] The debate on the origins, nature, composition, and settlements of these groups is one of the most fiercely disputed in scholarship on this period; see Pohl and Reimitz 1998; Heather 2005; Goffart 2006; Halsall 2007; Meier 2019. The present author favours the view that the original groups following Alaric, Geiseric, or Theoderic the Amal were a motley crew of soldiers and their families from widely different ethnicities. Yet these men did eventually develop a new ethnicity aligned towards their leaders and successors in the process.

to Italy, with transalpine *reges* going their own way. Very few contemporaries in Italy noticed that the world had changed either in 476, when the Italian field commander deposed yet another local usurper, or in 480, when the last legitimate western emperor was assassinated in Dalmatia. Western emperors were gone, but their army, staff and church remained resilient under Odoacer (Chapter 4). When Theoderic conquered Italy in 489–93, late Roman Italy finished its trajectory from *imperium* to *regnum*.

Ostrogothic Italy was no longer an integral part of an empire that allowed its emperor in Constantinople to extract resources from it (especially recruits and taxation). Yet there was a profound belief among contemporary authors in Italy that they were firmly part of the Roman world. Ostrogothic Italy was not just any *regnum* like those in Africa or the former western transalpine provinces. It contained assets that none of these could boast: the preservation of its prefecture and accompanying bureaucratic infrastructure, the Roman senate, and the Amals' prerogative to appoint western consuls, which encouraged local elites to join forces with the monarchy. The result of this was that Theoderic could count on the presence and support of a civilian bureaucracy that none of his peers among Merovingian Franks, Gibichung Burgundians, Balthi Visigoths or Hasding Vandals could rival. It is telling that among the first three of these several *reges* issued their own law codes, whereas Theoderic never felt the need to do so. After all, his *regnum* was the most Roman of all. Indeed, some things did not change at all. Stuart McCunn explains that, despite the vagaries of the fifth century, cities and their councils remained instrumental in the running of the government's writ on a local level (Chapter 6). And on a cultural level, as Adrastos Omissi and Peter Van Nuffelen demonstrate, it was very hard for the newly emancipated Italy to escape the shadow of Rome, as it continued to loom large in the writings of court poets (Chapter 16) and historiographers (Chapter 17). Still, Roman Italy experienced its last phase of unity under the Amals: a unity Italy would not experience again until the *Risorgimento*.[18]

The downfall of Theoderic's daughter Amalasuentha in 535 ushered in conflicts with the eastern Roman court that ultimately led to the destruction of the Ostrogothic kingdom. Justinian's Gothic War was the longest ongoing war that the Italian peninsula ever experienced until the present day. It unravelled much of its urban infrastructure, and the foundations of what made it recognisably Roman in the process. Equally significant, Justinian's Pragmatic Sanction in 554 dissolved the former western imperial *fiscus*, thereby preventing future possibilities of a revived *Hesperium Regnum*. The aftermath of the Gothic War also paved the way for the fragmentation of the political landscape. The arrival of Lombards broke the peninsula's imperial spine, and resulted in new entities being carved out along Italy's internal geographical divisions, such as the Exarchate of Ravenna, the emerging papacy or autonomous city states such as Naples. By the time Gregory the Great died in 604, even Rome's senate had ceased to be.[19] Ancient Italy slowly became Medieval.

---

[18] The question of unity has been one of the most prominent themes through Italy's history. Italian unification has rarely been achieved in the three thousand years since the name *Italia* was first recorded. As Wickham 1981, 1, already observed, it is not a coincidence that even the name of Italy's Communist magazine was not, contrary to so many other of its international siblings, 'The Worker', 'The People', 'Tomorrow' or even 'Truth', but . . . *l'Unità*.

[19] Salzman 2021, ch. 7.

Late Roman Italy in the Wider Debate

This volume reassesses one of the most fundamental transformations in ancient history, centred on a pivotal region: the transition from 'empire' to 'kingdom' in Italy c.250–500. To date, there exists no scholarly work covering this topic. That is not to say that the history of Italy between the Principate and the Ostrogothic era has lacked scholarly attention. One can go back as far as the late nineteenth century for the first volumes of Thomas Hodgkin's *Italy and Its Invaders*, or seminal studies in the twentieth century such as Lellia Cracco Ruggini's *Economia e società nell'Italia Annonaria*.[20] But as late as 1981, Chris Wickham had to point out that even early medieval Italy was usually studied as 'an appendage of the North', while he sought to study it on its own merits.[21] Still, no previous book has ever provided such attention to the whole of Italy for the era of AD 250–500.[22] In contrast to several other key western regions of the late antique world, which have seen extensive revision in recent scholarship, we still lack a proper study on Italy in this era.[23] This omission is surprising, and not only because of the dramatic events the peninsula and its islands experienced, from its 'provincialised' demotion (c.285–395), to a new imperial hub kept afloat by cannibalising other provinces' resources (c.395–475), to an autonomous kingdom governed by non-Roman rulers as part of an eastern Roman 'commonwealth' (c.476–535). Even more so, because it is the best-documented western region in the entire period of c.250–500. We possess a wealth of literary sources (e.g. letter collections, chronicles), administrative sources (e.g. inscriptions, law codes), and material sources (e.g. coins, monumental art). Late Roman Italy's surviving urban fabric is unmatched by anything else in the west and still yields new finds year after year, as Neil Christie makes clear (Chapter 11). Nevertheless, the lacuna in scholarship remains. Most recent scholarship pertaining to this topic and period usually focuses on either the city of Rome or the reign of Theoderic.[24]

A wealth of sources, and an omission of scholarship on late Roman Italy notwithstanding, the larger history of Italy as part of the (western) Roman Empire in this period has of course witnessed incredible revision since Hodgkin's day. Well into the

---

[20] Hodgkin 1892–1896; Cracco-Ruggini 1961.
[21] Wickham 1981, 8.
[22] For early Imperial Roman Italy, see the various chapters in Cooley 2016. Despite the collection being titled a *Companion to Roman Italy*, out of twenty-five chapters the entire period of AD 300–550 is relegated to a single chapter. Arnaldi and Marazzi 2017 provide a solid introduction to the history of Italy, from the crisis of the Roman Empire in the third century until the Norman conquest of southern Italy in the eleventh century. Delogu and Gasparri 2010 touches on several important aspects of Italy in the fifth century. However, it does not take Italy as its exclusive focus of attention, and one also comes across various chapters dealing with North Africa, Northern Gaul and Spain. Ostrogothic Italy has received tremendous scholarly attention in recent decades. The most thorough and best recent introduction is Arnold et al. 2016.
[23] E.g. Africa: Merrills 2004; Gaul: Diefenbach and Müller 2013; Illyricum: Poulter 2007; Spain: Bowes and Kulikowski 2005. Despite the immensely complicated material and textual record, recent studies on Britain in this era abound galore.
[24] Rome: Curran 2000; Grig and Kelly 2012; Machado 2019; Salzman 2021. Theoderic: Moorhead 1992; Ausbüttel 2012; Arnold 2014; Wiemer 2018.

last century it was fashionable to approach this period as one of 'Decline and Fall', disregarding this phase of the Roman world as 'le Bas Empire', or occasionally even abhorring its demographic changes as an 'Ausrottung der Besten', of which Italy was always regarded as a prime victim. None of these verdicts have universally persisted into the twenty-first century.[25] Santo Mazzarino, one of Italy's finest Roman historians in the twentieth century, already wrote in 1942 that we can never return to the Gibbonian model.[26] For a very long time, Mazzarino's optimism seemed justified, with the advent of the 'late antiquity' paradigm. First coined by Alois Riegl and Josef Strzygowski at the dawn of the 1900s, further developed by Henri Pirenne during the Interbellum, ultimately to be entrenched by Peter Brown and his school, late antiquity has proved to be an enduring periodisation (though one for which the boundaries remain disputed).[27] It is no coincidence either that art historians were the first ones to reappraise this period in the light of its material culture, as Miriam A. Hay remarks (Chapter 15), nor that Peter Brown enforced his argument about the splendour of the 'World of Late Antiquity' with nearly 150 illustrations. While the 'late antiquity' paradigm has always had a strong eastern focus, Italy – and especially Ravenna – always found a place of pride in it.[28] By 1996, Glen Bowersock even felt confident enough to declare the Fall of Rome a 'Vanishing Paradigm'.[29] Yet, with the turn of the current century, the 'Fall' struck back with a vengeance in scholarship. Since Peter Heather and Bryan Ward-Perkins published their respective works in 2005, the debate has not stopped on the Gibbonian question regarding what factors contributed to the end of empire in the West during the fifth century. For Italy, Alaric's sack of Rome in 410 even prompted no less than three international conferences and volumes as part of its 2010 'anniversary'.[30] As Andrew Gillett has pointed out in an excellent survey of the landscape, one cannot read these works and ignore their dialogue with our contemporary world.[31]

An alternative approach to these vexing issues is by recognising that various regions in an imperial superstructure could individually be affected very differently by the same phenomenon. Regional approaches help shed further light on the trajectory of empire in this transformational period.[32] This has already been made abundantly clear by work on the other major regions of the Roman West, especially Africa, Britain, Gaul and to a lesser extent Spain. By focusing on one major region in particular, such as Italy, and using an unconventional chronology (c.250–500), this volume seeks to break the gridlock in this debate and shift it in other directions.[33] It will be demonstrated, as one of our authors once stated elsewhere, that 'in 500, a "Roman" Italy

---

[25] Gibbon 1776–1788; Seeck 1897–1920; Stein 1947.
[26] Mazzarino 1990 [1942], 239.
[27] See the various articles in the *Journal of Late Antiquity*'s 2008 maiden issue.
[28] Deliyannis 2010.
[29] Bowersock 1996.
[30] Van Nuffelen 2015.
[31] Gillett 2017.
[32] See also Wickham 2005 and Halsall 2007 for this approach.
[33] To a certain extent, this is also the aim of Salzman 2021, yet more narrowly focused on the city of Rome.

still existed'.³⁴ This work consciously positions itself in the field of late Roman studies and only to a lesser extent in that of late antiquity, where cultural, religious and social history has always received more attention. Here the Roman Empire remains the primary framework of reference. Given the era under consideration, this volume thus has an emphasis on the political, without eschewing cultural, economic, religious and social matters.³⁵

A regional study of this period helps us to reframe questions about the trajectory of the late Roman Empire that have previously been framed on models of catastrophe, continuity or transformation. As will become clear throughout this work, each chapter provides the reader with both a general outline and the latest state of research on key issues, while simultaneously adding a fresh perspective on long-standing problems in a surprisingly neglected area. Attention is given to both macro-developments (such as Edward M. Schoolman's chapter on environmental change (Chapter 10)) and micro-studies (such as Jessica van 't Westeinde's chapter on the interaction of religious communities in small towns (Chapter 14)). This volume also offers unique chapters on topics such as that of Ulriika Vihervalli and Victoria Leonard on gendered violence (Chapter 8), or Niels P. Arends' on agrarian history-from-below (Chapter 9), which are rarely discussed in this genre.³⁶ While it tries to strike a balance between the various aforementioned domains, there is an emphasis on the political sphere and violent changes of this period, which loom larger than the more subtle changes in other areas. These are to underscore the many different facets of the transformation of Imperial Roman Italy into Ostrogothic Italy, yet without resorting to the catastrophist visions that one occasionally encounters in debates on the genesis of the post-Imperial polities in the West.

In contrast to some of the aforementioned literature, the majority of chapters do not focus on the city of Rome, since this has already been treated skilfully in other recent studies. The reign of Theoderic is only sporadically covered where vital, since we already have a wealth of recent studies available on this ruler. As a regional study, *Late Roman Italy* is in spirit akin to John Drinkwater and Hugh Elton's *Fifth-Century Gaul* and Andy Merrills' *Vandals, Romans and Berbers*.³⁷ It does not try to be a companion or all-encompassing study that touches upon every domain in the field.³⁸ Nor does

---

³⁴ Christie 2016, 148.
³⁵ For very recent and similar approaches, see Kulikowski 2016; 2019; Elton 2018. These works give full coverage of Later Roman Imperial history, with a strong emphasis on the political, institutional and military background, yet they also pay sufficient attention to economy, society and religion, especially the rise of Christianity and its interweaving with the governmental fabric.
³⁶ Arnold et al. 2016 is an admirable exception.
³⁷ Drinkwater and Elton 1992; Merrills 2004.
³⁸ In this regard, I very much sympathise with Riehle 2020, who conceded that his volume '[s]hould be understood as a companion in the proper sense: it does not aim to cover all relevant aspects and issues pertinent ... in the manner of an exhaustive handbook, but rather as an eclectic guide giving orientation, raising questions, and providing inspiration. Several important subjects ... as well as further case studies ... were part of the original publication plan but did not materialize. It is hoped, however, that this somewhat fragmented picture will not encroach on the usefulness of this volume but will, on the contrary, instigate others to explore those areas that have remained at the periphery or are absent from the volume.'

it offer a conventional narrative. Instead, it offers new insights on the various domains affected by the evolution of Imperium to Regnum in what was once the heart of the empire. As many contributors note, the late Fergus Millar once claimed that 'Italy has no history under the empire'.[39] With that he meant that it had no narrative history, at least for the period he examined from Augustus to Constantine I. This volume will show that there are countless histories still to be told, from rustic to ruler, woven against the tableau of the late Roman Italian peninsula and its islands.

Bibliography

Arnaldi, G. and F. Marazzi (2017) *Tarda Antichità e Alto Medioevo in Italia*, Rome.
Arnold, J. J. (2014) *Theoderic and the Roman Imperial Restoration*, Cambridge.
Arnold, J. J., M. S. Bjornlie and K. Sessa (eds) (2016) *A Companion to Ostrogothic Italy*, Leiden.
Ausbüttel, F. (2012) *Theoderich der Große*, Darmstadt.
Bowersock, G. W. (1996) 'The Vanishing Paradigm of the Fall of Rome', *Bulletin of the American Academy of Arts and Sciences* 49 (8): 29–43.
Bowes, K. and M. Kulikowski (eds) (2005) *Hispania in Late Antiquity: Current Perspectives*, Leiden.
Cameron, A. (2011) *The Last Pagans of Rome*, Oxford.
Christie, N. (2016) 'Late Roman and Late Antique Italy: from Constantine to Justinian', in A. E. Cooley (ed.) *The Blackwell Companion to Roman Italy*, Chichester, 133–53.
Cooley, A. E. (ed.) (2016) *The Blackwell Companion to Roman Italy*, Chichester.
Cracco-Ruggini, L. (1961) *Economia e società nell' 'Italia Annonaria': rapporti fra agricoltura e commercio dal IV al VI secolo d.C.*, Milan.
Croke, B. (2010) 'Reinventing Constantinople: Theodosius I's Imprint on the Imperial City', in S. McGill, C. Sogno and E. Watts (eds) *Later Roman History and Culture, 284–450 CE*, Cambridge, 241–64.
Curran, J. (2000) *Pagan City and Christian Capital: Rome in the Fourth Century*, Oxford.
De Blois, L. (2018) *Image and Reality of Roman Imperial Power in the Third Century AD*, London.
Delogu, P. and S. Gasparri (eds) (2010) *Le trasformazioni del V secolo: l'Italia, i barbari e l'Occidente*, Turnhout.
Deliyannis, D. (2010) *Ravenna in Late Antiquity*, Cambridge.
Dey, H. (2011) *The Aurelian Wall and the Refashioning of Imperial Rome, AD 271–855*, Cambridge.
Diefenbach, S. and G. M. Müller (eds) (2013) *Gallien in Spätantike und Frühmittelalter*, Berlin.
Drinkwater, J. and H. Elton (eds) (1992) *Fifth-Century Gaul: a Crisis of Identity?* Cambridge.
Elton, H. (2018) *The Roman Empire in Late Antiquity*, Cambridge.
Erdkamp, P. (2019) 'War, Food, Climate Change, and the Decline of the Roman Empire', *Journal of Late Antiquity* 12 (2): 422–65.
Gibbon, E. (1776–1788) *The History of the Decline and Fall of the Roman Empire*, ed. H. Trevor-Roper (1993–1994), New York.
Gillett, A. (2017) 'The Fall of Rome and the Retreat of European Multiculturalism: a Historical Trope as a Discourse of Authority in Public Debate', *Cogent Arts and Humanities* 4 (1): 1–13.
Goffart, W. (2006) *Barbarian Tides: the Migration Age and the Later Roman Empire*, Philadelphia.
Grig, L. and G. Kelly (eds) (2012) *Two Romes: Rome and Constantinople in Late Antiquity*, Oxford.
Halsall, G. (2007) *Barbarian Migrations and the Roman West, 376–568*, Cambridge.
Harper, K. (2017) *The Fate of Rome: Climate, Disease, and the End of an Empire*, Princeton.

---

[39] Millar 1986, 295.

Heather, P. (2005) *The Fall of the Roman Empire*, Oxford.
Hodgkin, T. (1892–1896) *Italy and Her Invaders*, 4 vols, 2nd ed., London.
Kulikowski, M. (2016) *Imperial Triumph: the Roman World from Hadrian to Constantine (AD 138–363)*, Cambridge, MA.
Kulikowski, M. (2019) *Imperial Tragedy: from Constantine's Empire to the Destruction of Roman Italy (AD 363–568)*, Cambridge, MA.
Machado, C. (2019) *Urban Space and Aristocratic Power in Late Antique Rome: AD 270–535*, Oxford.
Maier, F. K. (2019) *Palastrevolution: der Weg zum hauptstädtischen Kaisertum im Römischen Reich des vierten Jahrhunderts*, Paderborn.
Mazzarino. S. (1990 [1942]) *Stilicone: la crisi imperiale dopo Teodosio*, Rome.
Meier, M. (2019) *Geschichte der Völkerwanderung*, Munich.
Merrills, A. (ed.) (2004) *Vandals, Romans and Berbers: New Perspectives on Late Antique North Africa*, Aldershot.
Millar, F. (1986) 'Italy and the Roman Empire, Augustus to Constantine', *Phoenix* 40 (3): 295–318.
Moorhead, J. (1992) *Theoderic in Italy*, Oxford.
Pohl, W. and H. Reimitz (eds) (1998) *Strategies of Distinction: the Construction of the Ethnic Communities, 300–800*, Leiden.
Poulter, A. (ed.) (2007) *The Transition to Late Antiquity, on the Danube and Beyond*, Oxford.
Riehle, A. (2020) 'Byzantine Epistolography: a Historical and Historiographical Sketch', in A. Riehle (ed.) *A Companion to Byzantine Epistolography*, Leiden.
Salzman, M. R. (2021) *The Falls of Rome: Crises, Resilience, and Resurgence in Late Antiquity*, Cambridge.
Seeck, O. (1897–1920) *Geschichte des Untergangs der antiken Welt*, Berlin.
Sessa, K. (2019) 'The New Environmental Fall of Rome: a Methodological Consideration', *Journal of Late Antiquity* 12 (1): 211–55.
Stein, E. (1947) *Histoire du Bas-Empire*, vol. 1, *De l'État romain à l'État byzantin (284–476)*, trans. J.-R. Palanque, Amsterdam.
Stover, J. and G. Woudhuysen (2022) 'The Poet Nemesianus and the *Historia Augusta*', *JRS* 112.
Van Nuffelen, P. (2015) 'Not Much Happened: 410 and All That', *JRS* 105: 322–9.
Ward-Perkins, B. (2005) *The Fall of Rome and the End of Civilization*, Oxford.
Wickham, C. (1981) *Early Medieval Italy: Central Power and Local Society, 400–1000*, New Jersey.
Wickham, C. (2005) *Framing the Early Middle Ages: Europe and the Mediterranean 400–800*, Oxford.
Wiemer, H.-U. (2018), *Theoderich der Große: König der Goten, Herrscher der Römer*, Munich.
Wijnendaele, J. W. P. (2019) 'Late Roman Civil War and the African Grain Supply' *Journal of Late Antiquity* 12 (2): 298–328.

Part I

Political Developments

1

ITALY FROM THE CRISIS OF THE THIRD CENTURY TO THE TETRARCHY

Umberto Roberto

Italy in the Third Century: A Political and Cultural Anomaly in the Roman Empire

IN ITALY, THE PERIOD between Gallienus and the end of the Tetrarchy marks the final stage in a long process of administrative and political 'normalisation' compared to the situation in the other provinces. For over three centuries, Italy had remained an anomalous territory under Roman rule. In the period between Trajan and the Severi, the imperial government had taken various measures in the attempt to bring the administration of juridical and financial matters in the region into order. Yet these were only exceptional or limited steps. Italy remained an anomaly, a territory exempt from the kind of government policies applied to the provinces: no taxes or governor were imposed on the Italians. In a landmark contribution of 1986, Fergus Millar raised some crucial questions concerning the governing of Italy. With respect to many aspects, significant steps forward have been made in the research. However, we still need to more closely examine certain fundamental issues related to the capacity of imperial power to influence the life of municipal communities, and to replace through its action the relations of solidarity and patronage between local aristocracies and the senatorial aristocracy of Rome.[1] With the reforms introduced by Diocletian and Constantine, the role played by Rome and Italy within the Roman Empire changed for good. The imperial authorities gained direct control over a territory where Rome – the metropolis and ancient capital of the empire – coexisted in a condition of autonomy and immunity, with numerous urban communities governed by their own aristocracies and connected to the Roman senatorial aristocracy through ancient bonds of patronage.[2]

---

[1] See Millar 1986, 310; 318: 'How, by whom, and in what ways was power exercised? Did Italy live, in a more specific sense than the provinces, within the decision-making structures of the Roman *res publica*, or under the jurisdiction of its magistrates? Or was it the Emperor to whom cities and individuals turned? . . . Italy thus still presents fundamental puzzles. Firstly, can it really be true that there was no significant exchange of economic and human resources between Italy and the Empire of which it was a part? And, secondly, if the state did not exercise power and physical force there, who did?'

[2] Concerning the first part of the third century see, e.g., the recommendations of Maecenas to Augustus in Cassius Dio 52.22. See in general Chastagnol 1987; Eck 1979; Simshäuser 1980; Giardina 1997a; see also Porena 2006a.

There is no doubt that the repercussions of the third-century crisis accelerated this process of 'normalisation'. In the period between Gallienus and Carinus, Italy was a politically troubled area, marked by military instability in the north and ridden with processes of dissolution that affected its alleged cultural identity.[3] Obviously, there never was an Italian 'nation' within the Roman Empire; indeed, before the unification attempt made by Rome, the region even lacked any distinguishing traits that could be traced back to a shared Italian identity. The Italic peoples varied considerably in terms of language, culture, society and economy. Besides, as Andrea Giardina has clearly demonstrated, the process of cultural unification launched after the Roman conquest was conditioned, and compromised, by the fact that Rome had already created a Mediterranean empire before conquering the whole of Italy. As the capital of a vast, universal empire, Rome could not limit its role to that of the capital of Italy. As a consequence, in the Imperial age Italian identity developed asymmetrically under Rome: it remained an incomplete identity.[4] The sources confirm that it is impossible to attribute a single identity to Roman Italy between the first century BC and the third century AD. Despite the 'propaganda' efforts made by certain intellectuals, it is necessary to speak of different identities, which often cannot even be defined in terms of ethnicity, but which are rather limited to local communities, which continued to survive even under the rule of Rome. Regional characteristics were not erased, but remained prominent even in Late Antiquity, according to what Santo Mazzarino has described – in relation to other regions of the empire – as the phenomenon of 'democratisation of culture in Late Antiquity'. One significant piece of evidence comes from late antique Etruria: Etruscan endured for centuries in the Tuscan countryside, along with ways of thinking and cultural forms that can be traced back to the ancient, pre-Roman past.[5]

I will anticipate that the process of provincialisation brought about by the Tetrarchy is an administrative fact, which had no effect on the cultural fragmentation of the various peoples inhabiting the peninsula. On the contrary, in its laying out of the various territories and even in its choice of often perfectly neutral names for the new provinces, the imperial government would appear to have emphasised the evanescence of strong and indispensable identity-defining traits in Roman Italy. An interesting example of the fact that the Tetrarchs did not take account of previous cultural-geographical paradigms is the establishment of 'Greater Liguria', a territory encompassing Aemilia and Liguria, thereby ignoring the Po River as a boundary and including within the same administrative area both the stretch of Liguria south of the Po and the Celtic area north of the river.[6]

---

[3] As far as imperial intervention in administration and politics is concerned, four *correctores totius Italiae* are known in the period between Caracalla and Aurelian: see Giardina 1993; Porena 2006a, 1316.
[4] See, in general, Giardina 1997b; 2010. See also Humphries 2000, 548; Carlà-Uhink 2017.
[5] On Etruria in Late Antiquity see Mazzarino 1980a; Cracco Ruggini 2015. On the cultural identity of the Venetia-Histria see Mazzarino 1980b, 214–57. On Campania see Savino 2005. In general, for Sicily see Cracco Ruggini 1980.
[6] See Porena 2004, 541–2; 2013, 332.

'Rome Is Where the Emperor Is': Gallienus in Northern Italy

In the emergency context of the third-century crisis, the transformation of the status of Italy within the empire also coincides with the evolution of the role of the city of Rome with respect to the imperial authorities. The historian Herodian repeatedly refers to the changes underway at his time, c.250. He imagines a hypothetical dialogue between the young prince Commodus and Pompeianus, a friend of his father Marcus Aurelius. After the death of Marcus, Commodus was anxious to return to Rome. Pompeianus suggests delaying the departure:

> My son and my master, it is quite reasonable for you to want to go home; all of us are equally consumed by anxiety to see those we left at home. But the more important, urgent work here restrains our desires. You will have your enjoyment of the pleasures of the city after this for the rest of your life. Furthermore, Rome is where the emperor is. (trans. Whittaker)[7]

'Rome is where the emperor is': For the emperors after Marcus Aurelius and the Severi, Rome cannot mean just the city on the banks of the Tiber. It must rather coincide with any place where the *princeps* happens to be residing with his army. Maximinus Thrax confirms this evidence, as he delayed his entry into Italy until the revolt of the senate forced him to 'descend' into the peninsula with his army.[8]

At the time of the third-century crisis, Rome even lost its role as the only seat of residence of the emperor in Italy. Gallienus was forced to remain in northern Italy in order to defend the Po valley against the mounting threat of barbarian incursions. The famous inscription found on an altar dedicated to the Victory from Augsburg reveals just how serious a threat this was. According to the text in the inscription, at the end of April 260 an imperial army obtained victory over barbarians. The Iuthungi were ambushed by troops led by Marcus Simplicinius Genialis, on their way back from an expedition in the Po valley. The Iuthungi were carrying huge amounts of plunder, along with a column of civilian captives who had been enslaved and were being taken into the *Barbaricum*. Genialis had success in freeing the captives (*excussis multis milibus Italorum captivorum*).[9] The Augsburg inscription provides only one among many examples of the perils that loomed over Italy from the Danube area. In more general

---

[7] See Herodian 1.6.4–5: "ποθεῖν μέν σε", ἔφη, "τέκνον καὶ δέσποτα, τὴν πατρίδα εἰκός· καὶ γὰρ αὐτοὶ τῶν οἴκοι ὁμοίᾳ ἐπιθυμίᾳ ἑαλώκαμεν· ἀλλὰ τὰ ἐνταῦθα προυργιαίτερα ὄντα καὶ μᾶλλον ἐπείγοντα ἐπέχει τὴν ἐπιθυμίαν. τῶν μὲν γὰρ ἐκεῖσε καὶ ὕστερον ἐπὶ πλεῖστον αἰῶνα ἀπολαύσεις, ἐκεῖ τε ἡ Ῥώμη, ὅπου ποτ' ἂν ὁ βασιλεὺς ᾖ. See on this text Galimberti 2014, 73–4. Herodian's *History of Empire after Marcus* was probably written in the period between the reign of Philip (244–9) and Decius (249–51): see Zimmermann 1999, 285–302; Galimberti 2014, 10. Sidebottom 1997 places Herodian under the reign of Gallienus. According to Polley 2003, Herodian wrote his *History* in 240s or the very early 250s, and certainly before 253.
[8] See Christol 1990; Marotta 2016a.
[9] See *AE* 1993, 1231. See Bakker 1993; König 1997; Drinkwater 2007, 53–71.

strategic terms, the Po valley offered an easy passage to Gaul or the heart of Illyricum. It was time for the imperial government to remedy the situation, and Gallienus acted accordingly. This all went to the benefit of Milan, which within a few years – along with the nearby city of Ticinum – became an imperial seat and administrative and military centre, with its own mint. The military emergency and growing presence of the army and of bureaucratic offices set Milan on the path to becoming an imperial 'capital', clearly in opposition to Rome. The polarity between these two cities is one of the defining traits of late antique Italy.[10]

Aurelian, Rome and the Senatorial Aristocracy

In the process of development of a new political, administrative and economic order in Italy, a very important role was played by Emperor Aurelian. In 271 the Iuthungi invaded the Po valley once more. Aurelian marched against the barbarians, but was defeated near Placentia. The Roman senate and people reacted to the news of his defeat in northern Italy with bitter disappointment. In Rome sedition against the imperial government took root. This situation shocked Aurelian, who reacted by adopting a policy that reflected a traditional view of the relation between Rome, the emperor and the senatorial aristocracy.[11] As the *Historia Augusta* recalls (*Vita Aureliani* 21), the emperor opted for an approach based on moderation and concord. To prove that the imperial government was concerned about Rome's safety, Aurelian ordered huge walls to be built. Most importantly, he confirmed the need to ensure that the metropolis would benefit from the inflow of taxes from central and southern Italy. These financial resources were intended to support the vast population of Rome and meet its needs in terms of consumption. However, Aurelian's conception of imperial authority soon made any genuine form of collaboration with the senate very difficult. As also suggested by a fragment from Peter the Patrician, Aurelian foreshadowed the Tetrarchy in basing the legitimacy of his power on direct divine appointment: on a gift or 'grace' – *charisma* – that made any form of protest, opposition or even attempt at usurpation futile.[12] In this respect, Aurelian paved the way for Diocletian and Constantine, and offers an

---

[10] See Mecella 2021, 68–81; on Gallienus' military strategy in Italy see De Blois 1976, 30–6, 84–5; see also Cracco Ruggini 1984, 17; Dietz 2012, 33–7. In general on the crisis during the reign of Gallienus see also De Blois 2018, ch. 2.3.

[11] See Hartmann 2008, 312–14. For the Roman reaction to the news of Aurelian's defeat near Placentia see Dmitriev 2004, 575.

[12] See *Anonymus post Dionem*, fr. 10.6 Mü. (= Petrus Patricius) = *Excerpta de Sententiis* 178: ὅτι Αὐρηλιανὸς πειραθείς ποτε στρατιωτικῆς ἐπαναστάσεως ἔλεγεν ἀπατᾶσθαι τοὺς στρατιώτας, εἰ ἐν ταῖς αὐτῶν χερσὶ τὰς μοίρας εἶναι τῶν βασιλέων ὑπολαμβάνουσιν· ἔφασκε γὰρ τὸν θεὸν δωρησάμενον τὴν πορφύραν (καὶ ταύτην ἐπεδείκνυ τῇ δεξιᾷ) πάντως καὶ τὸν χρόνον τῆς βασιλείας ὁρίσαι· καὶ οὐ πρότερον ἀπέστη πρὶν ἂν εἰς τοὺς ἀρχηγοὺς τῆς στάσεως πεντήκοντα ἐξεδίκησεν; trans. Banchich 2015, 131: 'Aurelian once learned of a military mutiny and said that the troops were mistaken if they supposed that the fates of the emperors were in their hands. For he said that God had bestowed the purple (and this he displayed in his right hand) and had totally determined the duration of his reign. And he did not depart before he had punished about fifty instigators of the revolt.' See also Marotta 2016b.

intimation of the difficult relationship that was to mark the engagement between late antique emperors and the senate of Rome, down to the choices of 476. The city – understood as the civic body comprising the senate and the urban population – was not the most suitable place for flaunting this imperial power legitimised by divine will. As far as the imperial administration in Italy is concerned, Aurelian followed the traditional policy of his predecessors. Esuvius Tetricus' office represents a very interesting example of this traditional behaviour. According to the sources (*Hist. Aug.*, *Aur.* 39.1; Aur. Vict. *Caes.* 35.5), after his defeat Tetricus was appointed *corrector Lucaniae* by Aurelian. On the contrary, a passage of *Historia Augusta, Tyranni triginta* 24.5, claims that Tetricus was appointed *corrector totius Italiae*.[13]

Bearing Aurelian's vision in mind, which still respected the privileged role of Rome and Italy compared to the provinces, it may be argued that Aurelian did not really foreshadow Diocletian's reform in subdividing Italy into small provincial districts. Tetricus became *corrector totius Italiae*; and the particular importance assigned to his role in Lucania by certain sources is probably due to the prominence of this region as a source of food supplies for Rome, based on Aurelian's food distribution programme.[14]

'Two Italies': Emperor Probus' Vision of a Bipolar Region

It was probably Probus who accelerated the transformation of Italy into a politically and administratively bipolar region. In his reign, possibly as early as 279, we find two *correctores Italiae* of senatorial rank, exercising an ordinary office at the same time. One of the two *correctores* operated south of the Po, and was also in charge of the islands.[15] This subdivision reflects a split between at least 'two Italies', two macro-regions with different political, economic and social needs: a split which finally came to be defined

---

[13] See *Hist. Aug.*, *Aurel.* 39.1: *Tetricum triumphatum correctorem Lucaniae fecit, filio eius in senatu manente*; Aur. Vict. *Caes.* 35.5: *ita, ut rectore nullo solet, turbati ordines oppressi sunt, ipse post celsum biennii imperium in triumphum ductus Lucaniae correcturam filioque veniam atque honorem senatorum cooptavit*. See also Eutr. 9.13.2; Epit. de Caes. 35.7. See also *Hist. Aug.*, *Tyr. Trig.* 24.5: *pudore tamen victus vir nimium severus eum, quem triumphaverat, correctorem totius Italiae fecit, id est Campaniae, Samni, Lucaniae, Brittiorum, Apuliae Calabriae, Etruriae atque Umbriae, Piceni et Flaminiae omnisque annonariae regionis, ac Tetricum non solum vivere, sed etiam in summa dignitate manere passus est, cum illum saepe collegam, nonnumquam commilitonem, aliquando etiam imperatorem appellaret*.

[14] See Giardina 1997a, 274–89; Porena 2006a, 1316. On Lucania in Late Antiquity see Giardina 1997c, 149–52. In general, on the links between the south Italian economy and Rome in Late Antiquity see Barnish 1987; Lo Cascio 1999.

[15] See Chastagnol 1987, 348, who dates the two *correctores* in the period 281–2; Porena 2006a, 1317–20, with a detailed presentation of the inscription in honour of L. Aelius Helvius Dionysius (*CIL* 6.1673 + 31901a + 4730 = *ILS* 1211), which mentions his office of *corrector utriusque Italiae* in the period 288–92, when two *correctores Italiae* are already attested. On the inscription see also Giardina 1997a, 265–74. The inscription dedicated to T. Flavius Postumius Titianus (*AE* 1914.249 = *AE* 1918.124 = *AE* 1919.52 = IRComo p. 74, SN 01, from Como) provides a useful text to define the regions assigned to the *correctores Italiae* before Diocletian's reform: see Porena 2006a, 1320–5. See also Porena 2013, 331 and table 1 (*correctores Italiae*, 279–92).

in administrative and political terms with the reforms of Diocletian and Constantine.[16] The outcome of these reforms was the subdivision of Italy into various provinces, brought together under a single diocese governed by two *vicarii*. This process occurred in two stages. Between 293 and 298 Diocletian organised Italy as the *dioecesis Italiciana*, divided into twelve provinces that also included Sicily, Sardinia, the Alps and Raetia. This territory was further subdivided into two areas, the Annonaria region in northern Italy, and the Suburbicaria region in the centre and south. The boundary between the two areas coincided with the Esino and the Arno. At the head of the whole diocese Diocletian placed a single *vicarius Italiae*, who represented the praetorian prefect, based in Milan.[17] The 'Verona List', a document probably from the early reign of Constantine (314), reports the division of Italy into provinces in the tetrarchic age. Later, after his victory over Maxentius, Constantine was to create a second *vicarius urbis Romae* responsible for the *regio Suburbicaria*.[18]

It may be argued that the ancient opposition between the Po valley area and the Apennines finds expression in this division of Italy – which remained formally one – into the two Annonaria and Suburbicaria areas. However, this bipolar situation was chiefly due to political and economic requirements. On the one side stood urban northern Italy: a region made wealthy by its rural economy and by its location as a transit area for goods and people linking Gaul and Illyricum, yet at the same time exposed to significant threats, insofar as – especially from the age of Gallienus onwards – it bordered a frontier threatened by hostile peoples. On the other side stood central-southern Italy, which lived in a condition of direct political symbiosis with Rome, and of economic subordination to it. Throughout Late Antiquity, Rome was not economically self-sufficient. The size of its population, the monumental splendour of its buildings and the luxury-based economy of its senatorial aristocracy made it necessary for it to draw upon the resources of central and southern regions of Italy.[19]

The Provincialisation of Italy under Diocletian

The very introduction of taxation in Italy is a consequence of this new political and military situation. The presence of military units in the Po valley for defensive purposes and of a court in Milan made it necessary for the imperial government to levy some taxes. Money was required to pay officials and especially soldiers. The

---

[16] See Giardina 1997a.
[17] For a dating of the provincialisation to the years 292–4 see Porena 2006a, 1323–4.
[18] See Porena 2013, 333–4 and 346 n. 11; 2006b, 146–52. On the *Laterculus Veronensis* see also Jones 1954; Barnes 1982, 201–8. For the dating of the list see also Zuckerman 2002. A list of Italian provinces is also provided by the *Notitia dignitatum Occidentis* 1.52, 90; 2.6; 10. On the *Notitia* see Jones 1964, Appendix 2; Clemente 1968; Kulikowski 2000.
[19] On Italia Annonaria during the fourth century see Cracco Ruggini 1995 [1961]. On the social and economic relationship between Rome and Italia Suburbicaria see e.g. Giardina 1997a; see also the papers in Harris 1999; Giardina 2000; Savino 2005; Porena 2013. For the archaeological evidence see e.g. Marazzi 1998, 123–32; Christie 2016. See also Chapter 2 in this volume.

practical-minded Diocletian found it expedient to have the wealthy Italian aristocracy contribute to the defence budget. Consequently, it was not possible to maintain an anomalous position for Italy in the provincial model of the Roman Empire. Aurelius Victor describes this reform of Diocletian and the reaction in Italy. Judging from Aurelius Victor and the other sources at our disposal, it does not seem as though the extension of taxation to the whole of Italy in the time of Diocletian triggered any protests. If Italian aristocrats did not react, this was not simply for fear of a harsh response from the tetrarchic government. In terms of the way and form in which levies were imposed, the gradual collection of taxes ensured regular and predictable requests for fiscal contributions, whereas in the past such requests had been advanced abruptly and had therefore been perceived as far more onerous. More generally, the introduction of the provincial model in Italy, on the one hand, increased the possibility for senators to embark on a career as provincial governors in Italy; on the other, it strengthened the senators' hold over the *coloni* on their estates. The senatorial aristocracy, therefore, did not complain, because Diocletian's reform reinforced its authority in Italy.[20]

Competing Cultural 'Identities': On the Attitude of the Illyrian Emperors towards Rome and Italy

Economic and political reasons aside, it is possible to view the relation between the Tetrarchs and Italy, and the related political decisions, within the framework of a contrast between competing cultural 'identities'. In particular, like Aurelian, Probus and Carus before him, Diocletian belonged to the group of soldier emperors of Illyrian stock. This Illyrian background influenced his drastic behaviour towards Rome, Italy and the senatorial aristocracy.

As is widely known, one of the identity-defining traits most frequently attributed to the inhabitants of Roman Italy is their military prowess. In the Republican age the Italians were often portrayed as being brave and skilled at warfare; through their military virtue, hardened by *disciplina Romana*, they had helped Rome conquer its vast empire. At the time of Caesar and Augustus, in the literary genre of the *laudes Italiae* Italy is still celebrated for his centrality in the Roman world, for its military *virtus*, for its abundance and richness, for the religious behaviour of its inhabitants. In the third century a change occurred that was destined to become more entrenched in Late Antiquity: Italy came to be regarded as a land of peace, celebrated for its prosperity, the opulence of its cities and elites, and the industriousness of its inhabitants. What faded, by contrast, was the praising of the warlike and steadfast military character of the peoples of Italy. This primacy came to be assigned to other peoples within the

---

[20] See Aur. Vict. *Caes.* 39.31: *hinc denique parti Italiae invectum tributorum ingens malum. nam cum omnis eadem functione moderateque ageret, quo exercitus atque imperator, qui semper aut maxima parte aderant, ali possent, pensionibus inducta lex nova. quae sane illorum temporum tolerabilis in perniciem processit his tempestatibus.* See Porena 2003, 152–83; 2013, 331–4; on the relationship between *possessores* and *coloni* see Giardina 1997a, 289–300; see also Millar 1986, 297–8 with a different interpretation of Aurelius' text.

empire: to the Gauls, and especially to the Illyrians.[21] This is shown, for example, by another passage of Herodian, where the historian describes the reaction of the Italians in 193 to the news that Septimius Severus was approaching Italy with his army of Illyrian soldiers:

> After passing through Pannonia, Severus arrived at the Italian frontier before any news had reached them, and presented himself to the inhabitants as emperor before they had even heard that he was coming. The invasion of so large an army terrified the Italian cities when they heard the news, since the inhabitants of Italy had long ago abandoned armed warfare in favour of the peaceful occupation of farming. During the days of the Republic when the senate appointed army commanders to their posts, all Italians used to bear arms and gained control of lands and seas in wars against Greeks and barbarians. There was no corner of earth or region in the world, where the Romans did not extend their sway. But when Augustus established his sole rule, he relieved Italians of their duties, and stripped them of their arms . . . When therefore the Italians now heard the news of Severus' approach with a large army, they were naturally panic-striken at such an unusual event. Not daring to offer any opposition in his way, they went to meet him with garlands of laurels and opened wide their gates to admit him. (trans. Whittaker)[22]

Presenting the contrast between the panic-striken Italians and Severus' Illyrian army, Herodian celebrates the *virtus Illyrici*. At the end of the third century, the fact that the Tetrarchs and their most loyal men shared the same Illyrian identity is celebrated in panegyrics through references to the qualities distinguishing the inhabitants of this region. In the panegyric composed for the Augustus Maximian in 291, Mamertinus describes the emperor's homeland in accordance with the rules of the genre (*Pan. Lat.* 3(11).3.9):

---

[21] On this cultural development see Giardina 1997b, 32–8, 47. On military virtue – *virtus* – as a character of the Illyrian populations in Late Antiquity see Mecella 2019; see also Porena 2006c, 20–1; on the warlike character of the Gauls see Amm. Marc. 15.12.3. For Italy's prosperity and richness in Late Antiquity see e.g. *Pan. Lat.* 4(8).10.3; *Expositio totius mundi* 53–5; Ennod. *Vit. Epiph.* 138–9; Cassiod. *Var.* 8.33.3. On regular levies held in Italy in the second and early third century see Millar 1986, 308–9. For the consequences of the decision of Septimius Severus to exclude Italians from the Praetorians see Cassius Dio 74.2.4–6. On the *laudes Italiae* see Carlà-Uhink 2017, 164–74.

[22] Herodian 2.11.3–6: ὁ δὲ τὴν Παιονίαν διαδραμὼν ἐπέστη τοῖς τῆς Ἰταλίας ὅροις, καὶ τὴν φήμην φθάσας πρότερον ὤφθη τοῖς ἐκεῖσε παρὼν βασιλεὺς ἢ ἀφιξόμενος ἠκούσθη. δέος τε μέγα τὰς Ἰταλιώτιδας πόλεις κατελάμβανε πυνθανομένας τοσούτου ἔφοδον στρατοῦ. οἱ γὰρ κατὰ τὴν Ἰταλίαν ἄνθρωποι, ὅπλων καὶ πολέμων πάλαι ἀπηλλαγμένοι, γεωργίᾳ καὶ εἰρήνῃ προσεῖχον. ἐς ὅσον μὲν γὰρ ὑπὸ δημοκρατίας τὰ Ῥωμαίων διῳκεῖτο καὶ ἡ σύγκλητος ἐξέπεμπε τοὺς τὰ πολεμικὰ στρατηγήσοντας, ἐν ὅπλοις Ἰταλιῶται πάντες ἦσαν καὶ γῆν καὶ θάλασσαν ἐκτήσαντο, Ἕλλησι πολεμήσαντες καὶ βαρβάροις· οὐδέ τι ἦν γῆς μέρος ἢ κλίμα οὐρανοῦ ὅπου μὴ Ῥωμαῖοι τὴν ἀρχὴν ἐξέτειναν. ἐξ οὗ δὲ ἐς τὸν Σεβαστὸν περιῆλθεν ἡ μοναρχία, Ἰταλιώτας μὲν πόνων ἀπέπαυσε καὶ τῶν ὅπλων ἐγύμνωσε . . . ὅθεν τὸν Σεβῆρον προσιόντα πυνθανόμενοι τότε μετὰ τοσούτου στρατοῦ εἰκότως ἐταράττοντο τῷ ἀήθει τοῦ πράγματος· οὔτε δὲ ἀντιστῆναι ἢ κωλῦσαι ἐτόλμων, ὑπήντων δὲ δαφνηφοροῦντες καὶ πύλαις ἀναπεπταμέναις ἐδέχοντο.

for you were not born and raised in some quiet part of the world, a land enfeebled by luxury, but in those provinces whose border, exposed to the enemy (although a beaten one) and always arrayed in arms, has taught them the tireless habit of toil and patience, in provinces where all of life is military service (*omnis vita militia est*), whose women even are braver than the men of other lands. (trans. Nixon and Saylor Rodgers)[23]

Omnis vita militia est. The exaltation of life as *militia* is one of the hallmarks of the style of government favoured by Diocletian and his colleagues. And in the panegyrical literature in honour of the Tetrarchs this view is explicitly juxtaposed to a sort of transposition (*translatio*) of the military virtues from the Italians to the Illyrians. This is what the panegyrist Mamertinus affirms in his praise of Maximianus' origin from Pannonia (*Pan. Lat.* 2(10).2.2–4):

> Where, then, shall I begin? Shall I recall, indeed, the services of your native land to the State? For who doubts that for many centuries now, ever since its strength was added to the Roman name, while Italy indeed may have been mistress of nations by virtue of the antiquity of her glory, Pannonia has been in valor? (trans. Nixon and Saylor Rodgers)[24]

Diocletian confirmed this verdict through a clear decision he took at the time of his *vicennalia*. In keeping with tradition, he jointly celebrated the triumph over all the enemies of the empire and his *vicennalia*. At the beginning of 303 Diocletian was in Nicomedia, where the persecution of the Christians, the last enemies of the empire according to the Tetrarchs, began on 23 February, the day of the Terminalia. In mid-March 303 Diocletian set off from Nicomedia, heading west. However, he did not take the shortest route to Rome. On the contrary, he decided to travel by land through Illyricum, visiting the cities and the region which gave him his most loyal soldiers. In such a way, Diocletian celebrated his triumph and his twenty years of rule: this was an homage to the *virtus Illyrici* which had ensured the Tetrarchs' success. Diocletian only reached Rome in early November.[25]

Diocletian and the *libertas populi Romani*

In Rome the preparations for the great triumph had been going on for years. Their impact on the city's layout strikingly reveals the attitude towards Rome adopted by Diocletian

---

[23] *non enim in otiosa aliqua deliciisque corrupta parte terrarum nati institutique estis, sed in his provinciis quas ad infatigabilem consuetudinem laboris atque patientiae fracto licet oppositus hosti, armis tamen semper instructus limes exercet, in quibus omnis vita militia est, quarum etiam feminae ceterarum gentium viris fortiores sunt.* Later, see this theme also in Aur. Vict. *Caes.* 39.26: *his sane omnibus Illyricum patria fuit: qui, quamquam humanitatis parum, ruris tamen ac militiae miseriis imbuti satis optimi reipublicae fuere.*

[24] *unde igitur ordiar? commemorabo nimirum patriae tuae in rem publicam merita? quis enim dubitat quin multis iam saeculis, ex quo vires illius ad Romanum nomen accesserint, Italia quidem sit gentium domina gloriae vetustate, sed Pannonia virtute?*

[25] See Roberto 2014, 175–9; on Diocletian's route to Rome see also Kuhoff 2001, 230–2.

and the other Tetrarchs. Let us start from one important piece of evidence. As Lactantius states, Diocletian disliked Rome; in particular, he could not stand the Romans' *libertas*. During his long reign, he visited Rome only once, and then only for a few days:

> Diocletian proceeded at once to Rome in order to celebrate there his *vicennalia*. When this had been celebrated, he could not bear the independence of the Roman people, and just before 1 January when his ninth consulship was due to be conferred on him, he rushed from the city, impatient and weak in mind. (trans. Rees)[26]

The whole issue must be explained in the light of the overall conception of imperial power in the tetrarchic age. Like the third-century emperors before him, Diocletian regarded his power as being fully legitimised by the divine will. His subjects could only accept the charismatic investiture of the emperor. As one of the markers of this condition, Diocletian imposed an elaborate imperial ceremonial, introducing for example the *adoratio* of the purple. It is interesting to note that the first attestation of this practice is related to Diocletian and Maximian's encounter with their dignitaries in Milan in winter 290–1:

> What a thing that was, good gods! What a spectacle your piety created, when those who were going to adore your sacred features were admitted to the palace in Milan you both were gazed upon and your twin deity suddenly confused the ceremony of single veneration! No one observed the hierarchy of deities according to the usual protocol; they all stopped still to spend more time in adoration, stubborn in their duplicate pious duty. Yet this private veneration, as if in the inner shrine, stunned the minds only of those whose public rank gave them access to you. (trans. Nixon and Saylor Rodgers)[27]

Diocletian later imposed the ceremonial of *adoratio* even on the members of the Roman senate. An allusion to Diocletian's *phronēma* in Zonaras again brings up the political issue of the contrast between the monarchy and the *libertas* of the senators and people of Rome:

> Diocletian, when he had become elated and arrogant (μέγα φρονήσας) as a result, no longer tolerated being addressed by the senate as before, but made it a custom to receive obeisance (ἀλλὰ προσκυνεῖσθαι ἐθέσπισε). (trans. Banchich)[28]

---

[26] See Lactant. *De mort. pers.* 17.1–3: *hoc igitur scelere perpetrato Diocletianus, cum iam felicitas ab eo recessisset, perrexit statim Romam, ut illic vicennalium diem celebraret, qui erat futurus a.d. duodecimum Kalendas Decembres. quibus sollemnibus celebratis cum libertatem populi Romani ferre non poterat, impatiens et aeger animi prorupit ex urbe impendentibus kalendis Ianuariis, quibus illi nonus consulatus deferebatur. tredecim dies tolerare non potuit, ut Romae potius quam Ravennae procederet consul.* On Diocletian and the Roman *libertas* see Elbern 1990, 28–9; Roberto 2019.

[27] *Pan. Lat.* 3(11).11.1–3: *quid illud, di boni! quale pietas vestra spectaculum dedit, cum in Mediolanensi palatio admissis qui sacros vultus adoraturi erant conspecti estis ambo, et consuetudinem simplicis venerationis geminato numine repente turbastis! nemo ordinem numinum solita secutus est disciplina; omnes adorandi mora restiterunt duplicato pietatis officio contumaces. atque haec quidem velut interioribus sacrariis operta veneratio eorum modo animos obstupefecerat quibus aditum vestri dabant ordines dignitatis.* In general, on the religious and political concept of imperial power in the tetrarchic age see Kolb 2004; Marotta 2016b.

[28] Zonaras 12.31: οἷς ἐπαρθείς, ὁ Διοκλητιανὸς καὶ μέγα φρονήσας οὐκέτι προσαγορεύεσθαι παρὰ τῆς γερουσίας ὡς πρώην ἠνείχετο, ἀλλὰ προσκυνεῖσθαι ἐθέσπισε.

Given these excesses, Diocletian may be seen to have exercised a form of power that is the complete opposite of that of the *princeps civilis*, which – among other things – entailed a willingness on the emperor's part to cooperate with his most distinguished subjects. And among these, no doubt, were the representatives of the Roman senatorial aristocracy.[29]

Diocletian sought to limit the political role of the aristocracy and people of Rome, as far as possible. In particular, under Diocletian the senatorial aristocracy lost its strong political power, as members of the equestrian order were promoted to important administrative and military posts by the Tetrarchs. The imperial government was also concerned with administration and political control of the Italian provinces. Replacing the senators, equestrians were appointed as governors of the Italian provinces. In that way, the influence exerted by the senatorial aristocracy on municipal aristocracies was reduced.[30]

A New Polarity in Late Antique Italy: Milan and Rome

In addition to this political choice, Diocletian and Maximian downgraded the role of Rome within the empire. Until the late reign of Valentinian III (425–55), Rome lost its status as an imperial seat. Whenever he visited Italy, the Augustus of the West would reside either in Milan or in Aquileia. In particular, throughout the fourth century, Milan represents a model of provincial 'capital' and imperial residence in Italy in contrast with Rome, centre of the senate. Since the time of Maximianus' interventions, the polarity between Milan and Rome concerns, on the one hand, the urban aspect and topography of power and, on the other hand, the political function of both cities in the Italian *dioecesis*. In Milan the *vicarius Italiae* had his seat. He was the chief of the administration of the northern part of the *dioecesis Italiae* and was subordinate to the praetorian prefect. According to the sources, the population of Milan is depicted as devoted to the imperial power, submissive and active, clearly in opposition to the *libertas* and the civic pride of the senate and the people of Rome.[31] This condition is described in a famous passage on the meeting of Diocletian and Maximian in Milan in winter 290–1. As the Panegyrist states:

---

[29] Adoration in the sources: Jer. *Chron.* s.a. 296 (226 Helm); Aur. Vict. *Caes.* 39.4; Eutr. 9.26; Amm. Marc. 15.5.18 ('For Diocletian was the first to introduce the foreign and royal manner of adoration, when previously we have read that emperors were greeted like higher officials', trans. Rees). See also criticism in the *Historia Augusta*: *Alex. Sev.* 4.3, 18.1; *Maxim. Duo* 28.7. See Stern 1954; see also Tantillo 2014, 562–4.

[30] See Arnheim 1972, 39–48, a chapter significantly entitled 'Diocletian, Hammer of the Aristocracy'; but see De Giovanni 2008, 141–2; see also Cecconi 1994, 18–19; Porena 2018. For a general discussion of this problem see now Davenport 2019. For a list of the imperial governors in Italy under the tetrarchic government see Porena 2013, 346 n. 10.

[31] On the polarity between Milan and Rome in Late Antiquity see Roberto 2018. See also Cracco Ruggini 1990a; 1990b; Bauer 2011, 72–3. On Milan as imperial residence during the fourth century: Sannazaro 2016. During the tetrarchic age a representative of the imperial government in Rome was the *rationalis urbis Romae*: Porena 2006b, 136–7; the *vicarius urbis Romae* – and therefore the anomalous presence of two *vicarii* in a single *dioecesis* – is a later creation of Constantine. On the relationship between the *vicarius urbis Romae* and the urban prefect (*praefectus urbi*) see Sinnigen 1959. On Rome as imperial seat in the second half of the fifth century (until the end of the western empire) see Gillett 2001; Humphries 2012.

Even Rome herself, the mistress of nations, in a transport of extravagant joy at your proximity and in an attempt to get a glimpse of you from the summits of her own mountains, the closer to sate herself with your countenances, advanced as near as she could to get a look. Indeed she had sent the leaders of her Senate, freely imparting to the city of Milan, most blessed during those days, a semblance of her own majesty, that the seat of imperial power could then appear to be the place to which each emperor had come. (trans. Nixon and Saylor Rodgers)[32]

Secondly, under the Tetrarchs the city of Rome lost its military importance, whereas the troops of the imperial army were stationed in northern Italy, near Milan and Ticinum. Verona and Aquileia were the main strongholds in the Italian defence system. In addition to that, the border province of Raetia belonged to the military and administrative district of the Italian diocese (under the *vicarius Italiae*). Since Rome lost its role as residence of the emperor in Italy, Diocletian reduced the Praetorian Guard to a mere city garrison of Rome. The political influence of the guard was strongly minimised. Probably, Diocletian's aim was to transform the huge metropolis of Rome into a demilitarised city. This operation also provided an economic benefit resulting from the elimination of unnecessary military expenses.[33]

Another significant indication of Diocletian's impatience with the *libertas* of the senate and people of Rome comes from his invasive building policy in Rome. According to Lactantius:

To this can be added Diocletian's limitless passion for building – and in the provinces there was no less an exaction to raise workmen, craftsmen, wagons and everything required for building construction. (trans. Rees)[34]

---

[32] *Pan. Lat.* 3(11).12: *ipsa etiam gentium domina Roma immodico propinquitatis vestrae elato gaudio vosque e speculis suorum montium prospicere conata, quo se vultibus vestris propius expleret, ad intuendum cominus quantum potuit accessit. lumina siquidem senatus sui misit beatissimae illi per eos dies Mediolanensium civitati similitudinem maiestatis suae libenter impartiens, ut ibi tunc esse sedes imperii videretur quo uterque venerat imperator*. See also Porena 2013, 334, quoting a similar text in the description of Italy in the *Expositio*, 54–5: *post eam Campania provincia, non valde quidem magna, divites autem viros possidens et ipsa sibi sufficiens et cellarium regnanti Roma. et post eam Italia, quae et nominata verbo solum aut in nomine gloriam suam ostendit, multas et varias civitates habens et omnibus bonis plena . . . Italia ergo omnibus abundans insuper et hoc maximum bonum possidet: civitatem maximam et eminentissimam et regalem, quae de nomine virtutem ostentat et vocatur Roma . . . habet autem et senatum maximum virorum divitum: quos si per singulos probare volueris, invenies omnes iudices aut factos aut futuros esse aut potentes quidem, nolentes autem propter suorum frui cum securitate velle.*

[33] See Aur. Vict. *Caes.* 39.47: *hinc etiam quasi truncatae vires Urbis, imminuto praetoriarum cohortium atque in armis vulgi numero* (trans. Rees 2004, 95: 'for this reason too, Rome's forces were truncated, as it were, by a reduction in the number of praetorian cohorts and citizens bearing arms'). See also Dufraigne 2003, 189. As is well known, Maxentius reversed the policy of the Tetrarchs by increasing the military strength of the Praetorians once more. In 312 Constantine permanently disbanded the Praetorian Guard. For the military importance of the Po valley for Italy's defence in the tetrarchic age in clear opposition to the marginalisation of Rome see Porena 2006b, 152–4; Roberto 2013; see also Vannesse 2010, 109–58; and Chapter 7 in this volume. On Aquileia, an important stronghold guarding Italy against invaders from the north-east, see Janniard 2006.

[34] See Lactant. *De mort. pers.* 7.8: *huc accedebat infinita quaedam cupiditas aedificandi, non minor provinciarum exactio in exhibendis operariis et artificibus et plaustris, omnibus quaecumque sint fabricandis operibus necessaria.* On Diocletian's passion for building see also John Malalas 12.37 (μεγαλόψυχος πάνυ καὶ φιλοκτίστης). In general, on tetrarchic building policy in Rome see Bauer 2011.

The city centre had been partially destroyed in a serious fire in the time of Carus and Carinus.[35] In keeping with their political vision, Diocletian and Maximian were not content with merely restoring the ancient monumental layout – quite the contrary. Particularly in the area of the Roman Forum, which had been heavily damaged, they acted extensively, with the aim of setting the ground for their grand triumph. The political and symbolic value of this decision is evident. The most important space in the history of the city and its senate was entirely renovated. As a consequence, one of the most important spaces for the celebration of the *libertas* of the senate and people of Rome became a self-enclosed place, meant to serve as a stage for the exalting of the Tetrarchy. The new layout of the Forum was intended to evoke the collegial form of government adopted by the Tetrarchs and to express new strategies of representation for what was being presented as an everlasting and indestructible system of power. This was the setting for the main moments in the celebration of the *vicennalia* and the triumph. The Forum, therefore, continued to be at the centre of the life of the people and senate of Rome; yet participation in the rites and celebrations had to take place before the new lords of the empire, represented by the statues crowning the Forum's columns.[36]

Diocletian's Political Message in the Dedicatory Inscription of the *Thermae Felices Diocletianae*

Other areas of the city too were affected by the Tetrarchs' monumental building policy. In 298 work commenced, under Maximian's supervision, for the construction of the grand thermal baths in honour of Diocletian. It is important to focus on the dedicatory inscription for the baths, which by 25 July 306 had been inaugurated. As is well known, only a few fragments of the dedicatory inscription remain, but they confirm the reliability of the transcript made by the anonymous author of the *Itinerarium* of Einsiedeln (*CIL* 6.1130 cf. p. 845 = 6.31242 cf. p. 3071, 3778, 4326, 4340 = *ILS* 646):

> DD(omini) NN(ostri) Diocletianus et [[Maximianus]] Invicti
> Seniores Augg(usti) patres Impp(eratorum) et Caess(arum) et
> dd(omini) nn(ostri) Constantius et Maximianus Invicti Augg(usti) et
> [[Severus et]] Maximinus nobilissimi Caesares
> thermas Felices [Dio]cletianas quas
> [M]aximianus Aug(ustus) re[dien]s ex Africa sub
> [pr]aesentia maie[statis suae] disposuit ac
> [f]ieri iussit et Diocletiani Aug(usti) fratris sui
> nomine consecravit coemptis aedificiis
> pro tanti operis magnitudine omni cultu
> perfectas Romanis suis dedicaverunt.

---

[35] See *Chron. 354, MGH AA* 9.148; Altmayer 2014, 266–7; Bauer 2011, 10–12.
[36] See *CIL* 6.1203 = 31261; 1204 = 31262; 1205 = 31263 and L'Orange 1938; Kähler 1964; Coarelli 1999, 27–33; Bauer 2011, 57–65; Kalas 2015, 23–47. On the celebration on 20 November 303 see Kuhoff 2001, 230–45; Roberto 2014, 175–9; Bauer 2011, 65–70.

Our lords Diocletian and Maximian the unconquered senior Augusti, fathers of the emperors and Caesars, and our lords Constantius and Maximianus unconquered Augusti and Severus and Maximinus the most noble Caesars have dedicated to their own Romans the fortunate Baths of Diocletian, completed with every adornment, which Maximian Augustus, returning from Africa, under the presence of his majesty arranged and commanded to be made and consecrated in the name of his brother Diocletian Augustus, after buying out the buildings for the great scale of so large a project. (trans. Corcoran)[37]

In this area of Rome too, in order to lend the baths the kind of majestic character required by the celebration of the emperors, Maximian acted heavy-handedly. The measures taken were so drastic as to be recalled in the inscription: *coemptis aedificiis pro tanti operis magnitudine*. The memory of the expropriation of so many private buildings, which were lawfully purchased by the imperial government, is combined with that of the erasing of a significant stretch of Regio VI: a clearly political action. The baths were erected in an area of 13 hectares between the Quirinal and the Viminal hills. The expression is no doubt intended to celebrate the *magnitudo*, and hence generosity, of the imperial building work; but it also evokes the Tetrarchs' capacity – here as much as in the Forum – to renew cities' appearance at their own whim.

The political meaning of this operation is most powerfully revealed by another expression, a sort of *hapax legomenon*, to my knowledge, in the relations between imperial power and Rome. The Tetrarchs' generous gift is bestowed on *Romanis suis*. It is important to pay due attention to the 'political' weight of these words. The dedicator, which is to say the collegiate government of the second Tetrarchy, along with the *Seniores Augusti*, is addressing the population of Rome, yet without distinguishing – as would have been more customary and becoming – the traditional components of the civic body: the senate and the people of Rome. On the contrary, the inhabitants of Rome are addressed using a collective and politically levelling expression. Given that it was set on a building designed to remind everyone of the power of the Tetrarchy, the expression was intended to clarify in what way imperial power regarded the Romans and the city itself; and that is to say: as subjects – just like all other provincials. In my view, the expression does not merely convey closeness to or familiarity with the people of Rome. A deeper political level is at work here. The formula does not express any deference to the senate or the antiquity of the people of Rome. Rather, it completely downplays the political role of these actors with respect both to the governing of the city and to the empire as a whole. Like all other populations within the empire, the inhabitants of Rome owe obedience to Diocletian's regime. The meaning of the expression is further amplified by the magnitude of the undertaking, which has radically altered an area of Rome, without the senate and people being in any way involved in the redefinition of the urban space. As in the case of the provincialisation of Italy, there is an evident imbalance between the historical role of Rome and the

---

[37] Discussion by Corcoran 2017, 62. See also Bauer 2011, 25–6. On the text see Friggeri et al. 2001, 80–1; Crimi 2014, 57–67. On the *Thermae Felices Diocletianae* see Bauer 2011, 46–57; Friggeri and Magnani Cianetti 2014.

Tetrarchs' judgement. This inscription too testifies to the beginning of a new era: the ancient history of Rome, the history of its glorious senate and people, is obscured through the roughness and brutality typical of Diocletian's regime. The decision to address the Romans using the formula *Romanis suis* must be understood as another clear sign of Diocletian's hostility towards the Romans' *libertas*.[38]

Galerius populator Italiae

The Tetrarchs' attitude to the city also clearly emerges from an episode that occurred shortly after the dedication of the *Thermae Felices Diocletianae*. As is widely known, Constantine's decision to proclaim himself the successor of his father Constantius threw a cog into the wheel of the Tetrarchy, driving Maxentius to usurp power as well, proclaiming himself emperor at Rome. Galerius, Diocletian's political and spiritual heir, could not tolerate this and took resolute action. In the summer of 307, Galerius personally made his way down from Milan to launch an attack on Rome. According to Lactantius, the whole campaign was poorly orchestrated, chiefly because Galerius, an uncouth Illyrian emperor who had never set foot in Rome, had no idea of the vastness of the city. His behaviour in Italy betrayed his evil disposition:

> Meanwhile Galerius gathered his army and invaded Italy; he approached the city, intending to destroy the senate and butcher the people, but he found everything barred and defended. There was no hope of storming, attack was difficult, and he had too few forces to lay siege, for he had never seen Rome and assumed it was not much bigger than those cities he knew. (trans. Rees)[39]

Following the example of his predecessor (and political model), Galerius disliked Rome, his senate, his population (*ad urbem accedit senatum extincturus, populum trucidaturus*). However, having failed to seize Rome, he retraced his steps, laying to waste the area surrounding the Via Flaminia:

> Galerius had once taken the name of emperor; now he professed himself an enemy of the term 'Roman' and he wanted to change the title of the empire from 'Roman' to 'Dacian'. (trans. Rees)[40]

---

[38] See Roberto 2019; see also Bauer 2011, 56–7.

[39] Lactant. *De mort. pers.* 27.2: *ille interea coacto exercitu invadit Italiam, ad urbem accedit senatum extincturus, populum trucidaturus; verum clausa et munita omnia offendit. nulla erat spes inrumpendi, oppugnatio difficilis, ad circumsedenda moenia non satis copiarum, quippe qui numquam viderat Romam aestimaretque illam non multo esse maiorem, quam quas noverat civitates.* See also Zecchini 2011. On Galerius' hostility towards Rome see also Lactant. *De mort. pers.* 26.2: *cum statuisset censibus institutis orbem terrae devorare, ad hanc usque prosiluit insaniam, ut ab hac captivitate ne populum quidem Romanum fieri vellet immunem. ordinabantur iam censitores, qui Romam missi describerent plebem* (see Rees 2004, 112); *Origo Const.* 3.6: *Romam venit* (sc. Galerius) *minatus civitatis interitum* (see Aiello 2014, 166–9); Aur. Vict. *Caes.* 40.8–9; Zos. 2.10.3.

[40] See Lactant. *De mort. pers.* 27.7–8: *hoc modo se ad sedes suas recepit, cum Romanus quondam imperator, nunc populator Italiae, hostiliter universa vexasset. olim quidem ille ut nomen imperatoris acceperat, hostem se Romani nominis erat professus, cuius titulum immutari volebat, ut non Romanum imperium, sed Daciscum cognominaretur.* See also Corsaro 1978 on Lactantius' criticism of Galerius.

Also in this case, Lactantius chooses his words with care. In fact, this vast area surrounding the Via Flaminia is called by Lactantius *Italia*. Consequently, Galerius' hostility towards Rome, including its senate and people, accused of supporting the usurper Maxentius, appears to have been fully in line with that of Diocletian. This hostile attitude turned Galerius – the 'Dacian' emperor – from a Roman emperor into the 'devastator of Italy' (*cum Romanus quondam imperator, nunc populator Italiae*). The contrast between Italy (and Rome) and the Illyrian emperors which characterised the whole period of the Tetrarchy is drammatically confirmed by these events in 307.

Some Concluding Remarks

During the second half of the third century, the political attitudes of Gallienus, Aurelian and Probus towards Italy and Rome – and its powerful senatorial aristocracy – paved the way for Diocletian's and Constantine's reforms that completely changed the organisation and position of Italy in the Roman Empire. In the period between Gallienus and Probus, the transformation of Italy into a 'bipolar' region – according to a subdivision which reflects a split between 'two Italies' – foreshadows the creation of two macro-regions, Italia Annonaria, in Northern Italy, and Italia Suburbicaria, in central-southern Italy. Although these macro-regions were included in a single *dioecesis Italiciana* under Diocletian, the polarity between Annonaria and Suburbicaria – as well as the polarity between their respective major urban centres, Milan and Rome – represents one of the defining traits of late antique Italy. It is actually possible to consider this trait as a legacy of Late Antiquity destined to characterise Italian history through the centuries. The outcome of the reforms under Diocletian was the provincialisation of Italy, which was based on economic and fiscal motivations. However, despite the efforts to create a political and administrative uniformity in the peninsula, Diocletian's and Constantine's reforms emphasised the evanescence of strong identity-defining traits in Roman Italy. In fact, these reforms had no effect on the cultural fragmentation of Italy, which represents another long-lasting feature in Italian history far beyond Late Antiquity and the Middle Ages.

Bibliography

Aiello, V. (2014) *La Pars Constantiniana degli Excerpta Valesiana: introduzione, testo e commento storico*, Messina.

Altmayer, K. (2014) *Die Herrschaft des Carus, Carinus und Numerianus als Vorläufer der Tetrarchie*, Stuttgart.

Arnheim, M. T. W. (1972) *The Senatorial Aristocracy in the Later Roman Empire*, Oxford.

Bakker, L. (1993), 'Raetien unter Postumus: das Siegesdenkmal einer Juthungenschlacht im Jahre 260 n. Chr. aus Augsburg', *Germania* 71: 369–86.

Banchich, T. (2015) *The Lost History of Peter the Patrician: an Account of Rome's Imperial Past from the Age of Justinian*, Abingdon.

Banchich, T. and E. N. Lane (trans.) (2009) *The History of Zonaras: from Alexander Severus to the Death of Theodosius the Great*, London.

Barnes, T. D. (1982) *The New Empire of Diocletian and Constantine*, Cambridge, MA.

Barnish, S. J. B. (1987) 'Pigs, Plebeians and *Potentes*: Rome's Economic Hinterland, c.350–600 A.D.', *PBSR* 55: 157–85.

Bauer, F. A. (2011) 'Stadt ohne Kaiser: Rom im Zeitalter der Dyarchie und Tetrarchie (285–306 n. Chr.)', in T. Fuhrer (ed.) *Rom und Mailand in der Spätantike*, Berlin, 3–85.

Carlà-Uhink, F. (2017) *The 'Birth' of Italy: the Institutionalization of Italy as a Region, 3rd–1st Century BCE*, Berlin.

Cecconi, G. A. (1994) *Governo imperiale e élites dirigenti nell'Italia tardoantica: problemi di storia politico-amministrativa (270–476 d.C.)*, Como.

Chastagnol, A. (1987) 'L'administration du diocèse italien au Bas-empire' [1963], in A. Chastagnol, *L'Italie et l'Afrique au Bas-Empire: études administratives et prosopographiques. Scripta varia*, Lille, 117–48.

Christie, N. (2016) 'Late Roman and Late Antique Italy: from Constantine to Justinian', in A. E. Cooley (ed.) *A Companion to Roman Italy*, Chichester, 133–54.

Christol, M. (1990) 'Rome *sedes imperii* au IIIe siècle ap. J.-C.', *QCCCM* 2: 121–47.

Clemente, G. (1968) *La Notitia Dignitatum*, Cagliari.

Coarelli, F. (1999) 'L'edilizia pubblica a Roma in età tetrarchica', in W. V. Harris (ed.) *The Transformations of Vrbs Roma in Late Antiquity*, JRA Suppl. 33, Portsmouth, RI, 23–33.

Corcoran, S. (2017) 'Maxentius: a Roman Emperor in Rome', *AnTard* 25: 59–74.

Corsaro, F. (1978) 'Le "mos maiorum" dans la vision éthique et politique du "de mortibus persecutorum"', in J. Fontaine and M. Perrin (eds) *Lactance et son temps: recherches actuelles*, Paris, 25–49.

Cracco Ruggini, L. (1980) 'La Sicilia tra Roma e Bisanzio', in R. Romeo (ed.) *Storia della Sicilia*, vol. 3, Naples, 1–96.

Cracco Ruggini, L. (1984) 'Milano nella circolazione monetaria del Tardo Impero: esigenze politiche e risposte socioeconomiche', in G. Gorini (ed.) *La zecca di Milano: Atti del Convegno internazionale di studio, Milano, 9–14 maggio 1983*, Milan, 13–58.

Cracco Ruggini, L. (1990a) 'Milano da "metropoli" degli Insubri a capitale dell'impero: una vicenda di mille anni', in *Milano capitale dell'impero romano (286–402 d.C.)*, Milan, 17–23.

Cracco Ruggini, L. (1990b) 'Nascita e morte di una capitale', *QCCCM* 2: 5–51.

Cracco Ruggini, L. (1995 [1961]) *Economia e società nell''Italia Annonaria': rapporti fra agricoltura e commercio dal IV al VI secolo d.C.*, Bari.

Cracco Ruggini, L. (2015) 'La "Tuscia" tardoantica, terra di latifondi: fra tradizione pagana e cristianizzazione avanzante', in E. A. Arslan and M. A. Turchetti (eds) *Il ripostiglio di San Mamiliano a Sovana (Sorano – GR): 498 solidi da Onorio a Romolo Augusto*, Spoleto, 33–59.

Crimi, G. (2014) 'L'iscrizione dedicatoria delle Terme di Diocleziano', in R. Friggeri and M. Magnani Cianetti (eds) *Le Terme di Diocleziano/La certosa di Santa Maria degli Angeli*, Milan, 57–67.

Davenport, C. (2019) *A History of the Roman Equestrian Order*, Cambridge.

De Blois, L. (1976) *The Policy of the Emperor Gallienus*, Leiden.

De Blois, L. (2018) *Image and Reality of Roman Imperial Power in the Third Century AD: the Impact of War*, London.

De Giovanni, L. (2008) *Istituzioni, scienza giuridica, codici nel mondo tardoantico: alle radici di una nuova storia*, Rome.

Dietz, K. (2012) 'Zum Kampf zwischen Gallienus und Postumus', in T. Fischer (ed.) *Die Krise des 3. Jahrhunderts n. Chr. und das Gallische Sonderreich*, Wiesbaden, 29–62.

Dmitriev, S. (2004) 'Traditions and Innovations in the Reign of Aurelian', *CQ* 54: 568–78.

Drinkwater, J. F. (2007) *The Alamanni and Rome, 213–496: Caracalla to Clovis*, Oxford.

Dufraigne P. (ed. and trans.) (2003) *Aurélius Victor: Livre des Césars*, 2nd ed., Paris.

Eck, W. (1979) *Die staatliche Organisation Italiens in der hohen Kaiserzeit*, Munich.

Elbern, S. (1990) 'Das Verhältnis der spätantiken Kaiser zur Stadt Rom', *RQA* 85: 19–49.

Friggeri, R., M. G. Granino Cecere and G. Gregori (2001) *La collezione epigrafica del Museo Nazionale Romano alle Terme di Diocleziano*, Milan.

Friggeri, R. and M. Magnani Cianetti (eds) (2014) *Le Terme di Diocleziano/Il chiostro piccolo della Certosa Santa Maria degli Angeli*, Milan.

Galimberti, A. (2014) *Erodiano e Commodo: traduzione e commento storico al primo libro della Storia dell'Impero dopo Marco*, Göttingen.

Giardina, A. (1993) 'La formazione dell'Italia provinciale', in *Storia di Roma*, vol. 3.1, *L'età tardoantica: crisi e trasformazioni*, Turin, 51–68.

Giardina, A. (1997a) 'Le due Italie nella forma tarda dell'impero', in A. Giardina (ed.) *Società romana e impero tardoantico*, vol. 1, *Istituzioni, ceti, economie*, Bari, 1–30 = A. Giardina (1997) *L'Italia romana: storie di un'identità incompiuta*, Rome, 265–321.

Giardina, A. (1997b) 'L'identità incompiuta dell'Italia romana', in A. Giardina, *L'Italia romana: storie di un'identità incompiuta*, Rome, 3–116.

Giardina, A. (1997c) 'Allevamento ed economia della selva in Italia meridionale', in A. Giardina, *L'Italia romana: storie di una identità incompiuta*, Rome, 139–92.

Giardina, A. (2000) 'Considerazioni finali', in *L'Italia meridionale in età tardoantica: Atti del XXXVIII Convegno di Studi sulla Magna Grecia*, Naples, 609–25.

Giardina, A. (2010) 'Italy and Italians during Late Antiquity', in P. Delogu and S. Gasparri (eds) *Le trasformazioni del V secolo: l'Italia, i barbari e l'Occidente romano*, Turnhout, 101–22.

Gillett, A. (2001) 'Rome, Ravenna and the Last Western Emperors', *PBSR* 69: 131–67.

Harris, W. V. (ed.) (1999) *The Transformations of Vrbs Roma in Late Antiquity*, JRA Suppl. 33, Portsmouth, RI.

Hartmann, U. (2008) 'Claudius Gothicus und Aurelianus', in K.-P. Johne, with the collaboration of U. Hartmann and T. Gerhardt, *Die Zeit der Soldatenkaiser: Krise und Transformation des Römischen Reiches im 3. Jahrhundert n. Chr. (235–284)*, Berlin, 297–323.

Humphries, M. (2000) 'Italy, A.D. 425–605', in A. Cameron, B. Ward-Perkins and L. M. Whitby (eds) *The Cambridge Ancient History*, vol. 14: *Late Antiquity: Empire and Successors, AD 425–600*, Cambridge, 525–51.

Humphries, M. (2012) 'Valentinian III and the City of Rome (425–55): Patronage, Politics, Power', in L. Grig and G. Kelly (eds) *Two Romes: Rome and Constantinople in Late Antiquity*, Oxford, 161–82.

Janniard, S. (2006) 'La résistance d'Aquilée dans l'antiquité tardive, entre modèle littéraire et réalité (IIIe–Ve siècle)', in M. Ghilardi, C.-J. Goddard and P. Porena (eds) *Les cités de l'Italie tardo-antique (IVe–VIe siècle)*, Rome, 75–89.

Jones, A. M. H. (1954) 'The Date and Value of the Verona List', *JRS* 44: 21–9.

Jones, A. M. H. (1964) *The Later Roman Empire, 284–602: a Social, Economic and Administrative Survey*, 3 vols, Oxford.

Kähler, H. (1964) *Das fünfsäulendenkmal für die Tetrarchen auf dem Forum Romanum*, Cologne.

Kalas, G. (2015) *The Restoration of the Roman Forum in Late Antiquity: Transforming Public Space*, Austin, TX.

Kolb, F. (2004) 'Praesens Deus: Kaiser und Gott unter der Tetrarchie', in A. Demandt, A. Goltz and H. Schlange-Schöningen (eds) *Diokletian und die Tetrarchie*, Berlin, 27–36.

König, I. (1997) 'Die Postumus-Inschrift aus Augsburg', *Historia* 46: 341–54.

Kuhoff, W. (2001) *Diokletian und die Epoche der Tetrarchie*, Frankfurt am Main.

Kulikowski, M. (2000) 'The "Notitia Dignitatum" as a Historical Source', *Historia* 49: 358–77.

Lo Cascio, E. (1999) 'Canon frumentarius, suarius, vinarius: stato e privati nell'approvvigionamento dell'Vrbs', in W. V. Harris (ed.) *The Transformations of Vrbs Roma in Late Antiquity*, JRA Suppl. 33, Portsmouth, RI, 163–82.

L'Orange, H. P. (1938) 'Ein tetrarchisches Ehrendenkmal auf dem Forum Romanum', *MDAI(R)* 53: 1–34.

Marazzi, F. (1998) 'The Destinies of the Late Antique Italies: Politico-economic Developments of the Sixth Century', in R. Hodges and W. Bowden (eds) *The Sixth Century: Production, Distribution and Demand*, Leiden, 119–60.

Marotta, V. (2016a) 'Onnipresenza dell'imperatore e ubiquità dell'*Urbs*', in V. Marotta (ed.) *Esercizio e trasmissione del potere imperiale (secoli I–IV d.C.)*, Turin, 99–122.

Marotta, V. (2016b) 'Gli dèi governano il mondo: un conflitto ideologico tra III e IV secolo', in V. Marotta (ed.) *Esercizio e trasmissione del potere imperiale (secoli I–IV d.C.)*, Turin, 139–78.

Mazzarino, S. (1980a) 'Sociologia del mondo etrusco e problemi della tarda etruscità', in S. Mazzarino *Il basso impero: antico, tardoantico ed èra costantiniana*, vol. 2, Bari, 258–94.

Mazzarino, S. (1980b) 'Per una storia delle "Venezie" da Catullo al Basso impero', in S. Mazzarino *Il basso impero: antico, tardoantico ed èra costantiniana*, vol. 2, Bari, 214–57.

Mecella, L. (2019) '*Virtus Illyrici*: alle origini di un'identità controversa', in T. Gnoli and V. Neri (eds) *Le identità regionali nell'impero tardoantico*, Milan, 247–80.

Mecella, L. (2021) 'Milano e l'anarchia militare', in G. Albini and L. Mecella (eds) *Un ponte tra il Mediterraneo e il Nord Europa: la Lombardia nel primo Millenio*, Milan, 59–93.

Millar, F. (1986) 'Italy and the Roman Empire: Augustus to Constantine', *Phoenix* 40: 295–318.

Nixon, C. E. W. and B. Saylor Rodgers (eds) (1994) *In Praise of Later Roman Emperors: the Panegyrici Latini*, introd., trans. and historical commentary with the Latin text of R. A. B. Mynors, Berkeley.

Polley, A. R. (2003) 'The Date of Herodian's History', *AC* 72: 203–8.

Porena, P. (2003) *Le origini della prefettura del pretorio tardoantica*, Rome.

Porena, P. (2004) 'La Liguria nell'Italia provincializzata', in R. C. De Marinis and G. Spadea (eds) *I Liguri: un antico popolo europeo tra Alpi e Mediterraneo*, Milan, 541–5.

Porena, P. (2006a) 'Sulla genesi degli spazi amministrativi dell'Italia tardoantica', in L. Labruna, M. P. Baccari and C. Cascione (eds) *Cinquanta anni della Corte Costituzionale della Repubblica italiana*, vol. 1.2, *Tradizione romanistica e Costituzione*, Naples, 1315–76.

Porena, P. (2006b) 'L'Italia prima di Ponte Milvio e la carriera di "Caecilianus"', *Epigraphica* 68: 117–54.

Porena, P. (2006c) 'Riflessioni sulla provincializzazione dell'Italia romana', in M. Ghilardi, C.-J. Goddard and P. Porena (eds) *Les cités de l'Italie Tardo-antique (IVe–VIe siècle)*, Rome, 9–21.

Porena, P. (2013) 'La riorganizzazione amministrativa dell'Italia: Costantino, Roma, il Senato e gli equilibri dell'Italia romana', in A. Melloni et al. (eds) *Costantino I: Enciclopedia costantiniana sulla figura e l'immagine dell'imperatore del cosiddetto Editto di Milano 313–2013*, vol. 1, Rome, 329–49.

Porena, P. (2018) 'L'amministrazione palatina di Diocleziano e dei tetrarchi: *comitatus, consilium, consistorium*', in W. Eck and S. Puliatti (eds) *Diocleziano: la frontiera giuridica dell'impero*, Pavia, 63–110.

Rees, R. (2004) *Diocletian and the Tetrarchy*, Edinburgh.

Roberto, U. (2013) 'Aquileia tra Massenzio e Costantino: l'assedio della tarda estate 312', *Antichità Alto-adriatiche* 76: 129–43.

Roberto, U. (2014) *Diocleziano*, Rome.

Roberto, U. (2018) '*L'identità tetrarchica di Milano e l'Italia tardoantica*', in R. Passarella (ed.) *La chiesa di Milano prima di Ambrogio*, Milan, 25–53.

Roberto, U. (2019) '*Romanis suis*: i tetrarchi, la *libertas* dei Romani e l'iscrizione dedicatoria delle Terme di Diocleziano', in *Storici e storia da Costantino a Teodosio*, Bologna, 119–39.

Sannazaro, M. (2016) 'Milano e i Costantinidi', in O. Brandt and V. Fiocchi Nicolai (eds) *Costantino e i Costantinidi: l'innovazione costantiniana, le sue radici e i suoi sviluppi. Acta XVI congressus internationalis archaeologiae christianae, Romae 22–28.9.2013*, Vatican City, 405–30.

Savino, E. (2005) *Campania tardoantica (284–604 d.C.)*, Bari.
Sidebottom, H. (1997) 'The Date of the Composition of Herodian's History', *AC* 66: 271–6.
Simshäuser, W. (1980) 'Untersuchungen zur Entstehung der Provinzialverfassung Italiens', *ANRW* 2.2.13, Berlin, 401–52.
Sinnigen, W. G. (1959) 'The *Vicarius Urbis Romae* and the Urban Prefecture', *Historia* 8: 97–112.
Stern, H. (1954) 'Remarks on the *adoratio* under Diocletian', *JWI* 17: 184–9.
Tantillo, I. (2014) 'I cerimoniali di corte in età tardoromana (284–395 d.C.)', in *Le corti nell'alto Medioevo*, Spoleto, 543–84.
Vannesse, M. (2010) *La défense de l'Occident romain pendant l'Antiquité tardive: recherches géostratégiques sur l'Italie de 284 à 410 ap. J.-C.*, Brussels.
Whittaker, C. R. (1969) *Herodian: History of the Empire*, vol. 1, *Books I–IV*, Cambridge, MA.
Zecchini, G. (2011) 'Dall'imperium daciscum alla Gothia: il ruolo di Costantino nell'evoluzione di un tema politico e storiografico', in G. Zecchini (ed.) *Ricerche di storiografia latina tardoantica*, vol. 2, *Dall'Historia Augusta a Paolo Diacono*, Rome, 95–108.
Zimmermann, M. (1999) *Kaiser und Ereignis: Studien zum Geschichtswerk Herodians*, Munich.
Zuckerman, C. (2002) 'Sur la liste de Vérone et la province de Grande Arménie, la division de l'Empire et la date de la création des diocèses', in *Mélanges Gilbert Dagron, Travaux et Mémoires* 14, Paris, 617–37.

2

NEW PATHS TO POWER: THE BIPARTITE DIVISION OF ITALY AND ITS REALIGNMENT OF SOCIETY AND ECONOMY IN THE FOURTH CENTURY

Noel Lenski

The Administrative Reorganisation of Italy under the Tetrarchs and Constantine

FROM THE MIDDLE REPUBLIC, Rome had treated Italy differently from its *provinciae*.[1] This became especially evident in 167 BC when Italic land was proclaimed tax free, which gave it an economic edge that made it especially desirable for estate holders down to the late third century AD. Augustus maintained this privileged status even as he divided Italy into eleven districts (*regiones*) for purposes of administration. Trajan then further cemented the link between elite landholders and the Italian peninsula by requiring all senators, regardless of their homeland, to invest a defined quota of their net wealth in Italy. Nevertheless, like all territories of the empire, Italy manifested problems of territorial administration that demanded more central coordination than Augustus had created. Already in the second century, Hadrian is known to have assigned four *consulares* to hear judicial cases stretching across jurisdictions, and Marcus Aurelius regularised these in the form of four transregional *iuridici*.[2] Writing in the early third century, Cassius Dio would portray Agrippa in his fictional exhortation to Augustus as having recommended Italy be broken into districts to be ruled by governors, a reality Caracalla had already begun to enact by appointing occasional senatorial *correctores* to resolve problems with individual jurisdictions.[3] After defeating Tetricus in 274, Aurelian is said to have appointed this former rival as *corrector Lucaniae* (or perhaps *corrector totius Italiae*), and by c.279, Probus was appointing two *correctores Italiae*, one for territory north of the Po River and the other for all territories to its south. Probus may also have introduced more regularity to the system of extracting payments for supplying the army and city of Rome when the emperor or his armies

---

[1] The first part of this study is heavily influenced by the outstanding study of Porena 2013; compare Chastagnol 1963; Thomsen 1967, 196–260; Giardina 1986; 1997, 264–306; Ausbüttel 1988.
[2] Eck 1979, 247–66; compare Millar 1986.
[3] Cass. Dio 52.22.1–2 with Giardina 1997, 274–5; Porena 2013, 330.

were present.⁴ By the 280s, then, Rome's emperors had inched Italy closer and closer to provincialisation without pushing it over the edge.

Diocletian took the final step when he imposed regular taxes on Italy and divided it into twelve provinces, probably in c.292/3, in conjunction with his expansion of the imperial college. This is most plainly attested in Aurelius Victor:

> And ultimately the massive ill of tribute was imposed on part of Italy. For although all [of Italy] used to operate on the same payment scheme (*functio*), which was moderate, by which the army and emperor, who were present there a great deal of the time, could be supplied, a new law for tax payments (*pensiones*) was introduced. Which meant a system tolerable in its modesty from those days proceeded to become disastrous in these times.⁵

Italy was thus folded into the system of taxpaying territories. At the same time, it was divided into multiple provinces as part of a larger process of splitting existing provinces which resulted in a doubling of their total from c.50 to c.100 empire wide. Around the same time these new, smaller provinces were grouped into twelve greater administrative districts termed dioceses, each placed under the control of a *vicarius* (*agentes vices praefectorum praetorio*).⁶ Among these was Italiciana, a diocese which was considerably larger than the original Augustan territory of Italia, for it included the Alpine and Transalpine territories of Raetia and Alpes Cottiae as well as the islands of Sicilia, Sardinia and Corsica.

The new peninsular provinces were not fully coterminous with the old Augustan districts. This we learn from the only extant list of them from the immediate post-Diocletianic period, the Verona List (*Laterculus Veronensis*; Table 2.1), datable to c.314.⁷ Although its catalogue of Italian provinces is lacunose and marred by error, it can be reasonably reconstructed using independent testimony to offer a clear picture of the system established by Diocletian c.293. Building on arguments first advanced by Mommsen, Pierfranceso Porena has shown how the list was originally grouped to take account first of the relative rank of each province's governor (senatorial *correctores* coming before equestrian *praesides*) and second its inclusion or not in the original list of Augustan *regiones* (with new additions falling later).

---

⁴ Aurelian and Tetricus: SHA, *Aurel.* 39.1: *corrector Lucaniae*; compare Aur. Vict. *Caes.* 35.5; Eutr. 13.2; *Epit.* 35.7; see also SHA, *Tyr. Trig.* 24.5: *corrector totius Italiae*. Probus: Porena 2013, 331. See more on this crucial period at Porena 2006b.
⁵ Aur. Vict. *Caes.* 39.30–2. On the division into provinces, see Lactant. *De mort. pers.* 7.4 with Barnes 1982, 209–25; Porena 2013, 332–5; Roberto 2014, 135–6.
⁶ Zuckerman 2002 argued for the introduction of dioceses in 314, but a recently published fragment of Diocletian's currency edict already mentions them in 301, an indication that the traditional dating of c.293 should be preserved, Chaniotis and Fujii 2015. See especially Porena 2003, 152–86. See also Salzman 2021, 51–6.
⁷ Porena 2013, 333–4; compare Barnes 1982, 201–8; Zuckerman 2002.

Table 2.1 Restoration of *Laterculus Veronensis* 10, after Porena 2013, 334, tab. 3.

PROVINCE	GOVERNED BY (c.314)
Dioecesis Italiciana habet provincias numero XI‹I›	
[Campaniam]	Senatorial *corrector* (hosted in Rome, a unique privilege)
[Aemiliam et Liguriam]	Senatorial *corrector* (hosted in Milan, seat of the *vicarius Italiae*)
‹V›e[ne]tiam et Histriam	Senatorial *corrector*
Flaminiam et Picenum	Senatorial/Equestrian *corrector*
Tusciam et Umbr‹i›am	Senatorial *corrector*
Apuliam et Calabriam	Equestrian *corrector*
L‹u›caniam [et Bruttios]	Equestrian *corrector*
[Siciliam]	Senatorial *corrector* (added to Italia)
[Sardiniam]	*Praeses equestris* (added to Italia)
Corsicam	*Praeses equestris* (added to Italia)
Alpes Cotias	*Praeses equestris* (added to Italia)
Raetia[m]	*Praeses equestris* (added to Italia)

How precisely Maxentius exploited this new system after gaining control of Rome and Cisalpine Italy in October 306 we can no longer say. At a minimum, he is unlikely to have taken control of all of Diocletian's twelve provinces, for Raetia probably remained in Constantine's hands down to the eve of the Milvian Bridge in 312. Maxentius did, however, succeed in demonstrating how resilient Italy could be as an administrative and defensive unit, for he was able to defeat one Tetrarch (Severus), turn back another from an attack that reached Rome's walls (Galerius), and put a halt to a rebellion in Africa under the usurper Domitius Alexander.

It was with the resilience of Diocletian's new Italiciana in mind that Constantine set about further reorganising the diocese after defeating Maxentius in October of 312. His object was surely simultaneously to reduce the threat posed by a peninsular Italy that was, by all accounts, overly militarised without compromising the defensive structures put in place in northern Italy to protect it from foreign threats; to protect the food supply of the politically important yet perennially volatile Roman capital; and to maintain good relations with a senatorial aristocracy, clustered thickly in southern Italy, which had demonstrated discontent with the growing neglect it had received since the mid-third century. In a word, in the aftermath of Maxentius, Constantine needed to fortify the system against another revolt by the SPQR while continuing to profit from the wealth and political resources of Italy. He accomplished this using two primary strategies: first he demilitarised the peninsular part of Italy, and second he split it from northern Italy as an administrative unit.

As to the first, Constantine almost entirely declawed peninsular Italy by eliminating or transferring away its once sizeable garrison forces of c.13,000 soldiers:[8]

- He completely removed the ten praetorian cohorts (c.10,000 troops) from their barracks on the Viminal, presumably incorporating them into his mobile forces.
- He also removed Maxentius' special horse guard, the *equites singulares* (c.1,000), from their barracks at the Lateran.
- He removed the *Legio II Parthica* (c.2,000), stationed at the Castra Albana south of Rome, and eventually transferred it to Cefa in Mesopotamia (*Not. Dign. or.* 36.30).
- This left only c. 13,000 quasi-military personnel in Rome:
  - Seven cohorts of fire fighters (*vigiles*: c.7,000) – under the *praefectus vigilum*, answerable to the *praefectus urbi Romae* (*PVR*)
  - Three cohorts of police (*urbaniciani*: c.6,000) – under the *tribunus Fori Suarii*, answerable to the *PVR*.

Constantine's division of peninsular from northern Italy was very much part of the larger sweep of administrative reforms he introduced in the years between 312 and 337. Diocletian and the Tetrarchs had continued to treat praetorian prefects (*PPOs*) as combined military and civilian officers, but Constantine began systematically splitting these two roles, leaving *PPOs* only juridical and fiscal authority while turning over imperial guard duties to the new corps of *scholae palatinae* – under the *magister officiorum* – and military command to a new class of military officers (*magistri militum*). In so doing, Constantine diminished the potential threat posed by *PPOs* who, as recently as Maxentius, had been charged with the conduct of major military expeditions.[9]

For purposes of Italian administration, Constantine kept the single diocese of Italiciana initiated by the Tetrarchs but also split it into the two administrative spheres: the *Regio Annonaria* (Italia Annonaria), north of the Arno and Esino rivers, and *Regio Suburbicaria* (Italia Suburbicaria) to their south.[10] This made the northern ridge of the Apennines the effective dividing line between these two new districts, a line that some contemporary Italians would argue continues to divide the modern nation state. To manage the two districts, Constantine retained the tetrarchic *vicarius praefectorum praetorio per Italiam* (*vicarius Italiae*), who had already focused on the northern (frontier) portion of Italiciana but whose authority was now confined within the sphere of the *Regio Annonaria*. Constantine then transformed the old vice prefect of the Praetorian Guards in Rome (*agens vices praefectorum praetorio*) into a strictly civilian official, the *vicarius urbis Romae*, very much in the manner of other diocesan vicars. This resulted in the following bipartite scheme:

---

[8] Porena 2013, 336–8.
[9] See Aur. Vict. *Caes.* 40.18; Zos. 2.14.2–4, with *PLRE* 1, 'C. Ceionius Rufius Volusianus 4', 976–8; and *Pan. Lat.* 12(9).8.1–3; 4(10).25.4–7, with *PLRE* 1, 'Ruricius Pompeianus 8', 713. For Constantine's transformation of the praetorian prefecture, see Porena 2003. For the *scholae palatinae*, see Frank 1969. For an overview of these processes, see Kelly 2012.
[10] The legal sources tend to distinguish between, on the one hand, *Italia* or *Italiae regiones* (Annonaria), and on the other, *regiones urbicariae* (Suburbicaria); see Giardina 1997, 272–4.

- *Vicarius Italiae (Annonariae)* – manages Aemilia et Liguria, Venetia et Istria, Raetiae, Alpes Cottiae;
- *Vicarius Romae (Italiae Suburbicariae)* – manages Campania, Tuscia et Umbria, Flaminia et Picenum, Apulia et Calabria, Lucania et Brutii, Sicilia, Sardinia, Corsica.

The former is attested in operation already under Maxentius in the person of Caecilianus, *vic(arius) praef(ecti) per Ital(iam)* and first confirmed under Constantine in April 318 in the person of (Iunius?) Bassus, *vicarius italiae*.[11] The latter certainly appears in 318, when the *Chronicon Calendar of 354* reports that Iulius Cassius served in the stead of the *PVR* (*vice illius*) Septimius Bassus while Bassus was on embassy to the emperor; and the equestrian C. Caelius Saturninus may have held the post under the title *vicarius praeff(ectorum) praetorio in urbe Roma* as soon as 314.[12] *Italiciana* had thus become unique in the diocesan system as the only diocese to host two *vicarii*.

Porena has been able to catalogue detailed enough *fasti* of the earliest holders of these two offices to trace a history of the administrative development of Italiciana which can be mapped on to broader efforts by Constantine to establish lasting administrative structures as he gradually assumed control of the empire. Initially, Constantine instituted a tripartite system, probably during his stay in Rome following the Milvian Bridge in late 312 and early 313:

- The *PVR*, an officer established under Augustus with his powers increased by Septimius Severus,[13] witnessed a further increase in his authority over the *urbs Roma*: he could convoke the senate, set its agenda, offer court judgments *vice sacra* (in the emperor's stead), manage public building, oversee the distribution of public provisions (through the *tribunus Fori Suarii*, *rationalis vinorum* and *praefectus annonae*), and supervise policing within the walls of Rome and for up to 100 miles around it.[14]
- The *vicarius urbis Romae* (*VVR*) was responsible for overseeing the requisitioning, transport and warehousing of provisions from across Italia Suburbicaria for the *urbs Roma*.
- The *vicarius Italiae* was charged with provisioning imperial armies and administrators within the *Regio Annonaria* and overseeing transport when praesental or comitatensian armies passed through.

Constantine's brief flirtation with efforts to appoint his brother-in-law Bassianus as Caesar to rule over Italy in 315 would have altered this scheme, but the plan provoked conflict with Licinius and resulted in Bassianus' execution and the civil war that ended

---

[11] For Caecilianus, see *CIL* 11.831 = *ILS* 1218 with Porena 2006a. For Iunius Bassus, see *CTh* 9.8.1 with Porena 2012, 301–2. Porena 2014 makes a strong case that already in May 315 Flavius Ablabius is attested as *vicarius Italiae* at *CTh* 11.21.1.

[12] Iulius Cassius: *Chron. 354* s.a. 318 (*MGH AA* 9.67). Caelius Saturninus: *CIL* 6.1704 = *ILS* 1214 with Porena 2013, 336.

[13] *Dig.* 1.12.1; *Collatio legum Mosaicarum et Romanarum* 14.3.2; compare Peachin 1996, 189–91.

[14] Chastagnol 1960, 254–388 remains essential for its detailed explication of these duties.

in Constantine's takeover of Illyricum in 316.[15] A longer-lasting experiment may have followed Constantine's defeat of Licinius and assumption of sole rule in 324. Porena argues that the absence of attested *vicarii urbis Romae* and *Italiae* in the years between 326 and 337 may stem from an effort by Constantine to establish Italia as one of five new regional praetorian prefectures, which also included Galliae, Africa, Illyricum and Oriens.[16] Whether or not this theory stands the test of time, the system of Italian administration reverted to the tripartite scheme outlined above shortly after Constantine's death, for *vicarii urbis Romae* appear once again beginning in 340(?) with Iunius Tertullus, and *vicarii Italiae* in 341 with Crepereius Madalianus.[17] Both would have operated under the combined prefecture of *Italia Illyricum et Africa*, which was based in Sirmium and was one of four (sometimes three) regional prefectures that prevailed down to the reign of Theodosius I. Indeed, the *vicariatus Italiae* continues to be attested down to the early fifth century, when the *PPO Italiae Illyrici et Africae* was relocated from Sirmium to Ravenna, and even into the sixth, when it was moved to Genoa under the Byzantine exarchate; and both the *praefectus urbis Romae* and the *vicarius urbis Romae* also continue to be attested down to the end of the sixth century.[18] Meanwhile, fourth-century Italy witnessed further subdivision of its provinces, such that the Verona List's twelve grew to number seventeen by the time of the final redaction of the western *Notitia dignitatum* c.425.[19]

Between 293 and 313, then, Italy underwent a series of transformations along five primary trajectories. First, it was divided into provinces – twelve in number as attested in the Verona List of 314, growing to seventeen by the early fifth century. Second, like all provincial territory, it was taxed under the new *capitatio-iugatio* system. Third, it was incorporated into the diocesan system under the title *Italiciana*, a geographic unit that stretched from Calabria in the south to the Danube in the north and included the main Mediterranean islands of Sicily, Sardinia and Corsica – a massive territorial unit with an equally massive array of microclimates, agricultural regimes and security needs. Fourth, beginning under Constantine the peninsular part of Italiciana was split from the north to form the separate administrative units of Italia Suburbicaria and Italia Annonaria (Figure 2.1) – both part of the same diocese, but each with its own vicar, the former of whom was tasked with overseeing the provisioning of the capital, the latter with integrating northern Italy into the imperial and frontier defensive system. And fifth, the peninsular part of Italy was evacuated of imperial military forces, even while the north was reinforced against the frontier threats that had been growing since the mid-third century.

---

[15] *Origo Const.* 14, with Porena 2013, 335.
[16] Porena 2013, 340–1.
[17] *PLRE* 1, 'Iunius Tertullus 9', 884; *Chron. 354* s.a. 340 (*MGH AA* 9.68). *PLRE* 1, 'Lucius Crepereius Madalianus', 530; *CTh* 16.10.2 (a. 341).
[18] Diehl 1959, 161–2; Cosentino 2008, 128–9.
[19] *Not. Dig. occ.* 2.11–27: Venetia (et Histria – see *Not. Dig. occ.* 1.53), Aemilia, Liguria, Flaminia et Picenum Annonarium, Tuscia et Umbria, Picenum Suburbicarium, Campania, Sicilia, Apulia et Calabria, Lucania et Britii, Alpes Cottiae, Raetia Prima, Raetia Secunda, Samnium, Valeria, Sardinia, Corsica. On the date of the western *Not. Dig.*, see Neira Faleiro 2005, 41–3.

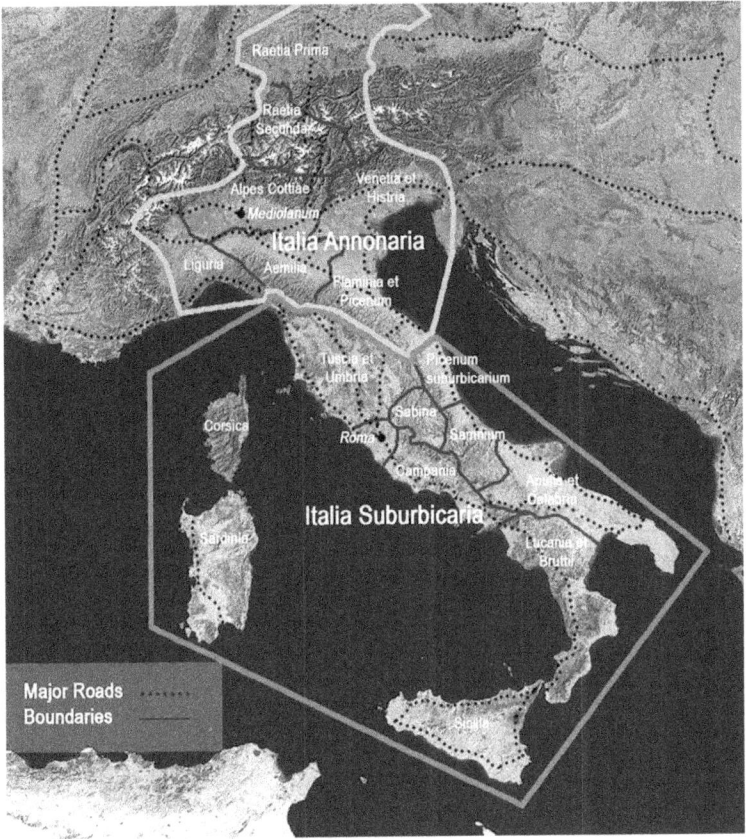

Figure 2.1 Schematic diagram of the *dioecesis Italiciana* in the early fifth century, with provincial boundaries and major roads (© Noel Lenski).

The Emperors' Presence in Italy in the Fourth Century

The provincialisation of Italy continued a process of normalising the region within the network of imperial territories that had been underway since the early second century, and its division into two halves followed patterns that came into focus in the third. But it is important to remember that both provincialisation and division were carried out in a fashion that reflected the topographic contours of the region. Although Cisalpine Italy had been united politically since the reign of Augustus, it always represented two topological units, with the north centred around the watershed of the Po valley and the south governed by the northern ridge of the Apennines. By acknowledging and reinforcing this distinction administratively, Constantine offered a road plan that led to the divergent political and historical development of Annonaria and Suburbicaria.

This happened first by further cementing the separate flow of traffic and communication across the two halves. The major roads of Suburbicaria were and always had been oriented along a north-west–south-east axis:

- The Via Appia: the city's oldest road, from Rome south through Campania and onward to Brundisium (Brindisi);
- The Via Aurelia: from Rome north-west along the Tyrrhenian coast;
- The Via Cassia: from Rome north through Umbria and Tuscia to Florentia (Florence) and Pisae (Pisa) on the Tyrrhenian Sea;
- The Via Flaminia: from Rome north-east, meeting the Adriatic at Fanum Fortunae (Fano) and Ariminum (Rimini).

Meanwhile, those of Annonaria were generally oriented east–west:

- The Via Postumia: across northern Italy from Aquileia to Genua (Genoa);
- The Via Iulia Augusta: from Genua west along the Mediterranean coast to Arelate (Arles);
- The Via Helvetica: from Placentia (Piacenza) through Augusta Praetoria (Aosta) and over the Alps to Vienna (Vienne) along the Rhône.

At the same time, the Via Claudia Augusta, from Mutina (Modena) north over the Reschen Pass to Augusta Vindelicorum (Augsburg) along the Danube frontier serves as a reminder that Annonaria was and always remained part of the empire's frontier defences. As such, northern Raetia – and thus the northern edge of Annonaria – was further interlinked with the empire's east–west networks north of the Alps along the Danube military road.

Constantine's administrative bifurcation of Italy further cemented these patterns of mobility. It took advantage of Annonaria's prevailing east–west flow of movement by incorporating the region more fully into the imperial traffic and supply system. At the same time, it exploited Suburbicaria's predominantly north-west–south-east network in order to allow peninsular Italy to thrive as an autonomous, but also anomalous unit. Recent work on Roman imperial networking and connectivity has stressed the fact that Rome was, by virtue of the topography and hodology of the Mediterranean basin, more closely networked for purposes of trade and transport with southern Italy, Sicily, Sardinia, Corsica and Africa Proconsularis than northern Italy. Constantine's new administrative division simply canonised this reality imposed by the region's geography of travel and transport.[20]

These roadways had, of course, been established long before the administrative reorganisation of Italy. But that reorganisation created systemic structures which reinforced and intensified the traffic patterns they governed so that the fourth century witnessed a wholesale reorientation of imperial traffic in and through Italy. This can be seen in graphic terms when one plots the number of months in which an emperor spent time in Italia Annonaria and Suburbicaria between 306 and 395. This is a period for which we have particularly robust information pertinent to imperial

---

[20] See Scheidel 2014, esp. 21: 'the case of Britain serves to illustrate the relative isolation of the Po valley, from which it was as expensive to reach Rome as from the British coast or (perhaps more realistically) from Middle Egypt'.

itineraries thanks to the subscriptions of the *Theodosian Code*.[21] At the most schematic level (Figure 2.2) it can be shown that, during this eighty-nine-year stretch, emperors were present in Annonaria during 3.6 times as many months as in Suburbicaria (347:97). If one limits the time horizon to the years following the death of Maxentius (October 312), who was the only emperor to take up permanent residence in Rome in the fourth century, that figure quadruples to 14.1 (324:23).

One can also visualise the data over a timescale (Figure 2.3), which offers a graphic representation of the manner in which imperial visits and residences in Annonaria are scattered with relative consistency across the century, while those to Suburbicaria (if we exclude the reign of Maxentius) tend to fall within the reigns of specific long-ruling emperors (Constantine I, Constantius II, Theodosius I) who managed the empire as supreme rulers, preferring not to share power with equal peers.

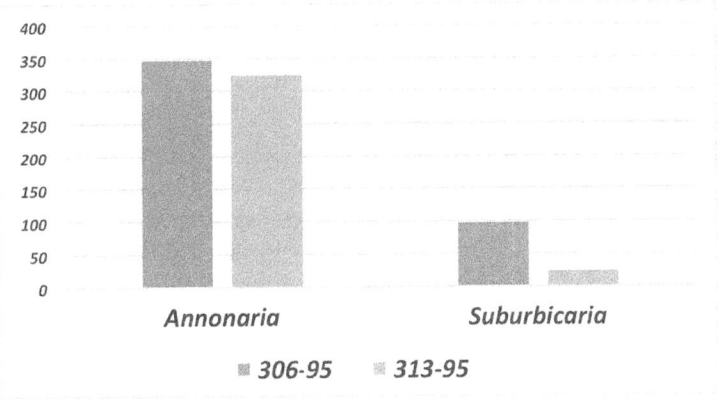

Figure 2.2 Total number of months when an emperor is present in Italy.

---

[21] The tables that follow were produced from a dataset derived primarily from Seeck 1919, with some supplements and corrections from Barnes 1982, 47–84; 1993, 218–28; and Schmidt-Hofner 2008b. To these it adds Julian's journey through Raetia in spring 361 (attested at Amm. Marc. 21.8.2–9.2 but not catalogued in Seeck) and those which can be inferred, (1) when Constantine II travelled from Naissus back to Trier after his promotion to Augustus in 337; (2) when Valentinian I travelled from Trier to Carnuntum in April 375. It follows McLynn 1994, 122 in assuming Valentinian II moved to Milan in early 381, even if he is first attested there in the laws in March 384 (*CTh* 13.1.12). It catalogues itineraries only of Augusti, not those of Caesares or Junior Augusti who did not have their own court (Gratian 367–75, Honorius 393–5). It includes the movements of usurping Augusti (but not Maximian after his return to power in 307–10). For the movements of Magnentius it follows Bastien 1983, 11–16. The temporal resolution is monthly, so that if an emperor is known to have spent any day during a month in a region, that month is counted as an integer. If more than one Augustus spent time in Italy simultaneously, each is counted – which means, for example, that 306 witnessed 24 months of imperial presence in Italy.

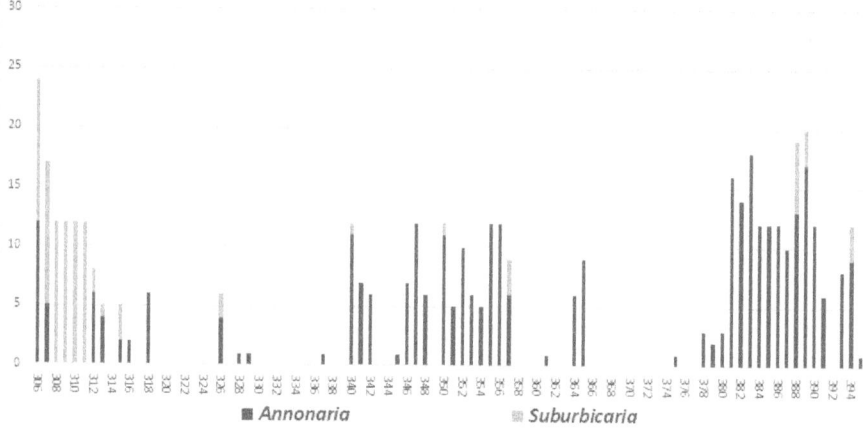

Figure 2.3 Total number of months when an emperor is present in Italy by year (months when more than one emperor is present in Italy are double counted)

Italia Annonaria was thus a regular part of the emperor's itinerary, even if Suburbicaria only rarely enjoyed imperial stays. This too was part of a trend that had increased over the imperial centuries. Thus the Severan emperors spent twenty-two of the forty-two years between 193 and 235 (52 per cent) in Rome, and even when absent they took up the practice of appointing deputies whom they left behind with the authority to offer judgment 'in the place of the emperor' (*vice sacra*).[22] In the mid-third century, when the imperial court became much more itinerant – primarily to deal with frontier crises and usurpations – emperors nonetheless engaged in what Caillan Davenport has called a 'balancing act', returning to Rome regularly to celebrate victories, manage state affairs and secure their hold on power:[23]

- Severus Alexander was in Rome 222–31, then headed east to fight the Persians, but returned to Rome in 233 to celebrate a triumph before heading to the northern frontier in 234.
- Pupienus and Balbinus were proclaimed in Rome in 238 and remained there the brief four months until both were killed by the Praetorians.
- Gordian III resided in Rome 238–42 while frontier wars were managed by his senatorial legate Tullius Menophilus, then headed to the East in 243 and died there in 244.
- Philip returned to Rome from the East in 244, headed north against the Carpi that same year, but returned in 247–8 to triumph, celebrate Rome's 1,000th anniversary, and probably also elevate his son Philip II to the throne.

[22] See Peachin 1996, 158–66.
[23] Davenport 2017, 27–34, with the details in the following list extracted from Halfmann 1986; Kienast et al. 2017.

- Decius was proclaimed in Pannonia in 249 but immediately came to Rome to shore up his power before heading north in 250 to fight the Goths, by whom he was killed in 251.
- Decius' son Hostilian remained in Rome in 250, was elevated to Augustus there, and remained until his death later that year.
- Valerian was proclaimed in Raetia or Noricum but returned to Rome in 253 and proclaimed his son Gallienus emperor that autumn. One or both then returned to Rome in 257 before Valerian headed east, never to return.
- Gallienus resided in Rome for most of 260–5 (apart from a brief visit to Greece), holding his decennalia there in 262.
- Claudius Gothicus probably spent the winter of 268/9 in Rome.
- Aurelian was proclaimed at Sirmium in 270 but immediately travelled to Rome and spent the winter there; he wintered in Rome once again in 271/2, when he began construction of the walls; he triumphed over Zenobia in Rome in 273, and again over Tetricus in Rome in 274.
- Tacitus was called to the throne from Campania and proclaimed by the senate in Rome in 275.[24]
- Probus visited Rome in 281 to triumph over the Germans and Blemmyes.
- Carinus is attested in Rome in 284, when he dedicated a bridge near Ostia and where his son Nigrinianus died.

Thus in the sixty-two years between 222 and 284, fourteen emperors visited Rome on at least twenty-six discreet occasions and spent parts of at least thirty-four years in the city.

This pattern of regular visits diminished greatly under the Tetrarchs, who largely avoided the capital. Diocletian first visited Rome in 303 to celebrate his twentieth year in power, and the unruliness of the city's inhabitants led him to leave the city hastily in midwinter and inaugurate his consulship for 304 in Ravenna.[25] He had been joined in Rome by Maximian, whose sphere of territorial responsibility included Italy, but who himself probably first visited Rome in 298 or 299, a decade and a half after coming to power.[26] After being forced to retire in 305, he chose to live in Campania rather than Rome, but his family appears to have resided in the city. It was there that his son Maxentius took advantage of the Romans' discontent with this neglect to secure his proclamation as emperor in October 306. In so doing, he was clearly tapping a neglected vein of political power that he continued to mine for the rest of his reign by abiding in Rome, lavishing the city with buildings, naming his son 'Romulus', and styling himself the CONSERVATOR VRBIS SVAE on coins and in inscriptions.[27] Rome had thus lost the drawing power it held in the third century but remained a potential source of political power for emperors into the fourth.

---

[24] Davenport 2014.
[25] Lactant. *De mort. pers.* 17.1–3; Barnes 1982, 56. See also Chapter 1 in this volume.
[26] *Pan. Lat.* 7(6).8.7, with Nixon and Saylor Rodgers 1994, 201; Davenport 2017, 34.
[27] Leppin and Ziemssen 2007.

This situation changed radically with Constantine's restructuring of Italy. Although Constantine visited the city twice in the first decade of his rule, imperial visits plummeted in the years to come, so that, in the eighty-three years between Maxentius' removal and the death of Theodosius I (312–95), Rome witnessed the presence of emperors – including usurpers – only nine discrete times and probably for a total of not more than seventeen months:[28]

- October 312–January 313: Constantine I, to triumph in the aftermath of defeating Maxentius;
- July 315–September 315: Constantine I, to celebrate his decennalia;
- July 326–August 326: Constantine I, to celebrate his vicennalia;
- Summer(?) 340: Constans (perhaps), to celebrate the defeat of Constantine II;[29]
- June 350: Nepotian, proclaimed emperor and executed in Rome;
- May 357: Constantius II, to triumph over Magnentius;
- Mid 388: Valentinian II, to facilitate the overthrow of Magnus Maximus by Theodosius I;
- June–August 389: Theodosius I, to triumph over Magnus Maximus;
- October 394: Theodosius I, to triumph over Eugenius.[30]

All but two of these occasions were ceremonial, meant to celebrate major imperial anniversaries or victories (or both). Apart from the feeble elevation of Nepotian to emperor in Rome in 350, the only real break from this pattern is represented by the period in 388 when, if Zosimus can be believed, Valentinian II was sent to Rome with a fleet by Theodosius, who was engaging Magnus Maximus by land in northern Italy – surely for the logistical purpose of securing Suburbicaria and its African grain supply, and the strategic purpose of surrounding Maximus' forces.[31] Otherwise, on the rare occasions when fourth-century emperors visited the capital, it was for purposes of symbolic communication, above all in the aftermath of civil wars.[32]

The fundamentally ceremonial nature of most of these visits is nowhere clearer than in Ammianus' description of Constantius II's triumphal entry in May 357. Its narration presents the author with a chance to offer an elaborate catalogue of the splendours of Rome, which he then turns upon the emperor himself, deploying their monumentality to diminish the figure whose achievements the event was meant to celebrate. Constantius is depicted as being carted through the city haughty and unwavering, like a human statue, but his efforts to overawe the *populus Romanus* with his stone-cold grandiosity crumble in the face of Rome's marvels, which leave him dumbstruck and

---

[28] For imperial visits to Rome in the fourth century, see Humphries 2003; 2015; Schmidt-Hofner 2012.
[29] Barnes 1993, 225 with 315 n. 47; compare Barnes 1975, 327–8.
[30] For the historicity of this much disputed visit, Cameron 1969, 248–65 remains decisive, *pace* Paschoud 1975; Döpp 1975. Cameron 2011, 121 himself denies a visit in 394 without further explanation or bibliography, most likely because the sources associated with that visit directly contradict his highly tendentious arguments on the battle of the Frigidus.
[31] Zos. 4.45.4 with Paschoud 1971–1986, 2.2.440–2; compare McLynn 1994, 292–4.
[32] The situation changed in the fifth century, and particularly after the death of Valentinian III, when emperors were regularly present in Rome; see Gillett 2001; McEvoy 2010; 2017; compare Humphries 2007.

humbled.³³ Nor is the critique limited to his demeanour, for Ammianus' overarching concern is with Constantius' presumptuous appropriation of triumphal rituals from a much worthier age:

> He had himself by no means overcome any foreign nation that was stirring up war nor even learned of the defeat of one by the valour of his generals, nor had he added territory to the empire, nor been seen as the leader or among leaders in the midst of perilous dangers; rather, he was making a display of his excessively distended parade, battle standards crusted in gold, and the comeliness of his entourage to a populace luxuriating in tranquillity, which neither expected nor desired ever to see these things or the like.³⁴

Ammianus, who had himself witnessed just such a triumph when Theodosius entered Rome after defeating Magnus Maximus in 389, was foregrounding his disgust at how the emperor was making a charade of what had once been a proud ritual in what had once been a proud city.

For all that Rome could no longer count on the regular presence of the emperor, it continued to host female relatives of the emperor even in the fourth century. Empresses who seem to have inhabited Rome over the long term include Maximian's wife, Eutropia, their daughter Fausta, the wife of Constantine, and her daughter, Theodora, the wife of Constantius I; their daughter Eutropia, Constantine's half-sister, the wife of Virius Nepotianus and mother of Iulius Nepotianus (usurping Augustus in 350);³⁵ Constantine's mother Helena, ex-wife of the Augustus Constantius I; Constantine's half-sister, Anastasia, married to the Roman senator Bassianus, whom Constantine attempted to appoint Caesar c.315; his daughter Helena, married to Julian; another daughter, Constantina, sister of Constantius II and wife of the Caesars Hannibalianus and later Gallus;³⁶ Laeta, the wife and then widow of Gratian; and, of course, Theodosius I's daughter Galla Placidia, half-sister of the Augusti Arcadius and Honorius and the mother of Valentinian III.³⁷ By allowing, perhaps also encouraging, their wives and daughters to establish their abodes in the queen city, the emperors were paying a kind of homage that bolstered their symbolic authority but also, to some degree, their political capital as well.

Just as striking are the many opportunities which the emperors themselves passed over to visit Rome: Valentinian I, who spent a year early in his reign in Annonaria (364/5) and passed through northern Italy one more time (375), and who conducted major investigations of the Rome's leaders and citizens for almost six years (369–75) never once visited the city; his son Gratian, whose reign brought détente and even

---

³³ Amm. Marc. 16.10.1–21; compare *Consularia Constantinopolitana* s.a. 357; *CIL* 6.41332, with analysis at Schmidt-Hofner 2012; Omissi 2018, 163–92.
³⁴ Amm. Marc. 16.10.2, my translation.
³⁵ *PLRE* 1, 'Eutropia 1', 316; 'Fl. Maxima Fausta', 325–6; 'Theodora 1', 895; 'Eutropia 2', 316; compare Barnes 1982, 33–7.
³⁶ *PLRE* 1, 'Fl. Iulia Helena 3', 410–11, with Drijvers 1992, 30–4; *PLRE* 1, 'Anastasia 1', 58; 'Helena 2', 409–10; 'Constantina 2', 222, with Lenski 2016, 399–400.
³⁷ *PLRE* 1, 'Laeta 1', 492; *PLRE* 2, 'Aelia Galla Placidia 4', 888–9.

rapprochement with the senate, spent something like thirty months of his reign in Annonaria (378, 379, 380, 381/2, 382/3), but seems never to have visited;[38] and the three usurpers Magnentius, Magnus Maximus and Eugenius (himself a senator of Rome) appear never to have entered the city during their reigns despite each having taken up defensive positions in northern Italy. Instead, the Roman senate was obliged to communicate with its emperors through embassies, often enlisting the urban prefect to travel to the emperor in hopes of winning his favour(s) from afar, in the manner of any other city of the empire.[39] Then too, emperors were uninterested in being interred in Rome after their death. Following the death of Maxentius, who had a mausoleum constructed on the Via Sacra near the Forum Romanum, no emperor chose to be buried there before Honorius began construction of his mausoleum near Old St Peter's in the early fifth century.[40]

This is hardly the first study in which the emperor's desultory presence in Rome over the course of the fourth century has been documented. It is, however, the first effort to compare this neglect with the relative frequency of visits to Annonaria. The extreme disparity is striking, not only because it reaffirms the ongoing importance of northern Italy as a critical node in the network of imperial connectivity, but also because it sets into stark relief the relative neglect of Rome. Here it should be recalled that every imperial visit to Annonaria could, in theory, have been extended with a journey south to the capital – much as happened throughout the third century and, arguably, even into the early reign of Constantine. Naturally, imperial journeys through Raetia (in the northern reaches of Italiciana) did not obviously entail a journey to Suburbicaria, but the emperors' many stays in Italy south of the Alps – particularly at Milan – could have ended in a visit to Rome with a little over two weeks of travel. The fact that so few did

---

[38] I follow Barnes 2000, 168–9 n. 17 in rejecting a visit in spring 376 posited by Seeck 1919, 248.

[39] Attested in 318, led by the *PVR* Septimius Bassus, to Constantine in Aquileia (*Chron. 354* s.a. 318 (*MGH AA* 9.67) with Chastagnol 1962, 70); in 340, led by the *PVR* Fabius Titianus, probably to congratulate Constans after his victory over Constantine II (*Chron. 354* s.a. 340 (*MGH AA* 9.68) with Chastagnol 1962, 109); in 351, led by Fabius Titianus, to negotiate with Constantius II on behalf of Magnentius (Zos. 2.49.1–2); twice in 352(?), led by Memmius Vitrasius Orfitus, to affirm support of Constantius II after his expulsion of Magnentius from Italy (*CIL* 6.1739–42 with Chastagnol 1962, 142); in 361, led by L. Aurelius Avienius Symmachus and Valerius Maximus to Constantius in the East to declare their allegiance to him against Julian, whom they then met at Naissus on their return journey (Amm. Marc. 21.12.24; compare *CIL* 6.1698= *ILS* 1257; Lib. *Ep.* 923, with Sogno 2006, 3–4); in 369/70, including Q. Aurelius Symmachus, to Valentinian I on the Rhine frontier (Seeck 1883, xlvi–xlvii; Matthews 1975, 32–3; Sogno 2006, 2–21; Humphries 2003, 34–6; Maier 2019, 287–99); in 371, led by Vettius Agorius Praetextatus, to mitigate Valentinian I's treason trials (Amm. Marc. 28.1.24–5; compare *CIL* 6.1777 = *ILS* 1258, with Lizzi Testa 2004, 219–305; Sogno 2006, 4–5); in 382, led by Symmachus, to Gratian in Milan, concerning the Altar of Victory (Symm. *Relat.* 3.1, 20); in 387, led by Symmachus, to Valentinian II to celebrate his consulship (Symm. *Ep.* 3.52, 63); 387/8, led by Symmachus, to deliver a panegyric to Magnus Maximus (Socrates, *Hist. eccl.* 5.14.5–9; compare Symm. *Ep.* 2.30–1 with Matthews 1975, 229–31; Cecconi 2002, 245–7; Humphries 2003, 36–8). These represent only a fraction of what must have been a much larger total; compare *CIL* 6.1698 = *ILS* 1257: (L. Aurelius Avienius Symmachus) 'performed multiple embassies at the behest of the Senate to the divine emperors' (*multis legat[io]nibus | pro amplissimi ordinis desideriis | apud divos principes functo*); *CIL* 6.1777 = *ILS* 1258: (Vettius Agorius Praetextatus) 'seven-times ambassador of the senate' (*legatus amplissimi ordinis septies*).

[40] Johnson 2009, 199–202.

is evidence that the symbolic and political geography of Italy had changed in the aftermath of Diocletian's provincialisation and particularly Constantine's division of Italy. Annonaria was now an integral piece of the imperial itinerary. Suburbicaria was not.

Alterations to the Landscape of Italian Politics

The provincialisation and division of Italy had distinct advantages for emperors. First and foremost, Diocletian's organisation of the region into provinces and imposition of taxes had the obvious benefit of rendering this richly productive territory liable to fiscal obligations. Constantine's bipartite division then created a northern district within the larger diocese that could, of itself, serve as a well-supplied conduit for imperial armies to move east–west across the region either north or south of the Alps. While the movement of large imperial entourages through Italy had formerly demanded extraordinary levies and put considerable strain on local communities,[41] the regularisation of the northern provinces of Italiciana into a single district straddling the Alps allowed armies to pass – with or without the emperor – along well-provisioned routes. It also allowed the richly productive Po valley to be tapped to supply the comparatively poorer northern reaches of Italiciana in Raetia. And it reintroduced military recruiting to Italy, whose supply of legionaries had largely ceased by the second century but revived in the fourth as citizens became eligible for recruitment. Thus, the future Saint Martin, who grew up in Ticinum (Pavia), was forced into the army as the son of a veteran; Symmachus' letters reveal deep concerns over the drain on his labour force caused by imperial levies; and the laws of the *Theodosian Code* make it clear that Italy was by no means immune to recruitment levies.[42]

Emperors also benefited from the division of Italy into two different defensive zones. Northern Italy became highly militarised, so that by the time of the composition of the western *Notitia dignitatum* in the early fifth century (but, in most instances, much earlier), it was outfitted with five arms factories (*fabricae*), at Concordia, Verona, Mantua, Cremona and Ticinum (*Not. Dig. occ.* 9.24–8). Along its northern frontier, Raetia was guarded by its own *dux limitum* (*Not. Dig. occ.* 1.43, 5.139) and had its own imperial treasury, at Augsburg, to supplement the two other treasuries in Annonaria at Milan and Aquileia (*Not. Dig. occ.* 11.27, 28, 30). By the fifth century, the region was also guarded by a *comes Italiae* (*Not. Dig. occ.* 28.1–6). In addition, Annonaria played home to imperial mints at Ticinum, Milan and Aquileia.[43] Suburbicaria, by contrast, had only one arms factory, at Lucca on the northernmost edge of the region (*Not. Dig. occ.* 9.29) and, after the death of Maxentius, one mint at Rome. Annonaria thus became an integral part of the empire's military and fiscal armature, while Suburbicaria became insulated from the military supply and communication network to its north.

Meanwhile the demilitarisation of Suburbicaria and particularly of Rome all but hobbled the city's ability to produce viable challengers to imperial power. The senatorial

---

[41] See Millar 1986, 305.
[42] On recruitment in the high empire, see Millar 1986, 308–9, with references. Sulp. Sev. *Vit. Mart.* 2; Symm. *Ep.* 2.52, 9.10. See also *CTh* 7.13.3–4, 15; 11.16.12, and Jones 1964, 614–17.
[43] Jones 1964, 435–7.

leadership of Italy had, after all, continued to spawn emperors throughout the mid-third century: Ti. Claudius Marinus Pacatianus (248); C. Vibius Trebonianus Gallus (251); and P. Licinius Valerianus (253).[44] Rome was regularly used as the staging ground for the elevation of the emperor's son: Philip II, Gallienus, Hostilian.[45] And the Roman senate itself put forward the Augusti Pupienus and Balbinus (238), Gordian III (238) and Tacitus (275), all senators.[46] Maxentius was thus in many ways continuing a tradition in launching his bid for empire from Rome, a fact not lost on Constantine when he determined to disband the Praetorians and other military units in late 312. From this point down to the radically changed circumstances of the 420s, only one emperor would arise out of Suburbicaria, and his example is indicative of Rome's disempowerment: in the absence of military forces, Nepotian hired gladiators to defend his claim to the throne but still met opposition from Magnentius' praetorian prefect Anicetus who, also lacking forces, assembled a citizen militia that struggled and failed to stop Nepotian; not wishing to abandon his military position in northern Italy, Magnentius solved the problem by dispatching a small force of imperial guardsmen to dethrone and decapitate the usurper after just twenty-seven days in power.[47] Rome had thus gone from being the default site of imperial accession in the first two centuries to being all but devoid of imperial claimants in the fourth.

At the same time as the reorganisation disempowered the *urbs Roma*, it also sealed off its often unruly populace from the emperor's immediate sphere of concern. Rome had, of course, cultivated a long tradition of political upheavals that could at times even threaten an emperor or members of his family. These included mass protests against Macrinus during birthday celebrations for his son Diadumenianus at the Circus Maximus in 217 that seriously weakened his power; at least two public disturbances during the reign of Maximinus; the revolt of the senator Iulius Valens Licinianus against Decius in 250; the unrest following the death of Gallienus that led senate and people to execute his slaves, an imperial official and his relative Marinianus in 268; the revolt of the moneyers of Rome's mint under Aurelian, which resulted in armed combat in the streets and the deaths of thousands in 271; and the famous unrest of 303 which drove Diocletian out of the city on the eve of his consulship.[48] Maxentius' proclamation was, of course, itself the result of a Roman uprising, but it by no means guaranteed Maxentius control over the city. Grain shortages in the wake of Domitius Alexander's usurpation in Africa led to rioting that forced the deployment of the Praetorians and resulted in the deaths of some 6,000 citizens.[49]

---

[44] Syme 1983.
[45] Details at Kienast et al. 2017, 192, 198, 209. See also Quintillus, Kienast et al. 2017, 224.
[46] Details at Kienast et al. 2017, 183, 185, 187, 193, 200, 205, except on Tacitus, for whom see Davenport 2014.
[47] Zos. 2.43.2–4; Aur. Vict. *Caes.* 42.6–8; Jer. *Chron.* s.a. 350; Oros. 7.29.11. On imperial proclamations in Rome in the fifth century, beginning with Valentinian III's elevation in 425, Lenski forthcoming; compare Feeney 2020, 291–336.
[48] Macrinus: Cass. Dio 79(78).20.1–3. Maximinus: Hdn. 7.7.1–2, 8.6.8. Licinianus: Aur. Vict. *Caes.* 29.3; Cyprian, *Ep.* 55.9.1–2; compare *Epit.* 29.5. Marinianus: Zonar. 12.26; Aur. Vict. *Caes.* 33.31. Aurelian, sources at Watson 1999, 236. Diocletian: Lactant. *De mort. pers.* 17.3, with Chapter 1 in this volume.
[49] *Chron. 354* (*MGH AA* 9.148); Zos. 2.12, 14; Aur. Vict. *Caes.* 40.17–19; *Epit.* 40; compare Lenski 2012, 65; Wijnendaele 2019, 302–4.

Even Constantine, who worked assiduously to cultivate the city, was greeted with rioting during his vicennalian visit in 326, most likely connected with his refusal to perform sacrifices on the Capitoline.[50] Discontent may also have been stoked, however, by announcements that he was constructing a 'second Rome' on the Bosporus, which would receive its own *senatus* as well as the entirety of the Egyptian grain supply that had formerly fed Rome. This as much as anything explains the shifts Constantine made in the administration of Suburbicaria, whose surplus food production was now directed quite purposefully to the city of Rome. Little wonder, then, that Constantius' visit in 357 was orchestrated with special attention to supplies, as attested in an inscription honoring the *praefectus annonae* Attius Caecilius Maximilianus, 'by whose diligence and foresight the food supply (*annona*) was managed for the populace and a massive military force during the arrival (*adventus*) into *urbs Roma* of Our Lord Constantius, the greatest victor and triumphator, eternal Augustus'.[51] The best guarantee against discontent among the perennially restive Roman populace for an imperial visit was to feed the beast.

Added to the mix in the fourth century was unrest over religion, a reality only exacerbated by the rise to prominence of Rome's powerful ecclesiastical apparatus. Conflicts already arose shortly after the death of Constantine when Pope Julius I (s. 337–52) provoked Constantius II by welcoming the exiled Athanasius of Alexandria to Rome in 342, while Constans still ruled the West. The resultant strain between eastern and western bishops – and courts – set the stage for the failed Council of Serdica the following year. After Constantius gained control of Rome in 352, he continued the conflict with Julius' successor Liberius (s. 352–66), whom he exiled in 355, only to be forced to recall him two years later under pressure brought to bear by the urban populace during his 357 visit.[52] But Felix, who had been chosen to replace Liberius in 355, continued to challenge Liberius' authority after his return. When Felix died in November 365 and Liberius in September 366, their two factions put forward duelling candidates to fill the Roman bishopric: Damasus (s. 366–84), favoured by partisans of Felix, and Ursinus, favoured by those of Liberius. The story is preserved in lavish detail in documents transmitted in the *Collectio Avellana* and has been analysed with great acumen by Rita Lizzi Testa and, in this volume, by Sam Cohen.[53] To summarise the events, after Ursinus was consecrated in the Basilica of Julius in Trastevere, Damasus promptly assaulted the church using armed toughs; shortly thereafter Ursinus was himself ordained at the Lateran Basilica, which his partisans controlled (September/October 366); after convincing the *PVR* Viventius and the *praefectus annonae* Iulianus to exile Ursinus, Damasus sought to consolidate his position by attacking the Ursinian stronghold at the Basilica

---

[50] Zos. 2.30.1; Lib. *Or.* 19.19, 20.24 with Wiemer 1994.

[51] *CIL* 6.41332: [c]uius diligentia ac provisione | [a]dventu ad urb(em) Romam d(omini) n(ostri) | [C]onstanti maximi victoris | [a]c triumf(atoris) semper Aug(usti) | [an]nona populo et fortissimo | [mil]iti adfatim subministrata est; compare Mazzarino 1974.

[52] Details at Barnes 1993, 138–9, esp. Amm. Marc. 15.7.6–10; *Collectio Avellana* 1.3 (*CSEL* 35.1: 2).

[53] *Coll. Avell.* 1–2a, 5–13 (*CSEL* 35.1: 1–46, 48–58), with Lizzi Testa 2004, 129–70; Chapter 13 in this volume. Further sources at Amm. Marc. 27.3.11–13, 27.9.9; Jer. *Chron.* s.a. 366; Socrates, *Hist. eccl.* 4.29.1–6; Sozom. *Hist. eccl.* 6.23.1–2; Rufinus, *Hist. eccl.* 11.10; Sulp. Sev. *Chron.* 2.39.5.

of Liberius (modern S. Maria Maggiore), where 160 people lost their lives over three days of fighting; in September 367 Ursinus and his partisans were allowed to return to the city by an edict of Valentinian issued to the *PVR* Praetextatus; but Damasus' influence allowed him to secure another edict expelling Ursinus from the city once again in November 367. At first the Ursinians were allowed to reside and congregate outside the walls, but further agitation led Valentinian to ban the Ursinians from a twenty-mile perimeter around Rome; by January 369, another conflict and massacre occurred at the Church of Saint Agnes on the Via Nomentana, leading to house arrest for Ursinus in Gaul which lasted down to 371/2.

Three things of importance for this study stand out in these documents. First, to believe the Ursinian version as transmitted in a document preserved under the title *Quae gesta sunt inter Liberium et Felicem Episcopos*, Damasus' partisans consisted of hired charioteers (*quadrigarii*), gladiators (*arenarii*), ditch-diggers (*fossatores*) and slaves (*familiares*) armed with axes (*secures*), arena swords (*gladii*) and clubs (*fustes*), against followers of Ursinus, who were underequipped members of the *plebs urbana*.[54] Regardless of the accuracy of the testimony, it highlights how the absence of trained soldiers and military equipment prevented civic violence from exploding to a level that could threaten the state, but also inhibited the state's imposition of a quick resolution. Secondly, the documents show how the *PVR* and the *VVR* were expected to cooperate in managing the conflict over the years during which it simmered: because the *PVR* had jurisdiction only within the city and for 100 miles around, he had to work in lockstep with the *VVR* to maintain order in the remainder of Suburbicaria. This explains why the *Collectio* preserves sets of paired imperial orders which repeat virtually the same instructions to the *PVR* and *VVR* in 368 (Olybrius and Aginatius) and 371 (Ampelius and Maximinus), for Rome and Suburbicaria had been welded into a single administrative machine the management of which necessarily involved synchrony between these two officials.[55] Finally, the documents show how the emperor could use this new administrative arrangement to remain at arm's length from urban conflicts, allowing such low-level disorder to smolder under local supervision without committing his own military forces or squandering his own political capital.

While the emperor benefited from cordoning off the behemoth that was Rome, Annonaria benefited from the much more regular presence of the emperor and the expenditure and attention this involved. We have already seen that three mints and four arms factories were opened, providing an increase in the regional money supply and in urban employment. As imperial 'capitals' in northern Italy, Milan and Aquileia saw building booms both in civic and in ecclesiastical architecture.[56] Milan in particular witnessed unprecedented growth as it came to serve as the primary residence of

---

[54] *Coll. Avell.* 1.5–7, 6–7 (*CSEL* 35.1: 2–3, 49–50).

[55] *Coll. Avell.* 8–9, 11–12 (*CSEL* 35.1: 50–4); compare 1.6 (*CSEL* 35.1: 3), and see 13 (*CSEL* 35.1: 54–8), which shows Gratian continuing to deal with the conflict in late 378 by ordering the *VVR* to maintain a hundred-mile radius around Rome free of Ursinian partisans, thus beyond the jurisdiction of the *PVR*. See Chastagnol 1962, 170–88 on dates. On the relationship between *PVR* and *VVR* see Sinnigen 1959. On the hundred-mile limit, see Rivière 2009.

[56] On Aquileia, see Lenski 2016, 148, 189–90.

emperors in Italy from the reign of Maximianus into the early fifth century, when it was replaced by Ravenna in this role.[57] Milan also played home to the many administrators and officeholders operating around the new *vicarius Italiae*.[58] Church leaders as well gained in power and prestige through cooperation – sometimes also conflict – with the emperors so regularly in their midst. Ambrose of Milan is the most obvious example, but others included, in a previous generation, Eusebius of Vercelli as well as Dionysius and Auxentius of Milan, and in a later, Chromatius of Aquileia, Gaudentius of Brescia and Maximus of Turin.[59]

Meanwhile, Suburbicaria witnessed a profound reshuffling of power and resources in a series of tradeoffs that benefited the SPQR far more than it cost them. First and foremost, the food supply of the *urbs Roma* was put on a solid footing in a new imperial environment where the capital was no longer the primary concern of the empire nor, after the dedication of Constantinople in 330, the only city with a supply system fully integrated into the fiscal apparatus.[60] For this it benefited greatly from the relative agricultural abundance of the Italian peninsula, which had long been recognised but was now fully mobilised to feed the *urbs sacra*. Providing for Rome's caloric needs was greatly aided by Aurelian's choice to reform the distribution system to include not only the traditional oil and grain (now converted to baked bread), but also free pork; this was further supplemented at some point before the early fourth century with the addition of price-controlled wine. A huge percentage of the urban populace (probably 50 per cent) was now fed on a nutrient-rich array of foodstuffs that central and southern Italy were well equipped to supply.[61] Tuscia, Bruttii and Campania in particular were famous for their wine production, and Lucania and Samnium for pork.[62] The relative proximity of these regions to Rome reduced transport costs and made pork provisioning possible given that the animals needed to be brought to the city on the hoof. Moreover, the inclusion of Sicily and Sardinia into Suburbicaria helped cushion the loss of Egyptian grain that came with the rise of Constantinople.

By removing the soldiery – and himself – from Suburbicaria, the emperor also cushioned the imperial state from the shocks and volatility inherent in the management of Rome's food supply. To be sure, the capillary details of food distribution

---

[57] Krautheimer 1983, 69–92; Sordi 2008, 113–23; Sena Chiesa and Biscottini 2012; Roberto 2018. During this same period, Milan is regularly compared with Rome as the seat of emperors in official rhetoric, *Pan. Lat.* 11(3).12.1–5, 12(9).7.5–7; Auson. *Ordo nob. urb.* 44–5.

[58] Roberto 2018. See also Cracco Ruggini 1990.

[59] Lizzi 1989; Barnes 1993; McLynn 1994; Liebeschuetz 2005. See also Chapter 12 in this volume.

[60] On the Roman food supply in Late Antiquity, see Chastagnol 1960, 297–334; Jones 1964, 695–705; Tengström 1974; Barnish 1987; Sirks 1991; Schmidt-Hofner 2008a, 313–26; Linn 2012; Vera 2015.

[61] On pork: SHA, *Aurel.* 35.2, 48.1; Aur. Vict. *Caes.* 35.7; *Epit.* 35.7; *Chron. 354* (*MGH AA* 9.148), with Chastagnol 1960, 325–30; Sirks 1991, 361–87; Schmidt-Hofner 2008a, 315–20. On wine: Chastagnol 1960, 322–5; Sirks 1991, 391–4. On oil: Vera 2015, 171–4.

[62] *Expositio totius mundi* 54–5: *Calabria, quae frumentifera cum sit, habundat in omnibus bonis. post hanc Brittzia, et ipsa obtima cum sit, negocium emittit vestem byrrum et vinum multum et obtimum. post Brittziam Lucania regio obtima et ipsa omnibus habundans et lardum multum foras emittit . . . post enim Campania . . . cellarium regnanti Roma[e]*. For archaeological confirmation of large-scale wine production in late antique Calabria and Bruttium see Arthur 1989.

remained in the hands of the *praefectus annonae*, but the pressures of supplying the system with foodstuffs were shifted to the *VVR*, and the political consequences of shortages now rested squarely on the shoulders of the *PVR*. The burdens must have been tremendous. Using details provided by Ammianus and the letters of Symmachus, Lellia Cracco Ruggini and Hans Peter Kohns have constructed what must be a nearly complete catalogue of Roman food crises between 353 and 402 which can be summarised thus:[63]

- 353–5: riots and the expulsion of foreigners from the city over shortages in the wine supply (Amm. Marc. 14.6.1; Lib. *Or.* 11.174);
- 356–7: riots over shortages in the wine supply (Amm. Marc. 15.7.3);
- 359 or 360: unrest over grain shortages caused by interruptions in African shipments (Amm. Marc. 19.10.1–4);
- 361: shortages in the grain supply caused by the conflict between Julian and Constantius force Julian to grant extraordinary supplements from the imperial patrimony (*Pan. Lat.* 3(11).14.1–6; Amm. Marc. 21.7.2–5);
- 368: riots over the papal succession are compounded by unrest over grain shortages (*Coll. Avell. Ep.* 10 (*CSEL* 35a.51–2));
- Likely 374/5: uprisings over wine provisioning lead to attacks against the ex-*PVR* Avianius Symmachus (Amm. Marc. 27.3.4);
- 376: a grain shortage arises, perhaps related to the Firmus revolt in Africa the previous year (Ambr. *Off.* 3.46–8; compare Symm. *Ep.* 1.5; *CTh* 1.6.7 (13 July 376));
- 382: a grain shortage in Africa causes panic in Rome (Symm. *Ep.* 4.74);
- 383: a drought across the Mediterranean and a Nile failure lead to grain shortages (Symm. *Relat.* 3.15–17; *Ep.* 2.6–7, 52; Ambr. *Ep.* 73(18).20–1; Prudent. *C. Symm.* 2.910–1063);
- 384: a panic over the food supply leads to the mass expulsion of foreigners and pleas for imperial intervention (Ambr. *Off.* 3.43–5, 49–51; Symm. *Relat.* 9.7, 18, 37; compare Amm. Marc. 14.6.19; 28.4.32);
- 385–6: shortages arise due to speculation in the grain market (Symm. *Ep.* 2.55);
- 395–6: Gildo cuts off the African grain supply, leading to grain shortages that are blamed by the plebs on the *PVR* (Symm. *Ep.* 4.18; 5.47; 6.1, 12, 14, 18, 21, 22, 26; 7.68);[64]
- 397–8: Gildo cuts off the African grain supply again, forcing Stilicho to convey grain from Sardinia, Gaul and Spain (Symm. *Ep.* 4.54, 9.42; *Chron. Gall. 452* 36 (*MGH AA* 9.650); Claud. *Gild.* 17–127; *Cons. Stil.* 3.307–9; 3.91–105; *Eutr.* 1.399–409; *AE* 1926.124);
- 399–400: problems with the *arca vinaria* lead to shortages in the wine supply (Symm. *Ep.* 7.96).

---

[63] Cracco Ruggini 1961, 152–76; Kohns 1961. See also Erdkamp 2002 on the political economy behind these incidents of unrest.

[64] On the chronology of the Gildo revolt, see Seeck 1883, lxvii–lxxi. On shortages during the Gildo uprising, see especially Wijnendaele 2019, 308–12; compare Wijnendaele 2017.

This catalogue documents disturbances over the food supply in twelve of forty-nine years (25 per cent). Moreover, a careful look at the sources indicates that in almost every instance, such shortages were caused by problems of politics, administration or shipping, rather than the environment. Meanwhile, Cracco Ruggini's catalogue indicates that Annonaria experienced food crises only three times in this same period, in 378/9, 388 and 405–6.[65] Food crises were thus an acute problem primarily in Rome and Suburbicaria. This was surely one of the primary reasons why emperors preferred to avoid the city and leave it to its senators to manage.

That the senate did indeed bear the brunt of urban anger over food shortages and other forms of urban unrest in the fourth and early fifth centuries can be seen in the number of times that mobs threatened senators, and especially the *PVR*, with violence, and the number of occasions on which senators dug into their pockets to bail out the city from provisioning crises:

- In 365 an angry mob was barely stopped from burning the house of the *PVR* C. Ceionius Rufius Volusianus Lampadius (Amm. Marc. 27.3.8);
- In 366, the *PVR* Viventius fled the city in fear during the first wave of the Damasus and Ursinus uprising (Amm. Marc. 27.3.12);[66]
- In some year thereafter (likely 374/5), angry mobs burnt the house of the ex-*PVR* L. Aurelius Avianius Symmachus over rumours that he had refused to sell his wine at state-regulated prices (Amm. Marc. 27.3.4);[67]
- In 376 a special contribution from the senators was needed to relieve the grain shortage (Ambr. *Off*. 3.46–8);
- In 383/4 the senate debated whether to provide extraordinary payments to relieve shortages again, but demurred (Symm. *Relat*. 37.2; *Ep*. 2.7);
- In 396, the shortages occasioned by the Gildo revolt forced Q. Aurelius Symmachus and other senators to consider fleeing the city (Symm. *Ep*. 6.21), but they later resolved to provide extraordinary provisions out of pocket;
- In 398, Symmachus fled the angry populace for reasons we can no longer establish (Symm. *Ep*. 6.66; 8.64, 65; 9.81);
- In 408, during Alaric's first siege, tensions over food shortages combined with anger over efforts to confiscate money to pay off Alaric induced the urban populace to stone the *PVR* Gabinius Barbarus Pompeianus to death (*Vita Melaniae Latina* 34.1–3 (p. 214–15 Laurence)); to relieve the siege, the senate provided the massive ransom demanded by Alaric (Olympiodorus fr. 7.2 Blockley; Zos. 5.29.9).

---

[65] Cracco Ruggini 1961, 99, 158–9, 163, 170. Each can be connected with periods of extreme demand for military provisioning: 378/9 coincides with the movement of armies through northern Italy before and after the battle of Adrianople; 388 with Magnus Maximus' residence in Italy in advance of his final conflict with Theodosius I; and 405–6 with Stilicho's war with Radagaisus. I thank J. W. P. Wijnendaele for pointing this out.

[66] Orlandi 2017 has demonstrated that Iunius Pomponius Ammonius replaced Viventius after his premature departure from office in the wake of the conflict between Damasus and Ursinus.

[67] See esp. Lizzi Testa 2004, 326–72.

Rome's senators thus lived under constant pressure – and fear – lest food shortages or other sources of discontent provoke violence which could affect their persons or property. The cordoning off of Suburbicaria and its transference into the control of Rome's senate brought with it not just heightened risks but also tremendous opportunities for reward. These were manifested on both an economic and political level. As to the former, the senatorial aristocracy of Rome had always favoured landholding in Italy, and this preference continued even after the removal of tax exemption from Italic land under the Tetrarchs. Symmachus, whose portfolio we know best, had estates in Mauretania, Sicily, Samnium, Apulia and especially Campania, where we learn of properties at Baiae, Bauli, Capua, Cora, Cumae, Formiae, Lucrina, Naples, Praeneste, Puteoli and Tarracina.[68] This concentration of properties in southern Italy, Sicily and Africa was normal for Roman senators and made sense not just for convenience of visitation and supervision but also because it permitted senators to tie their estates into the integrated economy of Suburbicaria.[69] Tremendous sums were to be made in the industry that was supplying the megalopolis of Rome with its daily bread – and meat and wine. In fact, by Olympiodorus' report, the richest senatorial incomes of late fourth-century Italy amounted to 4,000 pounds of gold annually plus a third as much in kind, and even modest senatorial households could expect to earn 1,000 pounds per year.[70] Some of this was made selling grain, oil and wine at state-controlled prices, but there was also a free market that generated much higher returns.[71] There were even fortunes to be made in pork, as Sam Barnish has shown using textual and archaeological evidence from Lucania et Brutii and Samnium.[72] And with state requisitions, considerable returns could be reaped by officeholders and bureaucrats in the commutation (*adaeratio*) of in-kind obligations to cash, and the reverse process.[73] Indeed, money could be made all up and down the system, as indicated by a series of eight inscriptions copying a list of *annona* cheaters posted by the *PVR* Tarracius Bassus in 375/6.[74] From the richest to the poorest, the empire's capital proved to be a spectacular generator of money capital.

Moreover, the late antique administrative reforms and particularly those instituted by Constantine also brought with them political benefits on two primary levels: first, the creation of Suburbicaria, which transformed southern Italy into the closed system

---

[68] Details at Seeck 1883, xlv–xlvii; Matthews 1975, 24–6.
[69] Giardina 1981; 1997, 282–300; Vera 1986; Volpe 1996; Sfameni 2006; Weisweiler 2011.
[70] Olympiodorus fr. 41.2 Blockley; compare Harper 2015.
[71] Giardina 1981; compare Banaji 2016, 63–74. On the connection between surplus agricultural production and the generation of wealth for the senatorial elite, see Weisweiler 2021.
[72] Barnish 1987.
[73] Mazzarino 1951, 187–206; Vera 2015, 175–8. See, for example, the efforts by Julian (*CTh* 14.4.3 (9 December 362)) and his *PVR* Apronianus (*CIL* 6.1770 = 31927; 1771) to reform the pork levy to avoid profiteering; compare Amm. Marc. 26.3.6. Julian's law implies that Apronianus' subordinates had been complicit in the schemes. And see Symm. *Ep.* 9.42, attempting to clear the reputation of the *PLRE* 2 Turranius Decentius Benignus, from charges he had profited from his management of the *annona* while serving as *praeses Sardiniae*.
[74] *CIL* 6.41329 = 31893 = *ILS* 6072; 6.1766 = 41328 = 31894.

of subsistence and security we have outlined, created a closed – if not impenetrable – political incubator that proved capable of hatching the careers of a whole new generation of senatorial elites; second, Constantine's redesign of career paths through which he maintained a division between equestrian soldiers/bureaucrats and senators by birth while granting access into the senate for the former as a consequence of their office (*honorati*) allowed him and his successors to solve the age-old problem of rewarding high performers from outside the aristocracy while continuing to cultivate it.[75] The result was the creation of a series of regional spheres within which aristocrats could build their careers by amassing governorships near their homes in Gaul, Asia Minor, Syria and especially – the richest and most prestigious territory of all – southern Italy.[76]

As part of this third shift, Constantine's reforms in Italy were particularly complex because they had to work within a system of officeholding that had a history stretching back to the fifth century BC. With respect for these traditions, he retained the by now ancient urban offices of quaestor and praetor, which granted access to the senate of Rome, but he downgraded the suffect consulship, which after 313/14 no longer counted towards iterations of the ordinary consulship, but became instead a strictly urban office. Suffect consulships continued to be used, much as they always had been, to increase the supply of 'exconsuls' for consular and proconsular governorships, but after 314, they were now generally omitted from honorific and funerary inscriptions as a mere pro-forma part of an Italian senatorial career.[77] At the same time, Constantine reversed the trend begun in the third century and taken to its height in the tetrarchic period of excluding senators by birth from provincial governorships. Instead he began inserting Roman senatorials into the – now strictly civilian – posts created for *consulares* and *correctores* in the new Italian provinces. Over time, he also increased the number of provinces governed by senatorial officeholders both within Italy and beyond it by adding Achaea to the list of proconsular governorships[78] (alongside Africa and Asia) and by adding Numidia, Byzacena, Belgica Prima, Pannonia Secunda, Campania, Aemilia et Liguria, Sicilia, Bithynia et Pontus, Europa et Thracia, Syria Coele and Phoenice to the list of consular governorships.[79]

This process had the result that Suburbicaria became a seedbed for Italian senatorial careers. To demonstrate this, we have catalogued and aggregated data for all holders of Italian governorships in *PLRE* 1.[80] In the instances of those who governed equestrian provinces (Sardinia, Corsica, Alpes Cottiae, Raetia) as *praesides*, the source record usually offers insufficient information to allow us to reconstruct their background and

---

[75] On Constantine's reforms to Roman career structures, see Salway 2006; Dillon 2015; Davenport 2019, 553–606.
[76] On late antique governors see Cecconi 1994, 133–69; Slootjes 2006.
[77] Salway 2015.
[78] Dated c.317 at Davenport 2013.
[79] Barnes 1982, 161–6; compare Arnheim 1972, 52. The upgrading of provinces to senatorial rank continued throughout the fourth century; see Davenport 2019, 586–600.
[80] I follow the *fasti* at *PLRE* 1.1092–8, with reference to Chastagnol 1963 and to the revisions proposed by Barnes 1982, 161–6; Ausbüttel 1988, 166–75; Cecconi 1994, 209–24; compare Cecconi 1998, 176–9. I also build in the revisions to the career of Iunius Bassus 14 suggested at Porena 2012.

subsequent careers.[81] But for those who held senatorial governorships in the remaining provinces of Italiciana, we have sufficient traces to outline more robust prosopographies. The first thing one notices from this data (Table 2) is that the vast majority of those known to have held at least one Italian governorship and at least one higher office held their first (or only) known governorship in Suburbicaria (41) and not Annonaria (4). Furthermore, certain provincial governorships were much more likely to lead to higher office than others, especially those of Campania (11), Tuscia et Umbria (8) and Sicilia (6).

Equally striking is the correlation between the place of origin of the holders of Italian governorships and the provinces they governed (Table 3). Of the 39 holders of Italian governorships whose origins are known or can be deduced, most (31) were from Rome (22) or southern Italy (9), with only 2 north Italians and 7 from other regions. Italian governorships were thus largely reserved for the Italians of Suburbicaria. Those of south Italian origin are especially noteworthy in that all but one whose home cities are known held governorships in their provinces of origin, while the lone exception, Paulinus of Nola, came from an Aquitanian family which owned an estate

Table 2.2 First known or only known governorships of those who held an Italian governorship and at least one subsequent office (284–395).

Province	First known governorship	Only known governorship	Total
Italia Annonaria			4
Aemilia et Liguria	1	1	2
Venetia et Istria	0	2	2
Alpes Cottiae	0	0	0
Raetia	0	0	0
Italia Suburbicaria			41
Campania	7	4	11
Flaminia et Picenum	3	1	4
Tuscia et Umbria	5	3	8
Apulia et Calabria	3	0	3
Lucania et Brutii	2	3	5
Sicilia	3	3	6
Sardinia	1	1	2
Corsica	1	1	2

[81] A notable exception is *PLRE* 1, 'Maximinus 7', 577–8, who was equestrian *praeses* of Corsica and Sardinia before becoming senatorial *corrector Tusciae et Umbriae*, then *praefectus annonae*, *VVR* and *PPO Galliarum* under Valentinian I.

in Campanian Fundi, where he had spent time as a boy.[82] In other words, their political careers were built in their own backyards. Furthermore, the vast majority (15/18) of those who held an Italian governorship and then a governorship outside of Italy (and especially one of the three proconsular governorships, 11/13) were from Rome. Fourth-century emperors from Constantine onward thus seem to have intended to exploit the new provincial structures of Italy to reward the Roman aristocracy with plum positions close to home and, at times, the premier governorships in the empire.

Indeed, Italian governorships regularly opened the path to high office, especially the urban prefecture, but also positions such as praetorian prefect, *vicarius* and other high-level posts in the consistory (*quaestor sacri palatii, comes sacrarum largitionum*). Of the 61 individuals known to have held at least one Italian governorship and some higher office, 21 served as *PVR*, 14 as *consul ordinarius*, 14 as *PPO* and 18 as *vicarius*. This group also proves a point asserted long ago by John Matthews with regard to Q. Aurelius Symmachus: most senators did not amass large portfolios of governorships on their way to high office.[83] Of the 22 individuals known to have held an Italian governorship and subsequently been appointed *PVR* in *PLRE* 1, 10 held just one governorship, 8 held two, and 4 held three. One governorship was, in other words, perfectly sufficient to power the career of a traditional senator to higher office.

Table 2.3 Geographical distribution of governorships for individuals (n = 39) with known geographic origin who held at least one Italian governorship.

	Governorship in Suburbicaria	Governorship in Annonaria	Proconsul Africae	Proconsul Asiae or Achaeae	Other
Romans (n = 22)	21	6	7	4	4
South Italians (n = 9)	12	0	0	0	0
North Italians (n = 2)	1	2	0	0	0
Non-Italians (n = 7)	9	0	2	0	1
Total governorships held	43	8	9	4	5

---

[82] *PLRE* 1, 'Alpinius Magnus 8 *signo* Eumenius', 534–5, of Lilybaeum, *consularis* (*Siciliae*); 'Volusius Venustus 5', 949, of Canusium, *corrector Apuliae et Calabriae*; 'Iulius Claudius Peristerius Pompeianus 7', 713, of Lilybaeum, *consularis Siciliae*; 'Anicius Paulinus 12', 678, of Capua, *proconsul Campaniae*; 'Anicius Auchenius Bassus 11', 152–4, of Beneventum, *proconsul Campaniae*. 'Meropius Pontius Paulinus 21', 681–3, *consularis Campaniae*, compare Trout 1999, 272–87. More on regionalism and Italian governorships at Arnheim 1972, 155–9; Ausbüttel 1988, 122–5; Cecconi 1994, 136–56.

[83] Matthews 1975, 13–30.

Table 2.4 Higher imperial offices known to have been held by individuals in *PLRE* I who held at least one Italian governorship (n = 46).

	PVR	*Consul ordinarius*	PPO	*Vicarius*	Other
Appointments	31	16	18	17	9
Individuals	26	15	14	17	8

And power it did, as can be seen from Table 4. The pattern is also discernible from the correlation between Italian governorships and the ordinary consulship. Of the 222 possible ordinary consulships available by western reckoning between 284 and 395, only 31 did not go to emperors or their relatives, generals, career bureaucrats (or to post-consulates or individuals whose career and background are now obscure to us).[84] Of these – essentially senatorial – consulships, 3 (10%) went to eastern senators,[85] 5 (16%) to Italian senators who jumped straight to one of the three proconsulships,[86] 2 (6%) to those who held a non-Italian governorship and some other high office,[87] 2 (6%) to those who immediately held high bureaucratic office,[88] 4 (13%) to those whose family connections appear to have landed them the ordinary consulship with no previously known imperial office,[89] and the remaining 15 (48%) went to individuals who had held at least one Italian governorship.[90] There was, of course, no guaranteed path to the consulship for any but emperors and their family members. Nevertheless, the surest starting point for senators with ambitions to hold the highest honour in the empire was to have held an Italian governorship.

Conclusion

For all that the Tetrarchs and Constantine had saddled the senators of Italy with tremendous burdens and risks, they had also afforded them tremendous opportunities to build wealth, power and prestige. The net result was a western senatorial aristocracy

---

[84] These numbers derive from Bagnall et al. 1987 but, for ease of calculation, include only consuls recognised in Rome from the beginning of each year.
[85] 358 Censorius Datianus; 384 Flavius Clearchus; 391 Flavius Eutolmius Tatianus.
[86] 322 Petronius Probianus; 322 Amnius Anicius Iulianus; 325 Sextus Anicius Paulinus; 334 Anicius Paulinus Honorius; 371 Sextus Claudius Petronius Probus.
[87] 347 Vulcacius Rufinus; 349 Aconius Catullinus.
[88] 311 Aradius Rufinus; 358 Neratius Cerealis.
[89] 317 Ovinius Gallicaus; 345 Nummius Albinus; 395 Anicius Hermogenianus Olybrius; 395 Anicius Probinus.
[90] 298 Virius Gallus; 301 T. Flavius Postumius Titianus; 311 and 314 C. Ceionius Rufius Volusianus; 316 Vettius Rufinus; 332 Maecilius Hilarianus; 333 Domitius Zenophilus; 331 Iunius Bassus; 337 T. Fabius Titianus; 340 L. Aradius Valerius Proculus Populonius; 343 M. Maecius Memmius Furius Baburius Caecilianus Placidus; 355 Q. Maesius Egnatius Lollianus; 379 Q. Clodius Hermogenianus Olybrius; 391 Q. Aurelius Symmachus; 394 Virius Nicomachus Flavianus. Of these, 9 also held the proconsulship of Africa, which was held by a total of 13 fourth-century consuls, making it the most common stepping stone on the way to the consulship.

that thrived both economically and politically. This has been recognised in scholarship beginning in the 1960s and continuing up to the present,[91] although – except in Italian scholarship – the success of southern Italy and its senators has only rarely been connected with the administrative restructuring described here. The Tetrarchs' elimination of tax-exempt status from Italy had deprived the region of a major economic advantage, and Constantine's removal of military garrisons shifted many of the burdens of managing the *urbs sacra* more squarely onto the shoulders of the senatorial elite. In return, the division of Italy into provinces provided an array of political posts for Italians from which they could construct prestigious and meaningful careers. Moreover, the creation of a diversified supply stream for the capital's populace primed through fiscal stimulus from the emperor provided the means for the SPQR to amass considerable wealth.

Constantine's division of Italy also had the consequence of directing its two halves along very different paths. Annonaria became a conduit for imperial traffic, both north and south of the Alps. The new provisioning system allowed emperors to treat the northern half as an integral part of the frontier defence system and thereby to integrate it into the military highways along which they could pass with large armies without overtaxing the provisioning system. Along the way, many rulers took up residence there over the long or short term, and this increased imperial attention often had positive effects on the creation of infrastructure and the level of imperial expenditure. Meanwhile Suburbicaria became a sort of closed system structured around the empire's queen city. It developed its own self-sustaining provisioning system, reinforced by grain from Africa – but no longer Egypt after the elevation of Constantinople to the status of 'Second Rome' by 330. The absence of military forces created new security challenges for the Suburbicarian region, which needed to be managed through a series of compromises made between the emperor, the senatorial elite, their rent-paying tenants and the massive population of Rome. In exchange, this same elite was given new opportunities for career-building by the transformation of its own south Italian homeland into the staging ground for their political ambitions. This same territory was exploited with new efficiency as a generator of wealth, for senatorial landholders were able to convert the *urbs Roma*'s voracious appetite – whetted by the addition of meat and wine to its already rich menu and by the folding of southern Italy into its market basket of suppliers – into a powerful moneymaking machine.[92]

Bibliography

Arnheim, M. T. W. (1972) *The Senatorial Aristocracy in the Later Roman Empire*, Oxford.
Arthur, P. (1989) 'Some Observations on the Economy of Bruttium under the Later Roman Empire', *JRA* 2: 133–42.

---

[91] See especially Arnheim 1972; Matthews 1975; Salzman 2002; and more recently Weisweiler 2021; Machado 2019.

[92] I should like to thank Jeroen Wijnendaele for his invitation to contribute to this important collection and for his learned and helpful comments on my chapter. I was also greatly assisted by the careful readings and learned suggestions of Kevin Feeney, Sam Cohen, Laurent Cases, Michele Salzman, John Weisweiler and the anonymous reader for Edinburgh University Press.

Ausbüttel, F. M. (1988) *Die Verwaltung der Städte und Provinzen im spätantiken Italien*, Frankfurt am Main.
Bagnall, R. S., A. Cameron, K. A. Worp and S. R. Schwartz (1987) *Consuls of the Later Roman Empire*, Philological Monographs of the American Philological Association 36, Atlanta.
Banaji, J. (2016) *Exploring the Economy of Late Antiquity: Selected Essays*, Cambridge.
Barnes, T. D. (1975) 'Gratian and Constans in Rome', *HSCP* 79: 325–33.
Barnes, T. D. (1982) *The New Empire of Diocletian and Constantine*, Cambridge.
Barnes, T. D. (1993) *Athanasius and Constantius: Theology and Politics in the Constantinian Empire*, Cambridge.
Barnes, T. D. (2000) 'Ambrose and Gratian', *AntTard* 7: 165–74.
Barnish, S. J. B. (1987) 'Pigs, Plebeians and Potentates: Rome's Economic Hinterland, c.350–600 A.D.', *PBSR* 55: 157–85.
Bastien, P. (1983) *Le monnayage de Magnence (350–353)*, Numismatique romaine 1, 2nd ed., Wetteren.
Cameron, A. (1969) 'Theodosius the Great and the Regency of Stilico', *HSCP* 73: 247–80.
Cameron, A. (2011) *The Last Pagans of Rome*, Oxford.
Cecconi, G. A. (1994) *Governo imperiale e élites dirigenti nell'Italia tardoantica: problemi di storia politico–amministrativa (270–476 d.C.)*, Biblioteca di Athenaeum 24, Como.
Cecconi, G. A. (1998) 'I governatori delle province italiche', *AntTard* 6: 149–79.
Cecconi, G. A. (2002) *Commento storico al libro II dell'Epistolario di Q. Aurelio Simmaco*, Biblioteca di studi antichi 86, Pisa.
Chaniotis, A. and T. Fujii (2015) 'A New Fragment of Diocletian's Currency Regulation from Aphrodisias', *JRS* 105: 227–33.
Chastagnol, A. (1960) *La préfecture urbaine à Rome sous le Bas-Empire*, Publications de la Faculté des lettres et sciences humaines d'Alger 34, 2nd ed., Paris.
Chastagnol, A. (1962) *Les fastes de la préfecture de Rome au Bas-Empire*, Études prosopographiques 2, Paris.
Chastagnol, A. (1963) 'L'Administration du diocèse Italien au Bas-Empire', *Historia* 12: 348–79.
Cosentino, S. (2008) *Storia dell'Italia bizantina, VI–XI secolo: da Giustiniano ai normanni*, Bologna.
Cracco Ruggini, L. (1961) *Economia e società nell' 'Italia Annonaria': rapporti fra agricoltura e commercio dal IV al VI secolo d.C.*, Studi Storici sulla Tarda Antichità 2, Bari.
Cracco Ruggini, L. (1990) 'Nascita e morte di una capitale', *QCCCM* 2: 5–51.
Davenport, C. (2013) 'The Governors of Achaia under Diocletian and Constantine', *ZPE* 184: 225–34.
Davenport, C. (2014) 'M. Claudius Tacitus: Senator or Soldier?', *Latomus* 73: 175–87.
Davenport, C. (2017) 'Rome and the Rhythms of Imperial Life: from the Antonines to Constantine', *AntTard* 25: 23–39.
Davenport, C. (2019) *A History of the Roman Equestrian Order*, Cambridge.
Diehl, C. (1959) *Études sur l'administration byzantine dans l'exarchat de Ravenne (568–751)*, New York.
Dillon, J. N. (2015) 'The Inflation of Rank and Privilege: Regulating Precedence in the Fourth Century AD', in J. Wienand (ed.) *Contested Monarchy: Integrating the Roman Empire in the Fourth Century AD*, New York, 42–66.
Döpp, S. (1975) 'Theodosius I. ein zweites Mal in Rom?', in A. Patzer (ed.) *Apophoreta für Uvo Hölscher zum 60. Geburtstag*, Bonn, 73–83.
Drijvers, J. W. (1992) *Helena Augusta: the Mother of Constantine the Great and the Legend of Her Finding of the True Cross*, Brill's Studies in Intellectual History 27, Leiden.
Eck, W. (1979) *Die staatliche Organisation Italiens in der hohen Kaiserzeit*, Vestigia 28. Munich.
Erdkamp, P. (2002) '"A Starving Mob Has No Respect": Urban Markets and Food Riots in the Roman World, 100 BC–400 AD', in Lukas De Blois and John Rich (eds) *The Transformation*

of *Economic Life under the Roman Empire: Proceedings of the Second Workshop of the International Network Impact of Empire (Roman Empire, c.200 BC–AD 476), Nottingham, July 4–7, 2001,* Amsterdam, 93–115.

Feeney, K. (2020) 'Roman Imperial Accession from Maximinus Thrax to Justinian (235–527 CE)', Dissertation, Yale University.

Frank, R. I. (1969) *Scholae palatinae: the Palace Guards of the Later Roman Empire*, Rome.

Giardina, A. (1981) 'Aristocrazie terriere e piccola mercatura: sui rapporti tra potere politico e formazione dei prezzi nel tardo impero romano', *QUCC* 7: 123–46.

Giardina, A. (1986) 'Le due Italie nella forma tarda dell'impero', in A. Giardina (ed.) *Società romana e impero tardoantico*, vol. 1, *Istituzioni, ceti, economie*, Rome, 1–30.

Giardina, A. (1997) *L'Italia Romana: storie di un'identità incompiuta*, Rome.

Gillett, A. (2001) 'Rome, Ravenna, and the Last Western Emperors', *PBSR* 69: 131–67.

Halfmann, H. (1986) *Itinera Principum: Geschichte und Typologie der Kaiserreisen im römischen Reich*, Heidelberger Althistorische Beiträge und Epigraphische Studien 2, Stuttgart.

Harper, K. (2015) 'Landed Wealth in the Long Term: Patterns, Possibilities, Evidence', in P. Erdkamp, K. Verboven and A. Zuiderhoek (eds) *Ownership and Exploitation of Land and Natural Resources in the Roman World*, Oxford, 43–61.

Humphries, M. (2003) 'Roman Senators and Absent Emperors in Late Antiquity', *AAAH* 17: 27–46.

Humphries, M. (2007) 'From Emperor to Pope? Ceremonial, Space, and Authority at Rome from Constantine to Gregory the Great', in K. Cooper and J. Hillner (eds) *Religion, Dynasty and Patronage in Early Christian Rome, 300–900*, Cambridge, 21–58.

Humphries, M. (2015) 'Emperors, Usurpers, and the City of Rome', in J. Wienand (ed.) *Contested Monarchy: Integrating the Roman Empire in the Fourth Century AD*, New York, 151–68.

Johnson, M. J. (2009) *The Roman Imperial Mausoleum in Late Antiquity*, Cambridge.

Jones, A. H. M. (1964) *The Later Roman Empire, 284–602: a Social Economic and Administrative Survey*, Cambridge.

Kelly, C. (2012) 'Bureaucracy and Government', in N. Lenski (ed.) *The Cambridge Companion to the Age of Constantine*, rev. ed., Cambridge, 183–204.

Kienast, D., W. Eck and M. Heil (2017) *Römische Kaisertabelle: Grundzüge einer römischen Kaiserchronologie*, 6th ed., Darmstadt.

Kohns, H. P. (1961) *Versorgungskrisen und Hungerrevolten im Spätantiken Rom*, Antiquitas 6, Bonn.

Krautheimer, R. (1983) *Three Christian Capitals: Topography and Politics*, Berkeley.

Lenski, N. (ed.) (2012) *The Cambridge Companion to the Age of Constantine*, rev. ed., Cambridge.

Lenski, N. (2016) *Constantine and the Cities: Imperial Authority and Civic Politics*, Philadelphia.

Lenski, N. (forthcoming) 'The Late Roman Senate and Its Decrees – A Synthesis', in P. Buongiorno, N. Lenski and U. Roberto (eds) *Senatus Consulta nell'Impero Tardoromano*, Münster.

Leppin, H. and H. Ziemssen (2007) *Maxentius: der letzte Kaiser in Rom*, Mainz am Rhein.

Liebeschuetz, J. H. W. G. (2005) *Ambrose of Milan: Political Letters and Speeches*, Translated Texts for Historians 43, Liverpool.

Linn, J. (2012) 'The Roman Grain Supply, 442–455', *Journal of Late Antiquity* 5: 298–321.

Lizzi, R. (1989) *Vescovi e strutture ecclesiastiche nella città tardoantica (l'Italia annonaria nel IV–V secolo d.C.)*, Biblioteca di Athenaeum 9, Como.

Lizzi Testa, R. (2004) *Senatori, popolo, papi: il governo di Roma al tempo dei Valentiniani*, Munera 21, Bari.

McEvoy, M. (2010) 'Rome and the Transformation of the Imperial Office in the Late Fourth–Mid-Fifth Centuries AD', *PBSR* 78: 151–92.

McEvoy, M. (2017) 'Shadow Emperors and the Choice of Rome', *AntTard* 25: 95–112.

Machado, C. (2019) *Urban Space and Aristocratic Power Late Antique Rome: AD 270–535*, Oxford.

McLynn, N. B. (1994) *Ambrose of Milan: Church and Court in a Christian Capital*, Transformation of the Classical Heritage 22, Berkeley.

Maier, F. K. (2019) *Palastrevolution: der Weg zum hauptstädtischen Kaisertum im römischen Reich des vierten Jahrhunderts*, Geschichte und Archäologie 1, Paderborn.

Matthews, J. (1975) *Western Aristocracies and Imperial Court, A.D. 364–425*, Oxford.

Mazzarino, S. (1951) *Aspetti sociali del quarto secolo: ricerche di storia tardoromano*, Rome.

Mazzarino, S. (1974) 'Intorno alla carriera di un nuovo "Corrector" di Lucania e Britii e l'"adventus" di Costanzo II a Roma', in Santo Mazzarino (ed.) *Antico, Tardoantico ed èra costantiniana*, vol. 1, Rome, 197–220.

Millar, F. (1986) 'Italy and the Roman Empire: Augustus to Constantine', *Phoenix* 40: 295–318.

Neira Faleiro, C. (ed.) (2005) *La Notitia Dignitatum: nueva edición crítica y comentario histórico*, Nueva Roma 25, Madrid.

Nixon, C. E. V. and B. Saylor Rodgers (1994) *In Praise of Later Roman Emperors: the Panegyrici Latini. Introduction, Translation, and Historical Commentary, with the Latin Text of R. A. B. Mynors*, Berkeley.

Omissi, A. (2018) *Emperors and Usurpers in the Later Roman Empire: Civil War, Panegyric, and the Construction of Legitimacy*, Oxford.

Orlandi, S. (2017) 'Un prefetto urbano "ritrovato": Iunius Pomponius Ammonius', *ZPE* 204: 287–98.

Paschoud, F. (ed.) (1971–1986) *Zosime Histoire nouvelle*, 5 vols, Paris.

Paschoud, F. (1975) 'La fin du régne de Theodose et la "Histoire nouvelle" de Zosime et la source paienne de Eunape 1: le problème du voyage à Rome de Théodose en 394', in F. Paschoud (ed.) *Cinq études sur Zosime*, Paris, 100–24.

Peachin, M. (1996) *Iudex Vice Caesaris: Deputy Emperors and the Administration of Justice during the Principate*, Heidelberger althistorische Beiträge und epigraphische Studien 21, Stuttgart.

Porena, P. (2003) *Le origini della prefettura del pretorio tardoantica*, Saggi di Storia Antica 20, Rome.

Porena, P. (2006a) 'L'Italia prima di Ponte Milvio e la carriera di Caecilianus', *Epigraphica* 68: 117–54.

Porena, P. (2006b) 'Riflessioni sulla provincializzazione dell'Italia romana', in M. Ghilardi, C. J. Goddard and P. Porena (eds) *Les cités de l'Italie tardo-antique, IVe–VIe siècle: institutions, économie, société, culture et religion*, Collection de l'École française de Rome 369, Rome, 9–21.

Porena, P. (2012) 'I dignitari di Costantino: dinamiche di selezione e di ascesa durante la crisi del sistema tetrarchico', in G. Bonamente, N. E. Lenski and R. Lizzi Testa (eds) *Costantino prima e dopo Costantino – Constantine before and after Constantine*, Munera 35, Bari, 293–319.

Porena, P. (2013) 'La riorganizzazione amministrativa dell'Italia: Costantino, Roma, il senato e gli equilibri dell'Italia romana', in A. Melloni et al. (eds) *Costantino I: Enciclopedia costantiniana sulla figura e l'immagine dell'imperatore del cosiddetto Editto di Milano 313–2013*, vol. 1, Rome, 329–49.

Porena, P. (2014) 'Ancora sulla carriera di Flavius Ablabius prefetto del pretorio di Costantino', *ZPE* 190: 262–70.

Rivière, Y. (2009) 'Compétence territoriale, exercice de la coercition, et pouvoirs juridictionnels du préfet de la ville (Ier–IVe siècle ap. J.-C.)', *MedAnt* 12: 227–56.

Roberto, U. (2014) *Diocleziano*, Rome, 2014.

Roberto, U. (2018) 'L'identità tetrarchica di Milano e l'Italia tardoantica', in R. Passarella (ed.) *Milano e la Chiesa di Milano prima di Ambrogio*, Milan, 23–53.

Ross, A. (2021) 'Envisioning *adventus*: Ammianus between Panegyric and Polemic', *Journal of Late Antiquity* 14: 97–116.

Salway, B. (2006) 'Equestrian Prefects and the Award of Senatorial Honours from the Severans to Constantine', in A. Kolb (ed.) *Herrschaftsstrukturen und Herrschaftspraxis: Konzepte, Prinzipien und Strategien der Administration im römischen Kaiserreich. Akten der Tagung an der Universität Zürich, 18.–20.10.2004*, Berlin, 115–35.

Salway, B. (2015) 'Redefining the Roman Imperial Elite in the Fourth Century AD', in P. Briks (ed.) *Elites in the Ancient World*, Szczecińskie Studia nad Starożytnością 2, Krakow, 199–220.

Salzman, M. R. (2002) *The Making of a Christian Aristocracy: Social and Religious Change in the Western Roman Empire*, Cambridge, 2002.

Salzman, M. R. (2021) *The Falls of Rome: Crises, Resilience, and Resurgence in Late Antiquity*, Cambridge.

Scheidel, W. (2014) 'The Shape of the Roman World: Modelling Imperial Connectivity', *JRA* 27: 7–32.

Schmidt-Hofner, S. (2008a) *Reagieren und Gestalten: der Regierungsstil des spätrömischen Kaisers am Beispiel der Gesetzgebung Valentinians I.*, Vestigia 58, Munich.

Schmidt-Hofner, S. (2008b) 'Die Regesten der Kaiser Valentinian und Valens in den Jahren 364 bis 375 n. Chr', *ZRG* 125: 498–602.

Schmidt-Hofner, S. (2012) 'Trajan und die Symbolische Kommunikation bei kaiserlichen Rombesuchen in der Spätantike', in R. Behrwald and C. Witschel (eds) *Rom in der Spätantike: historische Erinnerung im städtischen Raum*, Stuttgart, 33–59.

Seeck, O. (ed.) (1883) *Q. Avrelii Symmachi qvae svpersvnt*, MGH AA, vol. 4, Berlin.

Seeck, O. (1919) *Regesten der Kaiser und Päpste für die Jahre 311 bis 476 n. Chr.: Vorarbeit zu einer Prosopographie der Christlichen Kaiserzeit*, Stuttgart.

Sena Chiesa, G. and P. Biscottini (2012) *Costantino 313 d.C.: l'editto di Milano e il tempo della tolleranza*, Milan, 2012.

Sfameni, C. (2006) *Ville residenziali nell'Italia tardoantica*, Munera 25, Bari.

Sinnigen, W. G. (1959) 'The *Vicarius Urbis Romae* and the Urban Prefecture', *Historia* 8: 97–112.

Sirks, A. J. B. (1991), *Food for Rome: the Legal Structure of the Transportation and Processing of Supplies for the Imperial Distributions in Rome and Constantinople*, Amsterdam.

Slootjes, D. (2006) *The Governor and His Subjects in the Later Roman Empire*, Mnemosyne Suppl. 275, Leiden.

Sogno, C. (2006) *Q. Aurelius Symmachus: a Political Biography*, Ann Arbor.

Sordi, M. (2008) *Sant'Ambrogio e la tradizione di Roma*, Rome.

Syme, R. (1983) 'Emperors from Etruria', in G. Alföldi and J. Straub (eds) *Bonner Historia Augusta Colloquium 1979/1981*, Bonn, 333–60.

Tengström, E. (1974) *Bread for the People: Studies of the Corn-Supply of Rome during the Late Empire*, Stockholm.

Thomsen, R. (1967) *The Italic Regions, from Augustus to the Lombard Invasion*, C&M Dissertationes 4, Copenhagen.

Trout, D. (1999) *Paulinus of Nola: Life, Letters, and Poems*, Berkeley.

Vera, D. (1986) 'Forme e funzioni della rendita fondiaria nella tarda antichita', in A. Giardina (ed.) *Società romana e impero tardoantico*, Bari, 367–447 and 723–60.

Vera, D. (2015) 'Constantino, l'Africa e i privilegi dell'Italia: osservazioni sulla redistribuzione statale nel IV secolo', in J. Vilella Masana (ed.) *Constantino, ¿el Primer Emperador Cristiano? Religión y política en el siglo IV*, Barcelona, 163–80.

Volpe, G. (1996) *Contadini, pastori e mercanti nell'Apulia tardoantica*, Munera 6, Bari.

Watson, A. (1999) *Aurelian and the Third Century*, London.

Weisweiler, J. (2021) 'Capital Accumulation, Supply Networks, and the Composition of the Roman Senate, 14–235 CE', *P&P* 2021: 4–44.

Weisweiler, J. (2011) 'The Price of Integration: State and Elite in Symmachus' Correspondence', in P. Eich, S. Schmidt-Hofner and C. Wieland (eds) *Der Wiederkehrende Leviathan: Staatlichkeit und Staatswerdung in Spätantike und früher Neuzeit*, Heidelberg, 343–73.

Wiemer, H.-U. (1994) 'Libanios und Zosimus über den Rom-Besuch Konstantins I. im Jahre 326', *Historia* 43: 469–94.

Wijnendaele, J. W. P. (2017) 'The Career and "Revolt" of Gildo, *comes et magister utriusque militiae per Africam*', *Latomus* 27: 385–402.

Wijnendaele, J. W. P. (2019) 'Late Roman Civil War and the African Grain Supply', *Journal of Late Antiquity* 12: 298–328.

Zuckerman, C. (2002) 'Sur la *Liste de Vérone* et la province de Grande Arménie: la division de l'Empire et la date de création des diocèses', in *Mélanges Gilbert Dagron, Travaux et Mémoires* 14, Paris 617–37.

3

COURT, CRISIS AND RESPONSE: ITALY FROM GRATIAN TO VALENTINIAN III

Mark Humphries

Introduction

IN A CELEBRATED STUDY of Roman Italy from Augustus to Constantine, the late Fergus Millar drew a stark contrast between Italian history before and after the end of the Republic: 'Italy during the period of the Roman Monarchy and Republic has a history; one which offers us enormous challenges and problems, but still a history: . . . Italy under the Empire has no history. That is to say, it has no narrative history.' While he admitted that narrative history was out of vogue when he was writing in the mid-1980s, he nevertheless lamented that

> the absence of a narrative – of any narrative at all which is in any way focused on Italy – has robbed us of historical questions; since there is no narrative history we have been unable to put any coherent questions to such archaeological, epigraphic, and literary evidence as we have, because we do not know what historical evolution it is which we are trying to explain.[1]

Millar went on to delineate various ways in which integration into the empire impinged on Italy, particularly in terms of the imposition of taxes, the establishment of new tiers of administration, and the presence in Italy of military forces. The evidence for these processes is clearest for the north, especially for the third century onwards; but in many ways, he concluded, imperial 'Italy still presents fundamental puzzles.'[2]

For the period covered by this chapter (indeed, by this volume as a whole) the very opposite may be said to be true. There is no shortage of narrative, encompassing various types of upheaval, whether political, military or administrative. Recent studies of the late fourth and fifth centuries have re-emphasised the importance of political institutions: for example, François Chausson on the role of women in imperial succession, or Meghan McEvoy on child emperors and their courts;[3] meanwhile, scholars such as Christine Delaplace and Guy Halsall have sought to impose unity on the political

---

[1] Millar 1986, 295.
[2] Millar 1986, 318; see also Chapter 5 in this volume.
[3] Chausson 2007; McEvoy 2013a. For political institutions more generally, see Errington 2006.

and military history of the late Roman and immediately post-Roman West.[4] Yet, in many of these studies, Italy is the stage on which other histories (that of the court or that of the generals) is played out, rather than a focus of analysis in its own right. The aim of this chapter (as with others in this volume) is to put Italy back at the centre of the analysis.

This renewed emphasis on institutions and events reflects how narrative history is enjoying a resurgence by comparison with when Millar was writing. It has emerged from the shadows of *longue durée* chronologies, represented for Late Antiquity by the epic sweep of works such as those of Peter Brown. As Averil Cameron noted in her preface to the English translation of Giusto Traina's study of the year 428, this revival 'encourages us to focus again on chronology' and highlights an appreciation of 'the unexpected juxtapositions of history, [and] the crucial role of events, expected or not'.[5] Moreover, a return to a tighter focus in terms of time frame serves to highlight just how different Italy in the late empire is from Italy under the Principate. There is, in contradistinction to the apparent (though, of course, never complete) shapelessness of early Imperial Italian history, a clear historical trajectory, signalled in this volume's theme of 'the transition from *imperium* to *regnum*'. And yet, the challenges to analysis remain undiminished. In part this is owing to the complexity and unevenness of the sources; but it also reflects how the changing politics of the late empire impacted on Italy.

It is important, before proceeding further, to issue a note of caution: the various political, military and administrative problems afflicting Italy in between the succession of Gratian in November 375 and the murder of Valentinian III on 16 March 455 had been presaged by difficulties in the later third and fourth centuries.[6] The particular challenges of military upheaval that we find in this period, of both civil war and invasion, echo developments stretching back to the late Antonine and Severan periods, as demonstrated by events such as the incursion of the Marcomanni and Quadi into northeastern Italy in the 160s and the siege of Aquileia in 238 during the civil war between Maximinus Thrax and his senatorial rivals Pupienus and Balbinus.[7] These upheavals were largely, although not wholly, concentrated in the north, and their impact on central and southern Italy seems to have been much less profound.[8] Nevertheless, in terms of direct imperial intervention in Italy as a whole, it seems reasonable to assume that the division of Italy into provinces in the early fourth century reflects the outcome of a series of haphazard developments stretching back to the Hadrianic period that sought to provide for Italian communities mechanisms for recourse to imperial authorities.[9] For all that, however, the period straddling the later fourth and early fifth centuries does seem to have an unusual concentration of upheavals, in terms both of both the local impact of episodes of civil war and invasion, and of Italy's place in the empire.

---

[4] Delaplace 2015; Halsall 2008; compare Elton 2018.
[5] Averil Cameron, Preface, in Traina 2009, x.
[6] See Chapters 1 and 2 in this volume.
[7] Second-century invasions: Amm. Marc. 29.6.1; third-century civil wars: Sotinel 2005, 8–10.
[8] For military dispositions, see Millar 1986, 301.
[9] Millar 1986, 296–8 and 313–17.

In what follows, I will take as my focus interactions between the imperial administration and Italy, seeing things, as it were, from the perspective of the imperial court and how it responded to various challenges confronting Italian society. I will begin by reviewing the changing patterns in the presence of the imperial court in Italy as an indicator of imperial priorities and responses to various Italian crises. Next, I will examine in more detail how emperors and their bureaucrats met various challenges to Italian stability, examining administrative responses to such upheavals as Alaric's incursions into Italy and the apparently more remote, but no less real, threat posed by the Vandal conquest of Africa. A final section will consider Italy's place in an empire that was drifting apart into two increasingly distinct *partes*, East and West, and how the administrations of Honorius and Valentinian III sought to address the challenges presented by this geopolitical transformation.

The Imperial Court in Italy

As Bryan Ward-Perkins has observed in an important study of the fourth-century empire, the decision of emperors in that period to reside in a string of cities stretching from Trier on the Rhine frontier to Antioch in the East resulted in 'a most unusual empire', almost 'an empire turned inside-out', in which the long-established relations between centre and periphery were inverted.[10] Northern Italy played a role in this development, with cities such as Milan particularly, but also sometimes Verona and Aquileia, being favoured imperial residences from the third century and tetrarchic period onwards.[11] The division of Italy into two dioceses at the beginning of the fourth century, and visible in the *Notitia dignitatum*, reflected the north's place in imperial priorities.[12] The centre and south, along with the islands of Sicily, Sardinia and Corsica, became Italia Suburbicaria, with its administration subordinate to, and serving the needs of, the city of Rome. Northern Italy, by contrast, became Italia Annonaria, and was focused on the needs of the court and its apparatus. It was here that there were the greatest concentrations of troops and defensive dispositions (such as the *claustra Alpium Juliarum*), along with arms factories, treasuries (for military pay) and various mints, first at Ticinum/Pavia (from the 270s until the 320s, at which point its operations were moved to Constantinople) and Aquileia (c.294–c.425), and later at Milan (364–475) and Ravenna (from Honorius onwards).[13]

The period from the late fourth century to the mid-fifth brought with it further changes that made Italy even more central to imperial concerns, while also seeing a shift away from a primary concentration on Annonaria. An overview of the period from Gratian to Valentinian III will demonstrate this amply. What I offer first is a series of summaries of imperial activities in Italy (and, where relevant, adjacent regions)

---

[10] Ward-Perkins 2014, 112–22.
[11] Cecconi 1994, 109–11; compare Sotinel 2005, 17–24, on the relative importance of Aquileia.
[12] The base data is usefully compiled in the lengthy first footnote in Ruggini 1961, 1–4; for broader discussion, see Giardina 1986, 1–36.
[13] See Chapter 7 in this volume. Arms factories: *Not. Dign. occ.* 9.23–9. Treasuries: *Not. Dign. occ.* 11.26–30. Mints: Hendy 1986, 371–95; for mints and regional status: Cecconi 1994, 52–3 (on Aquileia).

proceeding reign by reign.[14] At the outset of this period, we have an emphatically mobile court led by emperors active in various aspects of civil and military government, meaning that the movement of the court is a good guide to imperial priorities. It is sometimes assumed that the death of Theodosius signalled a decisive shift towards a more static court, with emperors who often acceded to the throne as children and were much less active in terms of personal leadership; but as I hope to show now, for Italy that is not the whole picture, and the various officials who made up the imperial court were still concerned to demonstrate an interest in effective governance.[15]

First, under Gratian, we see a gradual shift from a concentration on Gaul, which had characterised most of his father's reign, in favour of northern Italy.[16] In no small measure this must be related to the upheavals following the Gothic victory at Adrianople in 378, which provoked considerable anxiety in Italy, separated from the Balkans by only the Julian Alps.[17] Even if administrative arrangements were put in place to allow Theodosius I to take responsibility for resolving the crisis,[18] the focus of Gratian's activities now shifted decisively towards northern Italy. From 375 to early 378, he was to be found exclusively in Gaul; then he moved east towards the Balkans for the aborted campaign with Valens; from 379 he adopted a new strategy, spending the summer in Italy (or the western Balkans) and the winter in Trier, until 381, when there was no return to Gaul and the emperor spent the whole period from March 381 to June 383 in northern Italy. He now resided mainly at Milan, but made regular excursions to Aquileia,[19] with occasional presences (as a result of these travels) at Brescia, Padua and Verona; there is, additionally, a brief foray to Viminacium on the Danube in July 382, which falls shortly before the resolution of the crisis.[20] Then, after June 383, he was forced to return north to face the usurpation of Magnus Maximus.

Maximus' seizure of the north-western provinces meant that Gratian's half-brother Valentinian II spent all of his time (until Maximus' invasion of Italy in 387) in northern Italy, mainly at Milan, but also at other centres, particularly Aquileia (every year 384–6), but also occasionally at Verona (385) and Ticinum (386). Maximus' activities in Italy in 387–8, insofar as we can recover them, concentrated on Milan and Aquileia, the latter particularly in the context of the civil war with Theodosius in the summer of 388.[21]

For the next few years, Theodosius remained in Italy, seeking to restore order after the region's dalliance with the usurper. He resided chiefly at Milan, with visits also

---

[14] The basic point of reference for any such reconstruction remains Seeck 1919. Some of his reconstructions have been challenged, for example, in an important reconsideration of the period after 395 by Gillett 2001. These works should be assumed as underlying the following discussion.

[15] The most important recent study of these youthful emperors and their courts is McEvoy 2013a; for a study of the impact on the East, see Destephen 2016, 157–69.

[16] For a revision of Seeck's reconstruction of Gratian's itineraries, see Barnes 1999.

[17] Ambr. *Exc. Sat.* 1.31 laments Italy's vulnerability: *si nunc urgeri Italiam tam propinquo hoste cognosceres, quantum ingemisceres, quam doleres in Alpium vallo summam nostrae salutis consistere lignorumque concaedibus construi murum pudoris!* Date (autumn 378): McLynn 1994, 69 n. 56.

[18] Errington 1996, 22–7.

[19] E.g. in 381: *CTh* 15.10.2, 15.7.8. For Gratian at Aquileia: Duval 1976, 260–2.

[20] Viminacium: *CTh* 12.1.89, 1.10.1.

[21] *Pan. Lat.* 2(12).38.4–39.2; Sulpicius Alexander *ap.* Gregory of Tours, *Hist.* 2.9 (F1 in Van Hoof and Van Nuffelen 2020, 84–90). For Valentinian II and Maximus in northern Italy: Duval 1976, 262–7.

to Rome in 389 (the occasion for Pacatus' panegyric) and Verona in 390.[22] When he returned to the East in 391 he passed through Concordia and Aquileia. The pattern of Theodosius' presences in northern Italy broadly resembles that set by Gratian after 379. Yet Gaul remained a priority: a court nominally headed by Valentinian II had been established outside Italy, in Gaul, and it would be there that he would meet his death in 392.[23] Of the activities of the usurper Eugenius who overthrew him, he too stayed briefly at Milan, prompting the city's bishop Ambrose to vacate the city so that he should not meet with the rebellious ruler.[24] With the return of Theodosius to the West, Milan once more became the favoured residence for the remaining months of the emperor's reign.[25]

Following Theodosius' death on 17 January 395 and the succession of Honorius as western emperor, the court becomes almost permanently settled in Italy, although some members of the elite, such as Constantius III, spent time in Gaul, where rival courts are also established under a string of usurpers in the early 400s.[26] As had been the case since 379, Milan served as the main centre for the imperial court until 402, although the habit visible under Gratian and Valentinian II of excursions eastwards to Venetia is visible also in 397 (Padua in September), 399 (Brescia, Verona, Padua, Ravenna and Altinum between July and September) and 400 (Brescia, Altinum and Aquileia in August and September). Following Alaric's first incursion into Italy, there is a shift from Milan to Ravenna, where the court is attested by 6 December 402.[27] Ravenna remains the focus of court activities for the next few years, except for a visit to Rome in 404, and two more visits to the ancient capital in 407–8;[28] 408 also saw a brief imperial return to the western reaches of the Po valley, with laws even issued from Milan in September.[29] This could point to a reversion to earlier habits, but Alaric's second invasion of Italy that year seems to have confined the court for the foreseeable future to Ravenna, and Gillett is surely right to see the occupation of Ravenna in 408 as the decisive shift in the location of the court.[30] It is at Ravenna and nearby Rimini that

---

[22] On Theodosius' Italian residence, see Omissi 2018, 268–90.
[23] For Valentinian's last years (advancing the argument that sending him to Gaul effectively sidelined him), see McEvoy 2013a, 93–9.
[24] Paulin. *Vit. Ambr.* 26–7, 31.
[25] I am sceptical of any visit by Theodosius to Rome between his victory over Eugenius on 5–6 September 394 and his death at Milan on 17 January 395, although the detail makes little difference to the broader argument presented here. The case for Theodosius' putative visit to Rome late in 394 depends primarily on a positive affirmation by the notoriously problematic Zosimus (4.59.1), a dizzying set of reconstructions from the text of Theodoret (again, hardly the most reliable witness) and inferences drawn from Claudian, Prudentius and others. The 394 visit was rejected as a confusion with the much more securely attested visit of 389 by Ensslin 1953; but its historicity was accepted as genuine by Cameron 1969, 247–80; more recently, Lejdegård 2002, 46–52, accepted that Theodosius visited in 394, but argued Honorius did not accompany him. For the problematic nature of the sources for the war against Eugenius, see Errington 2006, 253–8.
[26] Kulikowski 2000; for Spanish events: Arce 2005, 31–72.
[27] Gillett 2001, 137.
[28] For the character of Honorius' visits: McEvoy 2013a, 172–4.
[29] *CTh* 11.28.4 (13 September 408), 9.42.20 (24 September 408); Gillett 2001, 138.
[30] Gillett 2001, 141.

Alaric negotiated with Honorius' representatives during the Gothic siege of Rome and Portus.[31] Ravenna remained the chief centre for the court down to Honorius' death in 423, but there were also important expeditions to Rome in 414 and 416; Rome was also the location of a dynastic tomb begun by Honorius at St Peter's.[32]

Following the usurpation of John (423–5) and the establishment of Valentinian III in Italy, this oscillation between Ravenna and Rome continued, with Rome occasionally taking the upper hand, particularly after 440 and also for important ceremonial occasions, such as his elevation from Caesar to Augustus on 23 October 425, and, perhaps, his quinquennial consulships in 430 and 435.[33] We rarely hear of Valentinian's court elsewhere than at Ravenna or Rome, and the only two instances are in the context of major political events. The first comes at the very beginning of his reign, in summer 425, when the court was established at Aquileia for a number of months following the overthrow of John, and when his ministers (and emphatically not the infant emperor himself) issued various laws in an effort to reassert legitimate government after John's usurpation. The second, in autumn 437, saw the emperor travel to Constantinople to marry his cousin, Eudoxia; precise details of his route on the outward and return legs of this journey cannot be reconstructed with confidence. So far as we can tell, the last five years of Valentinian's reign were spent continuously at Rome, where he can be observed flexing his political muscle, orchestrating the murder of his *magister militum* Aëtius in 454, before being himself murdered on 16 March 455.

I have spent some time setting out these movements in detail because they reveal a number of significant trends in terms of intraregional relationships. One, as several scholars have noted, is the resurgence in Rome's profile in imperial affairs after 395. But an overview of imperial activities that stretches back to the reign of Gratian (and even earlier) suggests that we can delineate the evolution of a more complex pattern of imperial actions in Italy.

In the first place, the reign of Gratian showed every sign of continuing well-established traditions of imperial presences in Italy. Since the late third century, imperial activities largely concentrated on frontier provinces, so visits to Italy were largely concentrated in Annonaria, particularly at Milan and Aquileia, with occasional trips south to Rome for ceremonial assertions of imperial authority, particularly at imperial anniversaries or after episodes of civil war (as can be seen, for instance, in Constantius II's Roman *adventus* of 357, as well as in earlier visits by Diocletian and Maximian and by Constantine).[34] This showed every sign of continuing under Gratian, even if he did not, as was once supposed, visit Rome.[35]

A second stage in the process can be identified midway through Gratian's reign. In the late 370s and early 380s, and presumably in response to Gothic instability in the Balkans, there was a decisive shift towards northern Italy as the focus of imperial activities, with a particular concentration on residences along an axis stretching

---

[31] See below, n. 45.
[32] Expeditions: Gillett 2001, 138. Tomb: McEvoy 2013b.
[33] For this, and what follows, see Humphries 2012, 161, 165–6.
[34] Humphries 2015; see also Chapter 2 in this volume.
[35] A visit was postulated by Barnes 1975; in a later study (Barnes 1999), he rightly rejected the source for the visit (the *Parastaseis syntomoi chronikai*) as late and unreliable.

between Milan and Aquileia. This remained the pattern under those of his immediate successors who were based in Italy. There were still occasional visits to Rome, as in 389 to reassert authority there after Italy's brief dalliance with Magnus Maximus, and by Honorius in 404, after the upheavals of Alaric's first invasion of Italy. After an interval between Valentinian II's death and the overthrow of Eugenius in 394, the cities along the Milan–Aquileia axis resumed their earlier importance. The shift to Ravenna in 402 might at first have been ephemeral given the return to Ticinum and Milan in 408. What is most striking is the precipitous decline of Gaul in imperial priorities, after the successive residences there of emperors such as Maximian, Constantius I, Constantine I, Constans, Julian as Caesar, Valentinian I and, for the first half of his reign, Gratian. There were, of course, efforts to establish an imperial administration in Gaul: that is precisely what Magnus Maximus had done,[36] and perhaps he might have returned there (but his death in Italy makes that an insoluble speculation); at any rate, we can see an attempt to reassert an imperial presence in Gaul with Theodosius I's establishment of Valentinian II at Trier and later Vienne.[37]

A third stage is visible after the Goths' second incursion into Italy, when we see another shift, this time towards an axis between Ravenna and Rome. At first Ravenna is the dominant partner, even if Rome remained the location of choice for ceremonial events and burials in the imperial mausoleum at the Vatican. Increasingly, though, Rome becomes more important as the reign of Valentinian III progresses, and particularly from the early 440s onwards. Having established this framework, let me now attempt to put some analytical flesh on its bare bones.

Emperors, Invaders and Responses to Crisis

In terms of making sense of these imperial activities, it helps to situate them in the context of the various serious threats to Italian security, arising from both internal conflicts and invasions from outside. The closing decades of the fourth century had been marked chiefly by instability caused by civil war, against Maximus in 388 and Eugenius in 394. But after 400 there was a notable upswing in terms of the frequency of episodes of uncertainty. These include the incursions of Alaric in 401–402/3 and 408–10 leading to the sack of Rome (and its aftermath, including the sacking of Rhegium vividly evoked by Rufinus,[38] before the move to Gaul); the invasion of Radagaisus in 405/6, which caused considerable disruption in Tuscany; the fallout from the destruction of Stilicho in 408; the attack on Italy mounted by the *comes Africae* Heraclianus in 413;[39] the disruption that attended the usurpation of John in 423 and his violent overthrow by eastern forces sent by land and sea two years later; the confrontation between count Boniface and Aëtius at Rimini in 432;[40] the threat of seaborne attacks on peninsular Italy and the islands after the Vandal conquest of Africa and the fall of Carthage in the

---

[36] Harries 1978, esp. 37–8.
[37] Seeck 1919, 274, 276, 280; McEvoy 2013a, 93–7.
[38] Rufinus, *praef.* Origen, *Hom. in Numeros.*
[39] See Wijnendaele 2017.
[40] Wijnendaele 2015, 100–1.

430s; the brief expedition into northern Italy by Attila's Huns in 452;[41] and the Vandal sack of Rome following Valentinian III's death in 455.[42]

Such challenges to Italian security required a variety of responses. In some cases these were military, although the character of the sources means that the nature of individual actions (e.g. those of Stilicho described by Claudian) is often more obscure than we might wish.[43] At times, though, military achievements could be quite considerable, as Jeroen Wijnendaele has argued in connection with Stilicho's defeat of Radagaisus' Goths at Faesulae in 406, in terms of both the scale of the victory itself and the Gothic retainers who now flocked to Stilicho's side.[44] Beyond military action, the court also sought diplomatic resolutions to some crises. Alaric negotiated with Honorius' representatives at Rimini and Ravenna on no fewer than three occasions during his second Italian expedition.[45] The most celebrated example is the embassy comprised of the distinguished senators Gennadius Avienus and Trygetius alongside bishop Leo of Rome dispatched to treat with Attila in northern Italy in 452.[46]

There is also evidence of administrative responses, in which the government sought to expiate the worst effects of upheaval. Our glimpses of such activities generally come from legal sources, and we need to be sensitive here to the problems caused by imperfect survival.[47] Even so, the laws shed interesting light on a number of challenges under Honorius. A law of early December 408, issued by Honorius at Ravenna to Theodorus, praetorian prefect (for the second time) of Italy and Illyricum, refers to various recent upheavals resulting from barbarian incursions, and deals in particular with complex arrangements for the ransoming of captives.[48] The law might refer to circumstances not in Italy but rather in adjacent Illyricum, since both came under Theodorus' jurisdiction, and another law issued to him at roughly the same time more explicitly refers to disruption caused by barbarian raids in Illyricum and the displacement of populations there.[49] But the proximity of Illyricum across the Julian Alps and the Adriatic meant that affairs there were of concern to Italian populations. Interestingly, the law proposes that a leading role in the recuperation of captives be taken by local Christian clergy (*Christianae sacerdotes, vicinorum et proximorum ecclesias retinentes*), and Italian churchmen certainly expressed an interest in such matters. Ambrose of

---

[41] Duval 1976, 291–6.
[42] See Chapter 4 in this volume.
[43] This is particularly true of Stilicho's achievements as described by Claudian: for example, his poem *De bello Gothico*, written to celebrate Stilicho's victory at Pollentia in 402, contains just seventeen vague and allusive lines (580–97) on the confrontation itself
[44] Wijnendaele 2016, 267–84.
[45] First with Jovius, *PPO Italiae*, at Rimini: Olympiodorus fr. 8.1 Blockley; and then twice before Ravenna, before and after the elevation of Priscus Attalus to the purple: Philost. *Hist. eccl.* 12.3–4.
[46] Prosper, *Chron.* 1367.
[47] Salway 2013, §16.
[48] The most complete version of the text is preserved as *Const. Sirm.* 16, which gives the date of 3 December 408 (*data III Non. Decemb.*); other versions survive as *CTh* 5.7.2 (date given as 11 December: *iii id. Dec.*), *Brev.* 5.5.2 (10 December: *iv id. Dec.*); the version in *CTh* was the basis for *CJ* 1.4.11 (a brief excerpt) and 8.50.2. On the difficulties of identifying the recipient: *PLRE* 2, 'Theodorus 9', 1086–7.
[49] *CTh* 10.10.25 (10 December 408): *cum per Illyrici partes barbaricus speraretur incursus . . . Illyricianos omnes.*

Milan had dealt with the ransoming of captives, presumably in Illyricum during the Gothic crisis of 376–82.[50]

Later (and this time definitely in Italy), during similar upheavals caused by barbarian invasions (*conturbatio procellae barbaricae*), perhaps indicating the sack of Rome in August 410, the fate of one captive exercised the concern of bishop Innocent I (401–17) of Rome.[51] During these uncertain times, a Roman woman called Ursa had been carried off into captivity; when she returned to Rome some unspecified time later, she discovered that her husband, Fortunius, had given her up as irretrievably lost and had married a certain Restituta. Ursa appealed to Innocent, who wrote to Probus, a Roman aristocrat (and perhaps the individual who had been western consul in 406) regarded as having some clout in the matter, urging him to pressure Fortunius into returning to his first wife. While it is debatable whether this intervention represents Innocent flexing his social influence 'in the light of the weakness of Honorius' regime after Alaric's invasion',[52] the bishop's intervention clearly shows that the problems of what to do about those carried off as prisoners by invaders very certainly impinged upon Italy. Other sources confirm a picture of difficult times in the context of Alaric's invasion. It was in this context that the wealthy aristocrat Melania the Younger and her husband Pinianus abandoned their Italian estates and made for Africa.[53] A law of Valentinian III, issued 451, sheds further light on the issue, implying that Alaric's incursions into Italy caused hardships that compelled some decurions to sell property.[54] Another of Honorius' extant laws, from May 413, appears to reflect the upheavals caused by Gothic activity in southern Italy after the siege of Rome. It instructs the praetorian prefect Johannes to alleviate tax burdens from regions particularly affected, namely Campania, Etruria, Picenum, Samnium, Apulia, Calabria, Bruttium and Lucania.[55]

We are on rather firmer ground, however, for the reign of Valentinian III, since a number of his *leges novellae* attest to his administration's response to problems caused in Italy by the Vandal conquest of Africa, which culminated with the capture of Carthage in 439.[56] There may already be a hint of looming difficulties in the first *novella*, a law of 8 July 438. It remits debts owing from tax arrears for the most recent year in the tax cycle, extending its provisions to Italy, the islands and, even at this

---

[50] Ambr. *Off.* 2.15.70–1 and 28.136–43; discussion in Lizzi 1989, 28–30. For the wider phenomenon: Klingshirn 1985, esp. 184–7.

[51] Innocent I, *Ep.* 36. For what follows, see the major treatments in Dunn 2007; Sessa 2011; 2012, 139–47.

[52] As argued by Dunn 2007, 107. For a more restrained interpretation, seeing the letter as a rhetorical bid by Innocent to claim authority in domestic matters, see Sessa 2012, 127–73.

[53] Gerontius, *Vita Melaniae* 19; Clark 2021, 98–113.

[54] *N. Val.* 32.5 (451): *statuo itaque a tempore, quo Italiam Alaricus intravit, nullam moveri quaestionem his, quae curiales taliter de facultatibus propriis vendiderunt.*

[55] *CTh* 11.28.7: *idem aa. Iohanni praefecto praetorio. Campaniae Tusciae Piceno Samnio Apuliae Calabriae, sed et Brittiis et Lucaniae ex omni praestationis modo, quem antiqua sollemnitas detinebat, quattuor partes iubemus auferri, ita ut ex indictione decima quinque annorum indulgentia contributa partem solvant publicae functionis. ad reparationem sane cursus intra indulgentiae tempus quidquid fuerit postulatum, id solum conferri censuimus. Dat. VIII id. mai. Ravennae Lucio v. c. cons.* (8 May 413).

[56] It should be noted, however, that no western laws *at all* survive from the years in which the *Theodosian Code* was being compiled (429–37): Salway 2013, §18.

late stage in the Vandal conquest, Africa. A remark in the preamble about 'the condition of present affairs' (*praesentium rerum condicio*) perhaps alluded to the upheavals attending the Vandal advance.[57]

The next law to address this matter was issued on 24 January 440 to the praetorian prefect of Italy, Petronius Maximus.[58] As with the law of July 438, it was concerned with defining the limits of exemptions from tax arrears, but took a slightly less generous line than the earlier law, in that it insisted that the tax burden be shared as equally as possible, and that excessive remissions of arrears to some would only cause the burden to fall more heavily on others. This seems to present a government anxious about its tax base. But altogether more importantly, the law is issued from Rome, and provides the first evidence for the presence of Valentinian and his court in the old capital since the visit in 425–6 at the time of his elevation to the throne. That the court should suddenly relocate to Rome in the course of the winter, and do so in the months following the fall of Carthage, is suggestive that the new strategic disposition in the Mediterranean resulting from the Vandal ascendancy in Africa was a cause of this new pattern in imperial behaviour. The next set of laws appears to confirm this hypothesis.

The next law in the sequence was issued at Rome on 3 March.[59] It dealt with a series of issues that were seemingly affected by growing insecurity. The preamble and first clause addressed the rights of Greek traders (*panatapolae*) to operate at the city of Rome in spite of the protestations of local shop owners (*tabernarii*). That this was a product of unusual circumstances, rather than merely a disinterested effort to impose equal trading opportunities, is implied by some of the language used, specifically its insistence that 'during these critical times the City may be inhabited by a greater multitude' (*in rebus suspectis a maiore multitudine civitas possit habitari*): does the law envisage refugees coming to the city? The second clause similarly responds to local anxieties by clarifying that no Roman citizen or guild member should fear compulsory conscription into the army; nevertheless, they should be prepared to be pressed into sentry duties in defence of the city's walls and gates, and in this respect should abide by the orders of the urban prefect. The third clause picks up this issue, ordering that the urban prefect should oversee the restoration of the city's defences, and that no one should be exempt from assisting with this project. A similar concern with the upkeep of the urban fabric is visible in the final clause of the law, which made provision for the upkeep of the city's aqueducts. That these provisions were a product of uncertain times is by turns implicit and explicit in what the emperor was made to say in the law. While the provision for the maintenance of the aqueducts was stated to have been made to preserve Rome's status (*pro tuendo statu venerandae urbis*), the rest of the law makes it clear that the emperor was concerned chiefly about matters of security that were causing anxiety in the city: contingencies must be put in place to feed a likely

---

[57] N. *Val.* 1.1, §1: *in quartam usque indictionem per omnes provincias atque insulas Italiae, per Africam vero tertiae indictionis debita titulis fiscalibus eximantur*. For 438, Prosper, *Chron.* 1332 mentions raids on Sicily by barbarian 'pirates' – but an earlier entry in his *Chronicon* (1330) implies that these were distinct from the bulk of the Vandal army. For problems of piracy in these years, see Wijnendaele 2015, 107–8.

[58] N. *Val.* 4.

[59] N. *Val.* 5.

influx of new inhabitants; the prefect should oversee the city's defences; and widespread fears of compulsory conscription into the military needed to be scotched.

Further indications that the law was addressing an anxious population come from its address and opening lines. It was not addressed to any particular magistrate, although the second and third clauses clearly envisioned a major role for the urban prefect in overseeing the city's defences; instead, the law was addressed simply *ad populum* – which in context of where the law was issued and the rhetoric adopted in it can only mean the *populus Romanus*. Furthermore, the preamble began with an elegant rhetorical statement of Rome's importance to the emperor.[60] Two aspects are particularly striking: first, the emphasis on Rome's fortunes is stressed by having the words *urbs Roma* placed first in the sentence, right at the opening of the law; secondly, the preamble's language that stressed the emperor's veneration of Rome's status (*veneamur*) was mirrored in the closing clause in the justification offered for restoring the aqueducts (*venerandae urbis*). The law stressed the emperor's determination that the city should continue to enjoy peaceful conditions (*quies*). But this was more than just rhetoric: the emperor's presence in the city could be seen as providing ample demonstration of his need to see to its safety and supply in uncertain times.[61]

Just over two weeks later, on 20 March, Valentinian issued another law from Rome.[62] Its concern was with recruitment to the army, and particularly the problem with deserters; it was addressed, appropriately enough, the *magister militum* Sigisvult,[63] who would be mentioned also in a law issued in June of the same year as overseeing the coastal defences of Italy.[64] The law is linked to expressions of concern about the tax base found in Valentinian's other legislation, such as the laws of July 438 and August 439. It expressed concerns about deserters hiding out on agricultural estates, and that landowners might protest at their removal, owing to the pressure they felt to produce enough crops to be able to pay their taxes. In response, the tenor of the law was firm. The preamble expressed the emperor's frustration at having to restate the law on furnishing recruits, while the first clause concluded by stating that any estate managers knowingly harbouring deserters should receive capital punishment; the third clause prescribed a fine of ten pounds of gold for local magistrates (and their staff) who connived at such practices; and the concluding fourth clause enjoined Sigisvult to publish the law 'by the customary edicts throughout all the municipalities of the provinces' (presumably the provinces of Italy) so that nobody could plead ignorance of the emperor's wishes (*quam legem ne quis se ignorasse confingat, per omnes provinciarum civitates edictis sollemnibus divulgabit*). But Valentinian and his administrators were conscious that the law might be open to abuse, so the second clause ordered an amnesty of thirty days for recruits living on estates to come forward.

---

[60] 'Our constant care for the city of Rome, which we justly venerate as the head of our empire, abides with us, to such an extent that we make wise provision in all ways for her peace and abundance' (*urbis Romae, quam merito caput nostri veneamur imperii, in tantum nos cura non deserit, ut quieti eius atque abundantiae modis omnibus consulamus*).
[61] Humphries 2012, 161, 178.
[62] N. Val. 6.1.
[63] PLRE 2, 'Sigisvult', 1010.
[64] N. Val. 9.

After this law in late March, there is no further surviving legislation from Valentinian until 4 June, when a law was addressed to the praetorian prefect Petronius Maximus.[65] By this stage, the emperor and his court had returned to Ravenna, presumably having made a satisfactory display of the *cura urbis Romae* that had been signalled in the law of 3 March. Now the emperor's attention was once again focused upon tax payments. The law was directed against the unscrupulous activities of *palatini*, officials charged with the collection of tax arrears: Valentinian decreed that they were not to extract anything beyond what was specified in the taxation accounts. Moreover, in order to secure a restoration of order to tax collections, Valentinian specified those officers of state who should be involved in the scrutiny required to end such corruption. These included the 'counts of the two treasuries' (*inlustres viri comites utriusque aerarii*), namely the *comites rei privatae* and *sacrarum largitionum*, provincial governors (in Italy, we may assume) and the praetorian prefect himself, who through posting the law would make it known to the provincials (*programmate suo in cunctorum provincialium iubebit ire notitiam*), a provision which echoed the instructions for publication issued to Sigisvult in the law of 20 March.

Later in the month, on 24 June, Valentinian, still based in Ravenna, issued a law that dealt with the right to bear arms during a period of uncertainty, and which would be the most unambiguous so far about the crisis resulting from the Vandal capture of Carthage.[66] It made explicit reference to the Vandal threat: 'Geiseric, the enemy of our people, is reported to have set forth from the port of Carthage a large fleet, whose sudden excursion and ill-omened depredations must be feared by all shores' (*Gensericus hostis imperii nostri non parvam classem de Karthaginensi portu nuntiatus est eduxisse, cuius repentinus excursus et fortuita depraedatio cunctis est litoribus formidanda*). That fear was genuinely widespread: later in the text it was noted that, owing to the clement weather of the sailing season, it would be impossible to predict exactly where along the Italian coast the Vandals might attack (*tamen quia sub aestiva navigandi opportunitate satis incertum est, ad quam oram terrae possint naves hostium pervenire*). The emperor sought to reassure his audience that a massive effort was being marshalled to defend Italy: the *magister militum* Sigisvult would deploy *milites* and *foederati* throughout the towns and coastal areas of Italy; the other chief commander Aëtius was expected to arrive soon (from Gaul, presumably) with substantial forces; and perhaps most enticingly, an expedition to counter the Vandal assault could be expected from Theodosius II in the East.[67] Although the law was issued from Ravenna, it was addressed more generally, in terms that parallel the law of 3 March, to the Roman people (*ad populo Romano*). Moreover, in a move to reassure the recipients of the law of his continued solicitude, Valentinian added a personal salutation in his own handwriting to his 'most beloved

---

[65] N. *Val.* 7.
[66] N. *Val.* 9.
[67] *Et quamvis clementiae nostrae sollicitudo per diversa loca praesidia disponat atque invictissimi principis Theodosii patris nostri iam propinquet exercitus et excellentissimum virum patricium nostrum Aetium cum magna manu adfore mox credamus cumque vir inlustrissimus magister militum Sigisvuldus tam militum atque foederatorum tuitionem urbibus ac litoribus non desinat ordinare.*

Roman people'.[68] The emperor might now have relocated to Ravenna, but his care for Rome was ever present, just as he had promised in the law of 3 March.

This relatively copious stream of legal evidence begins to dry up after mid-440, but two further laws are pertinent to understanding the imperial court's response to the Vandal threat. The first law is, unfortunately, impossible to date exactly, because it breaks off mid-clause, and is therefore missing its dating formula; nevertheless, the fact that it is issued yet again to Petronius Maximus as praetorian prefect means that it certainly belongs to 440–1.[69] Enough of it survives to show how Valentinian's administration was continuing to respond to the crisis. By now the focus of Geiseric's attack (described in the preamble as a noxious disease, to which Valentinian's law now offers a cure) had become clear: Sicily. The law offered a significant remission of taxes from areas under attack, to a seventh of the usual rate. The text goes on to mention a number of towns, Syracuse, Catania, Aetna, Lilybaeum, Thermae and Soluntum, but breaks off before indicating any special provision being made for them.[70] All of them are on the coast, save for Aetna, which lay on the southern slopes of the volcano. Other sources imply that the Vandal devastation was profound,[71] which offers sufficient justification for the leniency that the emperor displays in these tax remissions.

The final law to be considered here was issued from Ravenna on 14 March 441, again to Petronius Maximus as prefect.[72] It dealt with the fiscal and other liabilities of aristocrats (*inlustres*) and clergy holding land. Again, it insisted that burdens should be shared equally, and specifically mentions that lower-grade taxpayers risk becoming exhausted if the wealthy evade or avoid taxation (preamble). More importantly for my purposes here, the law frankly admitted to the difficulties of the times. It mentioned how taxes that supported a number of defensive activities – road maintenance, arms manufacture, restoring defences and the provision of food, and other activities for public defence (*quo instauratio militarium viarum, quo armorum fabricatio, quo murorum refectio, quo apparatus annonae, quo reliqua opera, per quae ad splendorem defensionis publicae pervenitur*) – were a pressing concern during present difficulties (*sub difficultate autem praesentis temporis*). And it ended by hoping that the combined efforts of rich and poor would help in the current crisis (*ut sero saltem difficultati rerum devotio locupletum pariter ac pauperum iustis aequata partibus libentius obsecundet*).

The picture that emerges from the legislation issued by Valentinian III allows us to see in some detail the nature of the court's response to Italian vulnerabilities in the wake of the fall of Carthage – it is certainly much more comprehensive than the one we have for the period of crisis under Honorius. The challenges facing Valentinian's administration

---

[68] *Et manu divina: proponatur amantissomo nostro populo romano*. This can be compared with the personal greeting (*bene valere te cupimus*) offered by Theodosius II to Egyptian officials in the response to the famous petition (*P. Leiden Z*) of Appion bishop of Syene, Kentasynene and Elephantine sometime between 425 and 450. Discussion in Porten 2011, 441–2; Millar 2006, 22–3, 34, 63, 168–9.

[69] N. Val. 1.2.

[70] *Syracusanus vero Catinensis Aetnensis Lilybitanus Thermitanus Soluntinus* . . . For analysis, see Wilson 1990, 330–1 and 418 n. 13.

[71] E.g. Cassiodorus, *Chron.* 1235 (ed. Mommsen) on 440: *Gensericus Siciliam graviter affligit*. For other sources, see Wilson 1990, 418 nn. 10–15.

[72] N. Val. 10.

largely concerned securing the tax base (and ensuring that tax was extracted equitably) and making provisions for defence. But the response also demanded the emperor's personal touch; it is interesting to note how quickly Valentinian's court made it to Rome after the fall of Carthage: Geiseric had taken the capital of Africa in October 439; by the following January, Valentinian's court was in Rome. And even when the court returned to Ravenna in the summer, the personal greeting in the law of 24 June suggests that the emperor's officials were concerned that his personal solicitude should continue to be demonstrative.

Similar preoccupations can be found in Valentinian's laws from the remainder of his reign, even after treaty arrangements were reached with the Vandals in 442.[73] The challenges of securing the tax base remained a recurring problem,[74] as was the financial hardship of African provincials dispossessed by the Vandals.[75] In the context of Attila's invasion, we find Valentinian seeking to impose order on exactions in southern Italy.[76] But we also find the emperor legislating for a wide range of other concerns: not the least of his (or his advisers') objectives will have been to show that orderly government should continue to operate, even in the face of crisis. Further light on the legacy of these upheavals is shed in papal correspondence. The Hunnic incursion plainly saw captives taken, and the question of how to redeem them once more raised its head as it had done in 408–10. Yet again we have an intervention from the Roman bishopric: six years after the invasion, Leo, who had served as part of the imperial delegation to Attila, wrote to bishop Nicetas of Aquileia offering guidance on the restoration of married women carried off by the barbarians.[77]

Italy between East and West

The first half of the fifth century had seen Italy confronted by serious challenges to its security; at the same time, its command of resources was diminishing as not only large swathes of Africa, but also other territories beyond the Alps periodically fell out of control of the court based in Italy. Yet another factor bearing on Italian fortunes in this period is the division of imperial responsibilities between East and West. Although Malcolm Errington is surely right to emphasise that the roots of the division stretched back further than the accession of Arcadius and Honorius in January 395,[78] there can

---

[73] Treaty: Prosper, *Chron.* 1347; Vict. Vit. 1.13. The most important modern discussion is Modéran 2002; useful summaries in Lancel 2002, 279–81; Merrills and Miles 2014, 61–6.
[74] E.g. the conduct of *palatini* remains a concern for the emperor in N. *Val.* 7.2–3, dating to 442 and 447 respectively.
[75] N. *Val.* 12 (443), 34 (451).
[76] N. *Val.* 36 (452). The context is clear enough from the opening of the preamble, which refers to Aëtius' diligence *inter bellicas curas et obstrepentes lituos*.
[77] Leo I, *Ep.* 159; discussion in Sessa 2011, 423–9.
[78] An early assertion of the significance of 395 is found in Marcell. Com. s.a. 395.3: *Arcadius et Honorius germani utrumque imperium divisis tantum sedibus tenere coeperunt*. For a classic modern statement of its permanency: Bury 1923, 1.2: 'the division of the Empire into two geographical portions, and eastern and a western, under two Emperors, a division which had been common during the past century, was finally established'. For argument that the division was a practical reality in the previous thirty years, see Errington 2006, 1, 3–9, 90–108, 147–8. For wider critique of the trope of imperial division, see Sandberg 2008.

be no doubt that the late fourth and first half of the fifth century saw the emergence of a pattern of relationships between the *partes imperii* that impacted directly upon Italy. This is most often understood in political terms, whether it be the rivalry of Stilicho and the eastern administration in 395–408,[79] the eastern intervention in 425 that led to the establishment of Valentinian III on the throne,[80] or the series of exchanges between Italy and Constantinople in 437–8 that saw the marriage of Valentinian III to Eudoxia and the promulgation of the *Theodosian Code* for the West.[81] The years around 440 represent a high-water mark for East–West cooperation, to the extent that Valentinian's law of 24 June 440 included an expectation that Theodosius II would send aid from the East. This was not a wholly unrealistic prospect: a decade earlier eastern forces under the leadership of Aspar had assisted the West against the Vandals and had held Carthage for a time.[82] An eastern fleet was dispatched to Sicily in 441, although our source, Prosper, sniffs that it was more of a burden than a help.[83] In any case, the army sent with this fleet was soon recalled to assist eastern forces against the Huns in the Balkans.[84] For the short term, the treaty of 442 reduced the necessity of further joint imperial action. Even so, ostentatious displays of western harmony with the East continued: in 448, for instance, Valentinian ratified for the West the validity of those *leges novellae* that Theodosius had issued in his *pars imperii* in the years since the publication of the Code.[85]

While East–West cooperation persisted beyond the period of interest to this chapter, and was manifested in episodes such as naval operations against the Vandals or the elevation of Anthemius, there are also hints that the relationship was under strain. When Priscus of Panium accompanied an embassy to the court of Attila in 449, he encountered there an embassy from the western Romans, an indication that Italy and Constantinople were pursuing discrete Hunnic policies; indeed, Priscus routinely talks of *hesperioi Romaioi*, 'western Romans', in contrast to those ruled from Constantinople, which appears to point towards divergent destinies.[86] The death of Theodosius II and the succession of Marcian in 450 provided further causes of tension: it took Valentinian III – now technically senior Augustus, but not consulted on the matter by authorities in the East – some two years before he acknowledged the legitimacy of his new eastern colleague.[87] Of course, in the interim, communications between Italy and the East continued via other channels, as is abundantly demonstrated by the participation of papal representatives at the Council of Chalcedon in 451, and the correspondence of Pope Leo with the eastern court.[88]

---

[79] Still classic: Mazzarino 1990, 47–71.
[80] Humphries 2012, 164–6; Van Nuffelen 2013, 130–52.
[81] Matthews 2000, 1–9.
[82] *PLRE* 2, 'Fl. Arbabur Aspar', 164–9, at 166. For the campaign, Wijnendaele 2015, 95–6.
[83] Prosper, *Chron.* 1344: *Siciliae magis oneri quam Africae praesidio fuere.*
[84] Prosper, *Chron.* 1346.
[85] *N. Val.* 26.
[86] Priscus fr. 11.2 Blockley. See also Chapter 17 in this volume.
[87] Humphries 2012, 173.
[88] The following letters were addressed directly to Marcian before the rapprochement of 452: Leo, *Epp.* 82–3, 89–90, 94.

Leo's correspondence with Constantinople is a reminder that connections between East and West were well established and interactions could continue regardless of awkward administrative divisions. Even so, there are hints that Italy's place in divisions between East and West was not always clear. This much is suggested by a law enacted by Honorius' government in 398 that sought to compel Jews in Apulia and Calabria in southern Italy to participate in curial liturgies in their communities.[89] The reason for its enactment was that south Italian Jews had been appealing to a law issued in the East (*lege, quae in Orientis partibus lata est*) that had exempted Jewish elites from such service on the basis of earlier legal precedents. To Honorius' ministers, this was insupportable: it represented a threat to the smooth governance of Honorius' part of the empire (*lege cessante, quam constat meis partibus esse damnosam*) and should therefore be ignored. Most discussion of this ruling has centred on whether the eastern law can be identified with a law of Arcadius of 1 July 397, which had sought to confirm privileges issues by Constantine I, Constantius II, Valentinian I and Valens and exempt Jewish religious officials from compulsory public services.[90] But the law is also instructive of the messiness of the division between the *partes imperii*, and how it could be confounded by human interactions across their boundaries. In terms of human geography, Apulia and Calabria were close, as they always had been, to the East; this may have been the case particularly for the region's Jews, who had long-standing connections with the East through the annual collections they made on behalf of the Jewish patriarch.[91] For Honorius' government, however, the dynamics of such interactions mattered much less than the threat they posed in this instance to the territorial and legal integrity of his *pars imperii*; we should not forget either that the law belongs to a period when relations between the *partes* were under considerable strain, to the extent that eastern appointees to the consulship were not recognised in the West in 399 and 400.[92] This case is instructive as an early example of the challenges that arose in connection with Italy's place in the separation of East and West.

Conclusions

The period examined in this chapter saw a profound shift in Italian fortunes. For about a century up to the death of Valentinian I, Italy had enjoyed peace, interrupted only by episodes of civil war, particularly those between Constantine and Maxentius in 312 and Constantius II and Magnentius in 351. After 375, however, both the Po valley and the peninsula became increasingly more vulnerable, and with this came a shift in imperial activity across the region. Under Gratian, a region hitherto marginal to – or transitional in – imperial activity became increasingly central, as the emergence

---

[89] *CTh* 12.1.158. For more detailed discussion of this law, see Humphries 2022 [2016].
[90] *CTh* 16.8.13; with discussion in Linder 1987, 212–13.
[91] This too was a topic that caused Honorius' court anxiety: such payments were outlawed in 399 (*CTh* 16.8.14), but the prohibition was later rescinded in 404 (*CTh* 16.8.17); for discussion, see De Bonfils 2012, 233–43; cf. Linder 1987, 215–16, rejecting any East–West tension as a factor in these laws. On the wider profile of Jewish communities in southern Italy at this period, see Chapter 14 in this volume.
[92] Bagnall et al. 1987, 332–5.

of a Gothic problem in the Danubian provinces caused imperial priorities to focus along an axis from Aquileia to Milan. This arrangement, and the priorities it implied, endured until Alaric's second incursion into Italy in 408–10. Now there began a shift away from that East–West axis to a North–South one that prioritised links between Ravenna and Rome. In part, this reflects a retreat of Roman power beyond the Alps, and a reorientation of imperial priorities towards Italy. This shift was made more decisive when the Vandal acquisition of Africa made the Italian coast open to attack, effectively turning the Mediterranean into a frontier zone for the first time since the Punic Wars. Valentinian III's legislation of the late 430s and early 440s demonstrates a decisive shift in imperial strategic priorities. Concurrently, it was also increasingly via more southerly channels, across the southern Balkans and the Adriatic Sea, that interactions between Italy and Constantinople now occurred, because the land routes along the Danube had been increasingly cut off by Gothic and Hunnic occupation.

We have here clear signs of the geopolitical fragmentation of the empire: it was, moreover, affecting Italy's relations with other regions too. In the aftermath of the invasions and usurpations of the first decade of the fifth century, Gaul and Spain were effectively independent of Honorius for several years; at the same time, Britain slipped from imperial control. Afterward, the ties that bound the north-western provinces to Italy were significantly weaker than had been the case under Valentinian I and his predecessors. While the reigns of Avitus (455–6) and Majorian (457–61) would see a final attempt to reforge the ancient connections between Italy and Gaul, those interactions were beginning to crumble. It is telling that Sidonius Apollinaris in his panegyric of Majorian delivered in 458 complained about the neglect of Gaul by Italian-focused elites as beginning precisely in the reign of Gratian, and continued by his successors.[93] With emperors stuck in Italy, Gaul had languished; now, with Majorian on the throne and present in Gaul, that long neglect seemed at an end.[94] The dream was to be short-lived: Majorian's reign ended in ignominy at an executioner's hand in northern Italy in the summer of 461, after a planned invasion of Africa had come to naught in the previous year. Ricimer, the *magister militum* who had unmade Majorian, now chose in his stead an aristocrat from Lucania in southern Italy, Libius Severus, who would rule for four years as his puppet emperor. This brief oscillation between Italy and Gaul had ended in Italian interests winning out. Thus, it affirms what we have seen generally in this period: a shift in strategic geopolitics away from transalpine Europe and towards the Mediterranean.[95]

---

[93] Sid. Apoll. *Carm.* 5.354–7: *ex quo Theudosius communia iura fugato | reddidit auctoris fratri, cui guttura fregit | post in se vertenda manus, mea Gallia rerum | ignoratur adhuc dominis ignaraque servit*. Commentary in Green 2022, 73, 98.

[94] Sid. Apoll. *Carm.* 5.363–7: *princeps haec omnia noster | corrigit atque tuum vires ex gentibus addens | ad bellum per bella venit; nam maximus isse est, | non pugnasse labor. terimus cur tempora verbis? | pervenit et vincit*. See further Green 2022, 99.

[95] I am grateful for Jeroen Wijnendaele's invitation to contribute, both to the conference on which this volume is based and to an earlier workshop on food supply and the military in Late Antiquity, as well as his editorial good sense. Audiences in Ghent and Cambridge offered helpful feedback on earlier versions of this paper, as did groups in London, Oxford and Maynooth when presented with a related paper; my excellent and collegial neighbours in Cardiff, Shaun Tougher and Nic Baker-Brian, also helped supply materials I could not otherwise access. Trenchant comments from a 'Reviewer 2' (thankfully not 'stopped' in my case) helped improve the final version. Whatever virtues this chapter possesses owe everything to this generous assistance.

Bibliography

Arce, J. (2005) *Bárbaros y romanos en Hispania, 400–507 A.D.*, Madrid.
Bagnall, R. S., A. Cameron, S. Schwartz and K. A. Worp (1987) *Consuls of the Later Roman Empire*, Atlanta.
Barnes, T. D. (1975) 'Constans and Gratian at Rome', *HSCP* 79: 325–33.
Barnes, T. D. (1999) 'Ambrose and Gratian', *AntTard* 7: 165–74.
Bury, J. B. (1923) *History of the Later Roman Empire from the Death of Theodosius I to the Death of Justinian*, 2 vols, London.
Cameron, A. (1969) 'Theodosius the Great and the Regency of Stilico', *HSCP* 73: 247–80.
Cecconi, G. A. (1994) *Governo imperiale e élites dirigenti nell'Italia tardoantica: problemi di storia politico-amministrativa (270–476 d.C)*, Biblioteca di Athenaeum 24, Como.
Chausson, F. (2007) *Stemmata Aurea: Constantin, Justine, Théodose*, Rome.
Clark, E. A. (2021) *Melania the Younger: from Rome to Jerusalem*, New York.
De Bonfils, G. (2012) 'I rapporti legislativi tra le due *partes imperii*', in S. Crogiez-Pétrequin and P. Jaillette (eds) *Société, économie, administration dans le Code Théodosien*, Villeneuve d'Ascq, 233–43.
Delaplace, C. (2015) *La fin de l'Empire romain d'Occident: Rome et les Wisigoths de 382 à 531*, Rennes.
Destephen, S. (2016) 'La naissance de Constantinople et la fin des voyages impériaux (IVe–Ve siècle)', *AntTard* 24: 157–69.
Dunn, G. D. (2007) 'The Validity of Marriage in Cases of Captivity: the Letter of Innocent I to Probus', *EThL* 83: 107–21.
Duval, Y.-M. (1976) 'Aquilée sur la route des invasions (350–452)', *AAAD* 9: 237–98.
Elton, H. (2018) *The Roman Empire in Late Antiquity: a Political and Military History*, Cambridge.
Ensslin, W. (1953) 'War Kaiser Theodosius I. zweimal in Rom?', *Hermes* 81: 500–7.
Errington, R. M. (1996) 'Theodosius and the Goths', *Chiron* 26: 1–27.
Errington, R. M. (2006) *Roman Imperial Policy from Julian to Theodosius*, Chapel Hill.
Giardina, A. (1986) 'Le due Italie nella forma tarda dell'impero', in A. Giardina (ed.) *Società romana ed impero tardoantico*, vol. 1, *Istituzioni ceti economie*, Rome, 1–36.
Gillett, A. (2001) 'Rome, Ravenna, and the Last Western Emperors', *PBSR* 69: 131–67.
Green, R. (2022) *Sidonius Apollinaris: Complete Poems*, Translated Texts for Historians 76, Liverpool.
Halsall, G. (2008) *Barbarian Migrations and the Roman West, 376–568*, Cambridge.
Harries, J. D. (1978) 'Church and State in the *Notitia Galliarum*', *JRS* 68: 26–43.
Hendy, M. F. (1986) *Studies in the Byzantine Monetary Economy, c.300–1450*, Cambridge.
Humphries, M. (2012) 'Valentinian III and the City of Rome (AD 425–55): Patronage, Politics, and Power', in L. Grig and G. Kelly (eds) *Two Romes: Rome and Constantinople in Late Antiquity*, New York, 161–82.
Humphries, M. (2015) 'Emperors, Usurpers, and the City of Rome: Performing Power and Contesting Monarchy from Diocletian to Theodosius', in J. Wienand (ed.) *Contested Monarchy: Integrating the Roman Empire in the Fourth Century AD*, New York, 151–68.
Humphries, M. (2022 [2016]) 'The Emperor, the Jews, and the Anatomy of Empire', *Hermathena* 200–1: 129–47.
Klingshirn, W. E. (1985) 'Charity and Power: Caesarius of Arles and the Ransoming of Captives in Sub-Roman Gaul', *JRS* 75: 183–203.
Kulikowski, M. (2000) 'Barbarians in Gaul, Usurpers in Britain', *Britannia* 31: 325–45.
Lancel, S. (2002) *Victor de Vita: histoire de la persecution vandale en Afrique*, Paris.
Lejdegård, H. (2002) 'Honorius and the City of Rome: Authority and Legitimacy in Late Antiquity', Doctoral dissertation, Uppsala.

Linder, A. (1987) *The Jews in Roman Imperial Legislation*, Detroit.
Lizzi, R. (1989) *Vescovi e strutture ecclesiastiche nella città tardoantica (L'Italia Annonaria nel IV–V secolo d.C.)*, Bibliothea di Athenaeum 9, Como.
McEvoy, M. (2013a) *Child Emperor Rule in the Late Roman West, AD 367–455*, Oxford.
McEvoy, M. (2013b) 'The Mausoleum of Honorius: Late Roman Imperial Christianity in the City of Rome in the Fifth Century', in R. McKitterick, J. Osborne, C. M. Richardson and J. Story (eds) *Old St Peter's Rome*, Cambridge, 119–36.
McLynn, N. B. (1994) *Ambrose of Milan: Church and Court in a Christian Capital*, Berkeley.
Matthews, J. (2000) *Laying Down the Law: a Study of the Theodosian Code*, New Haven.
Mazzarino, S. (1990) *Stilicone: la crisi imperiale dopo Teodosio*, repr. Milan.
Merrills, A. and R. Miles (2014) *The Vandals*, Chichester.
Millar, F. (1986) 'Italy and the Roman Empire: Augustus to Constantine', *Phoenix* 40: 295–318.
Millar, F. (2006) *A Greek Roman Empire: Power and Belief under Theodosius II*, Berkeley.
Modéran, Y. (2002) 'L'établissement territorial des Vandales en Afrique', *AntTard* 10: 87–122.
Omissi, A. (2018) *Emperors and Usurpers in the Later Roman Empire: Civil War, Panegyric, and the Construction of Legitimacy*, Oxford.
Porten, B. (2011) *The Elephantine Papyri in English*, 2nd ed., Documenta et Monumenta Orientis Antiqui: Studies in Near Eastern Archaeology and Civilisation 22, Atlanta.
Ruggini, L. (1961) *Economia e società nel 'Italia Annonaria': rapporti fra agricoltura e commercio dal IV al VI secolo d.C.*, Milan (repr. Bari, 1995).
Salway, B. (2013) 'The Publication and Application of the *Theodosian Code*', *MEFRA* 125 (2), doi: https://doi.org/10.4000/mefra.1754.
Sandberg, K. (2008) 'The So-Called Division of the Roman Empire in AD 395: Notes on a Persistent Theme in Modern Historiography', *Arctos* 42: 199–213.
Seeck, O. (1919) *Regesten der Kaiser und Päpste für die Jahre 311 bis 476 n. Chr.*, Stuttgart.
Sessa, K. (2011) 'Ursa's Return: Captivity Remarriage, and the Domestic Authority of Roman Bishops in Fifth-Century Italy', *JECS* 19: 401–32.
Sessa, K. (2012) *The Formation of Papal Authority: Roman Bishops and the Domestic Sphere*, Cambridge.
Sotinel, C. (2005) *Identité civique et Chistianisme: Aquilée du IIe au VIe siècle*, Rome.
Traina, G. (2009) *428 ad: an Ordinary Year at the End of the Roman Empire*, trans. A. Cameron, Princeton.
Van Hoof, L. and P. Van Nuffelen (2020) *The Fragmentary Latin Histories of Late Antiquity (AD 300–620): Edition, Translation, and Commentary*, Cambridge.
Van Nuffelen, P. (2013) 'Olympiodorus of Thebes and Eastern Triumphalism', in C. Kelly (ed.) *Theodosius II: Rethinking the Roman Empire in Late Antiquity*, Cambridge, 130–52.
Ward-Perkins, B. (2014) 'A Most Unusual Empire: Rome in the Fourth Century', in C. Rapp and H. A. Drake (eds) *The City in the Classical and Post-classical World*, Cambridge, 109–29.
Wijnendaele, J. W. P. (2015) *The Last of the Romans: Bonifatius – Warlord and Comes Africae*, London.
Wijnendaele, J. W. P. (2016) 'Stilicho, Radagaisus, and the So-Called "Battle of Faesulae"', *Journal of Late Antiquity* 9: 267–84.
Wijnendaele, J. W. P. (2017) 'The Manufacture of Heraclianus' Usurpation (413 C.E.)', *Phoenix* 71: 138–56.
Wilson, R. J. A. (1990) *Sicily under the Roman Empire: the Archaeology of a Roman Province, 36 BC–AD 535*, Warminster.

4

THE FINAL WESTERN EMPERORS, ODOACER AND LATE ROMAN ITALY'S RESILIENCE

Jeroen W. P. Wijnendaele

A MID-SIXTH-CENTURY ITALIAN HISTORIOGRAPHER wrote the following about the year 476:

> The emperor Zeno remembered the affection felt for him by the senate and people; and therefore showed himself so generous to all that he earned the gratitude of every one. He upheld so well the senate and people of Rome, that statues were even erected to him in various parts of the city. His times were peaceful.[1]

Very few things are as good a sign to herald the restoration of imperial authority as the erection of an emperor's statue. This passage serves as a deliberate counterweight to that oft-quoted passage in the surviving fragments of Malchus, concerning the Roman senate's embassy to Zeno on behalf of Odoacer to request the dissolution of western emperorship.[2] These two stories are not mutually exclusive. We know that after Julius Nepos' murder in 480, there were to be no more official western Augusti. Yet as far as Italy is concerned, the period of 476 onwards was a period of prosperity spent under the aegis of empire, after a quarter-century of mayhem and misery. For this chapter, therefore, I want to give a brief survey of the period 455–93, with a special focus on the final western emperors and Odoacer.[3] It is not the aim to cover every aspect of these men's background or government, but rather to focus on their relationship with the Italian field army and the impact their interaction had on Italy. I will not go over the well-known tribulations of the downright dearth of sources we have at our disposal, never mind their fragmentary and opaque deficiencies. Instead, I want to immediately advance two theses in this chapter. Firstly, that the murders of Aëtius and Valentinian III did not necessarily mean the terminal haemorrhage of imperial power in the West, as eastern sources like to portray, and as has often been regurgitated in

---

[1] *Anon. Vales.* 2.9.44 (trans. Rolfe).
[2] Malch. fr. 14 (Blockley 1983 henceforth).
[3] Unless one is willing to hark back to Cantarelli 1896, very few works cover this specific period and region. More profitable are choice chapters in Henning 1999 and MacGeorge 2002. McEvoy 2017 is the most recent contribution on the final emperors, with special emphasis on their relationship with Rome. Elton 2018 and Kulikowski 2019 provide solid general accounts.

modern scholarship.⁴ The majority of Valentinian's successors fought tooth and nail to restore the position of western emperor as leader of government.⁵ Yet this very ambition often clashed with that of the senior commanders of the Italian field army. This turned out to be the major determinant directing the dissolution of the western imperial office. The second thesis flowing out of this is that the actual end of western emperorship in 480 meant the salvation of Italy. Paradoxically, nothing demonstrates this better than Odoacer's war with Theoderic, which despite its viciousness also serves as a testament to the recovery and resilience of late Roman Italy, on the eve of its transformation into a *regnum*.⁶

Petronius Maximus

As is well known, the murder of Valentinian III in 455 did have grave ramifications for the Imperial West. It meant the end of the Theodosian dynasty and introduced a new era of domestic insecurity. For Italy, this all started with the wedding plans of Petronius Maximus, the orchestrator of Valentinian's assassination and his self-proclaimed successor.⁷ In order to strengthen his claim to the throne, Maximus forced his predecessor's widow to marry him, while his son Palladius married her daughter Eudocia.⁸ The latter marriage proved to be a fatal mistake, for it meant that Maximus violated the western treaty with Geiseric, since Eudocia had been promised to Geiseric's heir Huneric as part of the treaty of 442. Now that the terms of this treaty had been breached, Geiseric seized upon the opportunity to exact retribution. He set sail with his army to Rome, which he duly sacked, after which he returned to Africa with substantial booty and several prize hostages including the dowager empress, her two daughters and Aëtius' younger son Gaudentius.⁹ Meanwhile, Maximus panicked, tried to flee the city, and was brutally killed. Maximus' death has often been interpreted as the result of a popular riot.¹⁰ Instead, it seems more likely that Maximus was betrayed by the imperial bodyguard, probably at the instigation of Majorian.

---

⁴ See the verdicts of Priscus fr. 30.1 (Blockley 1983 henceforth) and Marcell. Com. s.a. 454.2. Far too many modern scholars still see follow this verdict in regards to Aëtius, but for a more critical assessment see Moss 1973; Delaplace 2015, ch. 8; Wijnendaele 2017.
⁵ To use the expression of Halsall 2007, 281.
⁶ I adapt Salzman 2021's use of 'resilience' here. While, in late antique studies, resilience has been mainly used in environmental debates, it can be profitably used for political and social history as well. Resilience is here understood as the 'marshalling of resources to reorganize and restore social formations, even in the face of fractures and swerves' (Salzman 2021, 18).
⁷ *PLRE* 2, 'Petronius Maximus 22', 749–51; Czuth 1983; McEvoy 2013, 298–300.
⁸ Hyd. 155(162) (ed. Burgess 1993 henceforth). Oost 1968, 305, believed that Palladius married Valentinian's younger daughter Placidia, since Maximus 'would not have been so foolish as to break with her prospective father-in-law [Geiseric]'. However, Conant 2012, 28 n. 37, convincingly shows that Palladius married Eudocia. It is worthwhile to note that Maximus did not consider breaking off Olybrius and Placidia's betrothal. In the long run it would have been much safer to have Palladius marry Placidia. Given that Maximus and Olybrius belonged to the same network, however, this option was probably not open to a usurper needing support from his own power base.
⁹ Prosper, *Chron.* s.a. 455.1.
¹⁰ Jones 1964, 240; Loyen 1967, 55; Oost 1968, 307; Clover 1978, 176; O'Flynn 1983, 105; Collins 1999, 89; Gillett 2003, 87; Halsall 2007, 255; McEvoy 2013, 325.

The fact that Geiseric met no serious opposition and was even able to sack Rome over a two-week period raises questions about the state of the city's defences. Only a few months earlier, Valentinian had still been training there with elite soldiers.[11] Less than a year later, the army suddenly resurged, scoring victories over the Vandals along the great western islands.[12] So, where had these troops gone? Even Maximus would have had the good sense to have kept some sort of praesental army relatively near for his protection. The most plausible explanation is that someone withdrew the protection of these troops from Maximus at a key moment and that Maximus decided to flee not just because of the approach of Geiseric, but because he realised that a large portion of his troops would not stay to defend him. The sources are clear that his own troops played at least some role in his final moments. Prosper describes how Maximus was killed by royal 'servants' (*famuli*), a term sufficiently vague to include perhaps *buccellarii* or *domestici*.[13] One also notes that Hydatius specifically claims that he was killed as a result of a popular riot and military revolt, that is, that there was definitely a military element to his death.[14] Meanwhile, John of Antioch remarks that Maximus was deserted by his bodyguard at the end, and while he does not identify the precise status of the individual who threw the fatal rock at him, he is just as likely to have been one of these deserters as anyone else.[15] Finally, Sidonius remarks that Maximus had not been in control of the soldiers at the time of his death,[16] and, while not always reliable about fifth-century western events, Jordanes reports that Maximus was slain 'by a Roman soldier'.[17]

The new emperor had evidently not succeeded in gaining the confidence of his palatine forces, some of whom may have remained loyal to Majorian, a former contender for the throne after Valentinian's murder.[18] Majorian is not known to have held any command under Maximus, and it may be assumed that the latter did not wish to give a major command to his only rival. It is possible, therefore, that Majorian had already been stirring up dissent among the *domestici* responsible for Maximus' protection and had withdrawn troops loyal to him from Rome as soon as Maximus became emperor, a common warlord tactic in this era.[19] Maximus had always been a civilian aristocrat prior to his emperorship and did not demonstrate great leadership in the

---

[11] Priscus fr. 30.1.
[12] Sid. Apoll. *Carm.* 2.367; Hyd. 170(177); Priscus fr. 31.1.
[13] Prosper, *Chron.* s.a. 455.1.
[14] Hyd. 155(163).
[15] Joh. Ant. fr. 201.
[16] Sid. Apoll. *Epist.* 2.13.5.
[17] Jord. *Get.* 235.
[18] Priscus fr. 30.1.
[19] Oppedisano 2013, 59–69, rightly refutes older Italian scholarship, which envisioned a grand collusion to bring down Maximus between the Italian field army and Geiseric. However, he absolves Majorian from any involvement in Maximus' demise, on the argument that he was not in control of all soldiers in Rome. I agree it is safer to respect the sources and see the imperial bodyguard as having contributed to Maximus' downfall, which facilitated Geiseric's attack. However, Majorian need only have withdrawn soldiers loyal to him, and stir up dissent among others, to let Maximus be swept away by further events. This would have been reminiscent of Aëtius' tactics in bringing down the *magister militum* Felix in 430; see Wijnendaele 2017.

advent of Geiseric's attack. At that point, disgruntled bodyguards deserted and perhaps even killed him.

Avitus

The Vandal sack of Rome meant the heartland of the Imperial West was threatened for the first time since the treaty of 442. Geiseric went on to conquer the last imperial possessions in Africa and launched massive raids throughout the Mediterranean.[20] All major western islands, save Sicily, soon found themselves under Vandal occupation.[21] Surprisingly, however, the next western emperor was proclaimed in Gaul. On 9 July 455, Eparchius Avitus, the only known *magister militum* of Maximus, was hailed as emperor with the support of the Gallic army, the local aristocracy and the Aquitanian Goths.[22] He crossed over to Italy on 21 September, where he was quickly able to establish himself because of his Gothic troops.[23] The fact that Avitus even maintained his own Gothic guard in Italy suggests he did not trust the imperial guard, who had failed to avert the murder of the two previous emperors. Nevertheless, he did make some effort to win the support of the Italian field army. Although Rome had been completely at the mercy of Geiseric in 455, the new rising star of the Italian field army Ricimer was able to inflict crushing defeats on the Vandals in both Sicily and Corsica in 456.[24] Clearly, the Italian field army was still a capable force to be reckoned with. Avitus had sent Ricimer to Sicily for this task as *comes*, and another source states that Majorian held the rank of *comes domesticorum* during Avitus' reign.[25] Given their close ties, it is possible he had appointed both men as *comites domesticorum*.[26] However, Avitus appointed his own Gallic supporters as his *magistri militum*, and this may have been a source of discontent within the Italian field army. Avitus' position in Italy steadily weakened throughout the rest of the year. A famine struck the peninsula, and this was probably aggravated by the lack of imported African grain due to Geiseric's hostilities.[27] The recent sack of Rome also meant that the treasury was in such a deplorable state that Avitus was forced to sell bronze obtained from public works to pay off his Gothic guards.[28] Most significantly, Avitus was never able to win over the Italian elites to his side. He appointed several Gauls to key palatine offices, but this only offended the Italian elites who saw these as their monopoly. For them, the new emperor remained

---

[20] Vict. Vit. 1.13.
[21] Clover 1999; Merrills and Miles 2010, 129–40.
[22] *PRLE* 2, 'Eparchius Avitus 5', 196–8; Sivan 1989; Harries 1994, 54–81.
[23] Joh. Ant. fr. 202.
[24] Hyd. 169(176), 170(171); Sid. Apoll. *Carm.* 2.367.
[25] Ricimer: Hyd. 169(176); Majorian: *Chron. Gall. 511* 68 (627–8) (ed. Burgess 2001 henceforth).
[26] Meyer 1969, 6.
[27] Joh. Ant. fr. 202.
[28] Burgess 1987, 336 n. 5, already observed the stark contrast between Petronius Maximus' coinage and that of Avitus. During a reign of scarcely seventy-seven days, Maximus managed to issue a massive output of gold coins (thirty-three different issues at Rome, twenty-eight at Arles). During his reign of nearly a year, there is only one known and underweight issue by Avitus.

an outsider relying on barbarian support.[29] Eventually, the army in Italy cast off its allegiance and rose up in revolt in late 456.

Majorian and Ricimer initiated their revolt in September as the sailing season drew to a close and thus reduced the possibility of Vandal raids. They will also have been encouraged by the departure of Avitus' Gothic troops from Italy. Their first act was probably usurping the high command of the field army. Avitus' *magister militum* Remistus was killed near Ravenna on 17 September.[30] When Avitus received word of his main general's death, he took an army in all haste with him from Arles to reassert his control over Italy, but was defeated at Placentia one month later.[31] The sources are in conflict about the circumstances of Avitus' deposition.[32] The most likely outcome is that he was forced to abdicate and was consecrated as a bishop, but conveniently died shortly afterward. Yet far more significant than the nature of Avitus' ultimate fate is that of his downfall. The battle of Placentia was the first time since Gratian's downfall in 383 that a western field army had taken up arms to bring down its incumbent emperor. More crucially, this was the first time a western Roman army brought down an emperor without immediately replacing him with a candidate of their own choice. Instead, it would take more than a year before Majorian proclaimed himself Augustus.[33]

Majorian

The question of Majorian's and Ricimer's official positions after Avitus' fall, and their relationship, is a thorny one. One western source states that both became *magistri militum* in February 457.[34] Some regard the new eastern emperor Leo I as responsible for these appointments, yet it is more likely that Majorian and Ricimer had simply usurped these ranks during their rebellion against Avitus.[35] Majorian eventually became emperor, but the sources are divided over the date of his elevation. One chronicle states that he was elevated on 1 April 457, another that he only became Augustus on 28 December 457.[36] This date is to be preferred, because Majorian issued his first *novella* shortly afterwards, in which he expressed the common trope of *recusatio imperii*. It is often assumed that Leo endorsed Majorian as Augustus. However, two eastern sources state that Leo made Majorian Caesar, and this discrepancy could explain the dating problem.[37] By February 457, there had been an interregnum of five

---

[29] Sivan 1989, 89; Harries 1994, 80; Henning 1999, 35; MacGeorge 2002, 191.
[30] *Addit. Prosp. Haun.* s.a. 456; Fast. Vind. Prior s.a. 456. Theoph. a.m. 5948 is surprisingly enough the only eastern source to record Remistus' murder.
[31] Hyd. 176(183); Priscus fr. 32; *Chron. Gall. 511* 68 (627–7); Gregory of Tours, *Hist.* 2.11.
[32] For the debate, see Mathisen 1985; Burgess 1987; Mathisen 1991.
[33] Despite his brief reign, Majorian has received decent coverage in various articles and chapters, especially by Gerry Max and Ralph Mathisen. With Oppedisano 2013, we finally have a dedicated monograph.
[34] Fast. Vind. Prior. s.a. 457.
[35] *PLRE* 2, 'Maiorianus', 703; Demandt 1970, 673; Max 1979, 234; O'Flynn 1983, 107. Barnes 1983, 268, for the suggestion of the two warlords usurping these commands.
[36] 1 April 457: Fast. Vind. Prior. s.a. 457; 28 December 457: *Auct. Prosp.* s.a. 457.
[37] Marcell. Com. s.a. 457; Jord. *Rom.* 335.

months since Avitus' fall – the longest period without any western emperor so far. Yet Majorian waited until 28 December 457 before he finally took the title of Augustus. It seems likely that Leo had originally appointed him Caesar in April 457, but that Majorian was not satisfied with this, and kept negotiating until it became clear that he would not receive eastern support as Augustus. A few days before the year was about to end, and Majorian intended to take his first consulship, he then proceeded to claim the title regardless.[38]

Majorian has often been seen as a puppet of Ricimer when he ascended the throne, or at least the weaker partner in their collaboration, while Ricimer then became the *generalissimo* on whose power Majorian depended.[39] Ricimer's later reputation as kingslayer and kingmaker, due to his role in the downfall of Avitus, Majorian and Anthemius, whilst also having aided the elevation of Majorian, Libius Severus and Olybrius, has influenced scholars retrospectively to see his dominance in Italy starting in 456. There are several arguments against this view, and that his hegemony has to be postponed until Majorian's death, that is, that Majorian remained the dominant partner. Firstly, Ricimer does not feature prominently in the sources until his murder of Majorian. He is not directly attested before his victories in 456, and is not known to have conducted any military operations during Majorian's reign: Majorian himself, or other commanders, conducted the necessary military operations. Secondly, Majorian had a more prominent track record at the time of his elevation. He had already fought with distinction in Gaul a decade before Ricimer's victories. In 455, he was considered important enough to become *comes domesticorum*. That Valentinian III considered Majorian worthy of his daughter's hand, and that his widow backed his bid for the throne, again underlines Majorian's prominence before Ricimer had even appeared on the scene.

Majorian ensured that Ricimer could not become a *generalissimo* by deliberately exercising his personal right to appoint a variety of commanders to the campaigns fought in his name. Already during the spring of 457, he sent a force under a certain Burco to northern Italy that defeated 900 Alamanni.[40] This success was repeated during the summer of 458 when his soldiers defeated a Vandal raid in Campania.[41] This pattern recurs through Majorian's reign, with other commanders such as Aegidius in Gaul, Nepotianus in Spain and Marcellinus in Sicily.[42] More crucially, Majorian could

---

[38] A breakdown in relations is evident from Majorian's refusal to acknowledge Leo's emperorship and consulship in his first edicts issued in 458 (*N. Maj.* 1–2). However, after some time Majorian recognised Leo (*N. Maj.* 3–7), while the latter recognised western consuls appointed by Majorian (Bagnall et al. 1987, 454–7). Jones 1964, 323 observes that it was a common tactic of both Leo and his successor Zeno to appoint rivals as Caesar while playing for time. Leo probably did this with Majorian to keep him subordinate, given that neither had any great claim to legitimacy.

[39] Oost 1968, 306; O'Flynn 1983, 109; Williams and Friell 1999, 261 n. 9; Liebeschuetz 2007, 482; Lee 2013, 94; McEvoy 2013, 325; Salzman 2021, 162–3.

[40] Sid. Apoll. *Carm.* 5.373–9.

[41] Sid. Apoll. *Carm.* 5.388–440. Ricimer cannot have been in charge of this force, since Sidonius never refers to it in a later survey of his victories.

[42] The epitaph for the otherwise unattested Constantius Heros (*ILCV* 66) most likely was also set up for a commander who served under Majorian. See Wijnendaele and Hanaghan 2021.

trust these men to carry out campaigns in the field without turning against him or each other (a very familiar feature of the first half of the fifth century).[43] Ricimer's loyalty was guaranteed by granting him the most significant generalship and additional honours, such as the title of *patricius* and the western consulship of 459.[44] Yet Majorian had already emphasised in his first *novella* his care of military affairs. In this way, Majorian ensured that he personally remained the supreme commander and thus became the first western emperor since Theodosius I to maintain equilibrium between his various generals. More importantly, Majorian managed to combine the two portfolios that had been separated since the death of Theodosius I: that of supreme commander of the armed forces and that of head of state.

He spent the rest of his reign strengthening his military authority as emperor. Most of 458 was dedicated to the preparations of campaigns to regain the allegiance of the western transalpine provinces and ultimately to invade Vandal Africa. To this end, he did not take up residence in Rome, as had the previous three emperors, but instead installed himself at Ravenna, where he issued no less than seven *novellae* during 458.[45] Majorian's presence in this city is best explained by his need to construct a new fleet and assemble additional troops. Ravenna's closer proximity to both Gaul and Illyricum made it preferable to Rome for both these reasons. When Majorian finally crossed the Alps into Gaul in late 458, it was at the head of an army which included many war bands originating from Illyricum in the aftermath of the disintegration of Attila's empire. Majorian probably took the field into western Illyricum, attracted the service of several of these, and then used them to pacify remaining Huns.[46] As a result of this subjugation, Majorian was able to divide their spoils among the rest of his troops. One cannot overestimate the significance of war booty in an economy of violence during an era where the state's finances were dwindling.[47] Majorian seems to have pursued the same tactic as warlord commanders had done in the 420s: to expand both his military and economic resources by means of aggressive military campaigns. This reduced threats from his eastern frontier and reinforced his authority as supreme commander, while Ricimer was left in charge of the Italian field army.

After having prepared this army, Majorian then crossed the Alps into Gaul, which was in a state of anarchy, but which he managed to pacify with a combination of diplomacy and show of arms. From 17 April 459 to 28 March 460 he is attested at Arles, where he rearranged Gallic affairs to his satisfaction. The emperor then entered Spain in May 460. Majorian's itinerary so far was exceptional. Not since Magnus Maximus (383–8) had a western emperor campaigned in both Illyricum and Gaul.

---

[43] Wijnendaele 2016; 2018.
[44] *N. Maj.* 1. Too much has been made in the past of Majorian styling Ricimer here as *parens*. In fact, half of the *Constitutiones Sirmondianae* feature emperors from Constantine I to Theodosius II addressing their praetorian prefects as such. To the best of my knowledge, nobody has ever dared suggesting that because of this we should regard Ablablius or Felix as Constantine I's puppet masters.
[45] *N. Maj.* 1–7. Gillett 2001, 150–1, demonstrated that Majorian is never known to have visited Rome when he was emperor.
[46] Sid. Apoll. *Carm.* 5.503–5; Wijnendaele and Hanaghan 2021, 269–71.
[47] Wijnendaele 2018, 438–40.

More extraordinarily, the last Augustus to have both visited the Iberian provinces and campaigned in Africa was the Tetrarch Maximian in the 290s. By travelling through Gaul and Spain, Majorian reasserted personal control over these regions and fostered links with the various polities before his invasion of Africa.[48] In this way, he consolidated the strength of the western imperial office. Alas, as is well known, this all became void when the Vandals sabotaged his fleet and he was forced to retreat back to Gaul, and then to Italy, where he learned the consequences of his policies.

Ricimer had Majorian killed near Derdona in northern Italy on 7 August 461.[49] Was he too independent as emperor, and did Ricimer fear that he would become a threat to him? Did Ricimer wish to undo Majorian because he did not support his campaigns outside Italy? Was Majorian's treaty with Geiseric the breaking point in their relationship? These are some of the explanations given in the past for Ricimer's volte-face in 461, yet they all start from the premise that Ricimer enjoyed an all-powerful position within Majorian's government and was at liberty to dispose of him at his own volition. Ricimer had hitherto been subordinate to Majorian. As for the precise cause in the breakdown in relations between Majorian and Ricimer, it probably had very little to do with Majorian's treaty with Geiseric, given that this was agreed during the summer of 460, while Majorian only returned to Italy a year later, having first re-entered Gaul, where he resided at Arles.[50] It then took Ricimer another four months to elevate Libius Severus as the next emperor.[51] Despite Majorian's long absence from Italy, Ricimer did not have a candidate ready to replace him, a situation which eerily reminds us of the death of Valentinian II and Arbogastes' elevation of Eugenius.[52] Indeed, the emperor was clearly not aware of any growing tensions between him and Ricimer, since he demobilised his army of Danubian auxiliaries when returning to Italy. Hence the evidence suggests that Ricimer's decision to move against Majorian was relatively sudden and opportunistic rather than long planned.

The emperor had been absent from Italy for three years. During this time, Ricimer strengthened his control over the regional field army.[53] His other key supporters were probably members of the Italian and Roman senatorial aristocracy (Hydatius' *invidorum concilio*).[54] They can hardly have approved of the emperor's prolonged absence, limiting their opportunities to profit from imperial patronage and hold palatine offices. Furthermore, the grand Vandal campaign had cost them dearly, with promises of higher taxes to come. That this campaign had then ended 'on shameful terms' will surely have incensed them. Last but not least, a further insult to their parochial sentimentalities was his allocation of the western consulship of 460 to a Gaul.[55] When Majorian arrived in

---

[48] Sid. Apoll. *Carm* 5.353–60 explicitly disparaged the Theodosian dynasty's neglect of Gaul.
[49] Fast. Vind. Prior. s.a. 461. Chron. Gall. *511* 72 (635–6); Marcell. Com. s.a. 461; Jord. *Rom*. 335.
[50] Sid. Apoll. *Epist*. 1.9.
[51] Fast. Vind. Prior. s.a. 461.
[52] Croke 1976.
[53] At the time of Majorian's elimination, Ricimer had already accumulated enough wealth to suborn Marcellinus' 'Scythian' soldiers in Sicily. Priscus fr. 38.1 explicitly states that Marcellinus could not compete with Ricimer's wealth.
[54] Hyd. 205(210); Salzman 2021, 165.
[55] Bagnall et al. 1987, 454–5.

Italy, Ricimer had him ambushed. Five days passed between Majorian's capture and his eventual murder. John of Antioch claims that Ricimer first stripped Majorian of his imperial symbols, suggesting that the general formally 'abolished' Majorian's emperorship, and then eliminated him as a private citizen.[56] This was a major departure from the conduct of previous leading *magistri militum* in the fifth century. Ricimer's execution of Majorian heralded the final disintegration of the western Roman army as an imperial force outside Italy, as the subsequent events of 461 were to show.

Libius Severus

Majorian's death meant the fragmentation of military authority and the effective disintegration of the western Roman army as a supraregional force.[57] Outside Italy, warlord commanders rejected Ricimer's hegemony and went their own way, such as Aegidius in Gaul, Marcellinus in Dalmatia and Nepotianus in Spain. Meanwhile in Italy, a series of western emperors continued to reside during the next fifteen years, yet henceforth they either reigned as puppets of the warlord commanders of the regional field army, or as their rivals. None of Majorian's successors ever regained full control of the army in Italy, let alone those forces outside the peninsula which had taken orders from him previously. Meanwhile, Geiseric continued to promote the interests of Olybrius as his candidate for the western throne, and raided the Italian littoral.[58] Ricimer's elevation of Libius 'Serpentius' Severus resolved few of these issues. Severus himself is a blank, besides the fact that he was a senator who hailed from Lucania (a region vulnerable to Vandalic raids), and Constantinople flat out refused to recognise him.[59] The Italian field army still performed admirably in its land defence of the peninsula, as demonstrated by Ricimer's victory at Bergamo over an invading Alan army under their *rex* Beorgor in 464.[60] Yet its naval resources were utterly crippled, as noted by contemporaries.[61] This was the inevitable result of Geiseric's sabotaging one of Majorian's fleets near Alicante, but also because of Marcellinus heisting the other one during his retreat from Sicily, due to Ricimer suborning his auxiliaries.[62] As a naval warlord based in Dalmatia,

---

[56] For an interesting precedent, see Alaric's treatment of Priscus Attalus in 410 (Sozom. *Hist. eccl.* 9.8; Zos. 6.12.3).

[57] Wijnendaele 2018, 429–32.

[58] Priscus fr. 38.2; Clover 1978.

[59] Cassiod. *Chron.* s.a. 461. Oost 1970 goes to the fullest extent possible in any reconstruction of Severus' background, with the paucity of material available. Woods 2002 remains valuable for Severus' coinage and the question of Ricimer's hegemony.

[60] Fast. Vind. Prior. s.a. 464; Cassiod. *Chron.* s.a. 464; Marcell. Com. s.a. 464.

[61] Priscus fr. 39.1 explicitly states that during the reign of Libius Severus, the western government struggled against the Vandals 'by their lack of a fleet'.

[62] Priscus fr. 38.1. Previously, Ricimer had possessed the naval means to score a victory over the Vandals near Corsica. Majorian had also expanded the west's naval capacities by the construction of two new fleets for his Vandal campaign (Sid. Apoll. *Carm.* 5.441–5). Geiseric captured Majorian's main fleet in Spain, but another fleet must have been present with Marcellinus near Sicily. He had presumably travelled with it to Sicily in the first place, so this was probably the fleet traditionally based at Ravenna. When Marcellinus retreated to Dalmatia he took this fleet with him and crippled Italy's naval capacity. Therefore, 461 meant the end not only of the western Roman army as a unified force, but also of its navy.

Marcellinus turned out to be the only military actor capable of successfully combating the Vandals, as evidenced by his independent victory over them in Sicily in 464.[63] Throughout this period, the island became contested territory with sporadic Vandal occupation, while Corsica and Sardinia remained firmly part of Geiseric's domain.[64] Individual military successes by renegades, however, did little to alter the larger geopolitical challenges Italy faced. When Libius Severus died in 465, with or without a little help from his friend Ricimer, Italy entered its longest interregnum.

Anthemius

It took sixteen months, featuring undoubtedly plenty of shuttle diplomacy between Ricimer and Leo I, before a new western emperor was hailed. Ultimately, Anthemius arrived in Italy with impeccable credentials from the East, conveniently backed up by a personal treasury and sizeable army.[65] One can acknowledge that Anthemius' imperial credentials were in fact even better than Leo's, and that this was the prime reason for the latter shipping him off to Italy, whilst also recognising that Leo could not have given the West a more competent emperor. Furthermore, Anthemius was the only western emperor who ever received full eastern recognition after Valentinian III's demise, and was treated as a partner in the imperial college.[66] In many ways, Anthemius' emperorship mirrored that of Majorian. Both had been career officers hailing from families with a track record of service going back to the late fourth century.[67] Both had been contenders for imperial office on earlier occasions, due to their ties with respective previous dynasties. Both took their role as supreme commander of the western army seriously, and pursued a policy of tackling Geiseric, the most significant obstacle to the restoration of western imperial authority beyond Italy. Yet, regarding Italy, Anthemius had clearly learned from Majorian's mistakes. Throughout his reign, Anthemius never left the peninsula and instead took up residence in Rome, after his arrival and acclamation as Augustus on 12 April 467. Equally importantly, he carefully fostered relations with the senatorial elites, some of whom backed him until the end. Similarly, Anthemius was at pains to set up a rapprochement with Ricimer. A decade after the elevation of Majorian, Ricimer's position as uncrowned ruler of the Italian field army could not be ignored.[68] This is nowhere more apparent than in Sidonius' speeches. In his panegyric to Majorian of late 458, Sidonius only describes Ricimer anonymously in two lines as Majorian's brother-in-arms under Aëtius. In contrast, he devotes five lines to another unnamed *magister militum* whose martial prowess is

---

[63] Hyd. 223(227).
[64] Clover 1999; Caliri 2016.
[65] *PLRE* 2, 'Anthemius 3', 96–8; O' Flynn 1991; Roberto 2015; Oppedisano 2020.
[66] This is amply demonstrated by eastern coinage, and by mutual recognition of the twin regimes' consuls during his reign. Anthemius also received the unprecedented honour that century to hold a sole consulship as western emperor in 468 (Bagnall et al. 1987, 470–1).
[67] On Anthemius' pedigree, see Roberto 2015, 4–7.
[68] In an interesting slip of the tongue, Marcell. Com. s.a. 464 erroneously describes him as *Ricimere rege*.

favourably compared to renowned Republican commanders.[69] By way of comparison, in his panegyric to Anthemius in 467, Sidonius explicitly named Ricimer and praised him in thirty lines, effectively crafting a miniature panegyric inside the main panegyric. A few years later, Ricimer was regarded as *qui tunc secundis ab Anthemio principe habenis rempublicam gubernabat*.[70] Words of praise were accompanied with words of vows, as Anthemius gave his daughter Alypia in marriage to the Suevo-Gothic general (a decision he infamously regretted years later during a heated exchange with the bishop of Pavia).[71]

There is no need to cover in detail Anthemius' 'fourth Punic War' (to quote Emile Félix Gautier), the epochal event of his reign.[72] Regarding Italy, a few things stand out. The swashbuckling warlord Marcellinus had received overall command of the western army, and did an admirable job evicting Vandal garrisons from Sardinia and Sicily.[73] He probably commanded far more men than his personal Dalmatian force for such an operation, fitting with his position as Anthemius' second praesental *magister militum* and the targeted objectives. In the aftermath of the eastern Roman armada's cataclysmal rout near Carthage, however, some of these proved to be of questionable loyalty given how they ended up murdering Marcellinus in Sicily.[74] In contrast to Majorian, the failure of the African campaign did not spell the immediate end of Anthemius, who continued to reign for four more years. This is a telling indication that he was still a force to be reckoned with in Italy, and continued to enjoy the support of local elites, despite ongoing Vandalic raids.[75] Yet the writing was on the wall.

While Gallic and Aquitanian Gothic elites started casting off their allegiance, Anthemius executed his *magister officiorum* Romanus on treason charges in 470.[76] Alas, Romanus was an ally of Ricimer, who in retaliation departed to Milan with an army of 6,000 men, previously called upon to serve against the Vandals.[77] This number is, in fact, our only indication of the size of Italian armies in these decades, and a credible one it is. An effective stalemate ensued for the next year, during which Epiphanius had to parley between the 'skin-clad Goth' and the 'Greekling' emperor.[78] The saint's life betrays the visible anxiety of the Ligurian elites and, together with Ricimer's decision to fall back on this region, might imply that Anthemius enjoyed an even higher number of troops. That during this stand-off he was able to send his son Anthemiolus at the head of an army, on an ill-fated expedition to salvage what was left of the imperial toehold in southern Gaul, seems to indicate as much.[79] Yet the dismal failure of this

---

[69] Ricimer under Majorian: Sid. Apoll. *Carm.* 5.266–8. Ricimer under Anthemius: Sid. Apoll. *Carm.* 2.352–80.
[70] Ennod. *Vit. Epiph.* 51.
[71] Sid. Apoll. *Epist.* 1.5.10; *Carm.* 2.484–6.
[72] Heather 2005, 399–406; Merrills and Miles 2010, 121–3; Janniard 2020.
[73] Fast. Vind. Prior. s.a. 468; Cassiod. *Chron.* s.a. 468; Marcell. Com. s.a. 468; Proc. *Bell.* 3.6.25.
[74] Cassiod. *Chron.* s.a. 468; Marcell. Com. s.a. 468.2.
[75] Halsall 2007, 273.
[76] Cassiod. *Chron.* s.a. 470.
[77] Joh. Ant. fr. 207.
[78] Ennod. *Vit. Epiph.* 53, 68.
[79] *Chron. Gall. 511* 76 (649).

ultimate imperial transalpine campaign paved the way for Ricimer's showdown. The latter's choice of Milan as headquarters was an unusual one in the fifth century, given that the city had not served as a residence of government since Alaric's first incursion in 401, and was not to do so again afterwards.[80] Nonetheless, Milan was within striking distance of Ricimer's Burgundian allies, who joined forces in his march on Rome. Anthemiolus' defeat probably meant that Anthemius could no longer field an army able to match Ricimer's, unlike Avitus, who had at least fought a head-on confrontation in 456. Instead, Anthemius used the men at his disposal to make his stand at Rome, which withstood a siege for four months.[81] It is a woeful symbol of the western Roman Empire's swansong that the only occasion in the century the *urbs* was able to mount a proper defence was against its own army.[82] When Ricimer's troops broke through, the city suffered looting, while his nephew Gundobad hunted down Anthemius. The emperor had deplorably disguised himself as beggar, seeking sanctuary in a church at Trastevere to no avail, dying as he did at the hand of Gundobad.[83] The many curses Anthemius had previously uttered against Ricimer during Epiphanius' parley did work their magic, though. A month later, Ricimer started coughing up blood and joined Anthemius in the grave.

Olybrius, Glycerius, Julius Nepos and Romulus Augustulus: The Last Shadow Puppets

After Anthemius' demise, Italy entered a veritable state of anarchy, with emperors such as Olybrius, Glycerius, Nepos and Romulus coming and going, until the field army acclaimed Odoacer as *rex* in 476.[84] At the very least, the army still managed to carry out its task of defending the peninsula. For reasons unknown, but perhaps owing to the evident grasp their Burgundian rival Gundobad held over the western courts of Olybrius and Glycerius, the Aquitanian Goths launched an attack across the Cottian Alps in 473. Their force was commanded by a certain Vincentius, an erstwhile *dux Hispaniarum* who had come to terms with the futility of imperial transalpine office-holding, and had distinguished himself in taking by storm the last imperial cities of Tarraconensis for Euric.[85] Vincentius was sent to Italy *quasi magister militum*, which might imply that Euric intended to set him up as 'his' commander of the peninsular army, since the Aquitanian Gothic *reges* never appointed *magistri militum* otherwise.

---

[80] Paul. Diac. *Hist. Rom.* 15.3 describes Ricimer as 'governing Liguria', which is probably a reflection of his regional hegemony. For Milan and northern Italy as Ricimer's *Hausmacht*, see Anders 2010, 279–82.
[81] Another indication of Petronius Maximus' failing leadership that he could not do in 455, what Anthemius was able to do nearly two decades later.
[82] Making its omission in Petersen 2013's catalogue of late antique sieges rather curious.
[83] *Chron. Gall. 511* 650; John Malalas 375; Joh. Ant. fr. 209.1; Paul. Diac. *Hist. Rom.* 15.4.
[84] MacGeorge 2002, 293, rightly describes the period of 471–7 as a continuous power struggle or even civil war. The reigns of these men are utterly brief and ill documented, though one could go back as far as Cantarelli 1896 and Hossner 1900 for a collective treatment. Some aspects have received more detailed scrutiny in Kent 1966; Clover 1978; Gusso 1992; Nathan 1992.
[85] *Chron. Gall 511* 79 (652).

We will never know, since the operation came to naught and Vincentius was vanquished by local forces.[86] In the same year, a different Gothic army from Pannonia crossed the Julian Alps. Glycerius bought these off and passed the buck to Gaul, where they vanish from the record.[87] The political chaos plaguing Italy is well reflected in the consulships. After Anthemius' death, not a single western consul was designated for the rest of the decade.[88] Not surprising, since none of his successors managed to reign in Italy for more than a single year. It is perhaps not coincidental that the next western consulship was only designated again in 480 – the same year Nepos died as last legitimate western emperor. Before Nepos' demise, Odoacer had decided that the peninsula no longer needed a western emperor. This also eliminated the possibility of becoming a *generalissimo*, since the two positions had been intrinsically linked. As head of the army, he still desired recognition from the eastern court, and he affirmed Italy's position as part of the empire during subsequent negotiations. However, his position as *rex* of the army, and the dissolution of the western imperial office, underlines the fact that the imperial army in Italy had become a personal force under the control of a warlord commander.[89] Thereby, Odoacer finally formalised a de facto state of affairs that had been affecting Italy since Majorian's death. This was the game-changer that Italy required to catch a second lifeline, as will become clear.

Odoacer and Theoderic

Counterintuitively, we have to wait until Theoderic's invasion of Italy to assess the profound impact of the events of 476–80 on Italy.[90] The war itself was extraordinary in its intensity, geographical scale and duration. It raged from the Cottian and Julian Alps in the north to Sicily in the south. More importantly, it lasted from 489 to 493, making it the longest-running continuous conflict Roman Italy had had to endure since the days of the second Triumvirate half a millennium earlier. By 489, the eastern emperor Zeno had become fed up with Theoderic the Amal, who for over a decade had both fought for Zeno as *magister militum*, and against Zeno as a roaming warlord when his terms were not met, or when he realised that the eastern emperor was downright duplicitous in his dealings. The simplest compromise to break this stalemate was to give Theoderic sanction to move his forces to Italy and take over Odoacer's position, regardless of whether the emperor or the Goth had taken the initiative for such a gambit, or its outcome.[91]

---

[86] *Chron. Gall 511* 80 (653).
[87] Jord. *Get.* 284.
[88] Bagnall et al. 1987, 480–93.
[89] Wijnendaele 2018, 445.
[90] We are in the dark for most of Odoacer's governance of Italy in the 480s, though he clearly enjoyed good relations with the senatorial aristocracy and the bishops of Rome; see Stein 1949, 39–54; Chastagnol 1966; Pietri 1981; Salzman 2021, 224–30. In spite of the comparatively rich source survival, the 489–93 war has been relatively understudied. For some background, see Moorhead 1992, 17–31; Ausbüttel 2012, 43–63; Wiemer 2018, 180–92.
[91] Moorhead 1984.

Odoacer and Theoderic's armies met near the Isonzo River, where western and eastern imperial armies had fought each other to the death at the Frigidus a century earlier. Odoacer had dug himself in there with his troops. Ennodius claims that all Theoderic had to do was show up to induce his adversary to flight.[92] Other sources, including Cassiodorus, however, indicate that this was the first set-piece battle between both commanders on 28 August 489.[93] Eventually, Odoacer decided to withdraw and reassemble his armies in the Po valley, where the two armies clashed again at Verona on 30 September. Even the pro-Amal sources state the battled raged for a long time with great slaughter on both sides.[94] Once again Odoacer had to yield, and this time he fled to Ravenna, at which point part of his troops surrendered to Theoderic. Theoderic sent a mixed force, including the surrendered army, to Ravenna with the expectation of closing the campaign. Yet Odoacer's turncoat general Tufa turned turncoat once more, handed over Theoderic's officers to Odoacer, and the latter took the field again in 490.[95]

The damage sustained at Verona must have been substantial, because Theoderic was either in no position to offer battle or deemed it wiser to retreat and fortify his position at Pavia. Meanwhile, Odoacer gradually took control again over northern Italy and now started to besiege Theoderic. In what must have seemed like a *deus ex machina* moment, Theoderic's position was relieved in the nick of time due to the arrival of an Aquitanian Gothic army. A third set battle was fought near the Adda River on 11 August 490, between Theoderic and Odoacer, and once again the latter lost and retreated to Ravenna. Yet again, this did not spell the end of the war. It took three more years before Odoacer finally yielded at Ravenna, making this the longest siege of the fifth century, and very likely all of Late Antiquity.[96] Yet even during that time he carried out sallies against Theoderic's besieging army.[97] Meanwhile, Gundobad pillaged Liguria, the Vandals crossed into Sicily, and Theoderic lost control over his allied auxiliaries near Pavia.[98] Theoderic had to slowly deal with all these challenges piecemeal, and take one city after the other, until he was able to construct a fleet and cut off supplies from Ravenna. Eventually, a treaty was negotiated between the two parties on 5 March 493, where Odoacer and Theoderic were supposed to have joint rule in Italy – until, ten days later, the Amal personally murdered his adversary.

What can this bare-bones account tell us about Odoacer's reforms and their impact on Italy? Quite a lot actually. Let's start with strategy. Ever since the Frigidus in 394, late Roman Italy's frontier security had been in tatters. Traditionally, this was based on two principles: firstly, any enemy that was deemed a potential threat to Italy

---

[92] Ennod. *Pan.* 8.38.
[93] Cassiod. *Chron.* s.a. 489; *Anon. Vales.* 2.11.50; *Auct. Havn.* s.a. 490.
[94] Cassiod. *Chron.* s.a. 489; *Anon. Vales.* 2.11.50; *Auct. Havn.* s.a. 490.
[95] *Anon. Vales.* 2.11.51.
[96] The concise treatment of Petersen 2013, 481, does little justice to the scale of operations involved at Ravenna.
[97] *Anon. Vales.* 2.11.54; *Auct. Havn.* s.a. 491.
[98] Gundobad in Liguria: Ennod. *Vit. Epiph.* 172. Vandals in Sicily: Cassiod. *Chron.* s.a. 491. Unruly allies: Fast. Vind. Prior. s.a. 493; *Auct. Havn.* s.a. 493.

should be halted at the gates or preferably beyond.[99] Thus, the emperors Constantius II and Gratian had both pre-emptively and reactively campaigned in Raetia against Alamanni. Similarly, throughout the late third and fourth centuries, civil wars between western and eastern emperors were usually fought in the Balkans, which in this era truly functioned as the highway to the danger zone. This also ties into the suspicious coincidence that during his march on Italy, Theoderic's forces were ambushed by the Gepids.[100] Whether Odoacer was behind this cannot be proven, but it could align both with Ennodius' statement that the former had summoned kings to his aid, and with late Roman strategies in defending Italy.[101] The fact that Odoacer was willing to halt Theoderic at the Isonzo is equally significant. Ever since Alaric's first march on the peninsula in 401, almost any invading force in the fifth century had to be fought inside Italy's borders.[102] In 401, Alaric easily crossed the Timavus and struck all the way to Milan. In 405, Radagaisus' forces crossed the Alps and penetrated as far as Florence. In 408, Alaric advanced at leisure throughout northern and central Italy. In 425, the eastern Roman Army swiftly moved through northern Italy, and so did Attila in 452. Odoacer was Italy's first leader to make a stand at the gates since the Frigidus.

This brings us to the second principle, namely that should an enemy break though the Alpine passes, then the next step was to settle the conflict in the Po valley. This is why the famous, but overrated, battle of the Milvian Bridge really was an afterthought, because Maxentius had already lost the war for Italy at Turin and Verona against Constantine's invading forces.[103] This was indeed the second step Odoacer pursued by repositioning his forces for a second battle at Verona, and a third one at the Ada. His repeated defeats have been often taken for granted, but they should not. The post-Imperial West was a world where defeat in a single pitched battle could mean the fall of a *regnum*. This is what happened when the Suevic *rex* Rechiar crossed swords with the Aquitanian Goths at the Urbicus in 455, lost and saw his hegemony over the Iberian peninsula crumble. Equally, Clovis' victory at Vouillé in 507 meant the end of Gothic Aquitania, and it took the Visigoths half a century to rebuild a new *regnum* around Toledo. Even the Vandals in Africa, who under Geiseric had consistently defied the unified might of both imperial governments, were brought down with two battles during a single season in 534. Not so Odoacer. Not only did he have the resources to keep putting boots on the ground, but also to retain the loyalty of many soldiers through years of adversity. This tenacity and allegiance requires emphasis. Despite more than three years of war and three defeats in pitched battles, Odoacer

---

[99] On Late Roman Italy's defensive systems prior to Alaric's invasion, see Vannesse 2010 and Chapter 7 in this volume.

[100] Ennod. *Pan.* 7.28–34.

[101] Ennod. *Pan.* 8.36. The fact that Odoacer held Dalmatia gave him open communication lines to other Danubian polities. We possess many details of the geographical reach of the war of 489–93, but none of these pertain to Dalmatia. This may suggest that Theoderic had not tried taking the region before pushing on to Italy, as the eastern Roman army had done against the usurper John in 424, or against the Ostrogoths in 536 – probably because he did not have enough forces to spare. On Dalmatia's position in this era, see now Sarantis 2019.

[102] See also Chapter 3 in this volume.

[103] Kulikowski 2013.

still had a sizeable force in Ravenna that allowed him to carry out sallies and that Theoderic could not just bribe or overcome, as for instance Ricimer had done with the remaining forces of Anthemius during his siege of Rome in 472.[104] This suggests that the Italian *rex* inspired great loyalty, which is confirmed in other places.

Once the war was done, Theoderic had considered taking revenge on Sicilian communities, most likely because they had supported Odoacer.[105] It is probable that supplies from Sicily, and perhaps Dalmatia as well, had allowed Odoacer to last as long as he did in Ravenna. Theoderic had also considered revoking the citizenship of all Roman senators who had not explicitly supported him.[106] Another famous case is that of Liberius, who only yielded when he heard the news that his lord Odoacer had perished, implying that he may have held a military command.[107] When Odoacer was dead, Theoderic organised a massacre of Odovacrian soldiers.[108] Finally, the fact that Theoderic had to dirty his own hands by personally murdering Odoacer smacks of great insecurity, something which we can only compare with Diocletian's murder of Aper or Valentinian III's of Aëtius.[109] All of this suggest that Theoderic was far from in control in 493.[110] The Amal monarch had his work cut out for him the following years in establishing his dominion.

Late Roman Italy's Resilience

The tenacity of Odoacer and the Italian field army during 489–93, despite defeat after defeat, seems extraordinary compared to the provincial civil wars of previous decades. Yet they flow from two key policies that Odoacer had enacted at the very start of his governance: the dissolution of western Roman emperorship, and peace with its neighbours. The decision to no longer have a separate western emperor meant the salvation of Italy in the short-to-middle term since it stopped the downward spiral of infighting over command of the field army that had kept recurring in the past twenty years.[111] Immediately afterwards, he came to terms with the Vandals and the Aquitanian Goths.[112] Until Theoderic's invasion, he brought thirteen years of peace to Italy, which had not happened since the death of Gratian a century earlier. In a century dominated

---

[104] *Anon. Vales.* 2.11.54.
[105] Cassiod. *Var.* 1.3.3.
[106] Ennod. *Vit. Epiph.* 122.
[107] Cassiod. *Var.* 2.16.
[108] Anon. Val. 2.11.56.
[109] Anon. Val. 2.11.55.
[110] Lafferty 2013, 6, rightly describes Theoderic as the one capitulating at Ravenna in 493. After all, Odoacer had not technically surrendered; he had negotiated a deal whereby both men were to share authority over Italy, probably because Odoacer still held enough sway. Even Ennod. *Pan.* 9.49–53 is extremely circumspect about the vicissitudes of the war between Theoderic's victory at Verona in 489 and Odoacer's demise in 493. Tellingly, Agnellus 39 mentions how it was Theoderic's armies that were starving in front of Ravenna's gates before the negotiations.
[111] This is not to say that leaving Romulus' throne vacant was the eureka solution that immediately resolved all tensions, since Odoacer still had to execute noblemen such as Brachila in 477 (*PLRE* 2, 'Brachila', 241) and Adaric in 478 (*PLRE* 2, 'Adaric', 7).
[112] Treaty with Geiseric: Vict. Vit. 1.14. Treaty with Euric: Proc. *Bell.* 5.12.20.

by intermittent warfare and violence, especially during its third quarter, we should not underestimate what kind of a boon this was.[113] Of all western provinces, Italy retained the strongest bureaucratic system. The *Vita Epiphanii* complains about an 'evil' praetorian prefect of Odoacer who wished to impose stringent taxes, but this in itself is a testimony that the fiscal cogs kept turning.[114] All this time, the revenue of the united peninsula, soon followed by Sicily and Dalmatia, was finally flowing again into the coffers of Ravenna uninterrupted and on a larger scale than any of the competing *regna* in Gaul, Spain or even Africa could achieve.[115] This brings us to the army.

Especially when talking about armed forces, this was a crucial period to rebuild. It is not a coincidence that the eastern Roman field army in the Balkans waited ten years after the defeat of Adrianople until it organised a major offensive again. Similarly, it is also not coincidental that under Odoacer the western imperial army, because that is what it still was, was able to successfully go on the offensive again outside Italy for the first time since Majorian. It was able to conquer Dalmatia after the murder of Julius Nepos.[116] When rumours reached him of a potential Rugian invasion in 487, he struck first and inflicted crushing defeats on them in Noricum, dismantling their *regnum* in the process.[117] The resilience of his army has already been demonstrated in its ability to withstand several defeats and a three-year-long siege at Ravenna against Theoderic. In fact, if it had not been for the intervention of the Aquitanian Goths in 490, Theoderic might very well have been the one having to come to terms with Odoacer, besieged as he was at Pavia. We should treat both armies as veteran imperial forces, given their *modus operandi*, previous service and track record. The innate prosperity of Italy is visible in other ways as well.

Odoacer could afford to give the throwaway emperor Romulus an annual pension of 6,000 solidi.[118] Even as late as 489, he could reward his *comes domesticorum* Pierius with estates in Sicily and Dalmatia, generating 690 solidi per annum.[119] Finally, around the same time he had forwarded his spoils of war from the conquered Rugians to Zeno's court.[120] All of this belies Ennodius' claim that the long years of peace had bankrupted Italy.[121] Late Roman panegyric usually is founded on the principle that if an adversary's accomplishments cannot be ignored or denied, the best one can do is to utterly invert them.[122] As a point of comparison, Claudian's panegyrics have long

---

[113] It is known.
[114] Ennod. *Vit. Epiph.* 107.
[115] Africa was more prosperous than any of the western polities during Geiseric's raiding era (455–74), yet all of his successors faced fierce raids from the native Mauri tribes. By 500, Theoderic could even impose his hegemony over Thrasamund, by sending 5,000 retainers to the region on the occasion of the latter's marriage to Amalafrida (Proc. *Bell.* 3.8.11–14).
[116] Cassiod. *Chron.* s.a. 481; Fast. Vind. Prior. s.a. 482; *Auct. Havn.* Prior. s.a. 482.
[117] Eugipp. *Vit. Sev.* 44.4–5.
[118] *Anon. Vales.* 2.8.38.
[119] *P. Ital.* 10–11.
[120] Joh. Ant. fr. 214. On this episode, McCormick 1977 remains seminal.
[121] Ennod. *Pan.* 6.23.
[122] Even after fifteen years, Odoacer had to be explicitly and repeatedly named in the panegyric for Theoderic, and the war against him receives more space than any other event. This is the best testament that he could not be ignored. For a similar analysis of Magnus Maximus' portrayal in Pacatus' panegyric for Theodosius I, see Lunn-Rockliffe 2010.

obscured that his patron Stilicho had been part of an invading force that had battered the western Roman army into submission at the Frigidus, with all the problems that entailed when he had to lead this very same army a year later.[123] Ennodian and Cassiodoran rhetoric has also masked the reality that Theoderic came to Italy as an eastern invader as well.[124] It was Theoderic, not Odoacer, who suddenly brought hardship, devastation and famine after thirteen years of peace. Small wonder many Italians were not waiting to accept him with open arms.

Conclusion

An obvious feature of this era is the ubiquity of warfare and violence that affected most of the Italian peninsula, and the islands, especially during the third quarter of the century. Rome was sacked twice (455 and 472), but there were also battles, sieges or other military operations at Bergamo (457 and 464), Campania (458), Placentia (456 and 476), Ravenna (476, 490–3), Pavia (476 and 490) and Verona (490), and naval operations near Corsica (456), Sardinia (468) and Sicily (456, 465, 468), without even considering the incessant Vandal raids along the Italian littoral and islands. The majority of this warfare was generated through internecine rivalry between emperors and generals, even though none of these matched the ferocity of Geiseric's sack of Rome or Theoderic's invasion. Secondly, it has to be emphasised that the imperial army in Italy had become the prime arbiter of politics, yet without wishing to take on the responsibility of governance until there was no longer an alternative by 476.[125] Indeed, Majorian was the only man who had no desire to act as the Italian army's puppet, but had also held a significant command in it prior to becoming emperor. The other emperors of this period were either military outsiders, such as Avitus from Gaul, Anthemius from Constantinople or Nepos from Dalmatia; beholden to the dominant *magister utriusque militiae* regardless of background, such as Libius Severus, Olybrius, Glycerius or Romulus; or the senatorial oddity Petronius Maximus. We may even wonder how much agency the Italian army's senior commanders themselves possessed. Ricimer has often been seen as putting the defence of Italy above all other priorities. This is probably right, but one might ask how much this was of his own volition.[126] Pressure from the peninsula's landed senatorial elites who staffed the civil administration was a factor, as exemplified by their collusion with Ricimer in bringing down Majorian. Yet the most decisive factor in this was probably the Italian field army itself. Ever since the rise of Stilicho in 395, northern Italy had witnessed the largest concentration of field armies of all

---

[123] McEvoy 2013, 154–5.
[124] I am very sympathetic to Arnold 2014's efforts to rehabilitate Theoderic the Amal as a restorer of the Imperial Roman West. However, Arnold 2014, 29–36, is too beholden to Ennodian rhetoric in accepting the latter's dismal view of Odoacer's government and resistance.
[125] On this point, I depart from McEvoy 2017's otherwise splendid analysis, which sees the majority of 'shadow emperors' as either military men or men appointed by the military. Whatever military qualities they had, Avitus, Anthemius and Julius Nepos were brought to the imperial purple *in spite of* the Italian field army.
[126] Recent German historiography, as exemplified by Stickler 2002 and Anders 2010, has been acutely sensitive to the constraints under which some of these *generalissimos* were able or unable to operate.

western regions.[127] Geiseric's conquest of Carthage in 439 meant that this army became even more tied down to the peninsula. As the decades progressed, we may envision more and more local recruitment, unless one is willing to imagine that the field army became composed of non-Roman outsiders exclusively, which the evidence does not bear out.[128] One may wonder whether it was this field army who came to associate the defence of the empire simply with that of Italy.[129]

A second point of consideration in the logical evolution of Odoacer's request to dissolve western emperorship is the pressure of Italy's elites to prioritise their diocese above the rest of the empire. From the Tetrarchy until the death of Valentinian I, Italy had lost its former privileged position in the empire.[130] Yet from Gratian's residence at Milan in the early 380s onward, Italy's aristocracy started turning back the clock against the rhythm of imperial government that had seen western emperors playing a careful balancing act between residing in Gaul, Italy and Illyricum.[131] As the fifth century dawned and western emperors entrenched themselves again in the peninsula, their security, and by extension Italy's, was prioritised at the expense of all other provinces.[132] When there were no more western provinces to cannibalise, it became clear that Italy had to start footing its own bill. To accomplish this, it had to stop the downward spiral of violence that had principally been caused by the tug-of-war for supremacy between the western emperor and his *magister utriusque militiae*. The answer to this question was to leave both offices vacant. And by doing so, Odoacer brought salvation to late Roman Italy. Once a rapport was established with all neighbours, Italy received unbroken peace for thirteen years, allowing the recovery and resilience of the unified peninsula and its army, as demonstrated by the swift annexation of Dalmatia, the destruction of the Rugian *regnum* in Noricum, and defiance in battle to Theoderic for more than three years.[133] The fact that the Italian field army survived three defeats and withstood an unprecedented three-year-long siege of Ravenna is in itself a testament to its imperial veteran structure, when

---

[127] See Chapter 7 in this volume.

[128] This is one of the few points regarding military affairs in Italy where Philip Rance (Chapter 7) and I cordially disagree in this volume. For more discussion of local recruitment, see Wijnendaele and Hanaghan 2021.

[129] That is not to ignore the increased presence of field units predominantly composed of Goths, Heruls, Rugians or Scirians formerly under Hunnic dominion but recruited by Majorian in 458, on which see also Janniard 2020. It cannot be a coincidence that precisely these were the primary factions urging Odoacer to champion their rights against Orestes, nearly two decades later when they were reaching veteran status. It would go far beyond the aims of this chapter, but in the perennial discussion since Goffart 1980 about whether Odoacer's soldiers received shares of land or taxes, one may wish to consider this: if they had received land, they would have had an extra incentive in fighting as tenaciously as they did for Odoacer – and by extension their property – against Theoderic.

[130] See Chapters 1 and 2.

[131] Even during the 440s, when the court still maintained tenuous control over large parts of Gaul, Spain and Dalmatia, a bronze statue was awarded to Aëtius whose many victories in Gaul were claimed *ob Italiae securitatem* (CIL 6.41389)

[132] The obvious exception to this pattern is Majorian. Yet one could say that his campaigns to reassert imperial authority over Gaul, Spain, and Africa, were just as much in Italy's interest.

[133] For a similar case of what a resilient Italy could accomplish alone, see Noel Lenski's remarks in Chapter 2 on Maxentius being able to defeat Severus, deflect Galerius and Licinius, and destroy Domitius Alexander.

compared with other western polities, for whom defeat in a single pitched battle meant the destruction of their *regnum*. And by 500, Italy was finally ready to become the linchpin of Theoderic's western Roman commonwealth.[134]

Bibliography

Anders, F. (2010) *Flavius Ricimer: Macht und Ohnmacht des weströmischen Heermeisters in der zweiten Hälfte des 5. Jahrhunderts*, Frankfurt.
Arnold, J. J. (2014) *Theoderic and the Roman Imperial Restoration*, Cambridge.
Ausbüttel, F. (2012) *Theoderich der Große*, Darmstadt.
Bagnall, R. S., A. Cameron, K. A. Worp and S. R. Schwartz (1987) *Consuls of the Later Roman Empire*, Philological Monographs of the American Philological Association 36, Atlanta.
Barnes, T. D. (1983) 'Late Roman Prosopography: Between Theodosius and Justinian', *Phoenix* 37: 268.
Blockley, R. C. (1983) *The Fragmentary Classicising Historians of the Later Roman Empire*, vol. 2, Liverpool.
Burgess, R. W. (1987) 'The Third Regnal Year of Eparchius Avitus: a Reply', *CP* 82 (4): 335–45.
Burgess, R. W. (1993) *The Chronicle of Hydatius and the Consularia Constantinopolitana*, Oxford.
Burgess, R. W. (2001) 'The Gallic Chronicle of 511: a New Critical Edition with a Brief Introduction', in R. W. Mathisen and D. Shanzer (eds) *Society and Culture in Late Antique Gaul: Revisiting the Sources*, Aldershot, 85–100.
Caliri, E. (2016) 'Orizzonti Mediterranei nel V secolo: la Sicilia, i Vandali e Odoacre', in C. Giuffrida and M. Cassia (eds) *Silenziose rivoluzioni: la Sicilia dalla tarda antichità al primomedioevo*, Catania, 137–59.
Cantarelli, L. (1896), *Annali d'Italia: dalla morte di Valentiniano III alla deposizione di Romolo Augustolo (anni 455–476)*, Rome.
Chastagnol, A. (1966) *Le Sénat romain sous le règne d'Odoacre: recherches sur l'épigraphie du Colisée au Ve siècle*, Bonn.
Clover, F. M. (1978) 'The Family and Early Career of Anicius Olybrius', *Historia* 27 (1): 169–96.
Clover, F. M. (1999) 'A Game of Bluff: the Fate of Sicily After AD 476', *Historia* 48 (2): 235–44.
Collins, R. (1999) *Early Medieval Europe 300–1000*, 2nd ed., London.
Conant, J. (2012) *Staying Roman: Conquest and Identity in Africa and the Mediterranean, 439–700*, Cambridge.
Croke, B. C. (1976) 'Arbogast and the Death of Valentinian II', *Historia* 25 (2): 235–44.
Czuth, B. (1983) 'Petronius Maximus – Kaiser der italischen Senatorenaristokratie (455)', *Oikumene* 4: 253–8.
Delaplace, C. (2015) *La fin de l'Empire romain d'Occident: Rome et les Wisigoths de 382 à 531*, Rennes.
Demandt, A. (1970) 'Magister Militum', *RE* Suppl. 12, Stuttgart, 553–790.
Elton, H. (2018) *The Roman Empire in Late Antiquity: a Political and Military History*, Cambridge.
Gillett, A. (2001) 'Rome, Ravenna and the Last Western Emperors', *PBSR* 36: 131–67.
Gillett, A. (2003) *Envoys and Political Communication in the Late Antique West (AD 411–533)*, Cambridge.

---

[134] Earlier versions of this chapter were presented at Ghent, Leeds and Los Angeles. I would like to thank Jon Arnold, Shane Bjornlie, Guy Halsall, Ralph Mathisen, Walter Pohl, Umberto Roberto, Tina Sessa and Giusto Traina for generous feedback on these occasions.

Goffart, W. (1980) *Barbarians and Romans, A.D. 418–584: the Techniques of Accommodation*, Princeton.
Gusso, M. (1992) 'Sull'imperatore Glycerio', *Studia et documenta historiae et iuris* 58: 168–93.
Halsall, G. (2007) *Barbarian Migrations and the Roman West, 376–568*, Cambridge.
Harries, J. (1994) *Sidonius Apollinaris and the Fall of Rome, AD 407–485*, Oxford.
Heather, P. (2005) *The Fall of the Roman Empire*, Oxford.
Henning, D. (1999) Periclitans res publica: *Kaisertum und Eliten in der Krise des Weströmischen Reiches 454/5–493 n. Chr.*, Stuttgart.
Hossner, K. (1900) *Die letzten Kaiser des romischen Abendlandes: Anthemius, Olybrius, Glycerius, Julius Nepos und Romulus Augustulus*, Bielitz.
Janniard, S. (2020) 'Objectifs et moyens de la politique militaire d'Anthémius', in F. Oppedisano (ed.) *Procopio Antemio, imperatore a Roma*, Bari, 229–55.
Jones, A. H. M. (1964) *The Later Roman Empire, 284–602: a Social, Economic, and Administrative Survey*, Oxford.
Kent, J. P. C. (1966) 'Julius Nepos and the Fall of the Western Empire', *Corolla Numismatica Memoriae Erich Swoboda Dedicata*, 146–50.
Kulikowski, M. (2013) 'The Failure of Roman Arms', in J. Lipps, C. Machado and P. von Rummel (eds) *The Sack of Rome in 410 ad: the Event, Its Context and Its Impact*, Wiesbaden, 77–83.
Kulikowski, M. (2019) *Imperial Tragedy: from Constantine's Empire to the Destruction of Roman Italy, AD 363–568*, Cambridge, MA.
Lafferty, S. (2013) *Law and Society in the Age of Theoderic the Great: a Study of the Edictum Theoderici*, Cambridge.
Lee, A. D. (2013) *From Rome to Byzantium, AD 363 to 565*, Edinburgh.
Liebeschüetz, J. H. W. G. (2007) 'Warlords and Landlords', in P. Erdkamp (ed.) *A Companion to the Roman Army*, Malden, MA, 479–94.
Loyen, A. (1967) *Recherches historiques sur les panégyriques de Sidoine Apollinaire*, Rome.
Lunn-Rockliffe, S. (2010) 'Commemorating the Usurper Magnus Maximus: Ekphrasis, Poetry, and History in Pacatus' Panegyric of Theodosius', *Journal of Late Antiquity* 3 (2): 316–36.
McCormick, M. (1977) 'Odoacer, Emperor Zeno and the Rugian Victory Legation', *Byzantion* 47: 212–22.
McEvoy, M. A. (2013) *Child-Emperor Rule in the Late Roman West, AD 367–455*, Oxford.
McEvoy, M. A. (2017) 'Shadow Emperors and the Choice of Rome (455–476 AD)', *AntTard* 25: 95–112.
MacGeorge, P. (2002) *Late Roman Warlords*, Oxford.
Mathisen, R. W. (1985) 'The Third Regnal Year of Eparchius Avitus', *CP* 80 (4): 326–35.
Mathisen, R. W. (1991) 'The Third Regnal Year of Eparchius Avitus: the Interpretation of the Evidence', in R. W. Mathisen, *Studies in the History, Literature and Society of Late Antiquity*, Amsterdam, 163–6.
Mathisen, R. W. and D. Shanzer (eds) (2001) *Society and Culture in Late Antique Gaul: Revisiting the Sources*, Aldershot.
Max, G. E. (1979) 'Political Intrigue during the Reigns of the Western Roman Emperors Avitus and Majorian', *Historia* 28: 225–37.
Merrills, A. H. and Miles, R. (2010) *The Vandals*, Malden, MA.
Meyer, H. (1969) 'Der Regierungsantritt Kaiser Majorians', *Byzantinische Zeitschrift* 62: 5–12.
Moorhead, J. (1984) 'Theoderic, Zeno and Odovacer', *Byzantinische Zeitschrift* 77 (2): 261–6.
Moorhead, J. (1992) *Theoderic in Italy*, Oxford.
Moss, J. R. (1973) 'The Effects of the Policies of Aetius on the History of Western Europe', *Historia* 22: 711–31.
Nathan, G. (1992) 'The Last Emperor: the Fate of Romulus Augustulus', *C&M* 43: 261–71.

O'Flynn, J. M. (1983) *Generalissimos of the Western Roman Empire*, Edmonton.
O'Flynn, J. M. (1991) 'A Greek on the Roman Throne: the Fate of Anthemius', *Historia* 40 (1): 122–8.
Oost, S. I. (1968) *Galla Placidia Augusta: a Biographical Essay*, Chicago.
Oost, S. I. (1970) 'D. N. Libivs Severvs P. F. AVG', *CP* 65: 228–40.
Oppedisano, F. (2013) *L'impero d'Occidente negli anni di Maioriano*, Rome.
Oppedisano, F. (ed.) (2020) *Procopio Antemio: Imperatore di Roma*, Bari.
Pietri, C. (1981) 'Aristocratie et société cléricale dans l'Italie chrétienne au temps d'Odoacre et de Théodoric', *Mélanges de l'école française de Rome* 93 (1): 417–67.
Petersen, L. I. R. (2013) *Siege Warfare and Military Organization in the Successor States (400–800 AD)*, Leiden.
Rolfe, J. C. (ed. and trans.) (1939) *Ammianus Marcellinus: History*, vol. 3, Cambridge, MA.
Roberto, U. (2015) 'Politica, tradizione e strategie familiari: Antemio e l'ultima difesa dell'unità dell'impero (467–472)', in U. Roberto and L. Macella (eds) *Governare e riformare l'impero al momento della sua divisione: Oriente, Occidente, Illirico*, Rome, 163–96.
Salzman, M. R. (2021) *The Falls of Rome: Crises, Resilience, and Resurgence in Late Antiquity*, Cambridge.
Sarantis, A. (2019) 'Justinian's *Novella* 11: Memory and Political Propaganda in the Build Up to the Gothic War', *Early Medieval Europe* 27 (4): 494–520.
Sivan, H. S. (1989) 'Sidonius Apollinaris, Theodoric II, and Gothic-Roman Politics from Avitus to Anthemius', *Hermes* 117 (1): 85–94.
Stein, E. (1949) *Histoire du Bas-Empire*, vol. 2, *De la disparition de l'Empire d'Occident à la mort de Justinien (476–565)*, Amsterdam.
Stickler, T. (2002) *Aëtius: Gestaltungsspielräume eines Heermeisters im ausgehenden Weströmischen Reich*, Munich.
Vannesse, M. (2010) *La défense de l'Occident romain pendant l'Antiquité tardive: recherches géostratégiques sur l'Italie de 284 à 410 ap. J.-C.*, Brussels.
Wiemer, H.-U. (2018) *Theoderich der Große: König der Goten, Herrscher der Römer*, Munich.
Wijnendaele, J. W. P. (2016) 'Warlordism and the Disintegration of the Western Roman Army', in J. Armstrong, Jeremy (ed.) *Circum Mare: Themes in Ancient Warfare*, Leiden, 185–203.
Wijnendaele, J. W. P. (2017) 'The Early Career of Aëtius and the Murder of Felix', *Historia* 66 (4): 468–82.
Wijnendaele, J. W. P. (2018) 'Generalissimos and Warlords in the Late Roman West', in T. Ñaco Del Hoyo and F. López-Sánchez (eds) *War, Warlords and Interstate Relations in the Ancient Mediterranean*, 429–51.
Wijnendaele, J. W. P. and M. P. Hanaghan (2021) 'Constantius *Heros* (*ILCV* 66) – an Elegiac Testimony on the Decline of the Late Roman West', *Chiron* 51: 257–76.
Williams, S. and Friell, G. (1999) *The Rome That Did Not Fall: the Survival of the East in the Fifth Century AD*, London.
Woods, D. (2002) 'A Misunderstood Monogram: Ricimer or Severus?', *Hermathena* 172: 5–21.

Part II

Institutions

5

Administering Late Roman Italy: Geographical Changes and the Appearance of Governors

Daniëlle Slootjes

Introduction

While gradually acquiring territories during the Republic, Roman government started to develop an imperial administration that was able to reach the local level of cities via a hierarchical system of officials.[1] By the late third and early fourth centuries, the emperors Diocletian (284–305) and Constantine I (306–37) set in motion a series of reforms that resulted in a more complex, hierarchical and multi-layered system of administrative units: an almost doubling of the number of provinces and the creation of dioceses and prefectures. These administrative changes led to a significant increase in the number of officials.[2] Due to the sheer size of empire and of the bureaucratic apparatus, the instruments available for the realisation of the splitting of provinces and the creation of new administrative units were still fairly limited. As the evidence indicates, it took years, if not decades, for all these new units to be completed at an empire-wide level.[3] Regional differences undoubtedly played a part in the pace of the actual realisation of the alterations in certain areas of the empire. Some scholars such as Frank Kolb have argued for a tetrarchic planned experiment for these administrative changes, whereas others such as Elio Lo Cascio observe a lack of a prearranged and well-thought-out design.[4] Ultimately, though, the nature of and practical steps within the decision-making process behind this large-scale administrative operation and its impact on the empire's inhabitants remains difficult to detect.[5]

The Italian peninsula, traditionally the heartland of the empire, experienced perhaps the most drastic transformation.[6] Whereas other territories of the empire had

---

[1] Cities remained the backbone of the provincial administration. Liebeschuetz 2001, 2; Brown 2012, 6.
[2] Jones 1964, 42–7, 373–7; Barnes 1982; 1992; Migl 1994; Palme 1999, 95–8; Kulikowski 2004, 69–71; Feissel 2004, 108–10; Slootjes 2014; 2020.
[3] The formation of prefectures as territorial units was part of a development that followed over the course of the fourth century. See Barnes 1982; Migl 1994, 161–208.
[4] Kolb 1987; Lo Cascio 2005, 170–1.
[5] Slootjes 2014; compare also Slootjes 2020. Sipilä 2009 can be considered a first serious attempt to understand different factors influencing the imperial decision-making process.
[6] Lo Cascio 2005, 166 and 172, for the argument that perhaps at the periphery of the empire the administrative changes were more innovative than at the centre.

always had provinces and were used to a certain level of Roman control, the Italian peninsula had enjoyed a particularly exceptional status within the empire. Why it became incorporated into the regular administrative structures of the empire as a series of provinces remains somewhat unclear, but various ingredients seem to have played a role.[7] The city of Rome had started to lose its convenience in terms of a military strategic location for the emperors, even though symbolically it was still its undisputed capital. With this decrease in importance as a prime location for imperial presence, the exceptionality of the Italian peninsula might have been diminished as well. Furthermore, one might also argue for a close connection between the provincialisation of Italy and a reform of the financial system of the empire, in particular of the taxation, for which not only a general census of the population but also a land survey was conducted.[8] In other words, the imperial government ended up with a detailed map of all the territory in Italy which could then have facilitated the creation of new provinces. The census would have registered the boundaries of the landholdings of the elite and most likely of the territories of cities as well. These recent recorded boundaries might no longer have matched previously designated *regio* boundaries which had of course been created several centuries earlier. Indeed, over the centuries Italy had further developed into a highly urbanised region, which must have influenced the designation of new administrative units.[9] This possible mismatch in certain areas would explain why the boundaries of the newly created provinces in Italy did not necessarily overlap with the boundaries of previous *regiones*.

Thus, the peninsula ended up being divided into a series of new provinces which became part of the diocese of Italiciana. The diocese was separated into Italia Annonaria and Italia Suburbicaria, a unique division not found in any of the other dioceses. So far, modern scholarship has paid little attention to the effect of these general administrative changes on the Italian peninsula in the late third and early fourth centuries.[10] This chapter analyses two aspects that characterised the provincial administration and their governors in late Roman Italy. First, it will offer a geographical perspective on the effect of the administrative changes in Italy. While in previous centuries Italy had consisted of *regiones*, from the early fourth century onwards the peninsula was divided into new provinces and thus officially incorporated into the larger system of provincial government. These new provinces, together with the already existing provinces in the Alpine region and the islands Sardinia, Corsica and Sicily, formed the new diocese of Italiciana. In terms of the geographical arrangement of the new administrative system, not all Italian provinces matched the previous *regiones*. By way of zooming in on various regions and new provinces, I will attempt to shed some light on various political and geographical factors that influenced the decision-making processes of the new provinces.

---

[7] Dio Cass. 52.22.1–6 for, as Lo Cascio 2005, 165–6 has pointed out, 'anachronistic anticipations' in the fictitious dialogue between Maecenas to Agrippa on possible ways of dealing with Italy from the administrative point of view.

[8] Lo Cascio 2005, 175–80.

[9] See also Chapter 2 in this volume on this issue. Both urbanisation and the influence of the geography of the Italian peninsula should be taken into account further when analysing the creation of the new provinces.

[10] For one of the few valuable and recent analyses on the administrative changes in Italy, see Porena 2013.

Second, the administrative transformation of the Italian peninsula into a series of provinces meant that the Italian provinces and their communities were confronted with the presence of governors and their attempt to 'control' the provinces. What was the effect of the arrival of governors at local level? I will focus particularly on the recruitment of governors in the Italian provinces, as many of them came from Italy, even though officially they were not allowed to rule a province they originated from. Furthermore, the group of governors was not homogeneous, either in terms of status and rank, or in the type of career they eventually pursued. Who were these men, and how were they positioned within the expanding system of an increasing number of imperial offices that were needed to keep the enlarged late antique administrative system operational?

Boundary Awareness in the Roman World

Before turning to the geographic transformation of fourth-century Italy, some remarks on geographical awareness in antiquity are in order. For us, geographical transformation leads to questions on the boundaries of the former provinces or *regiones* of Italy. Which boundaries changed or were newly created? In our modern western world, we are used to frontiers and borders that we can often clearly point to and even visibly cross.[11] No man's land is typically not part of the daily perception of our world. In antiquity, territories' boundaries were often more fluid, not always clearly marked or even always known. Consequently, in trying to understand the geography of the Roman provinces, two issues need to be kept in mind. First, the ancient evidence often lacks precise information on the boundaries of local communities and provinces, which makes it difficult in certain regions of the empire to draw an accurate map of a province and thus of the empire at large. If one compares different modern maps of the Roman provinces that currently exist, it is striking how mapmakers have chosen very different locations for some of the provincial boundaries.[12] Lack of precise knowledge certainly plays a role here, but it is also a sense of apparent modern satisfaction with a rough outline of the provincial boundaries that does not really encourage us to search for more accurate information on the boundaries.[13]

Second, even though we do not precisely know where the provincial boundaries were, people in the ancient world were certainly aware of the extent of their city territory or their province. In part, this awareness should be connected to the necessity and value of administrative and juridical boundaries.[14] Several modern studies on boundary

---

[11] See Green and Perlman 1985, 4, on the difference in meaning of 'frontiers' and 'boundaries', which in modern studies are often used as if they are similar. Whittaker 1994.
[12] See for instance maps 100 and 101 of the *Barrington Atlas of the Greek and Roman World* (Talbert 2000), maps 2 and 3 in volume 12 of the *Cambridge Ancient History* (Bowman et al. 2005), and the maps on p. 176–7, 206–7, 224–5 in the Neue Pauly *Historischer Atlas der antiken Welt* (Wittke et al. 2012).
[13] Though obviously difficult, it would be worthwhile to conduct a project that would reassess all the currently known and unknown provincial boundaries of the Roman Empire.
[14] Richardson 2011 for a brief examination of the political and territorial meaning of (*fines/termini*) *provinciae* in the period of the Roman Republic. Compare Hesberg 1995 on the meaning of provinces. In this contribution I will use both 'boundary' and 'border' interchangeably to indicate the physical demarcations of the Late Roman provinces, dioceses and prefectures.

markers and boundary disputes have demonstrated that both central and local civic authorities were able to identify the specific locations of the borders between different communities and different provinces.[15] This implies not only a general awareness and knowledge of the location of boundaries; the fact that communities quarrelled about them shows their importance.[16]

For this contribution on late Roman provinces in Italy, both these two issues play a role. For the geographical makeup of several provinces, especially in the northern part of the Italian peninsula, it is difficult to establish their boundaries. Notably, however, for the imperial officials having authority within these provinces it appears less important to know the precise physical boundaries.

A Geographical Perspective on the Provinces of Late Antique Italy

Unlike the other parts of the empire, Italy had not been divided into provinces, but into so-called *regiones* from the reign of Augustus onwards.[17] Even though it is not quite clear what the function of these *regiones* was – perhaps they were needed for the census – they seem to have been mostly based on the geography of the landscape or on previously existing and older cultural boundaries.[18]

Italy's exceptional status without provinces and thus without governors had led to other forms of interaction between the local communities of the Italian peninsula and the imperial government. Whereas provincial communities elsewhere would have turned to Roman governors in times of crisis or need for restorations or any other type of support, Italian communities would most likely turn to a senatorial or equestrian patron from Rome or – since Trajan's rule – to so-called *curatores rei publicae* for support.[19] In other words, the direct link with the authorities in Rome was represented by individual and private members of the elite more than official representatives of the Roman government.

Modern scholars point to the first signs of some sort of provincialisation of Italy at the beginning of the third century, when the emperor Caracalla appointed so-called *correctores Italiae* in several *regiones* of Italy in support of local administrations.[20] Perhaps

---

[15] Aichinger 1982; Burton 2000; 2002a; 2002b; Elliott 2004.
[16] Whereas in the case of boundary disputes within a province, governors were often asked to pass judgment, in the case of disputes that involved the provincial borders, emperors seem to have sent special legates of *iudices* to bring such conflicts to an end. See for instance Elliott 2004, nos 84 (boundary dispute between Vienna in Gallia Narbonensis and Axima in Alpes Graiae et Poeninae in AD 74) and 95 (six boundary markers indicating the demarcation between Thracia and Moesia Inferior, dated to AD 135).
[17] For an overview of the developments in Italy during the early empire, see Cooley 2016, chh. 6 and 7, 103–32.
[18] Ausbüttel 1988, 86; Christie 2006, 64, for the argument that Italians most likely felt more attachment to their local community than to the unit of their *regio*.
[19] Ausbüttel 1988, 27–33, on *curatores rei publicae*, and 40–7, on city patrons. Cf. Eck 1979, 190–246; Porena 2013, 330. On the phenomenon of patrons in Italian communities, see Nichols 1980.
[20] Lo Cascio 2005, 167. Against Eck 1979, 247, who argues for the appointment of *iuridici* under Marcus Aurelius as forerunners of regionalisation of Italy, which eventually leads to provincialisation.

a division of Italy into a *pars annonaria* and *suburbicaria* might be traceable to the decades previous to Diocletian's rule.[21] However unclear the developments in the early third century might have been, Diocletian's reforms led to major changes in the existing administrative arrangements of the Italian peninsula. Officials with the title of *corrector Italiae* seem to have disappeared. Instead, *correctores* of specific areas and governors especially with the title of *praeses* emerged as the leading officials.[22]

From *regiones* to Provinces and Dioceses

The administrative transformation of the Italian peninsula of the late third and early fourth centuries should be understood as a development that took various steps over several decades. Two distinct processes can be discerned. There was the shift from *regiones* into provinces as well as the creation of the diocese of Italiciana with its two parts, Annonaria and Suburbicaria.[23] Although scholars disagree about the date of creation of the dioceses, I follow the scholarship that argues that the provincial reforms did not take place simultaneously with the dioceses.[24]

To comprehend which provinces were created, information from the Verona List (which seems to present us with an incomplete list of Italy) and the early fifth-century *Notitia dignitatum* needs to be combined.[25] As said, the shift from *regiones* to provinces cannot be regarded as a simple procedure by which each existing *regio* turned into a province with precisely the same boundaries. Based on the Verona List and scattered prosopographical evidence for governors in the early fourth century, Ausbüttel concluded that Diocletian created seven provinces on the Italian peninsula: Campania (containing Latium and Samnium as well), Tuscia et Umbria, Flaminia et Picenum, Lucania et Bruttium, Apulia et Calabria, Aemilia et Liguria and Venetia et Histria.[26] However, in a recent analysis, Porena – in regarding the list of the Italian provinces in the Verona List as seriously corrupt – argued for a larger number of smaller provinces and fewer combinations of regions into single provinces.[27] However it may be, by the end of the fourth century and into the fifth century, the *Notitia dignitatum* lists

---

[21] Ausbüttel 1988, 87–93; Porena 2013, 330–3. See Chapter 1 in this volume for further discussion on this issue.

[22] Before Constantine, governors with the title *consularis* seem rare. Perhaps a certain Olympiades (*PLRE* 2, 'Olympiades', 642) was *consularis* of Umbria somewhere between 284 and 303, but otherwise the evidence seems to point mostly to *correctores* and *praesides*. Compare Ausbüttel 1988, 92–3.

[23] Christie 2006, 65.

[24] Noethlichs 1982; Ausbüttel 1988, 94; Migl 1994; Zuckerman 2002; Lo Cascio 2005, 172–3. However, Porena 2013, 332, argues for a more simultaneous process, as he assumes that the creation of the dioceses should be placed somewhere between 293 and 298, which might be confirmed by an inscription from Aphrodisias recently discussed by Chaniotis 2015. See both Zuckerman 2002 and Wiewiorowski 2015, 52–77, for extensive discussions on this issue.

[25] Jones 1964, appendix II, 'Dioceses and provinces', 1451. The information from the Verona List on the administrative structures of Italy is notoriously unreliable, as known data about several provinces seems to be missing. Also, Ausbüttel 1988, 94.

[26] Ausbüttel 1988, 92–3; Christie 2006, 65.

[27] Porena 2013.

seventeen provinces for the Italian peninsula.[28] In addition, in the early decades of the fourth century the diocese of Italy started to function as well, which was a unison of provinces already in existence before the late third century with provinces that had been newly created based on the *regiones*. Some of the territories of previously existing provinces were reorganised into smaller territories (such as Raetia, for instance), while others continued within their former geographical domain (such as Alpes Cottiae, Sicilia, Sardinia and Corsica). By the end of the fourth century, the overview of the provinces and governors of the diocese of Italy is as shown in Table 5.1.

Table 5.1 Provinces and governors of the diocese of Italy at the end of the fourth century.

Italia Annonaria (capital Mediolanum, led by a *vicarius Italiae*)		
Province	**Rank of governor**	**Geographical territory**[a]
1. Alpes Cottiae	*praeses*	Already existing province, though western part of the province seems to have been transferred to Alpes Maritimae
2. Liguria[b]	*consularis*	Former *regio* Liguria
3. Raetia I[c]	*praeses*	Mostly western part of former province Raetia
5. Raetia II	*praeses*	Mostly region Vindelica (north-eastern part of former province Raetia plus small part of western part of the province Noricum)
4. Aemilia	*consularis*	Part of *regio* Aemilia (without the eastern coast)
6. Flaminia et Picenum Annonarium	*consularis*	Former northern part of *regio* Picenum plus the eastern coast of *regio* Aemilia plus a small part of Umbria; until c.350/2 under *correctores*
7. Venetia et Histria	*consularis*	Seems the same as former *regio*; until c.370 under *correctores*

---

[28] See Ausbüttel 1988, 102, for the notion that most of the provincial changes in territories took place during the reign of Theodosius and Honorius. A division of Flaminia et Picenum into Flaminia et Picenum Annonarium and Picenum Suburbicarium seems to have taken place at some moment post-364, and perhaps even more precisely between 413 and 418. See for the arguments on this split Ausbüttel 1988, 99–101. Tuscia and Umbria were kept together in the fourth century, but ancient evidence – as Ausbüttel 1988, 101, argues – points to a division into Tuscia Annonaria and Tuscia Suburbicaria in the fifth or sixth century.

Italia Suburbicaria (capital Rome, led by *vicarius Vrbis Romae*)		
Province	**Rank of Governor**	**Geographical territory**
1. Sardinia	*praeses*	Former province
2. Corsica	*praeses*	Former province
3. Tuscia et Umbria	*consularis*	Central part of *regio* Umbria plus most of the *regio* Etruria
4. Picenum Suburbicarium	*consularis*	Former southern part of *regio* Picenum
5. Valeria[d]	*praeses*	Newly created province in the late fourth century in the territory of Picenum
6. Campania	*consularis*	Former *regio* Campania, without Rome
7. Samnium[e]	*praeses*	Approximately former *regio*
8. Sicilia	*consularis*	Former province
9. Lucania et Brutii	*corrector*	Approximately former *regio*
10. Apulia et Calabria[f]	*corrector*	Approximately former *regio*

[a] Based on the information from the Verona List, the *Notitia dignitatum*, as well as modern maps of ancient Italy such as those in the *Barrington Atlas* (Talbert 2000) and the Neue Pauly *Historischer Atlas* (Wittke et al. 2012). See Jones 1964, appendix III, 1451–61; Chastagnol 1963, 355–72; Barnes 1982, 208, 218–19.
[b] Ausbüttel 1988, 98. Aemilia et Liguria were split into two somewhere between 385 and 397. See also Cecconi 1998, 158–9.
[c] The division of Raetia can perhaps be dated to the years just before the middle of the fourth century. In describing the year 354, Amm. Marc. 15.4.1 speaks of two provinces. Chastagnol 1963, 358; Ausbüttel 1988, 95–6. The capital of Raetia I was Curia Raetorum (modern Chur) and that of Raetia II was Augusta Vindelicum (modern Augsburg).
[d] Valeria was probably created in the late fourth century. One of its first appearances in the ancient sources is *CTh* 9.30.5 of 399. Ausbüttel 1988, 98–9.
[e] The date for the creation of Samnium has caused much scholarly disagreement, though it was likely a date before 357. See Ausbüttel 1988, 96–8, for some arguments on the date of creation.
[f] See Chelotti and Mennella 1994, 171–2, for epigraphic attestations of governors of Apulia and Calabria in the fourth and fifth centuries.

Notably, in terms of the geographical arrangement of the provinces, the new division of Italy represents a mixture of both already existing provinces and the so-called *regiones* of Italy. As said, not all the previous *regiones* boundaries were taken over. Some of the provinces were set up in such a way that they represent a deliberate step away from the already existing *regio* boundaries. For instance, why would the western part of Noricum be assigned to Raetia, and why was the central part of the *regio* Umbria combined with most of the *regio* of Etruria into the province Tuscia et Umbria? What could have been the reasoning behind these particular geographical and administrative choices? Who made these choices? Are these the results of developments in previous centuries? In general, we would like to know more about the factors that influenced the design of new administrative units, be they provinces or dioceses. The most obvious factors, as is also to be expected, must have been geographical, military strategic, political and perhaps even economic in nature.[29] In addition, regional differences or local peculiarities must have been taken into account as well. As mentioned before, the census that was probably held in the late third century might have led to new local boundaries that then were taken as new provincial boundaries. Unfortunately, little to no information on the decision-making process behind this operation into provinces and dioceses has come down to us, which seriously hinders our understanding of the transformation. The following brief case study on northern and north-western boundaries of the Italian diocese, represented by the provinces Raetia, Aemilia et Liguria and Alpes Cottiae will be offered as an illustration of the interpretative difficulties modern scholars experience. It will bring to light various geographical and political complexities that must have been part of this large-scale administrative operation. Moreover, it will also demonstrate how the new geographical and administrative arrangement of late antique Italy was closely connected to the provinces and dioceses adjacent to the Italian peninsula.

The Northern and North-Western Boundaries of Late Antique Italy

The creation of the diocese of Italy, which combined territories of previously existing provinces and former *regiones*, led to an administrative change that now connected the Italian peninsula to the northern frontier line of the empire through its northern boundary of Raetia.[30] At its northern side Italy was thus no longer safely locked in or protected by a buffer of provinces. Would this make the peninsula more vulnerable? Or should we see this is as a purely administrative change, that would lead to the most practical administrative units from the perspective of provincial and diocesan government? The *vicarius Italiae* who had his seat in Mediolanum would be mostly responsible for the civil administration of his diocese (together with the provincial governors), whereas the frontier defences were led by military officials and, for that region in particular, the *dux Raetiae*.[31] The frontier defence of this area had proven to be of vital importance for keeping enemies from moving into the Italian peninsula. Especially in the last decades of third century, Raetia had experienced serious problems at its frontiers, when Alamanni threatened to enter northern Italy. Various emperors such as Gallienus, Aurelian and Probus had to fight against them, the latter consequently organising new defences.[32]

---

[29] See Cherf 1987.
[30] One look at the various maps such as those in the *Barrington Atlas* (Talbert 2000) or the Neue Pauly *Historischer Atlas* (Wittke et al. 2012) shows how messy and insecure our knowledge on the boundaries of Raetia is, as on each map they are placed in different locations.
[31] *Not. Dign. occ.* 35. On the *limes* forts, see the extensive studies by Garbsch 1970 and Schönberger 1985.
[32] Kreucher 2003, 145–8; Wilkes 2005, 223–8; Drinkwater 2007, 177–216.

The western frontier of the diocese of Italy – the borders of Aemilia et Liguria and Alpes Cottiae – adjoined the diocese of Galliae and that of Viennensis. In previous centuries, this western Alpine region had been formed – in geographical order from north to south – by the three provinces Alpes Graiae et Poeninae, Alpes Cottiae and Alpes Maritimae.[33] The provincial changes of the late third and early fourth centuries seem to have led to a geographical shuffle of these three provinces. By the time the provinces were organised into the dioceses, Alpes Graiae et Poeninae is still the northern most of the three, but seems to have been assigned some of the northern territory of Alpes Cottiae so that Alpes Graiae et Poeninae in this arrangement is connected to the northern boundary of Alpes Maritimae. Alpes Cottiae seems to have lost some of its central territory but also seems to have gained some southern territory, as it now borders on its western side the province of Alpes Maritimae almost all the way down to the Mediterranean coast. In the new allocation of the provinces into dioceses Alpes Graiae ended up in the diocese of Galliae, Alpes Cottiae in the diocese of Italiciana, and Alpes Maritimae in the diocese of Viennensis.[34]

Alpes Cottiae was a strategic location in terms of the passage through the Alps into the Italian peninsula.[35] Would that have been a reason to incorporate it into the Italian diocese? Remarkably, after the death of Constantine the Great in 337, in the division of the territories between his sons, Constantine II disconnected the province of Alpes Cottiae from its diocese Italiciana – which was under rule of Constans – and added it to his territory, which consisted already of the dioceses Britanniae, Galliae, Viennensis and Hispaniae.[36] Military-strategic considerations must have been part of the motivation for Constantine II to demand this province. As long as he was in command of Alpes Cottiae, he could swiftly move into Italy and the traditional heartland of the Roman Empire. In the year 340, Constantine II indeed made that rapid move into Italy, whereby civil war broke out between the brothers. Soon Constantine II lost his life, and Constans took control over the entire western territory of Constantine II. Unfortunately, we have no evidence for Alpes Cottiae in the decades to come, but by the time of the *Notitia dignitatum*, in the *Notitia occidentis*, it was listed again under the diocese of Italy.

The Impact of Empire: Governors in Late Roman Italy

By way of the transformation of the Italian *regiones* into provinces, the Italian peninsula became synchronised with the centuries-old administrative organisation of the

---

[33] Walser 1986; Christie 1991; Roncaglia 2013.
[34] At the end of the fourth century, the dioceses of Galliae and Viennensis were united into one diocese, called Septem Provinciae.
[35] Prieur 1968. See Bleckmann 2003, 247, for references to situations in which Alpes Cottiae and its passes over the Alps proved to be of essential strategic value.
[36] Of all the ancient sources, only Zonar. 13.5.1–4 mentions this particular addition of Alpes Cottiae to the territory of Constantine II. As a twelfth-century source, Zonaras was in time far removed from the fourth century AD, although Bleckmann has convincingly argued for an earlier fourth-century tradition for this particular passage in Zonaras which brings the work back to a time relatively close to the period under review. Bleckmann 2003, 230–1, see esp. n. 15. Also Bleckmann 1992.

empire at large. However, the situation in the newly created provinces must have been slightly different at the beginning of the fourth century than in the already existing other provinces of the empire. While in previous centuries emperors had sent *curatores* or *correctores* with special appointments to particular regions in Italy, now in the new Italian provinces for the first time local communities were confronted with the presence of a governor as permanent representation of the imperial government (even though, of course, individual governors had a relatively brief term of office). Traditionally, Italy's position had been one of exceptional status, exempt from land tax (*tributum soli*), as if it were a sort of unique extension of the city of Rome. Even though the cities on the Italian peninsula were no strangers to being held accountable by the imperial authorities, there was no tradition of being ruled by a governor as a Roman province.[37] Once the changes had been made by Diocletian and Constantine, the members of the local elites had to deal with the presence of a governor. The other provinces of the empire had had to deal with this arrangement of provincial governors already for centuries. Overall, however, for all provinces of the early fourth century an increased level of government control can be detected. In Italy this must have been the case because of the newly created provinces, while in the other provinces of the empire the splitting of many of the existing provinces into much smaller units would have led to an intensification of imperial administrative control.[38]

Different Status for the Italian Governors

In taking the provinces of the entire diocese of Italiciana into account, the overview in Table 5.1 shows a notable mixture of various types of governors: *correctores*, *praesides* and *consulares*.[39] Of the seventeen provinces of the entire diocese as catalogued in the *Notitia dignitatum*, eight started with the governor type *corrector*,[40] but by the late fourth century, only two were left in the south of the peninsula: in Lucania et Bruttii and in Apulia et Calabria.[41] All the other *correctores* in Italy had become *consulares*, which was the highest rank of governorship after the three proconsuls (Africa, Achaea and Asia) of the empire. *Correctores* were not new to the provinces, as from the emperor Trajan onwards, and later under Caracalla, they had been appointed occasionally as special senatorial legates taking up a sort of regular provincial office, even though we are not quite clear on their specific role and status. How are we to explain these switches in status of the Italian governors over the course of the fourth century? Based on the ancient evidence, these shifts did not take place at one particular moment for all the

---

[37] See Chapter 6 in this volume for further discussion.
[38] Liebeschuetz 1987, 466. Compare Slootjes 2006, 25.
[39] Slootjes 2006, 19, on the different terminology for governors.
[40] Liguria, Flaminia et Picenum Annonarium, Venetia et Histria, Tuscia et Umbria, Campania, Sicilia, Lucania et Brutii, Apulia et Calabria. See also *CTh* 1.16 and 22; *CJ* 1.40 and 45 on the duties of *correctores*.
[41] *Correctores* were not unique to Italy. By the time of the *Notitia dignitatum* there were three more *correctores*: one in Paphlagonia (in the diocese of Pontica), one in Augustamnica (in the diocese Aegyptus) and one in Savia (in the diocese of Pannonia).

Italian provinces.⁴² The transfer of the governor's status from a *corrector* to a *consularis* might be seen as an upgrade of the province's status as well as that of its governor.⁴³

Individual Governors and the Local Level

Based on the *Prosopography of the Later Roman Empire* with some addenda in more recent scholarship, for the seventeen provinces of Italy we have the names of more than 250 governors in the fourth, fifth and early sixth centuries, which means that Italy in late Antiquity is particularly well documented in terms of its officials.⁴⁴ At the same time, as Ausbüttel rightfully stated, it should also make us realise that we thus lack a lot of information on hundreds of governors who remain unknown to us.⁴⁵ This raises the issue of how representative the evidence is. Indeed, a cautious estimation of the seventeen Italian provinces for only the fourth century could potentially lead to about 850 governors, if one assumes that they would have on average a term of office of two years. Of course, many must have left already after a year, while others might have stayed longer, but with two years on average for the term of office that would lead to about 850 governors needed. As for the actual names we have of governors who were active in Italy, most of their evidence comes from honorary inscriptions, set up in local communities, or from the Theodosian law codes, in which a number of laws ended up being addressed to governors. Especially in the latter case, we mostly end up with no information other than their names and office.

The men appointed as governors in the fourth century cannot be seen as a homogeneous group. As said, in Italy, we find governors with the titles *corrector*, *praeses* and *consularis*;⁴⁶ these were all men with the rank *clarissimus* (the lowest rank in the later Roman Empire), indicating the beginning stage of an official's career. As is to be expected, governors never performed governorships of one province twice, and officially they were not allowed to govern the province they came from.⁴⁷ Even though there is barely any evidence for the origins of most of the governors in the Italian provinces, presumably in most cases they would have come from regions near the provinces where they ended up going for their term of office. For instance, Maecius Felix, who was governor of Samnium, was honoured in Venafrum, where he was also a patron and native of that town.⁴⁸

Governors seem to have taken two possible career paths. On the one hand, there is ample evidence for the category of governors who fulfilled one or more governorships but who never went beyond the level of governorships. On the other hand, there is the group of men for whom a governorship was a stepping stone in their civil

---

⁴² Chastagnol 1963, 355–72.
⁴³ See Chapter 2 in this volume for further discussion.
⁴⁴ Based on the *PLRE*, with additions by Ausbüttel 1988, 166–75; Cecconi 1998, 176–9.
⁴⁵ See Ausbüttel 1988, 107–8.
⁴⁶ Slootjes 2006, 19, for a schematic overview of ranks and titles of governors in the fourth century.
⁴⁷ Cass. Dio 72.31.1; *CTh* 8.8.6 (of 386); *CJ* 1.41 (of 610). Liebeschuetz 2001, 279; Slootjes 2006, 25–6, especially 26 n. 51 for various exceptions to the official regulations.
⁴⁸ *PLRE* 1, 'Maecius Felix 9', 333. *CIL* 10.4863. Ward-Perkins 1984, appendix 1, 232.

career, as they performed one or more governorships but then continued on into higher offices. For instance, Marcus Aurelius Consius Quartus Iunior was *corrector* of Flaminia et Picenum, *corrector* of Venetia et Histria, then *consularis* of Belgica Prima, before becoming *vicarius* of Hispania and finally *proconsul* of Africa.[49] Or, in the late fourth century, Caecina Decius Albinus was first *consularis* in Numidia Constantina, then *consularis* of Campania before he ended up as city prefect of Rome in 397.[50]

Governor's Duties

Governors in the new Italian provinces were expected to – and did – carry out the duties that governors in long-established provinces had already been performing for many centuries of Roman provincial government: to administer justice, to oversee local administration as well as to guarantee law and order in their province.[51] Furthermore, governors were expected to support local communities in times of need. For instance, when local public buildings were in need of restoration, governors were asked to support the renovation, not necessarily by giving money, but by allocating money to such a project. As Ward-Perkins argued, the ancient evidence – both inscriptions and legal sources – of the fourth century points to governors being expected to take up major public works instead of the local governments that would carry out such projects.[52] The epigraphic evidence offers many inscriptions that refer to all sorts of building and restoration projects that governors were involved in, such as the following:

> The Baths of Venus, damaged by the aging of a long period of time, Domitius Severianus, *vir consularis*, governor of Campania, built to its original appearance. Sentius Marcus, *vir consularis*, companion of the divine rulers, curator of Capua, Liternum, and Cumae, saw to the work and dedicated it.[53]

Ward-Perkins noted that the involvement of governors in major public works seems to be limited mainly to Campania and Samnium, at least based on the ancient evidence, and explains that in part as a reflection of the 'extreme conservatism of the areas influenced by the senatorial aristocracy of Rome'.[54] One of the differences between

---

[49] *PLRE* 1, 'Marcus Aurelius Consius Quartus Iunior 2', 757. Compare the remarkable career of Gaius Vettius Cossinius Rufinus (*PLRE* 1, 'Caius Vettius Cossinius Rufinus 15', 777), who was appointed as proconsul of Achaea sometime in 306 (but probably never took up the office because of the political situation), but is then found in a series of governorships in Italy as *corrector* of Campania, then *corrector* of Tuscia et Umbria and *corrector* of Venetiae et Histriae, before he moved on to the proconsulship of Africa, and subsequently became prefect of the city of Rome in 315–16.

[50] *PLRE* 1, 'Caecina Decius Albinus Iunior 10', 35–6.

[51] Slootjes 2006.

[52] Ward-Perkins 1984, 23–8.

[53] *Eph. Epigr.* 8.456 = Dessau 5693, *balneum Veneris lon[gi tempo]ris vetustate corruptum Domitius Severianus v.c., con[s.] Campaniae ad pristinam faciem [aedifi]cavit, curante hac dedicand[te] Sentio Marso v.c., comite divinor[um], curator Capuensium, Literni[norum] et Cumanorum.* *PLRE* 1, 'Domitius Severianus 8', 829; *PLRE* 1, 'Sentius Marsus 1', 562. Trans. Fagan 2002, 245. Cecconi 1998, 154. Cf. Ward-Perkins 1984, 21.

[54] Ward-Perkins 1984, 24–7.

the provinces of Italy and the other provinces of the empire was the relatively common presence of high-ranking members of the upper classes, senatorial and equestrian, already living in the provinces, with whom governors had to reckon and vice versa.[55]

As noted, cities gained an additional option for benefactions, both material and non-material. Governors could be asked to assign funds for building or rebuilding of public buildings. It also makes us wonder, to whom would the provincial population have turned in previous centuries when there were no provinces yet in Italy? Evidence points to many instances in which members of the senatorial order who had their estates in the area of particular cities would be asked for help, as illustrated quite clearly by men such as Pliny the Younger, whose patronage of Como was well known.[56] The arrival of governors presented a new source of potential benefactions for Italian cities, and a type of support that should be more evenly distributed over a province, or at least the support of an official who was supposed to distribute his attention evenly over his province, and not so selective as what might have been the case with individual senatorial patrons. In this sense, according to Ward-Perkins, governors filled a 'vacuum of power'.[57]

Apart from the expected duties of governors, we find epigraphic evidence for governors who helped local communities to publicly represent themselves, for instance in competition with other cities in their region, and in particular to make themselves positively known at the imperial court. As an example, the *corrector* of Lucania and Bruttium, Alpinius Magnus, honoured Helena, Constantine I's mother, with a statue and inscription in Salernum.[58] While this monument was a clear individual message by the governor to the imperial house, simultaneously it offered the city an opportunity to make Salernum known as housing such an important testimonial of loyalty to the emperor.

Honouring Governors

The permanent presence of governors on the Italian peninsula led to changes in public dedications. Whereas, before the fourth century, local honorary dedications were often addressed to the emperors and local members of the elite, a shift seems to have taken place by which imperial officials – governors in particular – were increasingly honoured at the expense of the emperors and local notables, because as Machado has argued, 'civic groups re-oriented their political allegiances'.[59] In other words, the number of local honorary monuments did not so much decline as become redirected to other honorees.

Officially, local communities were allowed to honour a governor with a statue only after his term of office and with imperial approval.[60] Plenty of examples have

---

[55] See Cecconi 1998, 157; Brown 1992, 22–3.
[56] Nicols 1980; Dix 1996.
[57] Ward-Perkins 1984, 16–17 and 23–8.
[58] *PLRE* 1, 'Alpinius Magnus *signo* Eumenius 8', 534–5. *CIL* 10.517, statue LSA-1847. See Machado 2018, 59, table 2 for an overview of governors as local dedicators.
[59] Machado 2018, 64 and 66.
[60] *CJ* 1.24.1 (from 398). Machado 2018, 66. See Slootjes 2006, 129–53 on honorary statues and inscriptions for late antique governors.

emerged of such honours. For instance, the *ordo et populus* of the community of Aesernia set up a statue for the governor Fabius Maximus, which was arranged by the curator and patron Aurelius Paulinianus, around 352/357.⁶¹ Or, in Puteoli, 'the most splendid *ordo* and the most respectable people (set this up) for Septimius Rusticus, *vir consularis*, governor of Campania, *provisor ordinis*, restorer of the baths, because of remarkable love'.⁶² Such monuments for governors were, of course, to honour the individuals who had been governors, but simultaneously they contained a strong message to the next governors or any other type of imperial official who might appreciate and strive for such a monument for themselves in the future. After all, obtaining public honour and glory was ingrained in the Roman elitist way of life.

When honorary inscriptions for governors – if they are not merely a list of the offices that they fulfilled – give some additional information, they can offer us a little glimpse of the actual effect of governors' presence at local level. On the one hand, one might argue that their presence was an additional layer of imperial control at local level which might have been experienced as burdensome by members of the local elite. On the other hand, there were also advantages to having a governor who could be asked for help. There are several inscriptions in which cities – sometimes represented by an individual – praise governors for their benevolence, for their support with public works such as baths or theatres, or for their integrity and sense of justice.⁶³ As for praise of justice, this must be linked to the duty of governors to manage important court cases in their provinces. In some cases the inscriptions honour them as city patrons.⁶⁴ Especially in the instances in which governors moved on to higher offices that brought them to the praetorian prefectures, the city prefecture or consulships, honorary inscriptions set up in cities in their former provinces must have been an advantageous and very public reminder of their connection to these cities and vice versa. Such inscriptions, often as part of a monument that also contained a statue, would not only be a valuable message to the person honoured and to those who would be able to help them advance their public career, but – as already said – most likely even more so to subsequent governors.

Governors in Italy beyond the Fourth Century

Military troubles and usurpations in Italy in the later fourth and especially the early fifth century must have led to a halt in the proper functioning of provincial government and

---

⁶¹ *PLRE* 1, 'Fabius Maximus 35', 587. *CIL* 9.2639 = ILS 1248. Ward-Perkins 1984, 16 and 25. See Ward-Perkins 1984, 231–3 and 234, appendix 1 with a list of late antique statues for governors.

⁶² *CIL* 10.1707 = *ILS* 5692, Puteoli. Rusticus, *PLRE* 1, 'Septimius Rusticus 3', 787. Cecconi 1998, 154; Fagan 2002, 245–6, on our lack of knowledge of the meaning of the title *provisor ordinis*.

⁶³ Caius Iulius Rufinianus Ablablius Tatianus (*PLRE* 1, 'Caius Iulius Rufinianus Ablablius Tatianus 4', 875–6); Marcus Maecius Memmius Furius Baburius Caecilianus Placidus (*PLRE* 1, 'Marcus Maecius Memmius Furius Baburius Caecilianus Placidus 2', 705–6); Caius Vettius Cossinius Rufinus (*PLRE* 1, 'Caius Vettius Cossinius Rufinus 15', 777); Marcus Aurelius Consius Quartus Iunior (*PLRE* 1, 'Marcus Aurelius Consius Quartus Iunior 2', 757); Lucius Turcius Apronianus (*PLRE* 1, 'Lucius Turcius Apronianus *signo* Asterius 10', 88–9); Iulius Eubulidas (*PLRE* 1, 'Iulius Eubulidas', 287); Barbarus Pompeianus (*PLRE* 1, 'Barbarus Pompeianus 4', 712–13); Virius Aedentius Aemilianus (*PLRE* 1, 'Virius Aedentius Aemilianus 4', 22).

⁶⁴ Virius Aedentius Aemilianus (*PLRE* 1, 'Virius Aedentius Aemilianus 4', 22), patron of Puteoli.

thus to a decrease in the number of governors. In general, we are badly informed about the continuation of the daily business of provincial government in times of crisis and military threats. In the *fasti* of the second volume of the *Prosopography of the Later Roman Empire* we not only find considerably fewer names of governors for Italia Suburbicaria and Annonaria, but the precise dating for their offices becomes increasingly insecure.[65] Furthermore, there are slightly more names for Suburbicaria than for Annonaria. This is to be expected, considering the chaotic and often unstable situation in the northern part of the peninsula. The career of Postumius Lampadius is illustrative of the tensions that members of the upper classes must have felt while they provided the emperors with their services.[66] Lampadius, a native of Capua, had fulfilled the office of *consularis* of Campania, for which he was honoured by his hometown as their patron, as *restitutor patriae* and *redintegrator operum publicorum*.[67] At some point between 403 and 408, he was promoted and acquired the position of city prefect under the emperors Arcadius, Honorius and Theodosius.[68] Notably, by 409 he was appointed praetorian prefect by the usurper Priscus Attalus, who was himself supported by the Gothic leader Alaric.[69] In other words, here we come across an official who – driven by ambition or fear – opted for continuation of service within the imperial government, even though the political situation was volatile and the imperial position of Attalus eventually proved to be untenable. At this early stage in the fifth century there would have been no reason to assume that administrative structures would break down.

A substantial part of the evidence for governors in the Italian peninsula in the first half of the fifth century comes from honorary inscriptions that present us with an image of governors that is similar to previous centuries: they are honoured for their official positions, for restoration projects and benefactions or as patrons. For instance, several cities in Campania (Abellinum, Puteoli, Beneventum) honoured Pontius Proserius Paulinus, who had been *consularis* of Campania in 409, was patron of Capua and whose family had patronage ties with Puteoli.[70] One governor emerges in the sources as the addressees of an imperial law. Rogatianus, the *consularis* of Tusciae Suburbicariae, was addressed by the emperors Leo I and Marjorian in 459 in a law on adultery.[71] Rogatianus had tried a case of adultery, but had subsequently written

---

[65] *PLRE* 2, *fasti*, 1278–9.
[66] *PLRE* 2, 'Postumus Lampadius 7', 656. *CIL* 6.9920, 10.1704, 10.3860 = Dessau 1276.
[67] *CIL* 10.3860 = Dessau 1276.
[68] See Slootjes 2020, 269–73 on the late antique governors for whom a governorship was merely a stepping stone into higher offices.
[69] *PLRE* 2, 'Priscus Attalus 2', 180–1. Zos. 6.7.1. *CTh* 9.38.12 might refer to Attalus as a tyrant. Thompson 1982; Chauvot 2017.
[70] *PLRE* 2, 'Pontius Proserius Paulinus 16', 848–9. *CIL* 10.1128, 10.1702–3; *AE* 1972, 143. Other examples of governors who were honoured at local level are for instance: Aemilius Rufinius, the *consularis* of Campania in the period 425–50 (*PLRE* 2, 'Aemilius Rufinus *signo* Euresius 15', 957); Flavius Liberalis, the *consularis* of Sicilia (*PLRE* 2, '(Flavius) Liberalis', 676); Cassius Ruferius, the *consularis* of Apulia and Calabria in the fifth or early sixth century (*PLRE* 2, 'Cassius Ruferius 2', 951–2); Iulius Agrius Tarrutenius Marcianus, who was *consularis Siciliae* before moving into higher offices in the early or middle fifth century (*PLRE* 2, 'Iulius Agrius Tarrutenius Marcianus 20', 718–19).
[71] *N. Maj.* 9. Compare *N. Maj.* 5 of 458, in which an unnamed *consularis* of Picenum is mentioned (*PLRE* 2, 'Anonymus 77', 1231).

a report to the emperors to consult them. The imperial answer led to an official legal pronouncement.

Both the honorary inscriptions for governors and Rogatianus' correspondence with and response from the emperors seem to point to a continuation of the long-established duties of governors, although the evidence remains thin. We might assume that in those provinces, in which it would have been possible to maintain Roman government by way of appointment of provincial governors, the administrative system most likely continued as it had for the previous centuries. Lack of evidence is not necessarily proof of breakdown of provincial government. At the same time, however, we also discern an emergence of increasing local responsibility for the well-being of cities and regions, as is demonstrated by McCunn in Chapter 6 in this volume.

Clearly, this is only a first step towards a more in-depth examination of the functioning of governors in the fifth century in Italy. Modern scholarship would profit from a more systematic analysis of the sources to reconstruct the way in which the imperial government continued or discontinued its administrative structures in the fifth century.

Conclusion

The provincial administrative changes that were set in motion under the emperor Diocletian had far-reaching consequences for the Italian peninsula. On the one hand, the Italian cities saw their status decreased by the additional layer of the provincial administration, with its new officials with whom they had to reckon. Whereas before they might have had a direct link or access to individual authorities in Rome – perhaps through patronage of senators – now presumably they were confronted with a governor who was supposed to be the mediator between Rome and the provincial cities. On the other hand, the presence of a governor gave them more direct access to the imperial administration, as a governor should have been approachable for every city, which made the local relation with the imperial administration less dependent on accidental local contacts of the elites. Overall, local communities were able to come to terms with the new situation, which was visible in their public dedication practices expressing their close ties to the presence of and dependence on the new type of imperial official at local level.

A governorship, however, in one of the newly created Italian provinces might not have been easy. In these Italian provinces, a high level of urbanisation as well as the proportion of members of the empire-wide elite (i.e. the members of the senatorial and equestrian order) being present at local level must have been quite different from the situation in the other provinces of the empire. The percentage of members of the senate who owned land and estates in the Italian countryside must have been proportionally high.[72] Consequently, their presence, and especially benefactions – also expected perhaps – must have been part of local city life for centuries already, perhaps more so than in other cities in the empire.

---

[72] Plin. *Ep.* 6.19: a third of their money in Italian lands in order to qualify for members of the senate.

Ultimately, the arrival of governors led to a standardisation of Italy in terms of provincial government. Governors of the newly created Italian provinces acted as the governors in the provinces of the other parts of the empire had done for centuries. Certainly, particular regions in Italy had unique features that governors had to take into account, but exceptional regional differences had also been part of provincial government for centuries. The Italian provinces turned out not to be so unique after all. As is often the case in the functioning of Roman administrative structures, the officials who represented Roman government and the provincial subject were indissolubly connected in a *do-ut-des* relationship.[73] Governors expected cooperation, loyalty and a smooth term of office, while provincials expected good government, benefactions and connections to the imperial level. Overall, as has become clear for the Italian provincial administration of the fourth and especially the fifth centuries, more scholarly analyses of the ancient material, for instance on the fiscal and judicial role of governors as well as their relationship with other higher officials present in Italy such as the *vicarii* and the praetorian prefect, are most welcome for deepening our understanding of Italy in the broader context of its position within the empire at large.[74]

Bibliography

Aichinger, A. (1982) 'Grenzziehung durch kaiserliche Sonderbeauftragte in den römischen Provinzen', *ZPE* 48: 193–204.

Ausbüttel, F. M. (1988) *Die Verwaltung der Städte und Provinzen im spätantiken Italien*, Frankfurt am Main.

Barnes, T. D. (1975) 'The Unity of the Verona List', *ZPE* 16: 275–8.

Barnes, T. D. (1982) *The New Empire of Diocletian and Constantine*, Cambridge, MA.

Barnes, T. D. (1992) 'Praetorian Prefects 337–361', *ZPE* 94: 249–60.

Bleckmann, B. (1992) *Die Reichskrise des III. Jahrhunderts in der spätantiken und byzantinischen Geschichtsschreibung: Untersuchungen zu den nachdionischen Quellen der Chronik des Johannes Zonaras*, Munich.

Bleckmann, B. (2003) 'Der Bürgerkrieg zwischen Constantin II. und Constans (340. n.Chr.)', *Historia* 52: 225–50.

Bowman, A., A. Cameron and P. Garnsey (eds) *The Cambridge Ancient History*, vol. 12, *The Crisis of Empire, A.D. 293–337*, 2nd ed., Cambridge.

Brown, P. (1992) *Power and Persuasion in Late Antiquity: Towards a Christian Empire*, Madison, WI.

Brown, P. (2012) *Through the Eye of a Needle: Wealth, the Fall of Rome, and the Making of Christianity in the West, 350–550 AD*, Princeton.

Burton, G. P. (2000) 'The Resolution of Territorial Disputes in the Provinces of the Roman Empire', *Chiron* 30: 195–215.

Burton, G. P. (2002a) 'The Roman Imperial State (A.D. 14–235): Evidence and Reality', *Chiron* 32: 249–80.

Burton, G. P. (2002b) 'The Regulation of Inter-community Relations in the Provinces and the Political Integration of the Roman Empire (27 BC–AD 238)', in V. B. Gorman and E. W.

---

[73] Slootjes 2016, 178–83.

[74] I thank Jeroen Wijnendaele and Noel Lenski for their valuable comments on an earlier draft of this contribution.

Robinson (eds) *Oikistes: Studies in Constitutions, Colonies, and Military Power in the Ancient World Offered in Honor of A. J. Graham*, Leiden, 113–28.

Cecconi, G. A. (1998) 'I governatori delle province Italiche', *AntTard* 6: 149–79.

Chaniotis, A. and T. Fujii (2015) 'A New Fragment of Diocletian's Currency Regulation from Aphrodisias', *JRS* 105: 227–33.

Chastagnol, A. (1963) 'L'administration du Diocèse Italien au Bas-Empire', *Historia* 12: 348–79.

Chauvot, A. (2017) 'Le triomphe d'Honorius et le châtiment d'Attale', *RH* 684: 739–74.

Chelotti, M. and G. Mennella (1994) 'Letture e riletture epigrafiche nella regio II', *ZPE* 103: 159–72.

Cherf, W. J. (1987) 'The Roman Borders between Achaia and Macedonia', *Chiron* 17: 135–42.

Christie, N. (1991) 'The Alps as Frontier (A.D. 168–774)', *JRA* 4: 410–30.

Christie, N. (2006) *From Constantine to Charlemagne: an Archaeology of Italy, A.D. 300–800*, Aldershot.

Cooley, A. E. (2016) *A Companion to Roman Italy*, Malden, MA.

Davenport, C. (2019) *A History of the Roman Equestrian Order*, Cambridge.

Dix, T. K. (1996) 'Pliny's Library at Comum', *Libraries and Culture* 31: 85–102.

Drinkwater, J. F. (2007) *The Alamanni and Rome (213–496): Caracalla to Clovis*, Oxford.

Eck, W. (1979) *Die staatliche Organisation Italiens in der hohen Kaiserzeit*, Munich.

Elliott, T. (2004) 'Epigraphic Evidence for Boundary Disputes in the Roman Empire', Dissertation, University of North Carolina.

Fagan, G. G. (2002) *Bathing in Public in the Roman World*, Ann Arbor.

Feissel, D. (2004) 'L'empereur et l'administration impériale', in C. Morrison (ed.) *Le monde byzantin*, vol. 1: *L'Empire romain d'Orient (330–641)*, Paris, 79–110.

Garbsch, J. (1970) *Der spätrömische Donau-Iller-Rhein-Limes*, Kleine Schriften zur Kenntnis der römischen Besetzungsgeschichte Südwestdeutschlands 6, Stuttgart.

Green, S. W. and S. M. Perlman (eds) (1985) *The Archaeology of Frontiers and Boundaries*, Orlando.

Hesberg, H. von (ed.) (1995) *Was ist eigentlich Provinz? Zur Beschreibung eines Bewußtseins*, Cologne.

Jones, A. H. M. (1964) *The Later Roman Empire: 284–602*, Baltimore.

Kaiser, R. (2008) *Churrätien im frühen Mittelalter: Ende 5. bis Mitte 10. Jahrhunderts*, 2nd ed., Basel.

Kolb, F. (1987) *Diocletian und die Erste Tetrarchie: Improvisation oder Experiment in der Organisation monarchischer Herrschaft?* Berlin.

Kreucher, G. (2003) *Der Kaiser Marcus Aurelius und seine Zeit*, Stuttgart.

Kulikowski, M. (2004) *Late Roman Spain and Its Cities*, Baltimore.

Liebeschuetz, J. H. W. G. (1987) 'Government and Administration in the Late Empire (to A.D. 476)', in J. Wacher (ed.) *The Roman World*, vol. 1, London, 455–69.

Liebeschuetz, J. H. W. G. (2001) *The Decline and Fall of the Roman City*, Oxford.

Lo Cascio, E. (2005) 'The Emperor and His Administration', in A. Bowman, A. Cameron and P. Garnsey (eds) *The Cambridge Ancient History*, vol. 12, *The Crisis of Empire, A.D. 293–337*, 2nd ed., Cambridge, 131–83.

Machado, C. (2018) 'Civic Honours and Political Participation in Late Antique Italy', *AntTard* 26: 51–71.

Migl, J. (1994) *Die Ordnung der Ämter: Prätorianerpräfektur und Vikariat in der Regionalverwaltung des Römischen Reiches von Konstantin bis zur Valentinianischen Dynastie*, Frankfurt am Main.

Nicols, J. (1980) 'Pliny and the Patronage of Communities', *Hermes* 108: 365–85.

Noethlichs, K. L. (1982) 'Zur Entstehung der Diözesen als Mittelinstanz des spätrömischen Verwaltungssytems', *Historia* 31: 70–81.

Palme, B. (1999) 'Die *Officia* der Statthalter in der Spätantike: Forschungsstand und Perspektiven', *AntTard* 7: 85–133.

Porena, P. (2013) 'La riorganizzazione amministrativa dell'Italia: Costantino, Roma, il Senato et gli equilibri dell'Italia Romana', in A. Melloni et al. (eds) *Costantino I: Enciclopedia costantiniana sulla figura e l'immagine dell'imperatore del cosiddetto Editto di Milano 313–2013*, vol. 1, Rome, 329–49.

Prieur, J. (1968) *La province romaine des Alpes Cottienes*, Villeurbanne.

Richardson, J. (2011) 'Fines Provinciae', in O. Hekster and T. Kaizer (eds.) *Frontiers in the Roman World: Proceedings of the Ninth Workshop of the International Network Impact of Empire (Durham, 16–19 April 2009)*, Leiden, 1–11.

Roncaglia, C. (2013) 'Client Prefects? Rome and the Cottians in the Western Alps', *Phoenix* 67: 353–72.

Schönberger, H. (1985) 'Die römischen Truppenlanger der frühen und mittleren Kaiserzeit zwischen Nordsee und Inn', *BRGK* 66: 322–497.

Sipilä, J. (2009) *The Reorganisation of Provincial Territories in Light of the Imperial Decision-Making Process: Later Roman Arabia and Tres Palaestinae as Case Studies*, Helsinki.

Slootjes, D. (2006) *The Governor and His Subjects in the Later Roman Empire*, Leiden.

Slootjes, D. (2014) 'Late Antique Administrative Structures: on the Meaning of Dioceses and Their Borders in the Fourth Century AD', in L. L. Brice and D. Slootjes (eds) *Aspects of Ancient Institutions and Geography: Studies in Honor of Richard J. A. Talbert*, Impact of Empire 19, Leiden, 177–95.

Slootjes, D. (2020) 'Governing the Empire: the Effects of the Diocletianic and Constantinian Provincial Reforms under the Sons of Constantine', in N. Baker-Brian and S. Tougher (eds) *The Sons of Constantine, AD 337–361: in the Shadows of Constantine and Julian*, London, 255–74.

Talbert, R. J. A. (2000) *Barrington Atlas of the Greek and Roman World*, Princeton.

Thompson, E. A. (1982) 'Zosimus 6.10.2 and the Letters of Honorius', *CQ* 32: 445–62.

Walser, G. (1986) *Via per Alpes Graias: Beiträge zur Geschichte des Kleinen St. Bernard-Passes in römischer Zeit*, Stuttgart.

Ward-Perkins, B. (1984) *From Classical Antiquity to the Middle Ages: Urban Public Building in Northern and Central Italy, A.D. 300–850*, Oxford.

Whittaker, C. R. (1994) *Frontiers of the Roman Empire: a Social and Economic Study*, Baltimore.

Wiewiorowski, J. (2015) *The Judiciary of Diocesan Vicars in the Later Roman Empire*, Poznań.

Wilkes, J. (2005) 'Provinces and Frontiers', in A. Bowman, A. Cameron and P. Garnsey (eds) *The Cambridge Ancient History*, vol. 12, *The Crisis of Empire, A.D. 293–337*, 2nd ed., Cambridge, 212–68.

Wittke, A.-M., E. Olshausen and R. Szydlak (2012) *Historischer Atlas der antiken Welt*, Der neue Pauly Sonderausgabe, Stuttgart.

Zuckerman, K. (2002) 'Sur la Liste de Vérone et la province de Grande Arménie, la division de l'Empire et la date de création des diocèses', in *Mélanges Gilbert Dagron, Travaux et Mémoires* 14, Paris, 617–37.

6

How the West Was Run: Local Government in Late Roman Italy

Stuart McCunn

Introduction

'No one can be unaware that decurions are the nerves of the State and the sinews of the cities.'[1] This was the verdict of the emperor Majorian in 458, but it represented a truth that stretched back into the early days when Rome was little more than a city state. The Roman Empire is often represented as a centralised dictatorship, but to its inhabitants it would have looked more like a distant executive with a laissez-faire approach to branch business. The heart of Roman administration was the city. It was city officials (decurions) who raised the taxes that supported Rome's armies, city officials who maintained the famous roads, and city officials who handled the minor trials that make up the majority of cases in any judicial system. For many residents, city officials were the highest authorities they were ever likely to come into contact with.

The city was one of the quintessential institutions of antiquity, and the absence of civic institutions on the same scale is one of the key markers of the rural-based power structures of the medieval period. Yet the timing and nature of the changeover is imprecise. The reforms instituted by Diocletian and Constantine towards the beginning of the period covered in this volume are often identified as the cause of failing cities. Yet so are the changes that came at the end of this period, the transition of Italy from Roman *imperium* to Ostrogothic *regnum*. Both claims cannot be true.

When we look at the changes the city underwent as it moved from the Classical Era into the Middle Ages we see that the transition from a city-based society under the control of short-term magistrates into a rural-based society under the control of landed aristocrats with undefined power limits was a gradual and nuanced affair. What do we mean by a classical city? Which changes can we consider to be decisive and which merely superficial? And how can we account for regional differences? Italy, the birthplace of the traditional Roman city, was on a very different trajectory from Gaul or Asia Minor. To understand the nature of late Roman administration we must look to the classical city itself. The trajectory of the Roman city can be traced through the magistrates who ran it – their backgrounds, powers and responsibilities. It can also be traced by looking at the competing power groups that confronted these magistrates.

---

[1] *N. Maj.* 7.1.

But ultimately, we need to understand the nature of the Roman city and how it adapted to the changed situation of Late Antiquity.

Early Municipal Government (First Century BC–Second Century AD)

Like Republican Rome, which was after all only the most successful city state on the peninsula, Italian cities under Roman rule were controlled by a class of elite families who maintained their status through wealth (particularly in land), patronage ties and control over local government. As with Rome, there was a certain degree of social mobility, and the old families could face serious competition from newcomers, but established names and lineages provided a significant advantage.[2] As in Rome, these ruling families maintained their authority through a combination of patronage ties and the holding of various offices. Magistrates were chosen by popular election, and service in such a magistracy made one a decurion and lifetime member of the *curia*, the town council that was the equivalent of the senate. Instead of consuls, the cities had shared magistrates who went by names such as *duoviri*, *quattorviri* or *decemviri*. In addition, every five years they had the opportunity to become a *quinquennalis*, the local equivalent of a censor. On the lower end of the magisterial scale were the aediles, who oversaw repairs and regulated the markets, and the quaestors, who managed the treasury.[3]

There are four key elements that defined these municipal magistrates:

1. They were elected positions. While hardly a fair democracy by modern standards, the electorate was composed of a significant portion of the population (generally all adult male citizens) and was the basis of a magistrate's legitimacy. That this was more than a mere rubber-stamping of preselected individuals can be seen by the often fierce rivalry seen in election sloganeering from Pompeii.[4]
2. The positions were collegial. In keeping with Republican ideals of sharing power, the chief magistrates always had one or more partners to reduce their potential for abuse. As their names suggest, there were two *duoviri*, four *quattorviri* and ten *decemviri*, but there were also two aediles, two quaestors and two *quinquennales*.
3. The positions were annual. Elections were held every year (their term began on 1 July in Nola and Pompeii, and early August in several cities with Sullan constitutions) and replaced the magistrates then in office.[5]
4. Their powers came from the office. While successful officeholders could bring their personal influence to bear as well, the government of the cities did not rely on irregular and personal power bases.

---

[2] Franklin 2001 provides a good prosopographical overview of the various families holding magistracies in Pompeii, the city for which we have the most detailed information.
[3] Good outlines of the municipal magistracies and their responsibilities can be found in Abbot and Johnson 1926, 59–68; Langhammer 1973, 62–188.
[4] See the list in Mouritsen 1988, 126–57, and analysis in Tacoma 2020, 61–95.
[5] Abbott and Johnson 1926, 331–2, 343–4.

The most detailed evidence for the operation of Roman cities comes from those who had charters that have survived. These charters identify the number and names of offices as well as the basic procedure for running the administration of the city. Our best-preserved example comes from Colonia Iulia Genetiva in Urso, where it was inscribed on nine bronze tablets (of which we have four) and displayed publicly. While Iberian, the city had a strongly Italian government since it was a colony of Roman veterans whose charter was drafted by Caesar and approved by the Roman senate.[6] The charter outlined a city government consisting of two *duoviri* and two aediles, each elected annually and taking office on 31 December. Each *duumvir* was assigned *apparitores* (aides): two lictors, an aide (*accensus*), two scribes, two summoners (*viatores*), a copyist (*librarius*), a crier (*praeco*), a haruspex and a flutist (*tibicinus*). Each aedile received a scribe, four public slaves, a crier, a haruspex and a flutist.[7] While *apparitores* were to be paid, the magistrates received nothing. In point of fact, they actually paid handsomely for the privilege. Also in Urso's charter is the proviso that the magistrates must provide games for the populace. Public funds were available for the purpose, 2,000 sesterces for *duoviri* and 1,000 for aediles, but the main cost would have been borne by the magistrates themselves, who were required to spend at least 2,000 sesterces out of their own pocket.[8]

Why would people want such positions if they were so great an expense? Decurions were entitled to certain benefits to distinguish them above common citizens, including preferential seating at the theatre. Officeholding also granted immunities. Serving magistrates were not allowed to be drafted into the army, nor were they required to perform menial labour. But the most important factor seems to have been prestige. A city leader was elevated above his peers and entitled to take public credit for building work in the form of inscriptions. The pride ex-*duoviri* felt can be seen by the number of inscriptions recovered boasting of their achievements.[9] Whatever their motivations, local elites spent large portions of their private fortunes conducting the business of the city. This was the basic requirement of Roman municipal government, which could otherwise hardly be self-supporting.

Like modern metropolitan areas, the reach of a city extended some distance beyond the city itself. Cities were not merely population centres or even administrative centres; they were essentially mini empires who ruled over their smaller neighbours. The region under the control of a city was called its *territorium*, and included a number of towns, villages and homesteads. These settlements answered to the municipal magistrates just as the city ultimately answered to Roman ones. Also a part of the city's domains were municipal lands whose rent provided a significant part of the city's income. Land and commercial taxes alongside tolls and fines made up the rest of the public revenue.[10] Generally speaking, cities like this were able to govern their own affairs without the aid of the central government.

---

[6] Crawford 1996, 395–8.
[7] *CIL* 2.5439 Urso 62.
[8] *CIL* 2.5439 Urso 70–1.
[9] E.g. the long list found in Forbis 1996, 105–232.
[10] Ausbüttel 1998, 69–74; Corbier 1991.

Munera et Curiales

While the late empire saw the radical restructuring of the upper levels of government into smaller provinces, dioceses and prefectures, the cities continued to function much as they had before. The traditional city magistracies were still present. *Duoviri* (often hidden under the generic *magistrati*), aediles and quaestors can be found in Italy until our epigraphic sources die off in the early fifth century.[11] Being *quinquennalis* could still be listed as the culmination of a long and successful municipal career.[12] Even some of the more Republican elements survived. The law codes only mention popular assemblies in relation to Africa, but from inscriptions we know they were present in Italy as well.[13] The *curia* also maintained its power. If anything, it was even stronger. The *curia* alone selected many of the new magistrates. Even the status of the decurions who made up the *curia* was on firmer footing. By the early third century non-decurions were prohibited from running for public office.[14] By the time of Constantine I, we find laws tying decurions to their father's status.[15] Those eligible for service on the *curia* now became a genuine class: the *curiales*.

Despite the force with which new laws proclaimed these changes, this was in many ways more of a semantic change than a real one. Digging deeper into the late Roman laws on curial service it becomes clear that it was not the person of the *curialis* who inherited decurion duties, but rather their land. If that land was lost then the individual would be removed from the album of the *ordo decurionum* and no longer subject to, or eligible for, the demands of office.[16] From the other end, sufficiently wealthy non-*curiales* could be drafted into the *curia*.[17] This can even be seen in the most prestigious *curia* of the ancient world: the Roman senate.[18]

Wealth had always been the basis of service on the *curia*. The charter of Urso required decurions to maintain sufficiently valuable property within a mile of the city in order to remain in the *ordo decurionum*.[19] Requirements in Tarentum were even stricter, requiring residence inside the city with a large house of no fewer than 1,500 roof tiles.[20] Late Roman property requirements were similarly precise. Constantius II

---

[11] There are twenty-three *duumvir* inscriptions known from Late Roman Italy, the latest being EE-08-01.648 (Antium) in 385. For the epigraphic habit in Italy see Witschel 2006, 359–67; Bolle 2017. See Bolle et al. 2017, more generally.

[12] CIL 9.259 (Genusia), 11.4094 (Ocriculum), 14.128 (Ostia); AE 1948.178 (Turris Libisonis).

[13] CTh 12.5.1; CIL 10.478 (Paestum); AE 1937.121 (Foruli). See Jacques 1984, 385–8 (this law); Lepelley 1979–1981, 1.140–9 (African assemblies); and Lewin 1995, 89–120 (assemblies generally). See also Lepelley 1992b, 64.

[14] *Dig.* 50.2.7. See Garnsey 1974, 241–50.

[15] CTh 12.1.7.

[16] The most obvious example are the laws demanding that decurions who joined the clergy surrender their land to heirs. See CTh 12.1.49, 12.1.59, 12.1.63, 12.1.99, 12.1.104, 12.1.115, 12.1.121, 12.1.163, 12.1.172; N. Val. 3.3.1.1.

[17] CTh 12.1.96, 12.1.133.

[18] Ausbüttel 1988, 16.

[19] CIL 2.5439 (Urso) 91.

[20] CIL 1.590 (Tarentum) 26–8; Crawford 1996, 301–12. See also Plin. *Ep.* 1.19.2 for the requirements in Comum.

established twenty-five *iugera* (a modest farm) as the minimum needed to serve on the council for those granted land on imperial estates.[21] A law of Valentinian III set 300 solidi as the minimum for Italy.[22] The significance of hereditary status was not that it restricted public service to the wealthiest inhabitants, but that it made the *curia* the gatekeeper to the magistracies rather than the other way round. Instead of being filled with elected magistrates, the *curia* was now the *source* of them.[23]

While the hereditary status of *curiales* was a formal recognition of existing practices, there were genuine changes to curial responsibilities. The insistence on the hereditary nature of curial membership was accompanied by a *requirement* that they undertake such service. Service on the *curia* became a *munus* (pl. *munera*): an obligation to provide service to the state with no financial compensation. Essentially, it meant being drafted into forced labour of one form or another. *Munera* applied to every level of society. Poorer citizens could be called on to perform manual labour in repairing roads or bridges. Often the term was used for taxes. *Curiales* served in municipal offices instead, supervising repair work or filling various necessary offices such as those of peacekeeper or judge.[24] A law of Constantine I held that those who fled municipal service were to be required to serve as *duumvir* for two full years, a threat which makes no sense if the position remained an honour.[25]

As with the hereditary nature of the office, the difference between this and earlier methods was mainly one of degree. The obligation for magistrates to hold games had always been a *munus*, and the expense had long been considered a burden.[26] The lower burdens were present as well. Urso's charter required all males between the ages of fourteen and sixty to help with construction or repair work for up to five days a year.[27] Even the compulsory nature of magistracies can be seen in the charter of Malaca (in Spain), which contains a provision for forcing men to submit themselves for election.[28] By the time of Marcus Aurelius compulsory officeholding was a subject for imperial law.[29] *Munera* had always been expensive, but now there were more of them. *Curiales* were expected to collect taxes, undertake repairs, run baths and host games. They were required to attend provincial councils and consult with the governor. They could be summoned to serve as envoys for the town, either to the imperial court or local powers. The frequency with which a *curialis* would undertake these *munera* would have varied depending on their status and location, but there is no doubt that they were common.

The expense of these *munera* has often been blamed for the decline of the curial class.[30] Yet, while keeping them tied to their office was certainly a preoccupation of

---

[21] *CTh* 12.1.33.
[22] *N. Val.* 3.1.3.
[23] Stahl 1978, 47–54.
[24] Petit 1955, 71–91; Jones 1964, 737–54.
[25] *CTh* 12.1.16.
[26] E.g. *CIL* 2.6278 (Italica); Cass. Dio 52.30.4. Plin. *Ep.* 10.113 may also refer to this (reading *inviti* for *invitati*), but see Garnsey 1974, 232.
[27] *CIL* 2.5439 (Urso) 98. See also Crawford 1996, 395–9; Laurence et al. 2011, 72–90.
[28] *CIL* 2.1964 (Malaca) 51. See commentary in Hardy 1912, 98–118.
[29] *Dig.* 50.1.38.6.
[30] E.g. Petit 1955, 45–62; Jones 1964, 737–51; Liebeschuetz 2001, 104–5.

the emperors, there is little to indicate that their departure was due solely or even primarily to bankruptcy. Most of the laws on this topic concern *curiales* who have fled *upwards*, not lost their position due to poverty.[31] Those who could afford to serve at the imperial court would not have been the poorest members of the curial class. Proximity to court may have helped the *curiales* of the northern region of Annonaria gain such important contacts, but that cut two ways: they could also be more easily located by their *curia* and forced to return to municipal service. Even with the other common method of escape, the church, it is clear that these laws are not primarily concerned with *curiales* who have sunk into poverty. Many of the decurions who abandoned their secular duties to be ordained were clearly holders of vast properties, as can be seen by the laws restricting the amount of land they could donate to the church.[32] It would not make much sense for the emperors to divide two thirds of such decurions' land among their heirs if the undivided lands in question were too small to bear the financial burden of service. If these men were fleeing their curial obligations it was not the money, but the time spent which they sought escape from.

The evidence that *curiae* were declining in size throughout the fourth century is also hard to find. Our two most detailed *alba decurionum* show no significant difference in size between early and later empire. An AD 223 album from Canusium had 164 names.[33] An album of 363/4 from Timgat in Africa had 168 names.[34] Any conclusions based on only two pieces of evidence can hardly be conclusive, but a clearer sign that the Italian curial class was not universally declining can be seen by the situation under Rome's successors. Under the Ostrogoths, Athalaric was able to say in passing that *curiales* were so abundant that the *curiae* would not miss a few.[35] The early Ostrogothic period was a rare time of stability for late antique Italy, but it is unlikely that the number of *curiales* could have risen so high if they had not been numerous beforehand.

The actual situation of *curiales* varied enormously. Landlocked cities like Nola must have had vastly different responsibilities from major ports like Naples, even though it was only 30 miles away. Some cities were struggling to survive. Formiae's *curia* was suffering from low numbers and poverty in the late fourth century.[36] In Salernum, the *curia* needed help because of the number of citizens deserting the city.[37] The *curiales* of Beneventum were broke. But even here the situation was not as dire as it may seem. The *curiales* of Beneventum had bankrupted themselves because they had spent all their money repairing the damage from an earthquake in 375.[38] Rather than being a sign of decline, the fact that so much money was available to the curial class at Beneventum shows that the city must have been doing pretty well before the disaster.

---

[31] Seventy-six of 192 of the laws in *CTh* 12.1 are dedicated to preventing decurions from escaping their *munera* by elevating their position. See Laniado 2002, 3–26.
[32] *N. Val.* 3.1.
[33] *CIL* 9.338 (Canusium). See also Mouritsen 1998.
[34] Chastagnol 1978, 33.
[35] Cassiod. *Ep.* 9.4.1.
[36] Symm. *Ep.* 9.136.
[37] *CIL* 10.520 = *AE* 2012.298 (Salernum).
[38] Symm. *Ep.* 1.3.4.

There seems no real reason to assume that the situation in Formiae or Salernum was more typical than that at Beneventum.

Centrally Appointed Rivals

This is not to say that there were no pressures being placed on *curiales*. While curial numbers were not declining radically, their influence was. The first and most obvious manifestation of this is the decreasing authority of the traditional magistracies. *Duoviri* and aediles continued to be appointed, but their powers were limited by new imperially selected officials. Wolf Liebeschuetz succinctly summarised the traditional view: 'The presence of imperial officials made the work of *curiales* and civic magistrates unattractive and hazardous, and by producing a flight from the councils, fatally damaged both *curiae* and cities.'[39] There is certainly some truth in this. Agents of the central offices were notorious for abuses since they were operating outside the eye of their superiors and there was little that the provincial authorities could do to restrain them. The emperors were continually issuing laws forbidding them from interfering with or even taking over municipal positions (especially those involved with tax collection). However, while imperial agents could damage municipalities, they had no interest in the permanent acquisition of local authority. If we are looking for imperial officials undermining the curial dominance of their municipalities, we need to examine the permanent representatives of the emperor. The story told is a lot more complicated than imperial interference damaging the cities.

Curatores (First Appeared c.105)

Curatores were the first of the supramagisterial municipal positions to appear. *Curatores rei publicae* were created by Trajan (98–117), and were most commonly found in Italy.[40] Sent to various cities, the *curator* had the authority to direct or cancel municipal projects and control the city's budget. This has often been treated as an example of imperial overreach reducing the independence of the city governments, although more recent studies have emphasised the helpful nature of the *curatores*.[41] Rather than imperial meddling, they represented a needed effort to restrain municipal excesses and help balance budgets. The people chosen for the post were frequently former decurions.[42] When the position began to expand from its original duties it turned in the direction of the *curia* rather than the centre. By the time of Gallienus, *curatores* were

---

[39] Liebeschuetz 2015, 33. See also Jones 1964, 737–62.
[40] Jacques 1984, 7–12.
[41] Eck 1979, 190–246; Camodeca 1980; Jacques 1984, 121–220. The alternative view was frequently expressed in older works (see Reid 1913, 471–4; Abbott and Johnson 1926, 200–1), but has been given a nuanced update in Stahl 1978, 128–31, where the *curator* is seen as a well-intentioned but ultimately destructive innovation.
[42] Jacques 1984, 571–661. While he was not a *curator*, a good example of the sort of problems *curatores* were tasked with solving can be seen in Book 10 of Pliny the Younger's letters.

undertaking roles in civic maintenance and building work that had previously been the purview of traditional magistrates.[43]

Under the Tetrarchy, the *curatores* became absorbed entirely into the municipalities. Instead of a mixed pool of candidates, tetrarchic *curatores* (*curatores civitatis*) came entirely from the curial class. While they were elected by the *curia*, the fact that they required the governor's approval allowed them to describe themselves as *sacro iudicio promoti* (promoted by imperial resolution).[44] Under Constantius II, the *curator* was considered the highest magistracy (even above serving as *quinquennalis*) of a long and successful municipal career.[45] Such a career was necessary to reach the post since it was only open to men who had already fulfilled all their civic *munera*.[46] In practice, this means that the post was dominated by the *principales*, who further enhanced their power over the remainder of the *curia* (see p. 141–2). Despite their prestige, *curatores* were not a universal component of Italian cities. Compared to regions like Africa, mentions of *curatores* are low.[47] Almost half (22/47) of Italian curatorial inscriptions come from the province of Campania. Another quarter can be found in Sardinia (7) and the area run by the urban prefect (5). In Alpes Cottiae, both Raetias, Valeria, Picenum Suburbicarium and Corsica there are no known *curatores* at all. This ratio does not line up entirely with the areas of greatest activity during this period. Annonaria, particularly the section near the imperial court, was a thriving region.[48] This likely represents the greater popularity of the post in the highly urbanised areas of central Italy.

Unfortunately, the title on *curatores* has not been preserved in the surviving manuscript of the *Theodosian Code*, so we cannot say with certainty what the emperors considered their function to be.[49] However, we do have evidence from the Ostrogothic period. Cassiodorus was praetorian prefect of Italy from 533 to c.538 and an influential secretary and royal letter-writer from as early as 507.[50] His letters (*Variae*) include a generic formula for appointing new *curatores*:

> And therefore, we wish that the care of this city pertain to you for the present indiction, so that you may wisely direct the honourable ranks of the *curia*, and you may cause regulated prices to be preserved for those who have an interest in them. Do not allow commerce to be only in the power of those selling; let fairness protect desired things in all matters. Indeed, this will even gather the most fulsome gratitude of the citizens if prices are maintained at a moderate level, so that you truly fulfil the duty of *curator* when your anxiety will be for the weal of all. Preserve, however, by our authority, the customary practices that your predecessors had in the same post.[51]

---

[43] *CIL* 9.1588 (Beneventum), 11.556 (Caesena), 11.3091/2 (Falerii); *AE* 1919.52 (Comum), 2016.415 (Lucus Feroniae); Eck 1979, 213, no. 80.
[44] *AE* 1940.48 (Suessa Aurunca).
[45] *CIL* 11.5283 (Hispellum).
[46] *CTh* 12.1.20.
[47] Camodeca 1980, 476.
[48] Secular inscriptions in general are more common in Suburbicaria, while Annonaria favoured religious ones. See Cecconi 1994, 177–81; Witschel 2006, 364–7.
[49] *CTh* 1.30.
[50] O'Donnell 1979, 20–32. See also Bjornlie 2013.
[51] Cassiod. *Var.* 7.12 (trans. Bjornlie).

From this formula it would seem that the *curatores* continued to handle civic finances, just as they had in the principate. The reference to directing the *curia* shows that this was still a curial post, indeed the highest in the city.

The high-water mark of Italian *curatores* was the early and mid-fourth century. There are only two attestations of a *curator* which can be securely dated after 380. The likeliest reason for the post's decline is that the *defensor civitatis* replaced the *curator* as many cities' chief magistrate. By the time of Cassiodorus cities only had one or the other, and since *curatores* are only mentioned once in his letters it is likely that the *defensor* was more common. Yet, if this is true, it is curious that inscriptions for the *defensor* should be so few as well. Only one can be securely identified after 370 and, curiously, the opposite side mentions a *curator*.[52]

The relationship of the *curatores* to the traditional municipal magistracies was complicated. Their initial role was strictly financial and left administration to the *curiae*, but they gradually grew to assume many of the duties previously held by the traditional magistracies. They had no colleagues or established terms of office.[53] That this change happened through the *curia* and the curial class meant that they never threatened to upend curial control of municipal government, but at the same time they did represent a trend of monopolising power among smaller groups that deprivileged lower *curiales*. The *curatores* represented new methods of government that eroded traditional magistracies.

Exactores (First Appeared c.303)

Exactor is the Latin word for debt collector and was used as such from the time of the Republic. From the third century on, *exactores* had become powerful but irregular representatives of the central government.[54] The standardised position called the *exactor civitatis* was an innovation of Diocletian and can be seen in Egyptian sources as early as 303.[55] Dating the position's appearance in Italy is impossible. There is only one Italian inscription referencing an *exactor*: a Gaius Caelius Censorinus held the post of *exactor auri et argenti provinciarum III* (*exactor* of gold and silver for the Three Provinces) under Constantine I.[56] Unfortunately, the Three Provinces was actually a region in Gaul, and since he was responsible for multiple provinces he must have been an imperial official and not an *exactor civitatis*. Lacking further data, we cannot say for certain whether this means the new model *exactor* was late to appear in Italy (perhaps only imported after Constantine's conquest of the East?) or whether documentation has merely not survived. Italy certainly had *exactores* later in the century, so the position was likely introduced empire-wide at the same time it appeared in Egypt.[57] Taxation officials were a novelty in Italy, and it seems unlikely that Diocletian would have created unique officials for that diocese while standardising the ones in Egypt.

---

[52] *AE* 1925.91 (Surrentum). Sadly, the inscription is only partial and the context has been lost.
[53] Eck 1979, 203.
[54] E.g. *CIL* 13.1807 (Lugdunum).
[55] Thomas 1959, 124.
[56] *CIL* 3732 = *ILS* 1216 (Atella).
[57] *CTh* 11.26.2, 12.10, 13.1.12, 13.5.17; Symm. *Ep.* 4.43, 6.38.2.

Exactores were the most important tax-collection officials in the municipalities. Like the *curatores*, the position initially began as an imperial appointment. We can see in a papyrus from 345 that the *exactores* were actually chosen by the central authorities and not the governors or *curiae*.[58] The pool of potential *exactores* would have been mainly curial, but the *curia* would not have had direct involvement in the process. By 384 the appointment process had turned into the same one used by *curatores*: the *curia* nominated an *exactor*, and the governor approved or rejected them. Unlike other novel positions, the *exactor* represented no threat to the authority of the existing magistrates. Since tax collection was not something that Italian cities had previously needed to worry about, the *exactor* was not stealing any existing functions. It did, however, have an impact on how the city was run. The *exactor*'s nominator was held financially responsible for his conduct, and this responsibility seems to have extended to the *curia* itself.[59] Unlike the *curatores*, every city needed an *exactor*. While they may have differed from earlier magistracies, the *exactores* were similarly bound to serve for a single year.[60]

The appearance of tax officials in Italy was a radical change, but *exactores* were always a curial post and apparently always intended as such. While the *exactor* represented a major addition to Italian administration, it did not represent a threat to the municipal government or social structure since it did not replace an existing position. The position continued into Ostrogothic times, but since *exactores* are never recipients of Cassiodorus' letters it seems that the position declined in importance during the fifth century.[61]

Defensores (First Appeared c. 364)

As with the previous two posts, the *defensor* was a local office with ties to the central government. Like the *curator*, it was intended to be an agent of the central authorities in and for the aid of the cities. Unlike the *curatores*, *defensores* were intended to serve as protectors: 'The entire populace (*plebs*) . . . shall be defended by the offices of [*defensores*] against the outrages of the powerful (*potentes*).'[62] As the law goes on to clarify, the *defensor* was meant to protect the populace from abuse by taxation officials. In tax conflicts or other minor cases such as rendering a verdict on a debt or recovering lost slaves, the *defensor* had judicial authority. For more serious cases he needed to refer cases to the governor.[63] Essentially, the *defensor* took over what was left of the judicial authorities of the *duoviri* and provided the cities with a dedicated judge so that taxpayers did not have to go all the way to the governor for the resolution of minor cases.

The goal for the *defensor* was laid out clearly in the law codes, but who was included in the *plebs* and who were the *potentes* they were meant to be protected against? We

---

[58] *P. Abinn.* 58.8–9; Thomas 1959, 131–2. But compare Bell et al. 1962, 118–19.
[59] *CTh* 12.6.20; Laniado 2002, 117–29.
[60] *CTh* 12.6.22.
[61] Cassiod. *Var.* 2.24.2, 5.39.13, 11.7.2, 11.8.4, 11.16.3, 12.8.2, 12.14.1.
[62] *CTh* 1.29.1: *Plebs omnis Illyrici officiis patronorum contra potentium defendatur iniurias*. The law concerns patrons but is included in the section labelled *De defensoribus civitatum*, so it is a reference to the *defensor*.
[63] *CTh* 1.29.2 = *CJ* 1.55.1. See also Schmidt-Hofner 2008, 71–80.

can get some idea of the targets of this legislation by looking at the people who were permitted to serve as *defensor*. The praetorian prefect was to select *defensores* from former governors, advocates, *agentes in rebus* and *palatini*, all representatives of the central authorities. Decurions and *officiales* of the prefect or governor were explicitly forbidden from this service.[64] Therefore, they must have been part of the *potentes*, or at the least people sympathetic to them. In other words, the *defensor* was not only not a curial post, it was anti-curial in focus.

Valentinian I's law of 364 seems to mark the introduction of the *defensor* into the Italian diocese.[65] At the least it indicated the expansion of the office, since all references that can be reliably dated come after this law. While new to the Western provinces, the position had existed in the East since the tetrarchic period.[66] Perhaps due to its late introduction, the *defensores* never seem to have become as important in the West. Italy and Africa are the only western regions where they are epigraphically attested. While the initial impetus for Valentinian's law concerned Illyria, most of the laws on the *defensor* are eastern. In fact, three of the five Italian laws addressing the position are part of the same law issued on 21 January 409.[67] The late fourth century was probably the high-water mark for the office. By 458, Majorian was complaining about the shortage of *defensores*, and Cassiodorus' letters only mention them for specific cities.[68] Their effectiveness against local interests also seems to have declined fairly quickly. By 386 the *defensor* had been turned from a counter to the *curiales* into a post chosen in consultation with the *curia*.[69] Our Italian inscriptions honouring *defensores* were mainly commissioned by the very *curiae* they were supposed to be guarding the populace from. A law of 409 has the *defensor* lumped in with *curatores*, magistrates and senators as regular municipal positions.[70]

By the time of the Ostrogoths, the *defensor* was all but indistinguishable from the *curator*. Cassiodorus' formula for the post comes immediately before that of the *curator* and contains few differences:

> And so, moved by the petitions of your fellow citizens, our authority grants you the title *defensor* of this city for the present indiction, so that you, who are solemnly announced by so important a name, would want to do nothing venal, nothing disreputable. Arrange commerce for the citizens according to the value of the day and with fair measure. Abide by the limits that you set, since it is not a burden to restrain the highest price for selling, unless the prices chastely preserve public statutes. For in a real sense, you fill the role of a good *defensor* if you neither suffer your fellow citizens to be oppressed by the laws nor to be consumed by want.[71]

---

[64] *CTh* 1.29.1, 1.29.3 = *CJ* 1.55.2.

[65] See Frakes 2001, 94–103, for the dating of this law. While the law in question concerned Illyricum, at this point the region was under the control of Probus, who was also the prefect of Italy.

[66] Frakes 2001, 15–42.

[67] *CTh* 1.55.8, 1.55.9, 9.2.5. The other two laws are *CJ* 1.55.7, *N. Maj.* 3.1.

[68] *N. Maj.* 3.1; Cassiod. *Var.* 2.17, 3.9, 3.49, 4.45, 4.49, 5.14, 7.11, 9.10. Cassiodorus' mentions of the *defensores* are invariably in connection with the *curiales*, *possessores* and other civic notables.

[69] *CTh* 1.29.6.

[70] *CTh* 9.2.5.

[71] Cassiod. *Var.* 7.11 (trans. Bjornlie).

The most important distinction between the two formulae is that the *curator* is explicitly identified with the *curia*, while the *defensor* seems (in theory) more of a free agent. The *defensor*, while frequently curial, was never as universally rationalised into curial careers.

As a new magistracy, the *defensor* shared key similarities with the *curator*. They served alone and their term of office was open-ended, although there was a five-year limit imposed after 385.[72] They were also, however rubber-stamped by the commission, the official appointees of the praetorian prefect. *Defensores* could also claim proudly that they were appointed 'by imperial command' (*iusso sacro*).[73] In practical terms, the establishment of the position as a rival to curial administration did not last. Senators and high officials from the central government could not reasonably be expected to provide a large enough pool of candidates for this office, and there was, as of yet, no real local alternative to curial government in the cities. Thus, the position was gradually absorbed into the existing curial career and lost much of its original function. It may be a sign of curial weakness that the *defensor* was never fully absorbed as earlier positions had been.

Local Rivals

While the *curiales* proved very successful at absorbing imperial appointments, they had more difficulty with local rivals. Imperial appointments posed little threat, because they lacked a power base of their own and needed to operate through the local *curia* in order to fulfil their role. A greater danger was the rise of local power groups who did not require the *curia* to function.[74] There were a number of these groups, some of whom eventually replaced the *curiales* and the entire classical system of city-based administration.

Principales

The *principales* were a natural development from the new stratification of citizens that followed from the grant of universal citizenship and growth in titles of the third century. As equestrian rank became increasingly insignificant, equestrians needed to find some new means of distinguishing themselves. Those participating in imperial service sought senatorial titles such as *vir clarissimus* and *vir illustris*.[75] Those who had more local ambitions became *principales*.[76] A *principalis* was not independent of the *curia*. Rather they were the top decurions and monopolised the chief magistracies. Gaius Matrianus Aurelius Antonius from Hispellum had a career that included the positions of aedile, quaestor, *duumvir*, *quinquennalis* and *curator*, but it was his status of *principalis*

---

[72] *CJ* 1.55.4.
[73] *CIL* 11.15 (Ravenna).
[74] See Bjornlie 2014 for a general overview.
[75] Jones 1964, 527–9; Davenport 2019, 570–3. But compare Bodnaruk 2017.
[76] Jones 1964, 731; Ausbüttel 1988, 18–19.

of which he was most proud.[77] While becoming a *principalis* required fulfilling the key magistracies, there was a sense of group identity within the larger curial community. An inscription from after 340 lists the *principales* of Puteoli after the *viri perfectissimi* but before the *splendissimus ordo* (*decurionum*) *et populus*.[78] *Principalis* tended to be passed down in family lines. An inscription of Lol(ius?) Cyrius from Velitrae (364–7) boasted that he was *principalis curiae* just like his father, grandfather and great-grandfather.[79] The position was also recognised by law. *Principales* who had completed their *munera* were granted the honorary title of *ex-comite*.[80]

The danger of *principales*, from the curial point of view, was that they tended to take all the oxygen out of the room. Libanius, writing in Antioch in the late fourth century, described how 'those who have performed lavish [*munera*] are able to shut up those who want to speak'.[81] The situation was no doubt similar in Italy. Indications of the growing power of the *principales* can be found from a law of Honorius mandating the fines due from those who continue in the Donatist heresy. Senators were fined thirty pounds of gold, *principales* twenty, and the average decurion only five.[82] The status of *principales* grew increasingly important during the fourth century until it reached the point where it was almost a magistracy of its own.[83] *Principales* controlled the album of the *ordo decurionum* and were expected to fill some of the higher taxation positions.[84]

In the sixth-century East, references to *curiales* were replaced with ones to *principales* (πρωτεύοντες), who now assumed the role once held by the *curia*.[85] This may represent the survival of the *principales* as a class, but it elevated them so high above the *curia* as to make the old councils irrelevant.[86] There is no sign that this was happening in Italy. Rather, the *principales* continued to dominate from within the *curia* as they had previously.

Honorati

The *honorati* were some of the most powerful local elites in late Roman Italy. They were enrolled in the senate, had powerful roles in the cities' administration and were immune from many *munera*.[87] As described by T. S. Brown, an *honoratus* was 'a person

---

[77] *CIL* 11.5283 (Hispellum).

[78] *CIL* 6.1691 (Rome).

[79] *CIL* 10.6565 (Velitrae). See also *CIL* 10.4755 (Suessa Aurunca).

[80] *CTh* 12.1.75, 12.1.109, 12.1.127.

[81] Lib. *Or.* 62.39 (trans. Rapp). See also Petit 1955, 323–4.

[82] *CTh* 16.5.52.

[83] Ausbüttel 1988, 19; Horstkotte 2000. Langhammer 1973, 253–7 goes so far as to call them magistrates. But compare Holum 1996, 621–2.

[84] *CTh* 8.15.5.1, 11.16.4; Lepelley 1979–1981, 1.202–5.

[85] *N. Just.* 128.16.

[86] Holum 1996, 619–26; Liebeschuetz 2001, 111–13. *Contra* Ganghoffer 1963, 147; Cameron 1976, 38, there is no evidence that the *principales* became entirely divorced from the *curia*.

[87] *CTh* 6.20.1 (senate); *CTh* 7.6.1, 12.6.4, *N. Maj.* 3.1 (administration); *CTh* 6.23.3, 6.26.3 (*munera*). See also Cecconi 2006b, 44–50.

with a legally superior status based on office-holding'.[88] The key issue which determines whether the *honorati* represented an outside threat to curial government is the question of their background. There are two broad viewpoints on this. According to one view, the *honorati* were mainly former officials of the central bureaux and governorships who now used their imperial connections to gain power in their local cities.[89] The other is that these were mostly former decurions who had completed their civic *munera*.[90] Both can be supported by the law codes, and indeed both must be true to some degree. The question is which group was predominant.

The most obvious reason for regarding the *honorati* as primarily ex-decurions is the relative number of such officials when compared to the central bureaux. There were perhaps 10,000 bureaucrats across the entire empire, and most of them would never have gained *honorati* status. Judging by the number of bishops, the Italian diocese had at least 250 cities in the sixth century, most of which were present by the fourth.[91] Dozens of decurions must have completed their service annually. Even though Italy hosted the western imperial bureaucracy after 381, ex-officials of the central government must have been substantially outnumbered by local ex-decurions. This is supported by the phrasing of laws. Laws directed at central officials exclude them from general obligations of *honorati*, while laws to *honorati* often specify that ex-imperial officials are exempt.[92] If ex-decurions were the less common figures, they could expect to be the exceptions, not the rule.

The status of an *honoratus*, unlike that of senator, was only hereditary in specific circumstances. While an *honoratus* could pass the rank of *vir clarissimus* on to his offspring, he could only do so to sons born after his elevation. Sons inherited the status their father held at the time of their birth. In the cities this meant at least twenty years' service. For bureaucrats in the central offices it could take more than forty.[93] In most cases their heirs were likely conceived before that time. While individual *honorati* were immune to many (but not all) curial obligations, their children would continue to provide the cities with manpower. The status of *honorati* was not that different from that of *viri egregii* in the late third/early fourth century.[94] As elite administrators elevated for completion of service, the *honorati* could never form a rival power base to the *curiales*.

Possessores

The *possessores* were a group that seems never to have been given a clear definition. The term means roughly what it does in English ('owners of property') and is intentionally vague in law. As Liebeschuetz observed, they were never a 'constitutional

---

[88] Brown 1984, 128.
[89] Brown 1992, 22–3; Liebeschuetz 2001, 105, no. 7.
[90] Chastagnol 1978, 24–5; Ruggini 1995, 109, no. 284.
[91] Lanzoni 1927, 1059, 1069.
[92] *CTh* 6.26.3, 6.27.13. The only exception is *CTh* 1.20.1, where *honorati* are glossed *ex curiae corpore* in the *interpretatio*.
[93] *CTh* 12.1.13 (decurions); Carney 1971, 9 (central offices).
[94] Davenport 2019, 565–570.

body of defined membership'.⁹⁵ Rather, they were a convenient way of describing wealthy landowners in the same way that we might use the word 'magnates' to refer to a variety of wealthy individuals. It is too simple to view the *possessores* as just a rural aristocracy taking power from a declining municipal one. As wealthy local elites with houses in the cities, their backgrounds were similar to those of the *curiales*. What distinguished *possessores* from *curiales* was less their wealth and more their lack of an obligation to serve on the *curia*.⁹⁶ The *possessores* occasionally met as a body, but that body was not the *curia*, nor was it one that met regularly at defined intervals.⁹⁷ That said, they, along with *honorati* and *curiales*, can be found at provincial councils.⁹⁸ Thus, they presented an alternative power base to the *curia*. This detachment from municipal government came at a cost: without curial exemptions, the *possessores*' land was liable for taxation. But this was evidently a price some were willing to pay, as we have the example of a curial in Ostrogothic Italy requesting the right to join the *possessores*.⁹⁹ The likeliest reason for this willingness to be subjected to taxation is that the *possessores* had found other methods of avoiding it (see below).

Ultimately, it was the *possessores* who succeeded the *curiales*. This had happened in the East by the early sixth century. Under Justinian, laws for the cities were addressed not to the *curia* but to the *possessores* (κτήτορες) and *habitatores* (οἰκήτροπες, meaning 'inhabitants').¹⁰⁰ In Italy, the process took perhaps another century. When Constans II visited Sicily in 663 the *possessores et habitatores* were the only local groups Paul the Deacon thought worth mentioning.¹⁰¹ In the sixth century, the *curiales* and *possessores* were more evenly matched. Our best evidence for them in Italy comes from Cassiodorus. By this time, letters to the city governments were often addressed to the *possessores et curiales* (or *possessores et defensores et curiales*).¹⁰² From that formulation alone it is evident that the *possessores* are a rival power group to the *curiales*. Athalaric was still able to describe *possessores* as being blissfully free from the kind of obligations that bound *curiales* and indeed subject to their potentially abusive authority, but this was an archaic or perhaps even humorous anachronism by his time.¹⁰³ Another letter of Cassiodorus makes clear that *possessores* were responsible for tax collection among their peers, and we have several letters giving them responsibility for repair work and collection of timber.¹⁰⁴

When we seek signs of this shift in western legislation, we can find very little evidence of change. It seems clear that the *curiales* retained their official responsibilities

---

[95] Liebeschuetz 2001, 114. See also Cecconi 2006b, 51–54. The claim of Ganghoffer 1963, 114–116, that the *possessores* were merely landless *curiales* must be rejected.
[96] There was great wealth disparity among *possessores* just as there could be among *curiales*. See Cassiod. *Var.* 5.14.2.
[97] Cassiod. *Var.* 3.44, 5.9.
[98] *CTh* 12.12.13.
[99] Cassiod. *Var.* 9.4.3. See Bjornlie 2014, 151–8 for discussion of *possessores* and taxation.
[100] *N. Just.* 128.16; See Liebeschuetz 2001, 110–15.
[101] Paul. Diac. *Hist. Lang.* 5.11.4.
[102] Cassiod. *Var.* 2.17, 2.25, 3.9, 3.49, 4.8, 4.11, 5.14.2, 6.24, 7.27, 8.31.
[103] Cassiod. *Var.* 9.4.3.
[104] Cassiod. *Var.* 5.14.2 (tax collection); 3.9, 3.44, 3.49, 5.9 (construction); 4.8 (timber).

throughout the period documented by the *Theodosian Code*. Nonetheless, the *possessores* do appear as a powerful interest group by the 390s. Initially, they seem to have been thought of as potential victims of *curiales* and imperial officials. One *defensor civitatis* in Italy referred to himself as *defensor* of the order of *possessores* and the people.[105] Another boasted of his generosity towards the *ordo*, *possessores* and citizens.[106] In 408, Honorius targeted *possessores* as foremost among those likely to acquire the property of people taken captive by the Goths. *Curiales* were hardly mentioned.[107] These notables were certainly among the groups that *curiales* had difficulty collecting taxes from. A tablet from the early 370s in the city of Trinitapoli demonstrates that many of the local *possessores* were interfering with the collection of taxes.[108] Likely many of them claimed *autopragia*, the right to collect and deliver their own taxes, as well as those of their tenants (*coloni*).[109] With the reach of the municipal authorities declining, some *possessores* were able to avoid taxes by simply keeping their properties distant from the city government.[110] At some point in the late fifth century, whether before or after the transition to *regnum*, *possessores* living close to the cities were co-opted into collecting such taxes from their peers.

While their ultimate fate was the same, Italian *curiales* held out much longer against the *possessores* than those in any other part of the empire. Although *possessores* had assumed some administrative powers, there is no sign that they had taken control of the nomination of magistrates the way they had in the East.[111] Italy's strong municipal traditions meant that *possessores* were only at the very beginning of their transformation by the end of the fifth century.

Bishops

One of the key features of the early medieval successor kingdoms is the important administrative roles assumed by bishops and churchmen. While the priestly assumption of some of the tasks of administration can be seen in the East by the early sixth century, it is difficult to detect in fifth-century Italy. We do have a single law giving western bishops a role in municipal government. In 409, Honorius ordered that *defensores civitatum* be chosen by a combined council of the *episcopi*, *clerici*, *honorati*, *possessores* and *curiales*. However, a subsequent law of Majorian stated that the selection was to be made by *municipes*, *honorati* and *plebs*.[112] It follows from this that if priests were given a role in choosing municipal officeholders, it was gone by mid-century.[113]

---

[105] *CIL* 10.4863 (Venafrum).
[106] *CIL* 11.15 (Ravenna).
[107] *CTh* 5.7.2.
[108] *AE* 1984.250 (Canusium).
[109] This practice was banned by Honorius in *CTh* 11.7.15, but this does not seem to have been effective, as Valentinian III had to issue a similar law forty-two years later (*N. Val.* 10.3) and we can still see it with senators in Ostrogothic Italy (Cassiod. *Var.* 2.24.4). See Marazzi 1998, 123–32.
[110] Bjornlie 2014, 155–8.
[111] *N. Just.* 128.16. See Cecconi 2006a (esp. 310–11) for post-curial positions in Italy.
[112] *CJ* 1.55.8; *N. Maj.* 3.1.
[113] Liebeschuetz 2001, 110; Rapp 2005, 288.

The far more likely explanation is that the law was edited when it was placed into the *Justinianic Code* (it does not appear in the Theodosian one) in order to fit it in with existing practice. A constitution of 505 lists the same groups as the elector of the *defensor*, and presumably this reflects sixth-century eastern practice.[114] Rather than look to that example, we should regard the situation recorded by Majorian as reflecting a closer match to early fifth-century practice. Thus, the argument that Italian bishops played any role in selecting municipal officials is unproven. If they played any role in municipal elections it would seem to have been as leaders among the *plebs* or *curiales* from which they originated.

Bishops could, of course, assume other important civil roles. Their use as envoys is well attested in the fifth century. The most famous example is Pope Leo leading the embassy that persuaded Attila to abandon his invasion of Italy, but this was hardly a unique occurrence.[115] Nearly half of Ennodius' *Life of St Epiphanius of Ticinum* is concerned with the various embassies he undertook on behalf of his congregation or important notables.[116] This included serving as an envoy at the imperial level. In 471 he was sent by Ricimer to negotiate with Anthemius, and in 475 he was sent by Julius Nepos on an embassy to the Gothic king Euric. Embassies had traditionally been led by important decurions or, on this level, senators or members of the administration. Sidonius treats the role of envoy as a great honour, sought after by the most powerful men in the community.[117] That bishops were increasingly gaining this role shows their expanding influence.

Bishops could also at times be given administrative roles usually reserved for *curiales*. Epiphanius was responsible for constructing the church at Ticinum, even using his own funds to finish it.[118] The Bishop of Vercellensis was given responsibility for completing the repairs of a local aqueduct.[119] Distribution of money was another task that might be assigned to a bishop: it happened in c.508 when Theoderic had his bishop Severus compensate locals for the property damaged by his soldiers marching to Gaul, and again in c.535/6 when Datius of Milan was given responsibility for distributing subsidised grain after an apparent crop failure.[120] In both examples the trustworthiness of the bishop is emphasised, which must have been an important factor when providing access to such large quantities of money. Bishops could also serve as community leaders. Maximus of Turin wrote several sermons in which he discourages his congregation from fleeing the city in the face of invasion.[121] One particularly dangerous innovation

---

[114] *CJ* 1.55.11. See Laniado 2006.
[115] Prosper, *Chron.* s.a. 452. See also Gillett 2003, 113–71. Leo may have played less of a role in this embassy than commonly thought, as he was accompanied by high-ranking imperial officials such as Avienus and Trygetius (who had earlier negotiated with Geiseric).
[116] Ennod. *Vit. Epiph.* 53–73 (Anthemius on behalf of Ricimer), 81–94 (Euric on behalf of Julius Nepos), 123–47 (Theoderic on behalf of Liguria), 148–77 (Gundobad on behalf of Theoderic), 183–91 (Theoderic on behalf of Liguria).
[117] Sid. Apoll. *Carm.* 7.458–86, *Epist.* 5.20. See also Gillett 2003, 108–12.
[118] Ennod. *Vit. Epiph.* 101.
[119] Cassiod. *Var.* 4.31.
[120] Cassiod. *Var.* 2.8, 12.27.
[121] Maximus of Turin, *Serm.* 85–6.

(from the standpoint of secular administrators) was that bishops controlled a parallel source of legal administration in the form of the episcopal *audientia*. This court could hear both clerical and secular cases, and there are several examples from the letters of Cassiodorus of the bishop serving in a judicial capacity.[122] Nonetheless, even with these examples the role played by bishops in civil administration was limited during this period.[123] When they did assume an administrative role, they never fully replaced but rather supplemented the wider pool of magistrates.

Imperium to *Regnum*

The final decades of the western empire saw the collapse of the central Roman state but not the end of Roman administration. The apparatus of the central state (the praetorian prefects, vicars, governors and their officials) survived and even flourished in Italy. City administration survived as well. Nonetheless, the fall itself brought with it administrative chaos. Invasions were highly disruptive to Roman administration. One result of Alaric's campaign was that most of Suburbicaria was unable to pay its taxes, and even two years after the Gothic departure, Honorius needed to write off all uncollected imperial income. Suburbicaria also lost Sardinia and Corsica to the Vandals in 456, and Rome itself was sacked in 410 and again in 455. Annonaria was subject to attacks as well, most notably the invasion of Attila in which Aquileia and Milan were sacked, which reached as far as the River Po and caused widespread famines.[124] Majorian's tax remission in 458 was likely connected to this since, as can be seen with Alaric, the effects of invasion could last for years afterwards.[125]

But the invasion that had the most negative and long-term impact on Italy was not even in the region but in Africa. Africa was one of the wealthiest regions in the west and provided a substantial portion of the empire's budget.[126] With Africa removed from the empire, the emperors recognised the need to increase the Italian tax base. Valentinian III even went so far as to cancel all tax immunities granted by previous emperors.[127] Yet, despite the tremendous need the imperial authorities had for tax revenue, recovering taxes from the cities was often impossible. There are nineteen tax remissions preserved from the fifth century.[128] The issuance of tax remissions was not unusual, but in the fourth century they were always for specific, often narrowly defined regions. We see Campania given a tax remission in 395 and 418, Rome was given one in 401, and all of Suburbicaria in 423.[129] The reluctance of emperors to forgo tax revenue can be seen most clearly by the remissions granted in response

---

[122] Cassiod. *Var.* 3.37, 3.45, 8.8, 8.24, 11.2; See also Chapter 12 in this volume, particularly p. 350.
[123] Ausbüttel 1988, 63–4.
[124] Hyd. 29(146). See Stathakopoulos 2004, 222–45.
[125] N. *Val.* 1.1, 1.3; N. *Maj.* 2.1.
[126] See the estimates in Elton 1996, 119–27; Heather 2005, 298, for the total military cost for Africa's loss.
[127] N. *Val.* 4.1, 5.1.4.
[128] *CTh* 11.28.3–17; N. *Val.* 1.1–3; N. *Maj.* 2.1; N. *Marc.* 2.1. See also Bjornlie 2014, 150–4, for a discussion of Ostrogothic and Late Roman tax remissions.
[129] *CTh* 11.28.2, 11.28.3, 11.28.12, 11.28.14. This is also in keeping with the policy of Theoderic, who granted a two-thirds tax remission to Liguria in 496 (Ennod. *Vit. Epiph.* 187–9).

to Alaric's invasion. Rather than a general remission for all Suburbicaria, Honorius excluded Valeria (presumably because the Apennines limited Alaric's incursions) and the islands.[130] By contrast, two of Valentinian III's remissions were general (438 and 450), as was Majorian's (458).[131]

An even larger problem was the general decline in the size and importance of cities. Archaeological evidence paints a clear picture of the decline of traditional cities throughout Late Antiquity. Public spaces stopped being maintained, secular inscriptions decreased, and there are signs of shrinking population density. Churches and other religious architecture took over many of the resources once dedicated to civic buildings.[132] The difference is starkest in Suburbicaria, where the population of Rome declined at an alarming rate. We know from the law codes that the city was receiving 8 million pounds of pork as part of their *annona* (imperially subsidised food supply) in 367, enough to feed around 320,000 people. By 452 that number had shrunk to 3.6 million pounds. By the early sixth century, Cassiodorus mentions a figure for the *annona* paid by Lucania and Bruttium that was a fifth of what it had been for the province in 452. If that figure is representative of *annona* payments overall, it could only have fed perhaps 30,000, less than a tenth what the city had been receiving a century and a half before.[133] The actual population must have been higher (although still probably not above the tens of thousands), but this clearly depicts a population in free fall.

Annonaria retained many cities well into the medieval period, but even there Lombard cities were not the same as classical ones.[134] The central authorities were powerless to prevent or explain the abandonment of cities for rural habitation. The only explanation they could imagine was flight from corrupt officials, and their only solution to promote curial offices more firmly. Majorian decreed that 'those persons who because of the outrages of the tax collectors seek rural habitations and solitude shall live under the protection of the *defensores* and thus shall restore themselves to the public view and to the view of the cities by means of residence in the domicile which they have again sought'.[135] Without a solution for the underlying issues, centralised policies could not work.

And yet, for all this, it is clear that the basic organs of government survived these crises and even the end of *imperium*. When we see Italy again through the letters of Cassiodorus, there were few incursions into the responsibilities held by *curiales*, and their continued prestige can be seen by papyri preserving the names of forty-eight

---

[130] *CTh* 11.28.7.
[131] *N. Val.* 1.1, 1.3; *N. Maj.* 2.1.
[132] For a good overview of the archaeological evidence, consult the footnotes in Liebeschuetz 2001, 94–7. Christie 2006, 214–63, provides a more nuanced account that denies the catastrophist viewpoint, but does not deny that cities changed radically and in many cases shrank in scale (see also Chapter 11 in this volume).
[133] Lo Cascio 2006, 59–61, based on *CTh* 14.4.4 (367), *N. Val.* 36 (452), Cassiod. *Var.* 11.39. Regarding the cause of this depopulation, it is worth noting that the figures for 452 are higher than those given for 419 (*CTh* 14.4.10), which suggests major population decline following Alaric's sack, followed by a modest recovery. The further decline of population during the sixth century can similarly be tied to warfare. According to Proc. *Bell.* 7.20.19 the population reached a low of 500 during the Gothic siege of Rome in 547.
[134] La Rocca 1992, 161–80.
[135] *N. Maj.* 3.1 (trans. Pharr).

curiales from Ravenna between 474 and 575.[136] Indeed, Italy seems to have fared better in this respect than any other region. Italy had been fortunate enough to survive the collapse of empire intact, in a way that no other western lands had. The division of a unified territory into separate feuding groups would have made the continuance of any sort of administrative structure difficult. When we look to the writings of Gregory of Tours (admittedly writing half a century after Cassiodorus) there is no mention of *curiae* or *curiales*. Instead, responsibility for tax collection in Gaul has been taken over by *comites* appointed by the Frankish king.[137] Nor is it seen in Visigothic Spain, when Erwig's tax legislation of 683 was addressed to *quisquis ille dux, comes, tiufadus, numerarius, vilicus aut quicumque curam publicam agens*.[138] *Curiales* seem to have declined in power even before the Visigoths formed an independent state. By 465, Pope Hilary was addressing the *honorati et possessores* of local cities with no mention of *curiales*.[139] The East was immune from most of this piecemeal disintegration, yet the end of curial dominance was if anything more extreme than in the West. Under Anastasius, chief curial officials were being replaced by central appointees like *vindices* or local magnates like pagarchs, who could serve for life.[140] By the time of Justinian, authors could speak of *curiae* in the past tense.[141] Only in Africa, also severed from Roman rule rapidly and intact, can curial structures be found comparable to those in Italy.[142]

If the curial role in municipal maintenance and local administration was declining, how can they have maintained their position in the hierarchy of provincial administration? The western empire simply had no alternative to *curiales* when it came to tax collection and the dissemination of laws. The western empire was invested in the existing structures, and its final decades did not offer the kind of stability that was required for the type of all-encompassing reforms that replacing them would involve. The *curiales* remained in charge largely due to administrative inertia. When the Ostrogoths took over and Italy returned to a period of relative peace, the weakened (but by no means dead!) *curia* was supplemented by *possessores* and, to a small degree, bishops. This effort to find a new equilibrium between local power groups was not inherently doomed. It was only after Justinian's reconquest and then the Lombard invasion that the *curia* began a precipitous decline.

The *curiales* remained in control of their cities throughout late Roman Italy. If their position was less secure by the fifth century, rival power groups had yet to do more than nibble at the edges of their authority and remained outside the official power structures. The *curiales* had proved remarkably resilient at absorbing rivals. Even when

---

[136] Ausbüttel 1987, 213–14. See also Brown 1984, 16–19, for the seventh century.
[137] Gregory of Tours, *Hist.* 4.2, 5.34, 9.30; cf. Loseby 2006, 84–93.
[138] *Concilium Toleti* 13.27. Alaric's *Breviarum* (506) preserved Roman laws on *curiales* but did not add new ones.
[139] Hilarius, *Ep.* 16 (465).
[140] See Haarer 2015 (general); Laniado 2002, 27–36 (*vindex*); Liebeschuetz 1974 (pagarch).
[141] Evagrius, *HE* 3.42 (144); John Lydus, *Mag.* 1.28; John Malalas 16.12 (400). The true situation was more complicated than this, since we have references to *curiales* as late as the late ninth century (*N. Const.* 2.46).
[142] See Lepelley 1979–1981, vol. 1. Lepelley originally viewed the survival of classical municipal administration as a uniquely African feature, but by Lepelley 1992a, he had changed his mind and found similar features in Italy.

specifically designed to counter curial groups, *iusso sacro* officials ended up working through them. Powerful groups from within the *curia* itself did gain some power at the expense of the rest, but they continued to operate through the *curiae*. It is true that the traditional magistracies declined in power and were eclipsed by new magistrates who lacked the traditional election by popular assembly, collegiality and annual terms. However, these new positions remained curial posts and continued to provide a strong, if different, power base for local elites. The fact that city administrations were able to survive the transition from *imperium* to *regnum* demonstrates their resiliency.

Bibliography

Abbott, F. F. and A. C. Johnson (1926) *Municipal Administration in the Roman Empire*, Princeton.
Ausbüttel, F. M. (1987) 'Die Curialen und Stadtmagistrate Ravennas im späten 5. und 6. Jahrhundert', *ZPE* 67: 207–14.
Ausbüttel, F. M. (1988) *Die Verwaltung der Städte und Provinzen im spätantiken Italien*, Frankfurt.
Ausbüttel, F. M. (1998) *Die Verwaltung des römischen Kaiserreiches*, Darmstadt.
Bell, H. I., V. Martin, E. G. Turner, and D. van Berchem (trans.) (1962) *The Abinnaeus Archive*, Oxford.
Bjornlie, M. S. (2013) *Politics and Tradition between Rome, Ravenna and Constantinople*, Cambridge.
Bjornlie, M. S. (2014) 'Law, Ethnicity and Taxes in Ostrogothic Italy', *Early Medieval Europe* 22 (2): 138–70.
Bjornlie, M. S. (trans.) (2019) *The Variae: the Complete Translation*, Oakland, CA.
Bodnaruk, M. (2017) 'Administering the Empire: the Unmaking of an Equestrian Elite in the 4th Century', in R. Varga and V. Rusu-Bolindeţ (eds) *Official Power and Local Elites in the Roman Provinces*, New York, 145–67.
Bolle, K. (2017) 'Spätantike Inschriften in Tuscia et Umbria: Materialität und Präsenz', in K. Bolle, C. Machado and C. Witschel (eds) *The Epigraphic Cultures of Late Antiquity*, Stuttgart, 147–212.
Bolle, K., C. Machado and C. Witschel (eds) (2017) *The Epigraphic Cultures of Late Antiquity*, Stuttgart.
Brown, P. (1992) *Power and Persuasion in Late Antiquity*, London.
Brown, T. S. (1984) *Gentlemen and Officers: Imperial Administration and Aristocratic Power in Byzantine Italy, A.D. 554–800*, Rome.
Cameron, A. (1976) *Circus Factions: Blues and Greens at Rome and Byzantium*, Oxford.
Camodeca, G. (1980) 'Ricerche sui curatores rei publicae', *ANRW* 2.13, Berlin, 453–534.
Carney, T. F. (1971) 'Byzantine Bureaucracy from Within', in T. F. Carney, *Bureaucracy in Traditional Society*, Lawrence, KS.
Cecconi, G. A. (1994) *Governo imperiale e élites dirigenti nell'Italia tardoantica*, Como.
Cecconi, G. A. (2006a) 'Crisi e trasformazioni del governo municipale in Occidente fra IV e VI secolo', in J. U. Krause and C. Witschel (eds) *Die Stadt in der Spätantike*, Stuttgart, 285–318.
Cecconi, G. A. (2006b) '*Honorati, possessores, curiales*: competenze istituzionali e gerarchie di rango nella città tardoantica', in R. L. Testa (ed.) *Le trasformazioni delle élites in età tardoantica*, Rome, 41–64.
Chastagnol, A. (1978) *L'album municipal de Timgad*, Bonn.
Christie, N. (2006) *From Constantine to Charlemagne: an Archaeology of Italy, AD 300–800*, Aldershot.
Corbier, M. (1991) 'City, Territory and Taxation', in J. Rich and A. Wallace-Hadrill (eds) *City and Country in the Ancient World*, London, 211–39.
Crawford, M. H. (ed.) (1996) *Roman Statutes*, London.
Davenport, C. (2019) *A History of the Roman Equestrian Order*, Cambridge.

Eck, W. (1979) *Die staatliche Organisation Italiens in der hohen Kaiserzeit*, Munich.
Elton, H. (1996) *Warfare in Roman Europe, AD 350–425*, Oxford.
Forbis, E. (1996) *Municipal Virtues in the Roman Empire*, Stuttgart.
Frakes, R. M. (2001) *Contra potentium iniurias: the Defensor Civitatis and Late Roman Justice*, Munich.
Franklin, J. L. (2001) *Pompeis difficile est*, Ann Arbor.
Ganghoffer, R. (1963) *L'évolution des institutions municipales en Occident et en Orient au Bas-Empire*, Paris.
Garnsey, P. (1974) 'Aspects of the Decline of the Urban Aristocracy in the Empire', *ANRW* 2.1, Berlin, 229–52.
Gillett, A. (2003) *Envoys and Political Communication in the Late Antique West, 411–533*, Cambridge.
Haarer, F. K. (2015) 'Developments in the Governance of Late Antique Cities', in U. Roberto and L. Mecella (eds) *Governare e riformare l'impero al momento della sua divisione: Oriente, Occidente, Illirico*, Rome.
Hardy, E. G. (1912) *Roman Laws and Charters*, Oxford.
Heather, P. (2005) *The Fall of the Roman Empire*, Oxford.
Holum, K. G. (1996) 'The Survival of the Bouletic Class at Caesarea in Late Antiquity', in A. Raban and K. G. Holum (eds) *Caesarea Maritima: a Retrospective after Two Millennia*, Leiden.
Horstkotte, H. (2000) 'Die principales des spätrömischen Dekurionenrates', *ZPE* 130: 272–8.
Jacques, F. (1984) *Le privilège de liberté: politique impériale et autonomie municipale dans les cités de l'Occident romain (161–244)*, Rome.
Jones, A. H. M. (1964) *The Later Roman Empire, 284–602*, Norman, OK.
Krause, J. U. and C. Witschel (eds) (2006) *Die Stadt in der Spätantike*, Stuttgart.
La Rocca, C. (1992) 'Public Buildings and Urban Change in Northern Italy in the Early Mediaeval Period', in J. Rich (ed.) *The City in Late Antiquity*, London, 145–60.
Langhammer, W. (1973) *Die rechtliche und soziale Stellung der Magistratus Municipales und der Decuriones*, Wiesbaden.
Laniado, A. (2002) *Recherches sur les notables municipaux dans l'Empire protobyzantin*, Paris.
Laniado, A. (2006) 'Le christianisme et l'évolution des institutions municipales du Bas-Empire: l'exemple du *defensor civitatis*', in J. U. Krause and C. Witschel (eds) *Die Stadt in der Spätantike*, Stuttgart, 319–34.
Lanzoni, F. (1927) *Le diocesi d'Italia dalle origini al principio del secolo VII*, Faenza.
Laurence, R., S. E. Cleary and G. Sears (2011) *The City in the Roman West, c.250 BC–c.AD 250*, Cambridge.
Lepelley, C. (1979–1981) *Les cités de l'Afrique romaine au Bas-Empire*, Paris.
Lepelley, C. (1992a) 'Permanences de la cité classique et archaïsmes municipaux en Italie au Bas-Empire', in M. Christol et al. (eds) *Institutions, société et vie politique dans l'empire romain au IVe siècle ap. J.-C.*, Rome, 353–71.
Lepelley, C. (1992b) 'The Survival and Fall of the Classical City in Late Roman Africa', in J. Rich (ed.) *The City in Late Antiquity*, London, 50–76.
Lewin, A. (1995) *Assemblee popolari e lotta politica nelle città dell'impero romano*, Florence.
Liebeschuetz, J. H. W. G. (1974) 'The Pagarch: City and Imperial Administration in Byzantine Egypt', *JJP* 18: 163–8.
Liebeschuetz, J. H. W. G. (2001) *The Decline and Fall of the Roman City*, Oxford.
Liebeschuetz, J. H. W. G. (2015) *East and West in Late Antiquity*, Leiden.
Lo Cascio, E. (2006) 'La popolazione', in E. Lo Cascio (ed.) *Roma Imperiale: una metropoli antica*, 17–69.
Loseby, S. T. (2006) 'Decline and Change in the Cities of Late Antique Gaul', in J. U. Krause and C. Witschel (eds) *Die Stadt in der Spätantike*, Stuttgart, 67–104.

Marazzi, F. (1998) 'The Destinies of the Late Antique Italies: Politico-economic Developments of the Sixth Century', in R. Hodges and W. Bowden (eds) *The Sixth Century: Production, Distribution and Demand*, Leiden, 119–60.
Mouritsen, H. (1988) *Elections, Magistrates and Municipal Élite*, Rome.
Mouritsen, H. (1998) 'The Album from Canusium and the Town Councils of Roman Italy', *Chiron* 28: 229–54.
O'Donnell, J. J. (1979) *Cassiodorus*, Berkeley.
Petit, P. (1955) *Libanius et la vie municipale à Antioche au IVe siècle après J.-C.*, Paris.
Pharr, C. (trans.) (1952) *The Theodosian Code and Novels, and the Sirmondian Constitutions*, Princeton.
Rapp, C. (2005) *Holy Bishops in Late Antiquity*, Berkeley.
Reid, J. S. (1913) *The Municipalities of the Roman Empire*, Cambridge.
Rich, J. (ed.) (1992) *The City in Late Antiquity*, London.
Ruggini, L. (1995) *Economia e Società nell' 'Italia Annonaria'*, Bari.
Schmidt-Hofner, S. (2008) *Reagieren und Gestalten*, Munich.
Stahl, M. (1978) *Imperiale Herrschaft und provinziale Stadt*, Göttingen.
Stathakopoulos, D. C. (2004) *Famine and Pestilence in the Late Roman and Early Byzantine Empire*, Burlington, VT.
Tacoma, L. E. (2020) *Roman Political Culture*, Oxford.
Thomas, D. (1959) 'The Office of Exactor in Egypt', *Chronique d'Égypte* 34: 124–40.
Witschel, C. (2006) 'Der *epigraphic habit* in der Spätantike: das Beispiel der Provinz *Venetia et Histria*', in J. U. Krause and C. Witschel (eds) *Die Stadt in der Spätantike*, Stuttgart, 359–411.

7

ARMED FORCES IN LATE ROMAN ITALY

Philip Rance

In 388/9, Symmachus, the distinguished senator, orator and *literatus*, departed Rome for one of his estates on the coast. Doubtless he sought to escape the disfavour into which he had fallen after openly supporting the now defeated usurper Magnus Maximus. In a letter to his close friend Nicomachus Flavianus, he reports the unpleasant discovery that awaited him, troops of the victorious Theodosius I billeted in his property: 'our estate at Ostia is beset by military assault. In vain I invoke the letter of the law ... What pains me is not fear of the damage but the insult to justice.' In backing the wrong side in a civil war, Symmachus had forfeited the immunities usually accorded to his privileged status.[1] In happier times a decade later, in 398, Symmachus, now rehabilitated, was contemplating another rural sojourn in Campania. A correspondent wrote to express concern about running into soldiers on the highway, specifically units returning northwards after suppressing a revolt in Africa. As any military presence in southern Italy was exceptional before the mid-fifth century, the very idea of troops in this region elicited Symmachus' disbelief: 'You appear to be joking with me when you write that you fear encountering soldiers under arms ... The whole of the Via Appia is devoid of all passing soldiers.'[2] Although relating to particular events during a crucial period of change, when a field army was first permanently stationed south of the Alps, these two contrasting episodes, involving a full house and an empty road, in some respects encapsulate characteristics of the evidence for armed forces in late Roman Italy. Symmachus' remarks especially convey the shifting visibility of troops throughout the late fourth and fifth centuries, a 'now-you-see-it, now-you-don't' army, which variously reflects fluctuations in the number, location and identity of military personnel, the fragmentary nature and mostly civilian perspectives of available sources, the diverse interactions between soldiers and urban and rural populations, and peculiarities of the geography, economy and political culture of the peninsula and its islands.

In the study of Roman imperial history, the army demands attention as the biggest employer, greatest consumer of goods and services, and most expensive item of state expenditure. Armed forces based in the Italian diocese from the late third to late fifth centuries were an integral and essential component of imperial government, supported

---

[1] Symm. *Ep.* 2.52: *urget Ostiense praedium nostrum militaris inpressio. nos legum inane nomen vocamus . . . interea mordemur non metu damni sed aequitatis iniuria.* See similarly 6.72: *siquidem Ostiense praedium nostrum frequens pulsat impressio.* See Sogno 2006, 72–3 for date and context. See generally below, p. 185–6.
[2] Symm. *Ep.* 7.38: *iocari mihi visus es, cum te scriberes obvia militum arma timuisse . . . caret Appia tota militibus transvectis omnibus.* See below, p. 163, 166 and 180–1 for the revolt of Gildo in 397–8.

by the demographic, economic and fiscal foundations of the society they defended and policed. Overall, this often poorly documented era is characterised by mounting insecurity and strained resources, and the dimly discernible profile of the army in Italy by the 470–80s had seemingly changed almost beyond recognition since the 270–80s. Nevertheless, heightened scholarly interest in the late Roman army over the last thirty years has loosened the tenacious grip of more simplistic 'decline-and-fall' preconceptions, partly by demonstrating the relative resilience of organisational structures and operational capabilities, while in particular challenging or nuancing long-prevailing assumptions about the 'Germanisation'/'barbarisation' of Roman military personnel, institutions and practices.[3] Although much of what is known – or believed – about armed forces in Italy is generally applicable empire-wide, and accepting that Italy-specific source material is comparatively meagre, it is possible to identify and discuss 'Italian' contexts and particularities. While the army is arguably of intrinsic interest, this institutional survey seeks to address aspects – political, socio-economic, cultural – that cohere with themes explored in other chapters. Its focus is the regional evolution and impact of a multifaceted organisation, and those internal and external factors that shaped its composition, behaviour and environments.

Historical and Geographical Contexts

During the first two centuries AD, the only armed forces permanently based in Italy were the ultimately ten *cohortes praetoriae* (or 'Praetorian Guard') and the *equites singulares augusti*, two elite palatine corps stationed at Rome.[4] In addition, the city's chief magistrate, the *praefectus urbi*, had at his disposal three *cohortes urbanae*, a metropolitan gendarmerie that exercised diverse policing functions.[5] Links between Italian society and provincial armies became attenuated: legionary recruitment declined sharply from the early second century, while the proportion of officers drawn from municipal elites steadily decreased into the third century.[6] Italians dominated the *cohortes praetoriae* until 193, when Septimius Severus reconstituted the corps using men drawn from Danubian legions.[7] In c.199 Severus also stationed *legio* II *Parthica* at Albanum, 25 km south-east of Rome, augmenting the centrally based internal-security forces, though over the following century its personnel served throughout the empire.[8] Although of waning political significance, detachments of *praetoriani* and *equites singulares* continued to accompany imperial expeditions into the 290s/300s.[9] Geostrategic considerations

---

[3] Foundational studies: Jones 1964, 607–86; Hoffmann 1969–1970. See selectively Elton 1996; Nicasie 1998; Whitby 2000; Le Bohec 2006; Lee 2007; Sabin et al. 2007; Rocco 2012.

[4] *Cohortes praetoriae*: bibliography in De la Bédoyère 2017. *Equites singulares*: Speidel 1994.

[5] *Praefectus urbi*: Jones 1964, 380, 689–92. *Cohortes urbanae*: Freis 1967. In contrast, the *cohortes vigilum*, a corps of firemen-cum-nightwatchmen at Rome, though sometimes classified as 'paramilitary', were not conventionally armed.

[6] Brunt 1974, 96–101.

[7] Durry 1938, 247–8, 381–6; Brunt 1974, 94–6; De la Bédoyère 2017, 223–4.

[8] Ritterling 1924, 1476–9.

[9] *Cohortes praetoriae*: e.g. *CIL* 8.21021 = *ILS* 2038 (297; Caesarea, Mauretania); Zos. 1.52.4, possibly 2.9.1. *Equites singulares*: Speidel 1994, 57–9.

periodically increased the military presence in northern Italy. Around 168–70, early in the Marcomannic Wars, Marcus Aurelius instituted a temporary special command in the north-eastern sector (*praetentura Italiae et Alpium*), probably involving two new legions.[10] The fortified river port of Aquileia emerged as a strategic bastion and logistical base, with a long-term garrison from 238.[11] Subsequently, to deter Alamannic incursions and/or potential aggression from rival regimes in Gaul, Gallienus concentrated cavalry and legionary detachments (*vexillationes*) around Milan (c.259/60–c.268).[12] These measures variously foreshadow developments under the Tetrarchy.

Diocletian's military-fiscal reforms, partly systematising third-century expedients, reconfigured relations between the army and Italian rural society. Beginning c.293, Diocletian abolished Italy's ancient land-tax exemption and imposed an empire-wide reformed tax system based on annual levies of agricultural produce (*annona*) and recruits (*tirones*). A broader process of 'provincialisation', which constituted Italia as a diocese (*dioecesis Italiciana*) comprising initially twelve, ultimately seventeen *provinciae*, introduced new administrative structures for transferring material and human resources from Italian taxpayers to the army.[13] Presiding over this bureaucratic apparatus, a praetorian prefect exercised overall responsibility for recruitment, remuneration and provisioning.[14] A particular regional factor was the senatorial aristocracy, whose predominant propertied interests in central-southern Italy and Sicily affected military procurement, especially conscription, even after this demilitarised core became exposed to hostilities from the 440s.[15]

In military-administrative terms, the Italian diocese, stretching from Sicilia to Raetia Secunda, was an artificial construct that disregarded natural-geographical confines.[16] Although Italia was notionally one diocese, Constantine's experiments with two subdiocesan jurisdictions from 312/13 became permanent bipartite governance under his successors. Italia Annonaria, embracing the Po basin, Alpine massif and upper Danube, was administered from Milan, directly by the praetorian prefect, when resident, but otherwise by a *vicarius Italiae*, who was primarily responsible for fiscal-logistical requirements of military personnel stationed in or passing through this crucial arterial zone between Gaul and Illyricum. Italia Suburbicaria, comprising the Apennine peninsula and islands, was administered by a *vicarius urbis* in Rome, with

---

[10] *CIL* 6.41119 = *ILS* 8977; SHA, *Marc.* 14.6, with Birley 1993, 155–8, 163–4, 250–1.
[11] *AE* 1934, 230 = 1973, 262 (238); *CIL* 5.899 = *ILS* 2324 (mid-third century), with Speidel 1990, 68–9: reading *ex(ercitus) aquil(iensis)*. See generally Pavan 1979; Lettich 1982, 78–80; Speidel 1990; Janniard 2006; Feugère 2013; Roberto 2014; Ricci 2014. Defences of Aquileia: Christie 2006, 291–5, with bibliography.
[12] The immediate and longer-term significance of these cavalry *vexillationes* has generated an extensive bibliography; see selectively Simon 1980; Bleckmann 1992, 226–37; Nicasie 1998, 36–8, 61–2, 257; Speidel 2008, 677–84.
[13] Jones 1964, 44–8, 373–5; Barnes 1982, 209–25; Porena 2003, 152–86; 2013, 332–6. See further Chapter 5 in this volume.
[14] Jones 1964, 370–2, 586–92; Porena 2003, 539–62.
[15] See below, p. 179–82.
[16] Dynastic disputes or usurpations briefly detached Raetia in 306–12 (Constantine/Maxentius: Zos. 2.14.1), 383–7 (Magnus Maximus/Valentinian II) and probably c.407–10 (Constantine III/Honorius: Burns 1994, 214). Similarly, Istria was detached from Italia by Licinius in 310–16/17: Picozzi 1976; Vannesse 2010a, 55–6; Roberto 2014, 138–40.

chiefly civil-fiscal responsibilities. While reflecting topographic contours and broader governmental concerns, this subdivision acknowledged the differing military presence in these two spheres.[17] In a parallel development, the protracted emergence of territorially defined praetorian prefectures under Constantine and his sons embedded the Italian diocese in a wider and often shifting military-administrative landscape, whereby from c.337 to c.344–7 and c.362 to c.395–9 ordinarily a single praetorian prefect, usually headquartered at Sirmium, oversaw a supraregional prefecture of Italy, Illyricum and Africa.[18] The partitioning of the prefecture of Illyricum, around 395–9, assigned the diocese of Pannonia (renamed Illyricum occidentale) to the prefecture of Italy and Africa, whose prefect only now resided permanently in Italy.[19] As Pannonia (at least partly) reverted to the eastern emperor in 437, if not before,[20] and the African diocese fell bit by bit under Vandalic control (429–c.455), Italia eventually became a unitary prefectural jurisdiction, though adjacent regions – Noricum, Dalmatia and south-eastern Gaul – remained closely linked to its military organisation.

While the Po basin was integrated, administratively and logistically, into the Danubian *limes*, modern geostrategic analyses have generally struggled to demonstrate grand-strategic 'defence in depth' across the Alpine zone, correlating threats to frontiers, axes of penetration and troop dispositions in northern Italy. Even systematic regional defence can be elusive.[21] Nevertheless, military infrastructure indicates efforts to control or monitor transalpine routeways into Italy, most extensively the *claustra Alpium Iuliarum*, between north-eastern Italy and Pannonia. This principally comprised a series of forts, fortlets, road stations and turreted cross-walls along the Via Gemina eastwards from Aquileia, through the lower-lying sector between the Julian and Dinaric Alps, almost to Emona/Ljubljana, and thence alternating walls and natural obstacles running southwards to Tarsatica/Rijeka on the Adriatic, effectively cordoning off Istria. Overall chronology is insecure: although certain forts may originate in the 270s–90s, no barrier wall is reliably dated before c.350, and some fortlets attest only short-term occupation thereafter. While future archaeological investigation might clarify their multiphase construction, operation and (never large) garrison, recent interpretations of purpose include regulating traffic, suppressing banditry and/or in-depth defence, especially once this subalpine corridor became a theatre of internal conflict (352, 361, 388, 394). Some installations were abandoned before c.390, others by c.410, but evidently posed no obstacle to invaders.[22] Elsewhere in the subalpine zone, material evidence for

---

[17] Porena 2013, 335–41; summarised by Lenski in Chapter 2 in this volume.
[18] Jones 1964, 101–2, 126, 370–1, 373; *PLRE* 1.1049–52; Porena 2003, 339–562, 571–4; Davenport 2020. A separate prefecture of Illyricum (comprising the dioceses of Pannonia, Macedonia and Dacia) was created c.344–7 but reincorporated with Italy and Africa in c.362. See Burns 1994, 45–52, 87–8 for the temporary transfer of Illyricum, wholly or partly, to Theodosius I during c.379–83.
[19] Partition of the prefecture of Illyricum in 390s: Burns 1994, 159–68, 175–8, who argues for 399.
[20] Conflicting evidence for the status of Pannonia during the first half of the fifth century: MacGeorge 2002, 32–41.
[21] Geostrategic analysis: e.g. Vannesse 2010a, 11–38, 159–422. See Christie 2007 for comparative analysis of regional defensive strategies in Pannonia and northern Italy.
[22] The bibliography is extensive; see selectively: Christie 2006, 324–6; Vannesse 2007; 2010a, 293–318; Kos 2012; 2013; Kusetič et al. 2014; Poulter 2013; Ciglenečki 2015; 2016.

military presence is sporadic, particularly at smaller outposts. For example, in the northern Adige valley, notably a necropolis at Pomarolo, finds of military artefacts indicate troops stationed on this strategic route in the early fifth century.[23] The existence of a *comes Italiae*, attested uniquely in the *Notitia dignitatum* (c.425), with responsibility for a *tractus Italiae circa Alpes*, suggests arrangements for peripheral or sectoral defence. The transmitted text assigns him neither troops nor *officium*, however, and almost everything about this – possibly already defunct – post remains conjectural.[24] Among those units that may have formerly belonged to such a territorial command are three consecutively numbered legions designated *Iulia Alpina*, originally *legiones limitanei* but upgraded to *comitatenses* by the latest redaction of the *Notitia*, although the origin of their regimental titulature has been disputed.[25]

If the primary purpose of any army might, understandably, be deemed 'defence', the question arises: against whom? Once Aurelian had terminated the periodic plundering of northern Italy by warrior bands of Alamanni and/or Iuthungi (259/60–70/1),[26] no intrusion by external barbarians is recorded for 130 years. In 405–6, a by-all-reports large confederation headed by Radagaisus caused widespread disruption.[27] Attila's invasion in 452 was of shorter duration, but possibly more destructive, especially to urban centres.[28] Over subsequent decades, obscure victories over small-scale and/or opportunistic incursions attest continuing defensive capabilities.[29] The exception to this pattern of aggression is the Vandals, whose capture of Carthage in 439 abruptly transformed Italy's south-western littoral and islands into a contested zone, escalating from pervasive raids upon Suburbicaria (440–1, 455–76) to recurrent occupation and eventual seizure of insular provinces.[30] In contrast, military dispositions in Italy more typically responded to threats from other imperial regimes, western

---

[23] Cavada 2002.
[24] *Not. Dign. occ.* 24: *comes Italiae*; previously registered at 1.31 (among *comites rei militaris*), 5.127 (among *comites limitum*). Conjectures: Jones 1964, 191–2; Christie 2007, 565–6; Poulter 2013, 111–12, 118–20; Ciglenečki 2016, 412–15. *PLRE* 2.500–1, 1297, speculatively assigns this office to 'Generidus 2'.
[25] *Legio* I *Iulia Alpina* (*Not. Dign. occ.* 5.107 = 257 = 7.34) and *legio* III *Iulia Alpina* (*Not. Dign. occ.* 5.99 = 248 = 7.35) are listed as respectively a *legio pseudocomitatensis* and *legio comitatensis* in the Italian field army; *legio* II *Iulia Alpina* (*Not. Dign. occ.* 5.108 = 258 = 7.60) occurs as a *legio pseudocomitatensis* in the field army of Illyricum. Disputed titulature: e.g. Ritterling 1924, 1404–5, 1456, 1493 believes these three legions originally formed the garrison of an Alpine province, probably Alpes Cottiae, and *Iulia* derives from the *nomen* of Constans (r. 337–50); Hoffmann 1969–1970, 1.204, 239 (with n. 305), 409 contends *Iulia Alpina* indicates that these units formerly served in the geographical zone of the Julian Alps (*Alpes Iuliae*).
[26] Drinkwater 2007, 44–79, with bibliography; Ricci 2014, 243–6.
[27] Janssen 2004, 187–93; Wijnendaele 2016a.
[28] Urban and rural destruction: Linn 2019, with bibliography. Prisoners: MacGeorge 2002, 202–3.
[29] In 457, on Majorian's orders, Burco defeated 900 Alamannic raiders at Campi Canini (Bellinzona): Sid. Apoll. *Carm.* 5.373–85, with *PLRE* 2.242–3, 'Burco'; Gusso 1996; Anders 2010, 266. In 464, Ricimer killed an Alanic *rex* Beorgor near Bergamo, though no context is specified: references in *PLRE* 2.224, 'Beorgor' (compare also Sid. Apoll. *Carm.* 2.379–80); differently interpreted with varying degrees of conjecture by Bachrach 1973, 33, 39; MacGeorge 2002, 228–31; Anders 2010, 161–2, 423, 452; Janniard 2020, 252 n. 95. In 473, Euric, *rex* of the Aquitanian Goths, sent Vincentius *quasi magister militum* to Italy, where he was killed by imperial forces: *Chron. Gall. 511* 653, with *PLRE* 2.60–1, 'Alla'; 1168, 'Vincentius 3'. See Chapter 4 in this volume.
[30] See, selectively, Aiello 2004; Merrills and Miles 2010, 109–24, 129–31, 134–6; Vannesse 2010c, 74–81; Modéran 2014, 184–200; Caliri 2014. See Chapter 4 in this volume.

and eastern, as the Po–Sava–Drava corridor became an arena for dynastic conflicts. From the early fourth century, Italy was 'invaded' far more often by imperial armies: Severus (307), Galerius (308), Licinius (310), Constantine I (312), Constantine II (340), Magnentius (350), Magnus Maximus (387), Theodosius I (388, 394), Constantine III (410), Heraclianus (413) and Theodosius II's forces (424–5). Whether Alaric is perceived as rebellious imperial commander or extrinsic barbarian *rex*-warlord, his two invasions (401–2, 408–10) also belong to this category insofar as his alternating imperial service and career-enhancing disruption operated entirely within Roman military-institutional and geographical frameworks.[31] From the mid-fourth century, successive eastern Roman interventions overthrew usurpers and/or (re)installed compliant regimes (352, 388, 394, 424–5, 467, 474) or reinforced western imperial forces in the Italian and/or African dioceses (410, 431–4/5, 441–2, 468). At an institutional level, these confrontations raise questions about how defeated western armies were reorganised, redeployed and/or integrated with eastern forces, especially in Italy after 388, 394/5 and 425.[32] In geopolitical terms, this pattern of intervention shows the degree to which Italy became a military-political annex of the eastern empire.

The evidence for armed forces permits partial answers to basic questions: who, where, when and, rarely, how many. Following the conflicts of the Tetrarchy, few troops were stationed in the peninsular between c.313–17 and c.370, and only from 394/5 was a field army based in northern Italy. It remains difficult to harmonise the testimony of fifth-century sources, which variously report large concentrations or dire shortages of troops, partly a reflection of actual fluctuations in military personnel and operational contexts, but also of differing evidential perspectives. In narrative histories, armies are most visible when concentrated for combat operations, as during Stilicho's counteroffensives against Alaric in 402 and Radagaisus in 406. Conversely, troops become largely invisible when dispersed in urban garrisons, whether implementing routine wintertime deployments or pursuing battle-averse defensive strategies, as during Alaric's protracted troublemaking in 408–10 and Attila's invasion in 452.[33] Correspondingly, the Vandals' assault on Rome in 455 encountered no coordinated resistance, yet Ricimer could assemble troops and vessels for counterstrikes in 456.[34] Furthermore, around the midpoint of these incursions, the *Notitia dignitatum*, reflecting administrative-documentary priorities in the mid-420s, locates in Italy a large field army, whose existence – if more than bureaucratic wishful thinking – would never otherwise be suspected.[35] The phenomenon of differential visibility extends to the character of imperial forces, particularly long-debated questions about recruitment, numbers and impact of 'barbarians'. Contemporary histories single out high-profile non-Roman contingents, large and small, contracted under various terms of service, which modern scholarship commonly (if not always accurately) terms

---

[31] See selectively: Liebeschuetz 1990, 48–85; 1992; Burns 1994, 151–68, 178–81, 187–97, 202–3, 214–15; Kulikowski 2002b; Janssen 2004, 215–20; Gheller 2017, 62–8; Wijnendaele 2018b, 263–8.
[32] See p. 162.
[33] Alaric in 408–10: Zos. 5.45.5–6, 46.5, 50.1. Attila in 452: Linn 2019, with bibliography.
[34] See below, p. 169.
[35] See below, p. 165–8.

foederati/'federates' – typically Goths, Huns and Alans engaged on account of tactical specialisms in mounted warfare. In contrast, the *Notitia*, registering only regular units, omits such troops, with implications for the size and composition of armed forces in Italy. Similarly, inscriptions can clarify the locations and histories of regular units, but *foederati* are absent from the epigraphic record. Archaeology elucidates other dimensions of the military presence, urban and rural, in both general distributive patterns and site-specific studies, usually through finds of military-related dress and equipment, often limited in number and inadequately provenanced. The eclectic *Mischkultur* of the late Roman army, reflecting diverse modes of recruitment and procurement, complicates interpretation of intrusive non-Roman artefacts.[36]

An Overview of Armed Forces in Late Roman Italy

The Tetrarchy to Honorius

Characterised by dynastic rivalries and regionalised armies, the tetrarchic period witnessed shifting concentrations of troops in Italy. Inscriptions and finds of *militaria* indicate a heightened military presence around Aquileia from the 290s, mainly *vexillationes* from legions stationed on the middle/lower Danube. Most studies credit Maximian with creating a nodal strategic reserve to control east–west (Pannonia to Gaul) and north–south (Noricum to Italy) arterial routes.[37] He could thence rapidly redeploy units to conflicts outside Italy, even as distant as Africa.[38] An alternative interpretation simply connects these troops to Maximian's frequent residence at Aquileia, accompanied by his *comitatus*, without grand-strategic objectives.[39] Subsequently, archaeologically attested troop dispositions in the north-eastern sector reflect anticipated hostilities in this territorial border zone, between first Maxentius and Licinius (308–12), then Constantine and Licinius (c.313–14).[40] Maxentius originally seized power with the support of the *cohortes praetoriae*, recently reduced and now of uncertain number or strength, along with those *equites singulares* then in Rome and, it seems, the *cohortes urbanae*.[41] Beyond these palatine troops, the composition of Maxentius' forces is less evident.[42] A significant proportion was reportedly recruited from the peninsula and islands as well as Africa; this would be a rare instance of a substantially 'Italian' army in Late Antiquity.[43] By a circuitous route, Maxentius also commanded former elements

---

[36] E.g. contributions in Buora 2002; Christie 2006, 307–8, 314; Vannesse 2010a, 262–72; Feugère 2013.
[37] Pavan 1979, 497–9; Lettich 1982, 78–80; Speidel 1990, 69–72; Roberto 2014, 140; Ricci 2014, 246–50.
[38] E.g. *CIL* 5.893 = *InscrAq* 2772: a cenotaph to a *miles* of *legio* XI *Claudia*, erected by comrades and citizens at Aquileia, following his death during Maximian's campaign in Mauretania in 297–8; see Hoffmann 1969–1970, 1.229; Šašel Kos 2016, 220. Speculation on a naval presence at Aquileia under the Tetrarchy: Vannesse 2010a, 56; Roberto 2014, 138, with bibliography.
[39] Pellizzari 2014, 147–9; Roberto 2014, 140; Ricci 2014, 246–9, 251.
[40] Vannesse 2007, 320; 2010a, 55–6; Roberto 2014, 138–40.
[41] Lactant. *De mort. pers.* 26.3; Aur. Vict. *Caes.* 40.5, 24–5; Eutr. 10.2.3–4; *Anon. Vales.* 3.6; Oros. 7.28.5; Socrates, *Hist. eccl.* 1.2.11; Zos. 2.9.3, 17.2. See Durry 1938, 88–9, 393–4; Freis 1967, 18; Speidel 1986.
[42] Roberto 2014, 135–7.
[43] Lactant. *De mort. pers.* 44.2; Zos. 2.15.2 (contrasting Maxentius' Italian/Roman troops with Constantine's 'barbarian' forces: 2.15.1).

of his father's *comitatus* – upon Maximian's retirement, these units had been reassigned to Severus, briefly legitimist western Augustus (306–7), but when he invaded Italy to enforce that claim in 307, bribery or dynastic sentiment induced these troops to go over to Maxentius.[44] Conversely, while historical sources lack detail, Constantine's invading army in 312 has been traced in funerary inscriptions to men of Rhine-based units who fell along the Via Flaminia.[45]

Following his victory, Constantine abolished the *cohortes praetoriae* and *equites singulares*, cashiering or reassigning their personnel, and razing their barracks and cemeteries to make way for new churches and dynastic mausolea.[46] This radical *damnatio memoriae* concluded a longer-term process: already Diocletian had in some way diminished the *cohortes praetoriae* and Galerius attempted their abolition.[47] The recently created *scholae palatinae* later assumed their functions as household troops, though currently these mounted guard units escorted emperors on campaign as elite combat troops. Aside from punishing Maxentius' prominent supporters, Constantine completed his predecessors' policy of dismantling the Severan-age super-garrison of Rome and thereby neutralising a source of political volatility.[48] It is plausibly assumed that Constantine also removed *legio* II *Parthica* from its base at Albanum, though there is no evidence that even its depot staff were still stationed in Italy.[49] Also unclear is the fate of the *cohortes urbanae*, last firmly documented c.317–37. Although their hierarchical titulature lingers as honorific distinctions into the 390s, they are conspicuously absent during civic and religious disturbances.[50] One *praefectus urbi*, Leontius (355–6), managed to quell rioting only through his own bravery and personal retinue, while the house of another, Lampadius (365), was spared destruction because his domestic servants and neighbours confronted the mob.[51]

---

[44] Lactant. *De mort. pers.* 26.4–8, 44.2; *Pan. Lat.* 12(9).3.4; Aur. Vict. *Caes.* 40.6–7; Eutr. 10.2.4 (= Joh. Ant. fr. 253 Roberto/195 Mariev); *Anon. Vales.* 3.6, 4.9–10; Oros. 7.28.7–8; Zos. 2.10.1–2. Hoffmann 1969–1970, 1.259–60 discusses possible epigraphic evidence for specific units.

[45] Historical sources: e.g. Zos. 2.15.1: diverse barbarian troops. Epigraphy: e.g. *legio* II *Italica Divitensium*, usually based at Divitia/Köln-Deutz: *CIL* 11.4787 = *ILS* 2777 (Spoleto) = *PLRE* 1.158, 'Baudio'; *CIL* 11.4085 (Otricoli); *AE* 1982, 258 (Otricoli); *CIL* 6.3637 = *ILS* 2346 = *ILCV* 462 (Rome). See Hoffmann 1969–1970, 1.177–8, 259; Scheithauer and Wesch-Klein 1990; Mennella 2004.

[46] *Pan. Lat.* 12(9).21.2–3; Aur. Vict. *Caes.* 40.25; Zos. 2.17.2; see Durry 1938, 393–6; Speidel 1986, 254–6; 1988; 1992, 279–89, 379–84, 387–9; 1994, 152–7. The statement of *Pan. Lat.* 12(9).21.2–3 that Constantine transferred unspecified troops to garrisons on the Rhine and Danube is often understood to relate to *praetoriani* but may in fact refer to regular units in Maxentius' army (compare *Pan. Lat.* 12(9).11.2–4): see Hoffmann 1969–1970, 1.259–60 for potential evidence.

[47] Aur. Vict. *Caes.* 39.47: Diocletian 'reduced the number of *cohortes praetoriae*', though in fact their number remained unchanged: see *AE* 1961, 240 = 1998, 467 (306; Granaione di Campagnatico, Tuscany). Lactant. *De mort. pers.* 26.3: Galerius 'had abolished' (or 'removed') the remaining *praetoriani*. See Durry 1938, 88–9.

[48] Porena 2013, 336–8.

[49] Ritterling 1924, 1479–82 for the far-flung campaigning of *legio* II *Parthica* (or detachments thereof) during the third century; also remarks of Speidel 1986, 256. *Not. Dign. or.* 36.30 lists a *praefectus* of *legio* II *Parthica* based at Cefa/Hasankeyf in Mesopotamia, but this unit probably descends from a third-century *vexillatio*, long predating Constantine's victory in 312.

[50] *CIL* 6.1156a (+ p. 4330) = 31248a = *ILS* 722 (317–37); Symm. *Relat.* 42 (384/5); *CTh* 6.27.8 (396); *CJ* 12.54.4. See Jones 1964, 692–3; Freis 1967, 18–22.

[51] Amm. Marc. 15.7.1–5, 27.3.8–9; *PLRE* 1.503, 'Leontius 22'; 978–80, 'Volusianus (Lampadius) 5'. On religious disorder see Chapter 13 in this volume.

Until the 370s, few troops were regularly stationed in the peninsula. When Constantine II invaded Italy from Gaul in spring 340, he rapidly overran the Po basin and reached Aquileia before his brother Constans, based at Naissus/Niš, transferred Danubian troops across the Alps, where they ambushed and killed Constantine.[52] In 350, supporters of the Gallic usurper Magnentius secured control of Italy between mid-January and late February seemingly without significant deployment of troops.[53] A countercoup staged by Nepotianus in June in Rome, reportedly using gladiators and criminal hirelings, was initially opposed only by citizens armed by Magnentius' *praefectus urbi*, while nearly a month passed before a detachment of Magnentius' forces arrived to squash the revolt.[54] From 351, north-eastern Italy briefly experienced a concentration of Magnentius' forces, and the *claustra* and northern plain were a theatre of conflict the following year.[55] With Constantius II resident in Milan from winter 354 to spring 357, north-western Italy became an operational base for campaigns against the Alamanni on the upper Rhine (355–7).[56] In 361, as Julian moved his army through the diocese, both sides of the Alps, to confront Constantius II, he reportedly deployed numerous troops in southern Sicily to oppose Constantius' forces in Africa.[57] Textual and archaeological evidence attests military activity in north-eastern Italy from the early 370s, indicative of perceived threats to this sector and/or logistical preparations for campaigns against Sarmatians and Quadi on the Danube.[58] Insecurity in the Balkans after 378 intensified barbarian inroads as far as the Julian Alps.[59]

Political and military events accentuated these developments. The frequent and prolonged presence of Gratian with substantial forces in north-western Italy between 379 and 383 enhanced the status of Milan as a military-administrative centre and a counterweight of military patronage relative to the Gallic capital at Trier.[60] When Magnus Maximus overthrew Gratian in Gaul in 383 and seized all transalpine provinces, the armed forces of Valentinian II's residual regime in Italy, though hugely outnumbered, acquired exceptional autonomy under their Frankish *magister militum* Bauto (c.380/1 to c.385–7).[61] Among the troops at Bauto's disposal are recorded 'Gothic' regulars and, at least occasionally, allied Huns, possibly reflecting his experience of Balkan warfare (380/1) and/or a general reorientation of recruitment

---

[52] Jer. *Chron.* 279.3/2356; Eutr. 10.9.2; *Epit. de Caes.* 41.21; Zonar. 13.5.7–13, with Seeck 1919, 189. See alternative analyses in Bleckmann 2003; Lewis 2020.

[53] Chronology in Beyeler 2011, 60–3, 134, 136, 358–9.

[54] Aur. Vict. *Caes.* 42.6–8; Zos. 2.43; Eutr. 10.11.2 (= Joh. Ant. fr. 260 Roberto/200 Mariev); Oros. 7.29.11; Socrates, *Hist. eccl.* 2.25.10; Sozom. 4.1.2.

[55] Numismatic evidence: Kos 2012, 278, 288; 2013, 250–2. Epigraphy: *AE* 1982, 383 (28 July 352, Aquileia). Hostilities in 352: Janniard 2006, 78–9; Vannesse 2007, 320–1.

[56] Seeck 1919, 200–3; Drinkwater 2007, 203–37, 242.

[57] Julian marches through Annonaria: Amm. Marc. 21.8–9. Sicily: Amm. Marc. 21.7.5.

[58] Vannesse 2007, 321–3.

[59] Ambr. *Exc. Sat.* 1.31; Amm. Marc. 31.16.7; Jer. *Ep.* 60.16 (396).

[60] Gratian three times quartered his troops in northern Italy: in June/July–August 379 when returning from Illyricum to Gaul; in April–June/July 380 en route to assist the eastern empire; and for more than two years from March 381 to June 383, when he campaigned against Alamanni in Raetia: Socrates, *Hist. eccl.* 5.6.2, 11.2; Sozom. 7.2.1, 4.1–2, 13.1. See Seeck 1919, 250–62; Hoffmann 1969–1970, 1.321, 476.

[61] McLynn 1994, 158–60, 164–5; McEvoy 2013, 66–8.

towards the Danube basin, now that Maximus monopolised the Rhineland. In addition, Arian/Homoian sympathies at Valentinian's court conceivably fostered a more sympathetic environment for Gothic soldiers at a time when the doctrinal stance at Constantinople was becoming overtly intolerant.[62] On Bauto's death, c.385–7, his subordinate Arbogast, another Frank, assumed command, without imperial authorisation, but with his troops' approval, perhaps signalling their communal self-identity or loyalties.[63] It is unclear, however, what happened to these forces when, seemingly unopposed, Maximus invaded Italy in mid-387 – did they flee from or flock to the usurper?[64] Nevertheless, when Theodosius reinstalled Valentinian II as his western colleague (388–92), Arbogast resumed his senior command. In their military authority and political behaviour, Bauto and Arbogast prefigure the 'generalissimos' of fifth-century Italy.[65] Ultimately, units stationed in the peninsula, readily or otherwise, sided with two usurpers, Maximus (387–8) and Arbogast's puppet emperor Eugenius (392–4), and were twice defeated in north-eastern Italy. How, on each occasion, the usurper's weakened or demoralised forces were treated or restructured – through amnesties, purges or transfers – remains largely conjectural.[66] Theodosius, resident in Italy in 388–91, reportedly incorporated Maximus' best troops into the eastern army.[67] These uncertainties undercut the military foundations of Honorius' regime after 395.

When Theodosius died in Milan in January 395, his expeditionary forces were wintering in Italy under Stilicho, *magister utriusque militiae* (c.393–408).[68] Following the demobilisation of some *foederati* and the return of most or all eastern regiments to Constantinople by autumn 395, it is unclear what troops remained, but over the following decade recruiting and retaining manpower consumed Stilicho's energies in improvised crisis management.[69] Already in 396, Stilicho tightened regulations

---

[62] Huns and Alans: Ambr. *Ep.* 30(24).8 (387). Gothic *tribuni* and soldiers: Ambr. *Ep.* 75A(21A).2; 76(20).9, 12, 16, 20. Campaign of 380/1: Zos. 4.33.1–2. See Hoffmann 1969–1970, 1.464, 475; McLynn 1994, 159–60, 182–4, 190–1.

[63] Eunap. fr. [58.2] (= Joh. Ant. fr. 280 Roberto/212 Mariev); Zos. 4.53.1–3 (compare 4.33.1–2).

[64] Zos. 4.42.5–43.1, noting (42.5) that Valentinian's forces were already strained by barbarian incursions into Pannonia. Maximus later believed he could suborn Theodosius' barbarian troops: Zos. 4.45.3.

[65] *PLRE* 1.95–7, 'Arbogastes'; 159–60, 'Bauto'. See O'Flynn 1983, 6–13; Liebeschuetz 1990, 9–10; Wijnendaele 2015, 12–16.

[66] Theodosius' widely reported clemency towards the defeated usurpers' troops in 388 and 394 combines panegyrical convention and pragmatic considerations; see sources and discussion in Hoffmann 1969–1970, 1.30 (esp. nn. 41–2), 479–80. Procedures for amnesty: e.g. *CTh* 7.18.9 (26 April 396) ratifies honourable and medical discharges obtained by soldiers 'during the time of the tyrant' (Eugenius).

[67] Zos. 4.47.2. In his analysis of the *Notitia dignitatum*, Hoffmann 1969–1970, 1.469–71, 480–7, 494 identifies in the two eastern praesental armies at least fifteen elite units (*palatini*) that, he argues, were transferred from the West in 388, though his argumentation partly relies on assumptions about regimental titulature that have since been disproved.

[68] Stilicho's military career: Matthews 1975, 253–83; O'Flynn 1983, 14–62; Janssen 2004; McEvoy 2013, 141–86; Poguntke 2016, 240–52; Wijnendaele 2016a; 2018b.

[69] Zos. 5.4.2 alleges that Stilicho retained the better-quality eastern troops in the West. See Hoffmann 1969-1970, 1.33–41, who seeks to identify such eastern units (in his view, fourteen in number) in the *Notitia dignitatum*.

governing recruitment and desertion, and apparently enlisted transrhenanian warriors as he inspected Rhineland defences.[70] His campaign in Greece in 397 and preparations to suppress Gildo's revolt in Africa in 397–8 prompted extraordinary recruiting measures in Italy that antagonised senatorial landowners.[71] Stilicho's obscure operations in Raetia in 401 also entailed enlistment of unspecified barbarians.[72] When Alaric invaded Italy in autumn 401, he encountered little active resistance, partly owing to Stilicho's absence, but also because imperial forces pursued a risk-avoidant strategy of attritional containment throughout the winter. In Raetia, Stilicho assembled reinforcements, comprising barbarians (possibly Alans), Raetian *limitanei* and, reportedly, troops from the lower Rhine and Britain, which he transferred to Italy in spring 402.[73] A force of allied Alans, commanded by Saul, figured prominently in combat operations.[74] Stilicho's victory in 402 induced some of Alaric's troops to switch sides.[75] Following Alaric's withdrawal in autumn 402, a spate of legislation concerned endemic desertion and a supplemental levy of recruiting-tax.[76] To confront Radagaisus in 405–6, Stilicho concentrated at Pavia an exceptionally large army, reportedly thirty units (*numeri*), augmented by diverse contingents of non-Roman allies/*foederati*: again Alans, also Huns, supplied by their ruler Uldin, and a war band led by Sarus, a Gothic dynastic renegade.[77] To secure additional recruits, Stilicho authorised emergency enlistment measures for civilians and even manumitted slaves.[78] This army, estimated at 15–20,000, possibly took the field only because it equalled or outnumbered Radagaisus' forces.[79] Again, after overcoming his opponents, Stilicho enlisted reportedly 12,000 high-status warriors from Radagaisus' following.[80]

---

[70] Recruitment and desertion: *CTh* 7.18.9 (26 April 396). Rhineland: Claud. *In Eutr.* 1.377–83; *IV cons. Hon.* 439–59; *Cons. Stil.* 1.188–236, with Cameron 1970, 96–7, 375–7; Hoffmann 1969–1970, 1.143, 168; Scharf 1995, 165, 171, 176–8.

[71] *CTh* 7.13.12–14 (397); Symm. *Ep.* 6.58.2, 62, 64.2 (397/8); 9.10 (397?). See below, p. 180–1.

[72] Claud. *BGet.* 400–3.

[73] Claud. *VI cons. Hon.* 458–62; *BGet.* 400–29, 450–78. See Hoffmann 1969–1970, 1.95–6, 143; Cameron 1970, 375–7; Burns 1994, 191–2; Vannesse 2010b, 104–5.

[74] Claud. *VI cons. Hon.* 223–6; *BGet.* 580–97; Oros. 7.37.2–3; Zos. 5.26.4. Wijnendaele 2016a, 273–80 differently interprets Oros. 7.37.3. It is unclear whether these Alans were newly recruited by Stilicho in Raetia (Claud. *BGet.* 400–3, 580–1) or had entered Italy with Saul in 394 (Zos. 4.57.2; Joh. Ant. fr. 280 Roberto/212.2 Mariev, with *PLRE* 1.809, 2.981; see also Claud. *IV cons. Hon.* 487, written 398), or both.

[75] Claud. *VI cons. Hon.* 127–32, 248–59, 309–15; *BGet.* 87–9.

[76] Desertion: *CTh* 7.18.11–14 (403). Supplemental levies: *CTh* 7.13.15 (402); 6.27.13 (403: referring to a recent levy). See below, p. 180–1.

[77] Oros. 7.37.12 (> Marcell. Com. s.a. 406.3 > Jord. *Rom.* 321); *Addit. Prosp. Haun.* (marg.) s.a. 405; *Chron. Gall. 452* 52; Zos. 5.26.3–5. See Cesa 1993, 206–8; Wijnendaele 2016a, 272–8. Veg. *Epit.* 1.20.2 (compare 3.26.36), here preferably dated to the 380s/90s, deems Goths, Alans and Huns as exemplars for contemporary imperial cavalry forces. The same trio occurs in near-contemporary sources: Amm. Marc. 31.16.3; Pacatus, *Pan. Lat.* 2(12).11.4, 32.4; Oros. 7.34.5 (> Marcell. Com. s.a. 379.2).

[78] Extraordinary recruitment: *CTh* 7.13.16–17 (406). Desertion: *CTh* 7.18.15 (406). See below, p. 186.

[79] Modern estimates: Wijnendaele 2016a, 270–1.

[80] Olymp. fr. 9; compare Zos. 5.26.5, whose wording 'whom he [Stilicho] brought into the Romans' alliance (*symmachia*)' may imply '*foederati*' status. See further bibliography in Wijnendaele 2018b, 270–4, who suggests that Stilicho may have recruited some of these troops as *buccellarii*.

Although these invasions dominate historical narratives, broader perspectives indicate military priorities and capabilities that transcend periodic emergencies. Throughout this period, Stilicho persisted with longer-term ambitions to seize the prefecture of Illyricum, deploying Alaric's forces as a vanguard in Epirus in 407.[81] When the usurper Constantine III, based at Arles by spring 408, became the greatest threat to Honorius' regime, an expeditionary army was assembled at Pavia, to be supplemented by Alaric's forces, now in Noricum. These preparations, barely two years after Radagaisus' incursion, occasioned no special legislation on recruitment or provisioning.[82] Furthermore, Stilicho could even contemplate taking an escort of four regiments to Constantinople in mid-408.[83] Stilicho's downfall in August, beyond its political consequences, affected the army in Italy at an institutional level. The mutiny orchestrated at Pavia and subsequent purge of Stilicho's supporters eliminated many higher-ranking personnel.[84] The coup also accentuated fault lines between 'regular' soldiers and those *foederati* associated with Stilicho's authority. When Stilicho convened the commanders of the *foederati* at Bologna to plan a response to the mutiny, it briefly seemed that their collective loyalty to him and distinct professional-ethnic identity might provoke a wider confrontation within the army, but events quickly exposed the relative isolation, numerical weakness and factional disunity of barbarian forces in Italy.[85] Soldiers quartered in north Italian cities then simultaneously massacred the resident wives and children of *foederati* and plundered their property, a stark expression of perceived factional, institutional and/or ethnic difference, whereupon many *foederati*, if not the 30,000 reported, quit Honorius' service and joined Alaric in Noricum.[86]

Stilicho's successors were unable to concentrate forces that could resist Alaric's second invasion in 408–10; the army assembled at Pavia in mid-408 presumably dispersed before he invaded in October. During the ensuing two-year military-political stalemate, while Alaric was free to manoeuvre, imperial forces remained in urban garrisons, occasionally cooperating but never achieving decisive numerical or tactical advantage.[87] Around Ravenna, Honorius had few troops he could effectively deploy or entirely trust.[88] Prominent among these were 300 Hunnic horse-archers.[89] As in 401–2 and 405–6, reinforcements had to be drafted into Italy, but now without access to transalpine manpower. In early 409, Honorius ordered Valens, a commander in Dalmatia, to

---

[81] Olymp. fr. 1.2 (= Sozom. 8.25.2–4 = 9.4.2–4); a confused version also in Zos. 5.26.1–2, also 27.1–3, 48.2, with *PLRE* 2.623–4, 'Jovius 3'. See Burns 1994, 193–7, 203. On Stilicho's eastern ambitions see further bibliography with critique in Wijnendaele 2018b, 263–5.

[82] Cesa 1993, 208–11; Burns 1994, 227–8; Wijnendaele 2018b, 265–8.

[83] Olymp. fr. 5.2 (= Sozom. 9.4.6).

[84] Olymp. fr. 5.2 (= Sozom. 9.4.7–8); Zos. 5.32.4–7, 35.4, 45.3; compare *CTh* 9.42.20–2 (408).

[85] Zos. 5.33.1–34.5. See Liebeschuetz 1990, 36–7; Cesa 1993, 209–13.

[86] Zos. 5.34.2, 35.5–6; compare Philost. *Hist. eccl.* 12.3, with Burns 1994, 218, 224–5; Wijnendaele 2018b, 270–2.

[87] Zos. 5.45.5–6, 46.5, 50.1.

[88] Military mutiny at Ravenna in 409: Zos. 5.47.1–48.1. Honorius doubtful of troops' loyalty: Sozom. 9.8.6.

[89] Zos. 5.45.6. Subsequently, in early 410, Sarus and his personal following of 200–300 joined Honorius at Ravenna: Olymp. fr. 6; Sozom. 9.9.3; Philost. *Hist. eccl.* 12.3; Zos. 6.13.2.

bring five units, comprising 6,000 high-quality troops. Dispatched to defend Rome, this force was ambushed by Alaric and destroyed.[90] Later that year, Honorius summoned '10,000' allied Huns and authorised large-scale logistical arrangements, though their arrival is never recorded. Preparing to abandon Italy in early 410, Honorius resolved to stay when six regiments, totalling 4,000 men, disembarked at Ravenna, sent by the eastern government in accordance with an agreement made with Stilicho (pre-August 408).[91] Despite losing control of much of the peninsula, Honorius was also able to remunerate troops in Italy from external sources of revenue.[92] The contemporary picture is further complicated by indications that some regular troops aligned with Alaric and his puppet emperor, Attalus, against Honorius in 409/10.[93]

The Notitia dignitatum

Despite the historical high drama of 408–10 and preceding crises, assessments of their impact on the army in Italy remain impressionistic, even though the next witness to diocesan military administration is the most detailed. The *Notitia dignitatum* places a large field army *intra Italiam*, consisting of forty-four units, mostly elite troops classed as *palatini*.[94] This is the second largest regional command in the empire, after Gaul (though smaller than the two eastern praesental armies combined). Seven cavalry regiments – six *vexillationes palatinae* and a *vexillatio comitatensis* – include some of the most prestigious regiments. Thirty-seven infantry units comprise eight *legiones palatinae* and twenty-two *auxilia palatina*, again including distinguished tetrarchic and Constantinian regiments, along with five *legiones comitatenses* and two *legiones pseudocomitatenses* (*limitanei* temporarily assigned to field commands).[95] The total establishment strength is estimated at c.25–30,000 men. If, as in any army, the names listed on the muster rolls (*matrices*, *matriculae*) of individual units never reached prescribed totals, and the number of men available for active duty was lower still, in Italy the high proportion of elite regiments and proximity to central authority may have militated against excessive shortfalls, corruption and absenteeism.[96] Also in Italy are five *scholae palatinae*, c.2,500 men, administered by the *magister officiorum*, now essentially ceremonial corps at imperial residences in Rome, Milan and Ravenna.[97]

---

[90] Zos. 5.45.1–2, 6.7.2, with *PLRE* 2.1137, 'Valens 2'.
[91] Huns: Zos. 5.50.1. Six eastern units: Sozom. 9.8.6; Zos. 6.8.2–3; a distorted version of the same in Socrates, *Hist. eccl.* 7.10; Proc. *Bell.* 3.2.36.
[92] E.g. Zos. 6.10.21: revenue from Africa.
[93] Sozom. 9.8.5.
[94] Jones 1964, 196–8; 3.367, table VIII; Hoffmann 1969–1970, Auszug, 14–15, 19 (emended text of *Not. Dign. occ.* 7); Vannesse 2010c, 70–3, 91–4.
[95] Cavalry: *Not. Dign. occ.* 7.158–65. Infantry: *Not. Dign. occ.* 7.2–39. The unit type of the *Victores seniores* (7.17) and *Placidi Valentinianici felices* (7.36) is not specified, but regimental titulature identifies both as *auxilia palatina*; see Scharf 2005, 178–9, with bibliography.
[96] The calculations of Jones 1964, 3.379, table XV, would equate to c.28,500 *comitatenses* in Italy.
[97] *Not. Dign. occ.* 9.4–8. See Jones 1964, 613–14; Frank 1969, 49–79, 99–125, 167–94; Hoffmann 1969–1970, 1.279–303, 310–311.

Chronological indicators suggest that this section of the *Notitia*, though originally drafted probably in 401, was updated to at least 425.[98] This is, ostensibly, a field army (re)constituted post-410, though when and how remain unclear, and successive contributions of Stilicho (395–408), Flavius Constantius (411–21) and/or Ardaburius (425) are inferred.[99] Some palatine units – *vexillationes*, *legiones*, *auxilia* – evidently belonged to the Italian field army pre-408. Five (three *legiones palatinae*, two *auxilia palatina*) are plausibly identified as units that participated in the 5,000-strong task force dispatched from Pisa against Gildo in 398.[100] The titulature of three other *auxilia palatina*, bearing the imperial cognominal epithet *Honoriani*, relates to a phase of programmatic regimental expansion dated to the mid-/late 390s.[101] This army may include units more recently transferred to Italy, such as the six dispatched from the East in 410 or unreported others in 424–5.[102] A unit named after Valentinian III, even if created or redesignated slightly earlier, cannot have joined the Italian army before the overthrow of the usurper John and installation of Valentinian in Rome in autumn 425; accordingly, this list took its final shape soon after another eastern Roman intervention and regime change.[103] Conversely, throughout the *Notitia* there is negligible evidence of units previously transferred out of Italy: among regimental titles that signify a unit's current or prior affiliation to a regional field army, just one unit, a *vexillatio comitatensis* stationed in Africa, is styled *Italiciani*, compared to at least twenty-four *Illyriciani* and sixteen *Gallicani*.[104] Overall, compared with other western regional commands, which

---

[98] Jones 1964, 3.347–58; Hoffmann 1969–1970, 1.7–53, 494–519; 2.207–15, with refinements by Zuckerman 1998b, 144–7 (*terminus post quem* of 398/9, arguing persuasively for 401); Scharf 2005, 3–4, 179.

[99] Differing assessments of chronological strata: Hoffmann 1969–1970, esp. 1.9–10, 22–4, 29–51; Liebeschuetz 1990, 41–2; Scharf 1995, 176–8.

[100] Claud. *Gild*. 415–23; Oros. 7.36.6 (5,000 men); Zos. 5.11.3. Claudian describes, in poetic idiom, seven participating infantry regiments (or detachments thereof), of which five are identifiable in the Italian field army listed in the *Notitia*: *Herculeam cohortem* = *Herculiani seniores* (*Not. Dign. occ.* 5.3 = 146 = 7.4); *Ioviamque cohortem* = *Ioviani seniores* (*Not. Dign. occ.* 5.2 = 145 = 7.3; also *AE* 1893, 122 = *ILCV* 551; *AE* 2002, 538 = 2011, 400); *Felix* [*cohors*] = *Felices iuniores* (*Not. Dign. occ.* 5.32 = 180 = 7.23); *dictaque ab Augusto legio* [VIII] = *Octavani* (*Not. Dign. occ.* 5.10 = 153 = 7.28); *clipeoque animosi teste Leones* = *Leones iuniores* (*Not. Dign. occ.* 5.27 = 172 = 7.19). See Hoffmann 1969–1970, 1.96, 105; Charles 2005, 283; Vannesse 2010a, 154–5, 373–6; 2010b, 101. Claudian also names: *Nervius* [*cohors*] and *Invicti*. If not referring to units since destroyed, the only likely correspondents in the *Notitia* are two *auxilia palatina* now listed in Spain: *Sagittarii Nervii* (*Not. Dign. occ.* 5.25 = 170 = 7.121) and *Invicti seniores* (5.34 = 182 = 7.125); see Hoffmann 1969–1970, 1.109–10.

[101] *Not. Dign. occ.* 5.51 = 200 = 7.24: *Atecotti Honoriani iuniores*; 5.55 = 204 = 7.26: *Mauri Honoriani iuniores*; 5.49/50 = 198/9 = 7.38: *Marcomanni Honoriani seniores/iuniores*. Date of creation: Hoffmann 1969–1970, 1.139, 143, 168–9, 365 (dating to 395–8); Scharf 1995, esp. 176–8 (dating to 396–7). *Honoriani* generally: Scharf 1994, 134–43.

[102] See above, p. 165. Hoffmann 1969–1970, 1.37, 47–8; Scharf 1994, 143–4.

[103] *Not. Dign. occ.* 7.36: *Placidi Valentinianici felices*. Hoffmann 1969–1970, 1.22, 169 maintains that this unit is an isolated addition to a pre-existing list. Scharf 2005, 179 argues that this regimental titulature cannot predate Valentinian's elevation as Caesar (October 424). See generally Scharf 1994, 143–4: eastern troops possibly left in Italy post-425.

[104] *Not. Dign. occ.* 7.180: *equites stablesiani Italiciani* in the army of the *comes Africae*. The prior presence of *equites stablesiani* in Italy during the tetrarchic period is documented epigraphically: *CIL* 5.4376 (Brescia); *AE* 1974, 342 (Aquileia); see Hoffmann 1969–1970, 1.148–9, 252, 263. I exclude units in the *Notitia* styled *Italiciani* where this titular component derives from the ancient *legio* II *Italica* rather than a recent regional affiliation to Italia (*Not. Dign. occ.* 7.44: *Secundani Italiciani*; 32.27: *Cuneus equitum Italicianorum*{,} *Secundarum*).

bear the impact of various crises of Honorius' reign, the army of Italy contains a far higher proportion of elite and long-established regiments, and was now perhaps the only command able to spare detachments for service elsewhere.[105]

The *Notitia* excludes 'non-regular' troops, typically non-Roman mounted formations: *foederati*, allies or diverse groups that elude generic definition or uniform terminology. Although employment of these troop categories in Italy fluctuated over the fifth century, the total number of soldiers and the proportion of cavalry units listed (16 per cent) would accordingly be higher.[106] Distinct from older, generalising paradigms of 'barbarisation', the issue here is not 'ethnicity': many non-Romans, unremarkably, enlisted as long-service regulars in *comitatenses* or *palatini*, where they were functionally indistinguishable from Roman recruits.[107] Of interest, rather, are motivations for and implications of 'irregular' modes of recruitment. Latin *foederati* (Greek: *symmachoi*) had long signified troops supplied under treaty (*foedus/symmachia*) by external allies, serving under their own leaders and not subject to Roman discipline. While this usage persisted, from the late fourth/early fifth century the same terminology seemingly applied also to tribal groupings settled by agreement within the empire or, specifically, to contingents they furnished. This vocabulary was in turn loosely extended to heterogeneous war bands enlisted in differing contexts and with varying remuneration and maintenance, whereby in some cases the Roman state exercised greater control and scrutiny, presaging a protracted and poorly documented regularisation of *foederati* as 'foreign legions' designed to accommodate itinerant groups or individual warriors.[108] Certain barbarian troops, notably Hunnic horse-archers, were valued for weaponry skills and/or tactical specialisms, in accordance with centuries-old traditions of Roman military eclecticism.[109] More generally, in circumstances that urgently required additional troops – invasions, civil wars or expeditionary armies – enlistment of barbarians, under various terms of service, offered shortcuts to trained soldiers, while *ad hoc* employment reduced costs proportionate to the finite fiscal-demographic resources of Italy.[110] At the same time, however, some senior Roman commanders, particularly Stilicho and Aëtius, were alert to the power-political implications of longer-term exploitation of non-Roman manpower.[111]

As Italia Annonaria included Raetia, the armed forces of the Italian diocese also comprised *limitanei*. Units assigned to the *dux Raetiae primae et secundae* in the *Notitia* appear to be largely unchanged since the tetrarchic era.[112] Archaeological studies delineate interrelationships between fortifications and infrastructure, military

---

[105] Jones 1964, 355.
[106] Hoffmann 1969–1970, 1.193–4; Liebeschuetz 1990, 32–4, 37; *contra* Elton 1996, 93.
[107] Hoffmann 1969–1970, 1.81–3, 132–73; Elton 1996, 134–52; Vannesse 2010c, 70–2; Rocco 2012, 313–31.
[108] Olymp. fr. 7.4 remarks on the shifting application of the term *phoideratoi* in the reign of Honorius; see also *CTh* 7.13.16 (406) (*foederati*); August. *Ep.* 220.7 (427, referring back to c.417) (*foederati*), compare 185.1.1 (417) (*Gothi*); Zos. 5.26.4 (*symmachikon*), 5 (*symmachia*), 33.1–2 (*barbaroi symmachoi*), 34.2–5. The limited and ambiguous evidence is susceptible to multiple interpretations, e.g. Jones 1964, 159–60, 199–203, 611–13, 663–6; Elton 1996, 91–4; Scharf 2001, 8–50; Stickler 2007.
[109] E.g. Zos. 5.45.6: the combat capabilities of 300 Hunnic horse-archers in Honorius' service in 409–10.
[110] Liebeschuetz 1990, 33–4; Elton 1996, 228–9.
[111] See below, p. 170–3.
[112] *Not. Dign. occ.* 35 (compare 1.43, 5.139).

presence, civilian settlements, and migration, involving increasing recruitment of transdanubian manpower, though interpretation remains fraught with difficulties.[113] Some *comitatenses* listed *intra Italiam* periodically operated in Raetia – and, more rarely, in Noricum – as in 430–1, when Aëtius defeated Iuthungi and subjugated obscurely reported provincial rebels.[114] Conversely, though barely traceable, Raetian *limitanei* possibly served in peninsular Italy in exceptional circumstances, as in 402.[115]

The *Notitia* lists *in Italia* four praefectural commands of 'fleets' (*classes*). Two *praefecti classis*, as traditionally, were based at Misenum and Ravenna (or Classe), and two smaller flotillas at Aquileia and on Lake Como. Unclassified *milites* at Ravenna apparently functioned as dock guards.[116] Some (or perhaps all) of these *praefecti* exercised broader curatorial authority over their respective municipalities.[117] In Raetia, a corps of boatmen (*barcarii*) was headquartered at Brigantium/Bregenz on Lake Constance. The various lacustrine facilities were probably concerned with transportation and surveillance.[118] The size, organisation and capabilities of naval forces by c.400 remain obscure.[119] In the fourth century, regional maritime operations are occasionally recorded.[120] Shipping performed primarily logistical functions, notably conveyance of expeditionary forces, especially to Africa (398, 424/5, 427–8, 431), though details are scarce.[121] Large-scale troop shipments depended on temporary requisitioning of commercial cargo vessels

---

[113] Keller 1986; Burns 1994, 112–47, 178–81; Mackensen 1999; 2018.

[114] *AE* 1994, 1326 (Augsburg), with Scharf 1994, 144–5; see also Sid. Apoll. *Carm.* 7.233–5; *Chron. Gall. 452* 106; Hyd. 83(93), 85(95); *CIL* 6.1724 = *ILS* 2950; possible archaeological evidence in Burns 1994, 135. See generally Stickler 2002, 189–90; Wijnendaele 2017c, 478–9.

[115] Claud. *BGet.* 414–15. Jones 1964, 3.365, table VII, identifies the *Pontinenses*, a *legio pseudocomitatensis* listed in the Italian field army (*Not. Dign. occ.* 5.113 = 263 = 7.39), as a unit formally stationed at Pons Aeni (Pfaffenhofen am Inn) on the border of Raetia II and Noricum Ripense. Similarly, Burns 1994, 192 suggests that an *auxilium palatinum* named *Raeti* (*Not. Dign. occ.* 5.43 = 191 = 7.44), stationed in western Illyricum, may originate in Stilicho's transfer of Raetian *limitanei* in 401/2, but such an upgrading of *limitanei* to *palatini* would be unparalleled. Alternatively, Hoffmann 1969–1970, 1.149–50, 168 dates the creation of the *Raeti* and a group of similarly named *auxilia palatina* to the reign of Valentinian I.

[116] Classes: *Not. Dign. occ.* 42.2–11; compare Veg. *Epit.* 4.31; Zos. 6.8.2. Milites: *Not. Dign. occ.* 42.6.

[117] *Not. Dign. occ.* 42.7, 9 records that *praefecti classis* based at Ravenna and Como are 'with responsibilities for the same city' (*cum curis eiusdem civitatis*), but this authority is not specified for *praefecti* at Misenum or Aquileia. This divergence may be due to omission; a similar formula is attested with respect to a late fourth-/fifth-century *praefectus* at Misenum: *CIL* 10.3344 = *ILS* 5902: *Fl. Mariano v.p. praef(ectus) classis et curatori reip(ublicae) Misenatium* (see *PLRE* 1.559, 'Marianus 3').

[118] Lake Constance: *Not. Dign. occ.* 35.32, with archaeological literature in Burns 1994, 122. Lake Como: Claud. *BGet.* 319–21 (Stilicho in 401). Archaeological evidence from northern Italian lakes: Christie 2006, 313–14; 2007, 570–3, with bibliography.

[119] Reddé 1986, 573–82; Elton 1996, 97–9; MacGeorge 2002, 306–11; Charles 2005, 275–80.

[120] E.g. Naval operations in the Adriatic in 388: Ambr. *Ep.* 40(32).22; Oros. 7.35.3; Zos. 4.45.4–47.1; followed by military action on/off Sicily: Ambr. *Ep.* 40(32).23. See Hoffmann 1969–1970, 1.478–9. Operations in the Adriatic in 424: Olymp. fr. 43[2] = Philost. *Hist. eccl.* 12.13; Socrates, *Hist. eccl.* 7.23 (= Joh. Ant. fr. 289 Roberto/221 Mariev).

[121] Transhipment of Stilicho's forces from Adriatic ports to Greece in 397: Claud. *IV cons. Hon.* 460–5; Eunap. fr. 64.1 (= Joh. Ant. fr. 282 Roberto/215.2 Mariev); Zos. 5.7.1. Expedition to Africa in 398, sailing from Pisa via Sardinia: Claud. *Gild.* 480–526; Oros. 7.36.5. Some of these troops returned to Italy via a more southerly port: Symm. *Ep.* 7.38 (398): troops traversing Campania after Gildo's defeat. In other cases, it is not certain that Italy was the/a point of embarkation: e.g., in 373, *comes* Theodosius' expedition to Mauretania embarked at Arles: Amm. Marc. 29.5.5, 7.

and/or shipbuilding.¹²² Naval forces acquired greater significance once the Mediterranean ceased to be *mare nostrum* following the Vandals' seizure of Carthage in 439, notably Ricimer's defence of Sicily and victory over a sixty-ship Vandal expedition on/off Corsica in 456, though the nature of combat – nautical, terrestrial or both – remains ambiguous.¹²³ Majorian's construction of a reportedly 300-ship armada in 458–60, on the Adriatic and Tyrrhenian coasts, was an exceptional initiative, even if treachery off Spain thwarted his offensive against the Vandals.¹²⁴ Thereafter shortages of vessels and crews constrained even defensive operations.¹²⁵ Based in Dalmatia, Marcellinus possessed some naval capability, enabling him, if correctly recorded, to drive the Vandals from Sicily in 464/5, but the extent and nature of his 'fleet' can only be conjectured.¹²⁶ Nor is anything known of the naval forces he commanded off Sardinia and Sicily during joint East–West Roman operations against the Vandals in 468, though his access to eastern Roman resources has been plausibly assumed.¹²⁷

Military Command, Authority and Retinues

A striking feature of armed forces in Italy, and the West generally, is their centralised command and its military-political implications. While the titles of *magistri* or army commanders vary across documentary contexts, by 400 contrasting structures emerged in the two halves of the empire. In the East, five *magistri* commanding praesental and regional armies were equal in rank, if not precedence, and directly subordinate to central government, resulting in a horizontal diffusion of military authority. In the West, where older (Constantinian) bureaucratic distinctions persisted, ordinarily a single *magister* (*peditum/utriusque militiae*) *praesentalis*, commanding the Italian field army, was also supreme commander of all western troops, via a *magister equitum* in Gaul, *comites rei militaris* in Africa, Illyricum and Britannia, and *duces* in frontier zones. A second *magister* (*equitum*) *praesentalis*, notionally equal in rank but in reality subordinate, was sometimes appointed in Italy, during episodes of military crisis or political tension.¹²⁸ The powers of the senior *magister* were extensive. His *officium* probably issued all officers' commissions (*epistulae*), an important source of patronage and fees, which in the East was a prerogative of several civilian bureaux.¹²⁹ The senior bureaucratic staff of most comital and ducal *officia* were annually seconded from the *officium* of one or

---

¹²² Charles 2005, 280–97 (treating events of 397–8 in isolation).
¹²³ Priscus fr. 31.1; Sid. Apoll. *Carm.* 2.367–70; Hyd. 169–70(176–7). See MacGeorge 2002, 184–8; Anders 2010, 89–93.
¹²⁴ Construction: Sid. Apoll. *Carm.* 5.441–8; Priscus, fr. 36.1 and 2 (= Joh. Ant. fr. 295 Roberto/226 Mariev). Capture: Hyd. 195(200); *Gall. Chron. 511* 634; Marius Avent. s.a. 460.2.
¹²⁵ Priscus fr. 39.1, referring to c.462–5; compare Sid. Apoll. *Carm.* 2.386.
¹²⁶ Hyd. 223(227), if not a misdated record of Marcellinus' prior command in Sicily from c.458–60 to 461/2 (Priscus fr. 38.1); see Kulikowski 2002a, 180, 186; MacGeorge 2002, 49–51.
¹²⁷ Events of 468: *PLRE* 2.710, 'Marcellinus 6'; Kulikowski 2002a, 188–9; Janniard 2020, 230–3, 240–4. Marcellinus' 'fleet' and possible forces: MacGeorge 2002, 53–5; Anders 2010, 468–9; Janniard 2020, 243–4, 252.
¹²⁸ Jones 1964, 174–5, 191–2; O'Flynn 1983, 4–5; Burns 1994, 98–101, with bibliography. See *fasti* in *PLRE* 1.1112–14, 2.1288–9.
¹²⁹ Jones 1964, 641.

other of the *magistri militum praesentales*.[130] Less formally, emplacement of associates and supporters, sometimes reinforced by kinship or marriage, created pervasive cliental networks and loyalties that rooted a *magister*'s influence throughout the armed forces and even civil administration.[131] Although precursors may be discerned in Bauto and Arbogast, Stilicho's long-unchallenged 'regental' authority magnified this magistral office into the seat of real power, which was later enhanced with the dignity of *patricius*. Control of this paramount *magisterium* – rather than usurpation of imperial office – became an intensified focus of senior officers' competitive ambitions, leading to occasional military unrest on Italian soil, particularly between 422/3 and 432/3.[132]

The most influential 'generalissimos' were those able to amplify their office through prestige, talent, wealth and/or connections. In particular, Stilicho and Aëtius tapped different sources of non-Roman manpower to enhance both Roman military capabilities and their own pre-eminence in ways that reconfigured the institutional dynamics of imperial armed forces. Besides short-term enlistment of barbarian groups amid specific crises, Stilicho exploited the fissile instability of tribal conglomerations and personal followings to absorb elements of Alaric's (402) and Radagaisus' forces (406).[133] Furthermore, evolving cooperation with Alaric after 402 reveals Stilicho's appreciation of the potential value of Alaric's troops for projected operations in Illyricum (402–5 to 407) and Gaul (408).[134] In contrast, Aëtius exploited contacts with the barbarian world originating from his prior experience as a guest-hostage among the Huns. He first sought to purchase Hunnic assistance in 424/5 as an emissary of the usurper John, then beleaguered by eastern Roman forces. On returning with a large army of Huns, and finding John already deposed, Aëtius leveraged this military-demographic resource to secure a senior command in Valentinian III's regime.[135] Subsequently, Aëtius' 'special relationship' with Hunnic elites and control of Hunnic troops, notably in Italy in 433 and in Gaul c.435–9, became a pillar of his military-political dominance. Whether these Huns were technically *foederati*, allies or/and *bucellarii* is less important than the personal dimension of Aëtius' command.[136] For both Stilicho and Aëtius, in different ways, barbarian troops constituted an integral strike force within a field army and a component of a personalised power base. Such direct relationships between an extrinsic ethnic-professional subset and their commander-paymaster (rather than the emperor), fusing loyalty and mutual self-interest, blurred

---

[130] *CTh* 1.7.3 (398), with references in *Not. Dign. occ.* in Jones 1964, 175 n. 2.

[131] Stilicho's supporters and clients: see above, p. 163–4. *Magistri militum* and patronage: Anders 2010, 135–7, 140–2. Marriage links among the military aristocracy: Demandt 1980; Wijnendaele 2015, 48–53, 107; 2017a, 440–3.

[132] The invasion of Italy by Heraclianus, *comes Africae*, in 413 has also been characterised in these terms rather than as 'usurpation': Wijnendaele 2017b, with bibliography.

[133] Alaric: Claud. *VI cons. Hon.* 127–32, 248–59, 309–15; *BGet.* 87–9. Radagaisus: Olymp. fr. 9; Zos. 5.26.5. See above, p. 163–4.

[134] Burns 1994, 192–7.

[135] Philost. *Hist. eccl.* 12.14; Prosper, *Chron.* 1288; Gregory of Tours, *Hist.* 2.8. See Stickler 2002, 32–5, 87–8, 106; McEvoy 2013, 244–6.

[136] E.g. Jones 1964, 199 ('contingents obtained under treaty', 'auxiliaries'); Liebeschuetz 1990, 42 ('federates'); 1993, 270–2 (usually '*bucellarii*' but occasionally 'federates'); Stickler 2002, 55–6, 88–9, 106–14 ('Auxilien').

distinctions between state-salaried soldier and personal retainer, or 'army' and 'retinue'. This phenomenon, however, was fluctuating and opportunistic rather than progressive and unilinear. Stilicho's close, but brief, association with certain *foederati* could not prevent his eclipse in 408, but did ensure that they and their families shared his downfall.[137] Correspondingly, as Aëtius' deployment of Huns is last attested in 439, it seems that, for whatever reason, this source of manpower was no longer available.[138]

On a smaller scale and more intimate level, a further extension of the personalisation of recruitment is discernible in a proliferation of armed retainers or bodyguards, employed primarily by senior military officers, but also civilian officials and magnates (though neither category is attested in Italy).[139] While Roman sources variously label such attendants, modern scholarship prefers the term *buc(c)ellarii*, commonly understood as 'hardtack-men' or 'biscuit-men', a derisive coinage purportedly referring to their receipt of army field rations without regular military status, though the derivation harbours uncertainties. Rarely attested in the fifth century, this term subsequently became a prevailing semi-technical designation.[140] While the phenomenon is traceable to the 380s, this terminology clearly emerges during Honorius' reign, when non-Roman warriors were already prominent, if not predominant, in these roles.[141] As fifth-century evidence is meagre, most of what is known or believed about *buccellarii* relates to the sixth-century eastern empire, though the broader applicability of this documentation is assumed rather than demonstrable. Privately recruited and, at least in the first instance, paid and maintained by their commander-employer, *buccellarii* apparently received state 'rations' (*annonae*) and state-manufactured equipment. Even if their employer was thus more the conduit than the source of their remuneration, personal interaction fostered patron–client relationships.[142] While some, especially older scholarship perceives *buccellarii* as an intrinsic threat to state governance, fifth-century prohibitive legislation – none of which relates to Italy – addressed unauthorised, particularly civilian-employed retinues, rather than the practice itself. On

---

[137] See above, p. 163–3.
[138] It is uncertain whether the Huns in Aëtius' service in Gaul in c.435–9 reflect initial *amicitia* with Attila (r. 434–53) or, on the contrary, comprised renegade groups displaced by Attila's ascendancy: see Stickler 2002, 111–14.
[139] Diesner 1972; Liebeschuetz 1990, 43–7; Schmitt 1994; Whitby 1995, 116–19; Sarris 2006, 162–75; Wijnendaele 2018b, 271–4.
[140] Olymp. fr. 12 derives *buccellarius* from a mocking reference to *buccellatum*, 'hardtack' issued as field rations; if correct, '*buccellatarius*' would be expected. Later Byzantine sources disagree regarding the terminological morphology and significance; see Schmitt 1994, 149–52, 158 (derivation from *buccellum/ buccella*, a variety of bread); Sarris 2006, 163, 170–1. Alternative designations in fifth-century contexts: e.g. August. *Ep.* 220.6 (*homines armati*); Prosper, *Chron.* 1375 (*amici, armigeri*); Hyd. 154(162) (*familiares*); Zos. 5.11.5 (*doryphoroi*), 34.1 (*prosedeuontes*); Marcell. Com. s.a. 455.1 (*satellites*); Cassiod. *Chron.* 1262 (*amici*).
[141] Olymp. fr. 7.4: *buccellarii* both Romans and Goths 'in the time of Honorius'. See Zos. 5.11.5: Stilicho's guards in 398; 5.34.1, 3–4: Stilicho's Hunnic retainers and other attendant 'barbarians' in 408. A prior occurrence of the term *buccellarii* in regimental titulature at *Not. Dign. or.* 7.25 has not been satisfactorily explained.
[142] Schmitt 1994, 152–66; Whitby 1995, 117–18. With differing emphasis, Lenski 2009, 158–66 argues for the semi-dependent status of *buccellarii*.

the contrary, imperial authority arguably benefited from and relied on an officially sanctioned reservoir of privately organised or 'subcontracted' manpower.[143] Such retinues afforded commanders or freelance military entrepreneurs some independence of action but were typically far too small to ensure lasting influence without wider support or resources. An extreme case is the maverick Gothic nobleman Sarus, recruited by Stilicho in 405/6.[144] As the *magister*'s authority crumbled in 408, Sarus ostentatiously broke with Stilicho, slaughtering his guards and seizing his baggage.[145] During the ensuing turmoil, being both estranged from Honorius and hostile to Alaric, Sarus remained unaligned for over a year, as he and his 200–300 retainers sustained themselves in Picenum. Rejoining Honorius' forces at Ravenna in 410, he frustrated peace negotiations by leading his retinue against Alaric's army.[146] Again falling out with Honorius in 412, Sarus quit Italy, reportedly accompanied by just twenty-eight retainers, to seek his fortune – and find a heroic death – in Gaul.[147]

In Italy, *buccellarii* become more visible in the decade following the death of Constantius III in 421, when Castinus, Felix, Aëtius and Boniface intermittently contended for high command.[148] In 422/3, Ravenna witnessed street fighting between Galla Placidia's barbarian retainers, acquired through successive marriages to Athaulf and Constantius, and supporters of Honorius (or, in fact, Castinus).[149] It is often inferred, on circumstantial grounds, that the engagement between Boniface and Aëtius near Rimini in 432 primarily or exclusively involved large personal retinues, operating, it would seem, in a parallel dimension to official army structures.[150] It is further conjectured that Boniface previously acquired *buccellarii* through marriage to his second wife Pelagia, daughter of a Gothic nobleman, in c.422; if so, this would reinforce the impression of armed 'muscle' as a common currency of military aristocrats, with implications for the widowed Pelagia's post-432 remarriage to Aëtius.[151] Some of Boniface's retainers in turn probably passed to his son-in-law Sebastianus.[152] During

---

[143] Schmitt 1994, esp. 155–6, 168–71; Whitby 1995, 116–18. Legislation: see below, p. 188–9.

[144] *PLRE* 2.978–9; Wijnendaele 2019. Recruitment: Oros. 7.37.12 (> Marcell. Com. s.a. 406.3 > Jord. *Rom.* 321). Varying opinions on Sarus' prior history: Jones 1964, 186, 200; Liebeschuetz 1990, 38–9; Wijnendaele 2016a, 274–5, 278–80. The broader phenomenon of 'independent military contractors': Mathisen 2019, 146–8.

[145] Zos. 5.30.3, 34.1.

[146] Olymp. fr. 6; Sozom. 9.9.3; Philost. *Hist. eccl.* 12.3; Zos. 5.36.2–3, 6.13.2, with Wijnendaele 2019, 279–84.

[147] Olymp. fr. 18; Sozom. 9.15.3.

[148] Stickler 2002, 26–58; Wijnendaele 2015, 43–74, 96–103; 2017b.

[149] Olymp. fr. 38, with Stickler 2002, 26–8; Wijnendaele 2015, 55.

[150] Evidence for Boniface's armed following is extremely slim and imprecise: August. *Ep.* 220.6 (427). Successive studies infer *buccellarii*: e.g. Diesner 1972, 338–41; Liebeschuetz 1993, 269–71; Elton 1996, 212; Wijnendaele 2015, 100–8. See more circumspect remarks by Schmitt 1994, 161–2. Scharf 2001, 31–2 identifies Boniface's forces as primarily *foederati* under his command in Africa, as documented at August. *Ep.* 220.7; compare 185.1.1 (417) (*Gothi*); Possid. *V. Aug.* 28.12; Olymp. fr. 40. The proposal of Ibba 2016, 530–4, 543 that Boniface's *foederati* were local Mauri further complicates this picture.

[151] *PLRE* 2.224–5, 'Beremud'; 856–7, 'Pelagia 1'; 1155, 'Verimodus', with Diesner 1972, 339–42; Liebeschuetz 1990, 43; Gil Egea 2003, 496–503; Wijnendaele 2015, 48–53, 107.

[152] Hyd. 89(99); *Suda* θ 145 = Priscus fr. [4], with Diesner 1972, 336, 341–3; Wijnendaele 2015, 105–8; alternatively Scharf 2001, 32.

his two-decade ascendancy, Aëtius maintained a significant personal retinue, though it remains hard to quantify or categorise. It is glimpsed after his murder in 454, when Valentinian III sought to integrate the general's following into elite regular units (*palatini*). While Valentinian deemed it expedient to recall from retirement Majorian, a former subordinate of Aëtius, to facilitate this transition, the very notion that Aëtius' murderer could thus reassign his retainers arguably delimits their number, loyalty and corporate identity.[153] Whatever the wider success of this scheme, the two former *buccellarii* of Aëtius who slew Valentinian in 455 had already entered that emperor's personal service; the assassins' motive was less vengeance for a late employer than opportunities offered by a change of regime.[154] Similarly, shifts of allegiance motivated by money signal underlying pecuniary motives (even if modern scholars assiduously avoid the term 'mercenary'): in 461/2 Ricimer neutralised a force that Marcellinus commanded on Sicily by enticing 'his Scythian attendants', who formed the majority, to enter his own service with higher pay.[155]

Transformation of Armed Forces in Italy from the 420s to 470s

The large, mostly elite Italian field army listed in the *Notitia* is not easily located in near-contemporary events. Where was it – and what was it doing – during John's usurpation (423–5), when John so lacked troops that he sought Hunnic assistance?[156] Some commanders in Italy, notably Castinus, supported or acquiesced in John's rule, though a reported conspiracy by dismissed generals signals disaffection.[157] If in fact Aëtius and Boniface contested north-central Italy with massed *buccellarii* in winter 432/3, this army presumably stayed in winter quarters.[158] But it is also absent in the aftermath: fleeing to the Huns in Pannonia, Aëtius returned to Italy in 433 with Hunnic troops and secured his reinstatement, while the imperial government requested military assistance from the Goths settled in Aquitaine, apparently in vain.[159] If there was a large, regular army in Italy in the 420s–30s, it was remarkably inert or apolitical.

It is likewise difficult to discern Italian *comitatenses/palatini* in military operations during Valentinian III's reign. The Ravennate government dispatched troops to subjugate Africa in 427–8, but, excepting a contingent of 'Goths', their number, character

---

[153] Sid. Apoll. *Carm.* 5.306–8; *PLRE* 2.702–3, 'Maiorianus'.
[154] Prosper, *Chron.* 1375; Priscus fr. [30.1] (= Joh. Ant. fr. 294.1 Roberto/224.3–4 Mariev). See Diesner 1972, 345–7; Schmitt 1994, 156, 160, 170; Stickler 2002, 81–2.
[155] Priscus fr. 38.1, with *PLRE* 2.709, 'Marcellinus 6'; Kulikowski 2002a, 177–8, 185; MacGeorge 2002, 46–8. See generally Wijnendaele 2018a, 438–40 on the 'economy of violence'.
[156] Hunnic assistance: above, p. 170. Some Italian *comitatenses* may have been engaged in operations to secure Africa in 424/5: Prosper, *Chron.* 1286; *Chron. Gall. 452* 96, 98, with Stickler 2002, 31–2; Wijnendaele 2015, 62–4.
[157] Castinus, probably *magister militum praesentalis*: Prosper, *Chron.* 1282, 1288, with *PLRE* 2.269–70, 'Castinus 2'; Wijnendaele 2015, 67–8. Dismissed generals: Olymp. fr. 43[2] (= Philost. *Hist. eccl.* 12.13).
[158] The fighting occurred during the especially harsh winter of 432/3: *Chron. Gall. 452* 110.
[159] Prosper, *Chron.* 1310; *Chron. Gall. 452* 112–13, 115; *Chron. Gall. 511* 587–8; see Stickler 2002, 55–6, 88, 106–9.

and provenance remain conjectural.[160] Another unspecified task force 'from Rome' joined an eastern Roman expedition against the Vandals in 431.[161] More optimistically, units of Italian *palatini* have been detected in a fragmentary inscription in Raetia, conjecturally associated with Aëtius' campaign against Iuthungi in 430.[162] Similarly, with varying degrees of confidence, personnel of three units listed *intra Italiam* in the *Notitia* may be documented epigraphically at Salona in Dalmatia, in at least one case postdating that document's latest redaction.[163] Accordingly, during the later 420s and 430s, units/detachments of the field army potentially served in or were transferred to Africa, Raetia-Noricum or Dalmatia. In response to early Vandalic raids, Valentinian's *novellae* of 440–4 sought to exact recruits rather than money from estates in Suburbicaria, an extraordinary measure resisted by landowners and ultimately unenforceable owing to insufficient revenue.[164] In 440, some regular soldiers and *foederati* were redeployed to coastal localities in Suburbicaria. Contemporaneous innovations in military-fiscal bureaucracy may indicate a preponderance of barbarian *foederati*.[165] An epic-verse account of imperial forces intercepting a Vandalic-Moorish raiding party in Campania around mid-458 may exemplify new dispositions or tactics, but its accuracy and typicality are uncertain.[166] Also in 440, a relaxation of ancient legal prohibitions on private citizens bearing arms acknowledged the inadequacy of military resources.[167] Although authorities in Italia had previously armed civilians during emergencies, this measure

---

[160] Evidence and literature in Wijnendaele 2015, 69–86. Goths: Possid. *V. Aug.* 17.7, 18.12.

[161] Proc. *Bell.* 3.3.35, with *PLRE* 2.166.

[162] *AE* 1994, 1326 (Augsburg), with Scharf 1994, identifying *Pannoniciani seniores*, an Italy-based *legio palatina* (*Not. Dign. occ.* 5.6 = 149 = 7.7), and *Anglevarii/Angrivarii*, an *auxilium palatinum* previously stationed in the East (*Not. Dign. or.* 5.18 = 59) but, in Scharf's view, recently (post-425) transferred to Italy. The presence of the *Angrivarii* in the western empire is supported by *ILJug* 2164 = Marin et al. 2010, 720–1, no. 400 (Salona), but context and chronology remain uncertain.

[163] The evidence relates to one *vexillatio palatina* and two *auxilia palatina*. *CIL* 3.14704 = Marin et al. 2010, 313–14, no. 97 (431–70 AD): [e]*x vexill*[*atio*]/*n*(*e*) *equi*[*t*(*um*) *Va*]/[*len*]*tin*[*ianen*(*sium*)] (compare *Not. Dign. occ.* 6.10 = 52 = 7.165: *equites constantes Valentinianenses*); *CIL* 3.9539 = *ILJug* 2498 = Marin et al. 2010, 593–5, no. 287 (400–500 AD): *Maurorum i*[*un*(*iorum*)] (compare *Not. Dign. occ.* 5.55 = 204 = 7.26: *Mauri Honoriani iuniores*); *CIL* 3.9538 (add. p. 2139) = *ILCV* 0543 = Marin et al. 2010, 849–50, no. 478 (350–500 AD): *de numero Ata*[*cottorum*] (compare *Not. Dign. occ.* 5.51 = 200 = 7.24: *Atecotti Honoriani iuniores*). See Janniard 2010.

[164] Conscription: *N. Val.* 6.1 (20 March 440), 6.2 (25 May 443). Exemptions: *N. Val.* 5.1.2, 4 (3 March 440). Supplemental commuted recruiting levies: *N. Val.* 6.3 (14 July 444). See below, p. 181–2. In addition to the new Vandal threat (explicitly mentioned *N. Val.* 9.1 (24 June 440)), this legislation also coincides with the curtailing of Aëtius' access to Hunnic manpower by 439: Jones 1964, 201.

[165] *N. Val.* 9.1 (24 June 440): *milites* and *foederati*, with Scharf 2001, 32–4. The provisioning of unprecedented coastal garrisons of *foederati* in Suburbicaria has been connected with the *fiscus barbaricus*, an obscure treasury department uniquely attested in 443/4 in *P. Ital.* 1 (Tjäder), lines 61–2 (445/6), which records a quantity of wheat and barley paid by a Sicilian estate into this 'barbarian account', but the exiguous evidence allows multiple interpretations. See recently Savino 2017, with bibliography.

[166] Sid. Apoll. *Carm.* 5.385–440; compare semi-legendary Greg. Mag. *Dialog.* 3.1; Paul. Diac. *Hist. Rom.* 14.17–18. See Priscus fr. 39.1 for a later perception of Vandals targeting ungarrisoned settlements.

[167] *N. Val.* 9.1 (440). This enactment was reiterated, emended or rescinded by *N. Maj.* 8 (458–9), of which only the title survives.

inspired local self-defensive initiatives – Cassiodorus later boasted that his grandfather had thus 'freed Brutti and Sicily from Vandalic incursions by armed resistance'.[168]

In some respects, the dearth of evidence for the conscription or deployment of *comitatenses/palatini* after the mid-440s, compared to the high profile of non-Roman contingents, is consistent with the long-term evolution and documentation of late Roman armies.[169] In Italy, this evidential pattern may suggest that, if not formally disbanded, *comitatenses/palatini* ceased to play decisive or offensive roles, while *foederati* and/or *buccellarii* became the dynamic elements of imperial armed forces, and even the primary means of sustaining military action, and thereby achieved political preponderance by the mid-470s. Military initiatives therefore relied mainly on diverse and extraneous barbarian troops. In 451, to confront Attila in Gaul, Aëtius reportedly crossed the Alps with 'a meagre force of *auxilia* without [regular] soldiers'.[170] During 458, Majorian began preparations to reconquer Africa by assembling large forces in north-western Italy, primarily drawing on transdanubian manpower released by the disintegration of Hunnic hegemony, which he transferred to Gaul and augmented with regional *foederati*.[171] Similarly, the troops Marcellinus then commanded in Sicily (c.458–60 to 461/2), whatever their status, were mostly 'Scythians', presumably Huns or Goths.[172] At the same time, however, an institutional 'army' is dimly discernible in successive power struggles within Italy. Becoming emperor in mid-455 with the support of the Aquitanian Goths, Avitus initially retained a Gothic contingent in Rome. Nevertheless, although ensuing events are disputed, the defeat of Avitus' 'allies' at Placentia in autumn 456 was clearly a victory for Italy-based forces led by Majorian, *comes domesticorum*, and Ricimer, *magister militum*.[173] Subsequently, although Majorian undertook ambitious transregional operations with barbarian expeditionary forces, once he 'dismissed his allies [or *foederati*] after his return' in 461, again Ricimer's executive control of troops in Italy ensured Majorian's deposition.[174]

Thereafter, Ricimer's lengthy tenure as *magister utriusque militiae et patricius* (457–72), combining command of a field army, regional defensive priorities and power-political

---

[168] Cassiod. *Var.* 1.4.14; *PLRE* 2.263–4, 'Cassiodorus 1'. Previous arming of civilians in the Italian diocese: e.g. Zos. 1.37.2 (259/60); 2.43.3 (350); *AE* 1993, 1231 (Augsburg 260–2). Temporary enlistment of civilians: *CTh* 7.13.17 (19 April 406).

[169] See above, p. 158–9 and 167.

[170] Sid. Apoll. *Carm.* 7.328–9. Scholarship generally discounts a report of Hyd. 146(154) that Aëtius counterattacked Attila's disease-stricken and starving forces in Italy in 452 'with *auxilia* sent by the emperor Marcian': see Linn 2019, 328 for varying opinions.

[171] Sid. Apoll. *Carm.* 5.363–5, 470–512; Priscus fr. 36.2 (= Joh. Ant. fr. 295 Roberto/226 Mariev); Proc. *Bell.* 3.7.4, 11. See Anders 2010, 143–9, 263–4, 266–7; Janniard 2020, 251–3.

[172] Priscus fr. 38.1; see above, p. 173. It is usually assumed that Marcellinus himself brought these 'Scythians' from Pannonia via Dalmatia to Sicily, but they may have been allocated to him by Majorian from the barbarian troops he had amassed in northern Italy.

[173] Goths: Sid. Apoll. *Carm.* 7.519–21; Hyd. 176(183); Priscus fr. [32] (= Joh. Ant. fr. 294 Roberto/225 Mariev), with numismatic evidence in Burgess 1987, 335 n. 5. Of the several, partly conflicting sources, only *Auct. Prosp. Havn.* s.a. 456.2 provides details of a battle, in which Ricimer 'with a great number of the army' overcame Avitus 'with a force of allies (*sociorum*)'. Chronological and historical complexities are discussed in Burgess 1987; MacGeorge 2002, 188–96; Anders 2010, 95–109, 266, 272.

[174] Priscus fr. 36.2 (= Joh. Ant. fr. 295 Roberto/226 Mariev). See MacGeorge 2002, 209–13; Anders 2010, 143–55.

self-interest, became one facet of a broader picture of territorialised 'warlordism' across the late/post-Roman West.[175] Explicit references to the army in Italy are rare and permit only cautious inferences about its size, character and factional affiliations. For much of the 460s, it seems that Ricimer's high-profile dominance, if not monopoly, of military authority and revenues, along with his kinship and marriage links to paramount barbarian lineages, attracted diverse warrior bands and individuals to Italy and into 'imperial'/his service, increasingly conflating state institution and patronal retinue.[176] Yet an evolving power struggle with the eastern imperial appointee Anthemius (467–72) exposed constraints to Ricimer's ascendancy, as substantial eastern forces accompanied Anthemius to Rome in 467.[177] These troops, at least initially, afforded Anthemius greater autonomy than puppet rulers typical of this era, though the duration of their deployment in Italy is uncertain.[178] In 470, when friction with Anthemius induced Ricimer to quit Rome for Milan, he 'summoned 6,000 men under his command for the war against the Vandals'.[179] Whether this rare but ambiguous numerical report refers to his entire forces or only those assigned to specific operations, Ricimer's withdrawal to the militarised sector of north-eastern Italy and the following stand-off suggest that he lacked decisive advantage.[180] The dispatch of a substantial part of Anthemius' troops under his son Anthemiolus to Gaul in 471, whether motivated by overconfidence or desperation, occasioned their defeat by the Goths near Arles and unbalanced the military-political contest in Italy.[181] With renewed hostilities in 472, Ricimer invested Rome with 'the multitude of his own barbarians', phraseology suggestive of personalised service, presumably *foederati* and *buccellarii*.[182] Although the siege

---

[175] O'Flynn 1983, 104–30; MacGeorge 2002, 173–268; Anders 2010, 264–9, 272–4. 'Warlordism': Wijnendaele 2016b; 2017a.

[176] Anders 2010, esp. 134–42, 269–79.

[177] Sid. Apoll. *Carm.* 2.540–1; Hyd. 230(234), with *PLRE* 2.96–8 for Anthemius' prior military career. See Henning 1999, 226–8, 237; MacGeorge 2002, 51–4, 234–5; Anders 2010, 196–8; Roberto 2013, 249–51; Janniard 2020, 244.

[178] In the absence of evidence, opinions differ widely regarding Anthemius' eastern forces after the collapse of the grand offensive against the Vandals in 468: e.g. Gillet 1999, 33–4: substantial eastern troops remained with Anthemius in Italy; Anders 2010, 208–9, 216–17, 265 n. 955, 269, 277, 434: (inconsistently) most or all eastern units withdrew leaving Anthemius with little or no military capability; Janniard 2020, 233–4, 238–9: all eastern forces withdrew, but by then somehow Anthemius – and not Ricimer – controlled the Italian field army or a significant part thereof. A letter of Sidonius (*Epist.* 2.1.4), stating that Anthemius has no military resources in Italy, is insecurely dated: Anders 2010, 209 locates the text to early 470, when this statement would be demonstrably untrue; Gillet 1999, 28, with further bibliography, argues for 472.

[179] Priscus fr. [62] (= Joh. Ant. fr. 299 Roberto/230 Mariev). The wording of the Greek text implies forces currently assigned to operations against the Vandals rather than a retrospective reference to previous Roman–Vandal conflicts.

[180] MacGeorge 2002, 245–53; Anders 2010, 279–82.

[181] *Chron. Gall. 511* 649; *PLRE* 2.93, 'Anthemiolus', with Anders 2010, 223–4; Janniard 2020, 237–8. Gallic military contexts: Gillet 1999, 33–5; Janniard 2020, 233–7.

[182] Priscus fr. [64.1] (= Joh. Ant. fr. 301 Roberto/232 Mariev); this text also refers to Ricimer's army as simply 'the barbarians'. See also John Malalas 14.45 (298.82–4 Thurn): 'a Gothic force'. See Schmitt 1994, 162; also Anders 2010, 134–42, 260–1, 271–2 for conjecture on Ricimer's wealth and personal following.

endured at least five months, with both sides summoning from Gaul reinforcements of indeterminate size and character, Ricimer seemingly controlled the only regional forces.[183]

Following Ricimer's death in August 472, his patrician title and military office passed to his nephew Gundobad, a Burgundian prince and former *magister militum per Gallias*, a quasi-hereditary transfer that accentuates the personal nature of command. The extent of Gundobad's authority and the continuing integrity of Ricimer's army are uncertain: Gundobad soon departed (473/4) to pursue kingship in Gaul, while eastern Roman forces sent to install Julius Nepos in 474 reportedly encountered no opposition.[184] By 474/5, the western court seemingly relied on contingents of smaller, predominantly East Germanic-speaking peoples or kin groups: Sciri, Heruli, Rug(i)i/Rogi and T(h)orcilingi, all former Hunnic subjects, who had recently arrived in Italy during the 460s or early 470s following displacement from the middle Danube.[185] It is thus less remarkable that the two foremost military figures in Italy in the mid-470s, Orestes, *patricius et magister militum* (475–6), and Odoacer, originated from Attila's inner circle.[186] The prominent role played by these ethnically defined troops in military unrest in 476 presumably reflects their prevailing influence over – and perhaps numerical preponderance within – the army. They seemingly discovered collective strength and opportunity under Odoacer, and it was a dispute over their remuneration and/or maintenance in 476 that occasioned the extinction of the western imperial office.[187]

Even allowing for the higher visibility of barbarian 'irregulars' in historical sources, 'regular' units cannot be securely distinguished after the 440s – irrespective of likely modes of recruitment or whether their personnel can be considered 'Roman', 'barbarian' or 'Italo-barbarian' – again, the issue is institutional, not ethno-cultural. It seems that 'federates', as both a tactical strike force and a foundation of senior officers' personal authority, absorbed fiscal and demographic resources, even if distinctions between 'regular' and 'irregular' soldiers diminished. Potential for subliminal continuity, however, is evidenced at the extremes of regimental precedence and professional environment within Italia. The attenuated survival of *limitanei* in neighbouring Noricum Ripense into the late 470s opens the possibility of a similar development

---

[183] Anthemius summoned Bilimer: Paul. Diac. *Hist. Rom.* 15.4, with *PLRE* 2.230. Ricimer summoned Gundobad: Priscus fr. [64.1] (= Joh. Ant. fr. 301 Roberto/232.1 Mariev); *Chron. Gall. 511* 650; John Malalas 14.45 (298.88–92 Thurn), with *PLRE* 2.525–5. See MacGeorge 2002, 178–9, 242, 269; Anders 2010, 224–6, 267–8, 278–9; Janniard 2020, 239, 245, 251.

[184] Priscus fr. [64.1] (= Joh. Ant. fr. 301 Roberto/232.2 Mariev); *PLRE* 2.524–5, 'Gundobadus 2'; 777–8, 'Nepos 3'. Varying views on Gundobad's military authority in Italy: O'Flynn 1983, 129–31; MacGeorge 2002, 178–9, 242, 269–75; Anders 2010, 240–1; Janniard 2020, 251.

[185] *Anon. Vales.* 37–8; *Auct. Prosp. Havn. ordo prior* and *post. marg.* s.a. 476.2; Jord. *Get.* 242, 291; *Rom.* 344; Proc. *Bell.* 5.1.3–8; Paul. Diac. *Hist. Rom.* 15.8–9. See MacGeorge 2002, 281–93; Porena 2012a, 255–62; Bjornlie 2014, 165–7; Janniard 2020, 253–4.

[186] *PLRE* 2.791–3, 'Odovacer'; 811–2, 'Orestes 2'; MacGeorge 2002, 276–93; Kim 2013, 96–105, 127–31 (with some caution); Janniard 2020, 252–4.

[187] See below, p. 184.

in Raetia.[188] Correspondingly, certain ceremonial corps, notably *scholae palatinae* and *protectores domestici*, persisted to at least 493. Thereafter, although questions remain unresolved, it seems that Theoderic effectively disbanded these corps or transformed placements into sinecures, granting their last or notional members honorific titles and pensions that were transmissible to their offspring. This titular residue of imperial armed forces in Italy persisted until Justinian's fiscal administration abolished these heritable pensionary payments in 540–1.[189]

Fiscal and Economic Impact

Diocletian's military-fiscal reforms recast relationships between Italian rural society and the army. Italy became subject to two regular property-based impositions: first, payment of *annona militaris*, typically foodstuffs, annually precalculated to meet soldiers' requirements; second, conscription (*praebitio tironum*), whereby landowners, individually or in consortia, provided recruits, usually from their tenantry. With progressive monetisation of the agrarian economy and increasing commutation (*adaeratio*) of state revenues and expenditure from in-kind to in-coin payments, levies of *annona* and *tirones* were gradually converted to monetary equivalents.

For much of the fourth century, *annona militaris* was collected in kind by provincial officials, who formed the link between landowners/-holders and the army's logistical staff, and then disbursed to soldiers as 'rations' (*annonae*) and fodder (*capitus*).[190] In Italy, the few troops stationed in the northern plain and its subalpine periphery between c.313–17 and c.370 were local consumers, while the transalpine administrative construct of Italia Annonaria channelled the agrarian wealth of the Po valley to less productive

---

[188] Eugipp. *Vit. Sev.* 4.1–4 (a *tribunus* commanding 'a very few' ill-equipped soldiers at Favianis/Mautern an der Donau), 20.1 (a *numerus* at Batavis/Passau-Altstadt); compare 22.4. In addition, a *dux Raetiarum* is recorded in the Ostrogothic kingdom; see Cassiod. *Var.* 1.11 (507–11); 7.4, with *PLRE* 3A.997, 'Servatus 2'. It remains uncertain whether and to what extent this apparent titular continuity signals the persistence of late Roman defensive arrangements; see Cecconi 2007, with older bibliography.

[189] Proc. *Anec.* 26.27–9. See Stein 1949–1959, 2.565; Jones 1964, 256 n. 45; Frank 1969, 193–4; Vitiello 2004, 98–106. In contrast, Halsall 2016, 186, 188 construes honorific titulature under Ostrogothic rule as evidence of institutional continuity. The sole apparent reference to *scholares* in sources of the Ostrogothic period is a *sextus scholari(u)s* in Cassiod. *Var.* 11.26 (c.533–8). Bjornlie 2019, 452 conceives this 'sixth scholarian' as an honorary 'position among the palace guardsmen', specifically in 'the sixth cohort of *scholarii*'. In fact, *scholares* were not cohortal and only five *scholae palatinae* are ever attested in Italy (*Not. Dign. occ.* 9.4–8). The designation *sextus scholarius* is otherwise identified as an unrelated clerical grade in the *officium* of the praetorian prefecture, to which this section of the *Variae* (11.17–32) is devoted: Stein 1922, 32–8; *PLRE* 3A.758, 'Iustus 1' (excluded from *scholarii* at 3B.1520). In addition, Bjornlie 2016, 50, 53–4, observing that the *Variae* refer to *domestici* mostly 'in strictly honorary terms', correctly identifies one instance of *domestici* with real administrative functions assigned to the staff of provincial *comites* at *Var.* 9.13 (c.526/7); these Bjornlie assumes to be necessarily members of the palatine corps of (*protectores*) *domestici*. However, the term *domesticus* is widely used in late Roman military and civilian bureaucracy to designate diverse officials functioning as senior staff officers and personal assistants, including in provincial *officia*: Jones 1964, 598, 602–3; Schmitt 1994, 154; Rance 2007, 400; and specifically on *Var.* 9.13: Gračanin 2016, 232–3, 247–8, citing older bibliography.

[190] On *annona* see Chapter 9 in this volume.

limital provinces.[191] Geostrategic centrality and agricultural productivity made northern Italy a well-provisioned artery and logistical base for simultaneous or sequential operations on the Rhine and Danube.[192] From the mid-390s, the Po emerges as a likely conduit for provisioning *comitatenses/palatini* and *foederati* billeted in cities along its basin, including Pavia, Piacenza, Cremona, Mantua, Verona and Bologna.[193] Commutation occurred faster and more comprehensively in the western empire, where *scholae, palatini* and *comitatenses* were entitled to receive *annonae* in coin by 396. In the East, in contrast, *comitatenses* ordinarily drew *annonae* in kind into the sixth century. The differential pace and scope of commutation may reflect the readiness of western governments to concede – or inability to refuse – soldiers' preferences for cash payments. As commutation of land tax in Italy became universal by 458, whenever the praetorian prefecture required foodstuffs for the army, it resorted to *coemptio* or compulsory purchase. Although, in essence, an accounting mechanism whereby the value of requisitioned produce was deducted from a current or future tax liability, the procedure could variously disadvantage food-producers through below-market price fixing, disproportionate or unseasonal demands, and haulage costs. Previously an exceptional expedient, *coemptiones* became a routine method of military provisioning into the Ostrogothic period.[194]

Particular characteristics of Italian society shaped the socio-economic impact of recruitment. Certain recruiting methods are barely traceable. Some voluntary enlistment is presumed.[195] Sons of soldiers and veterans were hereditarily obliged to serve, if physically able. Legislation enforces this requirement even in the Suburbicarian provinces, which otherwise enjoyed a privileged status with respect to regular conscription (see below).[196] This category of recruit is sparsely recorded and unquantifiable; it traditionally includes St Martin, an officer's son raised at Pavia. The legal hereditary obligation seemingly lapsed during the fifth century.[197] The primary mode of recruitment was annual selective conscription or *praebitio tironum*, though its effects on rural populations are difficult to gauge.[198] By the mid-fourth century, privileged landed interests and monetisation of the economy combined to turn *praebitio* into a

---

[191] Difficulties of provisioning in Raetia: e.g. *CTh* 11.16.15 (382), 18 (390), 19.4 (398); August. *De civ. D.* 18.18.10.

[192] See Chapter 2 in this volume. See Vannesse 2010a, 159–86 on the evidence of milestones across northern Italy.

[193] Henning 1999, 54–5; MacGeorge 2002, 168–9, 176; Anders 2010, 279–82.

[194] Jones 1964, 207–8, 460–1, 629–30; Banaji 2001, 51–60; Tedesco 2016, 143–8.

[195] Jones 1964, 617. Italy-specific legislation: *CTh* 7.2.2 (10 July 385) on verifying the status of volunteers.

[196] *CTh* 7.22.1 (319): to *corrector Lucaniae et Bruttiorum*; reiterated 7.13.4 (367): to *vicarius urbis Romae*, and thus applicable to Suburbicaria. *CTh* 7.13.3 (367), concerning the height of unspecified recruits, is excerpted from the same law as 7.13.4; compare the same issue explicitly relating to veterans' sons in *CTh* 7.22.8 (372).

[197] St Martin: Sulp. Sev. *Vit. Mart.* 2. The latest extant laws referring to obligatory enlistment of veterans' sons are *CTh* 7.20.12.pr. (30 January 400) and 7.18.10 (17 May 400), both issued in Milan and addressed to Stilicho. For veterans in Italy see below, p. 182–3.

[198] Jones 1964, 614–19; Brunt 1974, 114–15; Brandt 1988, 69–78; Elton 1996, 128–54; Nicasie 1998, 83–96; Zuckerman 1998a; Carrié 2004; Lee 2007, 79–85. Comparative historical perspectives: Whitby 1995, 63–8.

'recruiting tax', whereby landowners could retain agricultural labour by paying a sum (*aurum tironicum*) in lieu of each recruit. Governmental authorities increasingly preferred commutation as a means of financing voluntary enlistment, whether of Roman citizens or non-Roman warriors from peripheral cultures.[199] Indeed, panegyrists praise the avoidance of recruiting levies in Italy.[200] Furthermore, perhaps two-thirds of the Italian diocese did not ordinarily furnish recruits. Properties of current and retired senior civil and military officials and court dignitaries were entirely exempt.[201] Only monetary payments were required of leaseholders of imperial patrimony (*res privata*).[202] More importantly, this privilege was accorded to all properties in the Suburbicarian provinces, where senatorial estates dominated the agrarian economy.[203] Accordingly, although conscription was imposed on Italy from the Tetrarchy, in the central and southern peninsula and islands this was typically a fiscal levy and, overall, a tradition of military participation or martial identity never emerges, at any social level. The record of senior officers native to Italia is correspondingly negligible.[204] Ammianus disparages Italian manhood, claiming that in Italy, but never in Gaul, draft-dodgers, termed *murci* ('clippers'), evaded service through self-mutilation. Early legislative countermeasures indeed concerned hereditary enlistment of veterans' sons in Suburbicaria, though such evasion evidently became a wider phenomenon.[205]

Major troop concentrations in northern Italy from the 390s created a new military-legislative environment. Problems of manpower prompted recurrent legislation (397, 402–3, 406–7).[206] While its content and reiterative urgency reveal systemic vulnerabilities, exceptional countermeasures to unfolding crises potentially belie the longer-term functioning of the system. Scholarship has connected the first spate of laws, June–November 397, with preparations to suppress Gildo's revolt in Africa (397–8), though this legislative sequence may reflect broader strains exacerbated by Stilicho's operations

---

[199] The expression '*aurum tironicum*' is a modern terminological convention unattested in any ancient Latin text. The origin of commutation (*adaeratio*) of recruits is uncertain and disputed. The earliest evidence adduced is Amm. Marc. 19.11.6–7, relating to 359, which implies a well-established practice. See Delmaire 1989, 322–7; Giglio 1990, 84–100; Carrié 2004, 383; *contra* Zuckerman 1998a, who argues for Valens' innovation.

[200] Claud. *BGet.* 400–4, 463–8 (forces raised by Stilicho against Alaric in 401/2), with Cameron 1970, 376–7. Compare Pacatus, *Pan. Lat.* 2(12).32.3 (Theodosius I's campaign preparations in 389).

[201] *CTh* 7.13.15 (6 December 402); 6.27.13 (1 July 403); 7.13.18 (22 March 407); 6.26.14 (15 October 407(412)); 11.18.1 (15 February 409(412)); 6.30.20 (7 June 413); 6.23.2 (9 March 423).

[202] *CTh* 7.13.2 (31 January 370); 11.16.12 (18 March 380); 7.13.12 (17 June 397), 14 (12 November 397).

[203] *CTh* 11.16.12 (18 March 380), concerning *res privata*, but affirming that *suburbicariae partes* are altogether exempt from demands for actual recruits (*exactio tironum*). See similarly 7.13.2 (31 January 370), specifying that liability of *res privata* to conscription depends on whether a property is located in one of two categories of province: 'those provinces in which recruits in person (*corpora*) are demanded' or a province 'in which a money value (*pretia*) is requested'.

[204] See a rare instance in *ILCV* 66, with *PLRE* 2.319–20, 'Constantius 9'; Wijnendaele and Hanaghan 2021.

[205] Amm. Marc. 15.12.3. On *murcus* see Rance 2022, 112–14. Legislation: *CTh* 7.22.1 (319): addressed to *corrector Lucaniae et Bruttiorum*; reiterated 7.13.4 (367): *vicarius urbis Romae*; but see also 7.13.5 (368/370): *praefectus praetorio Galliarum*; 7.13.10 (381): *praefectus praetorio Illyrici*.

[206] Cesa 1993, 204–5; Scharf 1995, 171–5; Vannesse 2010b.

in Greece in 397.²⁰⁷ Three edicts evince the government's intention to exact recruits by suspending exemptions, but influential interest groups evidently resisted and extracted concessions. The first edict temporarily nullifies the immunity of *res privata* from furnishing recruits. The second implies a prior attempt to levy recruits from senatorial estates but, yielding to senators' petitions, concedes an alternative option of commutation. The third effectively rescinds the first by extending commutation to perpetual leaseholders of *res privata*. In parallel, Symmachus' correspondence of 397–8 expresses senatorial anxieties about conscription in Italy and alludes to a deputation from Rome to the emperor in Milan.²⁰⁸ Overall, the reaction of propertied classes indicates both the novelty of conscription and the government's inability to enforce it.²⁰⁹ Later military edicts arising from the invasions of Alaric (401–2) and Ragadaisus (405–6) reflect different stages of crisis response. Of six edicts promulgated in 402–3, following Alaric's withdrawal, four address desertion,²¹⁰ while two concern supplemental levies of commuted recruiting tax imposed upon *honorati* (honorary dignitaries).²¹¹ In contrast, in 406, as hostile forces ravaged Italy, two edicts authorised large-scale enlistment of civilian volunteers and even slaves through drastic expedients;²¹² another reaffirmed measures against desertion and consequent lawlessness.²¹³ While emergency extension of military eligibility to slaves is eye-catching and exudes desperation, collectively the laws regarding deserters specify mundane but meticulous investigative, judicial and penal procedures at provincial level that assume functioning legal-administrative machinery of some complexity.

Subsequent legislation attests enduring senatorial hostility to *praebitio* and increasing governmental difficulties in juggling sources of men and/or money. Alaric's progress through Suburbicaria in 410, hitherto untouched by war, inflicted long-term fiscal-demographic strains on the region's ability – or willingness – to fulfil military-fiscal

---

[207] *CTh* 7.13.12 (17 June 397), 13 (24 September 397), 14 (12 November 397). The first edict in fact predates Gildo's revolt (autumn 397). See nevertheless e.g. Jones 1964, 183–4, 364–5; Matthews 1975, 268–9; Vannesse 2010b, 100–1. One also struggles to connect the exceptional recruiting measures prescribed in these edicts and the rather unremarkable 5,000-strong task force actually dispatched in February/March 398, comprising at least seven elite regiments (or detachments thereof): see above, p. 166.

[208] Symm. *Ep.* 6.58.2, 62, 64.2 (397/8). Opinions differ as to whether Symmachus refers to the extant legislation of 397 (thus Roda 1989 [1993]; Zuckerman 1998a, 104–5; Vannesse 2010b, 100–1) or a subsequent and otherwise unattested recruiting tax on senators' domestic slaves in 398 (Jones 1964, 184, 365, 614; Matthews 1975, 269; Lenski 2009, 152–3). Symm. *Ep.* 6.64.2 mentions commutation at 5 pounds of silver per recruit, which, at recently adjusted rates (*CTh* 13.2.1 (19 February 397)), equates precisely to the 25 solidi per recruit specified in *CTh* 7.13.13 (24 September 397).

[209] Landowners' hostility to conscription generally: e.g. Amm. Marc. 19.11.7; *CTh* 7.13.8 (380); Veg. *Epit.* 1.7.8–9; Symm. *Ep.* 9.10.2 (397?); see Jones 1964, 364–5; Matthews 1975, 268–9, 277; Roda 1989 [1993]; Zuckerman 1998a, 104–5. See also tightening of recruitment procedures and discipline in *CTh* 7.20.12 (30 January 400); 7.18.10 (17 May 400).

[210] *CTh* 7.18.11 (24 February 403); 7.18.12 (25 July 403); 7.18.13 (2 October 403); 7.18.14 (2 October 403).

[211] *CTh* 7.13.15 (6 December 402); 6.27.13 (1 July 403); compare 7.13.18 (22 March 407), referring to previous and future levies. See Jones 1964, 466, 616.

[212] *CTh* 7.13.16 (17 April 406); 7.13.17 (19 April 406): offering cash bounties to citizens who enlist for the duration of the emergency and likewise manumission to slaves, especially those of soldiers, *foederati* and *dediticii*. See Jones 1964, 614; Vannesse 2010b, 103–4; Lenski 2009, 153–4.

[213] *CTh* 7.18.15 (24 March 406).

obligations.[214] Further supplemental recruiting levies upon *honorati* imply the inadequacy and/or irregularity of *praebitio*.[215] When Vandalic raids first afflicted Suburbicaria, entrenched proprietorial interests again emerged. Valentinian III's *novellae* of 440 and 443 imposed on senators and all landowners, specifically in Suburbicarian provinces, an obligatory duty (*munus*) of furnishing recruits. Anticipating their reluctance to relinquish agrarian labour even when under attack, these enactments equate non-compliance or obstruction with harbouring a deserter or 'un-Roman' activity, punishable by severe penalties.[216] A *novella* of 444, however, concedes that the treasury now lacks sufficient revenue to meet projected military expenditure and resorts to another supplemental recruiting levy upon *honorati*, the last recorded.[217] Shortly afterwards, following a remarkable admission of the state's inability to feed and clothe existing soldiers, let alone new recruits, from current tax revenue, a further enactment imposed a 4 per cent universal sales tax (*siliquaticum*) to finance the army.[218] It has been inferred that ultimately, following land grants to his troops from c.476, Odoacer abolished *praebitio*, as a means of courting senatorial support.[219]

Before 476, little evidence for soldiers' owning or holding land relates to Italy. Judicial precedent prohibited soldiers from purchasing land in a province where they currently served, ostensibly because agricultural responsibilities might obstruct military duties, but no legal impediment prevented soldiers from renting local land or acquiring it by non-commercial means (inheritance, marriage, gift), purchasing land in other provinces or possessing land upon enlistment.[220] If valid parallels can be drawn with papyrological documentation from fourth-/fifth-century Egypt, properties of current and former soldiers were individually modest and collectively formed a small proportion of overall landownership.[221] Military landholding was most common among veterans, whose discharge privileges (after 20 or 24 years of service) usually included a tax-exempt arable allotment, typically on neglected or abandoned land (*agri deserti*). Extant legislation last refers to such pensionary land grants in 364, and the practice evidently lapsed between the Theodosian (438) and Justinianic codes (529).[222] The scant legislative evidence for veterans in Italy

---

[214] Tax remissions: *CTh* 11.28.7 (8 May 413); 11.28.12 (15 November 418). See also *CTh* 7.13.20 (8 February 410), imposing a supplemental levy of recruiting tax on *honorati* of specifically Sardinia, Corsica and Sicily, as being unaffected by recent warfare in Italy.

[215] *CTh* 7.13.20 (8 February 410); 11.18.1 (15 February 409(412)); 6.26.14 (15 October 407(412)); 6.30.20 (7 June 413); 6.23.2 (9 March 423); compare 7.13.22 (26 February 428): Africa.

[216] *N. Val.* 6.1 (440), 2 (443).

[217] *N. Val.* 6.3 (444).

[218] *N. Val.* 15 (444); see Jones 1964, 205, 351, 432, 435, 826.

[219] Stein 1949–1959, 1.85, 2.43; Chastagnol 1966, 55–6.

[220] Prohibition on soldiers purchasing land: *Dig.* 49.16.9.pr.–1, 13.pr.–3. Soldiers possessing land is implied or assumed in *CTh* 7.1.3 (349), 20.4.pr. (325). In the eastern empire, soldiers were later forbidden from being primary leaseholders (*conductores*): *CJ* 4.65.31 (458).

[221] Bagnall 1992; Rance 2018, 403–4, 413–14.

[222] *CTh* 7.20.3 (320), 8 (364). Furthermore, *CTh* 7.11 (368) permitted veterans to cultivate additional waste lands, as a grant of usufruct, free from claims by absentee landowners. See Jones 1964, 635–6, 653–4, 813; Rance 2018, 400–1.

predates 400 and, perhaps against expectations, mostly relates to Suburbicaria.[223] Fourth-/fifth-century veteran communities of *comitatenses/palatini* near northern garrison towns are easily conceivable, but the epigraphic record, also largely pre-400, is meagre outside the hinterland of Aquileia, while decreasing visibility of 'regular' troops renders assessment of their socio-economic significance entirely conjectural.[224] *Limitanei* in Raetia may have acquired privileged proprietorial rights to agrarian lands near their forts, as documented for eastern *limitanei* by the 420s, but the relevant legislation is Constantinopolitan in origin and context.[225]

The resettlement of barbarian prisoners of war and surrendered groups, variously termed (*laeti, gentiles, dediticii*) and under varying conditions, connects military service, landholding and the rural economy in Italy.[226] The *Notitia dignitatum* lists fifteen *praefecti Sarmatarum gentilium*, praefectural jurisdictions over colonies of Sarmatians: thirteen in the *territoria* of cities and towns across northern Italy, two at unspecified locations in Apulia et Calabria and Lucania et Brutti.[227] The *Notitia* records in Gaul corresponding settlements of *Sarmatae gentiles* and other barbarians classified as *laeti*, likewise administered by *praefecti*.[228] Scholarship links the colonies in Italy to reportedly vast numbers of Sarmatian men, women and children resettled by Constantine in Italy and Balkan provinces around 334.[229] Such land grants, on *agri deserti*, combined revitalisation of agriculture with provision of recruits.[230] Similarly, Ammianus records that Alamanni captured beyond the Raetian *limes* in 370 were deported to Italy and allocated districts in the Po valley, while Goths and Taifali defeated in Thrace in 377 were assigned to cultivate lands around Modena, Reggio Emilia and Parma. In both cases, Ammianus implies purely agricultural labour, but the possibility of military obligations cannot be excluded.[231] A law of 400, issued in Milan and addressed to Stilicho,

---

[223] Suburbicaria: *CTh* 7.22.1 (319); 9.30.1 (364); 7.13.3–4 (367). A longer enactment preserved in 7.22.2 is of disputed date, but the addressee Severus is more plausibly identified as the *vicarius Italiae* in 318 (*PLRE* 1.836, 'Severus 25'), with jurisdiction over Annonaria, than the *praefectus urbi* of 326 (*PLRE* 1.834, 'Severus 16'); see thus Seeck 1919, 166.

[224] Aquileia: *CIL* 5.1636 = *ILCV* 3349 = *InscrAq* 2925; *CIL* 5.8276 = *InscrAq* 2926. Concordia: explicit *veteranus*: *CIL* 5.8744; *CIL* 5.8751 = *ILCV* 555–6, both *Mattiaci iuniores*; *CIL* 5.8724 = *ILS* 829; *CIL* 5.8749 = *ILS* 432, both unspecified units. See Hoffmann 1969–1970, 1.63, 77–8 (nos 28–9), 80, 110–11. Possible *veterani* by context: *CIL* 5.8755 = *ILCV* 515; *ILCV* 501, both *Leones seniores*. These epitaphs may relate to discharges following Theodosius' victory in 394, from units that were only briefly in Italy. Elsewhere in Italy: *CIL* 6.32984, 32986 (both fourth century; Rome); *CIL* 9.5900 = *ILS* 8250 = *ILCV* 810 (c.400–30; Ancona).

[225] *CTh* 7.15.2 (423): concerning alienation of lands allocated to border forts (*castelli*), issued in Constantinople but in the name of both eastern and western Augusti; *N. Theod.* 24.4 (443): regulating proprietorial rights of *limitanei* to *agri limitanei* in Oriens. See Jones 1964, 649–54, 661–3; Whitby 1995, 111–14. A similar context may apply to *CTh* 2.23.1 (423), addressed to an otherwise unrecorded Crispinus, *comes et magister equitum* (*PLRE* 2.329), in which Honorius apparently extended or affirmed the right of serving soldiers to appropriate vacant public land in perpetuity. Jones 1964 omits this law.

[226] See generally Liebeschuetz 1990, 11–16; Elton 1996, 129–33.

[227] *Not. Dign. occ.* 42.45–63 (with Seeck's apparatus criticus). See Roberto 2022.

[228] *Not. Dign. occ.* 42.33–44 (*laeti*), 64–70 (*Sarmatae gentiles*).

[229] Euseb. *Vit. Const.* 4.6; *Anon. Vales.* 32.

[230] Jones 1964, 620; Cracco Ruggini 1984, 25–6, 31–2, 36–8; Marcone 1994, 249–50; Vannesse 2010c, 68.

[231] Amm. Marc. 28.5.15, 31.9.4. One of the aforementioned Sarmatian settlements, if correctly identified, was also at Reggio Emilia: *Not. Dign. occ.* 42.60, with Seeck 1875, 237–8.

lists *laetus, Alamannus, Sarmata* among several sociodemographic categories subject to conscription into regular units.[232] Other legislation alludes to *laeti* within the praetorian prefecture of Italy and Africa, but their identity and location remain unknown.[233] A *novella* of 465, regulating unlawful unions between *laeti* and *coloni* or slaves, appears again to prioritise landowners' access to labour over potential military manpower.[234] Italian place names have suggested other, possibly fourth-/fifth-century military colonies of Germanic, Alanic and Oghuric groups, but the toponymic evidence, and especially its chronology, remains very insecure.[235]

If these settlements had negligible impact on Italy's demography, they testify to availability and usefulness of land as a means of maintaining soldiers. Such considerations underlay unprecedented events in 476, when diverse barbarian troops who then predominated in – if not entirely comprised – the field army, demanded land grants or, according to the sole, late account, 'the third part' of 'all the lands in Italy'.[236] Whether or not their demand was so formulated or inspired by prior arrangements for settling *foederati* in Gaul, it may essentially reflect the government's inability to remunerate or support soldiers by other means. Although much remains obscure, Odoacer seemingly secured power by implementing a partitive allotment of land (or land-based revenues) in selected districts, primarily in northern Italy, the long-term militarised zone. After 489, Theoderic dispossessed Odoacer's supporters of these properties to reward and/or maintain his own followers. Scholarship has long debated connections with a tripartite fiscal assessment in the Ostrogothic kingdom, though recent studies have exposed its doubtful relevance to soldiers' landholdings.[237]

The industrial impact of the army in Italy is most evident in *fabricae* or arms manufactories, administered by the *magister officiorum*. The *Notitia* records *fabricae* at six northern Italian towns, each, as in other dioceses, specialising in particular armaments: Concordia (arrows), Verona (shields and weaponry), Mantua (armour), Cremona (shields), Pavia (bows) and, just inside Suburbicaria, Lucca (swords).[238] Another at Salona, in western Illyricum, probably supplied the same distributive network.[239]

---

[232] *CTh* 7.20.12.pr. (30.01.400): 'any *laetus*, Alamannus, Sarmatian, vagrant or son of a veteran or anyone of any other group (*corpus*) who is subject to the draft (*dilectus*) and ought to be enrolled in the finest legions (*legiones*)'.

[233] Italy and Africa: *CTh* 13.11.10 (399): 'laetic lands' (*terrae laeticae*); 7.20.12.pr. (400). See previously *CTh* 7.20.10 (369), referring to *praepositi* of *laeti*, addressed to Probus (*PLRE* 1.736–40, 1050, 'Probus 5'), praetorian prefect of Italy, Illyricum and Africa.

[234] *N. Sev.* 2.1 (465), issued in the name of the late Libius Severus, but presumably sanctioned by Ricimer.

[235] E.g. Bachrach 1973, 33–41, 69–71, with some imagination, conjectures Alanic colonies across northern Italy; his arguments are rehearsed by MacGeorge 2002, 231; Anders 2010, 162, 260. See further Mastrelli 1978, 35–7; Restelli 1984.

[236] Proc. *Bell.* 5.1.3–8, 28. On the barbarian groups reported see above, p. 177.

[237] The bibliography is extensive; see selectively Porena 2012a; 2012b; Bjornlie 2014, 160–7; more recently Bjornlie 2016, 49–54; Halsall 2016, 176–83 (largely reviewing older debates).

[238] *Not. Dign. occ.* 9.24–9. See Jones 1964, 578–9, 834–7; James 1988; Christie 2006, 309–14; Rocco 2012, 209–17.

[239] *Not. Dign. occ.* 9.22. See Janniard 2010 for the fourth-/fifth-century military presence at Salona. If this *fabrica* was still functioning in the 460s, during Marcellinus' semi-autonomous command of Dalmatia, it may account for a tradition that his forces were especially well equipped: *Suda* ε 3748 = Dam. *Isid.* fr. 156 Zintzen/69C Athanassiadi.

These *fabricae* appear to be mostly tetrarchic establishments, possibly in some localities, such as Concordia, developing pre-existing manufacturing traditions.[240] Although armaments workers (*fabricenses*) were hereditary state employees subject to military-style compulsion, procurement and haulage of raw materials, transportation of arms, and associated services must have affected urban economies, even if some activities were undertaken as *munera* rather than private enterprise. Correspondingly, though evidence is slim and scattered, the long-term presence of naval facilities and personnel presumably shaped the economy and cultural complexion of harbour towns like Misenum and Classe, as well as smaller coastal or insular bases.[241]

Sociocultural Impact

Soldiers' activities and behaviour, on and off duty, intruded upon civilian lives and spaces, public and private. Empire-wide, soldier–civilian interactions occurred in diverse scenarios arising from military assistance to civil authorities and 'policing' functions.[242] In most cases, Italy-specific evidence is unavailable, partly reflecting the modest military presence before 394/5, and even though soldiers' professional environments range between the palatine milieu of *scholae* and the frontier cultures of *limitanei*, but the slim record permits some comparative observations. The sudden and protracted influx of victorious eastern Roman forces in 388–91 and from 394/5 initially entailed improvised arrangements while logistical infrastructures were established. Contemporaries complain of troops lodged on rural or suburban estates.[243] Legislation imposed menial obligatory services (*munera sordida*) on the populace to ensure procurement and haulage of provisions.[244] By the early 400s, it seems that most or all *comitatenses/palatini* and *foederati* were seasonally or semi-permanently billeted in northern Italian cities.[245] Although billeting was a perennial source of antagonism, specific problems arising from this newly militarised urban landscape cannot be detected in billeting-related laws promulgated from Milan or Ravenna in the 390s–400s; perhaps any difficulties were addressed at a provincial or municipal level.[246] An increasing proportion of non-Roman troops possibly aggravated military–civilian

---

[240] Cresci Marrone 2001; Di Filippo Balestrazzi and Vigoni 2016.
[241] Christie 2006, 313–17.
[242] Rance 2018, 422–7, with bibliography.
[243] See above, p. 153. Also Symm. *Ep*. 9.48: soldiers billeted on the estate of a deceased *consularis* at Ariminum/Rimini. See further Roda 1989 [1993].
[244] E.g. *CTh* 7.5.1 (13 September 399), 2 (24 March 404), with Scharf 1995, 174.
[245] E.g. regular troops: Zos. 5.35.5, 45.6; *foederati*: Zos. 5.34.2, 35.5–6. Epigraphic evidence: *AE* 1979, 235 appears to place at least a detachment of *schola tertia scutariorum* at Arretium/Arezzo in early 407 (see further below, n. 248). Two fifth-century epitaphs of men serving in the *schola gentilium* (*seniorum*), one a senior officer, buried in Florence may belong to the same period: *CIL* 11.1708, 1711 = *ILCV* 562, 563; *PLRE* 2.767, 'Mundilo'; 987, 'Segetius'. By way of comparison, Ennod. *Vit. Epiph*. 112 describes Theoderic's troops packed into billets in Pavia during winter 489/90.
[246] *CTh* 7.8: of the fourteen billeting-related laws preserved from between 383 and 435, only six were issued in the western empire. Of these, four (7.8.7, 9, 10, 12) relate exclusively to Africa. The remaining two applicable to Italy (7.8.6, 11) concern accommodation of civilian officials. See generally Jones 1964, 631–2; Lee 2007, 165–75.

relations, though soldier–'host' relationships were varied and complex.[247] Epigraphic evidence for soldiers' children may signal longer-term residence and social integration.[248] Operational concentrations of troops prompted laws addressing social and environmental consequences.[249]

Meagre evidence for the army's role in suppressing armed violence embraces diverse phenomena. In Suburbicaria high levels of social control may have restrained organised criminality.[250] War, famine and economic hardship unsurprisingly provoked or exacerbated brigandage.[251] Trans-/subalpine districts were traditionally prone to banditry, and historical precedent suggests that soldiers stationed in *claustra* policed those routes.[252] The potential scale of lawlessness is illustrated in 407/8: as Sarus' forces retired from Gaul over the Cottian Alps, *bacaudae* – variously identified as outlaws, private militia and/or army deserters – compelled him to relinquish his booty in return for safe passage.[253] Throughout Italy, however, soldiers themselves could be the malefactors. Laws concerning 'brigands' (*latrones*) and 'plunderers' (*populatores*) of travellers or property presume likely involvement of soldiers, typically deserters, but even veterans.[254] Particularly following the crises of 401–2 and 405–6, marauding bands of deserters menaced northern Italy.[255]

While in the eastern empire soldiers often intervened in Christian theological disputes and ecclesiastical politics, in the different doctrinal climate of Italy such coercive roles were rare.[256] Even when contested episcopal elections in Rome provoked factional rioting in the 360s, no (para)military response is recorded.[257] Exceptionally, in 385–6, interconfessional rivalries in Milan between Arian/Homoian elements of Valentinian II's court and the zealously Nicene bishop Ambrose involved confrontations between Ambrose's congregation and primarily Arian/Homoian Gothic soldiery.[258] Overall,

---

[247] E.g. McLynn 1994, 192–3 posits the possibility that the urban populace influenced the religious sensibilities of barbarian soldiers.

[248] E.g. *AE* 1979, 235 (6 February 407; Arretium/Arezzo): *schola tertia scutariorum*; *CIL* 5.1699 = *ILCV* 557 (late fourth century/early fifth century; Aquileia): *Moesiaci*. In both cases, a named female child is described as being 'of' (*ex/de*) the regiment, without naming the father.

[249] E.g. *CTh* 7.1.13 (27 May 391; Vincentia/Vicenza): pollution of watercourses. See generally Jones 1964, 629.

[250] E.g. *CTh* 9.30.1–2 (364), 3–4 (365), 5 (399): a series of laws narrowly restricting possession or use of horses in some or all Suburbicarian provinces in order to curb cattle rustling; *CTh* 15.15 (364): addressed to the governor (*consularis*) of Campania, qualifying authorised use of weapons of any kind.

[251] E.g. Symm. *Ep.* 2.22 (382–3); 5.18 (early 390s); 7.13 (402).

[252] E.g. *ILS* 2646 = *ILJug* 451 = *InscrAq* 2785 (later second century/early third century; Castra/Ajdovščina): *princeps* of *legio* XIII *Gemina* 'killed by bandits'. See Poulter 2013, 119–20; Šašel Kos 2016, 217.

[253] Zos. 6.2.5, with Wijnendaele 2019, 474–6.

[254] *CTh* 7.7.1 (28 April 323); 7.20.7 (11 August 326(353); *PLRE* 1.284–5, 'Evagrius 2'); 7.18.7 (12 July 383); 9.14.2 (1 July 391); compare 9.29.2 (27 February 391).

[255] *CTh* 7.18.14 (2 October 403); 7.18.15 (24 March 406); see above, p. 181. See generally Wesch-Klein 2004.

[256] E.g. Constantius II's arrest of dissenting bishops at the Synod of Milan in 355: Hil. *In Const.* 11; Ambr. *Ep. extra coll.* 14(63).68, with McLynn 1994, 13–21. See generally Lee 2007, 193–205; Vannesse 2009; Janniard 2018.

[257] Chapters 2 and 13 in this volume.

[258] These events are differently reconstructed by McLynn 1994, 170–218; Liebeschuetz 2005, 124–36; Nauroy 2009. Soldiers: Ambr. *Ep.* 75A(21A).2, 4, 29; 76(20).9–13, 16, 20–7.

pragmatism mitigated legislation disqualifying pagans and heretics from military service: reportedly Arbogast was a pagan, Stilicho an avid Nicene Christian, Ricimer an Arian/Homoian.[259] A law promulgated in 408 barred all but Nicene Christians from palatine service, but within months Honorius suspended its application in order to retain the services of Generidus, a valued pagan officer.[260] Nor did sectarian differences impede intermarriage among military elites.[261] That military – like civilian – aristocrats patronised religious foundations is unremarkable: thus c.428–30 Felix, *magister militum* (425–30), *patricius* and consul, with his wife Padusia, financed unspecified work in the Lateran basilica.[262] More interestingly, non-Roman military elites in later fifth-century Rome, beyond conventional manifestations of status through prestigious magistracies, dignities and marriages, emulated traditional patterns of religious-artistic patronage and civic display. Around 459–70, Ricimer sponsored the mosaic adornment of an Arian/Homoian church (now Sant'Agata dei Goti) on the lower Quirinal Hill.[263] A complementary case is Valila, also known as Theodovius, *magister militum* in the 470s, whose Germanic name and military title alone distinguish him from the senatorial cultural milieu.[264] In 471, he founded and richly endowed a Nicene church on his estate at Tibur/Tivoli.[265] When he died (pre-483), he bequeathed an aristocratic *domus* on the Esquiline Hill to Pope Simplicius (468–83), with instructions that he consecrate its aula as a church dedicated to St Andrew.[266] The relative proximity and differing doctrinal affiliations of Ricimer's and Valila's churches on the Quirinal-Esquiline plateau, adjoining a neighbourhood in which Germanic soldiery are supposed to have resided, may point to military aristocrats engaged in competitive euergetism or even confession-based clientelism.[267]

Italy offers little evidence for the blurring of military and civilian roles or identities that is often considered characteristic of the late/post-Roman West. Some items of soldiers' dress found favour outside military-cultural contexts, complicating interpretation of isolated archaeological finds.[268] Imitation of soldierly apparel in urban settings prompted prohibitive legislation: Theodosius banned senators from wearing 'military garb' (*habitus militaris*), specifically a heavy cloak (*chlamys*), while Honorius' severe proscriptions against boots, trousers and long hair in Rome similarly sought to eradicate

---

[259] Arbogast: Paulin. *Vit. Ambr.* 26, 31; Oros. 7.35.12 (see also *PLRE* 1.786, 'Rumoridus', another pagan *magister militum* of Valentinian II). Stilicho: August. *Ep.* 97.2 (408). Ricimer: Anders 2010, 317–29.

[260] *CTh* 16.5.42 (14 November 408); Zos. 5.46.2–5, with *PLRE* 1.500–1, 'Generidus'; Burns 1994, 237–8. See also *CTh* 16.8.24 (418) for Honorius' prohibition of Jews from future military service and dismissal of Jews currently in the armed forces.

[261] E.g. Wijnendaele 2015, 48–53, 107 on Boniface–Pelagia–Aëtius.

[262] *CIL* 6.41393 = *ILS* 1293 = *ILCV* 68; *PLRE* 2.461–2, 'Felix'.

[263] *ILS* 1294 = *ILCV* 1637, with MacGeorge 2002, 180–1; Mathisen 2009; Orlandi 2009; Anders 2010, 134–5, 317–18.

[264] *PLRE* 2.1147; Chastagnol 1966, 39–40, 79–80; Castritius 1972; Henning 1999, 92–3, 99, 255–7; Roberto 2013. His Roman name (Theodo{b}ius) and dignities were inscribed on a seat in the senatorial sector in the Colosseum: *CIL* 6.32169 + 32221 (c.476–83).

[265] *Carta Cornutiana* (ed. Duchesne 1886–1892, vol. 1, cxlvi–cxlvii).

[266] *CIL* 6.41402 = *ILCV* 1785; *Liber pontificalis* 49 (Duchesne, vol. 1, 249.2 with n. 2).

[267] Mathisen 2009, 318–20; Roberto 2013, 254–7.

[268] E.g. Buora 2020 on military and civilian wearers of 'Zwiebelknopffibeln' at Aquileia.

corrupting barbarian influences.[269] In two letters of Paulinus of Nola to Sulpicius Severus in 398–9, he deplores the attire of Severus' courier, who had arrived wearing a military-style tunic (*armilausa*) and army boots (*caligae*). Although Paulinus' sartorial diatribe articulates a particular monastic agenda, his remarks attest both civilian tastes for martial fashions and the disapproval they might arouse.[270] Contact between 'military' and 'civilian' cultural spheres took other forms. Although rarely reported in detail, triumphant spectacles paraded imperial troops, weaponry and insignia before urban audiences otherwise unused to seeing large numbers of military personnel.[271] Victory monuments and statues of generals exhibited idealised images of Roman warriors in public spaces.[272] Pictorial motifs in elite domestic and funerary decoration, even in a conspicuously 'non-military' province like Sicilia, imply martial associations and sensibilities that are otherwise untraceable.[273] At a literary-cultural level, and indicative of civilian-amateur efforts to engage with contemporary military issues, some scholars have wished to locate Vegetius' *Epitoma rei militaris*, a nostalgic prescription for selective army reforms, in fifth-century Italy, but the arguments are at best impressionistic. Among recent discussions of date (383–450), location and context, a majority favours composition in a Constantinopolitan setting.[274]

It seems, nevertheless, that bearing arms and armed violence essentially remained a monopoly of military personnel, excepting a temporary suspension of laws regulating civilian use of weapons in exceptional circumstances in the 440s, which itself implies governmental scrutiny and control.[275] Particularly from the 440s, legislation, mostly issued in Constantinople in response to specific eastern developments, periodically prohibited civilians from maintaining unsanctioned armed retinues, though the scale

[269] *CTh* 14.10.1 (382), 2–3 (399), 4 (416).
[270] Paulinus of Nola, *Ep.* 17.1, 22.1; see Rance 2015, 57–8.
[271] Descriptions of military processions in Rome (whether deemed technically *adventus* or *triumphus*): see especially in 357 (Amm. Marc. 16.10.1–13) and 404 (Claud. *VI cons. Hon.* 564–77); also in 312 (Nazarius, *Pan. Lat.* 4(10).30.5–32.1; Euseb. *Hist. eccl.* 9.9.9; *Vit. Const.* 1.39); 384/5 (Symm. *Relat.* 47.1–2); 389 (Pacatus, *Pan. Lat.* 2(12).47.3; Rufin. *Hist. eccl.* 11.17; Socrates, *Hist. eccl.* 5.14; Sozom. 7.14.7); 416/17 (Prosper, *Chron.* 1263). See McCormick 1986, 35–130, esp. 42–6, 51, 57–9, 80–91.
[272] Monumental depictions of soldiers: e.g. the arch of Constantine: see L'Orange and Gerkan 1939; Alföldi and Ross 1959. Statues of senior officers: e.g. equestrian statues of *comes* Theodosius dedicated by the senate: Symm. *Relat.* 9.4; 43.3 (384–5); *CIL* 9.333 = *ILS* 780 (Canusium/Canosa di Puglia, Apulia et Calabria). See also surviving dedications to statues of e.g. Stilicho (*CIL* 6.1730 + p. 4746 (398–9); 6.41382 (400); 6.1731 = 1195 + p. 4746 (405–6)), Merobaudes (*CIL* 6.1724 + p. 4743–4 (435); Sid. Apoll. *Carm.* 9.296–301) and Aëtius (*CIL* 6.41389 (437–45)) erected in Rome, though it is uncertain whether they were depicted in military or civilian garb.
[273] E.g. Pensabene 2014: the villa at Piazza Armerina; Jelusić 2017: the Villa Maria catacomb, Syracuse.
[274] See the survey of scholarship in Charles 2007, who constructs Vegetius as a western author writing in Italy in the 440s under Valentinian III. That scenario – in some respects the most problematic of all the options – has had negligible impact on subsequent research. An alternative view places Vegetius in a court milieu in the East, though disagreement persists regarding chronology: see prior studies cited by Charles 2007, 51–81, supplemented by Janniard 2008; Ortoleva 2009; Colombo 2019. All firm evidence for acquaintance with Vegetius' *Epitoma* before the seventh century is eastern or specifically Constantinopolitan: Reeve 2000, 246–9.
[275] See above, p. 174–5.

of this phenomenon is difficult to gauge.[276] In Italy, despite the collocation of landed magnates and numerous potentially freelance warriors, there is no corresponding evidence of aristocrats or landowners employing bands of *buccellarii*, large or small, nor of a general proliferation of paramilitary violence.[277] Even those studies determined to maximise and/or homogenise empire-wide evidence of 'landlord'–'warlord' synthesis and 'private forces' can cite no cases from Italy.[278] If this silence is not merely due to a dearth of judicial or tenurial documentation,[279] possible reasons include proximity to centres of power at Rome, Milan or Ravenna; the ability of military elites to monopolise recruitment; or the greater prestige and prospects of serving a senior officer or 'warlord'. One can perhaps already discern by the mid-fifth century an accommodation between the Italian civilian aristocracy and Germanic military elites that would underpin Ostrogothic rule.

Conclusion

As the limited evidence hardly sustains compelling or comprehensive theses, some thoughts and impressions must substitute for conclusions. The preceding institutional survey attempts to identify longer-term developmental factors and structural constraints, without discounting the potential significance of events and individuals. An outline of the military presence in Italy is clear: shifting strategic or dynastic-territorial troop concentrations under the Tetrarchy, followed by relative 'demilitarisation' between c.316/17 and the early/mid-370s, while from 394/5 a field army was permanently based in northern Italy. The subsequent evolution of those regional forces, within gradually shrinking operational horizons, poses important but unresolved questions, not least why 'regular' units of *comitatenses/palatini* fade from the historical record, leaving the large, mostly elite army catalogued in the *Notitia* as a mere spectre. One could point to privileged landed interests throughout Suburbicaria, which severely curtailed conscription in two-thirds of the diocese. Yet, in principle, military-fiscal revenues of Suburbicarian provinces financed regular recruitment – obligatory and voluntary – elsewhere, including the militarised provinces of Annonaria and among transdanubian peoples. Also unclear

---

[276] Eastern empire: *CTh* 7.1.15 (398): addressed to *dux Armeniae*; *N. Theod.* 15.2.1 (444): to praetorian prefect of Oriens, regarding a specific case at Emesa in Phoenice Libanensis; *CJ* 9.12.10 (468): to praetorian prefect of Oriens, with reference to Isaurians (*contra* Anders 2010, 215–16, this law could never be conceived as an attack on Ricimer's position in Italy). The only western-issued law is *N. Val.* 13.14 (445): responding to a delegation representing the now isolated provinces of the three Mauretaniae and Numidia.

[277] One potentially relevant Italy-related law deals with specific circumstances: *CTh* 15.12.3, issued in Rome in 399, forbids former employees of gladiatorial schools from entering the service of senators. In a satire on Rome in the late 380s, Amm. Marc. 14.6.16 alludes to urban aristocrats with large entourages of domestic servants (*familiares*).

[278] E.g. Whittaker 1993; Lenski 2009. See some corrective observations in Liebeschuetz 2007, 488–91.

[279] By way of comparative context, even in the rich papyrological documentation of Egypt, no record of *buccellarii* maintained on a private estate can be dated with certainty before the sixth century; see Schmitt 1994, 167–8 (citing *P. Ant.* II 103 with the date 475, but since redated to 580); Lenski 2009, 159–62; Sarris 2006, 162–74.

is the underlying impact of recurrent defeats in civil wars (388, 394, 424–5) upon the composition and integrity of armed forces in Italy, mirroring the political dependency of imperial regimes installed by eastern Roman armies. In addition, the relatively short and remote limital sector assigned to Italia precluded large-scale upgrading of *limitanei* into the field army, as documented in Gaul and elsewhere.

A shift towards 'irregular' modes of recruitment in Italy, specifically *foederati* and/ or *buccellarii*, apparently began as emergency expedients, notably by Stilicho (401–2, 405–6), but also Bauto (c.383–5), Honorius (409–10) and John (424–5). Expediency gave way to preference, perhaps as early as Stilicho, and certainly for Aëtius by the 430s. Contractual enlistment of external warrior groups simultaneously furnished shortcuts to effective strike forces and buttressed a commander's personal power base, elaborating inherent patronage networks, diverting military-fiscal resources, and merging state-salaried *milites* and privately contracted *satellites*. This recourse depended on diverse and unstable factors, including inter-regional 'market conditions': just as Attila's warrior coalition from the mid-430s monopolised Danubian/transdanubian military manpower, so its disintegration in the mid-450s unlocked or displaced freelance war bands. Overall, technical-terminological differences between *foederati*, *buccellarii* and other categories are less important than the commonalities of personalised recruitment and interdependence. Accordingly, for a field army comprising increasingly disparate forces, predominant military personalities became a unifying factor, as *empereurs fainéants* ceased to be viable foci of soldiers' loyalties. In Italy, this process is explicable less in Weberian terms of the state losing its 'monopoly of violence', once again fashionable in late Roman scholarship, and rather more akin to 'military rule', fluctuating in scope, intensity and participants, where even the overmightiest 'generalissimo' was constrained by army/court factionalism, resources and international events. In any case, state-sanctioned soldiery remained the primary instrument of armed coercion. If some recent studies may overrate the prevalence and significance of *buccellarii* even in military contexts, the inference that they embody a broader 'privatisation' of manpower and/or proliferation of paramilitary violence in Italy awaits demonstration. On the contrary, throughout Late Antiquity, the Italian aristocracy's lack of military capabilities and ambitions is striking, even when their properties later became the battleground of protracted East Roman–Ostrogothic conflict (535–54).

While emergent military-professional traditions or martial ethos are hard to discern in Italian society, armed forces in Italy correspondingly evince a weak institutional identity, beyond loyalty to particular commanders, at least compared to other regional field armies. One struggles to detect a notional *exercitus Italiae* – comparable to the well-attested institutional self-consciousness of, for example, the *exercitus Illyricianus* or *exercitus Gallicanus*, reflective of a rootedness in regional society through origin, kinship, property and culture. In comparison, the shifting configurations of military units documented in fourth- and especially fifth-century Italy, shaped by periodic unit transfers and successive eastern Roman interventions, appear rather artificial and deracinated, even before any reliance on a kaleidoscope of extrinsic barbarian 'irregular' forces. There are occasionally glimpses of the Italian field army's corporate self-identity and communal expression, notably – if ironically – in 476, but whether these were spontaneous or orchestrated remains unclear. Ultimately, the phrase *exercitus*

Italiae does occur, but not before the late sixth/seventh centuries, when it applies to the East Roman garrison, just as it was becoming embedded in Italian society and landholding.

Bibliography

Aiello, V. (2004) 'I Vandali nel Mediterraneo e la cura del limes', in M. Khanoussi, P. Ruggeri and C. Vismara (eds) *L'Africa romana. Ai confini dell'impero: contatti, scambi conflitti. Atti del XV convegno di studio, Tozeur, 11–15 dicembre 2002*, Rome, vol. 1, 723–39.

Alföldi, A. and M. C. Ross (1959) 'Cornuti: a Teutonic Contingent in the Service of Constantine the Great and Its Decisive Role in the Battle at the Milvian Bridge. With a Discussion of Bronze Statuettes of Constantine the Great', *DOP* 13: 169–83.

Anders, F. (2010) *Flavius Ricimer: Macht und Ohnmacht des weströmischen Heermeisters in der zweiten Hälfte des 5. Jahrhunderts*, Frankfurt am Main.

Arnold, J. J., M. S. Bjornlie and K. Sessa (eds) (2016) *A Companion to Ostrogothic Italy*, Leiden.

Arthur, P. (2002) *Naples. From Roman Town to City-State: an Archaeological Perspective*, Archaeological Monographs of the British School at Rome 12, London.

Bachrach, B. (1973) *A History of the Alans in the West*, Minneapolis.

Bagnall, R. S. (1992) 'Military Officers as Landowners in Fourth-Century Egypt', *Chiron* 22: 47–52.

Banaji, J. (2001) *Agrarian Change in Late Antiquity: Gold, Labour and Aristocratic Dominance*, Oxford.

Barnes, T. D. (1982) *The New Empire of Diocletian and Constantine*, Cambridge, MA.

Beyeler, M. (2011) *Geschenke des Kaisers: Studien zur Chronologie, zu den Empfängern und zu den Gegenständen der kaiserlichen Vergabungen im 4. Jahrhundert n. Chr.*, Klio Beihefte n.s. 18, Berlin.

Birley, A. (1993) *Marcus Aurelius: a Biography*, rev. ed., London.

Bjornlie, M. S. (2014) 'Law, Ethnicity and Taxes in Ostrogothic Italy: a Case for Continuity, Adaptation and Departure', *Early Medieval Europe* 22: 138–70.

Bjornlie, M. S. (2016) 'Governmental Administration', in J. J. Arnold, M. S. Bjornlie and K. Sessa (eds) *A Companion to Ostrogothic Italy*, Leiden, 47–72.

Bjornlie, M. S. (2019) *The Variae: the Complete Translation*, Oakland, CA.

Bleckmann, B. (1992) *Die Reichskrise des III. Jahrhunderts in der spätantiken und byzantinischen Geschichtsschreibung*, Munich.

Bleckmann, B. (2003) 'Der Bürgerkrieg zwischen Constantin II. und Constans (340 n. Chr.)', *Historia* 52: 225–50.

Bolla, M. (2002) 'Militari e militaria nel territorio veronese e gardesano (III–inizi V sec. d.C.)', in Buora 2002, 99–138.

Brandt, H. (1988) *Zeitkritik in der Spätantike: Untersuchungen zu den Reformvorschlägen des Anonymus De rebus bellicis*, Munich.

Brunt, P. A. (1974) 'Conscription and Volunteering in the Roman Imperial Army', *SCI* 1: 90–115.

Buora, M. (ed.) (2002) *Miles Romanus dal Po al Danubio nel tardoantico: Atti del Convegno internazionale Pordenone–Concordia Sagittaria, 17–19 marzo 2000*, Pordenone.

Buora, M. (2020) 'Militari e civili: raffigurazioni di portatori di "Zwiebelknopffibeln" in Aquileia', in M. Cadario and S. Magnani (eds) *Presenze militari in Italia settentrionale: la documentazione iconografica ed epigrafica*, Studi di Storia 20, Bologna, 151–64.

Burgess, R. W. (1987) 'The Third Regnal Year of Eparchius Avitus: a Reply', *CP* 82: 335–45.

Burns, T. S. (1994) *Barbarians within the Gates of Rome: a Study of Roman Military Policy and the Barbarians, ca. 375–425 A.D.*, Bloomington, IN.
Caliri, E. (2014) '*Piam manum porrigere defessis*: Sgravi fiscali sotto Valentiniano III e il problema del *fiscus barbaricus*', in V. Aiello (ed.) *Guerrieri, mercanti e profughi nel Mare dei Vandali: Atti del Convegno Internazionale (Messina 7–8 settembre 2009)*, Messina, 127–43.
Cameron, A. (1970) *Claudian: Poetry and Propaganda at the Court of Honorius*, Oxford.
Carrié, J.-M. (2004) 'Le système de recrutement des armées romaines de Dioclétien aux Valentiniens', in Y. Le Bohec and C. Wolff (eds.) *L'Armée romaine de Dioclétien à Valentinien Ier (Actes du Congrès de Lyon, 12–14 sept. 2002)*, Lyon, 371–87.
Castritius, H. (1972) 'Zur Sozialgeschichte der Heermeister des Westreiches nach der Mitte des 5 Jh.: Flavius Valila qui et Theodovius', *AncSoc* 3: 233–43.
Cavada, E. (2002) 'Militaria tardoantichi (fine IV–V secolo) dalla valle dell'Adige e dalle aree limitrofe: l'informazione archeologica', in Buora 2002, 139–62.
Cecconi, G. A. (2007) 'Funzioni e immagine del *dux Raetiarum*', in P. Desideri, M. Moggi and M. Pani (eds) *Antidoron: Studi in onore di Barbara Scardigli Forster*, Pisa, 17–32.
Cesa, M. (1993) 'Römisches Heer und barbarische Föderaten: Bemerkungen zur weströmischen Politik in den Jahren 402–412', *BJ* 193: 203–17. Also published, with minor variations, in F. Vallet and M. Kazanski (eds) (1993) *L'armée romaine et les Barbares du IIIe au VIIe siècle*, Rouen, 21–9.
Charles, M. (2005) 'Transporting the Troops in Late Antiquity: *Naves onerariae*, Claudian and the Gildonic War', *CJ* 100: 275–99.
Charles, M. B. (2007) *Vegetius in Context: Establishing the Date of the* Epitoma Rei Militaris, Stuttgart.
Chastagnol, A. (1966) *Le Sénat romain sous le règne d'Odoacre: recherches sur l'épigraphie du Colisée au Ve siècle*, Bonn.
Christie, N. (2006) *From Constantine to Charlemagne: an Archaeology of Italy AD 300–800*, London.
Christie, N. (2007) 'From the Danube to the Po: the Defence of Pannonia and Italy in the Fourth and Fifth Centuries AD', in A. G. Poulter (ed.) *The Transition to Late Antiquity: on the Danube and Beyond*, PBA 141, Oxford, 547–78.
Ciglenečki, S. (2015) 'Late Roman Army, *claustra Alpium Iuliarum* and the Fortifications in the South-Eastern Alps', in J. Istenič, B. Laharnar and J. Horvat (eds) *Evidence of the Roman Army in Slovenia*, NMS Catalogi et Monographiae 41, Ljubljana, 385–430.
Ciglenečki, S. (2016) '*Claustra Alpium Iuliarum, tractus Italiae circa Alpes* and the Defence of Italy in the Final Part of the Late Roman Period', *Arheološki vestnik* 67: 409–24.
Colombo, M. (2019) 'Nuove prove per la datazione di Vegezio sotto Teodosio II e la sua collocazione nell'impero romano d'Oriente', *Klio* 101: 256–75.
Cracco Ruggini, L. (1984) 'I barbari in Italia nei secoli dell'impero', in *Magistra Barbaritas: i Barbari in Italia*, Milan, 3–51.
Cresci Marrone, G. (2001) 'Lo stanziamento militare, la fabbrica di frecce e la comunità di commercianti orientali nella Concordia tardo antica', in P. Croce Da Villa and E. Di Filippo Balestrazzi (eds) *Concordia: tremila anni di storia*, Rubano, 245–9.
Davenport, C. (2020) 'The Dynamics of Imperial Government: Collegiality and Regionalism', in N. Baker-Brian and S. Tougher (eds) *The Sons of Constantine, AD 337–361*, Cham, 223–54.
De la Bédoyère, G. (2017) *Praetorian: the Rise and Fall of Rome's Imperial Bodyguard*, London.
Delmaire, R. (1989) *Largesses sacrées et res privata: l'aerarium impérial et son administration du IVe au VIe siècle*, CEFR 121, Rome.
Demandt, A. (1980) 'Der spätrömische Militäradel', *Chiron* 10: 609–36. Reprinted in A. Demandt (2013) *Zeitenwende: Aufsätze zur Spätantike*, Beiträge zur Altertumskunde 311, Berlin, 52–84.
Di Filippo Balestrazzi, E. and A. Vigoni (2016) 'Le *sagittae di Iulia Concordia*', in J. Horvat (ed.) *The Roman Army between the Alps and the Adriatic*, Ljubljana, 61–76.

Diesner, H.-J. (1972) 'Das Buccellariertum von Stilicho und Sarus bis auf Aetius (454/455)', *Klio* 54: 321–50.
Drinkwater, J. F. (2007) *The Alamanni and Rome 213–496 (Caracalla to Clovis)*, Oxford.
Durry, M. (1938) *Les cohortes prétoriennes*, BEFAR 146, Paris. Reprinted 1968.
Elton, H. (1996) *Warfare in Roman Europe, AD 350–425*, Oxford.
Feugère, M. (2013) 'Tra Costantino e Teodosio (IV–V secolo d.C.): osservazioni sui militaria di Aquileia', *Aquileia Nostra* 83/4: 319–46.
Frank, R. I. (1969) *Scholae Palatinae: the Palace Guards of the Later Roman Empire*, Rome.
Freis, H. (1967) *Die cohortes urbanae*, Cologne.
Gheller, V. (2017) *'Identità' e 'arianesimo gotico': genesi di un topos storiografico*, Bologna.
Giglio, S. (1990) *Il tardo impero d'occidente e il suo senato: privilegi fiscali, patrocinio, giurisdizione penale*, Naples.
Gil Egea, M. E. (2003) 'Warrior Retinues in Late Antiquity: the Case of Pelagia', *Studies in Latin Literature and History* 11: 493–503.
Gillet, A. (1999) 'The Accession of Euric', *Francia* 26: 1–40.
Gračanin, H. (2016) 'Late Antique Dalmatia and Pannonia in Cassiodorus' *Variae*', *Millennium: Jahrbuch zu Kultur und Geschichte des ersten Jahrtausends n. Chr.* 13: 211–73.
Gusso, M. (1996) 'Alle origini dei Grigioni: fatti d'arme combattuti sui Campi Canini, presso Bellinzona, nei secoli IV–VI d.C', *Prometheus* 22: 60–86.
Halsall, G. (2016) 'The Ostrogothic Military', in J. J. Arnold, M. S. Bjornlie and K. Sessa (eds) *A Companion to Ostrogothic Italy*, Leiden, 173–99.
Henning, D. (1999) *Periclitans res publica: Kaisertum und Eliten in der Krise des Weströmischen Reiches 454/5–493 n. Chr.*, Stuttgart.
Hoffmann, D. (1969–1970) *Das spätrömische Bewegungsheer und die Notitia Dignitatum*, Epigraphische Studien 7.1–2, 2 vols, Dusseldorf.
Horvat, J. (ed.) (2016) *The Roman Army between the Alps and the Adriatic*, Ljubljana.
Ibba, A. (2016) 'Bonifatius, *comes Africae*: notulae su alcuni passi controversi', in L. De Salvo, E. Caliri and M. Casella (eds) *Fra Costantino e i Vandali: Atti del convegno internazionale di studi per Enzo Aiello (1957–2013) (Messina, 29–30 ottobre 2014)*, Bari, 525–44.
James, S. (1988) 'The *fabricae*: State Arms Factories in the Later Roman Empire', in J. C. Coulston (ed.) *Military Equipment and the Identity of Roman Soldiers*, British Archaeological Reports International Series 394, Oxford, 257–331.
Janniard, S. (2006) 'La résistance d'Aquilée dans l'Antiquité tardive, entre modèle littéraire et réalité (IIIe–Ve siècle)', in M. Ghilardi, J. C. Goddard and P. Porena (eds) *Les cités de l'Italie tardo-antique (IVe–VIe siècle): institutions, économie, société, culture et religion*, Rome, 75–89.
Janniard, S. (2008) 'Végèce et les transformations de l'art de la guerre aux IVe et Ve siècles après J.-C.', *AntTard* 16: 19–36.
Janniard, S. (2010) 'Présence militaire aux IVe et Ve siècles', in E. Marin, N. Gauthier, F. Prévot (eds) *Salona*, vol. 4: *Inscriptions de Salone chrétienne IVe–VIIe siècles*, CEFR 194.4, Rome, 70–3.
Janniard, S. (2018) 'Les empereurs chrétiens et l'usage de l'armée pour réprimer les déviances religieuses aux IVe et Ve siècles', in S. Destephen, B. Dumézil and H. Inglebert (eds) *Le Prince chrétien de Constantin aux royautés barbares (IVe–VIIIe siècle)* (= TM 22.2), Paris, 399–413.
Janniard, S. (2020) 'Objectifs et moyens de la politique militaire d'Anthémius', in F. Oppedisano (ed.) *Procopio Antemio, imperatore e Roma*, Bari, 229–55.
Janssen, T. (2004) *Stilicho: das weströmische Reich vom Tode des Theodosius bis zur Ermordung Stilichos (395–408)*, Marburg.
Jelusić, M. (2017) 'Zu einem Schildzeichen der *Notitia dignitatum*: Neubewertung einer Grabmalerei mit der Darstellung des spätantiken Soldaten Flavius Maximianus aus der Villa Maria-Katakombe in Syrakus (reg. Siciliana/I)', *AKB* 47: 513–32.

Jones, A. H. M. (1964) *The Later Roman Empire 284–602*, 3 vols, Oxford.
Keller, E. (1986) 'Germanenpolitik Roms im bayerischen Teil der Raetia Secunda während des 4. und 5. Jahrhunderts', *JRGZ* 33: 575–92.
Kim, H. J. (2013) *The Huns, Rome and the Birth of Europe*, Cambridge.
Kos, P. (2012) 'The Construction and Abandonment of the *claustra Alpium Iuliarum* Defence System in Light of the Numismatic Material', *Arheološki vestnik* 63: 265–300.
Kos, P. (2013) '*Claustra Alpium Iuliarum*: Protecting Late Roman Italy', *Studia Europea Gnesnensia* 7: 233–61.
Kulikowski, M. (2002a) 'Marcellinus "of Dalmatia" and the Dissolution of the Fifth-Century Empire', *Byzantion* 72: 177–91.
Kulikowski, M. (2002b) 'Nation versus Army: a Necessary Contrast?', in A. Gillett (ed.) *On Barbarian Identity: Critical Approaches to Ethnicity in the Early Middle Ages*, Turnhout, 69–84.
Kusetič, J., P. Kos, A. Breznik and M. Stokin (eds) (2014) *Claustra Alpium Iuliarum: Med raziskovanjem in upravljanjem / Between Research and Management*, Ljubljana.
L'Orange, H. P. and A. von Gerkan (1939) *Der spätantike Bildschmuck des Konstantinsbogens*, Berlin.
Le Bohec, Y. (2006) *L'armée romaine sous le Bas-Empire*, Paris.
Lee, A. D. (2007) *War in Late Antiquity: a Social History*, Oxford.
Lenski, N. (2009) 'Schiavi armata e formazione di eserciti privati nel mondo tardoantico', in G. Urso (ed.) *Ordine e sovversione nel mondo greco e romano*, Pisa, 146–75.
Lettich, G. (1982) 'Concordia e Aquileia: note sull'organizzazione difensiva del confine orientale d'Italia nel IV secolo', *AAAD* 22: 67–87.
Lewis, W. (2020) 'Constantine II and His Brothers: the Civil War of AD 340', in N. Baker-Brian and S. Tougher (eds) *The Sons of Constantine, AD 337–361*, Cham, 57–94.
Liebeschuetz, J. H. W. G. (1990) *Barbarians and Bishops: Army, Church and State in the Age of Arcadius and Chrysostom*, Oxford.
Liebeschuetz, J. H. W. G. (1992) 'Alaric's Goths: Nation or Army?', in J. F. Drinkwater and H. Elton (eds) *Fifth-Century Gaul: a Crisis of Identity?* Cambridge, 75–83.
Liebeschuetz, W. (1993) 'The End of the Roman Army in the Western Empire', in J. Rich and G. Shipley (eds) *War and Society in the Roman World*, London, 265–76.
Liebeschuetz, J. H. W. G. (2005) *Ambrose of Milan: Political Letters and Speeches*, TTH 43, Liverpool.
Liebeschuetz, W. (2007) 'Warlords and Landlords', in P. Erdkamp (ed.) *A Companion to the Roman Army*, Oxford, 479–94.
Linn, J. (2019) 'Attila's Appetite: the Logistics of Attila the Hun's Invasion of Italy in 452', *Journal of Military History* 83: 325–46.
McCormick, M. (1986) *Eternal Victory: Triumphal Rulership in Late Antiquity, Byzantium, and the Early Medieval West*, Cambridge.
McEvoy, M. A. (2013) *Child Emperor Rule in the Late Roman West, AD 367–455*, Oxford.
MacGeorge, P. (2002) *Late Roman Warlords*, Oxford.
Mackensen, M. (1999) 'Late Roman Fortifications and Building Programmes in the Province of Raetia: the Evidence of Recent Excavations and Some New Reflections', in J. Creighton and R. J. A. Wilson (eds) *Roman Germany: Studies in Cultural Interaction*, JRA Suppl. 32, Portsmouth, RI, 199–244.
Mackensen, M. (2018) 'Organization and Development of the Late Roman Frontier in the Provinces of Raetia Prima et Secunda (ca. AD 270/300–450), in S. Matešic and C. S. Sommer (eds) *Limes XXIII: Proceedings of the 23rd International Limes Congress Ingolstadt 2015 / Akten des 23. Internationalen Limeskongresses in Ingolstadt 2015*, Mainz, 47–68.
McLynn, N. B. (1994) *Ambrose of Milan: Church and Court in a Christian Capital*, Berkeley.

Marcone, A. (1994) 'Dal contenimento all'insediamento: i Germani in Italia da Giuliano a Teodosio Magno', in B. Scardigli and P. Scardigli (eds) *Germani in Italia*, Rome, 239–52.
Marin, E., N. Gauthier and F. Prévot (eds) (2010) *Salona*, vol. 4, *Inscriptions de Salone chrétienne IVe–VIIe siècles*, CEFR 194.4, Rome.
Mastrelli, C. (1978) 'La toponomastica lombarda di origine longobarda', in *I Longobardi e la Lombardia: Saggi*, Milan, 35–50.
Mathisen, R. W. (2009) 'Ricimer's Church in Rome: How an Arian Barbarian Prospered in a Nicene World', in A. Cain and N. Lenski (eds) *The Power of Religion in Late Antiquity*, Farnham, 307–25.
Mathisen, R. W. (2019) 'The End of the Western Roman Empire in the Fifth Century CE: Barbarian Auxiliaries, Independent Military Contractors, and Civil Wars', in N. Lenski and J. W. Drijvers (eds) *The Fifth Century: Age of Transformation*, Bari, 137–56.
Matthews, J. F. (1975) *Western Aristocracies and Imperial Court*, Oxford.
Mennella, G. (2004) 'La campagna di Costantino nell'Italia nord-occidentale: la documentazione epigrafica', Y. Le Bohec and C. Wolff (eds.) *L'Armée romaine de Dioclétien à Valentinien Ier (Actes du Congrès de Lyon, 12–14 sept. 2002)*, Lyon, 359–69.
Merrills, A. and R. Miles (2010) *The Vandals*, Chichester.
Modéran, Y. (2014) *Les Vandales et l'Empire romain*, Arles.
Nauroy, G. (2009) 'La crise milanaise de 386 et les lettres d'Ambroise: Difficultés d'interprétation et limites d'un témoignage épistolaire', in R. Delmaire, J. Desmulliez and P.-L. Gatier (eds) *Correspondances: Documents pour l'histoire de l'Antiquité tardive*, Lyon, 227–58.
Nicasie, M. J. (1998) *Twilight of Empire: the Roman Army from the Reign of Diocletian until the Battle of Adrianople*, Amsterdam.
O'Flynn, J. M. (1983) *Generalissimos of the Western Roman Empire*, Edmonton, AB.
Orlandi, S. (2009) 'L'iscrizione di Flavius Ricimer in S. Agata dei Goti a Roma', in M. Rotili (ed.) *Tardo antico e alto medioevo: Filologia, storia, archeologia, arte*, Naples, 215–23.
Ortoleva, V. (2009) Review of M. B. Charles, *Vegetius in Context: Establishing the Date of the Epitoma rei militaris* (Stuttgart, 2007), *Gnomon* 80: 407–11.
Pavan, M. (1979) 'Presenze di militari nel territorio di Aquileia', *AAAD* 15: 461–513.
Pellizzari, A. (2014) 'Tra *adventus* imperiali e *bella civilia*: l'Italia Settentrionale e Aquileia nei *Panegyrici Latini* di età tetrarchico-costantiniana', in G. Cuscito (ed.) *Costantino il grande a 1700 anni dall' 'editto di milano' (Atti della XLIV Settimana di Studi Aquileiesi, 30 maggio–1 giugno 2013)*, Trieste, 145–60.
Pensabene, P. (2014) 'Pittura tardoantica a Piazza Armerina: gli spazi esterni e le tematiche militari come autorappresentazione del *Dominus*', in N. Zimmermann (ed.) *Antike Malerei zwischen Lokalstil und Zeitstil: Akten des XI. Internationalen Kolloquiums der AIPMA, 13.–17. September 2010 in Ephesos* (= *Archäologische Forschungen* 23 = ÖAW, Phil.-Hist. Kl. Denkschriften 468), Vienna, 147–55.
Picozzi, V. (1976) 'Una campagna di Licinio contro Massenzio nel 310 non attestata dalle fonti letterarie', *NAC* 5: 267–75.
Poguntke, A. (2016) 'Das römische Heermeisteramt im 5. Jahrhundert: Überlegungen zum Verhältnis zwischen Kaiser und Heermeister in Ost und West', in C. Föller and F. Schulz (eds) *Osten und Westen 400–600 n. Chr. Kommunikation, Kooperation und Konflikt*, Stuttgart, 239–62.
Porena, P. (2003) *Le origini della prefettura del pretorio tardoantica*, Rome.
Porena, P. (2012a) 'Voci e silenzi sull'insediamento degli Ostrogoti in Italia', in P. Porena (ed.) *Expropriations et confiscations dans les royaumes barbares: une approche régionale*, Rome, 227–78.
Porena, P. (2012b) *L'insediamento degli Ostrogoti in Italia*, Rome.
Porena, P. (2013) 'La riorganizzazione amministrativa dell'Italia: Costantino, Roma, il Senato e gli equilibri dell'Italia romana', in A. Melloni et al. (eds) *Costantino I: Enciclopedia costantiniana*

sulla figura e l'immagine dell'imperatore del cosiddetto Editto di Milano, 313–2013, vol. 1, Rome, 329–49.

Poulter, A. (2013) 'An Indefensible Frontier: the *claustra Alpium Iuliarum*', *JÖAI* 81: 97–126.

Rance, P. (2007) '*Campidoctores, vicarii vel tribuni*: the Senior Regimental Officers in the Late Roman Army and the Rise of the *campidoctor*', in A. S. Lewin and P. Pellegrini (eds) *The Late Roman Army in the Near East from Diocletian to the Arab Conquest*, British Archaeological Reports international series 1717, Oxford, 395–409.

Rance, P. (2015) '*Quam gentilitate appellant*. The Philological Evidence for Barbarians in the Late Roman Army: Germanic Loanwords in Roman Military Vocabulary', in T. Vida (ed.) with P. Rance (Eng. ed.), *Romania Gothica II. The Frontier World: Romans, Barbarians and Military Culture*, Budapest, 51–94.

Rance, P. (2018) 'The Army in Peace Time: the Social Status and Function of Soldiers', in Y. Stouraitis (ed.) *A Companion to the Byzantine Culture of War, ca. 300–1204*, Leiden, 394–439.

Rance, P. (2022) '*Simplicitas militaris*: Ammianus Marcellinus and *sermo castrensis*', in D. Woods and M. Hanaghan (eds) *Ammianus Marcellinus: from Soldier to Author*, Leiden, 83–139.

Reddé, M. (1986) *Mare nostrum: les infrastructures, le dispositif et l'histoire de la marine militaire sous l'empire romain*, Rome.

Reeve, M. D. (2000) 'The Transmission of Vegetius' *Epitoma rei militaris*', *Aevum* 74: 243–354.

Restelli, G. (1984) *Goti, Tedeschi, Longobardi. Rapporti di Cultura e di Lingua*, Studi Grammaticali e Linguistici 16, Brescia.

Ricci, C. (2014) '*Protendere per protegere*: Considerazioni sul carattere della presenza militare ad Aquileia tra Massimino e Costantino', in G. Cuscito (ed.) *Costantino il grande a 1700 anni dall' 'editto di milano' (Atti della XLIV Settimana di Studi Aquileiesi, 30 maggio–1 giugno 2013)*, Trieste, 239–54.

Ricci, C. (2018) *Security in Roman Times: Rome, Italy and the Emperors*, Abingdon.

Ritterling, E. (1924) 'Legio', *RE* 12.1: 1211–1328, 12.2: 1329–1829.

Roberto, U. (2013) 'Strategie di integrazione e lotta politica a Roma alla fine dell'impero: la carriera di Fl. Valila tra Ricimero e Odoacre', in N. Cusumano and D. Motta (eds) *Xenia: studi in onore di Lia Marino*, Rome, 247–61.

Roberto, U. (2014) 'Aquileia tra Massenzio e Costantino: l'assedio della tarda estate 312', in G. Cuscito (ed.) *Costantino il grande a 1700 anni dall' 'editto di milano' (Atti della XLIV Settimana di Studi Aquileiesi, 30 maggio–1 giugno 2013)*, Trieste, 129–43.

Roberto, U. (2022) 'Presenza e integrazione dei barbari nell'Italia del V secolo: il caso dei Sarmatae gentiles', in E. Possenti (ed.) *Presenze barbariche nel V secolo in Italia e regioni contermini*, Mantua, 15–32.

Rocco, M. (2012) *L'esercito romano tardoantico: persistenze e cesure dai Severi a Teodosio I*, Padua.

Roda, S. (1989 [1993]) '*Militaris impressio* e proprietà senatoria nel tardo impero', in *Hestiasis: studi di tarda antichità offerti a S. Calderone* (= *Studi tardoantichi* 4), Messina, 214–41.

Sabin, P., H. Van Wees and L. M. Whitby (eds) (2007) *The Cambridge History of Greek and Roman Warfare*, vol. 2: *Rome from the Late Republic to the Late Empire*, Cambridge.

Sarris, P. (2006) *Economy and Society in the Age of Justinian*, Cambridge.

Šašel, J. (1971) 'The Struggle between Magnentius and Constantius II for Italy and Illyricum', *Živa antika* 21, 205–16. Reprinted in J. Šašel (1992) *Opera selecta* (= *Situla* 30), Ljubljana, 716–27.

Šašel Kos, M. (2016) 'Cenotaphs and Unusual War-Time Deaths in the Southeastern Alps and Pannonia', in J. Horvat (ed.) *The Roman Army between the Alps and the Adriatic*, Ljubljana, 213–24.

Savino, E. (2017) 'Ancora sul *fiscus barbaricus*: una nota sulla storia della Sicilia nel V secolo', *DHA* 43: 147–52.

Scharf, R. (1994) 'Der Iuthungenfeldzug des Aëtius: eine Neuinterpretation einer christlichen Grabinschrift aus Augsburg', *Tyche* 9: 131–45.

Scharf, R. (1995) 'Aufrüstung und Truppenbenennung unter Stilicho: das Beispiel der Atecotti-Truppen', *Tyche* 10: 161–78.
Scharf, R. (2001) *Foederati: von der völkerrechtlichen Kategorie zur byzantinischen Truppengattung*, Tyche Suppl. 4, Vienna.
Scharf, R. (2005) *Der Dux Mogontiacensis und die Notitia Dignitatum: eine Studie zur spätantiken Grenzverteidigung*, Berlin.
Scheithauer, A. and G. Wesch-Klein (1990) 'Von Köln-Deutz nach Rom? Zur Truppengeschichte der *legio* II *Italica Divitensium*', ZPE 81: 229–36.
Schmitt, O. (1994) 'Die *Bucellarii*: eine Studie zum militärischen Gefolgschaftswesen in der Spätantike', *Tyche* 9: 147–74.
Seeck, O. (1875) 'Zur Kritik der *Notitia dignitatum*', *Hermes* 9: 217–42.
Seeck, O. (1919) *Regesten der Kaiser und Päpste für die Jahre 311 bis 476 n. Chr.*, Stuttgart.
Simon, H.-G. (1980) 'Die Reformen der Reiterei unter Kaiser Gallien', in W. Eck, H. Galsterer and H. Wolff (eds) *Studien zur antiken Sozialgeschichte: Festschrift Friedrich Vittinghoff*, Kölner Historische Abhandlungen 28, Cologne, 435–52.
Sogno, C. (2006) *Q. Aurelius Symmachus: a Political Biography*, Ann Arbor.
Speidel, M. P. (1986) 'Maxentius and his *equites singulares* in the Battle at the Milvian Bridge', *ClAnt* 5: 253–9.
Speidel, M. P. (1988) 'Les prétoriens de Maxence. Les cohortes palatines romaines', *MEFRA* 100: 183–6.
Speidel, M. P. (1990) 'The Army at Aquileia, the *Moesiaci* Legion, and the Shield Emblems in the *Notitia dignitatum*', *SJ* 45: 68–72.
Speidel, M. P. (1992) *Roman Army Studies*, vol. 2, Amsterdam.
Speidel, M. P. (1994) *Riding for Caesar: the Roman Emperors' Horse Guards*, Cambridge, MA.
Speidel, M. P. (2008) 'Das Heer', in K.-P. Johne with U. Hartmann and T. Gerhardt (eds) *Die Zeit der Soldatenkaiser, Krise und Transformation des römischen Reiches im 3. Jahrhundert n. Chr. (235–284)*, vol. 1, Berlin, 673–90.
Stein, E. (1949–1959) *Histoire du Bas-Empire*, ed. J.-R. Palanque, Paris, 2 vols.
Stein, E. (1922) *Untersuchungen über das Officium der Prätorianerpräfektur seit Diokletian*, Vienna. Reprinted 1967, ed. J.-R. Palanque, Amsterdam.
Stickler, T. (2002) *Aëtius: Gestaltungsspielräume eines Heermeisters im ausgehenden Weströmischen Reich*, Munich.
Stickler, T. (2007) 'The Foederati', in P. Erdkamp (ed.) *A Companion to the Roman Army*, Oxford, 495–514.
Tedesco, P. (2016) 'Economia monetaria e fiscalità tardoantica: una sintesi', *AIIN* 62: 102–47.
Vannesse, M. (2007) 'I *claustra Alpium Iuliarum*: un riesame della questione circa la difesa del confine nord-orientale dell'Italia in epoca tardoromana', *AN* 78: 313–40.
Vannesse, M. (2009) 'La religion dans l'armée romaine du IVe siècle: l'exemple d'Aquilée et de l'Italie du Nord', in C. Wolff (ed.) *L'armée romaine et la religion sous le Haut-Empire romain*, Paris, 459–63.
Vannesse, M. (2010a) *La défense de l'Occident romain pendant l'Antiquité tardive: recherches géostratégiques sur l'Italie de 284 à 410 ap. J.-C.*, Collection Latomus 326, Brussels.
Vannesse, M. (2010b) 'L'armée romaine en Occident sous Stilichon (395–408 ap. J.-C.): le témoignage des décrets impériaux', *Revue belge de philologie et d'histoire / Belgisch tijdschrift voor philologie en geschiedenis* 88: 99–112.
Vannesse, M. (2010c) 'L'esercito romano e i contingenti barbarici nel V secolo: il caso della difesa dell'Italia', in P. Delogu and S. Gasparri (eds) *Le trasformazioni del V secolo: l'Italia, i barbari e l'Occidente romano*, Turnhout, 69–85.

Vitiello, M. (2004) 'Teoderico a Roma: politica, amministrazione e propaganda nell' *adventus* dell' anno 500 (Considerazioni sull' "Anonimo Valesiano II")', *Historia* 53: 73–120.

Wesch-Klein, G. (2004) 'Hochkonjunktur für Deserteure? Fahnenflucht in der Spätantike', in Y. Le Bohec and C. Wolff (eds.) *L'Armée romaine de Dioclétien à Valentinien Ier (Actes du Congrès de Lyon, 12–14 sept. 2002)*, Lyon, 475–87.

Whitby, M. (1995) 'Recruitment in Roman Armies from Justinian to Heraclius (ca. 565–615)', in A. Cameron (ed.) *The Byzantine and Early Islamic Near East*, vol. 3: *States, Resources and Armies*, Princeton, 61–124.

Whitby, M. (2000) 'The Army c.420–602', in A. Cameron, B. Ward-Perkins and W. Whitby (eds) *The Cambridge Ancient History*, vol. 14: *Late Antiquity: Empire and Successors, AD 425–600*, 286–314.

Whittaker, D. (1993) 'Landlords and Warlords in the Later Roman Empire', in J. Rich and G. Shipley (eds) *War and Society in the Roman World*, London, 277–302.

Wijnendaele, J. W. P. (2015) *The Last of the Romans: Bonifatius – Warlord and comes Africae*, London.

Wijnendaele, J. W. P. (2016a) 'Stilicho, Radagaisus, and the So-Called "Battle of Faesulae" (406 CE)', *Journal of Late Antiquity* 9: 267–84.

Wijnendaele, J. W. P. (2016b) 'Warlordism and the Disintegration of the Western Roman Army', in J. Armstrong (ed.) *Circum Mare: Themes in Ancient Warfare*, Leiden, 185–203.

Wijnendaele, J. W. P. (2017a) 'The Career and "Revolt" of Gildo, *comes et magister utriusque militiae per Africam*', *Latomus* 27: 385–402.

Wijnendaele, J. W. P. (2017b) 'The Manufacture of Heraclianus' Usurpation (413 CE)', *Phoenix* 71: 138–56.

Wijnendaele, J. W. P. (2017c) 'The Early Career of Aëtius and the Murder of Felix', *Historia* 66: 468–82.

Wijnendaele, J. W. P. (2018a) 'Generalissimos and Warlords in the Late Roman West', in T. Ñaco del Hoyo and F. López Sánchez (eds) *War, Warlords, and Interstate Relations in the Ancient Mediterranean*, Leiden, 427–51.

Wijnendaele, J. W. P. (2018b) '"Dagli altari alla polvere": Alaric, Constantine III, and the Downfall of Stilicho', *JHA* 6: 260–77.

Wijnendaele, J. W. P. (2019) 'Sarus the Goth: from Imperial Commander to Warlord', *Early Medieval Europe* 27: 469–93.

Wijnendaele, J. W. P. and M. P. Hanaghan (2021) 'Constantius *Heros* (*ILCV* 66) – an Elegiac Testimony on the Decline of the Late Roman West', *Chiron* 51: 257–76.

Zuckerman, C. (1998a) 'Two Reforms of the 370s: Recruiting Soldiers and Senators in the Divided Empire', *REByz* 56: 79–139.

Zuckerman, C. (1998b) 'Comtes et ducs en Égypte autour de l'an 400 et la date de la *Notitia dignitatum orientis*', *AntTard* 6: 137–47.

Part III

Society, Economy and Environment

8

ELITE WOMEN AND GENDER-BASED VIOLENCE IN LATE ROMAN ITALY

Ulriika Vihervalli and Victoria Leonard

LIFE AS A FEMALE MEMBER of an elite family – imperial, senatorial, royal – led to a precarious existence in late Roman society, even with its benefits of privileges and power. Empresses were notable for their wealth as well as their influence in political and religious affairs, and particularly so in the eastern Mediterranean.[1] But gender-based violence often accompanied the careers of these influential women, who lived through rapid political changes, succession crises and wars. As the centre of the Roman Empire, Italy had enjoyed centuries of relative peace, but the late ancient period saw an upsurge in violence, conflict and unrest on the Italian peninsula. Women are particularly at risk and suffer disproportionately during disasters and conflict, with many of the factors associated with disasters – the separation of families, the collapse of social networks, the breakdown of norms and traditional beliefs, the destruction of infrastructure and economic transactional systems – increasing violence against women and children.[2] Conflict and unrest, therefore, has a gendered dimension; gender-based violence against women increases when their male relatives are involved in political and military conflicts, but the female experience of unrest is particular and discrete.[3] These female experiences of violence are, however, normalised by ancient and modern accounts alike, and violence against vulnerable groups has been subsumed in larger narratives of the empire's decline, fall or transformation. In response to this constructed absence, this chapter explores attempted and successful perpetration of gender-based violence against elite women, considering the extent and frequency of gender-based violence as a more general pattern in late Roman Italy between 250 and 500, and asking how far a consistent culture of risk saw unrest, conflict and gender-based violence as an expected constant rather than an abnormal state of affairs.

Gender-based violence is defined as violence that is directed against a person because of their gender. Both women and men can perpetrate and experience gender-based

---

[1] Holum 1982; Busch 2015; Hillner 2017; Vuolanto 2019.
[2] International Federation of Red Cross 2015, 17.
[3] Women in warfare 'who lost their lives or were raped during the sack of cities are as anonymous as the mothers and widows of the dead warriors', in Chaniotis 2008, 113. For women and violence in the Roman world, see Witzke 2016.

violence, but the majority of victims are women and girls.[4] The 1993 United Nations World Conference on Human Rights located gender-based violence as occurring in the family, within the general community, and perpetrated or condoned by the state.[5] It included domestic violence, rape and human trafficking in the definition.[6] The terminology of gender-based violence is important because it links different violences against women that together reflect and sustain structural gender power inequalities. A key methodological point is that gender-based violence is never an isolated or unrelated occurrence but is part of a wider societal pattern facilitated by a culturally embedded framework of institutional and structural sexism, misogyny, bias and discrimination. Violence against women is endemic in strongly patriarchal societies, and Roman society was quintessentially patriarchal.[7]

Our own historically based understanding of gender-based violence is as an umbrella term for many forms of abuse, including physical violence, such as assault, battery, murder, abduction, forced movement and captivity; sexual violence, including rape, sexual assault, forced pregnancy, premature marriage and sexual exploitation; and psychological violence, including coercion, defamation, harassment, economic abuse, intimidation, threats of violence and harm, manipulation and control, and the use of a child or children by a violent partner to control the mother or female relatives. Because gender-based violence is not confined to physical or sexual violence but encompasses forms of violence that are psychological, we also consider women's experiences of the murders of their male relatives and children. Examples of these forms of gender-based violence will be approached in four sections exploring the ancient evidence: (1) Pressure of Procreation and Marriage, Intimidation, Physical Harm and the Threat of Harm; (2) Pregnancy and Violence; (3) Abduction, Captivity and Rape of Elite Women; and (4) the Murder and Assassination of Women and Their Relatives.

Female agency is central to an understanding of the subjection of elite women to gender-based violence or their avoidance of it; women who cannot operate agency cannot protect themselves from persecution or attack. However, the complete removal of the agency of female subjects by ancient writers should be treated sceptically. Even where the ancient evidence seems to suggest that they have no agency, those subjected to or threatened with gender-based violence will be managing the situation and constantly risk-assessing for safety. For example, a lack of resistance to rape is a survival strategy and not an indication of complicity.[8] The fragmentary ancient evidence makes assessing the extent of control that elite women had over their own lives and of resisting gender-based violence particularly challenging. How far we can detect female agency through ideological representation and self-promotion in evidence such

---

[4] As defined by the European Institute for Gender Equality: https://eige.europa.eu/gender-based-violence/what-is-gender-based-violence. For further discussion of gender violence and violence against women and girls, see Elman 2013, 236–37; Lombard 2017.
[5] For the text of the Vienna Declaration and Programme of Action, see UN Doc. A/CONF.157/23 (1993).
[6] For further discussion of definitions, see Skinner et al. 2005.
[7] See Cantarella 2016. For patriarchy and history, see Bennett 2006.
[8] Möller et al. 2017.

as coins, dedicatory inscriptions and textual sources remains an open question.[9] Yet these activities do not exclude or contradict the endurance, survival or resistance of elite women in the face of gender-based violence. It is this complex, inconsistent and crucially women-orientated perspective that we can begin to uncover by considering late Roman Italy.

Gender-Based Violence in Late Ancient Studies: Framing the Field

In recent decades, the topic of violence in Late Antiquity has received increasing scholarly attention.[10] Yet an explicit focus on gendered violence, particularly violence perpetrated against women, girls and children, is almost entirely absent.[11] Although the evidence base for attitudes towards violence and disaster in late Roman society is considerable, critical understandings of how far unrest, conflict, sexual, domestic and gender-based violence contributed to an adverse environment for women have yet to be advanced, and the field is far from the recognition that cultural or traditional defences of male violence are indefensible.[12] Gendered violence has been dismissed in modern criticism, an approach that compounds rather than interrogates the embedded antipathy of ancient writers to detailing gender-based violence. Diffuse scholarly attention has been given to some aspects of gendered violence in ancient writers like Augustine of Hippo, through his attention to rape of women in the sack of Rome in 410, and his representation of the domestic abuse perpetrated by his father and suffered by his mother Monica, but there remains much potential for future research to expand upon.[13] More recently, less traditional approaches that take account of gender, consent, coercion and agency have begun to filter through, such as Mira Balberg and Ellen Muehlberger's excellent article on coercion in Late Antiquity.[14] Blossom Stefaniw has recently argued that patriarchy is a permanent and inescapable system, and that feminist historiography has to exist within the 'intimate wickedness' of persistent institutional misogyny, equating academic patriarchy with domestic violence.[15] There has been a noticeable turn towards thinking through the lens of gender-based violence and sexual violence in classics, where Graeco-Roman myths are reframed as

---

[9] For agency as a historical phenomenon, see Thomas 2016. For women on coins, see Brubaker and Tobler 2002; Angelova 2004. For inscriptions, see Trout 2013. See also the discussions in Brubaker and Smith 2004, and Cameron and Kuhrt 1993.
[10] Ando 1996; Cameron 2002 and 2008; Hahn 2004; Gaddis 2005; Drake 2006 and 2011; Stanton and Stroumsa 2008; Kahlos 2009; Sizgorich 2009; Athanassiadi 2010; Shaw 2011; Papaconstantinou et al. 2015.
[11] Notable exceptions include Dossey 2008; Hillner 2013; and Carucci 2018.
[12] Elman 2013, 238. Celene Lillie argues that 'evading and avoiding the reality of sexual violence ... is another way of perpetuating the structures and systems that promote, reward, and tolerate sexual violence'. Lillie 2018, 12.
[13] See Webb 2013; Clark 2015, 58–79; Barry 2020. On the rape of women during the Vandal sack of Africa through the letters of Leo I, see Ward-Perkins 2006, 13.
[14] Balberg and Muehlberger 2018.
[15] Stefaniw 2020, 264.

rape narratives, and the online journal *Eidolon* has provided a new platform for more radical approaches to gender and antiquity.[16] Conflict and unrest are pressure points for the perpetration of gender-based violence, but ancient military studies, described as 'the quintessentially patriarchal discourse', remain intractably resistant to considerations of gender, sexual violence and rape within warfare.[17] Kathy L. Gaca's research is an important corrective to the androcentric paradigm of ancient military studies. She argues persuasively that it is inadequate to regard ancient ravaging warfare 'simply as men's business of exercising lethal force on one another', and she foregrounds the wider context of warfare beyond the battlefield, including sexual violence and populace ravaging, which have particular consequences for women, girls and children.[18] But Gaca's work focuses on earlier periods of ancient history, and there has been no equivalent revisionist analysis for late ancient studies. Traditional historical approaches structured through male political rulership and the fall or transformation of empires are constituted so as to be nearly impenetrable to new insights. This chapter synthesises evidence for gendered violence in late Roman Italy and, in doing so, deconstructs the monodimensional understanding of violence in history that discounts gender.

Pressure of Procreation and Marriage, Intimidation, Physical Harm and the Threat of Harm

Betrothals and marriage alliances exposed women to the risk of gendered violence in antiquity, especially in the late Roman period, as elite marriages became increasingly restrictive against the political backdrop. The historical correlation between familial and kinship ties and the perpetration of violence against women, particularly through intimate partner violence, is evident but largely unrecognised.[19] Roman imperial marriage was a legal device exploited largely by men to exert influence, assert legitimacy and repress their competitors in politically fraught situations. Royal and imperial women were valued for marriage and procreation, and although a childless marriage could be sufficient to establish legitimacy, the reproductive capabilities of elite women nevertheless needed to be, and were increasingly, tightly controlled. Until the mid-third century, marriage alliances were insular and devised generally among the Roman aristocracy, but the political fragmentation of the Roman Empire in the post-Constantinian era polarised the question of legitimate imperial claims and bloodlines. As Meaghan McEvoy has argued, in the fourth and fifth centuries imperial women 'became increasingly difficult to place in marriages which would not be perceived as a threat by the reigning emperor'.[20] Marriage patterns of imperial women shifted away from localised aristocratic alliances to ties that could be exploited as a tool of international diplomacy, reflecting the political necessities of the time.[21] The

---

[16] Moretti et al. 2019; Herzog 2018.
[17] O'Gorman 2006, 193.
[18] Gaca 2016, 1041.
[19] For a preliminary analysis of historical intimate partner violence, see Roth 2014.
[20] McEvoy 2016, 173.
[21] See Becker-Piriou 2008.

changing face of late Roman imperial marriage increased the vulnerability of women and children to harm.

The pressure put on marriageable and fertile elite women was high: Constantius II's daughter Constantia was married in 374, around the age of 12, to facilitate the teenage western emperor Gratian in creating a much-needed link to the Constantinian dynasty – just as his father Valentinian I had formed a similar link through Justina.[22] Constantia spent her final years from 381 at the court in Milan before her death in 383 at the young age of 21 – the circumstances of her death are unknown.[23] The daughter of Valentinian III, Placidia, on the other hand, was contested territory in Ravenna in the 430s: her father anticipated that she would marry the future emperor Majorian, which went against the interests of the *magister utriusque militiae* Aëtius, who intended Placidia to marry his son Gaudentius instead. Placidia eventually married neither man, but an influential man of senatorial rank named Olybrius in 454–5.[24] Aëtius himself had similarly used marriage to generate power when he married Pelagia, the Gothic widow of Boniface, who allegedly had urged his wife to form this union with his enemy upon his death in 432 – we may again question who held the power in this situation.[25] Such elite women would have had an awareness of their unique positions as creators of alliances and heirs and must have anticipated such tensions, but this does not mean they welcomed marriages or that they were able to exert influence to their benefit amongst negotiations.

Questions of consent surround politically motivated marriages: if a woman was forced or harassed into a marriage, is this consent? The issue of marital consent is not only a modern concern and was addressed in Roman law: a woman had to agree to a marriage in order for it to be valid.[26] Although such legislation has been described critically as 'superfluous and irrelevant', given that women were expected to obey the *paterfamilias* with regards to marriage, women's consent appears to have been increasingly considered in the Imperial era.[27] In the late 440s the historian Priscus records that the intended union between the daughter of a wealthy Roman, Saturninus, and Attila the Hun's secretary, Constantius, fell through because Roman law required the woman to be willing to enter into the marriage, which the woman was not.[28] Furthermore, the popular Christian topos of young women defying family expectations by choosing dedicated continence over marriage arguably places some agency in their hands.

The obstacle of female consent, however, could be circumvented by child marriage, with the betrothed child having fewer capabilities for resistance. The betrothal and marriage of minors exploited the dependent and vulnerable status of children,

---

[22] Woods 2004.
[23] For Constantia, see McEvoy 2016.
[24] As observed by Oost 1964. For Olybrius, see Clover 1978.
[25] Marcell. Com. s.a. 432.3; see MacGeorge 2002, 183; Wijnendaele 2015, 107.
[26] *CTh* 3.10.1, 3.6.1 and 3.11.1. On women in Roman law, see Laiou 1993; Treggiari 1993; Evans Grubbs 1995; Arjava 1996 and 1998.
[27] Arjava 1996, 35; and for the growing attention paid to consent in Roman law, Kuefler 2007, especially 347–52.
[28] Priscus fr. 15.3. See *PLRE* 2, 'Saturninus 3', 979–80; 'Constantius 7', 317; 'Anonyma 21', 1240.

causing harm and suffering. The *magister utriusque militiae* Stilicho's two daughters, Maria and Thermantia, were both married to the young emperor Honorius to strengthen the alliance between the western emperor and Stilicho. In 398, Maria was married to Honorius and, when Maria died around 407–8, Honorius married Stilicho's second daughter Thermantia instead.[29] The historian Zosimus, drawing from the work of Olympiodorus,[30] gives the following account of these unions:

> When the marriage of Honorius to Maria was being arranged, her mother [Serena], seeing that the girl was not yet old enough to marry, was nevertheless unwilling to defer the marriage, although she realised that to give away her daughter to the marriage bed when she was too young was a crime against nature. So finding a woman who knew how to arrange such things, with her help she managed that her daughter should marry the emperor and even sleep with him, but that he should neither be willing nor able to fulfil his conjugal duty. The girl died still a virgin, and Serena, very properly anxious for royal grandchildren for fear her great power might be lessened, sought to join Honorius with her second daughter. This happened, but she died not long after, having had the same experience as her sister.[31]

The girls' years of birth are unknown, and while an age of 12 has been suggested for Maria,[32] she may have been even younger upon her marriage in 398 – the reluctance of the sources could imply an inappropriately young age. Her mother Serena was aware that Maria was too young for sex and the task of childbearing, and Zosimus recognises that to give such a child in marriage was to do injustice or commit wrongdoing to nature (φύσεως ἀδικίαν). Honorius was 14 at the time of the marriage, and Serena feared that he would deprive Maria of her virginity. Zosimus' language of wrongdoing and abuse of power reflects ancient awareness of the physical damage that penetrative sex can inflict on an unmatured female body. Serena sought to prevent this through unspecified methods, but neither she nor Stilicho was prepared to defer the marriage: politics overruled the physical and emotional welfare of the child. The poet Claudian describes Honorius as feverishly passionate for his new bride and states that Maria's womb was expected to grow with a *parvus Honoriades*.[33]

---

[29] For the marriages, see McEvoy 2013, 159–62, 177–80.
[30] For Olympiodorus and Zosimus' build-up of his work, see Matthews 1970, 79–97; Blockley 1981, 28–47.
[31] Zos. 5.28.1–3 (trans. Ridley 2017, 113). Mendelssohn 1887, 251: τοῦ γάμου τοῦ πρὸς Μαρίαν Ὀνωρίῳ ἐνισταμένου, γάμων ὥραν οὔπω τὴν κόρην ἄγουσαν ἡ μήτηρ ὁρῶσα, καὶ οὔτε ἀναβαλέσθαι τὸν γάμον ἀνεχομένη, καὶ τὸ παρ' ἡλικίαν εἰς μῖξιν ἐκδοῦναι φύσεως ἀδικίαν καὶ οὐδὲν ἕτερον εἶναι . . . γυναικὶ τὰ τοιαῦτα θεραπεύειν ἐπισταμένῃ περιτυχοῦσα πράττει διὰ ταύτης τὸ συνεῖναι μὲν τὴν θυγατέρα τῷ βασιλεῖ καὶ ὁμόλεκτρον εἶναι, τὸν δὲ μήτε ἐθέλειν μήτε δύνασθαι τὰ τῷ γάμῳ προσήκοντα πράττειν. ἐν τούτῳ τῆς κόρης ἀπείρου γάμων ἀποθανούσης, εἰκότως ἡ Σερῆνα βασιλείου γονῆς ἐπιθυμοῦσα δέει τοῦ μὴ τὴν τοσαύτην αὐτῇ δυναστείαν ἐλαττωθῆναι, τῇ δευτέρᾳ θυγατρὶ συνάψαι τὸν Ὀνώριον ἔσπευδεν. οὗ δὴ γενομένου τελευτᾷ μὲν ἡ κόρη μετ' οὐ πολύ, ταὐτὰ τῇ προτέρᾳ παθοῦσα.
[32] McEvoy 2013, 160.
[33] Claud. *Epith.* 1–46.

Maria and Honorius remained married until her death around 407–8. While the pair may have initiatially been sexually immature, Maria died in her late teens or early twenties, while Honorius was around 23 years of age. As Honorius entered his second marriage fully matured, even Serena, according to Zosimus, wanted children to be produced, as she wished to cement her own influence in the imperial court. Serena was a prominent figure in Italy; she was the adopted daughter of Theodosius I, well connected and had funded the building of shrines in both Milan and Rome.[34] Yet her position relied on the marriages of her daughters, and so she advocated for the union of Honorius and Thermantia. Thermantia was at this point most likely of an age more appropriate for childbearing. But her time as Honorius' wife cannot have been pleasant: within a year of the marriage came Stilicho's downfall, both of Thermantia's parents were executed, her brother Eucherius was assassinated, and Stilicho's supporters were massacred, leaving Thermantia with her support system obliterated. Honorius, who had authorised the execution of his wife's family, most likely cast her aside, and she died, childless, around 415.[35]

It is possible that Thermantia had remained a virgin. Arranged marriages could be accompanied by a mutual lack of interest, especially if the politics that forged them became obsolete. Several sources record Honorius as impotent or having chosen chastity, but this is difficult to reconcile with Serena's expectation of grandchildren or Claudian's description of Honorius' fiery passions, unless the rhetoric sought to compensate for Honorius' shortcomings.[36] A muddled legal dimension also marks Honorius' marriages to Stilicho's daughters – a legal issue that would have rendered any children produced in the second marriage illegitimate, as marrying a sister-in-law fell under the legal concept of incestuous marriages.[37] The lack of issue meant that the legitimacy of Honorius' children never arose, but these legal considerations emphasise that politically motivated marriages took place even if they were legally suspect but politically beneficial, and even if the marriages placed women under the threat of sexual violence and pregnancy before or during puberty. Such marriages also placed women in traumatising situations, including the husband's massacre of the wife's family. The threat of harm to women on the wrong side of marriage alliances was severe, as demonstrated also by the murder of Eutropia, the half-sister of Constantine, in the purge of opposition and overthrow of her son Nepotianus in 350 in Rome by Magnentius.[38]

The experiences of Maria and Thermantia are rarely considered in the schemes of Stilicho and his contemporaries, if they are mentioned at all. The issue of their consent is absent in all historical accounts, although Zosimus shows awareness of the detrimental

---

[34] *ILCV* 1801; Zos. 5.38.2–5.
[35] Zos. 5.44; Wijnendaele 2018.
[36] Impotence is suggested by Philost. *Hist. eccl.* 12.2; supporters of chastity include Oros. 7.37.11; Theodoret, *Hist. eccl.* 5.25.2, also see Marcell. Com. s.a. 408.
[37] A 355 law sent to Rome by Constantius forbade men from marrying their sisters-in-law, be that a former wife's sister or one's brother's wife. This same law also declared that children born of such unions were illegitimate (*CTh* 3.12.2 (355)). In the year of Thermantia's death – before or after is uncertain – the law forbidding a man from marrying two sisters was reissued at Constantinople, and Honorius' name was attached to the law; see *CTh* 3.12.4 (415).
[38] Athan. *Apol. Const.* 6; Zos. 2.43.2.

effects of early marriage, including coercion and sexual exploitation – perhaps echoing Olympiodorus' sentiments likewise. The procreative responsibilities of female children or teenage girls for the benefit of male hegemonic authority were bleak and brutal. However, it is possible to find female success amongst the considerable adversities of child marriage: Justina (d. 388) married the emperor Magnentius when she was still too young to have children, while her husband was decades her senior.[39] It should not be assumed that Magnentius and Justina's union was sexless because of her immaturity, and from any perspective the agency and consent of a child barely into puberty would have been non-existent. Magnentius committed suicide at the end of his failed usurpation in 353, some three years into the marriage. Yet this was the start rather than the end of Justina's career: she went on to exert great influence as the wife of Valentinian I, producing imperial heirs, and marrying her own daughter Galla to Theodosius I c.387 when Galla was aged between 13 and 17.[40] Justina had an acute political eye, and as a former child bride, viewed political marriages as a way of enforcing her own will. Perhaps her personal experience had shown her that women could operate and generate power from these unions, provided they survived them.

Pregnancy and Violence

Early marriage highlights the female body's capacity for childbearing, which was always potentially life threatening for women, whether young or old.[41] Women are made more vulnerable to harm through pregnancy and child-dependency, and elite women in particular were at risk of gender-based violence when pregnancy was perceived as a political threat. Rumours of violence surround the pregnancies of Helena, wife of the emperor Julian (360–3). Helena's marriage in Milan in 355 was intended to produce heirs with Constantinian lineage. She is subsequently recorded as being pregnant twice, and both times her children perished through nefarious means. Ammianus Marcellinus records that following Helena's first childbirth, a bribed midwife intentionally cut the newborn child's umbilical cord too short, killing the child.[42] The implication is that behind this scheming was Eusebia, the childless wife of Constantius II, who viewed any children by Helena and Julian as a threat to her own imperial interests.[43] Eusebia's role as a perpetrator of harm is cemented when, in 357, Helena travelled to Rome, pregnant for the second time within two years. Ammianus describes Eusebia's plot against Helena: '[Eusebia] herself had been childless all her life, and by her wiles coaxed Helena to drink a rare potion, so that as often as she was with child she should have a miscarriage.'[44] This narrative reveals how gendered violence does not necessitate male perpetrators and

---

[39] John of Antioch (fr. 187) records that Justina was too young to have children during her marriage. See further Chausson 2007, 100.
[40] Zos. 4.44.2–4.
[41] Dasen 2004 and 2011; Rawson 2011; Carroll 2018.
[42] Amm. Marc. 16.10.19.
[43] Tougher 2000.
[44] Amm. Marc. 16.10.18: *regina tunc insidiabatur Eusebia, ipsa quoad vixerat sterilis, quaesitumque venenum bibere per fraudem illexit, ut quotienscumque concepisset, immaturum abiceret partum.*

can involve women inflicting gender-based violence against other women. Helena's pregnancies may be cases of a stillbirth and a miscarriage without interference – neither would have been medically uncommon. The historicity of the poisonings has been questioned, although not all historians have dismissed these rumours.[45] If they are factual, Helena suffered targeted, cruel and traumatising violence; if fictional, Ammianus nevertheless testifies how pregnant elite women could become targets because of their unborn children, emphasising the vulnerability of not only the pregnant female body, but especially the pregnant, elite female body. Helena and her unborn children were at risk of violence, and she died in 360 after five years of marriage without issue.

Helena's own mother Fausta, Constantine I's wife, may also have died because of her procreative capacity. Her death is shrouded in mystery, but pregnancy and physical harm dominate the textualised rumours.[46] Fausta died in a bath or bathhouse in Rome in 326, and her husband was in some way responsible. She was murdered when Constantine's eldest son Crispus, from his first marriage, had been executed, and the deaths of the two are linked in the ancient sources, although these relations remain unresolved.[47] One tradition holds that Fausta was jealous of Crispus and wanted him dead, another that she was enamoured by him, and a third that Crispus had raped her. If Fausta and Crispus had a consensual affair, then we gain a glimpse of female agency, however fleeting, before Fausta's death.[48] According to some testimonies, Fausta killed herself when faced with interrogation, and another holds that Constantine's mother Helena had urged the emperor to avenge the death of Crispus, a further example of female-instigated gender-based violence. An alternative interpretation holds that Fausta was pregnant by Crispus and died following a botched abortion forced upon her by Constantine. Fausta's murder sits oddly with the image of the first Christian emperor, and it has baffled historians.[49] Although Constantine and Fausta's marriage was ostensibly amicable until her obscured death, all versions of events contain gender-based violence, whether that is rape, a forced abortion or adultery-related interrogation or suicide. Constantine had also been responsible for the death of her father. David Woods, who favours the narrative that pregnancy from adultery led to an abortion gone wrong, has argued that 'Constantine has been unfairly blamed for the execution of his wife', as Constantine had sought an abortion, not an execution.[50] However, if Constantine used his unquestioned authority over his pregnant wife to force her into a physically harmful, life-threatening medical procedure, Constantine is not absolved of culpability: forced abortion is gender-based violence in action.[51]

Between 250 and 500, imperial marriage in the Italian courts was a dangerous enterprise for women, premature or not. The ancient evidence is characterised by rumour, contradiction and a lack of transparency, which betrays the private and hidden

---

[45] See the discussion in Tougher 2000, 96–7.
[46] Fausta has been described as 'the most silent of all the silent women of Rome', in Harries 2014, 206.
[47] Zos. 2.29.2; Eunap. 9.3.
[48] On Fausta, see Drijvers 1992; Woods 1998. The rape charge is recorded in *Epit. de Caes.* 41.11–12.
[49] This ambivalence is perhaps first discernible in the representation of Constantine in Orosius.
[50] Woods 1998, 83.
[51] Pohlsander's analysis is similarly victim-blaming, and his conclusions are misogynistic. Pohlsander 1984.

environment in which violence against women, children and girls was perpetrated. But focusing on gender-based violence in women's experiences reveals how elite women were physically compromised, threatened and at risk of psychological harm, physical harm and death by the actions overwhelmingly of men, frequently acting out of political interests. The preservation of women's narratives in the ancient evidence reveals that reproductive coercion was a central aspect of gendered violence against women, where pregnancy, abortion and virginity were forced upon elite women.

The last of these – forced virginity – resulted in Valentinian III's sister Justa Grata Honoria (418–55) being caught in an affair with her property manager Eugenius and is testimony to celibacy as a method of oppression. This infamous episode from 440s Ravenna included Valentinian threatening to kill his sister, and Honoria being stripped of her title *Augusta*. It led to the executions of Honoria's lover and her attendant, and perhaps the murder of her child.[52] Instances such as these demonstrate how restrictive and manipulative gendered violence was inflicted on some of the most politically influential women of the time. The mobilisation of the tools of patriarchy, particularly the shaming of women through accusations of adultery and *stuprum*, remained effective throughout the Roman period.[53] However, virginity could be a method through which agency was exercised for elite women. The eastern empress Pulcheria, the older sister of Theodosius II and the de facto ruler in his childhood, dedicated herself to virginity at the age of 14, placing herself beyond the demands of marriage and the dangers of pregnancy. The benefit to her was noted contemporarily: 'to avoid all cause of jealousy and intrigue, [Pulcheria] permitted no man to enter her palace'.[54] By choosing to become a consecrated virgin, Pulcheria, in effect, took control of her future, exercising her right to renounce sex and her own fertility, in order to protect herself and her family's imperial interests. Pulcheria also recruited her younger sisters into vows of virginity.[55]

Pulcheria did not invent the exercise of power through virginity, however; earlier examples stem from the western courts in Trier and Milan. Valentinian I's two daughters Grata and Justa appear to have been consecrated virgins, as attested by Ambrose of Milan.[56] The remaining daughter of Valentinian I, Galla, was married to Theodosius I by her former child-bride mother Justina in 387, after Magnus Maximus managed to push the imperial family out of Italy. The marriage was a carefully calculated political arrangement to ensure Theodosius' support for Valentinian II. Galla died in childbirth

---

[52] Jord. *Get.* 244, *Rom.* 328. The pregnancy is recorded in Marcell. Com. s.a. 434. For Honoria, see *PLRE* 2.569; Bury 1919; Busch 2015, 166–76. As noted by Kenneth Holum, 'ominous silence' surrounds the fate of the child that vanishes from the historical record, in Holum 1982, 1. For the political implications of what he terms the 'Honoria affair', see Meier 2017.

[53] The ancient concept of *stuprum* signified a sexual crime, but perhaps unsurprisingly given the requirements of shadowy euphemism, the complexity and plurality of the term make it difficult to define. For *stuprum*, see Fantham 1991; Laiou 1993; and Williams 2010, 103–36.

[54] Sozom. *Hist. eccl.* 9.1 (PL 67.1503): ὅπως μὴ ἄλλον ἄνδρα ἐπεισαγάγῃ τοῖς βασιλείοις, καί ζήλου καί ἐπιβουλῆς πᾶσαν ἀνέλῃ ἀφορμή.

[55] For Pulcheria's career, see Holum 1982, 79–111; 2004; Chew 2006; Busch 2015, 110–35.

[56] Ambr. *Ob. Val.* 36; Socrates, *Hist. eccl.* 4.31.17. On Grata, see *PLRE* 1.400; for Galla, see *PLRE* 1.382.

in 394, after the virginity of her two sisters had left her as the sole bargaining chip.[57] It is impossible to know if Grata and Justa had chosen virginity to circumvent the pressures of marriage and childbearing, or whether virginity was imposed on them to focus imperial legitimacy on Galla. Dedicated virginity was, nevertheless, a method that women could employ to escape the threat of or actual gender-based violence within marriage and childbearing. However, elite women could not mitigate against risk comprehensively, which becomes particularly apparent in their forcible removal from familiar surroundings through abduction, which exposed them to considerable harm.

Abduction, Captivity and Rape of Elite Women

Gender-based violence in late Roman Italy is particularly prevalent in accounts of warfare, most commonly in the capture of enemy women, followed by ransoming, enslavement, assault, sexual violence and death. Captivity occurred after raids, battles and sieges, which themselves were marked by rape and sexual assault.[58] Modern criticism generally holds that ancient and modern conceptions of rape are not directly analogous, and that *raptus* was treated as a crime against the male relatives of a female victim. Whilst late antique legal sources encompass a variety of actions within *raptus*, Judith Evans Grubbs defines it as the abduction of an unmarried girl by a man who is not formally betrothed to her.[59] It was assumed that sexual assault occurred while in captivity, and Roman law dictated that a husband could not accuse his wife returning from captivity of adultery.[60] Numerous contemporary accounts show that the abduction and ransoming of civilians was frequent during warfare in Italy in the fifth century,[61] while other narratives emphasise how escaping gender-based violence was a matter of luck: Constantius II's daughter Constantia was saved from near capture and enslavement in Pannonia in 374 following a raid of the Quadi, not because of her imperial connections, but by the swift actions of the local governor.[62]

Politically motivated rapes are also attested, where men of power raped the wives of their opponents. A dubious John of Antioch fragment states that Valentinian III had raped the wife of Petronius Maximus, which perhaps accounts for Maximus' treatment of Valentinian's widow Eudoxia (see below).[63] In writing his glorifying

---

[57] Zos. 4.57.3; Joh. Ant. fr. 187.
[58] For warfare and sieges, see Levithan 2013; Petersen 2013; Martinez Morales 2019; Vihervalli 2022. For abduction see Klingshirn 1985; Lenski 2011.
[59] Evans Grubbs 1989, 61.
[60] *Dig.* 48.5.14.7.
[61] Lamentations of wartime abductions in Italy are recorded in Innocent I, *Ep.* 36 (PL 20.602–3); Leo the Great, *Serm.* 78.4 (PL 54.418), *Serm.* 10.1–2 (CCSL 138.39–41), *Ep.* 159.1–5 (PL 54.1136); Peter Chrysologus, *Serm.* 103.7 (PL 52.489); Prosper, *Chron.* s.a. 455.
[62] Amm. Marc. 29.6.6–9. Ammianus' comment (29.6.8) reveals the ideology of personal and political shame that would have accompanied Constantia's capture: 'After the princess was saved by this fortunate chance from the danger of wretched slavery, which, if it had been impossible to ransom the captive, would have branded the state with the greatest disaster . . .' (trans. Rolfe 1952, 3.284–7); *hoc casu prospero regia virgine periculo miserae servitutis exempta, cuius ni potuisset impetrari redemptio captae, magnas inussisset rei publicae clades . . .*
[63] Joh. Ant. fr. 293.2.

Vita Constantini, on the other hand, Eusebius of Caesarea added to his tyrannical portraits of Maxentius and Licinius that both had raped the wives of senators and elite men, the former in Rome between 308 and 312, the latter in the eastern provinces between 314 and 324.[64] Whether historical or fictional, men were well aware that political hostility could be effectively enacted on the bodies of women. Capturing an elite woman enabled the captor's exploitation of her politically and economically as well as sexually, and instances of daughters and wives of emperors being abducted, married and impregnated while in captivity are historically attested. These types of abductions were wholly new – never before had imperial women been captured and forcibly moved, reflecting the shifting and politically fraught circumstances of late Roman Italy.

The most conspicuous example of female abduction was Galla Placidia, one of the few women whose life and career has been exclusively studied.[65] Placidia was the daughter of Theodosius I and sister of emperors Honorius and Arcadius, but she was not exempt from violent capture and compulsory marriage at the hands of Alaric's Goths following the sack of Rome in 410.[66] Placidia may have been in her early twenties when she was forcibly married to the Gothic leader Athaulf around 414 and had a son, Theodosius, in 415.[67] Athaulf had children and was married to an unnamed wife when he forcibly took Galla Placidia in marriage.[68] There is no further mention of Athaulf's first wife in the ancient evidence, and in a historical interpretation grounded in 'himpathy', modern scholars have assumed that she conveniently died, making the marriage (more) legitimate.[69] By the following year both Theodosius and Athaulf were dead, and Galla Placidia was 'returned' to her brother Honorius as part of the spoils of war, publicly and shamefully paraded through the streets like a prisoner of war.[70] Galla Placidia was a victim of war-ravaging, subjected to the same non-consensual capture, subjugation and sexual violence that women implicated in warfare in antiquity suffered.

Following Galla Placidia's marriage to Athaulf in 414, the marriage of imperial women to non-Roman leaders became a historical pattern in the fifth century. Justa Grata Honoria, after having been caught in her affair, avoided an unwanted marriage by finding an alternative partner, Attila the Hun. Eudocia, the granddaughter of Galla Placidia, married the Vandal king Huneric in the 460s.[71] Eudocia and her sister

---

[64] Euseb. *Vit. Const.* 1.33, 1.55. At *Vit. Const.* 1.34, Eusebius further includes an anecdote of a Christian prefect's wife committing suicide as she was about to be handed over to Maxentius for sexual violation.

[65] The two major works on Galla Placidia's life are Oost 1968 and Sivan 2011. Other biographies include Sirago 1961; Storoni Mazzolani 1975; and Salisbury 2015.

[66] See Oros. 7.40.2; Olympiodorus fr. 6; Prosper, *Chron.* s.a. 416; Marcell. Com. s.a. 410; Hyd. 36(44); Zos. 6.12.3. For discussion of Placidia's forced marriage, sexual violence and captivity, see Leonard 2019.

[67] The date of her birth is contested. See Sivan 2011, 12 n. 13. On the marriage between Placidia and Athaulf, see Cesa 1992–1993; Harlow 2004; Assorati 2016; and Leonard 2019.

[68] Olympiodorus fr. 10. See also Sozom. *Hist. eccl.* 9.8.2; Oros. 7.40.2; Zos. 5.37.1; Marcell. Com. s.a. 410; Jord. *Get.* 158.

[69] The term 'himpathy' was coined by Manne 2018. Olympiodorus fr. 26.1 also states that Athaulf's children by his first wife were killed after his death, but makes no mention of what had become of her.

[70] Olympiodorus fr. 26. For the reconstruction of Galla Placidia's return, see Leonard 2019.

[71] Becker-Piriou 2008 situates Placidia in a historical context that looks forward to the diplomatic role of imperial women, especially through marriage treaties between Romans and hostile non-Romans.

Placidia had been abducted as captives with the empress Eudoxia during the sack of Rome in 455 by the Vandal king Geiseric.[72] Placidia's value as a marital pawn in the ambitions of Aëtius and Valentinian III has already been observed, and she had presumably been married to Olybrius shortly before her abduction. Her mother Eudoxia, recently widowed after the murder of Valentinian III, was forced into marriage to her husband's successor Petronius Maximus, an alliance that was further strengthened by the marriage of her daughter Eudocia to Petronius' son Palladius.[73] Eudoxia is reported to have approached outsiders to help her, such as the Vandal king Geiseric, as Eudocia had been betrothed to Geiseric's son Huneric at around the age of 5, since the Romano-Vandal treaty of 442. This betrothal had necessitated the disposal of Huneric's existing wife, an unnamed Gothic princess who was the daughter of Theoderic I. In order to legitimate the divorce, she was accused of using poisons against Geiseric and punished by mutilation: her ears and nose were cut off, after which she was returned to her father shamed.[74] The violence and cruelty inflicted upon Huneric's first wife as a royal woman placed tension on Gothic–Vandal relations, and the episode must have been known in the Italian imperial courts. The authenticity of Eudoxia's desire to join her daughters and actively choose to become subject to hostile and violent men, particularly a devout Arian like Geiseric, should be treated with suspicion.

While in captivity in 460, Eudocia gave birth to a son, Hilderic. After the birth in 461, Eudoxia and Placidia were allowed to embark for Constantinople, where Placidia joined her husband Olybrius.[75] Eudocia remained in Carthage alone, without the support of her mother and sister. Nothing is known of her treatment, except that she remained there for sixteen years, and was finally allowed to leave for Jerusalem in 471–2, where she died soon after.[76] Like Galla Placidia, Eudocia was captured from the imperial courts of Italy, married into a barbarian royal family, and produced a child that consolidated the ties of kinship between a barbarian royal family and Roman imperial blood. In less sanitised terms, she was abducted, forcibly moved across international borders, raped and impregnated, and kept in captivity without agency. Eudocia died after spending about half of her life as a captive, and politically motivated male violence defined her entire existence, including her procreative capacity. Although Noel Lenski has described Eudocia's experiences as 'virtual sexual slavery', most scholarship has disregarded this reality.[77] Political hostility was repeatedly and consistently made manifest through the bodies of elite women.[78]

Galla Placidia and Eudocia are exceptional historical cases, representing the role of women in international politics at the highest level. As a result, assault and rape in their narrative experiences have traditionally been ignored. Their sexual and reproductive

---

[72] Kelly 2008, 177–89; Merrills and Miles 2010; Modéran 2014.
[73] Hyd. 155(162); Victor of Tonnena s.a. 455, 14; Proc. *Bell.* 3.4.36. The marriage of Palladius and Eudocia is recorded by Hyd. 155(162), in Burgess 1993, 105.
[74] For this episode, see Jord. *Get.* 36.184; Conant 2012, 24–5.
[75] Priscus fr. 38; John Malalas, *Chron.* 366; Theoph. a.m. 5949.
[76] Theoph. a.m. 5964; Zonar. 13.25.29. See also Conant 2012, 31–2.
[77] Lenski 2004, 120.
[78] MacKinnon 2007, 223.

relations have been romanticised to the limits of credibility, with legitimate heirs symbolising the convergence of Roman and barbarian *regna*. Their reality is unlikely to have been in any way romantic.[79] The Romans were fiercely opposed to abduction marriages, and the marked lack of criticism in the ancient evidence seeks to evade reality and smooth over the violence and degradation that was inherent to these women's experiences of captivity.[80] For contemporaries and historians picking up the narrative threads, it was easier to look the other way. For elite women these abductions reveal the extent of their limited agency in spite of their considerable prestige and lineage. This remained true in later contexts, as demonstrated by the forcible marriage of the Ostrogothic princess Matasuentha first to the Ostrogothic king Witigis and then to the Roman general Germanus in the mid-sixth century.

It is unclear if Eudoxia and her daughters were taken to Carthage in 455 by request or against their will. Eudoxia's appeal to the Vandals may be polemical, playing into the topos of the deceitful woman, or it may be a straightforward example of victim-blaming.[81] Eudoxia's situation in Rome would have been dire, and her risk-assessing would only have presented one potentially harmful situation as an alternative to another: Petronius Maximus had orchestrated the murder of her husband, while Geiseric was a potentially hostile alternative with a reputation for violence, as female mutilation in his court had shown. Ancient writers repeatedly blur historical fact and rumour in women's narratives, with elite women sending clandestine letters to barbarians and having secret affairs, all of which anticipates female blame. The misogyny that underpins the ancient evidence does not allow the analysis of female agency. Instead, we can conceive of rumours of female misbehaviour and narratives that invariably conclude with female punishment as a testament to the historic lack of safety of women – such anecdotes do not function rhetorically if they have no relevance to the context of gendered violence that they were written within. Women were persistently at risk in late Roman society, including elite and aristocratic women, whose status in reality offered no protection from the realities of male violence. We can see this in the later context of sixth-century Ostrogothic Italy with the murder of king Theoderic's daughter Amalasuentha. Procopius frames this murder as the emperor Justinian's motivation for the invasion of Italy in 535. Whilst Kate Cooper has understood that Procopius' narrative impulse to represent Amalasuentha's death as *casus belli* supersedes historical veracity, we can see continuity from the fifth century in narratives that make elite women complicit in political strategies of martial conflict, invasion and occupation.[82]

---

[79] Oost's understanding of Galla Placidia's experiences is idealising in the extreme. See, for example, Oost 1968, 94. Liz James adroitly observes that '[l]ove is an irrelevance; power, and the retention of power, are more plausible motives', in James 2002, 126.

[80] For abduction marriage, see Evans Grubbs 1989; Wilkinson 2012. Grey 2008; Sessa 2011; and Bjornlie 2014 have profitably directed attention to abduction and *raptio* in Italy and Gaul in the fifth and sixth centuries.

[81] This topos is similarly evident in Procopius' representation of Anicia Falcona Proba, who was responsible for the sack of Rome in 410 after she opened the gates to Alaric (*Bell*. 3.2.27).

[82] Cooper 2016, 296.

Murder and Assassination of Women and Their Relatives

This chapter has focused on elite women in late Roman Italy whose lives were marked, threatened or determined by gender-based violence, but who, with the exception of Fausta, survived it. Yet death was a frequent outcome of such violence. During Alaric's first siege of Rome around 408, Serena, the mother of Maria and Thermantia, was executed for her alleged involvement with the Gothic forces.[83] In 430, Padusia, the wife of the *magister militum* Felix, was assassinated in Ravenna on the steps of the Basilica Ursiana, for allegedly plotting against Aëtius with her husband and Grunitus the deacon.[84] Sunigilda, the wife of Odoacer, was either stoned or starved to death by Theoderic after his capture of Ravenna in 493.[85] The prospects of survival for elite women often followed the fate of their husbands: their fortunes rose or came apart together. Cornelia Salonina, the wife of emperor Gallienus, was likely executed after the death of her husband in the aftermath of the siege of Milan in 268.[86] Similarly, the emperor Maxentius' wife Valeria Maximilla vanishes from the historical record after the battle of the Milvian Bridge in 312.[87] While it is possible that these women were pardoned, murdering the female relatives of a defeated emperor is more widely attested, most notably in the beheadings of Prisca and Galeria Valeria in Thessalonica in 315.[88]

These vanishing women are attested throughout the late Roman period in Italy, disappearing into the tumults of the fifth century, as did Alypia, the daughter of the emperor Anthemius, who married Ricimer in 467.[89] An entirely political arrangement, Ennodius of Pavia records Anthemius' understanding of the marriage between Alypia and Ricimer as shameful, though necessary, for the imperial family.[90] As Alypia's father was reluctantly forced to create the union, it is likely that Alypia did not welcome it either. Sidonius Apollinaris was in Rome when the wedding took place and recorded the extravagant festivities as the entire population celebrated,[91] and a public procession featuring the bride and groom took place.[92] Although weddings were ostensibly opportunities for celebration, they were public manifestations of political alliances that

---

[83] PLRE 1.824; Zos. 5.38.1–5; Olympiodorus fr. 6. Giving this episode its due attention falls outside the scope of the current study, but see comments in Cooper 2007, 53–4. For Serena, see Busch 2015, 40–59.
[84] Prosper, *Chron.* s.a. 430 is the only of our sources that places Padusia in the conspiracy and gives her political agency in the affair. Other sources focus on Felix: Hyd. 84(94); Joh. Ant. fr. 201.3; Marcell. Com. s.a. 430.2; Agnellus 31. See also Wijnendaele 2017.
[85] Joh. Ant. fr. 214.
[86] PLRE 1.799; Zonar. 2.25. See also Aur. Vict. *Caes.* 33.6; Aur. Vict. *Epit.* 33.1.
[87] PLRE 1.576.
[88] Prisca was the wife of Diocletian, while Valeria was their daughter and wife of emperor Galerius. After Galerius' death, Maximinus Daia pressured Valeria into marriage, which prompted her to flee to Licinius with her mother (Lactant. *De mort. pers.* 41). Licinius eventually sentenced both women to death. They fled and hid in Thessalonica for a year and three months; they were eventually found and beheaded (Lactant. *De mort. pers.* 50–1). For Valeria, see PLRE 1.937; for Prisca, see PLRE 1.726. For Valeria's marriage to Galerius, see Amm. Marc. 19.11.4.
[89] Sid. Apoll. *Epist.* 1.5.10; *Carm.* 2.484–6. See MacGeorge 2002, 235–61.
[90] Ennod. *Vit. Epiph.* 67–70.
[91] Sid. Apoll. *Epist.* 1.9.
[92] On marital processions, see Treggiari 1993, 162–8; Hersch 2010, 140–4. Also compare the marriage of Constantius II and his unnamed bride, and the joyous festivities described in Euseb. *Vit. Const.* 4.49.

could be founded on a lack of female consent and the suppression of female agency, and that repositioned women in the way of potential harm. In 472, five years into the marriage between Alypia and Ricimer, and after losing a civil war against Ricimer, Anthemius was beheaded in Rome by Ricimer's nephew Gundobad acting under Ricimer's orders.[93] Anthemius was buried with honours, perhaps out of respect for Alypia.[94] Ricimer's death through illness a few weeks later meant that her father's murderer Gundobad became *magister militum* instead. At this point, the historical record on Alypia vanishes.

A prominent trend that can be identified in late Roman Italy and beyond is that with a change in political power, women aligned with male predecessors disappear. Final documentation in the ancient evidence records the murders of their male relatives, signalling psychological harm and a significant increase in physical vulnerability. The distinction between gender-based violence and political violence may be variable, but violence inflicted upon elite women always has a political dimension due to their status. The execution of women like Serena, even if perpetrated following ostensibly political accusations, contains an element of femicide that is voyeuristic. Women whose male relatives fell from power were usually reliant on the clemency of victorious men for their survival, and clemency was not usually given.

Despite familial murder and massacre, women did survive changes in political power in Italy between 250 and 500. In August 253, the emperor Gallus and his son Volusianus were killed in Interamna (modern Terni) by their own soldiers. The ancient evidence records the survival of the wife and mother, empress Afinia Gemina Baebiana, and her daughter, but the emotional trauma of the ordeal is not detailed.[95] Similarly, when Magnus Maximus was executed in Aquileia in 388, Ambrose of Milan tells us that his mother and daughters were spared.[96] Magnus Maximus' young son Victor, however, was executed shortly after his father's defeat.[97] It is impossible for historians to assess how many elite women were murdered following the downfall of male relatives, and whether their survival rates were inclining or declining in late Roman Italy, but the fear of violence and the proximity of death would have been a lived experience for many women.

Changing political circumstances were not adverse without exception for women, and occasionally female authority was augmented by the shifting political landscape. Herennia Etruscilla, wife of the emperor Decius, acted as a regent for her son after Decius' demise in 251, but after her regency she vanishes from records.[98] Aurelian's wife Ulpia Severina had coins issued in her image and may have briefly ruled in her own right after Aurelian's death in 275.[99] Power vacuums could be utilised by

---

[93] Joh. Ant. fr. 209.1; Priscus fr. 64.1; a further version is recorded in *Chron. Gall. 511* (650). See also Chapter 4 in this volume.

[94] Joh. Ant. fr. 209.1; MacGeorge 2002, 260.

[95] *PIR*² A 439.

[96] Ambr. *Ep.* 40.32.

[97] Zos. 4.47; Aur. Vict. *Epit.* 48.6; Oros. 7.35.10.

[98] For Decius, see Aur. Vict. *Caes.* 29; Eutr. 4.5; Amm. Marc. 31.13.13.

[99] '[W]e know very little about Ulpia Severina. No literary source betrays the slightest knowledge of her', in Watson 1999, 113.

women to promote themselves, but these instances are exceptional and sources on them obscure. Retiring from court or relocating could also offer new opportunities for elite women. The mother of the emperor Romulus Augustulus, perhaps called Barbaria, survived her husband Orestes' downfall and may have been instrumental in the foundation and flourishing of a monastic community near Naples. The identification of Orestes' wife as Barbaria, however, remains dubious.[100] Kreka, the widow of the assassinated Bleda, brother of Attila the Hun, went on to rule a village in her own right in the 440s, providing hospitality to the historian Priscus.[101] However, even where female political authority succeeded in flourishing, it was inevitably compromised and prematurely curtailed, and it is not well attested in the historical evidence.

Conclusions: Status, Violence and Female Experience

The structure of patriarchal ancient societies meant that the existence of women in late Roman Italy was fundamentally precarious. The fragmentary remains of women's experiences indicate that even the most privileged and successful of elite women were implicated; their high status increased the preservation of gender-based violence in the historical record but did not protect them from it. Although the ideological and political frameworks varied, gender-based violence perpetrated against women and girls from lower social demographics was not markedly different. There is evidently a positive correlation between the political centrality of women, their proximity to disaster, and gendered violence, which was precipitated by political crises, particularly warfare, conflicts of rulership, succession and foreign threat. Unstable political environments made elite women especially vulnerable as contests for authority were played out through them, particularly in their ability to produce heirs with an imperial claim. This inescapable burden of legitimate or illegitimate bloodlines could not be challenged or subverted to the advantage of elite women. From birth, they were bargaining tools in a way that laywomen were not; an elite woman's behaviour was heavily regulated, her agency was curtailed, and her womb was harnessed for procreation. Through numerous marriages, childbirths, through exiles and relocations, these women could be perceived as powerful and dangerous, but they were ultimately assets that needed to be tightly controlled to benefit male political interests. In the late Roman period, gendered violence perpetrated against elite women was characterised by reproductive coercion, involving impregnation, the prevention of reproduction, and abortion or infant murder.

This chapter has foregrounded the duality of elite women: whilst they divorced, remarried, relocated and held formal positions of power, their experiences and political careers were threatened and defined by gender-based violence. Nearly all of the women who achieved political successes in late Roman Italy between 250 and 500, holding power and producing coins in their name, and being revered as *Augustae*,

---

[100] Eugipp. *Vit. Sev.* 46.1–2; for this unnamed *illustris femina*, see *PLRE* 2.210; for problems in identification, see Šašel Kos 2008, 442, 446–7. See also Nathan 1992.
[101] Priscus fr. 11.2.

had been subject to gender-based violence. Despite this commonality, from ancient accounts to modern criticism, gender-based violence continues to be overlooked, elided and normalised, especially in scholarship on late Roman politics and warfare. Shining a spotlight on such violence reveals how the agency of elite women in Late Antiquity as powerful particularly in political and religious spheres has been exaggerated: this is not inauthentic agency as a result of false consciousness, it is often simply absent. Where women were able to exercise agency, it is important to recognise the constraints within which they operated, as well as the cost. Both the constraints and the cost in late Roman Italy were considerable in newly troubled circumstances: the abduction of women, their involuntary movement, and their forced marriages – including rape and impregnation – were unprecedented. By considering the evidence surrounding the elite women of late Roman Italy, we can begin to build a sense of women's lives during this tumultuous era: systemic violence and the threat of violence formed a significant part of female experience, which is readily evident whether we choose to observe it or not.[102]

Bibliography

Ando, C. (1996) 'Pagan Apologetics and Christian Intolerance in the Ages of Themistius and Augustine', *JECS* 4 (2): 171–207.

Angelova, D. (2004) 'The Ivories of Ariadne and Ideas about Female Imperial Authority in Rome and Early Byzantium', *Gesta* 43: 1–15.

Arjava, A. (1996) *Women and Law in Late Antiquity*, Oxford.

Arjava, A. (1998) 'Paternal Power in Late Antiquity', *JRS* 88: 147–65.

Assorati, G. (2016) 'Il matrimonio fra Ataulfo e Galla Placidia tra passi e diritto', in V. Neri and B. Girotti (eds) *La famiglia tardoantica: società, diritto, religione*, Milan, 269–82.

Athanassiadi, P. (2010) *Vers la pensée unique: la montée de l'intolérance dans l'Antiquité tardive*, Paris.

Balberg, M. and E. Muehlberger (2018) 'The Will of Others: Coercion, Captivity, and Choice in Late Antiquity', *Studies in Late Antiquity* 2 (3): 294–315.

Barry, J. (2020) 'So Easy to Forget: Augustine's Treatment of the Sexually Violated in the *City of God*', *Journal of the American Academy of Religion* 88 (1): 235–53.

Becker-Piriou, A. (2008) 'De Galla Placidia à Amalasonthe, des femmes dans la diplomatie romano-barare en Occident?', *RH* 647: 507–43.

Bennett, J. M. (2006) *History Matters: Patriarchy and the Challenge of Feminism*, Manchester.

Bjornlie, S. (2014) 'Law, Ethnicity and Taxes in Ostrogothic Italy: a Case for Continuity, Adaptation and Departure', *Early Medieval Europe* 22 (2): 138–70.

Blockley, R. C. (1981) *The Fragmentary Classicising Historians of the Later Roman Empire*, Liverpool.

Brubaker, L. and J. M. H. Smith (eds) (2004) *Gender in the Early Medieval World: East and West, 300–900*, Cambridge.

Brubaker, L. and H. Tobler (2002) 'The Gender of Money: Byzantine Empresses on Coins (324–802)', *Gender and History* 12.3: 572–94.

---

[102] The authors are sincerely grateful for the generous gift of expertise from Ellen Muehlberger, Julia Hillner and Jenny Barry, the participants of the Late Antiquity Reading Group at the University of Sheffield, and conference audiences at the universities of Tübingen and Ghent.

Burgess, R. W. (ed.) (1993) *The Chronicle of Hydatius and the Consularia Constantinopolitana*, Oxford.
Bury, J. B. (1919) 'Justa Grata Honoria', *JRS* 9: 1–13.
Busch, A. (2015) *Die Frauen der theodosianischen Dynastie: Macht und Repräsentation kaiserlicher Frauen im 5. Jahrhundert*, Stuttgart.
Cameron, A. (2002) 'Apologetics in the Roman Empire: a Genre of Intolerance?', in J.-M. Carrie and R. Lizzi Testa (eds) *'Humana sapit': études d'antiquité tardive offertes à Lellia Cracco Ruggini*, Turnhout, 219–27.
Cameron, A. (2008) 'The Violence of Orthodoxy', in E. Iricinschi and H. Zellentin (eds) *Heresy and Identity in Late Antiquity*, Tübingen, 102–14.
Cameron, A. and A. Kuhrt (eds) (1993) *Images of Women in Antiquity*, London.
Cantarella, E. (2016) 'Women and Patriarchy in Roman Law', in P. J. du Plessis, C. Ando and K. Tuori (eds) *The Oxford Handbook of Roman Law and Society*, Oxford, 419–31.
Carroll, M. (2018) *Infancy and Earliest Childhood in the Roman World: 'A Fragment of Time'*, Oxford.
Carucci, M. (2018) 'Domestic Violence in Roman Imperial Society: Giving Abused Women a Voice', in M. C. Pimentel and N. Simões Rodrigues (eds) *Violence in the Ancient and Medieval Worlds*, Leuven, 57–73.
Cesa, M. (1992–1993) 'Il matrimonio di Placidia ed Ataulfo sullo sfondo dei rapporti fra Ravenna e i Visigoti', *Romanobarbarica* 12: 23–53.
Chaniotis, A. (2008) *War in the Hellenistic World: a Social and Cultural History*, Oxford.
Chausson, F. (2007) *Stemmata aurea. Constantin, Justine, Théodose: revendications généalogiques et idéologie impériale au IVe siècle ap. J.-C.*, Rome.
Chew, K. (2006) 'Virgins and Eunuchs: Pulcheria, Politics and the Death of Emperor Theodosius II', *Historia* 55: 207–27.
Clark, G. (2015) *Monica: an Ordinary Saint*, Oxford.
Clover, F. M. (1978) 'The Family and Early Career of Anicius Olybrius', *Historia* 27: 169–96.
Conant, J. (2012) *Staying Roman: Conquest and Identity in Africa and the Mediterranean, 439–700*, Cambridge.
Cooper, K. (2007) *Fall of the Roman Household*, Cambridge.
Cooper, K. (2016) 'The Heroine and the Historian: Procopius of Caesarea on the Troubled Reign of Queen Amalasuentha', in J. Arnold, S. Bjornlie and K. Sessa (eds) *A Companion to Ostrogothic Italy*, Leiden, 296–315.
Dasen, V. (ed.) (2004) *Naissance et petite enfance dans l'Antiquité: Actes du colloque de Fribourg, 28 novembre–1er décembre 2001*, Fribourg.
Dasen, V. (2011) 'Childbirth and Infancy in Greek and Roman Antiquity', in B. Rawson (ed.) *A Companion to Families in the Greek and Roman Worlds*, London, 291–314.
Dossey, L. (2008) 'Wife Beating and Manliness in Late Antiquity', *P&P* 199 (1): 3–40.
Drake, H. A. (ed.) (2006) *Violence in Late Antiquity: Perceptions and Practices*, Aldershot.
Drake, H. A. (2011) 'Intolerance, Religious Violence, and Political Legitimacy in Late Antiquity', *Journal of the American Academy of Religion* 79 (1): 193–235.
Drijvers, J. W. (1992) 'Flavia Maxima Fausta: Some Remarks', *Historia* 41: 500–6.
Elman, R. A. (2013) 'Gender Violence', in G. Waylen, K. Celis, J. Kantola and S. Laurel Weldon (eds) *The Oxford Handbook of Gender and Politics*, Oxford, 236–58.
Evans Grubbs, J. (1989) 'Abduction Marriage in Antiquity: a Law of Constantine (*CTh* IX.24.I) and Its Social Context', *JRS* 79: 59–83.
Evans Grubbs, J. (1995) *Law and Family in Late Antiquity: the Emperor Constantine's Marriage Legislation*, Oxford.
Fantham, E. (1991) '*Stuprum*: Public Attitudes and Penalties for Sexual Offences in Republican Rome', *EMC* 35 (3): 267–91.

Gaca, K. L. (2016) 'Continuities in Rape and Tyranny in Martial Societies from Antiquity Onward', in S. L. Budin and J. MacIntosh Turfa (eds) *Women in Antiquity: Real Women across the Ancient World*, London, 1041–56.

Gaddis, M. (2005) *There Is No Crime for Those Who Have Christ: Religious Violence in the Christian Roman Empire*, Berkeley.

Grey, C. (2008) 'Two Young Lovers: an Abduction Marriage and Its Consequences in Fifth-Century Gaul', *CQ* 58 (1): 286–302.

Hahn, J. (2004) *Gewalt und religiöser Konflikt: Studien zu den Auseinandersetzungen zwischen Christen, Heiden und Juden im Osten des Römischen Reiches (von Konstantin bis Theodosius II)*, Berlin.

Harlow, M. (2004) 'Galla Placidia: Conduit of Culture?', in F. McHardy and E. Marshall (eds) *Women's Influence on Classical Civilization*, London, 138–50.

Harries, J. (2014) 'The Empresses' Tale, AD 300–360', in C. Harrison, C. Humfress and I. Sandwell (eds) *Being Christian in Late Antiquity: a Festschrift for Gillian Clark*, Oxford, 197–214.

Hersch, K. K. (2010) *The Roman Wedding: Ritual and Meaning in Antiquity*, Cambridge.

Herzog, R. (2018) 'Reading Consent into the Iliad: the Stakes of Writing from Briseis' Perspective', *Eidolon*, https://eidolon.pub/reading-consent-into-the-iliad-e2c42ae0b221.

Hillner, J. (2013) 'Family Violence: Punishment and Abuse in the Late Roman Household', in L. Brubaker and S. Tougher (eds) *Approaches to the Byzantine Family*, Farnham, 21–46.

Hillner, J. (2017) 'A Woman's Place: Imperial Women in Late Antique Rome', *AntTard* 25: 75–94.

Holum, K. G. (1982) *Theodosian Empresses: Women and Imperial Dominion in Late Antiquity*, Berkeley.

Holum, K. G. (2004) 'Pulcheria's Crusade A.D. 421–22 and the Ideology of Imperial Victory', *GRBS* 18: 153–72.

International Federation of Red Cross (2015) *Unseen, Unheard: Gender-Based Violence in Disasters Global Study*, Geneva, 1–51.

James, L. (2002) 'Goddess, Whore, Wife, or Slave: Will the Real Byzantine Empress Please Stand Up?', in A. J. Duggan (ed.) *Queens and Queenship in Medieval Europe*, Woodbridge, 123–40.

Kahlos, M. (2009) *Forbearance and Compulsion: the Rhetoric of Religious Tolerance and Intolerance in Late Antiquity*, London.

Kelly, C. (2008) *Attila the Hun: Barbarian Terror and the Fall of the Roman Empire*, London.

Klingshirn, W. (1985) 'Charity and Power: Caesarius of Arles and the Ransoming of Captives in Sub-Roman Gaul', *JRS* 75: 183–203.

Kuefler, M. (2007) 'The Marriage Revolution in Late Antiquity: the *Theodosian Code* and Later Roman Marriage Law', *Journal of Family History* 32: 343–70.

Laiou, A. E. (1993) *Consent and Coercion to Sex and Marriage in Ancient and Medieval Societies*, Washington, DC.

Lenski, N. (2004) 'Empresses in the Holy Land: the Creation of a Christian Utopia in Late Antique Palestine', in L. Ellis and F. L. Kidner (eds) *Travel, Communication and Geography in Late Antiquity: Sacred and Profane*, Aldershot, 113–24.

Lenski, N. (2011) 'Captivity and Romano-Barbarian Interchange', in R. W. Mathisen and D. Shanzer (eds) *Romans, Barbarians, and the Transformation of the Roman World: Cultural Interaction and the Creation of Identity in Late Antiquity*, Farnham, 185–98.

Leonard, V. (2019) 'Galla Placidia as "Human Gold": Consent and Autonomy in the Sack of Rome, CE 410', *Gender and History* 31 (2): 334–52.

Levithan, J. (2013) *Roman Siege Warfare*, Ann Arbor.

Lillie, C. (2018) *The Rape of Eve: the Transformation of Roman Ideology in Three Early Christian Retellings of Genesis*, Minneapolis.

Lombard, N. (ed.) (2017) *The Routledge Handbook of Gender and Violence*, London.
McEvoy, M. (2013) *Child Emperor Rule in the Late Roman West, AD 367–455*, Oxford.
McEvoy, M. (2016) 'Constantia: the Last Constantinian', *Antichthon* 50: 154–79.
MacGeorge, P. (2002) *Late Roman Warlords*, Oxford.
MacKinnon, C. (2007) *Are Women Human? And Other International Dialogues*, Cambridge, MA.
Manne, K. (2018) *The Logic of Misogyny*, Oxford.
Martinez Morales, J. (2019) 'Women on the Walls? The Role and Impact of Women in Classical Greek Sieges', in J. Armstrong and M. Trundle (eds) *Brill's Companion to Sieges in the Ancient Mediterranean*, Leiden, 150–68.
Matthews, J. F. (1970) 'Olympiodorus of Thebes and the History of the West (A.D. 407–425)', *JRS* 60: 79–97.
Meier, M. (2017) 'A Contest of Interpretation: Roman Policy toward the Huns as Reflected in the "Honoria Affair" (448/50)', *Journal of Late Antiquity* 10 (1): 42–61.
Mendelssohn, L. (ed.) (1887) *Zosimi Historia Nova*, Leipzig, 1887.
Merrills, A. H. and R. Miles (2010) *The Vandals*, Malden, MA.
Modéran, Y. (2014) *Les Vandales et l'Empire romain (édité par Michel-Yves Perrin)*, Arles.
Möller, A., H. P. Söndergaard and L. Helström (2017) 'Tonic Immobility during Sexual Assault: a Common Reaction Predicting Post-traumatic Stress Disorder and Severe Depression', *Acta Obstetricia et Gynecologica Scandinavica* 96: 932–8.
Moretti, K., A. Matz, D. Wright and S. Taborski (2019) 'The Leda Fresco: Rape or Romp? How to Talk about Consent and Art', *Eidolon*, https://eidolon.pub/the-leda-fresco-rape-or-romp-86c62f72a864.
Nathan, G. (1992) 'The Last Emperor: the Fate of Romulus Augustulus', *C&M* 43: 261–71.
O'Gorman, E. (2006) 'A Woman's History of Warfare', in V. Zajko and M. Leonard (eds) *Laughing with Medusa: Classical Myth and Feminist Thought*, Oxford, 189–208.
Oost, S. I. (1964) 'Aëtius and Majorian', *CP* 59 (1): 23–9.
Oost, S. I. (1968) *Galla Placidia Augusta: a Biographical Essay*, Chicago.
Papaconstantinou, A., N. McLynn and D. Schwartz (eds) (2015) *Conversion in Late Antiquity: Christianity, Islam, and Beyond*, Ashgate.
Petersen, L. I. R. (2013) *Siege Warfare and Military Organization in the Successor States (400–800 AD): Byzantium, the West and Islam*, Leiden.
Pohlsander, H. A. (1984) 'Crispus: Brilliant Career and Tragic End', *Historia* 33: 79–106.
Rawson, B. (ed.) (2011) *A Companion to Families in the Greek and Roman Worlds*, London.
Ridley, Ronald T. (2017) *Zosimus: New History*, repr., Leiden.
Rolfe, J. C. (ed. and trans.) (1952) *Ammianus Marcellinus*, 3 vols, London.
Roth, R. (2014) 'Gender, Sex, and Intimate-Partner Violence in Historical Perspective', in R. Gartner and B. McCarthy (eds) *The Oxford Handbook of Gender, Sex, and Crime*, Oxford, 1–18.
Salisbury, J. E. (2015) *Rome's Christian Empress: Galla Placidia Rules at the Twilight of the Empire*, Baltimore, MD.
Šašel Kos, M. (2008) 'The Family of Romulus Augustulus', in P. Mauritsch, W. Petermandl and R. Rollinger (eds) *Antike Lebenswelten: Konstanz, Wandel, Wirkungsmacht. Festschrift für Ingomar Weiler zum 70. Geburtstag*, Wiesbaden, 439–49.
Sessa, K. (2011) 'Ursa's Return: Captivity, Remarriage, and the Domestic Authority of Roman Bishops in Fifth-Century Italy', *JECS* 19 (3): 401–32.
Shaw, B. D. (2011) *Sacred Violence: African Christians and Sectarian Hatred in the Age of Augustine*, Cambridge.
Sirago, V. A. (1961) *Galla Placidia e la trasformazione politica dell' Occidente*, Louvain.
Sivan, H. (2011) *Galla Placidia: the Last Roman Empress*, Oxford.

Sizgorich, T. (2009) *Violence and Belief in Late Antiquity: Militant Devotion in Christianity and Islam*, Philadelphia, PA.
Skinner, T., M. Hester and E. Malos (2005) 'Methodology, Feminism and Gender Violence', in T. Skinner, M. Hester and E. Malos (eds) *Researching Gender Violence: Feminist Methodology in Action*, Cullompton, 1–22.
Stanton, G. N. and G. G. Stroumsa (eds) (2008) *Tolerance and Intolerance in Early Judaism and Christianity*, Cambridge.
Stefaniw, B. (2020) 'Feminist Historiography and Uses of the Past', *Studies in Late Antiquity* 4 (3): 260–83.
Storoni Mazzolani, L. (1975) *Galla Placidia*, Milan.
Thomas, L. M. (2016) 'Historicising Agency', *Gender and History* 28 (2): 324–39.
Tougher, S. (2000) 'Ammianus Marcellinus on the Empress Eusebia: a Split Personality?', *G&R* 47: 94–101.
Treggiari, S. (1993) *Roman Marriage: iusti coniuges from the Time of Cicero to the Time of Ulpian*, Oxford.
Trout, D. E. (2013) '*Fecit ad astra viam*: Daughters, Wives, and the Metrical Epitaphs of Late Ancient Rome', *JECS* 21: 1–25.
Vihervalli, U. (2022) 'Wartime Rape in Late Antiquity: Consecrated Virgins and Victim Bias in the Fifth-Century West', *Early Medieval Europe* 30 (1): 3–17.
Vuolanto, V. (2019) 'Public Agency of Women in the Later Roman World', in J. Rantala (ed.) *Gender, Memory, and Identity in the Roman World*, Amsterdam, 41–62.
Ward-Perkins, B. (2006) *The Fall of Rome and the End of Civilization*, Oxford.
Watson, A. (1999) *Aurelian and the Third Century*, London.
Webb, M. (2013) '"On Lucretia Who Slew Herself": Rape and Consolation in Augustine's *De ciuitate Dei*', *AugStud* 44: 37–58.
Wijnendaele, J. W. P. (2015) *The Last of the Romans: Bonifatius – Warlord and Comes Africae*, London.
Wijnendaele, J. W. P. (2017) 'Aëtius' Early Career and the Murder of Felix (c.425–430)', *Historia* 66 (4): 468–82.
Wijnendaele, J. W. P. (2018) '*Dagli altari alla polvere*: Alaric, Constantine III, and the Downfall of Stilicho', *JAH* 6 (2): 260–77.
Williams, C. (2010) *Roman Homosexuality*, Oxford.
Wilkinson, K. W. (2012) 'Dedicated Widows in *Codex Theodosianus* 9.25?', *JECS* 20: 141–66.
Witzke, S. S. (2016) 'Violence against Women in Ancient Rome: Ideology versus Reality', in W. Riess and G. G. Fagan (eds) *The Typography of Violence in the Greco-Roman World*, Ann Arbor, 248–74.
Woods, D. (1998) 'On the Death of the Empress Fausta', *G&R* 45: 70–86.
Woods, D. (2004) 'The Constantinian Origin of Justina', *CQ* 54 (1): 325–7.

9

LAND OF THE FREE? CONSIDERING SMALLHOLDERS AND ECONOMIC AGENCY IN LATE ANTIQUE ITALY

Niels P. Arends

TRADITIONALLY, THE ECONOMY OF late antique Italy has been studied from the perspective of large-scale landholdings. In that perspective, estates, culminating in the form of massive *latifundia*, dominate the Italian countryside.[1] However, while large landholdings were certainly a crucial part of the late antique world, and specifically its economy, the rural world consisted of many more relevant economic units. This chapter is concerned with the free smallholding farmer (the *liberi plebei*), rather than the large estate owner, that is to say, agriculturalists belonging to late Roman or 'barbarian' Italian communities in which the majority of member families lived by agricultural production on lands to which they had access rights.[2] Paradoxically, the small farmer has not received the same attention as the large-scale landowner, even though most of the land in the Roman and post-Roman world was occupied by the first.[3]

Without falling back into some kind of nativism that postulates supposedly isolated communities and uncontaminated expressions of culture, this chapter assesses the place of smallholders in a space – within an economy and society – that was not secluded from the outside world. Rather, I will emphasise that individual smallholders and farming communities in late antique Italy exercised a meaningful amount of agency in intermittently organising and orchestrating their economic operations, and that they were not, as is sometimes assumed, acting from a marginal position. Emphasis will be put on their economic agency, an analytical construct that allows us to better understand the complexity of smallholder economics and, by the same token, the late antique economy. By the use of this construct, I will show that smallholders in late Roman and Ostrogothic Italy were not consistently part of an economic

---

[1] Christie 2006, 405–9; using *latifundia* to describe the large estates of Late Roman Italy does not always make sense, however, considering that the majority of sources do not use the term. See Porena 2017.
[2] Mirković 1997, 22–4, 55, 70, 99, 106–7. I refrain from using the word 'peasant', for the same reasons as Faith 2020, 5–7.
[3] At times they are argued to have vanished after the Punic Wars. See Brunt 1971; Rosenstein 2004. Launaro 2012 has shown pretty decisively that this view is wrong. Especially in the historiography of the late antique and Byzantine East are they consistently marginalised. Amongst others, see Hirschfeld 1997; Villeneuve 1985; Tate 1992; Watson 2001; Kehoe 1988; 2007; 2015 should be seen as decisively opposite to this, as should Dossey 2010 and, to some extent, Grey 2011.

structure that could only and exclusively lead towards suppression. This is important, as currently the majority of economic relations in the countryside of the (Italian) late antique world have been explained in terms of a one-way asymmetry: the elite actor gains more than the small agriculturalist, and it is the gain of one over the other which constitutes this typical asymmetry.[4] Such a picture of economic relations seems overly simplified, and the relationship between smallholders, elite landowners and other economic actors are likely to have been much more complex. Indeed, without question, there were large areas in the late antique world where small-scale landownership subsisted in perpetuity side by side with large estates, which assuredly militates against the expectation that Italian smallholders were part of an economic structure that could only lead to subjugation.[5]

Lately, a re-examination of the Italian sources, especially the documentary materials, has resulted in two opposite views, with one emphasising a noticeably improved position of the rural working population, and the other vouching for continuity, claiming that elites only very minimally lost their grip on the lives of non-elites between the fourth and eighth centuries. As Marios Costambeys has noted, much of this debate is shaped by the choice of evidence scholars work with, i.e. putting more emphasis on charters or, conversely, on archaeological excavations.[6] A persistent underlying problem of this debate, however, is that its participants assume that the rural working population of late antique Italy underwent very similar experiences, with the result that they treat non-elites, undeservedly, as a homogeneous bloc. But the rural population was socially divided, between free and unfree, the very unfortunate and the more well-to-do, and, additionally, between smallholders, freedmen and slaves.[7] These divisions do not appear as clear-cut in our sources as we would like; and, even though legislators were keen to stress them, it is but the question if the general population respected such divisions or contemplated them in the very same way as their administrators did (or as we do nowadays). We should respect the possibility that the experience of individuals with a stronger claim to resources and, consequentially, freedom, had markedly different experiences from those who did not, even if these claims were only minutely different.

---

[4] See for example Alföldy 1991, 144–65. Again, I have to emphasise here the economic aspect of these relations. In the case of social or cultural relations, investigations have been much less pessimistic. See esp. Delmaire 1989, 679–82; Dossey 2010; Grey 2011; and Taylor 2017, with Grey 2011, 15 n. 40 giving a rundown of relevant works.

[5] The estates of the Apions in Byzantine Egypt already indicate a juxtaposition of small-scale landownership continuing to exist side by side with estates of the wealthiest people in the Roman Empire at that time. See Rathbone, 1991; Angold 1995, 325–9; Sarris 2012. Schmidt-Hofner 2017, 384 also argues that throughout the Mediterranean world there is enough evidence for the continued existence free smallholders. He argues that, while there was a fierce competition for land, it is questionable to conclude that large landowners accumulated land into their hands in very complete terms.

[6] Costambeys 2009, 95–6.

[7] On the presence of slaves in Late Antiquity, see Vera 1993, 160 and Brown 1984, 203 specifically for Italy; and Wickham 2005, 276–8 for a short synopsis of the debate in the broader sense, also including the East; and Banaji 2009, 71–3 stressing the strong prevalence of slavery on estates throughout antiquity and the Early Middle Ages.

I thus focus here on one of those groups, the smallholder. This prioritisation needs comment. More specifically, we should ask ourselves what we mean with 'smallholder'. Nowadays, anthropologists, economists and social historians generally characterise smallholders as free rural cultivators who practise intensive, permanent agriculture on relatively small farms, whereby the most important social and economic unit is the family household, capable of organising labour, exploiting resources and guiding consumption. The smallholder as defined here may be what Max Weber considered an *Idealtypus*.[8] Although broad, this is still a workable definition, as long as we understand and respect the many pitfalls our sources might have. In case of the documentary record, smallholders might in some instances be called *coloni* or *possessores*, while in other places they would be noted down as *rustici*, *operarii* and *mercenarii*. This is mostly the result of agriculturalists taking up various jobs in different localities due to crop cycles, new labour opportunities and various push and pull factors coming from outside the smallholder's household.[9] In each of these moments administrators and landlords might use different terminology to describe the farmer, and they would do so mostly on the basis of the work that he or she would do on *their* estates, not on that of others or the one owned by the farmer himself. Furthermore, while some of this terminology might originally have had very specific meanings, often the authors themselves are ambiguous as to their actual denotation.[10] In short: the legal categories given in our sources do not reflect the economic strategies taken by non-elites, nor do they specify them. This means that we will have to locate smallholders in frameworks of evidence that more often than not tell us more about legal constructs as used by late Roman officials and the clergy, rather than having access to a more straightforward approach that allows us to take from the sources what we need without much further thought. Archaeology is, of course, also not without its problems. How do we see that a site was worked by smallholders? Does it necessarily have to be a small site? Despite the many archaeological advances in terms of technique and technology, the issue of visibility remains a frustratingly apparent problem. For each source that I use it becomes clear why I believe it to say anything about smallholders, although often the reason comes down to a source or the author of a source discussing (or, in some cases, disputing) the actions of a smallholder. It must also be noted that, while most of us would normally associate smallholders with rural contexts, the division that we might call 'the urban–rural split' was not as apparent in these centuries as scholars at times assume it to be. There was not necessarily an absolute divide between these two domains; certainly, in the context of Late Antiquity, some argue that if there were divisions these must have become increasingly slim due to 'ruralisation'.[11] Whatever we believe, we encounter farmers who, rather clearly, did not live in fully

---

[8] Weber 1949 [1904], 90–107.
[9] Grey 2016, 281–2.
[10] Grey 2016, 282 gives the example of Cassiodorus' *Variae* 8.31, where it is not clear if the author means 'tenant' when he says *colonus*, or is actually just using it to denote agricultural activity. The latter seems more probable. The very same use can be seen in Paulinus of Nola, *Epistulae* 5.15, where *colonus* is used in a similar fashion.
[11] Bowden and Lavan 2014 for the question of how to define the countryside in the late antique context; for the ruralisation of Italy under the Ostrogoths, see Grey 2016, 264–9, who takes issue with this notion.

rural contexts, but seem to have roamed between town, city and countryside on a daily basis. Our sources, then, archaeological and documentary, often conceal a reality that is considerably more complex than what we might perceive at face value. Lastly, we should be wary of inventing social and economic institutions, norms and behaviour out of some of the suggestive encounters we might find; if anything, our sources call for a thorough and careful treatment.

In the first section, I briefly review some of the literature that has prepared the ground for thinking about the agency of smallholders and other rural non-elites in the late antique world, as well as summarising parts of the historiography that has focused on economic structures in terms of agency. One of the main objectives of that discussion, aside from evaluating the existing literature, is to show how economic agency can help us to give flesh to our portrayal of non-elites. My focus on economic agency is not a question of intellectual preference. Instead, I argue that it is a prerequisite to account for some of the evidence that we possess at the moment. I also argue that economic agency as understood by New Institutional Economics might not always convey the circumstances as they were, and that, in this case at least, it would best to approach economic ventures in the context of Amartya Sen's capability approach. I will not, as some might expect, give an extensive summary of the most important works on the state of agriculture in late antique Italy. It suffices to say that contributions by Federico Marazzi, Giuliano Volpe, Chris Wickham, Sauro Gelichi, Domenico Vera, Riccardo Francovich, Richard Hodges, Gian Pietro Brogiolo, Alexandra Chavarría Arnau and Neil Christie give the most comprehensive examinations of both the written and material record.[12] Throughout this chapter, I will repeatedly refer back to their works, question some and reaffirm others, as one would rightly expect. In the second part, I assess the economic agency of smallholders by looking at three topics that in my view tell us something about smallholder economics: choices of production; the capability to access and benefit from wider markets; and, lastly, the capability to use legal means as protection against predatory actions. Thereafter, I turn to a discussion of several archaeological case studies that provide tangible evidence for positions wherein Italian smallholders had – even if they were in the process of losing this – economic agency because of weakened or strengthened relations within and/or outside their community.

Ignorance and Reviving the Rural Non-elite

In his *Dialogi*, Gregory the Great notes how some of Italy's countrymen behaved or, rather, misbehaved. He speaks of the grave of St Laurence the martyr, and how a disrespectful farmer placed a chest of wheat upon the saint's burial place. Suddenly,

---

[12] I will not list each and every publication by these authors here, but merely those who offer their most recently given comprehensive surveys for the social and economic situation of Italy in these centuries: Wickham 1989; 2005, 203–10, 482–8; Marazzi 1998, 119–60; 2010; Francovich and Hodges 2003; Brogiolo et al. 2005; Brogiolo and Chavarría Arnau 2005; Christie 2006; Vera 2010; 2012; 2014; 2020, esp. 285–9; Gelichi 2012, 109–38; Volpe 2018, 5–52.

Gregory writes, a whirlwind came, overthrowing the chest and casting it far away from the graveyard. Everything else, miraculously, remained in its place.[13] In another story, a country fellow travels far to meet the famous preacher Constantius. Upon meeting the preacher, the country fellow cannot believe that the man standing before him, a tiny man, is the man he has heard so much about. The ignorant fellow's remarks do not upset Constantius, however: the preacher embraces the farmer and kisses him on the cheek.[14] At another point, Gregory describes a place near Cassino, where 'foolish' and 'simple' country people worshipped the god Apollo. Only after the priest Benedictus had set fire to the altar and the surrounding woods did these countrymen embrace the faith of Christ.[15]

Gregory's stories were not written in complete literary isolation. Many of his stories find precedents in the writings of preceding Italian bishops, such as Ennodius of Pavia, Maximus of Turin, Peter Chrysologus, Zeno of Verona, Gaudentius of Brescia, Paulinus of Nola and, to a certain extent, Ambrose of Milan.[16] When non-elite agriculturalists appear in their compositions, they always retain pejorative traits – vicious, dangerous, idolatrous, drunk and illiterate – and they are, as Jacques Le Goff argued, 'more animal than man'.[17] Although occasionally elite authors note the conscientious Christian values embodied by arduous agricultural labour, countrymen serve primarily a secondary role, merely used to highlight the good qualities of the holy man or

---

[13] Greg. Mag. *Dialog.* 1.4.
[14] Greg. Mag. *Dialog.* 1.5.
[15] Greg. Mag. *Dialog.* 2.8.
[16] Ennod. *Vit. Epiph.* 7–8; *Ep.* 6, 10; Maximus of Turin, *Serm.* 30–1 (sketches pagan rituals, and as Maximus is clearly expressing his words inside a rural church, this seems to apply to rustics in the vicinity), 71, 91, 106, 107, 108; Peter Chrysologus, *Serm.* 7.106 (where Chrysologus uses the image of a peasant as a contrast to the sophisticated); Zeno of Verona, *Serm.* 1.25.10 (see also Dölger 1937, who argues that the sermon is an indication of ongoing rural sacrifices); Gaudentius of Brescia, *Tractatus* 17; Paulinus of Nola, *Natalicia* 6.254–312, 9.549–91, 10.70–4, 10.164–6 describe the lives of farmers and tenants. Paulinus of Nola, *Nat.* 13.759, 761, 764, 766 and 776 are also used by Bocage-Lefebvre 2013 to describe the characteristics of the 'local population', what the author calls 'un monde paysan'. See Ebanista 2003; 2007; Lehmann 2004; Trout 2008; Yasin 2015. There are very few instances wherein Ambrose of Milan notes the bad habits of farmers in as clear-cut a manner as other late antique Church Fathers do. See Ambr. *Hel.* 8.27, wherein it is suggested that countrymen still drink and feast next to the graves of loved ones as pagans would do; Ambr. *Exp. Luc.* 9.23–33 notes tenants that killed the son of their master, but the affair focuses primarily on the moral violations of the Jews in the biblical past.
[17] Le Goff 1977, 87–101. Suffice to say that not all of these authors put identical amounts of emphasis on each of these traits. For instance, Paulinus of Nola's *Natalicia* is quite an exception, noting almost all immoral aspects of 'rural behavior', while Maximus of Turin focuses just on violence and idolatry. See Bocage-Lefebvre 2013 for an extensive treatment of the world of small farmers as portrayed in Paulinus of Nola's *Natalicia*; Lizzi 1990, 167–72 for idolatry by tenants on the estates of the wealthy. Telling might also be the letter of Ennodius to his 'friend' Asturius, a senator, who he imputes of becoming too 'wild', a result of his rural premises (Ennod. *Ep.* 1.24). Although the bishop only applies this behavioral transformation to his senatorial friend, here we might find exactly why the rural populace has a reputation of being 'wild' in the eyes of men like Ennodius: a wild environment creates wild people.

the patrician, those the ordinary rube did not possess.[18] As the complete opposite of the holy man, they are depicted as individuals who only with great difficulty would understand what they had done wrong, but despite their primitiveness, could still find salvation.[19]

Without going into why the depiction of late antique rural non-elites is remarkably different from comparable depictions centuries earlier, these late antique passages contain another substantial message.[20] They move from a claim about self-knowledge (the holy man) to a claim about passivity (the farmer). The texts therefore implicitly commit to the claim that if the late antique farmer is ignorant of his action, then he is not genuinely acting. Given that genuine agency requires that an agent is in control of the action, it would follow that most appearances of agency are illusory. The consistent portrayal of the passivity and 'ignorance' of non-elite agriculturalists in late antique sources such as Gregory's *Dialogues* has resulted in the fact that for decades the non-elite agriculturalist played a secondary role in the economic history of the later Roman Empire. A focus on the enterprises of the elite and an overall lack of interest in non-elites thus resulted in the neglect of a substantial and vital aspect of the late antique economy.[21]

It was long after the 'Marxist intellectual revolution' that rural non-elites finally received the attention they deserved.[22] Amongst others, Peter Garnsey, Dick Whittaker and Jerzy Kolendo showed what peasants ate, where they lived and how.[23] Together with the well-renowned *Journal of Peasant Studies*, their works gave way to an explosion of analyses focused on peasant life.[24] Though these works primarily navigated within an analytical framework that privileged problems of production, labour exploitation and extraction of surpluses, they have significantly improved our knowledge on the fates of rural non-elites in the late antique world, both East and West.

---

[18] Agricultural imagery employed to highlight Christian values: Maximus of Turin, *Serm.* 38, 66; Peter Chrysologus, *Serm.* 2, 5, 40, 43, 71, 118, 164 (where, together with *Serm.* 106 and 137, farming is used to the detriment of Judaism); Zeno of Verona, *Tract.* 1.36.1; 1. 13. 11; 1. 14.13; 2.27.2–3 (which concentrates mostly on the production of wine); Gaudentius of Brescia, *Tract.* 21; Ambr. *Spir.*; *Incarn.* 3.17.119; *Paen.* 2.1.3; *Off.* 1.4.16; 1.30.158 (which does not necessarily denote agriculture, yet speaks of 'food by labour'); 2.5.21; *Exh. virginit.* 14.83; *Vid.* 14.84; *Ep.* 18.20; *Virginit.* 1.9.45; 3.4.16; *Exc. Sat.* 2.51, 70; *Ep.* 17.14 (Symm. *Relat.* 3); Paulinus of Nola, *Nat.* 5, where St Felix lives as a farmer on a small piece of property, which is indicative of the holiness of the profession; for the religious fervour of farmers in Paulinus of Nola's *Natalicia* see Bocage-Lefebvre 2013, 211–13; for an interplay between divinity and agriculture in the letters of Ennodius of Pavia, see Kennell 2000, 52–60.

[19] Dio Chrys. *Or.* 7.44–7; Erdkamp 2005, 55–6.

[20] Writers from the elder Cato to Vergil and beyond harkened back to a Golden Age where small agriculturalists would set the moral tone of society, and *bonus agricola* and *bonus vir* were synonymous terms. This is, of course, almost completely a contrast to the later depictions of the small agriculturalist. See Garnsey 2004, 91–106.

[21] See Rostovtzeff 1926 and Weber 1976.

[22] See Bloch 1931; 1939–1940; Duby 1962; 1973; Thompson 1963; and Hilton 1975; 1976 for Marxist approaches.

[23] Kolendo 1962; 1973; 1976; Garnsey 1976; 1979; 1988; 1999; 2004; Whittaker 1988.

[24] MacMullen 1974; Lewit 1991; 2004; Kaplan 1992; Lo Cascio 1997; Van Ossel and Ouzoulias 2000; Banaji 2001, 190–212; Faure-Boucharlat 2001; Barceló and Sigaut 2004; Bowden et al. 2004; Wickham 2005; Christie 2006; honourable mentions: Jones 1963; Delano-Smith and Gadd 1986; Perkins and Attolini 1987; Bintliff and Snodgrass 1988; Motta 1997; Pettegrew 2001.

Two recent works, however, deserve separate recognition: Leslie Dossey's *Peasant and Empire in Christian North Africa* (2010) and Cam Grey's *Constructing Communities in the Late Roman Countryside* (2011). Both of these analyses emphasise the (overall) agency of rural non-elites in their late antique contexts. The authors describe that although in the late Roman Empire (North Africa in the case of Dossey, mostly eastern places in Grey's perspective) rural non-elites may have been burdened by both the state and powerful local figures, they were not powerless in any particular sense. Their studies, much unlike Chris Wickham's perspective, show that taxation was not their only concern: they cooperated with each other, exchanged goods and services, bargained with – and defied – patrons, landlords and officials.[25] Grey rightly notes: 'the factors motivating peasant households to undertake a particular course of action did not begin and end with the fiscal imperatives envisaged by the drafters and promulgators of the [imperial] legislation'.[26] These studies are important, in that they highlight the non-elite within a framework that does not readily accept the traditional view of small agriculturalists as being powerless. While neither study is particularly concerned with rural Italy, their focus on the opportunities that presented themselves in the late antique countryside as a result of fiscal, political and religious transformations opens the possibility to challenge the traditional view of the late antique agriculturalist as a class that is wholly typified by submission.[27]

Economic Agency, NIE and Capabilities

It must by now be clear that historians and archaeologists interested in the history of the ancient world, and Late Antiquity in particular, have paid increasing attention to the lives and struggles of non-elite actors and including those living in non-urban contexts. Although studies such as those from Grey and Dossey focus successfully on the agency of such individuals, and hence are very useful, at times it is unclear what kind of agency is at play. I suggest that we can move the debate on non-elites further by focusing on particular forms of agency, may it be political, social or economic forms. As noted at the beginning of this chapter, one of these, economic agency, could be helpful in redefining the relationship of non-elites with and within wider economic structures, and, following, make it easier to see divergences over time and space.

For the sake of clarity, it might be beneficial to give first a general definition of economic agency, as well as briefly commenting on its past usages.[28]

Because achieving general agency necessitates the use of economic resources, there are specialised economic types of agency, such as agency as a farmer, landowner or

---

[25] Wickham 2005.
[26] Grey 2011, 120.
[27] For the 'late antique serfdom' narrative, see Fustel de Coulanges 1885, which argues that there was no change in the labour organisation of the Late Roman colonate and Merovingian serfdom; Hilton 1976, 110–2; Barbero and Vigil 1978; Ste. Croix 1983, 155; against this, Reynolds 1994; and Carrié 1983; 1997; for a summary of the debate, Banaji 2011, 109–44.
[28] Good introductory works on economic agency: MacDonald 1984; Eisenhardt 1989; and Petersen 1993; Kiser 1999, 148–51 has a short summary on the different strands of research that use agency theory in economics.

official (in this context). While traditional economic thought, both implicitly and explicitly, contends that economic resources are frequently simply given to people, economic agency emphasises the importance of agency in both acquiring and maintaining resources. Even if a farmer receives land as a gift from a deceased family member, he is still a part of legal and informal organisations that require him to act appropriately in order to preserve the resource he has gained.

Only from this point of view can we express concerns about power dynamics between smallholders, major landowners and the state in terms of economic transactions. With this economic formulation, we leave open the possibility that there are other linked forms of agency (i.e. non-economic) that are required prerequisites for general agency. Similarly, there are non-economic types of agency that are required in order to obtain economic resources – for example, political or social resources. As a result, we might think of the late antique world as a place where resources are acquired, generated and preserved in order to gain a broad sense of agency and, as a result, a sense of autonomy and well-being.[29]

The concept of economic agency is anything but new. It has found its mark particularly in two theoretical frameworks, namely New Institutional Economics (NIE) and Amartya Sen's 'capability approach'. The first, like so many theoretical frameworks used by historians, has had its fair share of critique, especially by those who see its usage in historical research as 'too modernist'.[30] There are different strands to NIE, but at its core is the emphasis on the system(s) of rules, in the form of institutions, that influence (erratically) the habits, norms and demeanour of people who function under them. These can be explicit, as with law codes, or implicit, as is the case with norms or other unwritten social conventions.[31] For ancient historians, this analytical basis has been useful not only for making hypotheses about the importance of institutions in Greek, Roman and late Roman contexts, but also in our understanding of the behaviour of the individuals that function with them.[32]

---

[29] In more traditional economic theories, an actor's need for economic resources in order to have agency is mostly translated into an interplay between property rights, access to information and problems of control. See Berhold 1971; Ross 1973; Jensen and Meckling 1976; for a recent application of economic agency, see Claassen and Herzog 2019, 472–4; Htun et al. 2019; Portass 2021 is to my knowledge the only example of a historical analysis focused on a pre-industrial context that applies the concept of economic agency explicitly.

[30] For instance Vivenza 2012, 25: 'The basic principle that institutions are involved in economics as soon as transactions reach a relevant size (and cost) is acceptable; but to attribute "the fundamental assumption of scarcity" of neoclassical theory to ancient economic thought appears excessive'; and Bowes and Grey 2020, 635–6 with critique on the circularity of some arguments made by those who use NIE; see also Ankarloo 2002, which argues that NIE makes history a-historical, and, vice versa, history makes NIE non-economic.

[31] North 1981; 1990; Eggertsson 1990; Furubotn and Richter 1997; Williamson 2000; Brousseau and Glachant 2008.

[32] Kelly 2004; Kehoe 2007; Uhalde 2007; Scheidel et al. 2007; Bang 2009 for an extensive treatment of the use of NIE in research on the ancient economy; Dossey 2010; Scheidel 2012, 9–10, also with further reading in the footnotes; Temin 2012; O'Halloran 2019. See also Terpstra 2018, who debates the future of NIE for students of ancient economic history.

Economic agency, following NIE, can only exist when institutional arrangements allow the involvement of actors in the economy and, most importantly, when these rights are protected. This principle has been taken by Dennis Kehoe to argue for a more independent late antique peasantry than has commonly been accepted.[33] In his view, while late antique sources that make reference to small-scale farmers might indicate a complete subsidiary position with no access to legal rights, a closer reading of late Roman legislation shows a commitment by the Roman state to defend smallholders' ownership rights over tangible assets.[34]

Indeed, with the legal evidence we learn at the very least how authorities understood economic and social relations in the countryside. But these are almost exclusively defined in terms of legal rights and obligations, and, as such, say remarkably little about the actual capabilities of small landowners to use their assets.[35] Furthermore, institutional formation, in this case that of Roman farm tenancy, is explained in terms of voluntary contractual agreements based on the transaction costs minimisation principle, which, according to Kehoe, cannot only be usefully applied to the economic relationships observed in late Roman legal and tenurial documents, but is also helpful in explaining types of tenurial organisation that, if assessed within a neo-institutional framework, appear inefficient.[36] Here, the rules surrounding Roman farm tenancy, and the impact it has on the behaviour of economic actors, are causally associated with cost-benefit calculations of (more or less) rationally acting individuals. As a result, social relations are reduced to (contractual) exchange relations only, regardless of whether one is a tenant, a wage labourer or a landlord, who, so it seems, all attempt to minimise transaction costs irrespective of their social position. This cannot be the case: individuals are always part of a social whole and are moulded by the underlying social relations in respect to the relative social positions they occupy.[37]

Lately, Sen's 'capability approach' has been taken as an alternative to NIE.[38] If anything, its approach to social and economic issues is much broader, focusing not just on transaction costs but on 'capabilities'. Capability, here, Sen explains as a set of functioning vectors within the actor's reach. This depends on (1) a command over goods (or entitlements) and (2) a set of utility functions available to the person. In other words, persons are suggested to have a degree of choice both in relation to resources that one purchases or achieves command over, and in relation to how one utilises

---

[33] Kehoe 2007.
[34] More precisely, Kehoe 2007, 26: 'As I argue, the Roman government consistently protected the tenure rights of tenants on imperial estates, and this policy had important implications for tenure arrangements on private land.'
[35] Wickham 2005, 383–5 on the problems of legal sources.
[36] Kehoe 2007, 34.
[37] See also Basu et al. 1987 *contra* NIE: 'Individuals choose in the marketplace, in shops, in labour markets. They do not choose between institutions, customs, and social norms'; Meramveliotakis 2018, who argues that NIE is grounded on top of methodological individualism, and inaccurately discards wider social structures.
[38] Although not always completely as an alternative, as can be seen in Nambiar 2021, who argues that the capability approach would benefit from the conceptualisation of rules as understood by institutional economics.

these; most importantly, this approach also accounts for a set of social relations that can seriously restrict such actions and, hence, an actor's capability, thus giving attention to notions of power or coercion.[39] The concept of economic agency as used by followers of Sen's approach differs only minutely from the general characterisation as given above, namely in that it is more readily utilised as a practical concept that tests the potential for economic development.[40] In any case, this focus on a set of 'functionings' and/or 'capabilities' has been used in a number of historical studies, including those of archaeologists and ancient historians.[41] These have resulted in a more complete picture of the lives and capabilities of ancient actors, even those living in poor circumstances. Sen's capability approach, however, does not give a ready clear framework that tests, so to speak, the ability of historical actors akin to late antique smallholders to acquire resources as well as to keep them. How to analyse the 'economic capability' of such individuals?

Following the application of Sen's approach in modern economics and sociology, if we are to address such a capability, at a minimum it would need to address the following: (1) the ability to influence choices of production; (2) the ways in which smallholders are able to access and make use of local and supralocal markets; and (3) the ability of smallholders to defend their property or, more specifically, their right to access specific pieces of property.[42] These points of analysis do not presume that our smallholders operated like their modern counterparts, and are therefore a good point of departure in this investigation. Taken together, their assessment allows us to conceptualise the smallholders' ability to transform resources into improved conditions, may it be in material enrichment or in the development of a greater social position.

Obviously, for smallholders much depends on their initial social and economic position. Smallholders with significant endowments of land, moveable capital or strong social networks are in general better able to make favourable decisions than their less well-off counterparts.

Most of this chapter elaborates on the different aspects of smallholder economics as noted above. I have decided to look at the different types of evidence in parts, separating the written evidence from what archaeology has to offer. What I hope to show is that by looking at economic agency within a framework that stresses capability, the account on 'the fate of free farmers' moves beyond the intuitive examples that only focus on binary oppositions.

---

[39] Sen 1985, 201; 1987, 6–9, 17–18.

[40] Bebbington 1999, with further references; and Prendergast 2005 for a critical appreciation of Sen's work in the light of economic development.

[41] Nussbaum 1988; Taylor 2017; and Bowes and Grey 2020, 629–33 for ancient history; Hyams 2017 for medieval history.

[42] With 'choices of production' I mean the presence of freedom to choose the crops produced, or agricultural strategies to pursue. Helpful in this regard has been Sen 1992; as well as Michel and Randriamanampisoa 2017, who use Sen's capability approach to explain the presence (or absence) of agricultural diversification. For capabilities and access to resources see Berry 1989 and Blaikie 1989; and for capabilities in a framework of legal entitlement see Sen 1981 and Nussbaum 2003; Moser 1998 is also helpful in the case of the vulnerability of rural livelihoods in terms of assets.

The Textual Evidence

Judging from the traditional historiography on agricultural life in late antique Italy, the second to the end of the fourth century AD was characterised by an increasingly subjugated class of small landowners, that is, until the great 'watershed' of the fifth and sixth centuries, as argued by Chris Wickham; or, if we believe in continuity, structural change only occurred with the fracturing of the Carolingian government.[43] But for much of the fourth century, most agree, elites, which could be urban or rural-based, followed the logic of tax-farming: though large landholders weren't strictly invited to squeeze out the rural population, reality would often prove to be the opposite.[44] Such an image is easily accredited in the hagiographies and law codes of Late Antiquity, both of which adequately display a distaste for usury, the 'bondage' of agricultural workers to their lands, and the dissolution of their rights.[45]

Choices of Production

A bad harvest, sickness, a deceased family member or a misguided investment: an unfortunate event could seriously disturb the at times visibly fragile living conditions of a smallholder.[46] Events like these were readily exploited by landlords or neighbouring *potiores* through the offering of loans, which agricultural workers were often incapable of paying off.[47] For smallholders, however, there existed a plethora of strategies to follow so as to circumvent unnecessary risks. These are well known: working land in different areas; growing of different crops; running of plant-growing and stock-breeding simultaneously, and the like.[48] For most of these agricultural practices we have clear evidence coming from the Ravenna Papyri, documents originally written in a number of Italian places, before ending up in the hands of the clergy of the

---

[43] In more precise terms, it was argued that fiscal measures turned the rural populace, the working part that is, into a tool of elites. This idea was mainly the result of an emphasis on the almost disproportionate amount of (Late) Roman laws dealing with registered tenancy (above all *coloni*) and, more generally, the Late Roman state tying people to their occupation or place of origin, supposedly starting with Diocletian's tax reforms. See Jones 1964, 773, 795–803; 1974, 293–307; Scheidel 2000 gives an overview of the debate on the so-called 'colonate', as does Wickham 2005, 521–6; for the 'watershed' of the fifth and sixth centuries, see Wickham 2005, 517–88, where he also explains the 'peasant mode of production'; for change starting in the ninth century AD, Costambeys 2009, 95–6; Toubert 1973.

[44] Wickham 2005, 62–72 also argues that new agricultural techniques and practices made sure that the rural populace underwent further exploitation.

[45] Carrié 2017, 186; Ruggini 1961, 190–201, which includes enough references to primary sources concerned with usury. Most of these are conjoined with comments on the avarice of elites, as for example Gaudentius of Brescia, *Serm.* 13.21–3, which speaks of the strive for silver.

[46] Ruggini 1961, 466–89 gives an extensive list of food crises in late antique Italy. See also Noel Lenski's assessment of food shortages in Chapter 2 in this volume. Despite these crises, sick or clearly unwell agricultural workers only appear very occasionally in Italian sources. See for example Ambr. *Hex.* 3.37 and Cassiod. *Var.* 8.31, which might be indications for farmers dealing with malaria; for diseases in Late Antiquity more generally, see Harper 2019.

[47] Ambr. *Tob.* 80; Zeno of Verona, *Tract.* 1.3.5, 9.1.2, 15.6; Gaudentius of Brescia, *Serm.* 4, 8, 13; Maximus of Turin, *Serm.* 82, 101–2; see also Ruggini 1961, 25–6, 85, 190–201.

[48] Garnsey 1988, 47–50; Gallant 1991, 41–6; López-Sáez et al. 2019 for vegetational circumstances.

church of Ravenna. Other sources, such as collections of sermons or *epistolae*, similarly describe the variety of crops cultivated as well as the animals reared.[49] As Peter Garnsey noted in his phenomenal work *Food and Society in Classical Antiquity*, for pre-industrial farmers a strategy of diversification combined with land fragmentation 'makes very good sense' in the rugged, uneven landscape of (Greece and) Italy, with its great variety of topographies and microclimates.[50] No less must be true for the centuries under scrutiny here. Additionally, we can expect farmers to have actualised relationships of kinship and friendship by loaning fields or pooling labour to overcome scheduling bottlenecks at times of harvesting, repaying one another with surplus foodstuffs, or support at times of dearth. A division of labour along the lines of age and/or gender probably determined who in the household would be responsible for working specific fields or undertaking various tasks such as field clearing, planting, weeding and harvesting. Even so, the role of women or age in late antique agriculture is still very much underexplored.[51] Ambrose's *De virginibus* 1.8.40–1 alludes to the collection of honey by women; and Claudian's *De sene Veronensi* suggests that farmers worked the land no matter their age (what else would we expect?).[52] These sorts of interactions, which could have been made in annual terms or daily depending on the composition of the household, its location and time of the year, must have been essential to the domestic economy of each rural household.[53] Normally, this meant that farmers were unlikely to experience a very low return from their scattered assets; and, in principle, they could tolerate and absorb demands from outside up to a certain level without needing to make structural changes and adaptations.[54] Of course, this is all true supposing that smallholders were capable of withstanding the rapacious advances of neighbouring elites or kin. As Horden and Purcell famously enunciated: everything has to do with access.[55]

---

[49] Ravenna Papyri: *P. Ital.* 2: 'perseceto'; 3: 'lardi', 'anseres', 'galinas', 'lactis' (which indicates dairy cattle), and 'pullos'; 29, 30 and 33 display a wide variety of crops, trees, pastures and shrubs, noticeably the following: *pascuis, sationibus, sationalibus, vineis, arbusteis, arbustatis, arbustis, arboribus, arboribus arbustis pomeferis, fructiferis diversis generis limitibusque, ingressis, spatiis, campis, pratis, silbus, salectis* and *taleis olivarum*. These kinds of agricultural denotations can also be discerned in papyri written after 553. See *P. Ital.* 14–15, 17, 20, 35, 36, 37, 44, 46. For agriculture and animal husbandry in the sixth century, see Grey 2016, 270–7, referring primarily to Cassiodorus' *Variae*; for the sermons, see esp. Ambrose, which will become apparent on the following pages.

[50] Garnsey 1999, 25.

[51] Beaucamp 1999, 750.

[52] Ambr. *Virg.* 1.8.40–1. Claud. *Carm. min.* 10; some useful passages can also be found in Palladius' *Opus agriculturae*, wherein the author argues that women are particularly skilled in the collection and storage of acorns, as well as raising hens. I suspect similar divisions of labour to have occurred in Italy, yet evidence for it is, again, thin. See also Grey 2011, 42–3 on Palladius.

[53] Lirb 1993 argues explicitly for farmers exchanging draft animals; Grey 2011, 63–74.

[54] At the same time, the climatological changes and political upheavals experienced in Late Antiquity might mean that some farmers dealt with much tougher circumstances than previously experienced. There is increasingly more evidence for this; but, despite the efforts of many, it is not conclusive. See Squatriti 2016, 395–6 specifically for the rural population; Grey 2016, 285–9.

[55] Horden and Purcell 2000, 272.

Tenurial arrangements

Whether choices of production (and investment) fell to the smallholder ultimately rested on the existence of a relational contract (or *locatio conductio*) with a landlord, and, if it did, the provisos made therein. In the late antique world, and especially Italy, for landowners there existed a plethora of relational contracts to choose from, all of which would virtually dictate to what extent smallholders were capable of influencing choices of production.[56] We may expect smallholders to have worked as wage labourers, leaseholders, sharecroppers, and to take up similar roles simultaneously, while at the same time consenting to a variety of contractual conditions, which included advance payments, loans and different types of rent.[57] Within a given area contracts must have differed, all depending on the relative bargaining power of each individual smallholder as well as that of the landlord. Obviously, relations could change, e.g. with sharecroppers becoming wage labourers, leaseholders becoming sharecroppers, and so on. On the whole, then, Italy's late antique landscape presented many types of labour relations and contractual obligations, and that is, mostly, also what the sources seem to convey: Ambrose speaks of sharecroppers; one of the Ravenna Papyri, *P. Ital.* 2, shows leaseholds (with the local church collecting rents from tenants, and taxes from other holdings); another papyrus, *P. Ital.* 3, implies the combination of a leasehold (tenants paying rent in solidi) and a sharecropping contract at the same time; and the *Theodosian Code* speaks of wage labourers, while Gaudentius of Brescia alludes to it.[58] Recently it has been argued, primarily against views developed by Jean-Michel Carrié, that the use of *coloni* became much more important in Late Antiquity.[59] Next to this, some scholars argue that wage labour expanded concurrently, which, together with the entry of coinage into labour relations, would have made agricultural workers much more dependent on elites.[60] For Italy, the evidence might often be thin to make any conclusive argument, both in the qualitative and quantitative sense, but we cannot sidestep these discussions. The importance of *coloni* I will address later, as it is also related to the mobility of non-elites (as the laws concerned with it structurally emphasise the binding to *origo*), an issue that greatly affects our understanding of the participation of smallholders in wider economic structures. Nonetheless, I will comment on wage labour and coinage here, albeit briefly. As I showed above, wage labour does appear in our sources, but it does so very sporadically; it seems to me to be more logical to argue that it was just one way whereby landlords could manage their estates, with wage labourers being especially useful for seasonal work.[61] Undoubtedly, changing market conditions had an effect on the 'popularity' of this type of labour. For instance, the presence of migrants would have resulted in salaried, cheap labour. So, just as some form of labour, or management, must have become prominent in one

---

[56] Kehoe 2007, 95–109.
[57] Banaji 2001, 198–200.
[58] Ambr. *Noe* 109; on *P. Ital.* 2 see also Tedesco 2020, 355; *CTh* 10.10.23; Gaudentius of Brescia, *Serm.* 13.
[59] Carrié 1982; 1997.
[60] Banaji 2016, 75–7; Tedesco 2018, 424–5.
[61] Erdkamp 2005, 52–3.

region, its use might decrease in another.⁶² On coinage, there is a bit more evidence to use, which makes it possible for me to wholeheartedly disagree with the notion that the use of coinage in labour relations would necessarily lead to smallholders becoming more dependent. When coinage appears in the sources, we see smallholders using it to buy land, to buy commodities; and, as I argue later, there is also the possibility that they used it to discharge obligations. It thus offered a degree of flexibility in the use of their resources. In the case of rent payment, we may imagine two outcomes: well-to-do smallholders with access to assets capable of producing substantial amounts of produce benefited, as their income must, at times, have exceeded the monetary rent demanded from them; smallholders in less fortunate situations, however, might have been required to undertake additional obligations to pay their rents as elites could force low prices on to small producers at harvest, as well as charge exorbitant sums for their own goods in times of need.⁶³ The widespread use of coinage thus had concurrent effects: opening up the economy and giving smallholders the possibility to use this to their advantage, while simultaneously making it easier for elites to prey on the poor. The well-to-do became wealthier, the poor became poorer. Of course, these kinds of economic developments must have taken place primarily in the vicinity of significant commercial networks; I do not see why else there would be such an emphasis on coinage in the Ravenna Papyri.

Tenurial control

Another important matter is control.⁶⁴ Landlords, through their management and close supervision of smallholders, influenced the farming practices of their tenants. The opposite is, of course, also true: shrewd tenants took advantage of mismanagement on the part of their landlords. *P. Ital.* 1 and *P. Ital.* 3 are two sets of papyri that are strikingly similar in their structure but, conversely, show varying degrees of control. *P. Ital.* 1 consists of several letters written by Lauricius, *praepositus sacri cubiculi* to the church of Ravenna, all of which concern a patrimony on Sicily. Lauricius upholds communication with several of his *conductores* and *actores*, who, so the letters seem to convey, inform him about fiscal operations, e.g. the collection of rent of each and every *fundus* and *massa* the church of Ravenna possesses in this locality. They also show that one of the *conductores*, Sissinus, has gone to Ravenna to complain to Lauricius about the actions of the *tribunus* Pyrrus, who is responsible for collecting rents from the *conductores*. Apparently, Pyrrus neglects his duties, which makes the *conductores* ask Lauricius to send a new tribune.⁶⁵ Pyrrus was probably a landowner

---

⁶² Erdkamp 2005, 80. Though I would add to this that wage labour was probably more significant in areas where elites could be particularly resourceful and powerful, such as near urban areas, or, in any case, wherever elites gave a significant contribution to the vitality of commerce.

⁶³ See also Wickham 2005, 271, who notes that, while rents (just like taxes) might be assessed in money, it is questionable whether small farmers always had to ability to pay these in coin. Hence, the majority of smallholders must have paid their dues in kind, but the conversion that was needed as a result could have allowed defrauding by the use of 'unfair prices and false weights'.

⁶⁴ Wickham 2005, 270-1 on the interests of landowners in estate management; see also below, p. 237-8.

⁶⁵ *P. Ital.* 3.

very much unconcerned with the daily activities of the *conductores* – even less so with the smallholders working the estates. The correspondence between Lauricius and his men tells us of another problem, one regarding the *fundus* Partilaticus. This piece of property was once loaned by a tenant named Tranquillus, 'according to the bond of debt that you [the *conductor* of the estate, whose name is lost] brought with you, and that you handed over to Pyrrus yourself, under a certain prescription'.[66] It is clear that Tranquillus was not working it any longer, however, since some 'unknown persons' had 'acquired authorisation' over it.[67] Lauricius' response to this incident is telling. He urges that, first and foremost, the recipient of his letter, a *conductor*, pay his outstanding debts. It is only thereafter that he is allowed to investigate the incident enveloping the *fundus* – all at his own expense, however, as Lauricius makes clear.[68] This was a system plagued by corruption, fraud and indifference to the lives of the tenants working the estates; or, from the perspective of the top-level managers, to the issues experienced by the *conductores*. People often forsake their obligations, as *P. Ital.* 3 implies. We may safely assume that tenants regularly took over each other's plots, did not report their actions, and sold the crops harvested from their illegal properties to buyers other than their own landlords.

P. Ital. 3 lists the names of the tenants, their legal status, the rents paid, the foodstuffs produced; it is all very meticulously reported.[69] Especially striking is the homogeneity of the product, both in its quantities given and its contents, which reveals that despite the different types of tenancies presented here (*coloni, vilici*) the dues asked were relatively the same. The document has become especially famous because it also lists *operae*, labour duties, of three days a week.[70] There is little chance that the tenants that worked these estates had anything to say about the landholdings they leased, let alone about the crops they raised on them. Instead, at least for three days a week they performed labour services and produced exactly that which was needed. There is likewise no evidence of chief tenants unable to control the illegal activities of their inferiors. Everything suggests that there was a tight control on the economic ventures of the tenants who worked here.

We cannot go into every detail given in these papyri here. The inevitable aim of most landlords, it would seem, would be to depress almost all tenants to a uniform level of bare subsistence, the rare exceptions being those who were really large landholders

---

[66] My translation. *P. Ital.* 3: *ante omnia de fundo Pattilatico, quem Tranquillus in tempore, filius Gregori quondam, sub certa depectione fiduciae nexu obligaverat iuxta cautionem, quam tecum portaveras, quam ipsi Pyrro refudisti.*

[67] *P. Ital.* 3: *quorum personam ignoramus, dicitur occupatam elicita auctoritate.*

[68] *P. Ital.* 3: *ne in aliquo nobis aut secundae sententiae nostrae dispendium adferatur.*

[69] I cannot give the entirety of *P. Ital.* 3 here, but it suffices to say that it lists first the name of the property and the proprietor, thus: *Colonia Severiaca per Leonum et Achillem, Victurinum et Severum*; followed by the taxes paid: *praestat solidos numero V, tremisses II, siliquas G*; and finally the produce 'gifted' in *xenia: in xeniis anseres II, galinas XG, ova CLX, melis pondo CXXX.*

[70] The formulations given go as follows: *per ebdomada operas III*; See Wickham 2005, 278–9, which summarises the discussion on the *operae* in *P. Ital.* 3, arguing for a 'systemic break' between the control of labour as shown in *P. Ital.* 3 and on later bipartite estates, and also gives an extensive bibliography on the subject. The most important works in this case are Percival 1969; Toubert 1973; Vera 1986; and Pasquali 2008, 81–108; and Sarris 2006b, 412, who disagrees with Wickham's views.

in disguise – the *conductores*, for instance, as in *P. Ital.* 1, occupying holdings, perhaps at nominal rates to avoid taxes. And yet, though it would not do for the localities named in these documents to exaggerate the difficulties faced by landlords and *conductores*, there is a sense in which even their oppression may be seen to be precarious once we remember that its basis is in prestige and force, commodities subject to shifts or erosion.[71] If power in rural contexts was in essence quite customary and informal, it might, in turn, have been rather flexible in response to circumstances.[72] Thus, we may postulate the existence of well-to-do smallholders even in oppressive contexts, to the extent that exploitation was not uniform. In other words: the power of the landlord was not absolute. Much could be concealed from him. The fragmentation of landholdings undoubtedly contributed to this. Tenants often worked very small patches of land, interlaced with plots forming parts of other holdings, sometimes only marked off by small paths, some stones or markings made on trees.[73] It seems illogical that elite landholders would have had a trustworthy private servant in each and every locality; instead, they depended on chief tenants, for whom it was often not in their interest to report changes.[74] I would not go so far as to say that this was a problem everywhere. Pressure and control are, of course, very context-dependent. Domenico Vera argued that late Roman landowners gave up direct management completely during Late Antiquity, a theory that has justifiably been criticised by Jairus Banaji.[75] Control, and the economic agency of smallholders, we must expect, varied according to the degree of direct investment of landholders in their properties, as well as the 'logic of deployment'.[76]

Moments of functioning

Despite these brief moments of 'cracks in the system', where we see tenants accessing resources, albeit illegally, it is difficult to find instances where decision-making processes as from the viewpoint of the tenants themselves are highlighted. Instead, nearly all attention is given to the 'specialist' production of wine and cereals. Unsurprisingly, as both of these enjoyed great interest from the elite who sought to profit fully from them by controlling the flow of these products to the *urbs*.[77] There are some exceptions to the rule, however. It may be useful for our perception of agricultural strategies as used by smallholders, and hence their capabilities, to point our attention to one such exception, namely several passages from Ambrose's *De Noe*, *De virginibus* and *De virginitate*. In the first source, the bishop of Milan, considering himself an expert on the subject of cultivation, reacts with surprise at the total investment of some farmers in the production of wine, even when both the quality and price start

---

[71] Krause 1987, 233–43; see also Barzel 2002, 209–12.
[72] Kehoe 2007, 133–4.
[73] *CTh* 2.26.2, 9.1.1; *ET* 104, 105; Cassiod. *Var.* 3.52 for a dispute focused on boundary markers.
[74] The relationship between *conductores* and their landlords was often a hostile one, with the latter trying to dampen the prosperity of the former. See Lenski 2017, 120–4, 129–31.
[75] Vera 1983.
[76] Banaji 1992.
[77] Erdkamp 2005, 306–16; 2012, 257–62; Ruggini 1961, 56–146 on the grain market of late antique Italy specifically.

dropping drastically around the first half of the fourth century. Ambrose then exhorts that these individuals would be better off investing in the cultivation of grain, seeing it as the most critical foodstuff in their diet.[78] Subsequently, at separate moments throughout *De virginibus* and *De virginitate*, Ambrose states that farmers should devote themselves to harvesting a variety of crops, particularly fruit, olives, roses and the production of animal fodder.[79]

The passages are difficult to interpret due to their conspicuous moralising character. But they offer us evidence for moments of 'functioning', i.e. smallholders making decisions about the investment of their energy. In a hypothetical vein, let us imagine that Ambrose is telling us the truth in regards to the decisions made by these non-elite agriculturalists, and that they were, in fact, investing the larger part of their resources in a singular crop. The frustration of Ambrose over the choice of the crop in *De Noe* 109 suggests that the farmers (*cultores*, so *De Noe* 108) were free to decide what crop to cultivate, which could be indicating the presence of a sharecropping contract.[80] This information by itself indicates that we are dealing with smallholders here. If Ambrose was their landlord, he had every reason to be concerned: the less valuable the crop, the lower the price he could get for his share of the harvest.[81] The fact that at least some part of his buying power originated from the income derived from his rural properties meant that Ambrose might have been duly frustrated with the decisions made by these farmers.[82] Ambrose admits elsewhere that the *vindemiae expensae* weighed heavily on the total budget available to these farmers.[83] It is unclear what Ambrose exactly means with 'expenses' here, but we can assume that these involved more than the labour itself. The conventional Roman farm lease formulated that tenants provided moveable capital, including tools, draft animals and, when they had the funds to afford them, slaves.[84] Grape cultivation was considered much more labour-intensive than livestock farming, however, and more costly. The grapevine needed attention throughout the year; if left unattended it could seriously harm the precious soil.[85] Furthermore, it required tools and equipment that only the well-to-do farmers could afford.[86] These

---

[78] Ambr. *Noe* 109.
[79] Ambr. *Virg.* 1.45 and 3.17; *Virginit.* 34. See also Ruggini 1961, 180.
[80] Ambr. *Noe* 108 speaks of the master of the land (*dominus*) and the farmer (*cultoris*); *Noe* 109 notes that *iustus primum plantat*, by which he obviously means the cultivators, not the *domini*. See also Ruggini 1961, 180, who seems to think the same, although without explanation.
[81] We know that Ambrose owned property because of Paulin. *Vit. Ambr.* 1.39, even if he claims to have given away all of his property to the poor. His estates in Africa were administered by his brother Satyrus, judging from Ambr. *Exc. Sat.* 1.23. Whether Ambrose owned estates in Italy is less certain. In *Ep.* 75.33 he notes that he allows the emperor to take away his estates, even his patrimony, by which he could mean an Italian one; and Beraghi 1867 argues that the church of Sant'Ambrogio in Brugherio (Lombardy) was built on top of a villa owned by Ambrose.
[82] See also the same concern in Zeno of Verona, *Tract.* 1.5 and 4.14.
[83] Ambr. *Hex.* 4. 19.
[84] Kehoe 2007, 95–6; *ET* 150 indicates that farmhands, *rustici*, were able to own slaves: *nulli liceat invito [domino] rustico alieno operas aut obsequium imperare, nec eius mancipio aut bove uti, nisi hoc forte idem rusticus aut conductor ipsius, vel dominus sua voluntate praestiterit.*
[85] As Ambr. *Paen.* 1.17.96 shows.
[86] Erdkamp 2005, 75–6.

continuous investments meant that in the event of a bad year smallholders could face heavy overheads that possibly absorbed the whole of the profit – in all likelihood creating a potentially disastrous loss.[87] Considering the possible expenses implied by law codes, the heavy workload associated with viticulture, and the high taxes (*coemptiones, capitatio, iugatio*) pressed upon wine producers in this period of time, one can easily assume that smallholders profited only very minimally from the cultivation of wine grapes, if at all.[88]

Is it fair to label this as 'risky'? Normally, it is argued that a specialisation pathway forced upon smallholders, or used by them intentionally, results in an increased sensitivity to adverse environmental fluctuations that reduces the yields of crops produced, in turn making it more difficult to buy staples essential to the survival of the household and inviting predation. In the same vein, scholars often maintain that smallholders focused on diversification benefit not only from changing market opportunities – this 'spread of risk' is also crucial in moments of dearth. Anthropology has shown, however, that economic strategies such as these can go both ways, and that there are complementary explanations for both. For instance, it makes little sense to define diversification just as evidence for risk aversion. Farmers bent on diversification may use several of the plots they own to try out new crops (or techniques) with the sole aim of experimentation. Furthermore, farmers might have different types of land and be planting different crops on land with different characteristics – thus maximising expected profits in the process. So, in other words, behaviour ascribed to risk aversion may be the result of considerations that are, to us at least, not always readily apparent.

That means that choices of production ultimately depend on the combination of very specific circumstances that we find for each case – including the one sketched above. Differences in location, access to assets and social networks, household characteristics and other crucial variables mean that smallholders sometimes choose to follow a strategy that only makes sense when we consider a good number of these elements. It is impossible to generalise about the state of agriculture in Italy during the fourth and fifth centuries, and it is similarly a tall order to understand exactly why these smallholders choose to go for such an obviously bad investment – at least in the eyes of Ambrose, that is. On the other hand, it is clear that the region where these smallholders resided (northern Italy, somewhere around Milan presumably) was well known for its viticulture. Although the value of wine fell considerably from the third century

---

[87] Sessa 2018, 38–40; also Rossiter 2007, who uses Zeno of Verona, *Tract.* 2.27.2.

[88] Ruggini 1961, 37–66, 72–3 for the variety of taxes pressed upon cultivators, and a discussion on the suppressiveness of these. Needless to say, the most important sources on tax for Late Roman Italy come from codes of law (such as the famous law by Valentinian III on governmental officials abusing their power to charge more tax, *N. Val.* 1.3, which can also be found in the edition of the *Codex Theodosianus* used here, by Mommsen and Meyer); but sermons are also helpful (the most important ones are Maximus of Turin, *Serm.* 71; Ambr. *Exp. fid.* 1.12.84, although technically not a sermon). Ambrose is remarkably quiet about the collection of taxes considering he was (partly) responsible for it; see McLynn 1994, 5; Peter Chrysologus, *Serm.* 26.5, 28.2–3, 30.1–4, 54, 97.7, 105.4, 137.10, 168 are also helpful, as are the *Variae* by Cassiodorus; see Bjornlie 2014. In any case, complaints about taxation were widespread in Late Antiquity. For an extensive list of these see Demandt 1989, 248; and Wickham 2005, 62–4 with further references.

because of overproduction, and taxes on viticulture increased, the region continued to supply places near the Danube and the province of Illyricum, and intermittently others (such as Pannonia), for centuries, mainly because the region was crucial for the survival of the *annona* system.[89] Additionally, in spite of the fact that the price obtained for their products might have been low, the farmers were sure to offset their produce. And if not in the regions named above, the local populace seems to have been inclined to consume it: Ambrose is astonished to see not only the elite consuming wine but additionally the common populace.[90] Lastly, we should also not underestimate the effect of the reputation of certain products. There exists ample evidence to suggest that some places in the Mediterranean world were well known for their wares[91] – so famous that men like Ennodius exchanged constant letters with friends (in this case Agnellus) to ensure their collection.[92] Such fame, which might have worked very similarly to *publica fama*, must have impacted the demand for products at least to some extent.[93] For these reasons alone, specialisation does not always mean that farmers mostly have to 'rely on the vagaries of the market', as some suggest.[94]

This also means that efforts to understand the strategies of non-elites in rural contexts by the use of conventional economic analysis (prioritising the law of efficiency, or the minimisation of transaction costs, as explained earlier) at times yield inaccurate depictions because groups such as smallholders respond to economic incentives very differently than the capitalist firm on which models such as NIE are based. Economic anthropology has shown that smallholders regularly engage in high-risk strategies, basing their economic decision-making on the conditions of the market, and that, most importantly, the decisions they make in regards to their assets are based primarily upon moral frameworks which are conditioned by local contexts. The conditions of the wine market discussed above are one example.

The economic landscape that we encounter in our late antique sources is thus not a landscape defined by subsistence, an agricultural *modus operandi* which has already been greatly criticised in the context of pre-industrial smallholders, by a division of successful and unsuccessful smallholders due to the former prioritising diversification and the latter specialisation, with the latter ultimately becoming socially and economically dependent as a result of their chosen strategy, but by smallholders trying to understand their locality, figuring out the right choices of production, investing in assets, labour and one or several crops they deem most beneficial, so as to ensure and

---

[89] Overproduction: Plin. *Ep.* 4.6; Mart. 3.56 and 3.67. Continued production of wine in northern Italy (and the Danube region and Illyrica): Ruggini 1961, 179–80.

[90] For consumption of wine by all layers of society: Ambr. *Hel.* 25, 42, 46–50, 54, 62, 66–8; *Cain* 1.14; *Exp. Ps.* 1.46; *Ps.* 37.30; see also Ennod. *Carm.* 2.143 with a very similar observation.

[91] Lucania, for example, was quite famous for its pork sausage. See Barnish 1987; and Sessa 2018, 41–2; Cassiod. *Var.* 8.31 praising the horses from Bruttii, his native land. Italy continued to be quite famous for its wines more generally speaking. See Perkins 2000, 376. Sheep were of excellent quality from the countryside between the Apennines and the Adriatic. See Gabba and Pasquinucci 1979, 152–82.

[92] In this case the matter concerns a horse, apparently of the best quality as it comes from Ravenna. Ennod. *Ep.* 7.26.

[93] For *publica fama*, see Wickham 1998.

[94] Garnsey 1988, 56; Erdkamp 2005, 78.

develop their well-being.⁹⁵ Indeed, Ambrose's smallholders might have been the lucky ones in their locality. If they achieved being rather successful for a longer time, this must have been so because of a degree of agility and adaptability. There were people who did not succeed in that end. As a smallholder, there are of course reasons to try nonetheless, to take your chances, in the hope of getting the surplus you want – not merely to pay taxes or dues to the individuals that are keen to ask these, but to be able to buy artisanal products, clothing, utensils, tools, *ergo* a variety of goods, bits, bobs and trinkets, so that you can distinguish yourself from your neighbours, who, perhaps, may not be as bountiful.⁹⁶

The end of antiquity and microregions

Now, before I move to the issue of smallholders accessing local and regional markets, I want to address two points of debate, one in respect to the importance of state-subsidised ventures for the economic survival of smallholders, the other microregional. Scholars generally agree that Italy experienced the first signs of economic collapse in the first half of the fifth century, following the loss of the senatorial estates in Africa.⁹⁷ How much this event and the following structural weakening of the *annona* system impacted the overall economy of Italy, and smallholders specifically, wholly depends on the degree to which one connects Italy's economic prosperity to the survival of the fiscal enterprises of the state. Chris Wickham and Michael McCormick have argued that much of the late antique economy was dominated by state-subsidised movements of goods; any private economic enterprises formed merely an addendum to the importance of the *annonae*, and thus depended greatly on its survival.⁹⁸ Not everyone agrees with this view. Most recently it has been disputed by Jean-Michel Carrié, who asserts that most inhabitants of the late antique world relied on the open market and, more directly, on the private producers who sold their goods at local or regional markets (i.e. smallholders selling their goods at *nundinae* and private rural markets, to which we will come later).⁹⁹ Let us consider how the lives of the smallholders as sketched above, in Ambrose's *De Noe*, would fit in these opposing frameworks.

First, let me summarise in one sentence the purpose of the *annonae*. These were primarily used by the late Roman government, and to a lesser extent by Ostrogothic officials, to provide Italy's armies as well as a considerable part of the population of Rome with food and drink.¹⁰⁰ Now, as Lellia Ruggini has already shown for both the late Roman and Ostrogothic administrations, the central bureaucracy tended to switch the burden of providing provisions to both of these bodies, by way of

---

⁹⁵ Horden and Purcell 2000, 271–4.
⁹⁶ Wickham 2005, 699–700.
⁹⁷ Wickham 2005, 730.
⁹⁸ McCormick 2001, 83–119; Wickham 2005, 72–80, 693–720.
⁹⁹ Carrié 2012, 20–1, which borrows many of its views from Carandini 1983, 145–62; 1986, 10–19; Panella 1986, 444–46; 1993, 613–97; the debate is well summarised by Mark Whittow 2013, 137–43, who calls it a 'fiscalist' versus 'anti-fiscalist' debate.
¹⁰⁰ Sessa 2018, 148–52; Bjornlie 2014, 160.

coemptio, from one group of landowners in a particular area to another; these were also, so the sources convey, fairly irregular exactions.[101] The weight of these burdens thus changed in geographical terms, and it did so a considerable, erratic number of times.[102] There is zero evidence that this change of direction significantly impacted agricultural production in areas within Italy that were not, or from some point onwards, were no longer, connected to the state-subsidised systems of the *annonae*. Furthermore, Ruggini shows that between the fourth and fifth centuries there existed a class of large landowners which, by sending *mercatori* to markets and estates, tried to hoard as much grain, wine and pork as possible, with the intention of selling these goods for premium prices at times of dearth. These large landowners were not connected to the state; to the contrary, they sought to avoid contact with late Roman and Ostrogothic officials, where possible, with the sole purpose of tax evasion and forgoing civic obligations. They were, much to the annoyance of the general population, persistent in their economic goal and successful: even the state, at certain points, had to buy part of its needs from these proprietors; and, often, just to make sure the state's needs were met, officials could do nothing other than grant them tax exemptions.[103] The least this means is that there was a stratum of landowners which, in spite of the efforts of the state, and the collapse of state-subsidised ventures, continued to be able to buy and sell foodstuffs on a public market. In other words, when the *annonae* gradually ceased to exist, private individuals must have still been able to buy and sell products, which just by itself indicates the presence of a free market, able to function without the economic interventions of the state. With this in mind, Carrié's 'anti-fiscalist' depiction of the late antique economy seems to make significantly more sense than Wickham and McCormick's 'fiscalist' standpoint. Furthermore, Carrié's hypothesis would also explain some of the archaeological material that we encounter in Italy during these centuries. Take for example Helena Patterson and Paul Arthur's survey of ceramics in central and southern Italy.[104] They show that for the fourth and the fifth centuries the patterns of ceramic consumption are essentially the same: aside from locally produced ceramics, African Red Slip Ware (ARS), the presence of which is generally considered an indication of the *annonae*, appears consistently. Come the mid-fifth century, however, imported ARS disappears significantly, which, Wickham argues, 'must have been caused by the disruptions of the end of the *annona* in 439, rather than by changes in either production or demand'.[105] Yet what Patterson and Arthur also show is that standardised products made by both small local and large potteries continue to be available even after the disappearance of ARS; and, most strikingly, that the pottery industry even shows signs of increased vitality, which only begins to falter in the early to mid-sixth century.[106] Much as in Carrié's assessment of Egyptian evidence, we can also discern a variety of different

---

[101] Ruggini 1961, 207–22, esp. 210.
[102] Ruggini 1961, 219–21.
[103] Ruggini 1961, 96–145; Vera 1983; Cassiod. *Var.* 9.5; Symm. *Ep.* 6.12.
[104] Patterson and Arthur 1994.
[105] Wickham 2005, 730.
[106] Patterson and Arthur 1994, 423–5.

types and styles of ceramic, hinting at the possibility that its producers wished to attract buyers by giving them a variety of choices.[107] Thus archaeology, too, suggests that the breakdown of the *annona* system must not have greatly impacted agricultural production; that there existed a free market; and, most intriguingly, that the disappearance of a state-subsidised good might even have heralded an observably prosperous period for local producers.

In relation to the actual 'end' of the late antique economy, there can be considerably less discussion as regards the effects it had on the agricultural strategies of smallholders. The collapse or 'transformation' happened very gradually in Italy, starting in the sixth century, but was truly impactful come the seventh century – just after the period that we discuss here.[108] There have been many discussions on the fate of the late antique economy, with scholars pointing out a number of culprits. For Italy especially, a much-discussed candidate is the Gothic War, and the subsequent invasion of the Lombards; the impact of the two of them is still debated with much fervour.[109] Still, as Mark Whittow suggests, what must have caused the disappearance of economic growth in the late antique countryside – and this, I think, also holds true for Italy – must have been the lack of trust in the overall economy, as there was no longer a centralised state that would make (private) exchange work.[110] In terms of agricultural strategies as employed by smallholders, this must have meant that most small agriculturalists were now producing chiefly for home and local consumption, and only produced a few commodities for cash and market exchanges. Intense specialisation such as we see in *De Noe* 109 was probably rare at the end of the sixth century, with apparent exceptions in the politically more stable areas, i.e. around Rome and in the core areas of the Exarchate, which do show signs of continuity, as displayed by both the archaeological and documentary record.[111] That is not to say that smallholders stopped specialising completely: they still managed to make some of the goods they craved in the off season, get experience in the process, and sell these goods, in their own locality, to strangers and peddlers or in the close-by village, town or city, as some of the archaeological evidence we look at later on will show. But again, relatively speaking, only very few had access to specialised agriculture in the sense of what we encountered earlier. Now, this finally brings me to my second point, which is much briefer. There is a need for more systematic knowledge of livelihood strategies and their links to macroeconomic or macrosocial developments. The last decades have seen an uneven assessment of the many types of interaction between the late Roman and Ostrogothic government, its mid-level bureaucracy and rural households. Late Roman and Ostrogothic policies are only barely understood as to the changes in rural livelihood systems that they provoke.[112] This seems to me to be an area that would repay further research.

---

[107] Carrié 2012, 18.
[108] Wickham 2005.
[109] Christie 2006, 18–19, 34–50, with further bibliography.
[110] Whittow 2013, 155–60.
[111] Christie 2006, 402–96, again with further bibliography.
[112] Though Lafferty 2013, 234–40 comes close.

Access to Markets

In the last decades, two issues in particular have influenced how we are to understand the use of markets by non-elite agriculturalists: the legal binding of agricultural labour to the land, and the existence or nature of rural markets. Within debates that focus on these two topics, the conceptualisation of economic participation as experienced by smallholders ranges from characterisations highlighting complete economic isolation, structural dependence and hence little interaction with markets, to anything almost completely opposite.[113] This makes sense, seeing that the evidence left to us allows for very different interpretations. I will discuss each issue in turn, beginning with the so-called 'bondage' of non-elite agriculturalists to their holdings.

When it comes to the issue of bondage, I am not concerned with the question of whether restrictive laws were established on a fiscal imperative rather than aimed at altering the labour participation of Italy's population; in my view the first makes more sense, fitting nicely within an illustration of a late Roman state trying to cover its expenses, yet mostly unconcerned with the mediums through which the common populace pays its taxes.[114] Rather, I am interested in the mobility of rural non-elites 'on the ground', that is, to ask whether the sources addressing mobility restrictions should be taken at face value and, whatever the outcome may be, if this says anything useful about the capability of smallholders to use their economic assets, or produce, at markets.

Thinking about law

It remains the case that the weight of evidence on the so-called 'bondage of labour' comes from late Roman law. At least until the second half of the nineteenth century scholars tended to assume that these law codes reflected reality and that by the use of them, landlords, officials and other elites regulated almost all aspects of agricultural life.[115] Recent decades have seen the rise of a perspective that has veered almost completely to the opposite, being far more pessimistic about the impact of law 'on the ground'.[116] In the words of Jairus Banaji: 'Law is a dimension of reality, not a picture of it, and there is no reason to suppose either that people were fully aware of what the laws actually were ... or even that they were ever widely enforced.'[117] Conversely, the idea that both the late Roman government and its successors sought to force the agricultural population into submissive slave-like positions has also been challenged. For instance, one law issued by Constantine I in 332, frequently used as evidence to advocate for a pervasive social and economic development whereby *coloni* attained an increasingly worse social and economic position, had consistently been wrongly

---

[113] With Wickham 2005; Decker 2009; Dossey 2010; and Grey 2011 vouching for varying grades of independence of rural non-elites, and Sarris 2006a; 2006b; 2009; and Banaji 2009 critiquing it.
[114] On fiscal imperatives, see Banaji 2009, 119–24, esp. 121; Bransbourg 2015 on what he calls 'the limits of the tributarian regime', referring to the later Roman Empire.
[115] Saumagne 1937; Segrè 1947; Pallasse 1955; Finley 1980, 123–49.
[116] Wickham 2005, 383–84 is sceptical in regards to the usefulness of law, more than Banaji 2001.
[117] Banaji 2011, 121–2.

interpreted. Aleksandr Koptev has shown that the law spoke of tenants undergoing punishment 'as if they were slaves', instead of reducing *coloni* to a position of slavery as most scholars eagerly accepted.[118] Furthermore, the 'colonate', as the different legally determined groups of *coloni* are often referred to collectively, only started to exist as a real concept with the making of the *Codex Justinianus* in 534, which suggests that before the end of the sixth century *coloni* might not have been such an important, clear-cut group as had been thought before.[119]

As for the usefulness of these laws, they focus almost exclusively on 'the colonate', and only very occasionally do we catch a glimpse of agriculturalists not classified as part of this group. We may suggest that the 'other' group must then have been a part of this colonate, or that it was simply insignificant, but a close reading of several laws as well as *P. Ital.* 3 shows that this cannot have been the case. A law issued by Valentinian and Valens in 366 stipulates that if any person has the ownership of some piece of landed property, that person has to accept the responsibilities that come with the ownership of property, which includes the payment of taxes and, in the case of *coloni*, 'the duties of compulsory services [for those] who were born in their condition [that of *colonus*] and who are proved to have been enrolled on the tax lists on such lands'. Most importantly, the law states that persons that have possession of 'any small plot of land' and are 'enrolled under their own name in the tax lists' are excluded from this regulation. These individuals, on their part, are deemed responsible for paying their taxes in kind under the direction of the customary tax collector.[120] The law remains remarkably vague on the identity of these 'others', but it is obvious that these were people to whom the rules as described for *coloni* did not apply to. *P. Ital.* 3 is also instructive here. It lists several *coloni* that lease (parts of) *fundi*, but also several men who are not noted as such. Namely, Quintulus and Sabino, who lease the *colonia* (i.e. an estate) *Valeriaca*; Leo, Achilles, Victurinus and Severus, who lease the *colonia Severiaca*; and the presbyter Victor, who leases the *palude* ('marsh'), 'according to his own words (*quem sibi dicet*)'. Lastly, the document also shows that one particular *colonia*, named Candidiana, had not been cultivated yet; the administrators of the estates seem to have been looking for someone to do so.[121] For a document that is remarkably precise in respect to the names of the proprietors and their leaseholds, the types of land (*colonia, palude, saltus*), the amount of rent paid, as well as the produce 'gifted' (*in xeniis*), it would be peculiar for the author of *P. Ital.* 3 to merely forget to add the legal status of almost half of the individuals listed here. These were 'free' individuals, not *coloni*.

To suggest that there existed an independent stratum of free non-elite agriculturalists in Late Antiquity aside from the 'colonate' is nothing new, of course. It is not without reason that A. H. M. Jones treated 'the peasant freeholder' separately from *coloni*.[122] Yet scholars often readily assume that the laws concerned with the bondage of *coloni* are testament to the circumstances the entire rural population found itself in,

---

[118] Koptev 2009.
[119] Sirks 2008; see also Carrié 1982; 1983; 1997.
[120] My translations; *CTh* 11.1.14.
[121] *P. Ital.* 3.
[122] Jones 1964, 773–81, 795–803; Banaji 2011, 122 makes a similar observation.

for which there is practically zero evidence.[123] These generalisations are not helpful, as we might risk inferring a state of affairs that possibly never really existed.

So much for the 'colonate', and the ambiguities of laws that restrict movement. The basic ambiguity is that these laws are primarily aimed towards binding *coloni*, but not necessarily each and every non-elite agriculturalist. Of course, one could argue that these suggestions make no difference. Local powerful individuals could still force the majority of free smallholders to remain on their property, even if the law seems to exclude them. There is no doubt that many elites did. Having said that, our sources *do* hint at moments where non-elite agriculturalists were fully engaged in all the negotiation and involvement with forces entailed by broader economic systems.

Markets and movement

Farmers travelled the countryside of Italy quite extensively in Late Antiquity. This was clearly an important part of rural life. To give some illustrative examples: Paulinus of Nola speaks of the migration of a group of free labourers from Campania to Apulia, presumably seeking new beginnings; and of farmers that come to his church despite the cold weather.[124] The Ravenna Papyri often show how fragmented holdings necessitating movement between plots.[125] And the greater part of *rusticani*, *cultores* and *agricolae* mentioned in Ambrose's *De officiis ministrorum* seem to have been moving between the estates of different employers, looking for new opportunities.[126] No single factor can explain the majority of these cases; if anything, we can be sure that different forces often generated movement within a single area. We may safely assume that the greater part of the decisions made by individuals or households were strongly conditioned by economic hardship; the larger the famine, the more the *rusticana plebs* would move around.[127] Rural households experiencing structural hardship are far more likely to move than their well-to-do rural neighbours. Seeing as the late antique countryside of Italy was in a state of constant flux due to ecological deviations and social and political upheavals, the overrepresentation of distressed individuals within our sources should not surprise us.[128]

The more important are the moments where our sources do not focus on economic distress. As some sources show, small agriculturalists did sell their goods at rural markets, even if this was relatively speaking only a small amount of the total goods they could produce; again, to think of farmers only pursuing strategies of subsistence is unfair to the economic manoeuvring that pre-industrial smallholders conducted. This included the products they furnished next to their agricultural produce, such as pottery, fish and game. There is still an ongoing discussion on where exactly rural markets normally took place, but there is some consensus that they were, at least, seasonal, and

---

[123] Carrié 1997; Wickham 2005, 272.
[124] Paulinus of Nola, *Carm.* 20.312–37; and *Nat.* 6.44–81.
[125] *P. Ital.* 32, 33, 34, 35, 36, 37, 38–41.
[126] Ambr. *Off.* 3.51, 46, 47, 51; Ruggini 1961, 122–6, esp. 125.
[127] Symm. *Relat.* 3.15–17. No doubt 'the eating of roots' forced rural non-elites, certainly at one point, to start looking for foodstuffs outside their locality.
[128] Christie 1996.

commonly instigated by wealthy estate owners or merchants.[129] Importantly, field surveys suggest that rural inhabitants participated extensively in complex regional economies, the size of which supports the hypothesis that the rural market, or rural markets, were anything but insignificant.[130]

A famous example is the excavated fair at the Christian sanctuary of St Felix at Cimitile, in an agricultural area near Naples, which according to Paul Arthur, might have been instigated by Paulinus of Nola.[131] An equally famous case is the fair of St Cyprian, mentioned by Cassiodorus in one of his letters. It supposedly took place near the ancient sacred spring of Leucothea, near Consilium, in the Val di Tanagro.[132] Cassiodorus does not mince words when it comes to the variety of goods presented at the market, including products from Lucania, cattle from Campania, and 'other exports', as well as labour – all presented at different market stalls.[133] Another possible example might be the cave of St Michael Archangel, near San Nicandro Garganico, which, according to Paul Arthur, was the site of an important international fair.[134] True, the fairs of major trading cities must have dominated exchange over large surrounding areas.[135] But smaller, rural fairs were probably more convenient for rural buyers and sellers. They could be selling just their own produce, as one can rightly expect, or also the share they owed to their landlord, as Ruggini suspects.[136] These small markets, from which smallholders were able to sell their surplus, livestock or artisanal goods, were not only occasions for buying and selling, we must suppose.[137] They offered opportunities for social contact with people from outside the local world. We may assume that some attended these events even when they had no business to transact.

The experience of non-elite agriculturalists here, attending these fairs on a seasonal basis, must have been anything but parochial and circumscribed. For smallholders, the marketplace could permit investments into valued foodstuffs that could be transformed into staples. Conversely, the foodstuffs and attributes bought with staples or the money earned therefrom improved their social status through consumption and redistribution; and farmers likely stocked up some of their newly bought items or produce to function as buffers for moments of disaster in the near future.[138] On other occasions, markets also allowed smallholders to promote specialised skills, which could

---

[129] MacMullen 1970; Mitterauer 1973; Shaw 1981; De Ligt and De Neeve 1988; Hodges 1988; De Ligt 1993; Kaplan 1992, 94–5; Grey 2011, 29, 31, 52–7, 160.

[130] As Vera 2005, 34 already expected; the results of Castrorao Barba 2016 are quite decisive on this matter.

[131] For Cimitile see Vera 1983, 511; Arthur 2000, 422.

[132] Cassiod. *Var.* 8.33; Lafferty 2013, 160.

[133] Cassiod. *Var.* 8.33 seems to describe children being sold into slavery, but I would agree with Frayn 1993, 143 that it is actually describing the local hiring of labour.

[134] Arthur and Sindbaek 2007, 298.

[135] Though this is very context dependent. See Dossey 2010, 58, which shows very disconnected urban and rural markets. For Italy this seems less debatable. See Ruggini 1961, 112–47; also, Paulin. *Vit. Ambr.* 34 for a Libyan fair in Milan.

[136] Ruggini 1961, 133–6.

[137] Arthur 2000; see also *ET* 150, which implies that farmhands (*rustici*) could have full ownership over cattle (in this case oxen). Undoubtedly these kinds of resources were leased.

[138] Both Boethius, *Cons. phil.* 5. 1; and Zeno of Verona, *Tract.* 1.10.2, 1.14.3–5, 1.5.18 show men collecting valuables from the ground, which could have been used as buffers for later moments.

come in handy during moments of dearth. Skills, in this case, could mean the production of artisanal goods, such as pottery or cloth, but also the promotion of other competencies, such as nurturing children, or types of wage labour.[139] We may suspect also that agreements to hire labour or livestock might have been struck at local markets, and that, especially in the case of significant fairs, these provided the right commercial environment and amount of witnesses required for the creation of contracts.[140] Moreover, if there was significant specialisation by smallholders, they might have gone to different markets to sell different items.

Instructive here are also the Ravenna Papyri. These show tenants and small and large landholders actively participating in a land market wherein each of these groups not only occupy plots of land next to one another, but also sell the plots they own to their neighbours. Where non-elites appear, we see them selling and buying whole *fundi*, but also very small fractions of them, sometimes halves, thirds, sixths and even eighths.[141] The acquisitions that we see here were not merely purchases for the sake of purchase, or sales for the sake of selling. Rural households are not stable in the sense of the resources that they need or do not need; the birth of a family member might instigate members of the family to invest in the acquisition of another piece of land because of an extra mouth to feed. In the same way, the loss of moveable property, in the form of draft animals or dairy cattle, could push a family to sell a plot of land. These kinds of moments could motivate smallholders to invest in selling a bit more of their produce at the market, or entering into an extra contract of tenancy with a neighbour or landlord. It is only very sporadically that we encounter (economically) successful non-elite agriculturalists in our sources. The most intriguing case is perhaps one letter from Cassiodorus, wherein the Ostrogothic king Athalaric remarks the following: 'It is there that the rustics enjoy the fine food of the citizen, the poor man the opulence of the wealthy.'[142] We might not give much weight to such a comment; indeed, it is doubtful Athalaric had full knowledge of rural affairs in Bruttii.[143] On the other hand, he treated the situation very seriously, and I doubt that he would send a letter to Severus, *vir spectabilis*, with blatantly obvious exaggerations in it. The point is, smallholders have, as all economies and societies do, problems of matching supply in both the long and short run. While some were incapable of surviving these moments, others could be more fortunate. Local markets presented opportunities that allowed survival, allowing smallholders to sell off what could be sold. As Robert Portass notes about early medieval Iberia:

---

[139] *CTh* 9.31.1 for the 'rearing of children'.

[140] *P. Ital.* 7 shows two men, Volusanius and Luminosus, travelling outside of Ravenna to meet with Gundihild, *inlustris femina*, to take her testimony for the completion of a legal document. In this case we are dealing with the testimony of an elite individual, of course, and I doubt whether curial members would travel to dwellings of smallholders to take up testimonies for bills of sale. But we should not discount the possibility that bills of sale and labour contracts were made up at rural markets.

[141] As can be seen in *P. Ital.* 32, 33, 34, 35, 36, 37 and 38–41.

[142] Cassiod. *Var.* 8.31.

[143] Namely, that urbanites were fleeing the cities in Bruttii and taking up a country life. In basic terms, it would mean the rejection of certain obligations by *curiales* and *possessores*, as well as the circumvention of taxes. See Bjornlie 2014.

The peasantry also shaped its own present and future and often did so with considerable ingenuity considering the wider structural constraint that framed its existence ... Some peasants wanted to rise above their peers and succeeded in doing so; others must have failed; others, the least fortunate, merely wanted to survive. Some unsurprisingly, even wanted to make a profit ...[144]

While it is concerned with a context that existed some centuries later, I see no reason why much of this was not true for late antique Italy.

Defending Property and Rights to Property

There is no question that smallholders could be subjugated by elites. But the recurring tension between smallholders and outside forces for the time being, which is a leading theme in the historiography of Late Antiquity, is hardly explicable unless the non-elite rural population was an important and enduring force. It is worthwhile to analyse the character of resistance as used by non-elites and the legal protection they did or did not have access to, with the aim of discovering how smallholders could effectively resist encroachment from the outside. After all, continuing occupancy of land was critical for survival. In this part of the chapter, I will begin first with a short assessment of land rights and late Roman revenue policy, for it is crucial for our understanding of legal protection in this context, namely on what basis it was given. Thereafter I will look at what kind of transgressions smallholders had to endure, how legal policies changed in regards to these transgressions; and, lastly, the 'tools' smallholders could use to protect themselves in these moments of dearth.

Land rights in Late Roman policies

As I said, land rights are crucial in our understanding of the protection that smallholders could call upon. This is a very well-known story, but there may be benefits from telling it again as lucidly as possible, with an emphasis on the elements relevant to this chapter. There is one main issue, that is control. Land policies and laws related to the protection of farmers are primarily concerned with order in the countryside and with the timely and predictable furnishing of revenue to the state.[145] This does not mean that land policies were merely a form of coercion. Just as importantly, they offered a means of persuasion. The late Roman and Ostrogothic administrations wanted to support classes that would have an interest in collaborating with them and, where possible, would be able to check those who tried to resist or avoid their civic obligations.[146] The same administrations also intended to ensure (though we do not exactly know if they succeeded in this) basic levels of well-being in the rural population as a whole so as to avoid the costs and dislocation of famine, disease and desertion, and thus protect future state revenues. It is quite clear that the late Roman government was aware of the ever increasing burdens

---

[144] Portass 2021, 23.
[145] Kehoe 2007, 131–62.
[146] Brown 1992, 3–34.

placed upon agriculturalists, and that they actively sought to rectify and stabilise their economic position. In *CTh* 11.16.4 and 15.1.33, for example, tax collectors are told not to lay the burden of extraordinary public services or *superindictiones* on farmers, for they are already 'urgently occupied with their farm work'; *CTh* 11.27.2 confirms that many farmers suffered from a lack of sustenance, and were therefore assisted through the royal *fiscus* 'before they fall prey to calamity'; and *CTh* 14.4.5 tells of the reallocation of property to modest 'swine farmers' who had formerly lost it to 'all sorts of extraneous persons'. The same kind of urge to protect agricultural workforces can also be discerned in the *Edictum Theodorici*, albeit much less extensively.[147]

The basis of land policy was thus revenue settlement, as I stated earlier, meaning that the decision to protect smallholders came out of the same aspiration.[148] The tendency in late Roman Italy was for the government to reach down as near as possible to the actual cultivators for information about agriculture and landholding as well as to fix responsibility for the payment of land revenue. During much of the third, fourth and at least first half of the fifth century, this permitted not only a system of regulated revenue settlement based on assessments of agricultural output, but also legal protection to the cultivators involved in this system.[149] As Shane Bjornlie has shown, however, during the Ostrogothic period the government was increasingly unable to force regular payments of revenue – and we should expect that this failure to collect included a failure to uphold legal rights.[150] Protective measures started to be granted much more readily by local patrons, such as churchmen, well-to-do landlords and military figures, which, in turn, could expect the support of those they protected.[151]

Loss of property

Smallholders lost their property or access to property in a number of ways, but generally speaking, these critical moments can be divided into two groups. First, there was the option that smallholders encountered an outside actor who forcefully deprived them of their property or parts of it. To give an example, an excerpt from Cassiodorus' *Variae* concerns correspondence between Athalaric and Cunigast *vir illustris*.[152] The letter shows two men, Constantius and Venerius, complaining to Athalaric about being wrested from their farm by a vicious Goth named Tanca. Both Constantius and Venerius were men of modest background: it seems that they only possessed one farm, called Fabricula, and bore no extraordinary titles.[153] Before Tanca had assailed them, they had ownership over their property, the land as well as its livestock.[154] The absence of a patron (e.g. a local landlord) suggests that the men were rural *liberi plebei*,

---

[147] *ET* 150, on burdens illegally put upon rustics.
[148] Stathakopoulos 2005, 62–9.
[149] Goffart 1974, 71–2, 77, 81, 84–5; 87; Sirks 1993, 344; Banaji 2001, 211–12; Rosafio 2002, 12, 177–214; Koptev 2004, 287–8; Grey 2011, 192.
[150] Bjornlie 2014.
[151] Wickham 2005, 527–9; Grey 2011, 198–213; Rio 2017, 100–3.
[152] Cassiod. *Var.* 8.28.
[153] For the meaning of titles, see Schoolman 2017, 8.
[154] For late antique ownership see Crook 1967, 139–78, esp. 139–49; and Du Plessis 2015, 175–98, esp. 192–4.

rather than *liberi coloni*.[155] We have no knowledge of what happened to Constantius and Venerius. They might have succeeded in getting back their property, perhaps just as decidedly as the Gothic landlord Gundila was able to do in 557.[156] Or they lost it and were, unfortunately, forced to engage in a contract that reduced them to 'soil-bound' (*adscriptii*) *coloni*.[157] Now, these kinds of moments, where outsiders encroached upon the lands of smallholders, are not very difficult to find. Similar stories appear in thirteen other letters of Cassiodorus, three Ravenna Papyri, and they are at the centre of attention in numerous fourth- and fifth-century sermons and *epistulae*.[158] Aside from the encroachment upon property, the theft of moveable property and produce was a recurrent problem, as becomes apparent in several laws in the *Codex Theodosianus* and the *Edictum Theodorici*.[159] An illustrative example is the despondent story of a tenant in Paulinus of Nola's *Nat*. 6. The man, whose name is not mentioned, does not own the property he works on and, consequently, attaches great importance to his livestock, a pair of oxen. Both of the latter are stolen, much to the chagrin of the farmer. He then travels to the town of Nola to see St Felix, who he asks for help. The saint cannot conjure up the stolen oxen, however, as the farmer wants him to do. In the end the man aborts his contact with St Felix, after accusing him of being an accomplice of the thieves and even threatening him with blackmail.[160]

These kinds of transgressions, however, were not pre-eminently the product of 'lawless invaders' that operated outside of governmental structures. This brings me to the second group: many smallholders, on occasion, had to deal with the iniquity of Roman and, later on, Ostrogothic officials. A fourth-century law from Valentinian and Valens, while addressing the over-taxation of provincials, explicitly states that the 'connivance of favoritism' and 'ignoble pretence' of judges resulted in *decuriones* extorting from the poor.[161] The *decuriones*, a civil class tasked by the late Roman governments with collecting the taxes from urban and rural *plebeii*, were apparently quite fond of preying on small landowners and tenants, as various late Roman laws confirm.[162] They, together with other officials such as the *advocatus* (sometimes described as *patronus causarum*), could easily take advantage of smallholders in debt due to their privileged position as members of local town councils, which gave them, in addition to exceptional opportunities for extortion, a method to evade punishment.[163] The

---

[155] Mirković 1997, 6, 7, 110–20 for *coloni* statuses; rural patron–client contracts in Grey 2011, 123–37.

[156] P. Ital. 49: An *acclaratio in iure* with two sworn witnesses concerning the possessions of the Goth Gundila. The story is extraordinary, for Gundila loses his possession two times, yet succeeds in getting it back after travelling to Rome and asking the pope for help.

[157] Whittaker and Garnsey 1998, 322; Morony 2004, 168–9.

[158] Deprivation of landed property in Cassiod. *Var*. 1.18, 1.38, 3.18, 3.20, 3.37, 4.10, 4.32, 4.39, 4.41, 4.42, 4.44, 5.14, 5.24; deprivation of landed property in Ravenna Papyri: *P. Ital.* 7, 43 and 49; Cassiod. *Var*. 2.18, 3.14, 4.44, 9.2 and *Ep*. 3.4; for sermons and *epistulae* see nn. 16, 17 and 184.

[159] For the theft of livestock see Lafferty 2013, 237–9, with comparisons between the two legal codes; for produce specifically, *ET* 146.

[160] Paulinus of Nola, *Nat*. 6.219–312; see also a similar case in Maximus of Turin, *Serm*. 18 (theft of bullock) and 72 (cattle thieves).

[161] My translation; *CTh* 11.16.11.

[162] *CTh* 2.30.1, 7.21.2, 12.1.62, 12.1.97, 12.1.117, 12.1.118; *N. Maj*. 7.1.8, 7.1.15.

[163] For their privileged position see Garnsey 1968, with references to *decuriones* on p. 6, 10, 13, 15–17, 20–1.

large number of laws that address the extortion of provincials by *decuriones* and *advocati* suggests that this was primarily a problem among the lower-level bureaucracy. All the same, a flurry of edicts coming from Gratian, Valentinian II and Theodosius on the extortion of estates, tenants and smallholders by high officials (such as a 'Severinus', a *comes*) indicates that this was a problem gone rampant in all governmental spheres.[164] The many letters circulating between Theoderic and his servants on officials depriving 'provincials' of their property indicate that the issue persisted even after the last western emperors.[165] So, the deprivation of smallholders of their property by officials and non-officials was, at any rate, a consistent and vital problem, that most likely interfered notably with the government's aim of securing its revenue.

It is difficult to tell if the number of rapacious takeovers increased in Italy in the course of Late Antiquity. The legislation suggests they did, as can be seen in the increasingly harder punishments for *invasio*. For example, both the *Codex Theodosianus* and the *Edictum Theodorici* prohibited the transgression, and required stolen property to be returned to the dispossessed. Yet, in addition to returning property, Ostrogothic law ruled that the assailant was forced to pay twice the property's income 'for his insolence' (*pro tanta temeritate persolvat*).[166] The law shows that the effective consequences for *invasio* had become rather uncompromising; at any rate, it is a testament to the tenacious concern of both the late Roman and Ostrogothic government to protect tenants and smallholders against the avarice of others.[167]

Most takeovers must have been anything but sudden and precipitous, however, as they could often be the result of smallholders not being able to pay back debts, with the result that creditors took matters into their own hands.[168] Judging from the sermons and letters written by individuals such as Ambrose of Milan and Maximus of Turin, the main issue that smallholders had to deal with was debt claims.[169] This should not surprise us: in any agrarian society, small-scale farmers often require additional credit to achieve the production that allows them to meet their fiscal obligations, and provide for the nutritional needs of their household(s).[170] The attitude towards creditors and debtors of those in charge changed quite drastically between the third and first half of the sixth century. In 222 Alexander Severus guaranteed that a creditor could not fraudulently sell or invest a pledged piece of property or credit; if the creditor was not able to give back the property to the debtor, he had to provide the debtor with a property of his own.[171] Later, in 294, a law issued by Diocletian and Maximian made sure that in

---

[164] *CJ* 9.27.1–6.
[165] See also the many laws on property boundaries: *ET* 104, 105; *CTh* 2.57.1–5. For contextualisation, see the quarrelling *spectabiles* Leontius and Paschasius in Cassiod. *Var.* 3.52, wherein a local *agrimensor* checks for boundary stones and markers.
[166] Lafferty 2013, 160–1; see also the discussion on the (non-)use of the *ET* in the *Variae* in Bjornlie 2013, 222–4, esp. 223.
[167] See also the many laws on property boundaries: *ET* 104, 105; *CTh* 2.57.1–5.
[168] Ruggini 1961, 26.
[169] As Gaudentius of Brescia, *Tract.* 18.974 shows, *procuratori* would even trade the debt claims made upon farmers, a testament to the lucrative side of this business.
[170] Peebles 2010.
[171] *CJ* 8.29.1.

the case that a farmer owed anything to another proprietor, it was only by legal procedure that the payment could be made, ensuring that a farmer could not be permanently damaged by deceitful transactions.[172] A fourth-century law enacted by Constantine I gave small agriculturalists, free and unfree, protection from creditors by exempting their farm equipment from any form of a pledge.[173] Lastly, in 472, Leo I issued a law that insisted on the declaration of security transactions before a public authority, with the intention to solve the problem of unknown pledges.[174] As these examples show, laws with the aim to protect farmers had a long history, and it is possible that they went further back than the third century.[175] They are argued to have been the result of a period characterised by aggressive creditors, who started to secure their pledges in a number of ways – practices that were, so it seems, particularly abusive in comparison to the initial status quo.[176] Importantly, they show how the late Roman government generally aimed to put emphasis on the rights of debtors, rather than creditors.[177] After the end of western Roman emperorship, regulations took a different turn. Ostrogothic law, as presented in the *Edictum Theodorici*, treated debtors in a much less favourable way compared to late Roman law. For example, it granted creditors the right to claim pledged properties without the consent of the court.[178] And another law concerned with discouraging creditors to demand from debtors anything more than 1 per cent per month only punished lawbreakers by forfeiting the original debt; a law imposed in the *Codex Theodosianus*, by contrast, asked fourfold the original amount.[179] Sean Lafferty suggests that these laws were meant to encourage commercial activity by making the prospect of lending money more appealing.[180] While it may have had that impact, it could just as easily be meant to secure the privileged position of the municipal elite.[181] As Kehoe stated: 'some economic institutions . . . continued to exist because they were supported by groups that profited from them, even if they harmed the economy as a whole'.[182] For smallholders, the results of this 'legal swing' could have meant outright economic and social disaster. Because of the limited income-earning potential from their smallholdings, especially poor rural *liberi plebei* reached debt/equity ratios that were so high

---

[172] *CJ* 8.8.14.5.
[173] *CJ* 8.16.7.
[174] *CJ* 8.53.30.
[175] Schulz 1954, 403–5; Phillipson 1968, 1230–48; Kaser 1968, 130; see also the many other Late Roman laws that protect debtors in Kehoe 2007, 148–55.
[176] Lafferty 2013, 86–7.
[177] Later laws that favour debtors over creditors can be found in the *Codex Justinianus*: *CJ* 2.32, 4.15, 4.18, 4.32 and esp. *CJ* 8, which deals with most edicts regarding creditors and debtors (1–45; the rest, 46–58, is less useful); see also Ulpian's story in Justinian's *Dig.* 4.2.14. Here too the debtor is put in a preferable position. See also the recent volumes by Dari-Mattiacci and Kehoe (2020a and 2020b), and especially the chapter by Friedman (p. 328–45) in the same volume, which gives an overview on private property feuds in the context of Roman law.
[178] *ET* 124.
[179] *ET* 134; *CTh* 2.33.2.
[180] Lafferty 2013, 87.
[181] The Amals had made a point of favouring the municipal elite with public office; *ET* 124 and 134 could have been set up with similar considerations. See Bjornlie 2014, 187.
[182] Kehoe 2015, 89.

that they must have paid exorbitant costs for borrowing which impeded them from adequately securing essential consumption and productive needs.[183] In practice, this meant that the lower the smallholder household's wealth and risk-bearing ability, the higher the chance that its household members had to engage in social contracts similar to tenancy, as farmers had nothing else to offer besides their own labour.

Exploring ways forward

Thus far I have only paid attention to what could hurt smallholders by looking at codes of law, which gives us a fairly bleak image of rural life. We now have to consider what smallholders could do in those moments when individuals outside of their locality were taking away assets that were not legally theirs. Obviously, smallholders could fall back on the use of violence or the threat of it, as the nameless farmer does in Paulinus of Nola's *Nat.* 6. Aside from the last source, for late antique Italy there is only very little evidence of resistance by rural non-elites. To my knowledge we only have evidence in the form of very suggestive and incidental moments, such as when a praetorian prefect named Senator urges Valerian, *vir sublimis*, to repress the 'unruly movements of the cultivators', or when a certain Burco, in conflict with the church of Pavia, hits the then subdeacon Epiphanius on the head when the latter makes an enquiry about the conflict.[184] It all depends on how seriously we take these enigmatic comments, and to what extent we expect violent outbursts to have been a very common tool in the hands of the non-elite.[185] To be sure, when farmers used violence it was probably not akin to the very carefully thought out defiance that we can spot in other areas of the late antique and early medieval world, but rather some sort of despairing spasms as opposed to calculated forms of resistance.[186] We should also remember that violence is often the last option when lives are threatened: gossip, grumbling and satire were certainly part of the repertoire non-elites used against the actions of elites and other types of belligerents, and could be very effective.[187] Additionally, I doubt that all rural non-elites always defined themselves under all circumstances in terms of a binary opposition between themselves and their lords, as is often supposed. At moments when elites decide to suppress their non-elite neighbours more decisively, for instance by increasing the number of obligations or subtraction of goods, we must expect non-elites also to have started picking away at the assets of their similarly less well-off counterparts.[188] In any case, violence or the threat of it was

---

[183] Vera 1997 for calculations on what part of the population was above and below necessary subsistence levels.
[184] Cassiod. *Var.* 12.5; Ennod. *Vit. Epiph.* 7.
[185] On violence, see MacMullen 1974, 36–7; Wickham 2005, 71–2; Grey 2011, 152–3.
[186] Wickham 2005, 585.
[187] Scott 1985, 6–9; 1986, 14–17; Grey 2011, 84–90, also with useful further references in the footnotes; Wickham 1998 is also helpful in this regard.
[188] Banaji 2001, 194 gives the example of the successful villagers, Sakaon and Isidorus, that resisted the encroachments of large landholders in the region upon property in the village, while at the same time making use of their close-by neighbours with fewer resources at their disposal than them. This concerns an example situated within Egypt, but I doubt similar situations did not occur in the West.

certainly an option; but to argue that it occurred repeatedly must surely be open to question.

What about taking one's landlord or belligerent to court? Dennis Kehoe has argued that debtor-protection laws do not necessarily mean that the late Roman government was successful in holding in check the 'putative powers' of creditors, but that it at least must have provided 'some' protection to small landowners. The critical factor, Kehoe maintains, was the extent to which the court was involved to help debtors against creditors.[189] While it stands to reason, he does not set out on what variables the involvement of courts in such disputes depended. The first variable that mattered was, presumably, the relative location, and hence, the availability of courts to the rural population. Though we do not know exactly to what extent judicial courts reached into the countryside, for late Roman Italy it seems safe to assume that at least rural places near urban areas had access to these. In the case of more marginal places, on the other hand, there exists little evidence. We do know that both local officials and ecclesiastical personnel could function as intermediaries in these cases, which indubitably influenced the way in which non-elites were able to defend their case.[190]

For the Ostrogothic period the evidence is similarly thin.[191] If we assume that the Ostrogothic administrators had difficulty in controlling the countryside, as Bjornlie suggests, then that must inevitably have had consequences for the availability of courts as well. *ET* 52 includes the stipulation that in the absence of municipal officers, who witnessed transactions and legal cases, lawsuits had to take place in another municipality where such officers could be found. As Lafferty notes, the law could be an indication of the limited availability of civil magistrates, which presumably became a problem first in the periphery of Italy's rural landscape with the gradual break-up of the central government.[192] Conversely, a growing importance of decentralised tribunals managed by local elites, in whatever form, seems to make sense – especially considering the available early medieval (Italian) evidence that shows very similar circumstances.[193] But I have to stress here that these are very tentative suggestions; there is simply not very much documentary evidence that can confirm one proposition or another. Second, there is the issue of sufficient capital.[194] In the case of a relatively populated area, a small cultivator had to travel to the nearest central place, presumably a town, maybe even find lodgings, wait for his turn before the judge possibly with other prospective litigants, set a trial date with his opponent, have the case heard and finally return home with a verdict that may not be in the farmer's favour.[195] If the farmer had no close-by family to take care of his farm, he would also have to shut down work on his plot altogether when he was away. So not only would a smallholder have travel costs, but he would also have the cost of lost work. Sometimes, farmers were lucky enough to send someone in their stead, but that would mean offering the representative some

---

[189] Kehoe 2007, 154–5.
[190] Grey 2011, 141–2.
[191] Lafferty 2013, 101–55.
[192] *CTh* 8.12.1, 8.12.8 (415); Lafferty 2013, 115.
[193] Zeller et al. 2020, 99–100, 103–4, 106, 132, 159, 194–6, 199, 201, 206.
[194] Sessa 2018, 140.
[195] For court procedure and legal practice in Late Antiquity in general, see Humfress 2007.

recompense.¹⁹⁶ So, especially for farmers who were already greatly indebted, going to court was not just an issue of letting their voice be heard: it encompassed assessing the costs, risks and benefits. Third, the role of influence must be considered. There is very little direct evidence of individuals being strong-armed by those of greater influence into settling disputes under conditions unfavourable to themselves. However, we should not expect to find much evidence of such transactions – in such a society, it undoubtedly occurred, and not just due to threats of the opposing party: some judges were known to be corrupt, with the result that particular cases might have been decided even before the allegations were uttered.¹⁹⁷ Let us also keep in mind that the formalisation of land rights that occurred after some of these cases did not necessarily mean an uncontested possession of property in the future. Juridical capture or influence, especially in the presence of overlapping claims to land and contradictory institutions of land ownership and management, remained as possible channels for larger landholders operating outside the abstract idealisation of property markets embedded in the conceptualisation of private property.

There is no source from late antique Italy which shows smallholders actively participating in court in a very detailed manner, that is suing someone, travelling to court and so forth, as for example happens in Libanius' *Orationes*, or the wealth of sources that appear in the medieval West sometime later.¹⁹⁸ To my knowledge the only Italian sources that can be mentioned in this case are Symmachus, *Ep.* 7.56 (to Hadrianus, *Magister officiorum*), in which a *colonus* called Theodulus appeals a legal decision (but the exact legal procedure remains ambiguous), and *P. Ital.* 43, a bill of sale recorded in Ravenna in the year 542, in which the spouses Waduulfus and Riccifrida, two Goths, are recorded as selling and gifting pieces of *fundi* to Leo, quite possibly a person with elite aspirations, as compensation for his 'assistance', and more precisely because they lost in a legal dispute against him.¹⁹⁹ While Symmachus' letter is useful to understand the relationship between *colonus* and *dominus*, it does not say very much about the actual dispute that took place.²⁰⁰ *P. Ital.* 43, on the other hand, while similarly to Symmachus' letter not revealing that much, does leave room for some interpretation.

So, what happened? The fact that the author of *P. Ital.* 43 uses the terms *beneficiaris expulsi* and *pro certis laboribus expensisque propriis* indicates that Waduulfus and Riccifrida had been leaseholders of the *fundus* Raunis, and had been working on it.²⁰¹ They were tenants, most likely, and in any case smallholders with access to some type of land. At one point in time, they had asked Leo for help – perhaps to help harvest the yield from the *fundus* by lending some personnel or draft animals. We may assume that Leo obliged. After the partnership had taken place, the spouses were not able to pay Leo

---

¹⁹⁶ For beneficiaries or representatives, see *P. Ital.* 4–5, 7, 8, 10–11.
¹⁹⁷ As expressed by Lib. *Or.* 47.13–16.
¹⁹⁸ Lib. *Or.* 47.13–16.
¹⁹⁹ *P. Ital.* 43: *huic chartule damnate litis de una bem uncia fundi Raunis, que in centum triginta solidis Leoni viro honesto, naviculario solemni extimatione distracta est, et de uncia suprascripti fundi, que pro certis laboribus expensisque propriis ei suprascripto contala est.*
²⁰⁰ Grey 2004, 32; 2011, 127.
²⁰¹ *P. Ital.* 43: . . .[. . . .]*ciari* [.] *expulsi promittenties dare; pro certis laboribus* in n. 199.

back, which gave Leo a reason to sue them.²⁰² It is for the most crucial moments, the hearing of the witnesses, the arguments of Leo, and the defence of the spouses, that we lack the specifics. We never learn about the original contents of the agreement between Leo and the spouses. If Leo had held up his end of the bargain, then he had no reason to settle for anything less than the *fundus* or at least a good part of it, and was in a position of strength. We are left guessing that the spouses succumbed under the pressure from Leo and, perhaps, the statements of the witnesses he assembled. Although Waduulfus and Riccifrida were compensated for attending the lawsuit, they were not only forced to sell a part of their *fundus*, but had to 'gift' the rest of it as well. The spouses were left with virtually nothing, aside from several solidi.²⁰³ In all probability it was much less than they had hoped for.

The end of the document shows the witnesses that were present when the deal was sealed, who according to the scribe had been assembled by the spouses.²⁰⁴ Thus, we are allowed a glimpse into the social circle the spouses were part of. Bassus *vir clarissimus* is noted as the first witness. We do not know on what account he possessed his title; he could have earned it by office, or he could have inherited it.²⁰⁵ The fact that his social standing is offbeat in comparison to the rest of the witnesses could indicate that Bassus was a court official who signed the document in order to make it legal, instead of being used by the spouses as a witness for the court case; but it is just as reasonable to suggest that he owned the land of the two spouses as *dominus*, including the disputed *fundi*. Giberit, the next witness, is also an intriguing case: although his extended family (*comes* Cessi) seems to have been part of the higher echelons of North Italian elite society, he was 'just' a *vir devotus*. The other witnesses, Hilarus, Ardeca and Andreas, all bore the title of *vir honestus*, just like Waduulfus, which represented the lowest of elevated social stations.²⁰⁶ We may surmise that the witnesses listed here were not present during the actual court hearing itself, but I see no reason to believe that the spouses would have asked for different witnesses on the two occasions.

Why these people? As can be expected, the spouses did not base their identity solely on the legal titles (*vir honestus, honesta femina*) given to them. While some did so more than others, in pre-industrial societies non-elites interacted constantly with those living around them. Even the most impoverished were anything but solitary beings with minimal interest in mutual responsibility and obligations.²⁰⁷ At moments of crisis,

---

²⁰² And not the other way around, as Amory (1997, 436) suggests: 'He and his wife Riccifrida sued a shipbuilder named Leo for a payment outstanding on a sale of land.' Rather, I would follow Tjäder's (1982, 147) suggestion on the issue, that the spouses were indebted to Leo, and were obliged in court to give 1 ⅔ of the *fundus* Raunis, which was estimated at 130 solidi, to Leo, and another twelfth as compensation for certain work and personal expenses.

²⁰³ *P. Ital.* 43.

²⁰⁴ Witness list, *P. Ital.* 43: *Bassus vir clarissimus, filius quondam Alexandri. Hilarus vir honestus, qui commanet ad Frigiscus. Giberit vir devotus, gener Cessinis comitis. Ardeca vir honestus, qui commanet ad Frigiscus. Andreas vir honestus, qui commanet in domo Titiani quondam.* The scribe, a Mercator, indicates that the spouses had assembled the witnesses in the first couple of lines of the document.

²⁰⁵ See Schoolman 2017.

²⁰⁶ Schoolman 2017, 8.

²⁰⁷ Taylor 2017.

they turn to people near them, not caring much about social and economic inequality but about reliability. They associate themselves with individuals they know and trust, because of family relations, or religious, social and cultural commonalities.[208] Note that all of the individuals named on the witness list seem to have lived next to one another (perhaps except for Bassus and Cessi, as their place of residence is not provided).[209] Telling also are the titles *vir honestus* and *vir devotus*, used for almost all of the witnesses. As Pier Maria Conti already argued fifty years ago, these are commonly an indication for members coming from a modest military background.[210] We should not be surprised if the spouses knew most of the attendees on the basis of past, complementary experiences; and it is probable that some of these occurred during their service in the Gothic army. We may surmise, further, that these witnesses at one point in their lives had earned some land as compensation for their military service.[211] That land, needless to say, was critical to their survival. The loss of land to an outsider such as Leo did not only mean that the proprietor who used to own it potentially lost a significant part of his or her income, it also meant that these individuals were less likely to have sufficient funds to help others in their community. Against this background, we can imagine how the spouses, together with Giberit, Hilarus, Ardeca and Andreas, might have created an informal relationship aimed at insuring the weakest against ruin. The web of connections displayed here seems not only to have included everyday people, however. One could wonder how to interpret the words 'brother-in-law of *comes* Cessi', which appear in connection to Giberit.[212] Could it be that Giberit's input into the affair was based on the status of his extended family? Did Giberit urge the spouses to get Cessi involved in the conflict? Did Cessi ask anything in return for his indirect involvement? Unfortunately, the source gives no indication whatsoever.

The exact nature of elite involvement in legal cases between smallholders and elites or between smallholders individually is a significant question, however, and one that deserves attention. As the examples above show, a small proprietor might pull together individuals on the basis of kinship ties, perhaps even fictive kinship, or on the grounds of an 'employer–employee' relationship. As Giovanni Ruffini aptly states about the life of residents of the Egyptian village of Aphrodite: 'These people [non-elites] do look for help from those with higher status or rank, but they look first for anyone with information, with influence, with money, even if they have no status or rank to elevate them. They look horizontally before they look vertically.'[213] This observation also applies to legal disputes. One of the reasons that non-elites might be hesitant in approaching elites is the fact that the latter group tends to ask much more in return for their involvement, whereas people of similarly modest backgrounds do not have a

---

[208] Grey 2011, 98–120.
[209] See n. 204. Note the *ad Frigiscus* (twice), as well as the *qui commanet in domo Titiani quondam*.
[210] Conti 1971, 118–22; Amory 1997, 97; Brown 1984, 134; Schoolman 2017, 9.
[211] Which, of course, directly relates to the discussion of the Gothic *tertiae*, a discussion I will not go into here. See Halsall 2016, with the most recent discussion, giving also a summary of the debate thus far.
[212] *P. Ital.* 43: *Giberit vir devotus, gener Cessinis comitis*. It is, however, remarkable to see that the author of the document misspelled Giberit's name some sentences earlier: *ego Ghiveric vir devotus huic chartule damnate litis*.
[213] Ruffini 2018, 26.

proper amount of resources at their disposal to force relatively unequal deals. Elites can get away with this because there are many more non-elites with needs than there are potential patrons with assets. Thus, the bargaining power of the patron is by definition greater than that of his client.

Take, for example, both instances where Symmachus deals with disputes involving his tenants. In the first letter, it is quite clear that Symmachus is only helping the *colonus* working his fields, Theodolus, as he sees this first and foremost as an obligation and not because he genuinely wants to give his approval or support. The same is true in the second case, where Symmachus, though considerably frustrated with one of his estate managers, Amazonius, the person who informs him about the case, writes a letter regardless, through which he hopes to clear any charges put against a tenant named Ursus.[214] As Grey shows for these letters, as well as others of Sidonius Apollinaris, Paulinus of Nola and Ruricius of Limoges, they confirm that relationships between large landowners and their personnel were sometimes quite the opposite of the autarkic demeanour that the *agrimensor* Palladius recommends as to the management of labour. I would not say that this kind of attitude was completely the result of the alleged scarcity of labour in some places, as is hinted at in Ambrose's work and others when they describe abandoned landholdings, towns and *castellae*. But it must have had some kind of effect on the attitude of elites towards their 'dependents', at least in some areas of Italy.[215]

Thus far, most of our sources account for tenants and *coloni*, smallholders already in service of a landlord, and not, as we might hope to find, smallholders that had no direct or indirect ties to such individuals. There is precious little evidence regarding the interaction between elites and what we might call freeholders; still, it seems unlikely that these kinds of individuals never had any need for assistance. Smallholders, no matter whether they were already engaged in tenancy agreements or not, must have been aware of the possible support elites were able to give, who were well acquainted with the particularities of the legal apparatus. They might support the credibility of statements made by smallholders in court, or hire a person that could help smallholders with their defence, such as a *defensor*.[216] Smallholders might approach elites through their neighbours, or they would seek them out without the presence of a middleman. If the elite agreed to help the smallholder with his dispute, further favours were likely to be asked or offered at some later time. A smallholder would very likely reciprocate – at a time and in a context different from that of the acceptance of the favour, in order to de-emphasise the material self-interest of the reciprocate action – by bringing into cultivation another piece of land owned by the landlord, or by sending some members of the household to perform services. Smallholders would still retain their freedom with these sorts of social contracts, and although it added another obligation to the household, it potentially facilitated ongoing relations between farmer and elite, both of whom could call upon each other's services when necessary. This is not to deny that

---

[214] Symm. *Ep.* 7.56 and 9.2.
[215] Ambr. *Off.* 3.7.46; *Ep.* 17.15 (Memorial of Symmachus) or Symm. *Relat.* 3; Greg. *Dialog.* 3.33; Christie 1996; Brogiolo 1999; and Grey 2007 are useful for understanding these phenomena.
[216] That is, at least, what *CTh* 1.29.5 suggests, since it shows *patrocinium* (protection) granted to *rusticas*.

some elites exploited such agreements to the complete detriment of smallholders in a given locality; but from a practical point of view, where smallholders and elite would honour the agreement, it was an alliance benefiting both.

Smallholders and Material Culture

Archaeologists often wish to estimate the population of areas they have surveyed or of dwellings or sites they have excavated, usually in connection with an explanation for sociopolitical transformations, technological transitions or alterations in land use patterns. In those areas 'peasant studies' have come a long way since Garnsey's, Whittaker's and Kolendo's assessments of the subject. For the archaeology of late antique Italy specifically, the last decades have seen an astounding number of publications on the dwellings of non-elites, their relationships with towns, ceramic production and transformations coherent to politico-economic circumstances.[217] Despite these advancements, it often remains difficult if not impossible to find evidence for the many non-elite subcategories in the archaeological record. When we find an isolated farmstead near Rome, Palermo or Ravenna, is it possible to know if it belonged to a free smallholder, a tenant or some other group of non-elites? For centuries, the answer to that question was a simple 'no': a relic of the idea that archaeology could never be more than the physical description of unearthed things assumed to have been made by humans.[218] But roughly since the 1990s, archaeologists and historians have become more interested in identifying various social groups in the material record, as well as making bold statements about various types of material culture signifying social and economic conditions particular to such groups. For elites these types of assertions are, relatively speaking, only moderately difficult to make, considering they have often left a more easily distinguishable material culture than their more modest counterparts. Thus, the more intriguing are the moments when scholars claim to be able to identify quite specifically the social, spatial and economic relations of their dependents, as well as other rural non-elites in the archaeological record. In 1990, Lin Foxhall suggested that sites with significant architecture paired with limited amounts of crude, material culture are indicative of dependent tenancies; concomitantly, more and more scholars were convinced that slavery is discernible in the archaeological record by an 'absence' of material culture, or the complete absence of clearly distinguishable sites, conjoined with large amounts of fine wares in the vicinity.[219] In a few cases, scholars also argued that the right collection of remains represented *coloni*.[220] A more recent development

---

[217] Francovich and Hodges 2003; Brogiolo et al. 2005; Brogiolo and Chavarría Arnau 2005; and Christie 2006 are the most comprehensive surveys on these subjects, with Christie 2006, 412–62 with further references to notable publications relevant here.

[218] See Leach 1973; Foxhall 1990; Witcher 2006, esp. his section on 'dependency'.

[219] Foxhall 1990. See Coarelli 1982; 2005; Carandini 1985; Thompson 2003; Braconi 2005; Fentress 2005; Webster 2005; Petersen 2009; Heinen 2010; Severy-Hoven 2012; George 2013; Joshel and Petersen 2014; useful here is also the discussion on the status of the villagers (i.e. dependent or not) living in the Limestone Massif. For a 'short' synopsis of the debate, see Wickham 2005, 443–50.

[220] Witcher 2006; Ørsted 2004 infers the presence of *coloni* from landholding patterns.

shows, furthermore, that it is possible to theorise different stages of well-being, and most importantly, agency, with the right amount of evidence. Excavations at Pievina by Mariaelena Ghisleni and others, at Marzuolo by Anna van Oyen, and most recently at several sites in Tuscany as part of the Roman Peasant Project, by a team consisting of, amongst others, Kim Bowes, Cam Grey and Ghisleni, show not only 'resilient peasants' but signs of experimentation, human capital development, foresight planning, investment and 'distributed habitation'.[221] In some cases, the archaeological record suggests little to no interaction with elite actors, which, apart from leaving open the possibility that the individuals inhabiting such places were freeholders, shows that they were capable of managing their own assets, positively, without some kind of necessitated interference of the more well-to-do.[222] To this end, these authors interpret the archaeological record noticeably differently than most archaeologists thus far have done. This is, at the very least, a positive development in that the interpretation of material goes much further than simply ascribing it to 'non-elites' or 'elites' only. To put it in the words of Steve Roskams: 'We will only make progress via a critique of how evidence is gathered and interpreted.'[223]

Of course, putting a 'label' on material remains is not without its problems: there is no real basis for assuming a direct correspondence between particular material and social features, and in fact, a careful assessment of the archaeological evidence indicates considerable flexibility. Considering these restraints, Van Oyen, Bowes and Grey together have differing opinions on how the archaeological record does (or does not) reflect specific social categories. To begin with Van Oyen, in regards to Marzuolo she states that it is impossible to infer the legal status of the owners and labourers of the site from the archaeological remains alone.[224] Be that as it may, she then continues to argue that around Marzuolo smallholders, be they free or dependent, not only provided labour and a key consumption market, but held noticeable bargaining power in the local economy as well.[225] Here, the possibility that Marzuolo was worked by slaves is no longer considered, presumably on the basis of the evidence suggesting 'bottom-up' innovation, something which does not fit with the economic role of slaves, seeing that slaves are not very likely to innovate, except in the cases where landlords would supply them with the necessary tools to do so, a move which would be recognisable in the archaeological record through the appearance of characteristics generally ascribed to specialised workshops, such as shared production installations and clearly divided workspaces.[226] It is exactly this 'external investor' that makes no appearance – at least until a much later date, that is.[227] In the end, though Van Oyen is clearly indisposed

---

[221] Ghisleni et al. 2011; Van Oyen 2020; Bowes 2020, which also includes treatments of Marzuolo and Pievina. Distributed habitation is explained as the habit of non-elite agriculturalists to invest in many, small, specialised sites, necessitating continuous movement from place to place.

[222] Van Oyen 2020 suggests this especially, though not for the entire period that the site was in use; Bowes 2020 is more reserved.

[223] Roskams 2006, 487.

[224] Van Oyen 2020, 22.

[225] Van Oyen 2020, 37.

[226] Van Oyen 2020, 23.

[227] Van Oyen 2020, 22–7.

to 'label' her site, in the end, she appears to do so nonetheless. It was a group of smallholders that worked the lands around Marzuolo and experimented with pottery, not slaves. Bowes and Grey discuss the issue of discerning social relations from the archaeological record only slightly differently. Their interpretation of materials and sites found in Tuscany shows smallholders engaging in the same intensive practices commonly associated with elite landowners, though on a smaller scale.[228] At the same time, they discern a specialised management of multiple parcels simultaneously, together with a high degree of mobility between sites. As Bowes and Grey suggest, these indications cannot have been the consequence of activities done by slaves or tenants; rather, they are signs of smallholders directly and ardently managing their land, activities and labour.[229] They too recognise, however, that categories such as smallholder and tenant are not mutually exclusive, in that non-elite agriculturalists often pursue different economic strategies simultaneously, i.e. with smallholders working as tenants, wage labourers or even itinerant labourers. In the view of both Bowes and Grey, to know whether one site was worked by smallholders, tenants and so on is not a question impossible to answer, 'but they are not really the right questions'.[230]

But connections between configurations of material culture and features of social organisation should be pursued nonetheless, even if that means that the nature of the connection and the domain of its validity require more careful definition than is often recognised. We should do so primarily because it allows us to see detailed chronologies in terms of proprietary relationships, as for example has been shown by Van Oyen.[231] I recognise that it is principally impossible to see through the investigation of archaeological remains alone whether smallholders worked the land as tenants or wage labourers; in the case of relatively scarce amounts of material, it would be likewise impossible to see work done by slaves. But where we do find (enough) deposits, where we find a loose connection in the archaeological record, we should at least try to tighten it by revising the correlate, perhaps with a more precise specification of the material configuration used as evidence for the activities of specific groups, or of the social organisation behind them.

Following in the footsteps of Van Oyen, Bowes and Grey, if we work back from the data and humble our theoretical impulses, evidence for smallholders and complex patterns of decision can emerge. Their work suggests two important lines of investigation for examining the possible presence of smallholders. First, how does the site relate to sites around it; can we envision relationships between the inhabitants of the site under scrutiny and another; and does this relationship constitute one that is primarily exploitative, signifying the presence and/or investments of elites? Second, what kind of evidence do we possess for experimentation, human capital development, foresight planning and investment; and, if we do possess it, is it possible to discern periods of investment that have been instigated by external factors? By looking at the complex archaeology of communities, i.e. buildings, faunal assemblages, ecological and ceramic records, we get closer to the lives of smallholders as they lived them.

---

[228] Bowes 2020, 621.
[229] Bowes 2020, 624.
[230] Bowes 2020, 625.
[231] Van Oyen 2020.

In this part of the chapter, it is by no means my aim to incorporate all of the available archaeological evidence for smallholders in late antique Italy. That is quite impossible at the moment with the textual constrictions in mind (if not simply unfeasible due to the amount of material available). The focus is on several pieces of evidence from Liguria and southern Italy, because much of it has not been discussed to a great extent, while much of the evidence from Tuscany (and other places in central Italy) has been.[232] What I will do is show a variety of sites that demonstrate a range of economic orientations, with some clearly influenced by elite ventures, while others were not. The variety and complexity proposed by the reading of some of these locations indicate that rural non-elites were wholly capable of producing surpluses, both in terms of agricultural foodstuffs and ceramics, without the economic intervention of elites. I have also chosen to address sites for which it is impossible to discover whether they were inhabited by smallholders, while in practice they have been interpreted as such. By doing so, I demonstrate both the possible pitfalls as well as the possibilities when one tries to identify economic or social relations in the archaeological record. Lastly, while some of the evidence from Bowes, Grey, Van Oyen and Ghisleni might be applicable here, to them changes occurring in the late antique period are only of secondary importance due to the relative paucity of materials at their sites that can be dated to this period. That means that on the next pages I will not be using the sites they have examined.

Liguria

We begin with Liguria, which since the beginning of this century has seen an increase in excavations, many as the result of the ongoing expansion of northern Italy's cities. Recently, most of these sites have acquired more attention due to Ross Balzaretti's *Dark Age Liguria*, which displays Liguria's settlement patterns in the context of political and ecological changes in both Late Antiquity and the Early Middle Ages. Here I will mostly reassess his observations of several late antique rural establishments as excavated by others.[233] All of these go out of use before c.600 AD, which by itself has various implications – but for now it is helpful that this happens neatly within the time frame of our investigation.

The elite sites listed by Balzaretti that have been dated to Late Antiquity are almost exclusively located close to coastal settlements, overlooking the Ligurian Sea.[234] These locations were probably part of a much larger economic network, stretching inland as well as connecting to different mainland regions accessible by marine transportation. Though their elite proprietors had long been able to tap into the rich Mediterranean

---

[232] Tiber valley project publications; amongst others see Patterson 2004; Witcher 2005; Patterson 2007; Patterson and Coarelli 2008; Cascino et al. 2012; for the archaeology of non-elites more generally, see also Patterson 1991; Arthur 2004, 105–9; Christie 2006, 437–42; Decker 2009, 33–48; and Moreland 2010, 116–58.
[233] Balzaretti 2013, 35–62.
[234] Balzaretti 2013, 39.

network, following the third-century crisis most seem to have abandoned their investments in these quarters, permanently so at the end of the fourth century.[235] Simultaneously, and up to the sixth century, small rural establishments arise in the surrounding countryside, though increasingly much further away from the Ligurian coast.[236] Corti, the largest agricultural site in the hinterland of Pietra Ligure, apart from successfully securing its own subsistence, specialised in processing animal and agricultural products.[237] The number of products from Corti found elsewhere, as well as their type (the site produced olive oil in addition to raising cattle), suggests that the site (Balzaretti calls it a *vicus*) produced for the market – at least until the third and fourth centuries when pottery vessels attest the import of products from elsewhere.[238] From the fifth century onwards, the site becomes marshier, and much of its agriculture is abandoned. Only in the tenth century does agriculture return comparable to what had existed during the fourth century. As Balzaretti notes, the deterioration of the agricultural aptitude of the village can be explained by changing climatic conditions: apparently, from the fifth century onwards, cereals, vines and olives became increasingly difficult to grow.[239] Whether Corti's local population adapted to this ecological change as well as Edward M. Schoolman suggests in this volume for inhabitants of the Po plain (Chapter 10) is difficult to know. Their fate remains largely ambiguous.

A complete contrast to Corti is Savignone, another mid-slope site overlooking the river Scrivia, where excavations documented a small group of dry-stone walled and thatched houses, approximately thirty metres across.[240] The excavators found several hundred kilos of reused Roman roof tiles (*tegoloni*), the use of which is debated.[241] No local pottery was produced at Savignone, but many imported ceramics were found (fifth-/sixth-century *ceramica grezza*). Similar pottery was found in Ventimiglia and Luscignano in the Lunigania, together with imported *terra sigillata chiara* D and African amphorae of fourth-/fifth-century dates.[242] To many archaeologists, the presence of these imports seemed very much out of place (I will come back to this issue below) as they did not fit the crude lifestyle observable from the presence of relatively rudimental structures and close-by plant remains, namely rye, silver birch, elm and field maple, oak, hazel or chestnut, not very dissimilar to present vegetation cover.[243] Additionally, two coins were found, one of Theodosius I, the other unrecognisable.[244] They were both made of low-valued bronze. The site was probably occupied throughout the second and first centuries BC, then abandoned until the fourth century AD, when it was active until c.500. Later the site became agricultural land and was not reoccupied until modern times, even though it is near the current village site. Buildings very similar

---

[235] Bruun 2007, 201–17.
[236] Balzaretti 2013 calls them 'mid-slope inland sites'.
[237] De Vingo 2010, 82.
[238] Arobba et al. 2007, 91.
[239] Balzaretti 2013, 41–2.
[240] Fossati et al. 1976; Castelletti 1976; Cagnana 1994, 170.
[241] Mannoni 1983, 262.
[242] Fossati et al. 1976, 315–20.
[243] Fossati et al. 1976, 325; Castelletti 1976; Cagnana 1994, 170.
[244] Fossati et al. 1976, 314.

to those at Savignone were found at San Cipriano (Polcevera valley). Roof tiles produced in the suburbs of Genoa itself were again found.[245]

Two other late Roman sites bordering Liguria in the east seem to have had similar histories. In the 1970s at Gronda di Luscignano, east of Aulla in the upper Aulella valley, a small fourth- to sixth-century village was uncovered on top of an earlier site.[246] Again, pottery was found, dating to the fourth- to sixth-century period. Sites from other rural farmsteads in the region, near Savignone, San Cipriano and Filattiera, all show very similar circumstances.[247]

Another site in the east, Filattiera-Sorano, has been much more thoroughly excavated owing to its fame as the likely location of a fortification mentioned by the Greek author George of Cyprus in AD 610.[248] The 'Sorano part' of the excavations revealed a small village that existed between the first and sixth centuries, with houses built of timber and river cobble.[249] Ceramics were mostly of local production and functional, but some connections to coastal ports were evidenced in the third century with the presence of imported pottery. Although new buildings were made at the end of that century, the village declined drastically during the sixth century, with one burnt house producing some carbonised foodstuffs and remains of animals. Pigs, aged two to three years, seem to have been consumed during the fifth/sixth century, but they were never exported. It is possible that these served as a *dernier ressort* in case of bad harvests.[250] The site also turned up many cereal seeds, around 50,000, such as wheat, barley and foxtail millet. Furthermore, chestnuts were found, some peach stones, walnut shells and grape pips that had been pressed.[251]

The pressing question here, of course, is which of these sites were inhabited by smallholders. Judging by the materials found near the *vici* and several smaller dwellings, the sites can in effect be divided into three groups. The first group consists of only one site, Corti, which is characterised by its specialised production, namely that of olive oil, cattle and agricultural products. The second group is much larger. The sites of Savignone, Ventimiglia, Luscignano, San Cipriano, Gronda di Luscignano and Filattiera did not produce anything locally; imported ceramics were found at all of these places, and living quarters were made of crude materials. The only inconsistency is that at Savignone several small coins were found. The third group, like the first, is made up of only one site: Filattiera-Sorano. Excavation of it showed primarily evidence signifying production meant for local consumption; only very small amounts of imported pottery were found, together with a great number of cereals.

Corti, as noted, was the only site with a visibly extensive footprint outside of its close-by surroundings. It specialised in the production of olive oil, cattle and agricultural foodstuffs. The production of olive oil here might have been the result of the late Roman state's provisioning system, but the fact that amphorae were found near

---

[245] Cagnana 1994, 169–70; De Vingo and Frondoni 2003, 84.
[246] Davite 1988.
[247] Davite 1988, 401.
[248] Bullough 1956; Cagnana 1994, 174; George of Cyprus, *Descriptio orbis Romani* 958.
[249] Giannichedda 1998.
[250] Giannichedda 1998, 196–7.
[251] See also Giannichedda 1998, 198–212; and 2003.

rural places with no signs of military habitation suggests that it was produced primarily for the private market, and thus for private consumption.[252] Unlike the milling of grain, producing olive oil was a relatively cost-effective venture.[253] How exactly the inhabitants of Corti produced the oil is difficult to know, since the site shows no signs of specialised olive oil presses or other tools commonly used for extraction. It is likely that the oil was produced by crushing olives with stone rollers, paddles or mortar and pestle: in any case, tools that required less investiture. Olive oil required a large degree of marketing across time, as olive trees only offer good harvests every other year. While Ambrose urges farmers to invest in a variety of agricultural products, as we have seen earlier, non-elites would normally forgo specialised olive oil production, since it was notably market-dependent.[254] Indeed, Corti's inhabitants specialised in the production of other foodstuffs, which means that they were not entirely dependent on the production of olive oil; but the planning associated with the production and transportation of olive oil to quite a number of places was in all likelihood the result of direct investment by an established landowner or businessmen. At *villae* near Luni and Varignano very similar practices took place, and the fact that the economic ventures of Corsi seem to have collapsed precisely around the same time that other elite sites disappear suggests that they were strongly connected.[255] Corti's inhabitants might have been slaves, but the presence of an extensive material culture, as well as easily distinguishable sites, implies that the individuals working here were smallholders, and, perhaps, more specifically, tenants, who 'sold' their labour for supplemental income.

The second group (Savignone, Ventimiglia, Luscignano, San Cipriano, Gronda di Luscignano and Filattiera) are all very similar in that the 'buildings' found at these sites were made of relatively crude materials, while at the same time relatively elaborate *tegeloni* were found, together with some imported ceramics. As I already noted above, the material culture here is unusually conflicted. Tiziano Mannoni presented an interesting hypothesis, arguing that urban dwellers impoverished by the third-century urban crisis were forced to return to rural subsistence sites in the hills.[256] It is possible that the *stazioni a tegoloni*, the roof-tile sites, were the result of third-century urban dwellers moving into the hilly areas of Liguria. Balzaretti suggests that explanations for the conflicting material culture at these sites can be found by looking at more recently furnished dwellings characteristic of the region. There too the material culture 'displayed great contrast between the structural fabric and level of comfort and presence of objects from around the world'.[257] However, Balzaretti is unclear about the chronology of these 'other sites', and the fact that they were used even in the present day suggests to me that we are dealing here with a tradition not easily connected to the earlier sites. Rather, I would follow the suggestion of Mannoni, which is that the tiles were transported from their original locations (in this case near the coast) to inland

---

[252] Sessa 2018, 38.
[253] Erdkamp 2005, 106–14.
[254] Erdkamp 2005, 74–5.
[255] Balzaretti 2013, 40–1.
[256] Mannoni 1983, 254–65.
[257] Balzaretti 2013, 61.

areas. As Balzaretti notes, the *tegeloni* seem to have functioned as a 'layer' at these sites, possibly sustaining drainage; or they were used as platforms for construction.[258] Either way, the *tegeloni* now served a function that was unintended by the original producers, we may safely assume, and it seems probable to suggest that decisions regarding their use were made on an improvised basis, perhaps because the 'former urbanites' had been unable to fit them into the roofs of their new, haphazard constructions. On the other hand, it seems just as possible that the *tegeloni* did not originate from the coastal area, but that they were collected from *villae rusticae*, abandoned due to the third-century crisis. Whatever the case, a move of urban dwellers to inland regions would also explain the large number of imported amphorae. As no production centre of these goods has been attested further inland, it is likely that the inhabitants of these sites continued to have contact with the coastal area from which they, occasionally, collected supplements. What they sold in order to buy these amphorae is unclear, but obviously there was always the possibility of barter or the chance that the inhabitants of these *telegoni* sites produced agricultural foodstuffs which are now, unfortunately, lost to us. This hypothesis would also compare with Paolo de Vingo's and Alessandra Frondoni's revised settlement sequence, which shows late antique people repopulating the mid-slopes inland near Genoa.[259] Here, as at the sites spoken of above, individuals made use of pastures at higher elevations, a pattern that continued throughout the early medieval period until the eleventh century.[260] Now, supposing that these sites were inhabited by 'former urbanites', paired with the fact that no production facilities were found, seems to suggest that any connections to elites had now been severed – or at least they had become of only minor importance. Self-sufficiency conjoined with the occasional barter was the strategy followed here. It's highly doubtful whether the individuals living at these sites were socially dependent; at the same time, assuming that they were, indeed, free smallholders, they seem not to have managed their portfolio of land, activities and labour very effectively.

Lastly, we have Filattiera-Sorano. To summarise, again, the ceramics found here were mostly of local production and not exported, only a small amount of imported pottery was found, and foodstuffs encountered here were most likely meant for local consumption. Furthermore, the *vicus* evolved over the centuries in that it saw the construction of several new houses, which, together with the rest of the village, were for the greater part abandoned during the sixth century. Now, it is clear that activities and infrastructure at Filattiera-Sorano were never very greatly upscaled, since no specialist kilns were found, nor did the pottery produced here find its way to other sites. Nothing about the buildings encountered at the site was monumental, labour-intensive or meticulously planned, and the quality of the pottery shows likewise no signs of investment or standardisation. Rather, what likely happened was that the site's inhabitants produced pottery only for personal use, some of which they might have exchanged for ARS or the other types of pottery found here. Presumably, the inhabitants of Filattiera-Sorano engaged in 'economical farming', meaning that they invested in the

---

[258] Balzaretti 2013, 44.
[259] De Vingo and Frondoni 2003, 32–3.
[260] Christie 2006, 473–84 on hilltop sites, with further references.

survival of the site, but not in the sophisticated and responsive structures necessary for the movement of some of the goods they produced. The men and women living here were very likely to be independent farmers, free smallholders, up to the point that their village was destroyed.

Southern Italy

For southern Italy, as is the case with most of the traditional historiography concerning late antique economy, most excavations have concentrated on *villae*, and more precisely on the links between the crisis of villa settlement and the structural alteration of the countryside from the fifth to the sixth centuries.[261] Castrorao Barba has made an interesting contribution to this debate by employing an innovative quantitative and statistical approach in order to identify trends on the macro-regional level. According to his results, the fifth century appears as a turning point: 46 per cent of the villas in southern Italy (including Sicily and Sardinia) became abandoned at this time.[262] However, these deserted complexes were often reused for a variety of purposes, primarily for small (mainly timber-built) settlements, but sometimes also for the construction of necropolises, religious structures, workshops and production facilities.[263] The sixth century sees an even higher percentage of villa abandonment: only 14 per cent of sites recorded as *villae* in the fifth century remained in use. Again, the reuse of abandoned structures increases. Although Giuliano Volpe and Maria Turchiano have shown the refurbishment and embellishment of some of these *villae* by large landholders, suggesting that the 'villa system' lasted longer in southern Italy than anywhere else, their cumulative abandonment seems to have had differing results on the surrounding countryside.[264]

Recent excavations and surveys in Campania make for a particularly interesting case study. Here, the abandonment of *villae* seems to have had two results for the broader rural economy. In some areas, such as the middle and lower valley of the river Volturno, the *agri* of Capua and Pozzuoli, and the *ager* Falerno, this 'villa crisis' is matched by a general rarefication of both nucleated and scattered settlements, an overall decline in the number of sites that produced goods, and a reduction in long-range commercial exchanges.[265] Other contexts present a completely different picture: at least until the earliest sixth century, the available data indicate that rural areas around Naples, Avellino, Benevento and the plain of Alife were still thriving, supported by a network of towns and ports, which facilitated short- and long-range exchanges. It is here that the smaller structures, the so-called *fattorie* or 'farmsteads', and villages are

---

[261] Brogiolo 1996; Ripoll and Arce 2000; Francovich and Hodges 2003; Lewit 2003; 2005; Chavarría Arnau 2004; 2007; Brogiolo and Chavarría Arnau 2005, 49–68; Volpe and Turchiano 2010; Goffredo and Volpe 2018, 35–8.
[262] Castrorao Barba 2014.
[263] Lewit 2004.
[264] Volpe and Turchiano 2010.
[265] Arthur 2002, 83–108; Pagano 2009; see also Calzolari 1999 and Saggioro 2004 for very similar developments in northern Italy.

argued to have acquired, though gradually, increasingly autonomous positions.[266] The problem here, however, is that the decline of *villae* does not necessarily mean the rise of 'the smallholder', or that of the free, independent farming community. Most elites lived in cities, and the fact that several large *massae* continued to exist in southern Italy could indicate that the abandonment of these *villae* should not be seen as the departure of elites, but rather an increase in elites who managed their farms indirectly, or, perhaps, a concentration of property into the hands of the prosperous few.[267] Likewise, it can also be argued that the gradual impoverishment of elites mainly had results for the material culture that we find, and that while the distinction between elite and non-elite becomes increasingly difficult to see in the archaeological record, exploitative relationships remained.[268]

That said, two places excavated by a team led by Marisa Corrente show remarkable evidence for the activities of smallholders.[269] The first site, Lamiozza, was a small farmstead within the region of Luceria. It was occupied during the fourth and fifth centuries, comprising only two rooms built in rough stone and clay. One of the rooms was used for eating and sleeping, as suggested by the earthen floor and stove, while the second one was used exclusively for storage and, in all likelihood, artisanal activities.[270] The evidence therefore clearly indicates inhabitants of low status with limited capacity and meagre means of production. The fact that the site invested both in agriculture and crafts means that the inhabitants tried to spread risk to ensure subsistence needs. Remarkable is the material culture at the site: aside from local, regional and imported pottery (African *terra sigillata* C and D), excavations showed the presence of several iron tools, glass items and small wooden boxes, presumably used for the storage of precious goods. The large range of pottery, instead of groups of duplicates, indicates, importantly, that the site was not used for standard pottery production on demand, which would suggest elite intervention, but meant for the local market.[271] Furthermore, Lamiozza seems not to have been close to any of Luceria's possible elite establishments, such as towns and *villae*. Thus, the residents produced their own goods to gain access to broader markets in order to acquire supplemental goods. Pottery, tools and glass were some of those acquisitions, as the lack of an oven on site indicates that these must have been produced elsewhere.

The second site is the *vicus* of San Marchitto, near Ordona. The excavation of the local sepulchre revealed a small rural building that was built sometime at the end of the third century, and did not markedly change until the end of the fifth century. The thick walls of the complex were made from small and middle-large pebbles, bound together with clay and crudely made bricks. During these centuries the site experienced several phases, and in each of these phases, a new entrance was added to the building. Astonishingly, further excavation of the site revealed a number of burials

---

[266] Fariello and Lambert 2009; Ebanista 2009; Busino 2009; Savino 2009; Marazzi 2015.
[267] Vera 1999; Wickham 2005, 203–10.
[268] Lewit 2005.
[269] Corrente et al. 2012; Corrente and Cioce 2014.
[270] Corrente and Cioce 2014.
[271] Van Oyen 2020, 32–6.

that showed a small community of villagers, agriculturalists and shepherds that had led relatively healthy lives. Although several indicators of status differentiation were found by using post-mortem recognition, the community is best characterised as one based upon close reciprocal relationships with individuals on similar socio-economic levels. Similarly to Marzuolo, the village experimented heavily with ceramics. An imitation of an African oil lamp was found, as well as a number of badly made imitations of African *sigillata* D. Between the fifth and sixth centuries the village seems to have increased the production of ceramics, though only slightly. The kiln, which was already there from the beginning of the site, was not expanded, nor was another kiln added to the complex. During the same centuries, the site also experimented with ironworking, as is indicated by the several slags around the kiln. This suggests that the village started to make its own tools, presumably for agricultural use. The village traded some of its ceramics with outsiders, as small amounts of similar pottery have been found at close-by sites. The fact that the local town of Hedonia experienced a period of recession indicates that San Marchitto took over some of the town's economic vigour. Only at the beginning of the seventh century does the *vicus* scale up its production considerably, as suggested by the many elaborately painted ceramics of later dates. This could suggest that San Marchitto started to receive elite interest, but the lack of the introduction of a new kiln in this period could also suggest that the *vicus*' inhabitants became increasingly more efficient in the production of their pottery by developing labour.[272] As with Marzuolo, the site is indicative for smallholders experimenting with resources acquired around them, developing both skills and labour and, most importantly, successfully acquiring capital to ensure the village its subsistence needs.

We should be careful in applying the label 'smallholder site' to each and every small rural site in this area (or others), even if it 'ticks all the boxes'. A case in point is a site called San Biagio near Metaponto, the excavation of which showed a small structure, around 150 m², built in the second century and only abandoned in the early fifth. The complex consisted of several small storerooms for foodstuffs such as wheat, some of them simultaneously used for artisanal practices, and, remarkably, a small section of heated baths.[273] The site shows no signs of substantial surplus production; it seems only to have prioritised fulfilling the households' basic subsistence needs and, accordingly, had no clear connections with elite establishments. Roberto Goffredo and Giuliano Volpe remarked that the structure could have been inhabited by tenants, with the structure being part of a larger estate.[274] Though there is evidence of landlords providing their tenants with baths in the East, these were only located at city centres or larger semi-rural settlements.[275] There exists no evidence for this occurrence in the West. Goffredo and Volpe also recognised the possibility that the site could be evidence for well-to-do smallholders, 'middle-class' residents, who apparently had acquired enough funds and, importantly, time to invest in baths.[276] While that may be

---

[272] Corrente et al. 2012.
[273] Lapadula 2012.
[274] Goffredo and Volpe 2018, 30; see also Marazzi 2010, 681 regarding this middle class.
[275] John Chrysostom, *Hom. Act.* 17.
[276] Goffredo and Volpe 2018, 32.

true, the site could also have been inhabited by elite residents: again, it can be argued that well-to-do individuals, over the course of the fifth to seventh centuries, increasingly tended to occupy residences that were much less elaborate than the *villae* they occupied before.[277] Though it is evident that the owners of this area had acquired the necessary funds, physical capital and labour to maintain the quality of the building over a longer time, the site is a testament to many other 'small agricultural buildings' in the late antique Italian countryside of which the social relations remain largely contested.

Conclusion

This chapter has aimed to establish that smallholders in late Roman Italy were capable of using their economic (and to some extent social) resources in order to evolve their relative socio-economic position; it has also shown that smallholders were notably knowledgeable about their surroundings, using the landscape to great effect; capable of prioritising cost-effective strategies; defending their position by making use of cultural or kin-based relationships; and, above all, making choices of allocating time and effort, tools and land to specific uses in a context of resource availability. Smallholders, then, made economic decisions that are intelligible in rational, utilitarian terms. Thus, while the historiography of late antique Italy has often put significant emphasis on the docile character of the greater part of Italy's agricultural working population, including, most importantly, the legally free, both the documentary and archaeological record show consistent signs of their continuing importance, as well as unvarying signs of agency, particularly in relation to the economic resources they possessed or had access to.

When we think about late antique smallholders, we often imagine a community that is homogeneous, minimally active in trade, and unfavourably subject to outside influence. We often think that rural non-elites change for the worse when they become stratified or start producing for the market. However, there are no agrarian cultures that are completely egalitarian and secluded from the rest of the world. We do not have to work with absolutes. Families, villages and regions all have different levels of self-sufficiency and market relations. In late Roman Italy, just as in other agrarian societies dealing with socio-economic or political change, the gradual subjugation of one legally determined type of agricultural worker (say *coloni*) does not mean a similar kind of 'demise' of others. The sources suggest forms of interaction at each level of rural society. Even the most market-oriented individuals do not have to reject a certain amount of subsistence production *et vice versa*. Furthermore, by engaging in relations with kin and owner-proprietors, smallholders were able to secure and defend their access to economic assets.

Of course, there is no such thing as 'the late Roman smallholder', or 'the Ostrogothic smallholder'; we can safely assume that smallholders and their agricultural strategies were dependent on complex network relations, which, apart from the variation caused by ecological and geographical differences, were the result of political, social and economic considerations which went much further than the (visible) boundaries

---

[277] While the site was abandoned at the start of Lewit's 2005 time frame, that does not mean that the same should have occurred at Lucenia some decades before.

of each individual. Hence economic choices specifically depended upon a wide range of controls, related mainly to the extraction of rent and taxes, but also to interdependence within the local community. Each cultivator's responsibility, even for his day-to-day activities, was circumscribed in various ways because neither his holding nor his methods of production existed in isolation from the various structures that surrounded him. In some cases, smallholders were undoubtedly bound to provide labour for others, or hardly had any chance in accessing a free market in which to obtain labour themselves. Their choice of cash crops would depend not only on their own judgement but also on patterns of land use and water supply, judgements made by landlords and their chief tenants – often matters beyond their immediate control.

What this mostly boils down to is the question of whether a smallholder would be able to deny the claims of elites or other powerful actors in the first place. Evidently, a small farmer, who is in financial distress and often uninformed, is more prone to yield to pressure from local officials and large landowners and will thus often sustain a substantial loss. Even more so since his bargaining power is limited. On the other hand, smallholder households that could successfully transition from a mostly agricultural-dependent household to one in which non-agricultural income became more and more important probably had fewer problems with setting aside resources, and time, investing those not only in their own household but also in the community, and thus were able to deny elites their claim. Of course, this is impossible in those areas where the smallholder's household is initially too poor to even start spreading and investing its assets. Such households must have simply stagnated, or may have fallen into a poverty spiral.

But then again, with the sources in mind, is it fair to consistently characterise the late antique Italian smallholder as dependent and marginal? It is important to remember that both dependency and marginality are not just intellectual concepts; they are multidimensional, involving people at multiple levels of being and functioning.[278] It is the involuntary position and condition of a community (or individual) at the margins of political, social and economic systems that prevent them from adequately securing resources, services and assets as well as developing capabilities. They are, then, defined by their constrained freedom of choice. But in the case of our smallholders, and with the evidence in mind, it is difficult to suggest that they had no access to resources (land, labour, surpluses, pottery, tools), services (artisanal practices, taking up wage labour), or had little chance of using these to good effect.

The evidence thus calls into question assumptions about smallholder zones in Italy as marginal landscapes. Because of the common association of small agriculturalists with suppression, smallholder dwellings such as those at San Marchitto and Savignone are readily assumed to be poor farmers' houses, connected with marginality and a degree of insulation from broader forces of economic and social uncertainties in late antique Italy. Such assumptions reveal more about past and current attitudes towards smallholder environments and their agency than they inform about the experiences of people in the past. Given the dearth of archaeological information on these evidently

---

[278] Binder 2009; Braun and Gatzweiler 2014.

complex and variable sites, a real danger lies in complacency – we overlook the potential complexity of rural sites because we think we already know all there is to know. As Edward M. Schoolman shows in this volume (Chapter 10), archaeology allows us to see rural communities adapting, irrespective of some of the economic and political incentives that occur around them – even those made by the elite. Thus, while (legal) literary sources might indicate a principal problematic position for smallholders, our combined sources suggest the need for a more nuanced perception.

There remain, of course, loose ends. If we look beyond the incidental (and sometimes suggestive) moments of agency presented in our sources, our view is often murky and observations less certain than we would like them to be. Smallholders can be accommodated into arguments regarding economic or social agency, but we continue to know relatively little of them. Despite these uncertainties and lacunae, however, if we continue to gain more evidence from our resources, may it be through theoretical insights or through archaeological remains, we can be confident that the lives of these individuals, integrated into complex, longstanding and extensive social, cultural, political, economic and demographic systems, as well as their personal acts within these systems, become increasingly more elucidated.[279]

Bibliography

Alföldy, G. (1991) *Histoire sociale de Rome*, Paris.
Amory, P. (1997) *People and Identity in Ostrogothic Italy, 489–554*, Cambridge.
Angold, M. (1995) *Church and Society in Byzantium under the Comneni, 1081–1261*, Cambridge.
Ankarloo, D. (2002) 'The New Institutional Economics and Economic History', *Journal of Economic History* 57 (3): 718–21.
Arobba, D., F. Bulgarelli, C. Siniscalco and R. Caramiello (2007) 'Indagine paleobotanico su sedimenti di età altomedievale da livelli profondi dell'arenile di Pietra Ligure (Savona)', *Ligures* 5: 88–95.
Arthur, P. (2000) 'Medieval Fairs: an Archaeologist's Approach', in A. Buko and P. Urbanczyka (eds) *Archeologia w teorii i w praktyce*, Warsaw, 419–36.
Arthur, P. (2002) *Naples: from Roman Town to City-State*, London.
Arthur, P. (2004) 'From Vicus to Village: Italian Landscapes, AD 400–1000', in N. Christie (ed.) *Landscapes of Change: Rural Evolutions in Late Antiquity and the Early Middle Ages*, Aldershot, 103–33.
Arthur, P. and S. M. Sindbaek (2007) 'Trade and Exchange', in J. Graham-Campbell and M. Valor (eds) *The Archaeology of Medieval Europe*, vol. 1: *Eighth to Twelfth Centuries AD*, Aarhus, 289–310.
Balzaretti, R. (2013) *Dark Age Liguria: Regional Identity and Local Power, c.400–1020*, London.
Banaji, J. (1992) 'Historical Arguments for a "Logic of Deployment" in "Precapitalist" Agriculture', *Journal of Historical Sociology* 5: 379–91.
Banaji, J. (2001) *Agrarian Change in Late Antiquity: Gold, Labour, and Aristocratic Dominance*, Oxford.

---

[279] It is with the utmost appreciation of their criticism, support and patience that I thank Carlos Machado, Caroline Humfress, Dennis Kehoe and Jeroen Wijnendaele. I have asked for expert help of each of them, and have consistently been answered. It is my hope that the wonderful discussions that have led to this chapter will take place in the future also. Mistakes or infelicities that remain are, of course, mine alone.

Banaji, J. (2009) 'Aristocracies, Peasantries and the Framing of the Early Middle Ages', *Journal of Agrarian Change* 9: 59–91.
Banaji, J. (2011) 'Late Antiquity to the Early Middle Ages: What Kind of Transition?', *Historical Materialism* 19 (1): 109–44.
Banaji, J. (2016) 'The Economics Trajectories of Late Antiquity', in J. Banaji, *Exploring the Economy of Late Antiquity*, Cambridge, 61–88.
Bang, P. F. (2009) 'The Ancient Economy and New Institutional Economics', *JRS* 99: 194–206.
Barbero, A. and M. Vigil (1978) *La formacion del feudalismo en la Peninsula Iberica*, Barcelona.
Barceló, M. and F. Sigaut (2004) *The Making of Feudal Agricultures?* Leiden.
Barnish, S. J. B. (1987) 'Pigs, Plebeians and *potentes*: Rome's Economic Hinterland, c.350–600 A.D.', *PBSR* 55: 157–85.
Barzel, Y. (2002) *A Theory of the State: Economic Rights, Legal Rights, and the Scope of the State*, Cambridge.
Basu, K., E. Jones and E. Schlicht (1987) 'The Growth and Decay of Custom: the Role of New Institutional Economics in Economic History', *Explorations in Economic History* 24: 1–21.
Beaucamp, J. (1999) 'Women', in G. W. Bowersock, P. Brown and O. Grabar (eds) *Late Antiquity: a Guide to the Post-Classical World*, Cambridge, 749–51.
Bebbington, A. (1999) 'Capitals and Capabilities: a Framework for Analyzing Peasant Viability, Rural Livelihoods and Poverty', *World Development* 27 (12): 2021–44.
Berhold, M. (1971) 'A Theory of Linear Profit-Sharing Incentives', *Quarterly Journal of Economics* 85 (3): 460–82.
Berry, S. (1989) 'Social Institutions and Access to Resources', *Africa* 49 (1): 41–55.
Binder, C. (2009) 'Context Dependency of Valuable Functionings: How Culture Affects the Capability Framework', in E. Chiappero-Martinetti (ed.) *Debating Global Society: Reach and Limits of the Capability Approach*, Milan, 203–29.
Bintliff, J. and A. Snodgrass (1988) 'Off-Site Pottery Distribution: a Regional and Interregional Perspective', *Current Anthropology* 29: 506–13.
Biraghi, L. (1867) *Vita di Santa Marcellina*, Milan.
Bjornlie, S. (2013) *Politics and Tradition between Rome, Ravenna and Constantinople: a Study of Cassiodorus and the Variae, 527–554*, Cambridge.
Bjornlie, S. (2014) 'Law, Ethnicity and Taxes in Ostrogothic Italy: a Case for Continuity, Adaption and Departure', *Early Medieval Europe* 22 (2): 138–70.
Blaikie, P. (1989) 'Environment and Access to Resources in Africa', *Africa* 59 (1): 18–40.
Bloch, M. (1931) *Les caractères originaux de l'histoire rurale française*, Paris.
Bloch, M. (1939–1940) *Le société féodale*, Paris.
Bocage-Lefebvre, D. (2013) 'La représentation du monde paysan dans les *Natalicia* de Paulin de Nole', *Pallas* 92: 203–14.
Bowden, W. and L. Lavan (2014) 'The Late Antique Countryside: an Introduction', in W. Bowden and L. Lavan (eds) *Recent Research on the Late Antique Countryside*, Leiden, xvii–xxvi.
Bowden, W., L. Lavan and C. Machado (2004) *Recent Research on the Late Antique Countryside*, Leiden.
Bowes, K. (ed.) (2020) *The Roman Peasant Project 2009–2014: Excavating the Roman Rural Poor*, 2 vols, Philadelphia.
Bowes, K. and C. Grey (2020) 'Conclusions', in K. Bowes (ed.) *The Roman Peasant Project 2009–2014: Excavating the Roman Rural Poor*, vol. 2, Philadelphia, 617–40.
Braconi, P. (2005) 'Il Calcidico di Lepcis Magna era un mercato di schiavi?', *JRA* 18: 213–19.
Bransbourg, G. (2015) 'The Later Roman Empire', in A. Monson and W. Scheidel (eds) *Fiscal Regimes and the Political Economy of Premodern States*, Cambridge, 258–81.

Braun, J. von and F. W. Gatzweiler (2014) *Marginality: Addressing the Nexus of Poverty, Exclusion and Ecology*, New York.

Brogiolo, G. P. (ed.) (1996) *La fine del ville romane: trasformazioni nelle campagne tra Tarda Antichità e Altomedioevo. 1o Convegno Archeologico del Garda (Gardone Riviera 1995)*, Mantua.

Brogiolo, G. P. (1999) 'Ideas of the Town in Italy during the Transition from Antiquity to the Middle Ages', in G. P. Brogiolo and B. Ward-Perkins (eds) *Towns and Their Territories between Late Antiquity and the Early Middle Ages*, Leiden, 99–126.

Brogiolo, G. P. and A. Chavarría Arnau (2005) *Aristocrazie e campagne nell' Occidente da Costantino a Carlo Magno*, Florence.

Brogiolo, G. P., A. Chavarría Arnau and M. Valenti (2005) *Dopo la fine delle ville: le campagne dal VI al IX secolo; 11. Seminario sul Tardo Antico e l'Alto Medioevo, Gavi, 8–10 maggio 2004*, Mantua.

Brousseau, E. and J. M. Glachant (2008) *New Institutional Economics: a Guidebook*, Cambridge.

Brown, P. (1992) *Power and Persuasion in Late Antiquity: Towards a Christian Empire*, London.

Brown, T. S. (1984) *Gentlemen and Officers: Imperial Administration and Aristocratic Power in Byzantine Italy A.D. 554–800*, Rome.

Brunt, P. A. (1971) *Italian Manpower*, London.

Bruun, C. (2007) 'The Antonine Plague and the Third-Century Crisis', in O. Hekster, G. de Kleijn and D. Slootjes, *Crises and the Roman Empire: Proceedings of the Seventh Workshop of the International Network Impact of Empire (Nijmegen, June 20–24, 2006)*, Leiden, 201–17.

Bullough, D. A. (1956) 'A Byzantine (?) Castle in the Val di Magra: Surianum-Filattiera', *PBSR* 24: 14–21.

Busino, N. (2009) 'L'alta valle del Cervaro fra Tarda Antichità e Altomedioevo: dati preliminari per una ricerca topografica', in C. Ebanista and M. Rotili (eds) *La Campania fra Tarda Antichità e Alto Medioevo: ricerche di archeologia del territorio (Atti della Giornata di Studio)*, Richerche e studi 49, Cimitile (Tavolario), 129–52.

Cagnana, A. (1994) 'Considerazioni sulle strutture abitative liguri fra VI e XIII secolo', in G. P. Brogiolo (ed.) *Edilizia residenziale tra V e VIII secolo*, Mantua, 169–77.

Calzolari, M. (1999) 'Le operazioni militari a Ostiglia nell'autunno del 69 d.C.: problemi topografici', *Quaderni di archeologia del Mantovano* 1: 85–121.

Carandini, A. (1983) 'Pottery and the African Economy', in P. Garnsey, K. Hopkins and C. R. Whittaker (eds) *Trade in the Ancient Economy*, London, 145–62.

Carandini, A. (1985) 'Da villa perfecta', in A. Carandini (ed.) *Settefinestre, una villa schiavistica nell' Etruria Romana*, Modena, 107–37.

Carandini, A. (1986) 'Il mondo della Tarda Antichità visto attraverso le merci', in A. Giardina (ed.) *Società romana e impero tardoantico III: le merci, gli insediamenti*, Rome, 3–19.

Carrié, J. M. (1982) 'Le 'Colonat du Bas-Empire': un mythe historiographique', *Opus: International Journal for Social and Economic History of Antiquity* 1: 351–70.

Carrié, J. M. (1983) 'Un roman des origines: les généalogies du "colonat" du Bas Empire', *Opus: International Journal for Social and Economic History of Antiquity* 2: 205–51.

Carrié, J. M. (1997) 'Colonato del Basso Impero': la resistenza del mito', in E. Lo Cascio (ed.) *Terre, proprietari e contadini dell'Impero Romano: dall'affitto agrario al colonato tardoantico (Incontro studio di Capri, 16–18 ottobre 1995)*, Rome, 75–150.

Carrié, J. M. (2012) 'Were Late Roman and Byzantine Economies Market Economies? A Comparative Look at Historiography', in C. Morrisson (ed.) *Trade and Markets in Byzantium*, Washington, 13–26.

Carrié, J. M. (2017) 'The Historical Path of "Late Antiquity": from Transformation to Rupture', in R. Lizzi (ed.) *Late Antiquity in Contemporary Debate*, Cambridge, 174–214.

Cascino, R., H. Di Giuseppe and H. Patterson (2012) *Veii: the Historical Topography of the Ancient City. A Restudy of John Ward Perkins's Survey*, Archaeological Monographs of the British School at Rome 19, Rome.

Castelletti, L. (1976) 'Resti vegetali macroscopici da Refondou presso Savignone', *Archeologia Medievale* 3: 326–8.

Castrorao Barba, A. (2014) 'Continuità topografica in discontinuità funzionale: trasformazioni e riusi delle ville romane in Italia tra III e VIII secolo', *Post-Classical Archaeologies* 4: 259–96.

Castrorao Barba, A. (2016) 'Alcune statistiche sulle dinamiche cronologiche degli insediamenti secondari in Italia nella lunga durata tra età romana e Medioevo', in P. Basso and E. Zanini (eds) *Statio amoena: sostare e vivere lungo le strade Romane*, Oxford, 121–30.

Chavarría Arnau, A. (2004) 'Considerazioni sulla fine delle ville in Occidente', *Archeologia medievale* 21: 7–19.

Chavarría Arnau, A. (2007) *El final de las villas en Hispania (siglos IV–VIII)*, Turnhout.

Christie, N. (1996) 'Barren Fields? Landscapes and Settlements in Late Roman and Post-Roman Italy', in G. Shipley and J. Salmon (eds) *Human Landscapes in Classical Antiquity: Environment and Culture*, London, 254–83.

Christie, N. (2006) *From Constantine to Charlemagne: an Archaeology of Italy AD 300–800*, London.

Claassen, R. and L. Herzog (2019) 'Why Economic Agency Matters: an Account of Structural Domination in the Economic Realm', *European Journal of Political Theory* 20 (3): 465–85.

Coarelli, F. (1982) *Lazio*, Guide Archeologiche Laterza, Rome.

Coarelli, F. (2005) 'Aristonico', in B. Vergilio (ed.) *Studi ellenistici XVI*, Pisa, 211–40.

Conti, P. M. (1971) *Devotio e viri devoti in Italia da Diocleziano ai Carolingi*, Padua.

Corrente, M. and M. Cioce (2014) 'Piccoli e medi insediamenti rurale dell'Apulia centro-settentrionale nell'età tardoantica', in P. Pensabene and C. Sfameni (eds) *La villa restaurata e i nuovi studi sull'edilizia residenziale tardoantica*, Bari, 399–414.

Corrente, M., R. Cairoli, D. Marinelli, G. Miranda and A. Santarelli (2012) 'Le sepolture di San Marchitto (Ordona, FG): tipologie e ritualità funerarie di una communità rurale', in F. Redi and A. Forgione (eds) *VI Congresso Nazionale di archeologia medievale: sala conferenze 'E. Sericchi', Centro direzionale CARISPAQ 'Strinella 88', L' Aquila, 12–15 settembre 2012*, Florence, 544–50.

Costambeys, M. (2009) 'Settlement, Taxation and the Condition of the Peasantry in Post-Roman Central Italy', *Journal of Agrarian Change* 9 (1): 92–119.

Crook, J. A. (1967) *Law and Life of Rome, 90 B.C.–A.D. 212*, New York.

Dari-Mattiacci, G. and D. Kehoe (2020a) *Roman Law and Economics*, vol. 1: *Institutions and Organizations*, Oxford Studies in Roman Society and Law, Oxford.

Dari-Mattiacci, G. and D. Kehoe (2020b) *Roman Law and Economics*, vol. 2: *Exchange, Ownership, and Disputes*, Oxford Studies in Roman Society and Law, Oxford.

Davite, C. (1988) 'Scavi e riconizioni nel sito rurale tardo-antico di Gronda (Luscignano, MC)', *Archeologia medievale* 15: 397–406.

De Vingo, P. (2010) 'Archaeology of Power in the Rural Cemeteries of Western Liguria Maritima between Late Antiquity and the Beginning of the Early Middle Ages', in C. Ebanista and M. Rotili (eds) *Ipsam Nolam barbari vastaverunt: l'Italia ed il Mediterraneo occidentale tra il V secolo e la metà del VI*, Cimitile, 79–96.

De Vingo, P. and A. Frondoni (2003) 'Fonti scritte e cultura materiale del territorio fra Tardoantico e Altomedioevo in val Polcevera (GE): problemi aperti e prospettive di ricercar', in R. Fiorillo and P. Peduto (eds) *III Congresso Nazionale di Archeologia Medievale*, Florence, 32–6.

Decker, M. (2009) *Tilling the Hateful Earth: Agricultural Production and Trade in the Late Antique East*, Oxford.

Delano-Smith, C. and D. Gadd (1986) 'Luni and the Ager Lunensis 1986: the Roman Farmstead at Site 9', *PBSR* 54: 109–18.

Delmaire, R. (1989) *Largesses sacrées et res privata: l'Aerarium impérial et son administration du IVe au VIe siècle*, Rome.

Demandt, A. (1989) *Die Spätantike*, Munich.

Dölger, F. J. (1937) 'Das Sonnengleichnis in einer Weihnachtspredigt des Bischofs Zeno von Verona: Christus als wahre und ewige Sonne', *Antike und Christentum: Kultur- und religionsgeschichtliche Studien* 6: 1–50.

Dossey, L. (2010) *Peasant and Empire in Christian North Africa*, Berkeley.

Duby, G. (1962) *L'économie rurale et la vie des campagnes dans l'occident medieval (France, Angleterre, Empire IX–XV siècles): essai de synthèse et perspectives de recherches*, Paris.

Duby, G. (1973) *Guerriers et paysans, VII–XIIe siècle: premier essor de l'économie européenne*, Paris.

Du Plessis, P. (2015) 'Property', in D. Johnston (ed.) *The Cambridge Companion to Roman Law*, Cambridge, 175–98.

Ebanista, C. (2003) 'Dinamiche insediative nel territorio di Cimitile tra Tarda Antichità e Medioevo', in H. Brandenburg and L. Pani Ermini (eds) *Cimitile e Paolino di Nola*, Vatican City, 43–86.

Ebanista, C. (2007) 'Tra Nola e Cimitile alla ricerca della prima cattedrale', *Rassegna Storica Salernitana* 24: 25–119.

Ebanista, C. (2009) 'Dati preliminari sul territorio di Frigento fra Tarda Antichità e Alto Medioevo', in C. Ebanista and M. Rotili (eds) *La Campania fra Tarda Antichità e Alto Medioevo: ricerche di archeologia del territorio (Atti della Giornata di Studio)*, Richerche e studi 49, Cimitile (Tavolario), 103–27.

Eggertsson, T. (1990) *Economic Behavior and Institutions*, Cambridge.

Eisenhardt, K. M. (1989) 'Agency Theory: an Assessment and Review', *Academy of Management Review* 14 (1): 57–74.

Erdkamp, P. (2005) *The Grain Market in the Roman Empire: a Social, Political and Economic Study*, Cambridge.

Erdkamp, P. (2012) 'Urbanism', in W. Scheidel (ed.) *The Cambridge Companion to the Roman Economy*, Cambridge, 241–65.

Faith, R. (2020) *The Moral Economy of the Countryside: Anglo-Saxon to Anglo-Norman England*, Cambridge.

Fariello, M. and C. Lambert (2009) 'Il territorio di Abellinum in età tardoantica e altomedievale: dati archeologici e documenti epigrafici', in C. Ebanista and M. Rotili (eds) *La Campania fra Tarda Antichità e Alto Medioevo: ricerche di archeologia del territorio (Atti della Giornata di Studio)*, Richerche e studi 49, Cimitile (Tavolario), 25–6.

Faure-Boucharlat, E. (2001) *Vivre à la campagne au Moyen Âge: l'habitat rural du Ve au XIIe s. (Bresse, Lyonnais, Dauphiné) d'après les données archéologiques*, Lyon.

Fentress, E. (2005) 'On the Block: *catastae, chalcidica,* and *cryptae* in Early Imperial Italy', *JRA* 18: 220–34.

Finley, M. I. (1980) *Ancient Slavery and Modern Ideology*, New York.

Fossati, S., S. Bazzurro and O. Pizzolo (1976) 'Campagna di scavo nel villaggio tardoantico di Savignone (Genova)', *Archeologia medievale* 3: 309–25.

Foxhall, L. (1990) 'The Dependent Tenant: Land Leasing and Labour in Italy and Greece', *JRS* 80: 97–114.

Francovich, R. and R. Hodges (2003) *Villa to Village: the Transformation of the Roman Countryside in Italy, c.400–1000*, London.

Frayn, J. M. (1993) *Markets and Fairs in Roman Italy: Their Social and Economic Importance from the Second Century BC to the Third Century AD*, Oxford.

Friedman, D. (2020) 'Private Prosecution and Enforcement in Roman Law', in G. Dari-Mattiacci and D. Kehoe (eds) *Roman Law and Economics*, vol. 2: *Exchange, Ownership, and Disputes*, Oxford Studies in Roman Society and Law, Oxford, 327–44.
Furubotn, E. and R. Richter (1997) *Institutions and Economic Theory: the Contribution of New Institutional Economics*, Ann Arbor.
Fustel de Coulanges, N. D. (1885) *Le colonat romain: recherches sur quelques problèmes d'histoire*, Paris.
Gabba, E. and M. Pasquinucci (1979) *Strutture agrarie e allevamento transumante nell'Italia romana (III–I sec. A.C.)*, Pisa.
Gallant, T. (1991) *Risk and Survival in Ancient Greece*, Stanford.
Garnsey, P. (1968) 'Legal Privilege in the Roman Empire: Introduction', *P&P* 41 (1): 3–24.
Garnsey, P. (1976) 'Peasants in Ancient Roman Society', *JRS* 3 (2): 221–35.
Garnsey, P. (1979) 'Where Did Italian Peasants Live?', *PCPhS* 25: 1–25.
Garnsey, P. (1988) *Famine and Food Supply in the Graeco-Roman World: Responses to Risk and Crisis*, Cambridge.
Garnsey, P. (1999) *Food and Society in Classical Antiquity*, Cambridge.
Garnsey, P. (2004) *Cities, Peasants and Food in Classical Antiquity: Essays in Social and Economic History*, Cambridge.
Gelichi, S. (2012) 'Agricoltura e ambiente nell'Italia tardo-antica e altomedievale: un prospettivá archeologica', in P. Nann (ed.) *Agricoltura e ambiente attraverso l'èta romana e l'alto Medioevo: Atti della giornata di studio per il 50 anniversario della Rivista di storia dell'agricoltura, Firenze, 11 marzo, 2011*, Florence, 109–38.
George, M. (2013) *Roman Slavery and Roman Material Culture*, Toronto.
Ghisleni, M., E. Vaccaro and K. Bowes, with A. Arnoldus, M. MacKinnon and F. Marani (2011) 'Excavating the Roman Peasant I: Excavations at Pievina (GR)', *PBSR* 79: 95–145.
Giannichedda, E. (1998) *Filattiera-Sorano: l'insediamento dell'età romana e tardoantica. Scavi 1986–1995*, Florence.
Giannichedda, E. (2003) 'Insediamenti e culti in Lunigiana', in E. Giannichedda and R. Lanza, *Le ricerche archeologiche in provincial di Massa-Carrara*, Florence, 76–86.
Goffart, W. (1974) *Caput and Colonate: Towards a History of Late Roman Taxation*, Toronto.
Goffredo, R. and G. Volpe (2018) '*Per omnium villas vicosque cunctos*: Rural Landscapes in Late Antique Southern Italy', in P. Diarte-Blasco and N. Christie (eds) *Interpreting Transformations of People and Landscapes in Late Antiquity and the Early Middle Ages: Archaeological Approaches and Issues*, Oxford, 27–42.
Grey, C. (2004) 'Letters of Reccommendation and the Circulation of Rural Laborers in the Late Roman West', in L. Ellis and F. L. Kidner (eds) *Travel, Communication and Geography in Late Antiquity*, London, 25–40.
Grey, C. (2007) 'Revisiting the "Problem" of *agri deserti* in the Late Roman Empire', in *JRA* 20: 362–76.
Grey, C. (2011) *Constructing Communities in the Late Roman Countryside*, Cambridge.
Grey, C. (2016) 'Landowning and Labour in the Rural Economy', in J. J. Arnold, M. S. Bjornlie and K. Sessa (eds) *A Companion to Ostrogothic Italy*, Leiden, 263–95.
Halsall, G. (2016) 'The Ostrogothic Military', in J. J. Arnold, M. S. Bjornlie and K. Sessa (eds) *A Companion to Ostrogothic Italy*, Leiden, 173–202.
Harper, K. (2019) 'Invisible Environmental History: Infectious Disease in Late Antiquity', in A. Izdebski and M. Mulryan (eds) *Environment and Society in the Long Late Antiquity*, Leiden, 298–313.
Heinen, H. (2010) *Antike Sklaverei: Rückblick und Ausblick. Neue Beiträge zur Forschungsgeschichte und zur Erschliessung der archäologischen Zeugnisse*, Stuttgart.

Hilton, R. (1975) *The English Peasantry in the Later Middle Ages*, Oxford.
Hilton, R. (1976) 'A Comment', in G. Lefebvre, G. Procacci, J. Merrington, C. Hill, E. Hobsbawm, M. Dobb, P. Sweezy and K. Takahashi, *The Transition from Feudalism to Capitalism*, Lincoln.
Hirschfeld, Y. (1997) 'Farms and Villages in Byzantine Palestine', in *DOP* 51: 33–71.
Hodges, R. (1988) *Primitive and Peasant Markets*, Oxford.
Horden, P. and N. Purcel (2000) *The Corrupting Sea: a Study of Mediterranean History*, Oxford.
Htun, M., F. R. Jensenius and J. Nelson-Nuñez (2019) 'Gender-Discriminatory Laws and Women's Economic Agency', *Social Politics: International Studies in Gender, State and Society* 26 (2): 193–222.
Humfress, C. (2007) *Orthodoxy and the Courts in Late Antiquity*, Oxford.
Hyams, P. R. (2017) 'Medieval Attitudes to Poverty: Amartya Sen and Serfdom without Strings?', in M. C. Miller and E. Wheatley (eds) *Emotions, Communities, and Difference in Medieval Europe: Essays in Honor of Barbara H. Rosenwein*, London, 181–206.
Innes, M. (2006) 'Land, Freedom and the Making of the Medieval West', *Transactions of the Royal Historical Society* 16: 39–74.
Jensen, M. and W. Meckling (1976) 'Theory of the Firm: Managerial Behavior, Agency Costs, and Ownership Structure', *Journal of Financial Economics* 3: 305–60.
Joshel, S. R. and Peterson, L. H. (2014) *The Material Lives of Roman Slaves*, Cambridge.
Jones, A. H. M. (1964) *The Later Roman Empire, 284–602*, Oxford.
Jones, A. H. M. (1974) *The Roman Economy*, Oxford.
Jones, G. D. B. (1963) 'Capena and the Ager Capenas: Part II', *PBSR* 21 (18): 100–58.
Kaplan, M. (1992) *Les hommes et la terre à Byzance du VIe au XIe siècle*, Paris.
Kaser, M. (1968) *Das römische Privatrecht*, vol. 1: *Das altrömische, das vorklassiche und das klassische Recht*, trans. Rolf Dannenbring, London.
Kehoe, D. (1988) *The Economics of Agriculture on Roman Imperial Estates in North Africa*, Göttingen.
Kehoe, D. (2007) *Law and the Rural Economy in the Roman Empire*, Ann Arbor.
Kehoe, D. (2015) 'Property Rights over Land and Economic Growth in the Roman Empire', in P. Erdkamp, K. Verboven and A. Zuiderhoek (eds) *Ownership and Exploitation of Land and Natural Resources in the Roman World*, Oxford, 88–106.
Kelly, C. (2004) *Ruling the Later Roman Empire*, Berkeley.
Kennell, S. A. H. (2000) *Magnus Felix Ennodius: a Gentleman of the Church*, Recentiores, Ann Arbor.
Kiser, E. (1999) 'Comparing Varieties of Agency Theory in Economics, Political Science, and Sociology: an Illustration from State Policy Implementation', *Sociological Theory* 17 (2): 146–70.
Kolendo, J. (1962) *Kolonat w Afryce izymskiej w I–II wieku jego geneza*, Warsaw.
Kolendo, J. (1973) *Le traité d'agronomie des Saserna*, Wrocław.
Kolendo, J. (1976) *Le colonat en Afrique sans le Haut-Empire*, Paris.
Koptev, A. V. (2004) 'The Raptor and the Disgraced Girl in Sidonius Apollinaris' *Epistula* V', *AncSoc* 34: 275–304.
Koptev, A. V. (2009) 'The Colonate in the *Theodosian Code* and Its Interpretation in the Breviary of Alaric', in J. Aubert and P. Blanchard (eds) *Droit, religion et société dans le Code Théodosien: Troisièmes Journées d'Étude sur le Code Théodosien Neuchâtel, 15–17 février 2007*, Geneva, 261–85.
Krause, J. U. (1987) *Spätantike Patronatsformen im Westen des Römischen Reiches*, Munich.
Lafferty, S. D. W. (2013) *Law and Society in the Age of Theodoric the Great: a Study of the Edictum Theodorici*, Cambridge.
Lapadula, E. (2012) *The Chora of Metaponto 4: the Late Roman Farmhouse at San Biagio*, Austin.

Launaro, A. (2012) 'Why, What and How to Compare: Site Trends and Population Dynamics in Roman Italy (200 BC–AD 100)', in P. Attema and G. Schörner (eds) *Comparative Issues in the Archaeology of the Roman Rural Landscape: Site Classification between Survey, Excavation and Historical Categories*, Portsmouth, RI, 117–32.
Le Goff, J. (1977) *Pour un autre Moyen Âge*, Paris.
Leach, E. (1973) 'Concluding Address', in C. Renfrew (ed.) *The Explanation of Culture Change: Models in Prehistory*, Pittsburgh.
Lehmann, T. (2004) *Paulinus Nolanus und die Basilica Nova in Cimitile/Nola*, Wiesbaden.
Lenski, N. (2017) 'Peasant and Slave in Late Antique North Africa, c.100–600 CE', in R. L. Testa (ed.) *Late Antiquity in Contemporary Debate*, Cambridge.
Lewit, T. (1991) *Agricultural Production in the Roman Economy A.D. 200–400*, Oxford.
Lewit, T. (2003) 'Vanishing Villas: What Happened to Elite Rural Habitation in the West in the 5th–6th c.?', *JRA* 16: 260–74.
Lewit, T. (2004) *Villas, Farms and the Late Roman Rural Economy (Third to Fifth Century)*, Oxford.
Lewit, T. (2005) 'Bones in the Bathhouse: Reevaluating the Notion of Squatters Occupation in 5th–7th Century Villas', in G. P. Brogiolo, A. Chavarría Arnau and M. Valenti (eds) *Dopo la fine delle ville: le campagne dal VI al IX secolo. 11º Seminario sul Tardo Antico e l'Alto Medioevo (Gavi 2004)*, Mantua, 251–62.
Ligt, L. de (1993) *Fairs and Markets in the Roman Empire: Economic and Social Aspects of Periodic Trade in a Pre-industrial Society*, Amsterdam.
Ligt, L. de and P. W. de Neeve (1988) 'Ancient Periodic Markets: Festivals and Fairs', *Athenaeum* 3–4: 391–416.
Lirb, H. J. (1993) 'Partners in Agriculture: the Pooling of Resources in Rural *societates* in Roman Italy', in H. Sancisi-Weerdenburg, H. C. Teitler and J. C. Gieben (eds) *De agricultura: In Memoriam Pieter Willem de Neeve (1945–1990)*, Amsterdam, 263–95.
Lizzi, R. (1990) 'Ambrose's Contemporaries and the Christianization of Northern Italy', *JRS* 80: 156–73.
Lo Cascio, E. (1997) *Terre, proprietari e contadini dell'impero romano*, Rome.
López-Sáez, J. A., S. Pérez-Díaz, D. Galop, F. Alba-Sánchez and D. Abel-Schaad (2019) 'A Late Antique Vegetation History of the Western Mediterranean in Context', in A. Izdebski and M. Mulryan (eds) *Environment and Society in the Long Late Antiquity*, Leiden, 83–104.
McCormick, M. (2001) *Origins of the European Economy: Communications and Commerce, A.D. 300–900*, Cambridge.
MacDonald, G. M. (1984) 'New Directions in the Economic Theory of Agency', *Canadian Journal of Economics* 17 (3): 415–40.
McLynn, N. B. (1994) *Ambrose of Milan: Church and Court in a Christian Capital*, Transformation of the Classical Heritage 22, Berkeley.
MacMullen, R. (1970) 'Market-Days in the Roman Empire', *Phoenix* 24: 333–41.
Macmullen, R. (1974) *Roman Social Relations 50 BC to AD 284*, New Haven.
Mannoni, T. (1983) 'Insediamenti poveri nella Liguria di età romana e bizantina', *Rivista di Studi Liguri* 49: 254–64.
Marazzi, F. (1998) 'The Destinies of the Late Antique Italies: Politico-economic Developments of the Sixth Century', in R. Hodges and W. Bowden (ed.) *The Sixth Century*, Leiden, 119–60.
Marazzi, F. (2010) 'Città, territorio ed economia nella tarda antichità.', in G. Traina (ed.) *Storia d'Europa e del Mediterranea: il mondo antico*, vol. 3: *L'ecumene romana*, part 7: *L'impero tardo-antico*, Rome, 651–96.
Marazzi, F. (2015) 'Una valle italiana fra tarda antichità e alto medioevo: il tessuto insediativo rurale delle valle del Volturne (Molise-Campania) fra IV e XII secolo. Prospettive di mutamento nella

longue durée', in F. Marazzi (ed.) *Civitas aliphana: Alife e il suo territorio nel Medioevo*, Cerro al Volturno, 103–44.

Massabó, B. (1999) *Dalla villa al Villaggio. Corti: scavo di un sito archeologico di età romana e altomedievale lungo il metanodoto del Ponente Ligure*, Genoa.

Massabó, B. (2004) *Albingaunum: itinerari archeologici di Albenga*, Genoa.

Meramveliotakis, G. (2018) 'New Institutional Economics: a Critique of Fundamentals and Broad Strokes towards an Alternative Theoretical Framework for the Analysis of Institutions', *Asian Journal of Social Science Studies* 3 (2): 50–64.

Michel, S. and H. Randriamanampisoa (2017) 'The Capability Approach as a Framework for Assessing the Role of Microcredit in Resource Conversion: the Case of Rural Households in the Madagascar Highlands', *Oxford Development Studies* 46 (2): 1–21.

Mirković, M. (1997) 'The Later Roman Colonate and Freedom', *TAPhS* 87 (2): i–viii + 1–144.

Mitterauer, M. (1973) 'La continuité des foires et la naissance des villes', *Annales: économies, sociétés, civilisations* 28: 711–34.

Moreland, J. (2010) *Archaeology, Theory and the Middle Ages*, London.

Morony, G. M. (2004) 'Economic Boundaries? Late Antiquity and Early Islam', *JESHO* 47: 166–94.

Moser, C. (1998) 'The Asset Vulnerability Framework: Reassessing Urban Poverty Reduction Strategies', *World Development* 26 (1): 1–19.

Motta, L. (1997) 'I paesaggi di Volterra nel Tardoantico', *Archeologia medievale* 24: 245–67.

Nambiar, S. (2021) 'Capabilities and Communities: a Perspective from Institutional Economics', *European Journal of Development Research* 33 (6): 1973–96.

North, D. C. (1977) 'Markets and Other Allocation Systems in History: the Challenge of Karl Polanyi', *Journal of European Economic History* 6: 703–16.

North, D. C. (1981) *Structure and Change in Economic History*, New York.

North, D. C. (1990) *Institutions, Institutional Change, and Economic Performance*, Cambridge.

Nussbaum, M. (1988) *Nature, Function, and Capability: Aristotle on Political Distribution*, Oxford.

Nussbaum, M. (2003) 'Capabilities as Fundamental Entitlements: Sen and Social Justice', *Feminist Economics* 9 (2–3): 33–59.

O'Halloran, B. (2019) *The Political Economy of Classical Athens*, Leiden.

Ørsted, P. (2004) 'To Be a *colonus* or Not to Be: the Colonate in the Valley of Segermes (Roman Tunisia)', *Pallas* 64: 91–8.

Pagano, M. (2009) 'Continuità insediativa delle ville nella Campania fra Tarda Antichità e Alto Medioevo', in C. Ebanista and M. Rotili (eds) *La Campania fra Tarda Antichità e Alto Medioevo: ricerche di archeologia del territorio (Atti della Giornata di Studio)*, Richerche e studi 49, Cimitile (Tavolario), 9–21.

Pallasse, M. (1955) 'Les tablettes Albertini intèressant-elles le colonat romain du Bas-Empire?', *RD* 4 (33): 267–81.

Panella, C. (1986) 'Le merci: produzioni, itinerari e destini', in A. Giardina (ed.) *Società romana e impero tardoantico*, vol. 3: *Le merci, gli insediamenti*, Rome, 431–59.

Panella, C. (1993) 'Merci e scambi nel Mediterraneo tardoantico', in A. Momigliano and A. Schiavone (eds) *Storia di Roma*, vol. 3: *L'età tardoantico*, part 2: *I luoghi e le culture*, Turin, 613–79.

Pasquali, G. (2008) *Sistemi di produzione agraria e aziende curtensi nell'Italia altomedievale*, Bologna.

Patterson, H. (2004) *Bridging the Tiber: Approaches to Regional Archaeology in the Middle Tiber Valley*, Archaeological Monographs of the British School at Rome 13, Rome.

Patterson, H. (2007) 'The Tiber Valley Project: Archaeology, Comparative Survey and History', in J. Haldon (ed.) *The Logistics of Medieval Warfare*, Leiden.

Patterson, H. and P. Arthur (1994) 'Ceramics and Early Medieval Central and Southern Italy: a Potted History', in R. Francovich and G. Noyé (eds) *La storia dell'alto medioevo italiano (VI–X secolo) alla luce dell'archeologia*, Florence, 409–41.

Patterson, H. and F. Coarelli (2008) *Mercator placidissimus. The Tiber Valley in Antiquity: New Research in the Upper and Middle River Valley. Rome 27–28 February 2004*, Rome.

Patterson, J. (1991) '*Villae* or *vici*?', in G. Barker and J. Lloyd (eds) *Roman Landscapes: Archaeological Survey in the Mediterranean Region*, London, 117–79.

Peebles, G. (2010) 'The Anthropology of Credit and Debt', *Annual Review of Anthropology* 39: 225–40.

Percival, J. (1969) '*P. Ital.* 3 and Roman Estate Management', in *Hommages à Marcel Renard*, vol. 2, Brussels, 607–15.

Perkins, B. W. (2000) 'Specialized Production and Exchange', in A. Cameron, B. W. Perkins and M. Whitby (eds) *The Cambridge Ancient History*, vol. 14, *Late Antiquity: Empire and Successors, A.D. 425–600*, Cambridge, 346–91.

Perkins, P. and I. Attolini (1987) 'An Etruscan Farm at Podere Tartuchino', *PBSR* 60: 71–134.

Petersen, L. H. (2009) 'Clothes Make the Man: Dressing the Roman Freedman Body', in T. Fögen and M. Lee (eds) *Bodies and Boundaries in Graeco-Roman Antiquity*, Berlin, 181–214.

Petersen, T. (1993) 'The Economics of Organization: the Principal–Agent Relationship', *Acta Sociologica* 36 (3): 277–93.

Pettegrew, D. (2001) 'Chasing the Classical Farmstead: Assessing the Formation and Signature of Rural Settlement in Greek Landscape Archaeology', *JMA* 14 (2): 189–209.

Phillipson, D. E. (1968) 'Development of the Roman Law of Debt Security', *Stanford Law Review* 20: 1230–48.

Porena, P. (2017) 'Le dinamiche di formazione della rendita agraria nell'Italia settentrionale del IV secolo e la morale economica di Ambrogio', in R. Passarella (ed.) *Ambrogio e la questione sociale*, Milan, 61–85.

Portass, R. (2021) 'Peasants, Market Exchange and Economic Agency in North-Western Iberia, c.850–c.1050', *P&P* 255 (1): 5–37.

Prendergast, R. (2005) 'The Concept of Freedom and Its Relation to Economic Development: a Critical Appreciation of the Work of Amartya Sen', *Cambridge Journal of Economics* 29: 1145–70.

Rathbone, D. (1991) *Economic Rationalism and Rural Society in Third-Century ad Egypt: the Heroninos Archive and the Appianus Estate*, Cambridge.

Reynolds, S. (1994) *Fiefs and Vassals: the Medieval Evidence Reinterpreted*, Oxford.

Rio, A. (2017) *Slavery after Rome, 500–1100*, Oxford.

Ripoll, G. and J. Arce (2000) 'The Transformation and End of the Roman *villae* in the West (4th–7th): Problems and Perspectives', in G. P. Brogiolo, N. Gauthier and N. Christie (eds) *Towns and Their Territories between Late Antiquity and the Early Middle Ages*, Leiden, 63–114.

Rosafio, P. (2002) *Studi sul colonato*, Bari.

Rosenstein, N. (2004) *Rome at War: Farms, Families and Death in the Middle Republic*, Chapel Hill.

Roskams, S. (2006) 'The Urban Poor: Finding the Marginalised', in W. Bowden, A. Gutteridge and C. Machado (eds) *Social and Political Life in Late Antiquity*, Late Antique Archaeology 3.1, Leiden, 487–531.

Ross, S. (1973) 'The Economic Theory of Agency: the Principal's Problem', *American Economic Review* 63 (2): 134–9.

Rossiter, J. (2007) 'Wine-Making after Pliny: Viticulture and Farming Technology in Late Antique Italy', in L. Lavan, E. Zanini and A. Sarantis (eds) *Technology in Transition A.D. 300–650*, Leiden, 93–118.

Rostovtzeff, M. (1926) *The Social and Economic History of the Roman Empire*, London.
Ruffini, G. R. (2018) *Life in an Egyptian Village in Late Antiquity: Aphrodito before and after the Islamic Conquest*, Cambridge.
Ruggini, L. C. (1961) *Economia e società nell' Italia Annonaria: rapporti fra agricoltura e commercio dal IV al VI secolo d. C.*, Milan.
Saggioro, F. (2004) 'Late Antique Settlement on the Plain of Verona', in W. Bowden, L. Lavan and C. Machado, *Recent Research on the Late Antique Countryside*, Leiden, 505–34.
Sarris, P. (2006a) *Economy and Society in the Age of Justinian*, Cambridge.
Sarris. P. (2006b) 'Continuity and Discontinuity in the Post-Roman Economy', *Journal of Agrarian Change* 6 (3): 400–13.
Sarris, P. (2009) 'Introduction: Aristocrats, Peasants and the Transformation of Rural Society, c.400–800', *Journal of Agrarian Change* 9 (1): 3–22.
Sarris, P. (2012) 'Large Estates and the Peasantry in Byzantium c.600–1100', *RBPh* 90 (2): 429–50.
Saumagne, C. (1937) 'Du rôle de l'*origo* et du census dans la formation du colonat romain', *Byzantion* 12: 487–581.
Savino, E. (2009) 'L'area vesuviana in età tardoantica: modalità insediative e strutture produttive', in G. F. De Simone and R. T. Macfarlane (eds) *Apolline Project*, vol. 1: *Studies on Vesuvius' North Slope and the Bay of Naples*, Provo, 240–7.
Scheidel, W. (2000) 'Slaves of the Soil', *JRA* 13: 727–32.
Scheidel, W. (2012) 'Approaching the Roman Economy', in W. Scheidel (ed.) *The Cambridge Companion to the Roman Economy*, Cambridge, 1–24.
Scheidel, W., I. Morris and R. Saller (2007) *The Cambridge Economic History of the Greco-Roman World*, Cambridge.
Schmidt-Hofner, S. (2017) 'Barbarian Migrations and Socio-economic Challenges to the Roman Landholding Elite in the Fourth Century CE', *Journal of Late Antiquity* 10 (2): 372–404.
Schoolman, E. M. (2017) '*Vir clarissimus* and Roman Titles in the Early Middle Ages: Survival and Continuity in Ravenna and the Latin West', *Medieval Prosopography* 32: 1–39.
Schulz, F. (1954) *Classical Roman Law*, Oxford.
Segrè, A. (1947) 'The Byzantine Colonate', *Traditio* 5: 103–33.
Sen, A. (1981) *Poverty and Famines: an Essay on Entitlement and Deprivation*, Oxford.
Sen, A. (1985) 'Well-Being, Agency and Freedom: the Dewey Lectures 1984', *JPh* 82 (4): 169–221.
Sen, A. (1987) *Commodities and Capabilities*, New Delhi.
Sen, A. (1992) *Inequality Reexamined*, Oxford.
Sessa, K. (2018) *Daily Life in Late Antiquity*, Cambridge.
Severy-Hoven, B. (2012) 'Master Narratives and Wall Painting of the House of the Vetii, Pompeii', *Gender and History* 24: 540–80.
Shaw, B. D. (1981) 'Rural Markets in North Africa and the Political Economy of the Roman Empire', *AntAfr* 17: 37–83.
Sirks, A. J. B. (1993) 'Reconsidering the Roman Colonate', *ZRG* 123: 331–69.
Sirks, A. J. B. (2008) 'The Colonate in Justinian's Reign', *JRS* 98: 120–43.
Squatriti, P. (2016) 'Barbarizing the Bel Paese: Environmental History in Ostrogothic Italy', in J. J. Arnold, M. S. Bjornlie and K. Sessa, *A Companion to Ostrogothic Italy*, Leiden, 390–424.
Stathakopoulos, D. C. (2005) *Famine and Pestilence in the Late Roman and Early Byzantine Empire: a Systematic Survey of Subsistence Crises and Epidemics*, Aldershot.
Ste. Croix, G. E. M. de (1983) *The Class Struggle in the Ancient Greek World*, London.
Tate, G. (1992) *Les campagnes de la Syrie du Nord*, Paris.
Taylor, C. (2017) *Poverty, Wealth and Well-Being: Experiencing penia in Democratic Athens*, Oxford.

Tjäder, J. O. (1954) *Die nichtliterarischen lateinischen Papyri Italiens aus der Zeit 445–700*, vol. 3: *Tafeln*, Lund.
Tjäder, J. O. (1955) *Die nichtliterarischen lateinischen Papyri Italiens aus der Zeit 445–700*, vol. 1: *Papyri 1–28*, Lund.
Tjäder, J. O. (1982) *Die nichtliterarischen lateinischen Papyri Italiens aus der Zeit 445–700*, vol. 2: *Papyri 29–59*, Lund.
Tedesco, P. (2018) 'The Missing Factor: Economy and Labor in Late Roman North Africa (400–600 CE)', *Journal of Late Antiquity* 11 (2): 396–431.
Tedesco, P. (2020) 'What Made a Peasantry: Theory and Historiography of Rural Labor in Byzantine Egypt', *Journal of Egyptian History* 13: 333–79.
Temin, P. (2012) 'The Contribution of Economics', in W. Scheidel (ed.) *The Cambridge Companion to the Roman Economy*, Cambridge, 45–70.
Terpstra, T. (2018) 'Neo-institutionalism in Ancient Economic History: the Road Ahead', in C. Ménard and M. M. Shirley (eds) *A Research Agenda for New Institutional Economics*, Cheltenham, 233–40.
Thompson, E. P. (1963) *The Making of the English Working Class*, London.
Thompson, F. H. (2003) *The Archaeology of Greek and Roman Slavery*, London.
Toubert, P. (1973) *Les structures du Latium médiéval*, vol. 1, Rome.
Trout, D. E. (2008) 'Cimitile, Nola, and the Transformation of the City in Late Antiquity', in M. De Matteis and C. Ebanista (eds) *Il complesso basilicale di Cimitile*, Naples, 53–71.
Uhalde, K. (2007) *Expectations of Justice in the Age of Augustine*, Philadelphia.
Van Oyen, A. (2016) 'Historicising Material Agency: from Relations to Relational Constellations', *Journal of Archaeological Method and Theory* 23: 354–78.
Van Oyen, A. (2020) 'Innovation and Investment in the Roman Rural Economy through the Lens of Marzuolo (Tuscany, Italy)', *P&P* 248: 3–40.
Van Ossel, P. and P. Ouzoulias (2000) 'Rural Settlement Economy in Northern Gaul in the Late Empire: an Overview and Assessment', *JRS* 13: 133–60.
Vera, D. (1983) 'Strutture agrarie e strutture patrimoniali nella tarda antichità: l'aristocrazia romana fra agricoltura e commercio', *Opus* 2 (2): 489–533.
Vera, D. (1986) 'Forme e funzioni della rendita fondiaria nella tarda antichità', in A. Giardina (ed.) *Società Rinaba e impero tardoantico*, vol. 1, Rome, 367–447.
Vera, D. (1993) 'Proprietà terriera e società rurale nell'Italia gotica', in *Teoderico il grande e i Goti d'Italia: Atti del XIII Congresso internazionale di studi sull'alto Medioevo, Milano, 2–6 novembre 1992*, Spoleto, 133–66.
Vera, D. (1997) 'Padroni, contadini, contratti: realia del colonato tardoantico', in E. Lo Cascio (ed.) *Terre, proprietari e contadini dell'impero romano: dall'affitto agrario al colonato tardoantico*, Rome, 185–224.
Vera, D. (1999) '*Massa fundorum*: forme della grande proprietà e poteri della città in Italia fra Costantino e Gregorio Magno', *MEFRA* 111–2: 991–1025.
Vera, D. (2005) 'I paesaggi rurali nel Meridione tardoantico: bilancio consuntivo e preventive', in G. Volpe and M. Turchiano (eds) *Paesaggi e insediamenti rurali in Italia meridionale fra tardoantico e altomedioevo*, Bari, 23–38.
Vera, D. (2010) 'Schiavi della terra nell'Italia tardo-antico', in P. Galetti (ed.) *La tarda antichità tra fonti scritte e archeologiche*, Bologna, 15–34.
Vera, D. (2012) 'Questioni di storia agraria tardoromana: schiavi, coloni, *villae*', in *AntTard* 20: 115–122.
Vera, D. (2014) 'Imperial Estates in Late Roman Southern Italy: Land Concentration and Rent Distribution', in A. M. Small (ed.) *Beyond Vagnari: New Themes in the Study of Roman South Italy*, Bari, 285–93.

Vera, D. (2020) *I doni di Cerere: storie della terra nella tarda antichità (strutture, società, economia)*, Turnhout.

Villeneuve, F. (1985) 'L'économie rurale et la vie des campagnes dans le Hauran antique', in J. M. Dentzer (ed.) *Hauran I*, Paris, 63–136.

Vivenza, G. (2012) 'Roman Economic Thought', in W. Scheidel (ed.) *The Cambridge Companion to the Roman Economy*, Cambridge, 25–44.

Volpe, G. (2018) 'Storia e archeologia globale dei paesaggi rurali in Italia fra Tardoantico e Medioevo', in G. Volpe (ed.), *Storia e archeologia globale dei paesaggi rurali in Italia fra Tardoantico e Medioevo*, Bari, 5–52.

Volpe, G. and M. Turchiano (2010) 'The Last Enclave: Rural Settlement in the 5th c. in Southern Italy: the Case of Apulia', in P. Delogu and S. Gasparri (eds) *Le trasformazioni del V secolo: l'Italia, i barbari e l'Occidente romano*, Turnhout, 531–77.

Watson, P. (2001) 'The Byzantine Period', in B. MacDonald, R. Adams and P. Bienkowski (eds) *The Archaeology of Jordan*, Sheffield, 461–502.

Weber, M. (1949 [1904]) 'Objectivity in Social Science and Social Policy', in E. A. Shils and H. A. Finch (ed. and trans.) *The Methodology of the Social Sciences*, New York, 49–112.

Weber, M. (1976) *The Agrarian Sociology of Ancient Civilizations*, London.

Webster, J. (2005) 'Archaeologies of Slavery and Servitude: Bringing New World Perspectives to Roman Britain', *JRA* 18: 161–79.

Whittaker, C. R. (1988) *Pastoral Economies in Classical Antiquity*, Cambridge.

Whittaker, C. R. and P. Garnsey (1998) 'Trade, Industry and the Urban Economy', in A. Cameron and P. Garnsey (eds) *The Cambridge Ancient History*, vol. 13, *The Late Empire, A.D. 337–425*, Cambridge, 312–37.

Whittow, M. (2013) 'How Much Trade Was Local, Regional and Inter-regional? A Comparative Perspective on the Late Antique Economy', in L. Lavan (ed.) *Local Economies? Production and Exchange of Inland Regions in Late Antiquity (2013)*, Leiden, 133–65.

Wickham, C. (1989) *Early Medieval Italy: Central Power and Local Society, 400–1000*, Ann Arbor.

Wickham, C. (1998) 'Gossip and Resistance among the Medieval Peasantry', *P&P* 160: 3–24.

Wickham, C. (2005) *Framing the Early Middle Ages: Europe and the Mediterranean, 400–800*, Oxford.

Williamson, O. E. (2000) 'The New Institutional Economics: Taking Stock, Looking Ahead', *Journal of Economic Literature* 38: 595–613.

Witcher, R. E. (2005) 'The Hinterlands of Rome: Settlement Diversity in the Early Imperial Landscape of Regio VII Etruria', in P. Attema, A. J. Nijboer and A. Zifferero (eds) *Papers in Italian Archaeology VI: Communities and Settlements from the Neolithic to the Early Medieval Period. Proceedings of the 6th Conference of Italian Archaeology, Held at the University of Groningen, Groningen Institute of Archaeology, the Nertherlands, April 15–17 2003*, British Archaeological Reports International Series 1452 (I), Oxford.

Witcher, R. E. (2006) 'Agrarian Spaces in Roman Italy: Society, Economy and Mediterranean Agriculture', *Arqueología espacial (Paisajes agrarios)* 26: 341–59.

Yasin, A. M. (2015) 'Shaping the Memory of Early Christian Cult Sites', in K. Galinksy and K. Lapatin (eds) *Cultural Memories in the Roman Empire*, Los Angeles, 116–33.

Zeller, B., C. West, F. Tinti, M. Stoffella, N. Schroeder, C. van Rhijn, S. Patzold, T. Kohl, W. Davies and M. Czock (2020) *Neighbours and Strangers: Local Societies in Early Medieval Europe*, Manchester.

10

THE HUMAN LANDSCAPE AND PALAEOECOLOGY OF LATE ROMAN ITALY

Edward M. Schoolman

Introduction

IN THE 1860s while on assignment as ambassador to Italy, the American polymath George Perkins Marsh (1801–82) wrote *Man and Nature: or, Physical Geography as Modified by Human Action*.[1] Although relatively well received as a call for conservation following its publication in 1864 (and subsequent editions to 1885), the book was 'rediscovered' and became a foundational work for geography and environmental history in the United States in the middle of the twentieth century, noted for highlighting human drivers of ecological change.[2] Marsh's reflections on how humans shaped the natural world were formed initially from his experiences growing up in Vermont, but his time in Italy provided the opportunity to think comparatively between the New World and Old – an experience that had a significant influence on his views.[3] But it was not just the Italy of the nineteenth century that helped form his perspective; Marsh was also fascinated by Italy's history as the centre of the Roman Empire. He posited a geographically deterministic reason for its success, and saw in its decline and fall the failures of ecological conservation through the effects of incompatible and damaging economic and political motivations on the resiliency of agricultural production.

Marsh's interest in Rome was not simply a passing fancy; he introduced *Man and Nature* by opening with a vignette on the strengths and conditions of the Roman Empire, and from its very first pages explored three elements: 'Natural Advantages of the Territory of the Roman Empire – Physical Decay of that Territory – Causes of the Decay'. The fruits of this empire, notably its diverse set of landscapes, flora and fauna, were harnessed by human efforts with the results of a 'natural advantage', claimed by Marsh. In the last edition, he stated:

---

[1] Marsh 1864. The book was simultaneously published in London and New York in 1864, and reprinted in New York again a decade later with further notes. Although Marsh died in 1881, in 1885 the work appeared once more with further corrections and emendations under the title *The Earth as Modified by Human Action: a Last Revision of 'Man and Nature'*.
[2] Lowenthal 1953; Gade 1983. Recent work has revised the 'discovery' of Marsh in the 1950s, and suggests a longer and more continuous influence, especially in the field of geography: Koelsch 2012.
[3] Hall 1998, 93–7.

centuries of preserving labor were expelling the wild vegetation, and fitting the earth for the production of more generous growths. Every loaf was eaten in the sweat of the brow. All must be earned by toil. But toil was nowhere else rewarded by so generous wages; for nowhere would a given amount of intelligent labor produce so abundant, and, at the same time, so varied returns of the good things of material existence.[4]

In Marsh's argument, the physical decay that affected the landscape was as stark as the abundance that the Roman Empire once produced, marked by a decline in population and production. Echoing ancient and late antique sources on plague, crisis and calamity, he described a world of environmental degradation to the point of ceasing to support the empire it once so fruitfully maintained, that beginning 'about the commencement of the Christian Era' the lands were 'completely exhausted of their fertility, or so diminished in productiveness, as, with the exception of a few favored oases that have escaped the general ruin, to be no longer capable of affording sustenance to civilized man'.[5]

Although deterministic in his attitudes, Marsh did not entirely assign the cause of Rome's environmental decay to 'geological causes' – such as climate change, for example – as it was equally the fault of human actions and policies that forced Roman territories to 'relapse into their original state' of primeval wood, unprofitable 'forest growth' or 'dry and barren wilderness'. He wrote that

Rome imposed on the products of agricultural labor, in the rural districts, taxes which the sale of the entire harvest would scarcely discharge; she drained them of their population by military conscription; she impoverished the peasantry by forced and unpaid labor on public works; she hampered industry and both foreign and internal commerce by absurd restrictions and unwise regulations. Hence, large tracts of land were left uncultivated, or altogether deserted, and exposed to all the destructive forces which act with such energy on the surface of the earth when it is deprived of those protections by which nature originally guarded it, and for which, in well-ordered husbandry, human ingenuity has contrived more or less efficient substitutes.[6]

Simply put, without the efforts of man, the land lost its productivity and, in a vicious cycle, ceased to support civilisation.

These attitudes about human policies and activities as central to ecological degradation to the point of political or social collapse are not without other historical parallels, and would find many proponents today. Overexploitation of natural resources, mismanagement of water, and even inflexibility in the management of complex landscapes all might have consequence for the communities living and relying on the land. And indeed, one might see issues like taxation, excess conscription, compulsory servile

---

[4] Marsh 1885, 2.
[5] Marsh 1885, 4.
[6] Marsh 1885, 6–7.

labour on public works, and the abandonment of once-productive landscapes within texts produced by and about the late Roman Empire.[7] Yet Marsh could never have realised that between his observations of nineteenth-century landscapes and reading classical texts that new ways of extrapolating the history of the changing ecology in specific areas could be determined, offering paradigms that correlate human descriptions of activities with actual results on the land.

Marsh was of course not alone in his assessments. Ellsworth Huntington (1876–1947), a Yale historian and proponent of climate determinism, posited that the depletion of the soil through adverse agricultural practices, along with climate change (he suggests that 'by the seventh century . . . the Mediterranean lands and western Asia apparently became more arid than at any other known period'), were central to Rome's decline.[8] Emilio Sereni (1907–71), the communist and anti-fascist politician and agricultural historian, centred some of his arguments on the same sorts of deterministic assumptions about the late Roman period (without the scientific racism so prominent in Huntington's conclusions).[9] His 1961 *Storia del paesaggio agrario italiano* was celebrated soon after its publication, and reached anglophone audiences in 1997 as *History of the Italian Agricultural Landscape*.[10] Sereni's commitment to a Marxian framework, as Paolo Squatriti noted, was the book's greatest strength (and root of some of its weakness), but through this perspective Sereni came to understand 'the intimate connection between landscape and social and economic processes'.[11] Like Marsh and Huntington, Sereni viewed the period of the late empire as one of 'deterioration of the agricultural landscape', a phrase he used in his chapter on the very same period. Rather than taxation or the levying of troops, he posited that the deterioration was the by-product of 'a restriction of cultivated land, and a growth in the extent of land that was uncultivated or given over to pasture' with the expansion of the imperially sponsored *saltus*, or wooded pasture land.[12] Sereni was also specific on the effects of the 'invasions' beginning in 410 with the sack of Rome by Alaric's Goths and continuing into the tenth century in various waves, that these only exacerbated a Roman society 'falling into economic decline and torn by deep social divisions'.[13] While these invasions destroyed urban life and left cities as empty relics, he observed that the new rural landscape was one in which 'livestock and hunting prevailed over agriculture'.

These sweeping statements about decline and degradation, however, have not fared well. Revisiting literary and epigraphic sources, new archaeological excavations and surveys and novel methodologies applying palaeoecological records have rewritten

---

[7] Depending on discipline and perspectives, some of these issues have faded from scholarly focus while others remain current: for example, A. H. M. Jones advocated for both changing patterns of conscription and increased taxation as causes of decline. Jones 1955; 1959.
[8] Huntington 1917, 189. He further argued that the change in climate began c.250, and had an 'appreciable effect upon the energy and ability of the Roman people' due to their racial disposition (p. 207). On his theories as a part of the larger discourse of climate as an element of Roman decline, see Sessa 2019, 212.
[9] On the intellectual influences on Sereni's academic works, see Ferretti 2015.
[10] Sereni 1997.
[11] Squatriti 1999, 198.
[12] Sereni 1997, 44.
[13] Sereni 1997, 47.

much of what we understand about the interactions between humans and the late Roman landscape. First, general notions about the whole of the Roman Empire (as in the case of Marsh) or even Italy (as in the case of Sereni, whose later chapters make clear the substantial differences between areas of the peninsula) are almost impossible to make; both historical and archaeological records support the notion that, as summarised by Paul Arthur, 'a general pattern of rural occupation and land use valid for all of Italy' is incredibly hard to make.[14] Second, notions of decline of various types have been eroded by evidence for continuities or simply shifts in priorities that reshaped how land was managed. At social and cultural levels, this is manifest in the rise of 'Late Antiquity' as a periodisation, elevating transitions and transformations over declines and discontinuities; in terms of 'declines' in the landscapes, as Adam Izdebski has surveyed, examining the patterns of vegetation that flourished on the managed landscapes of the Roman world makes clear that 'it is impossible to detect a single trajectory that one could describe as irreversibly damaging the environment'.[15] The return to wilderness or rise of degradation that might have been reflected in top-down historical accounts is simply impossible to find either with a wide-angled lens or elsewhere in the ecological record.

Recent articles and collected volumes on landscape and environment have included studies that are highly focused around sites, local areas, regions, or centred on specific phenomena or methodologies, and in their resolution and specificity we can now begin to see many different types of changes across the varied landscapes that were part of the Roman world. These studies have included collections on rural landscapes in the post-Roman world,[16] a focus on various aspects of the environment or methodological approaches through the ancient Mediterranean,[17] and on site- or event-specific environmental phenomena in Late Antiquity.[18]

These examples represent a small portion of an ever increasing number of climatological and ecological records that are now being employed to make sense of the late Roman world. Some of these examples are at very large scales, such as the effects of certain dramatic or long-term changes in climate – like volcanic forcing or the Roman climate optimum – while others are far more local. In this contribution, I will concentrate on local conditions by presenting surveys of three regions (the eastern Po, the Rieti basin and Sicily) as broadly representative of northern, central and southern Italy, with the Po using primarily palaeoecological records extrapolated from fossilised pollens and similar data set against the contexts from written and archaeological sources. The interpretation of pollen data in this way is analogous to any other sort of historical record where context, scale and resolution all matter, as does the interdisciplinarity approach that is required. Specifically for this case, I am writing as a historian contextualising and bringing together the work of many scientists, often within frameworks and contexts clarified by archaeologists. The results of this foray into a

---

[14] Arthur 2004, 103.
[15] Izdebski 2018, 7.
[16] Christie 2004.
[17] Harris 2013.
[18] Izdebski and Mulryan 2018.

consilience-driven approach underscore that these regions differed in how their landscapes changed over the course of the late Roman period, sometimes dramatically.[19] These results also demonstrate not just the ways in which agriculture, open lands and woodlands were managed, but the strategies those living in these areas employed when faced with the changes and stresses of the late Roman period. Although their voices may be silent, this history reflects patterns of life of those living in rural contexts, outside of those whose lives and activities are more often recorded.

In reading the palaeoecological records of late Roman Italy, both Marsh and Sereni would have discovered that rather than decay and decline, the period from the first to the fifth century was remarkably stable in most areas despite political unrest, economic shocks and even changes in settlement patterns. Yet the world of late Roman Italy in 450 looked quite unlike that in 200: the changes in patterns of land management would have reinforced the human-centred perspective of Marsh, although likely to different conclusions, while buttressing the interrelationships between the economy, society and agrarian practices underscored by Sereni.

The Rieti Basin

Perhaps nowhere in central Italy can the ecological stability of the late Roman period be better observed than in the Rieti basin, an intermontane plain of 90 km^2 tucked between the Sabine hills and the Apennine mountains north-east of Rome, marked on its southern border by the ancient Via Salaria. Since the third century BC, the area had been dramatically reshaped by human actions, the first of which was the cutting of a channel through the limestone at the north end of the basin to drain the large, shallow lake (known as the Lacus Velinus) and creating a series of smaller bodies of water, meadows and cultivated lands around the Velino River.[20] This act of land reclamation was undertaken by the consul Manius Curius Dentatus in 271 BC, and it reshaped the hydrology of the basin, eventually leading to greater flows north during times of flood.[21] This condition eventually led to a millennium-long dispute between the citizens of Terni (a city at the confluence of the Velino and Nera rivers) and those of Rieti, the origins of which are articulated by Cicero in his *Letters to Atticus*.[22]

The drained land of the basin did not go unused, and the second century AD sees the area under full habitation. Archaeological evidence uncovered from a survey of the British School in Rome between one of the main lakes, Lago Lungo, and the foothills to its east, points to the occupation of several settlements and estates, some which had been consolidated into villas that remained in use throughout the entire period under

---

[19] The notion of consilience here is in research that balances archaeology, history and data from the natural sciences in meaningful ways: Izdebski et al. 2016; Haldon et al. 2018.

[20] This effort was known to Marsh: he refers to the 'celebrated cascade' formed by the cut of the Velino south of Terni, noting that the falls owe, if 'not their existence, at least their position and character, to the diversion of their waters from their natural beds into new channels, in order to obviate the evils produced by their frequent floods'. Marsh 1885, 402.

[21] Aldrete 2007, 186–7.

[22] Cicero served as advocate for Rieti in later aspects of the dispute: *Att.* 4.15.5.

discussion here. In the area covered by the survey of 22 square kilometers (representing just a small, but diverse, fraction of the region), ceramic evidence suggests that this area of the basin maintained twenty-six inhabited sites dating from the second and third centuries, but it witnessed a sharp drop in the number of sites in the period of the fourth to sixth centuries – a decline that corresponded to a decrease in the presence of imported wares. More succinctly, the survey observed that 'no imported pottery of any kind was found that could be dated unequivocally beyond the AD 440s' although there were clearly productions of various local ceramics.[23] Despite the material evidence for the loss of trade and the transformation of settlements between the third and sixth centuries, a fuller picture of the archaeological record points to a landscape that was still intensely utilised, with both pasture lands near the lakes and agriculture on the slopes of the lower basin.[24]

We do not have to rely solely on interpretations of material remains or on the sparse written descriptions. As part of a team of geographers, geophysicists, forestry specialists and historians, our recent work has included a focused reading of historical accounts and the survey's archaeological findings against a high-resolution history of the ecology of the basin left in the fossil pollen and spores found in the stratified sediment at the bottom of the basin's lakes, notably Lago Lungo.[25] These records stand as a proxy for the vegetation surrounding the basin, where changes in percentages of trees (serving to indicate woodland) or cereals and grasses (as representing more open landscapes dedicated to agriculture or pasture) point to different land management strategies. Combined with other data, they offer a view not only of the state of the environment, but the drivers of its change.

An examination of the history of the ecology of the basin through the pollen presents no evidence of a mid-Imperial-period agrarian crisis (like the one highlighted by Marsh) that seemed to have afflicted other areas in central Italy.[26] Research on the periodisation of the settlements beyond the immediate basin, such as the villas at San Lorenzo (Cittareale) to the east and Cottanello to the west, demonstrate Augustan-age villas partially abandoned in the third century, with renewed occupation from the fourth to the sixth century.[27] Further afield, archaeological evidence points to a

---

[23] Coccia and Mattingly 1992, 260.
[24] Coccia and Mattingly 1992, 274–5.
[25] On work relating to Lago Lungo, see Mensing et al. 2015; Mensing et al. 2018; Schoolman et al. 2019. Research on Lago Vientina at the northern edge of the basin between two upland areas has recently been undertaken, with the preliminary results suggesting that the area was also used intensively during the period from the third to the sixth century, but with different fluctuations indicative of different agricultural and land management practices. Dingemans 2019.
[26] As proposed by Gian Pietro Brogiolo, this 'crisis' appears in the framework of the occupation of villas in many parts of Italy, where villas were abandoned or greatly diminished in the second and third centuries, but with some recovery in the fourth followed by decline and re-adaption through to the sixth century: Brogiolo 1983. A number of other works have revisited this thesis over time adding significant nuance; for example, the final phases of villa occupation or abandonments are not necessarily economic, but rather 'political, socio-cultural, and conceptual' in parallel with changes in urban patterns: Lewit 2003, 267.
[27] Coarelli et al. 2012; Sfameni 2018.

settlement crisis that took hold in the *ager Cosanus* and areas around Cosa in southern Tuscany, perhaps related to economic changes and a decrease in wine exports.[28]

Instead, the pollen diagrams from Lago Lungo, the largest lake in the basin, present a view of a relatively consistent landscape balanced between forest and open spaces, with diversity in tree species, actively used meadows and pastures, and zones of agricultural activities, all under human management. Although there are some small shifts in percentages, these took place over decades, and for the most part the landscape remained consistent from the beginning of the first century to the sixth century. In Fig. 10.1, which depicts the common type of pollen diagram based on multiple core samples from Lago Lungo, the period from 250–500 depicts the stability of the landscape, clearest in signals for ferns and *Glomus* and *Sporormiella* spores, which are all indicative of animal husbandry activities. In this case, for nearly six centuries there is evidence of animals being raised along Lago Lungo at relatively consistent levels. The most interesting aspect here is that, while a balance between woodland and open landscapes was generally maintained (with a slow loss of woodland and expansion of pasture to the end of the third century), in the fifth century dominant tree species that occupied different ecological niches (beech and oaks) declined while grasses appeared in greater numbers.

The entire shift took place gradually over a century (and following a decrease in alder, a tree species that grows in marsh and riparian environments, that may have been related to greater drought conditions or other human efforts at hydrological

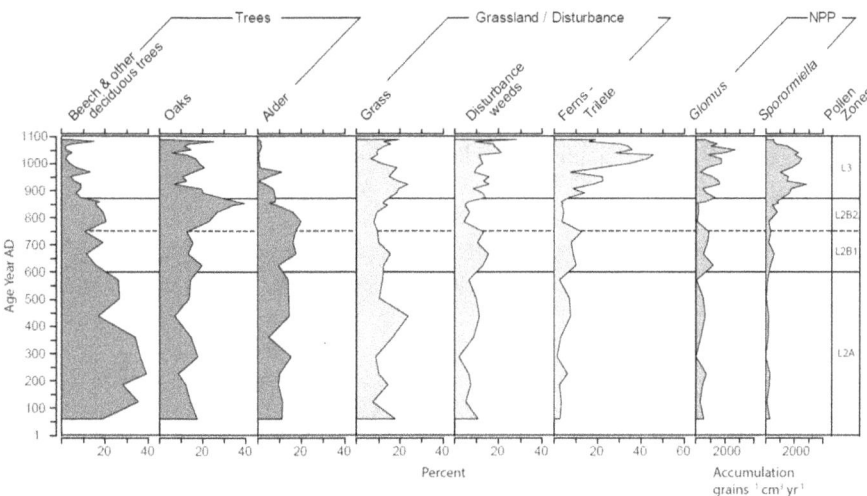

Figure 10.1 Summary pollen diagram and selected non-pollen palynomorphs (NPP) from Lago Lungo, Rieti basin. (Diagram by Gianluca Piovesan)

---

[28] Fentress and Perkins 2016, 496. Cosa remains a good parallel to Rieti, as both cities were closely interconnected to the hinterlands and were established under similar circumstances. Cosa was founded in 273 BC, just two years before the draining of the Velino.

management). The clearing of oaks and beech, and their temporary replacement of grasslands, seem to have been contemporary to the shifts in settlements, and more specifically, in both the declining quality of the ceramics of the 440s and threats of raids and political instability. Following the 450s, while settlements would remain abandoned and pottery would no longer be imported, the landscape would return to its pre-fifth-century state by the year 500.[29]

Later, more dramatic shifts underscore the fact that the Rieti basin does not witness the economic downturn visible in Cosa, or an unmanaged forest and 'dry and barren wilderness' as imagined by Marsh. Compared to later events, such as the demographic shocks of the Black Death and the coincidental cooling of the late antique Little Ice Age that indeed withdrew human management of the land, in the late Roman period the evidence demonstrates a persistence of a mixed landscape, not in a 'natural' state, but rather one that was carefully managed by the Romans living on the land who sought to maximise the benefits they could extract. Despite whatever political or economic tumult was affecting the area in the fifth century, as reflected in the shift towards a cleared landscape, the efforts of those working the land were supported by relatively stable climate patterns, temperatures and annual precipitation.

Sicily

Covering more than 25,000 km^2 and boasting several topographically distinct regions as it does, describing the managed landscapes of Sicily demands different tools and scales of interpretation. Unlike the small and relatively closed montane basin of Rieti, where the stratified pollen was collected at the edge of the lake, the sites of palaeoecological data in Sicily are found from across the island, often in areas with clear records of human habitation but without archaeological surveys and excavations (which have been focused elsewhere). Practically speaking, this makes the correlations between direct human activities and the history of land use more speculative. However, the rich evidence from the island makes it a valuable resource, especially when viewed comparatively across different sites and disciplinary foci – a practice made easier by new research efforts.[30]

While there are several locations that have been studied on a human time scale, one of the best examples reveals a pattern of slow deforestation in Sicily across the entire late Roman period (250–500). Lago di Pergusa, located in the centre of the island 5 km south of the city of Enna, has produced a record of the local vegetation that reflects cereal agriculture and the production of grapes and olives, along with other species.[31] Following the beginning of a more humid period after 450, rye

---

[29] The period after 550 would see less persistence of late Roman patterns in favour of a landscape with a greater emphasis on silvo-pastoralism, in which wooded areas coexisted with open spaces, and both served to support larger numbers of livestock (likely pigs). In the case of Rieti, see Schoolman et al. 2019. More generally, see Lewit 2009; Kreiner 2017.

[30] A survey of the research in general appears in Sadori et al. 2016.

[31] The most recent analysis of the evidence from Pergusa appears in Sadori et al. 2016. Previous analysis, although at a much greater chronological scale and focused on earlier periods, appeared in Sadori et al. 2008; Sadori et al. 2013. A discussion of the data from the lake in the context of nearby archaeological evidence appears in Montecchi and Mercuri 2018, 751–3.

becomes more prevalent, as part of a larger pattern of oaks and other tree species being replaced by plant species representative of more open landscapes.[32]

Not only does this pattern differ significantly from what was taking place in Rieti, the presence of rye at notable concentrations after 450 offers a remarkable window into the ways in which agricultural choices were part of larger 'ecological footprints' left by Rome as it underwent political and economic changes. Historians have offered conflicting versions of the appearance of this grain: in a larger consideration of ancient climate, Michael McCormick has posited that the increase in the cultivation of rye, which had been previously been valued for its cold-hardiness as a winter grain, may in fact be attributed to the crop's drought tolerance in a period with uncertain spring rains.[33] Yet, while many areas of the empire experienced patterns of drought and Europe was generally warming, the data is either especially localised (in the form of tree-ring dendrochronology) or part of multi-proxy studies with relatively low resolution.[34] Much of the evidence for climate patterns specific to Sicily is often extrapolated from fossil pollens, in which case it becomes very difficult to untangle the main drivers of landscape changes (human as opposed to climate). However, the data derived from isotopes supports the notion that for Sicily, the three-hundred-year period beginning in 450 was one of greater precipitation and relatively cooler temperatures favourable to intensification of agriculture.[35] In another recent study, Paolo Squatriti observes that the evidence from Pergusa 'complicates the "climatic hypothesis" for rye's ascendancy' because of the political stability and local climate of Sicily, and suggests that local agricultural strategies were at work. He argues that rye was established first as an alternative crop, then valued as a potential export to Constantinople.[36] While it is possible that in other regions of the empire rye emerged for its hardiness, this may be true in a broader sense, but in the case of Sicily other social and economic factors were at play.

Beyond the question of the development of rye as a staple grain, the long-term increase in grain over other taxa is visible not only in Pergusa but in other sites across Sicily, and traces an intensification of production that is also reflected in the island's archaeological record (at least in its inland areas).[37] Research undertaken on the lake of Gorgo Basso on Sicily's western coast has presented in general a case that mirrored Pergusa, with a decline in woodland species over the same period of roughly 200–600.[38] Given that Gordo Basso was somewhat far from other settlements (the closest major city was Selinus more than 20 km away, and a city that

---

[32] Sadori et al. 2016, 177–8.
[33] McCormick 2013, 82–3.
[34] The proxies for fourth-century warming are often quite geographically disparate, ranging from Greenland sea ice and various speleothems to Alpine dendrodata and glaciers. McCormick et al. 2012, 186.
[35] Erdkamp 2019, 452–3. This article also presents a clear and concise critique of the multi-proxy-driven methodology and the role of climate in Late Roman history.
[36] Squatriti 2018, 345.
[37] This intensification survived (and perhaps was perpetuated by) the Vandal raids of the fifth century, especially in inland areas. Vaccaro 2013, 265–72.
[38] Tinner et al. 2009. Gorgo Basso is one of four lakes within very close proximity of each other; these, along with another lake in southern Sicily, all bear witness to the fact that the landscape of pastures and fields began with the Bronze Age, marked by intense use of the landscape and the introduction of new species to the area (like chestnuts) in the period between 700 and 300 BC. Noti et al. 2009, 384.

reached its height at the end of the fifth century BC as a Greek colony), it reflects perhaps a more 'rural' context than Pergusa. Other studies of the sedimentary fossilised pollen are often presented with chronological resolutions too low to incorporate into historical and archaeological contexts, measured in scales of centuries or more rather than decades. Lago Preola, for example, has a decrease in wooded areas from roughly 1–500, with shrubs making up the majority rather than grasses, although the scale of recent studies there does not offer resolution that may foster greater analysis for this particular period.[39]

Returning to the site of Pergusa, its location offers another vantage point for understanding how patterns may have changed in land management. The lake is relatively close to one of the best-known late Roman settlements of Sicily, Piazza Armerina, and the nearby settlement of Villa del Casale, in which several recent palaeoecological studies have been undertaken, focused on pollen evidence from archaeological contexts rather than lake sediment.[40] But like those from the sedimentary lake cores, these studies have reconfirmed a late Roman landscape that was generally open rather than wooded, and became more so during this period. They also included a great diversity of plants, including several high-value cultivated species at Villa del Casale including olives, chestnuts and even ornamental varieties (although at very low percentages), while at Piazza Armerina pollen evidence further points to edible fruits, cereals and pasture, all markers of a 'non-urban but highly anthropized land'.[41]

The persistence of land use towards less forested areas, greater cultivation of grains, and areas for pasture across Sicily seems to be relatively unaffected by external disruptions, although Vandal raids beginning in 440, with intermittent occupation until 476, caused some small settlements to be abandoned. These events are described in the chapters by Mark Humphries (Chapter 3) and Jeroen Wijnendaele (Chapter 4) in this volume, but for the most part the archaeological and economic evidence suggests that in general the area remained healthy and productive.[42] This continuity is reinforced by the general patterns of occupation in Sicily's villas during this period. The work of Angelo Castrorao Barba has plotted two trends: the first was of a 'quantitative increase of the sites, growth of the size of some settlements at the expense of others no longer frequented and monumentalization of residential villas' in the fourth and fifth centuries, followed by new types of occupations and functionality at those same locations until the eighth century.[43] Until the sixth century, emphasis on agriculture and open spaces continued to be the dominant pattern in sites throughout Sicily; yet, as the rise in rye in the middle of the fifth century suggests, land was managed actively, with new crops being cultivated in response to changes in the broader economic, social and cultural contexts.

---

[39] Calò et al. 2012, 323–5.
[40] Montecchi and Mercuri 2018; Mercuri et al. 2019, 499.
[41] Mercuri et al. 2019, 30–1.
[42] Clover 1999; Merrills and Miles 2010, 129–39, esp. 131.
[43] Castrorao Barba 2016, 171.

The Po

Anchoring a massive basin, the Po River extends 650 km, passing from Turin in the Piedmont region on its way to the Adriatic, where it serves as the boundary between the Veneto and Emilia Romagna. Its history has shaped all of northern Italy, serving as both a route for transportation and source of irrigation. Simultaneously, the river was shaped by human activities which became the dominant driver of fluvial dynamics in the Roman period.[44] Given its extent and the various regions that were connected to the river, as with the case of Sicily, it is difficult to make the same kinds of specific cases. Furthermore, unlike the relatively stable lakes in Sicily and the Rieti basin, the course of the Po has changed regularly, especially in the delta regions on the Adriatic coast. But even further inland, the frequent carving of new channels has left few standing bodies of water undisturbed; in their place, the Po basin contained large areas of marsh and wetlands.

Despite these difficulties, some areas have produced pollen, measurable either from archaeological excavations or wetland pollen sampling, which shape our thinking about how this broad landscape extending from the northern foothills of the Apennines to the Alps may have been managed. Work on pollen samples from Modena (ancient Mutina) and its immediate hinterland has produced high-resolution records that enable palaeoenvironmental reconstructions.[45] Here, rather than witnessing the decreased forestation that was widespread in Sicily, the areas around the city changed in a very different way. Before the third century, the area was dominated by marshland with other areas of oak woods, patches of chestnut and fir, and cultivated grain; at the beginning of the third century, and continuing into the fifth and sixth centuries, woodlands increased and encroached upon the outskirts of the urban core.

Rather than human factors leading to the rise of woodlands, closer examination of the pollen data, specifically from the third to sixth centuries, suggests that unmitigated flooding and the expansion of wetlands were the primary drivers of this local change.[46] One of the more interesting results we see is that although major flooding had occurred, notably at the end of the third to the beginning of the fourth century, this only seemed to expand wetlands; the flooding at the end of the fourth century resulted in a very different response, one in which trees, especially the riparian and wetlands-dependent alder, increased substantially. While some studies of the growing backswamps around the Po of the fifth century allude to failures of human management in the wake of the political 'end' of the western Roman Empire, the populations of these areas adapted to the new environment by 'settling in positions of higher elevation around the swamp limits and using them for navigation as well as for silvopastoral sustenance practices'.[47] I would argue that the same could be said for late Roman Modena – rather than work to restore the earlier landscape, its inhabitants who laboured in the extra-urban rural lands may have adapted, and even preferred, this slightly more waterlogged countryside.

---

[44] Marchetti 2002. On the networks of Roman canals and their use for transport, see Lawrence 1999.
[45] Bosi et al. 2015.
[46] Bosi et al. 2019.
[47] Brandolini and Cremaschi 2018.

A short overview of other areas demonstrates, however, the exceptional diversity of land management techniques and preferences during the late Roman period. Like Modena almost directly to its south, the city of Mantua, on a tributary of the Po known as the Mincio, also left a record of its palaeoenvironment in the form of a historic lake. Its pollen illustrates a general pattern of Roman forest-clearing in favour of more open land, and after the sixth century, the 'recovery' of early medieval forest. Among some of the other interesting features, we find the appearance of chestnuts and rye in the late Roman period just as we did in Sicily.[48]

Although beyond the geographic purview of this contribution, other work on the Italian peninsula, such as in Tuscany, has continued to expand our understanding of the diverse ecological systems managed under the late Roman period. Work on Pisa and its harbour has brought to light both the effects and causes of catastrophic flooding in the late Roman period as well as new insights into the surrounding landscape as the waterways were affected by silt at the end of the fifth century and into the sixth century.[49] As the palaeoenvironment of other locations can be reconstructed for the late Roman period, these examples from the Po and Pisa will further tie together not only past agricultural practices, but the ways in which land management affected and was in turn influenced by geographic features – in these cases, rivers.

Conclusion

In concluding this chapter, it is worth making two points about what this kind of data offers. First, using past vegetation as a proxy for what existed in managed landscapes is helpful as a balance or corrective source to historical and archaeological assumptions, and more specifically, it offers a window into how those living on the land reacted to external pressures – political, economic or even from climate. Their story is one that is slowly being uncovered through and elevated in works like *The Roman Peasant Project* and Cam Grey's *Constructing Communities in the Late Roman Countryside*, for which continued analysis of archaeobotanical data adds to our understanding of their capabilities as communities.[50]

It is also worthwhile to note the resilience of the communities discussed here – those of inland Sicily or the Rieti basin or the hinterland of Modena; all faced significant pressures. In their responses, we can see the adoption of new agricultural products, continuity in the balances between open land and woods, and adaptation to radically changed landscapes all as part of the diversity of responses. More importantly, these are not top-down decisions, and although they may be influenced by economic or political incentives, they were still independent of them – a factor that contributes to this kind of rural and agricultural resiliency. This is not to say that there was not a rural aristocracy, or an urban one with rural holdings, but rather that the decline of those groups seems not to have had a significant impact on the ways in which the land was managed.[51] A

---

[48] Ravazzi et al. 2013.
[49] Benvenuti et al. 2006; Kaniewski et al. 2018; Sadori et al. 2015.
[50] Bowes 2020; Grey 2011.
[51] This would run counter to arguments made in Banaji 2011.

telling example of this kind of resiliency may be seen in the efforts to continue inhabiting the slopes of Mount Vesuvius: on the western flank at the site of Pollena Trocchia, not just after 79, but also after the eruptions of 472 and 512, in which settlements were rebuilt reusing visible and available materials in an area that had been totally destroyed by volcanic eruption.[52]

The second point about this data is that even within the last five years of collaborative projects and consilience-driven research, it is still possible to say that 'archaeobotanical research on Italian sites of Roman age is rather scarce and not systematic'.[53] Locating sites, taking core samples, counting pollen and measuring isotopes are all difficult and time-consuming, made more complicated by the necessity to work directly with historians and archaeologists. What has been presented here is just an incomplete snapshot, but one that suggests the possibilities that will emerge.

Finally, it is worth considering how more data about the late Roman environment, especially when considered locally or regionally, might influence not just the period from the crisis of the third century to the political decentralisation of the fifth century, but how factors changed in the sixth century as well. Over the past decade, the impact of the continent-wide late antique Little Ice Age, catalysed by volcanic climate forcing, and the arguably related epidemic of the Justinianic plague, have been seen as leading causes for the 'fall' of the western Roman Empire, or as having strained the eastern empire (notably in the work of Kyle Harper).[54] Yet, because of the interest in the plague and climate change, there has been far less work on the period of the Roman Empire before the sixth century. Looking towards this period, future collaborative research can offer remarkable stories of local resilience and continuity in the management and use of environmental resources in the face of multiple dramatic political, cultural and economic changes. In order to tell these narratives, however, written and archaeological evidence are insufficient on their own; these sources must be read against the history of the landscape preserved in the ecological record.

Bibliography

Aldrete, G. S. (2007) *Floods of the Tiber in Ancient Rome*, Baltimore.
Arthur, P. (2004) 'From Vicus to Village: Italian Landscapes, AD 400–1000', in N. Christie (ed.) *Landscapes of Change: Rural Evolutions in Late Antiquity and the Early Middle Ages*, Aldershot, 111–22.
Banaji, J. (2011) *Agrarian Change in Late Antiquity: Gold, Labour, and Aristocractic Dominance*, Oxford.
Benvenuti, M., M. Mariotti-Lippi, P. Pallecchi and M. Sagri (2006) 'Late-Holocene Catastrophic Floods in the Terminal Arno River (Pisa, Central Italy) from the Story of a Roman Riverine Harbour', *The Holocene* 16: 863–76.

---

[52] Scarpati et al. 2016.
[53] Sadori et al. 2015, 218.
[54] Harper 2017. Evidence of environmental data does not seem to fit this model, while recent reevaluations of the pandemic's effects have cast some doubt as to its impact: Mordechai et al. 2019. See also Sessa 2019.

Bosi, G., A. M. Mercuri, M. Bandini Mazzanti, A. Florenzano, M. C. Montecchi, P. Torri, D. Labate and R. Rinaldi (2015) 'The Evolution of Roman Urban Environments through the Archaeobotanical Remains in Modena – Northern Italy', *Journal of Archaeological Science* 53: 19–31.

Bosi, G., D. Labate, R. Rinaldi, M. C. Montecchi, M. Mazzanti, P. Torri, F. M. Riso and A. M. Mercuri (2019) 'A Survey of the Late Roman Period (3rd–6th Century AD): Pollen, NPPs and Seeds/Fruits for Reconstructing Environmental and Cultural Changes after the Floods in Northern Italy', *Quaternary International* 499: 3–23.

Bowes, K. (ed.) (2020) *The Roman Peasant Project 2009–2014: Excavating the Roman Rural Poor*, 2 vols, Philadelphia.

Brandolini, F. and M. Cremaschi (2018) 'The Impact of Late Holocene Flood Management on the Central Po Plain (Northern Italy)', *Sustainability* 10: 3968.

Brogiolo, G. P. (1983) 'La campagna dalla tarda antichità al 900 ca. d. C.', *Archeologia medievale* 10: 73–88.

Calò, C., P. D. Henne, B. Curry, M. Magny, E. Vescovi, T. La Mantia, S. Pasta, B. Vannière and W. Tinner (2012) 'Spatio-temporal Patterns of Holocene Environmental Change in Southern Sicily', *Palaeogeography, Palaeoclimatology, Palaeoecology* 323–5: 110–22.

Castrorao Barba, A. (2016) 'Sicily before the Muslims: the Transformation of the Roman Villas between Late Antiquity and the Early Middle Ages, Fourth to Eighth Centuries CE', *Journal of Transcultural Medieval Studies* 3: 145–60.

Christie, N. (ed.) (2004) *Landscapes of Change: Rural Evolutions in Late Antiquity and the Early Middle Ages*, London.

Clover, F. M. (1999) 'A Game of Bluff: the Fate of Sicily after A.D. 476', *Historia* 48: 235–44.

Coarelli, F., S. Kay, H. Patterson, L. Tripaldi and V. Scalfari (2012) 'Archaeological Fieldwork Reports: Excavations at Falacrinae (Cittareale, Rieti) 2011', *PBSR* 80: 362–5.

Coccia, S. and D. J. Mattingly (1992) 'Settlement History, Environment and Human Exploitation of an Intermontane Basin in the Central Apennines: the Rieti Survey 1988–1991, Part I', *PBSR* 60: 213–89.

Dingemans, T. (2019) *An Intersection of Climate, History and Landscape Use: 3000 Years of Central Italian Environmental Change*, Doctoral dissertation, University of Nevada.

Erdkamp, P. (2019) 'War, Food, Climate Change, and the Decline of the Roman Empire', *Journal of Late Antiquity* 12: 422–65.

Fentress, E. and P. Perkins (2016) 'Cosa and the *Ager Cosanus*', in A. E. Cooley (ed.) *A Companion to Roman Italy*, London, 476–501.

Ferretti, F. (2015) 'The Making of Italian Agricultural Landscapes: Emilio Sereni, between Geography, History and Marxism', *Journal of Historical Geography* 48: 58–67.

Gade, D. W. (1983) 'The Growing Recognition of George Perkins Marsh', *Geographical Review* 73 (3): 341–4.

Grey, C. (2011) *Constructing Communities in the Late Roman Countryside*, Cambridge.

Haldon, J., L. Mordechai, T. P. Newfield, A. F. Chase, A. Izdebski, P. Guzowski, I. Labuhn and N. Roberts (2018) 'History Meets Palaeoscience: Consilience and Collaboration in Studying Past Societal Responses to Environmental Change', *Proceedings of the National Academy of Sciences* 115: 3210–18.

Hall, M. (1998) 'Restoring the Countryside: George Perkins Marsh and the Italian Land Ethic (1861–1882)', *Environment and History* 4: 91–103.

Harper, K. (2017) *The Fate of Rome: Climate, Disease, and the End of the Empire*, Princeton.

Harris, W. V. (ed.) (2013) *The Ancient Mediterranean Environment between Science and History*, Leiden.

Huntington, E. (1917) 'Climatic Change and Agricultural Exhaustion as Elements in the Fall of Rome', *Quarterly Journal of Economics* 31: 173–208.

Izdebski, A. (2018) 'Setting the Scene for an Environmental History of Late Antiquity', in A. Izdebski and M. Mulryan (eds) *Environment and Society in the Long Late Antiquity*, Leiden, 3–16.
Izdebski, A. and M. Mulryan (eds) (2018) *Environment and Society in the Long Late Antiquity*, Leiden.
Izdebski, A., K. Holmgren, E. Weiberg, S. R. Stocker, U. Büntgen, A. Florenzano, A. Gogou, S. A. G. Leroy, J. Luterbacher, B. Martrat, A. Masi, A. M. Mercuri, P. Montagna, L. Sadori, A. Schneider, M.-A. Sicre, M. Triantaphyllou and E. Xoplaki (2016) 'Realising Consilience: How Better Communication between Archaeologists, Historians and Natural Scientists Can Transform the Study of Past Climate Change in the Mediterranean', *Quaternary Science Reviews* 136: 5–22.
Jones, A. H. M. (1955) 'The Decline and Fall of the Roman Empire', *History* 40: 209–26.
Jones, A. H. M. (1959) 'Over-Taxation and the Decline of the Roman Empire', *Antiquity* 33: 39–43.
Kaniewski, D., N. Marriner, C. Morhange, M. Vacchi, G. Sarti, V. Rossi, M. Bini, M. Pasquinucci, C. Allinne, T. Otto, F. Luce and E. Van Campo (2018) 'Holocene Evolution of Portus Pisanus, the Lost Harbour of Pisa', *Scientific Reports* 8: 11625.
Koelsch, W. A. (2012) 'The Legendary "Rediscovery" of George Perkins Marsh', *Geographical Review* 102: 510–24.
Kreiner, J. (2017) 'Pigs in the Flesh and Fisc: an Early Medieval Ecology', *P&P* 236: 3–42.
Lawrence, R. (1999) *The Roads of Roman Italy: Mobility and Cultural Change*, London.
Lewit, T. (2003) '"Vanishing Villas": What Happened to Élite Rural Habitation in the West in the 5th–6th c?', *JRA* 16: 260–74.
Lewit, T. (2009) 'Pigs, Presses and Pastoralism: Farming in the Fifth to Sixth Centuries AD', *Early Medieval Europe* 17: 77–91.
Lowenthal, D. (1953) 'George Perkins Marsh and the American Geographical Tradition', *Geographical Review* 43: 207–13.
McCormick, M. (2013) 'What Climate Science, Ausonius, Nile Floods, Rye, and Thatch Tell Us about the Environmental History of the Roman Empire', in W. V. Harris (ed.) *Ancient Mediterranean Environment between Science and History*, Leiden, 61–88.
McCormick, M., U. Büntgen, M. A. Cane, E. R. Cook, K. Harper, P. Huybers, T. Litt, S. W. Manning, P. A. Mayewski, A. F. M. More, K. Nicolussi, W. Tegel (2012) 'Climate Change during and after the Roman Empire: Reconstructing the Past from Scientific and Historical Evidence', *Journal of Interdisciplinary History* 43: 169–220.
Marchetti, M. (2002) 'Environmental Changes in the Central Po Plain (Northern Italy) Due to Fluvial Modifications and Anthropogenic Activities', *Geomorphology* 44: 361–73.
Marsh, G. P. (1864) *Man and Nature: or, Physical Geography as Modified by Human Action*, New York.
Marsh, G. P. (1885) *The Earth as Modifed by Human Action: a Last Revision of 'Mand and Nature'*, New York.
Mensing, S. A., E. M. Schoolman, I. Tunno, P. J. Noble, L. Sagnotti, F. Florindo and G. Piovesan (2018) 'Historical Ecology Reveals Landscape Transformation Coincident with Cultural Development in Central Italy since the Roman Period', *Scientific Reports* 8: 2138.
Mensing, S. A., I. Tunno, L. Sagnotti, F. Florindo, P. Noble, C. Archer, S. Zimmerman, F. J. Pavón-Carrasco, G. Cifani, S. Passigli, G. Piovesan (2015) '2700 Years of Mediterranean Environmental Change in Central Italy: a Synthesis of Sedimentary and Cultural Records to Interpret Past Impacts of Climate on Society', *Quaternary Science Reviews* 116: 72–94.

Mercuri, A. M., M. C. Montecchi, A. Florenzano, E. Rattighieri, P. Torri, D. Dallai and E. Vaccaro (2019) 'The Late Antique Plant Landscape in Sicily: Pollen from the Agropastoral Villa del Casale–Philosophiana System', *Quaternary International* 499: 24–34.

Merrills, A. and R. Miles (2010) *The Vandals*, Chichester.

Montecchi, M. C. and A. M. Mercuri (2018) 'When Palynology Meets Classical Archaeology: the Roman and Medieval Landscapes at the Villa del Casale di Piazza Armerina, UNESCO Site in Sicily', *Archaeological and Anthropological Sciences* 10 (4): 743–57.

Mordechai, L., M. Eisenberg, T. P. Newfield, A. Izdebski, J. E. Kay and H. Poinar (2019) 'The Justinianic Plague: an Inconsequential Pandemic?', *Proceedings of the National Academy of Sciences* 116 (51): 25546–54.

Noti, R., J. F. N. van Leeuwen, D. Colombaroli, E. Vescovi, P. Salvatore, T. La Mantia and W. Tinner (2009) 'Mid- and Late-Holocene Vegetation and Fire History at Biviere di Gela, a Coastal Lake in Southern Sicily, Italy', *Vegetation History and Archaeobotany* 18: 371–87.

Ravazzi, C., M. Marchetti, M. Zanon, R. Perego, T. Quirino, M. Deaddis, M. De Amicis and D. Margaritora (2013) 'Lake Evolution and Landscape History in the Lower Mincio River Valley, Unravelling Drainage Changes in the Central Po Plain (N-Italy) since the Bronze Age', *Quaternary International* 288: 195–205.

Sadori, L., G. Zanchetta and M. Giardini (2008) 'Last Glacial to Holocene Palaeoenvironmental Evolution at Lago di Pergusa (Sicily, Southern Italy) as Inferred by Pollen, Microcharcoal, and Stable Isotopes', *Quaternary International* 181: 4–14.

Sadori, L., E. Ortu, O. Peyron, G. Zanchetta, B. Vannière, M. Desmet and M. Magny (2013) 'The Last 7 Millennia of Vegetation and Climate Changes at Lago di Pergusa (Central Sicily, Italy)', *Climate of the Past Discussions* 9: 2059–94.

Sadori, L., C. Giraudi, A. Masi, M. Magny, E. Ortu, G. Zanchetta and A. Izdebski (2016) 'Climate, Environment and Society in Southern Italy during the Last 2000 Years: a Review of the Environmental, Historical and Archaeological Evidence', *Quaternary Science Reviews* 136: 173–88.

Sadori, L., E. Allevato, C. Bellini, A. Bertacchi, G. Boetto, G. Di Pasquale, G. Giachi, M. Giardini, A. Masi, C. Pepe, E. Russo Ermolli and M. Mariotti Lippi (2015) 'Archaeobotany in Italian Ancient Roman Harbours', *Review of Palaeobotany and Palynology* 218: 217–30.

Scarpati, C., A. Perrotta and G. F. De Simone (2016) 'Impact of Explosive Volcanic Eruptions around Vesuvius: a Story of Resilience in Roman Time', *Bulletin of Volcanology* 78: 1–6.

Schoolman, E. M., S. Mensing and G. Piovesan (2019) 'Land Use and the Human Impact on the Environment in Medieval Italy', *Journal of Interdisciplinary History* 49: 419–44.

Sereni, E. (1961) *Storia del paesaggio agrario italiano*, Bari.

Sereni, E. (1997) *History of the Italian Agricultural Landscape*, trans. R. Burr Litchfield, Princeton.

Sessa, K. (2019) 'The New Environmental Fall of Rome: a Methodological Consideration', *Journal of Late Antiquity* 12: 211–55.

Sfameni, C. (2018) 'La Sabina in età tardoantica e le nuove ricerche alla villa di Cottanello (RI)', in A. Castrorao Barba (ed.) *Dinamiche insediative nelle campagne dell'Italia tra Tarda Antichità e Alto Medioevo*, Oxford, 119–36.

Squatriti, P. (1999) 'Review of: *History of the Italian Agricultural Landscape* by Emilio Sereni, trans. R. Burr Litchfield', *The Historian* 62: 198–9.

Squatriti, P. (2018) 'Rye's Rise and Rome's Fall: Agriculture and Climate in Europe during Late Antiquity', in A. Izdebski and M. Mulryan (eds) *Environment and Society in the Long Late Antiquity*, Boston, 342–54.

Tinner, W., J. F. N. van Leeuwen, D. Colombaroli, E. Vescovi, W. O. van der Knaap, P. D. Henne, S. Pasta, S. D'Angelo and T. La Mantia (2009) 'Holocene Environmental and Climatic Changes at Gorgo Basso, a Coastal Lake in Southern Sicily, Italy', *Quaternary Science Reviews* 28: 1498–510.

Vaccaro, E. (2013) 'Patterning the Late Antique Economies of Inland Sicily in a Mediterranean Context', *Late Antique Archaeology* 10: 259–313.

11

CITIES AND URBAN LIFE IN LATE ROMAN ITALY: TRANSFORMATIONS OF THE OLD, IMPOSITIONS OF THE NEW

Neil Christie

Introduction

MANY OF THE CITIES PROLIFERATING in the Italian peninsula in the early Roman Empire were still active when Italy came to be ruled by Ostrogothic royalty and armies from the late fifth century AD. By then, many were the seats of bishops and a majority remained markets, acted as points of administration, and were foci for burial. Laws were still being promulgated, displayed and announced in the towns, and civic authorities functioned and oversaw, in diverse ways, the urban fabric. Yet this image must be recognised as a partial facade, since, jostling behind this apparent urban continuity, there is another image of substantial change and reorientation; and, in some cases, there is urban loss. Indeed, we must recognise a different, post-classical urbanism in progress by AD 500 – an urbanism that responded to social, economic, military and religious changes occurring across the wider empire since the mid-third century. This paper provides an overview of some of these changes, looking primarily at the physical evidence for diverse cities. Just what did these places look like? When did 'classical' monuments fail and change, and in what ways? How quickly did churches appear and where? How clear are the respective archaeologies? And how might we define 'post-classical' cityscapes? En route, we consider impacts on the inhabitants, from elites to urban poor, in terms of spaces frequented and lived in, and we ask how the dynamics of these centres evolved. While the City of Rome is a core locus of study, coverage here seeks to be broad, so as to understand sequences of urban physical and social change and response across the wider peninsula.

Historical and Archaeological Changes

While it is not necessary to revisit the politico-military events that impacted on Italy, the West and the wider empire across the period AD 250–500,[1] it is nonetheless

---

[1] For coverage, see this volume, Chapters 1–4; summary in Christie 2006, 21–34; 2016. On war and Rome: Lançon 2000, 35–44.

important to recognise the diverse readings of these vicissitudes. For some scholars, the civil wars and 'crisis' of the third century were hugely debilitating to the empire's economy and prompted changes in state attitude (more militarised), in elite outlook (reduced investment in urban life) and in urban direction (some adapt, some slip, internal emphases change). The fourth century still had civil conflicts, plus weaker frontiers, but political and economic stability overall provided some normalisation in civic life. The rise of the church added a new dimension that affected first the larger centres, but by the fifth century had impacted on most cities, with bishops and clergy increasingly the new civic face. Meanwhile, barbarian incursions and insertions into the western empire in particular meant a shrinking realm and ever reduced scope for display within towns (beyond the church), with emphasis otherwise much more on 'making do'.

While the texts centre on politico-military vicissitudes as well as on religious debates, civic inscriptions – in diminishing number compared to early imperial displays – point to commemorative works; alongside these, numbers of (often simple) Christian epitaphs rise.[2] Combined, these textual sources can paint somewhat conflicting images of urban damage and ones of continuity – such as sacks of cities and reduced elites, yet active bishops and busy cemeteries. Similarly, the laws in the *Codex Theodosianus* might imply thriving centres through reference to workers, slaves, officials, buildings, materials and food, yet the noises made by the promulgations also hint at struggling places – issues of runaway slaves, lack of building upkeep, reduced ability to pay taxes, reminders of public duties, etc.[3]

For long, the archaeological contribution to towns of the later Roman centuries looked to finding destruction layers and temple loss and highlighting Christian insertions; rather simplistic images of decay and depopulation were paraded, alongside generic references to city walls symbolising shut-in and insecure populations. Now, however, late Roman, early medieval and medieval sequences and material cultures are much better scrutinised, even if often their strata and signatures are fragmentary or harder to trace given damage from more substantial overlying medieval to modern constructions and interventions. Changes to housing in particular are now better explored, as are various early church phases. Some problems are, however, hard to resolve, notably where monuments have been long excavated, cleared and restored to their earlier imperial form, meaning that traces of their phases of decay, robbing and adaptation are frequently not available.[4]

---

[2] Changing epigraphic (and euergetistic) practice is summarised in Yasin 2009, 108–10.
[3] Detailed analysis offered in Honoré 1998.
[4] For Italy, an excellent example of the patchwork of old and recent archaeological information relating to a city's transformation is by Scampoli (2010, 41–134) for Florence. More broadly, see Augenti 2016, 27–81 on archaeologies of Italian cities across AD 400–1500; Brogiolo 2011, 33–76; plus papers in Carneiro et al. 2020 for wider surveys of western late and post-classical urban archaeology; and the recent analysis of cities in Late Roman Gaul and Spain by Esmonde Cleary 2013, 97–149. For advances in studying Late Antiquity more widely, see especially volumes in Brill's Late Antique Archaeology series, such as on housing (Lavan et al. 2007a), technology (Lavan et al. 2007b), social and political life (Bowden et al. 2006) and theory (Lavan and Bowden 2003) – each volume usually featuring many papers linked to urbanism.

Transformations of the Built Fabric

To understand how Italy's cities and their populations evolved across the late Roman period, we need to explore transformations across a range of elements: first, we consider the core public space of the forum, and then structures of entertainment, since these all formed foci of civic and elite investment and euergetism in the earlier imperial centuries. Next, changes in urban housing and, with this, material culture and building technologies are examined. Finally, two essential built components – churches and defences – are considered, both of which created core ingredients to an urban form that would endure into the Middle Ages.[5]

Capitolia and Fora

Key transitions in monumentality and in social and religious orientation in late Roman Italy are evident in the classical heart of the cities, namely the forum. Looking away from the larger centres, we can observe that components of the forum complex – basilica, Capitolium, imperial cult temple/shrine, market space – generally fail, fall into disrepair or see some repurposing (sometimes industrial) already in the fourth century.[6] Thus, at Agrigento in southern Sicily, decay and robbing of these public buildings, and a breakdown in the drainage system, occur around the end of the fourth century; rubbish is dumped around the so-called *Iseon* temple in the upper agora in the same period, alongside the collapse of part of the piazza's portico.[7] And at Grumentum in Basilicata, the well-equipped townscape falters in the fourth century as public spaces see neglect and as commercial and industrial units 'invade' these: thus, by the fifth century, busy metalworking activity occurred immediately east of the old forum's 'Temple C' (imperial cult), seemingly recycling materials (iron, bronze, lead) from the forum (Fig. 11.1).[8]

A recent overview[9] of selected north Italian *fora* identifies a variable pattern, but with a majority certainly still active in the late third century, with statue dedications at least revealing a level of civic vitality. However, such dedications could simply reflect (required) statements of loyalty to the emperors in periods first of state instability and then of state reinforcement. After 284, Milan became an imperial capital and a focus of investment, and imperial and military visibility was duly increased across the north. This brought different priorities, as witnessed in the creation of arms factories and in building or renewal of city defences (see below). In general, some maintenance and restoration of *fora* can be traced, and ceramic and coin evidence signifies frequentation and market activity. At Verona, for example, the ample late Roman and late antique

---

[5] Haug 2003 assesses various of these aspects for selected northern Italian cities. For a valuable comparison of urban archaeological sequences in Late Roman Hispania, see Diarte Blasco 2012, revealing, overall, slightly earlier changes to the urban fabric compared to Italy.

[6] A few fail before this, as claimed for Lucca – Abela 1998, 24.

[7] Rizzo 2014, 409–10.

[8] Bison et al. 2017; Brogiolo 2018, 4–5, questioning the 'authorities' who permitted or else prompted such exploitations of old public structures and spaces.

[9] Cavalieri 2015.

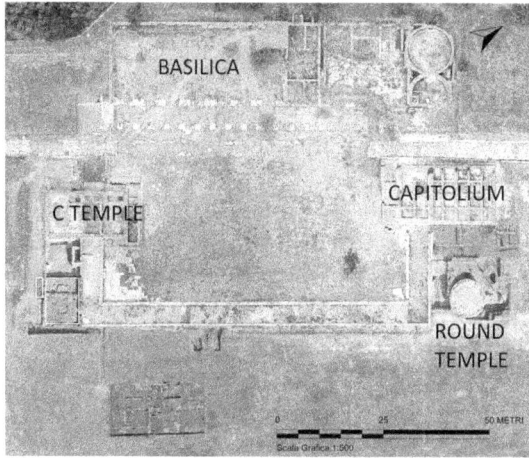

Figure 11.1 Grumentum: view of forum showing the location of the late Roman metal-workshop. (Image courtesy of Giulia Bison)

ceramic data imply healthy use of the forum and its environs into the sixth century, but with changes across time. While remains of a late fifth-century frieze point to a monumental fountain or *schola* of money-lenders hereabouts,[10] the archaeology points to a decay of core spaces from the later fourth century, notably the Capitolium temple, robbed for materials from the early fifth to sixth centuries.[11]

Often, sequences for forum complexes are not archaeologically secure, due to a lack of documentation and recognition of relevant data in early investigations and clearances; however, in various cases, these works (nineteenth- to mid-twentieth-century) did recover reused or discarded architectural materials which help discussion. In particular the evidence of inscribed statue bases guide on the ornamental face of these city cores in the late Roman period, as revealed by a comprehensive project, 'The Last Statues of Antiquity'.[12] This has shown how display of statuary remained fairly resilient, with over 480 bases recorded across Italy (though with almost half from Rome) for the time span AD 284–408.[13] These primarily honour imperial figures, but also record state officers (especially governors) and their efforts, and local elites; deities, by contrast, receive few dedications. Although original locations are not always known, findspots congregate in established areas, primarily among forum porticoes and at basilicas. Strikingly, most inscribed late Roman statue bases (and, probably, their statues too) were reworked earlier pieces: one base at Luni (Fig. 11.2) was reused three times, with new inscriptions cut on each of its faces – for statues (presumably

---

[10] Lusuardi Siena, in Cavalieri Manasse 2008, 215–31.
[11] Cavalieri Manasse 2008, 108–26. The forum cryptoporticus, however, seems only to have collapsed following an earthquake in c. AD 700.
[12] See project database at http://laststatues.classics.ox.ac.uk/.
[13] Machado 2016; Machado and Lenaghan 2016.

different ones) to Maxentius (AD 306–12), Galerius (c.300), Magnia Urbica, wife of emperor Carinus (c.284), and local patron and quaestor M. Pescennius.[14] Similarly, at Veleia, the pedestal for the mid-fourth-century statue of Constantius II reused one of Hadrian.[15]

Rome, unsurprisingly, as traditional seat of authority and imperial memory, offers prominent maintenance of the statue habit, albeit with a regular process of reuse of older bases and even statuary.[16] The *fora* remained the key locus of display (although texts do reference relocations of statues to better locations to ornament the city), with imperial officeholders the main dedicants. Levels of display diminish from the end of the fourth century, however, coinciding, arguably, with the final Christianisation of the city's senate and high aristocracy.[17] Strongly linked to Rome and her senatorial elite were the towns (and estates) of Campania, and this region generates a high proportion of statues (170 bases), honouring these local governors as well as emperors, across the fourth century and into the fifth.[18]

But while this traditional public exhibitionism endures well into the fourth century in some cities, there are strong indications that displays of statuary specifically within imperial cult sanctuaries faltered, perhaps in the face of growing episcopal authority from the mid-fourth century.[19] Striking is the collection of gilded bronze busts discovered at Brescia, attributable to emperors active in the north in the 260s–80s, such as Claudius Gothicus, Aurelian and Probus, plus a head of Septimius Severus

Figure 11.2 Luni statue base (reused) – *CIL* 11.6957c. (Image from Last Statues of Antiquity database)

---

[14] *CIL* 11.6957a–c; *LSA* 1618, 1619. Machado 2016, 47–8; Cavalieri 2015, 97–8, noting that this and ten other bases were employed as building material for the early fifth-century church.

[15] Cavalieri 2015, 96.

[16] Machado and Lenaghan 2016.

[17] See the extensive study on late antique statues in the Roman Forum by Kalas 2015, chh. 3 and 4, with comments on fifth-century works – these concentrating around the Senate House – on pp. 99–101. On statues more widely in the empire: Jacobs 2013, ch. 5. On late use, reuse or destruction, see Kristensen and Stirling 2016, 13–23.

[18] Machado 2016, 52–5. For funerary inscriptions and ongoing status definitions in late antique Campania, see Lambert 2008.

[19] On temple loss across the empire in this century, see Jacobs 2014.

Figure 11.3 Brescia: the stunning collection of gilded bronze later imperial busts found in the Capitolium area, now displayed at the Museo della Città, Santa Giulia. (Source: http://www.museiarcheologici.net)

(Fig. 11.3). These busts were found in the major clearance works of 1826, carefully concealed near the Capitolium, suggestive of deliberate safekeeping; the hoard included the famous, highly refined bronze first-century AD winged Victory statue.[20] The archaeology suggests the forum area fell into disuse in the second half of the fourth century, perhaps preceded by the decay of the nearby theatre; by the early fifth century, fairly basic houses and workshops were intruding on these spaces,[21] but by the same period churches had sprung up in the suburbs and the first intramural cathedral had been established.[22]

Dating the functional end of cult temples – imperial, state and of other divinities – is problematic archaeologically: even though the legislation against pagan worship and sacrifice grew louder across the fourth century, full bans were definitively made only towards the end of that century.[23] Yet church growth, imperial preference to the church and declining elite patronage meant life and funds were either slowly or suddenly sucked

---

[20] Discussed in Moreno 2002; Sansoni and Docchio 2005. See fine images at https://artsandculture.google.com/exhibit/brescia%E2%80%99s-winged-victory-fondazione-brescia-musei/rwIC6y5s2HsQLA?hl=en-GB.
[21] Brogiolo 1993, 73 and 115.
[22] Brogiolo 1993, 65–8, noting issues regarding the dating of the earliest episcopal church.
[23] See Jacobs 2014.

out of these cult sites. The noted relocation of statuary from some of these links into a recognition among some civic authorities (or individual officials) either of their artistic merit or a need to still honour old emperors. Yet aggressive attitudes by (Christian) authorities – a single strong-willed bishop, for example – could force temple closure and erasure of statuary, as evident in rural missionary acts in the Alpine regions, attested in letters by bishop Vigilius of Trento and sermons by bishop Maximus of Turin in the late fourth century.[24]

Archaeologically, however, slow decline, conscious neglect or acts of enforced decay/loss are hard to determine; in urban contexts such relevant deposits are much tougher to recover. One valuable guide outside of Italy is the Augusteum in Narona in modern Croatia, where deliberate casting down and beheading of statuary occurred, but without a precise chronology within the fourth century.[25] Evidence here was fuller because Narona is not overlain by a medieval and modern city. Some of the same potential lies in other 'failed' sites. Hence, back across the Adriatic, in Le Marche, the project team at Potentia (Fig. 11.4) used various strategies to understand the peaks and troughs within the 'lost' city, charting through surface data especially how, despite consistent site activity across the fourth and earlier fifth century, there was subsequent shrinkage to around the northern, forum area.[26] Excavations at the forum, meanwhile, showed 'partial abandonment, subdivision and encroachment on the sites of former grand buildings'; and 'by the end of the fourth century, the entire pagan temple complex was transformed: the temple itself was demolished, the surrounding portico closed off and the area in front of the temple levelled up to the base of the podium'.[27] Such works should not be viewed simply as destructive and signifying abandonment; rather they point to a still organised community, albeit one with modified needs.

Two other 'failed' cities can be cited here. First, Luna-Luni in Liguria, where prominent remains of the Capitolium and amphitheatre survive, and where extensive excavations since the 1970s have explored multiple facets of the town and environs. Luni was prominent in the early empire for exploitation of the fine white Carrara marble which adorned multiple monuments in Rome and Italy; economic downturn in the third century – marked by many civic authorities recycling/reusing building and decorative materials – saw Luni struggle, and a further blow came with a major late fourth-century earthquake. The latter is witnessed archaeologically in collapses, fractured walls and structural losses, which seemingly left a veritable 'ruinscape'.[28] And yet much of Luni fairly quickly resurfaces: an episcopal church of c. AD 400 exploits materials from demolished/damaged buildings (including statue bases from the forum, as noted above); the main road is cleared and resurfaced, again with recycled debris; and some private houses are rebuilt and expanded. Clearly local wealth persisted, presumably trade-connected, to enable this revival.[29] Recent investigations around the

---

[24] Lizzi 1990, 169–72. On the 'ends' of temples to Mithras, see Walsh 2019, noting a number enduring probably into the later fourth century.
[25] Marin 2001.
[26] Vermeulen 2012, 84.
[27] Vermeulen 2012, 86.
[28] Durante 2010, 81.
[29] Durante 2003, 204–10.

Figure 11.4 Aerial view of the 'lost' Roman city of Potentia, showing excavation zones near the West Gate and Forum. (Image courtesy of Frank Vermeulen and Cristina Corsi)

then redundant Capitolium reveal new domestic, as well as industrial, activity expanding into the zone, some houses even with bath suites and elaborate mosaics; and the renewed road extended over collapsed/levelled parts of the portico of the basilica.[30]

Second, Ostia, Rome's key port city in the Republic to mid-empire, which has seen very long-running excavation campaigns, but with variable levels of documentation. Recent studies have sought to understand its latest Roman phases better.[31] Indeed, while the late archaeology of some monuments, notably the main temples (Capitolium, Temple of Rome and Augustus), is problematic, revised readings of the epigraphic survivals show how the forum area retained a focal role into the fifth century, notably through erection (and relocation) of statuary, as indicated by inscriptions from two late fourth-century prefects of the *annona*.[32] This image of an ongoing, active 'civic centre' is enhanced by innovative re-excavation and detailed surface and elevation planning of sectors of the city core which had been exposed in earlier excavations and later restored (with many restorations now in a poor state).[33] The studies reveal early fifth-century works around the forum, its portico and walkways, and at

---

[30] Durante 2010, 82. On *domus* decay and renewal at Luni, see below.
[31] E.g. Boin 2013, 141–4, noting the types and records of archaeology – primarily of the early nineteenth century – available for the Capitolium.
[32] Boin 2013, 145–54. *CIL* 14.139, 173, 4721. See also the Last Statues of Antiquity database/catalogue.
[33] Lavan 2012.

the Forum Baths and its training ground. Reused material is a feature throughout, matching repairs to private *domus* and known stockpiling of architectural items (e.g. columns) in abandoned spaces; coins and ceramic finds show good activity across the period. The contrast comes with the later fifth century when there is stripping of materials from central public buildings, blockages of colonnades, and insertions of crude housing; nonetheless, this work still attests people working and living here, some perhaps employed by the bishops and, more widely, by the church.

Baths, Theatres, Amphitheatres

Baths remained active points of patronage in many late Roman Italian cities, and in Rome the massive public *thermae* of Diocletian and Constantine denote major expressions of investment in the water infrastructure still into the fourth century.[34] Since baths depended on functioning aqueducts and a large town population needed fresh water and working drains, so it is a positive sign for urban vitality to hear of ongoing bathing. Such is documented in restoration works in the Campania and Samnium provinces across the fourth century.[35] It is in the larger cities/capitals that baths appear still active into the fifth century, both public ones and private, smaller-scale units – Rome, Ostia, Milan and Aquileia can be cited – but here the state helped ensure aqueduct maintenance. The impression otherwise is a shrinking number of *thermae* elsewhere, in part due to a weakened economy, reduced elite base and perhaps even through Christian influence.[36]

The entertainment complexes met variable fates at variable times. The later third-century circuit walls at Verona and Rimini both, for example, incorporate the amphitheatre into the defences; Rome's Aurelianic Walls, likewise, encase on their eastern flank the Amphitheatrum Castrense and, nearby, the Claudia–Anio Novus aqueduct (Fig. 11.5).[37] These works presumably marked the close of games in these spaces (except in Rome, where games/animal hunts in the Colosseum, and probably also the Amphitheatrum Castrense, persisted fully into the fifth century)[38] and perhaps transitioned them into barracks, stores and/or training grounds. However, there is minimal archaeology to guide on these potential revised roles in the third and fourth centuries (and similarly for when some later become citadels). At Bologna, Rimini, Parma and Aquileia, theatres or amphitheatres seem redundant already in the third century and partially robbed – in the case of both Parma and Aquileia, perhaps as an emergency measure to help restore the old defensive circuit and to counter the

---

[34] See Rambaldi 2009, 200–4 on new and re-builds of baths in Rome in the mid- to late third century.

[35] Ward-Perkins 1984, 24–5, citing late fourth-century governors overseeing renewals in Anzio, Terracina, Puteoli, Sepino and Benevento.

[36] For Florence as one example of likely redundancy of baths by the second half of the fourth century, see Scampoli 2010, 75–8. For Spain, Diarte Blasco 2012, 265–7 identifies some loss of baths in the third century, but many persisted into the fourth century (with new ones occasionally added at capitals), but almost none beyond that. A valuable wider survey within Italy and other Mediterranean territories is Maréchal 2020.

[37] Dey 2011, 75–7.

[38] Orlandi 1999; Christie 2009, 223–4; Meneghini 2018, 12–3.

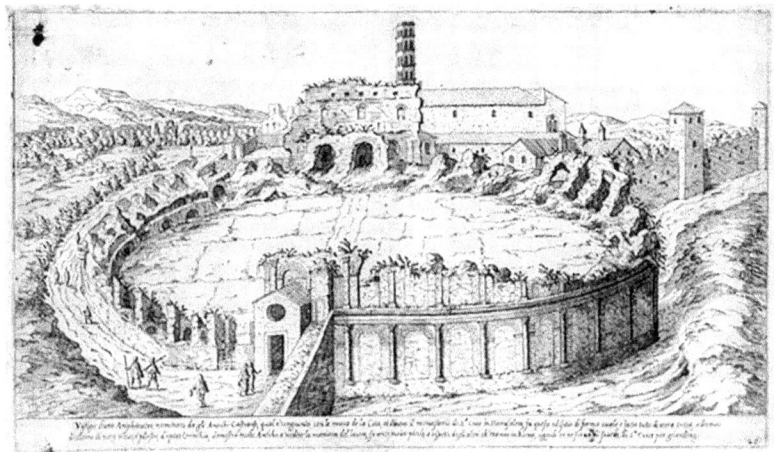

Figure 11.5 Rome's Amphitheatrum Castrense and associated line of the Aurelianic Walls, as drawn by Étienne Dupérac (1525–1604) and displayed at the Istituto nazionale per la grafica, Rome. (Source: Wikimedia Commons)

monuments' use by enemy forces.[39] To the mid-fourth century may be assigned the redundancy of the theatres at Turin and Ventimiglia. It is noticeable that at the late imperial residences, namely Milan, Aquileia, Rome and perhaps Ravenna, the circus became the main focus for spectacles; palaces were generally set alongside these. Arguably, if this became the favoured imperial entertainment venue, then that damaged further old-style euergetism by elites of/in theatres and amphitheatres after the earlier fourth century.[40] Exceptional, of course, is Rome's Colosseum, where epigraphic and some archaeological evidence identifies consistent imperial and senatorial efforts to restore the monument for celebrations across the fifth century, despite damage caused by earthquakes, neglect and sacks.[41]

Housing

In terms of housing, it is striking how, across many parts of Italy, elite or well-to-do *domus* begin to fail in the third and fourth centuries AD, either shrinking in on themselves, being quitted or part-quitted, or partitioned up into more workaday spaces/houses; alongside this, one can observe far fewer mosaics being laid after the third century.[42] On

---

[39] Rambaldi 2009, 213–5.
[40] On fates in Italy and more broadly, see Christie 2009; for Hispania, Diarte Blasco 2012, 270–87, with important discussion on evolving reuses.
[41] Rea 2002b; Orlandi 1999, with close reading of the epigraphic evidence; problematic is identifying the scale and quality of many of the documented repairs/restorations and the scale of damage caused by earthquakes, such as those of AD 429 and 443 – pp. 252 and 260.
[42] As one example, see Coralini 2010 for Forum Popili. At Lucca, various late Republican *domus* appear already abandoned by the third century – see Abela 1998, 25–7.

Sicily, at Agrigento, the owners of many quality peristyled properties in the 'Quartiere Ellenistico-Romano' district appear to have been struggling by c. AD 400, as shown by unrepaired mosaics, a use of beaten earth floors, blockings of peristyles, and dumping of rubbish in spaces. Various structures show collapse or burning down towards the mid- or later fifth century, which may be associated with Vandal raids on the site and region; few see any notable renewal, and instead 'poor' occupation prevails, on a reduced level, plus scattered burials into the post-Roman period.[43] In Lilybaeum, on Capo Boeo, some ornate *domus* appear to extend into the fifth century, to then be replaced by funerary activity; fifth-century houses likewise are attested at Syracuse in the Acradina district.[44] Few *domus*, however, retain their aristocratic luxury beyond this time, with subdivisions, poor materials, robbing or abandonment featuring strongly. A contrast lies with the wider Sicilian landscape where large rural villas, many ornately decorated and well equipped with baths, point to enduring aristocratic wealth and estate investment; but this denotes mainly senatorial wealth, and not local urban elites on display.[45]

One of the best-studied north Italian sequences is at Brescia, notably in the eastern intramural districts around Santa Giulia, located just east of the theatre and forum.[46] Excavation revealed two Roman *insulae* (dating from the later first century BC), with that at S. Giulia covering 120 × 90 m and occupied by a single substantial two-storey *domus*, with rooms organised around peristyles, one featuring a nymphaeum. The complex displayed good-quality wall frescoes and mosaic floors; this and a comparable one to the south at via Alberto Mario underwent minor structural modifications in the fourth century. For each, a dramatic transformation of space and function occurs from the first half of the fifth century: some rooms come to be divided by timber partitions which cut into the mosaic floors; hearths are set immediately on the old floors; other floors are covered by beaten earth or clay surfaces; decayed plaster accumulates; and some walls collapse or are robbed. Potentially these *domus* fell from single ownership to be occupied by various family units who carved out single- or double-roomed accommodation spaces; or else existing owners were struggling economically and failing to maintain old-style properties. While we note these deteriorations to the *domus* across the fifth century, the evidence does, at the same time, signify people still living in these domestic spaces. Brogiolo highlights Ennodius' reference to the billeting of Ostrogothic troops in Pavia in AD 489 as one scenario of house transformation: 'You would have seen the city teeming with vast throngs of troops, and huge *domus* cut up into the narrowest of huts.'[47] Comparable appears nearby Bergamo, featuring some *domus* being partitioned up in the fourth century, but potentially a few, such as the two traced under the cathedral, endured until the church took over those plots in c. AD 400.[48]

---

[43] Rizzo 2014, 409; Parello and Rizzo 2016, 55–8.
[44] Sami 2013, 29–31.
[45] Sfameni 2004, 337–43.
[46] Brogiolo 1999; on fourth- to sixth-century change, see Brogiolo 1993, 74–106.
[47] Brogiolo 1993, 74–5; 1999, 104. Ennodius, *Opera*, ed. F. Vogel, in *MGH AA* 7.98.
[48] Negri 2010, 199–206. See also Alba in Piemonte, with some *domus* intruding on public areas in the fourth century, and with one revealed under the cathedral; some saw robbing, and others partitioning in the later fourth and within the fifth century – Micheletto 2013, 40–4. For housing in north Italian examples, see Haug 2003; for wider studies on late antique housing, see papers in Lavan et al. 2007a.

There are, of course, cities where *domus* and mosaics persist – or, rather, resurface – as elite expressions, these often as indicators of state or senatorial investment in capitals or satellite centres (e.g. Ravenna and Rimini; Milan and Como). Thus we can observe in the case of Como the finely executed floor mosaic found in 1908 at via Perti, likely belonging to the second half of the fifth century, with its dominant panel of two antlered deer either side of a kantharos set under an arcade.[49] Although just one high-status remnant, this evidence fits with a strong body of around forty inscriptions and epitaphs from the city and environs of c. AD 425–525 showing the presence of *viri clarissimi* and *spectabiles*, whether resident senators, counts, court elites or even bishops.[50]

For Ravenna, the presence of the imperial and Gothic royal court is reflected in very high-status private residences for court functionaries and rich merchants among others: the best example is the Domus dei Tappeti di Pietra at via D'Azeglio, whose roots go back to Augustan times as two properties with a road between; these saw major upgrading in the fifth century followed by a sumptuous development in c. AD 500–30 merging the two *domus* and eliminating the road.[51] In nearby Rimini, there is comparable fifth-century investment in some *domus* (prominent being those in Piazza Ferrari and Palazzo Gioia), notably in the city's northern sector – linking to the main road and bridge, but also to the episcopal complex of S. Colomba.[52] The picture in some other urban zones of Rimini differed: some properties lay abandoned, robbed or semi-colonised by poor housing. This same mix of active and inactive space appears in other cities across the peninsula[53] and attests ongoing divisions of social status in these sites.

Textual documentation enables notable insights into the density and distribution of housing, not just of the elite, in Rome in the late empire. The 'Regional Catalogues' for the mid-fourth century, and the *Curiosum* and *Notitia urbis Romae* (both likely originating under Diocletian, then reworked by the mid-fourth)[54] guide on monuments, but also on dwellings across the city's districts: the catalogues notably indicate 1,790 *domus* and over 46,000 *insulae* and thus a maintained vast demographic.[55] Guidobaldi's detailed studies have pieced together textual and/or material (excavation, structures, finds) evidence for over 350 *domus* of the third and fourth centuries, enabling discussion on roots, forms, ownerships and neighbourhoods. A vast majority were not *ex novo*

---

[49] Flaminio 2015, citing comparanda and debates on religious connotations, especially for the 'Dionysiac' figure depicted under the right arch.

[50] Sannazaro 2015, 34–9. For Luni in eastern Liguria, following a later fourth-century earthquake, some *domus* were abandoned and robbed, but a few were rebuilt and even expanded: the Domus dei Mosaici now displayed a mosaic depicting Rome's Circus Maximus and featured its own baths – Durante 2003, 208–9.

[51] Cirelli 2008, 108–14; Montevecchi 2004. On possible furnaces and workshops at Classe supplying mosaic *tesserae* in this period, see papers by Chinni and Frantová in Cantone 2019.

[52] Negrelli 2008, 10–7.

[53] In the north, for example, at Aquileia – see Marano 2012, 578–80; Pesaro – Dall'Aglio and Di Cocco 2004, 69, with other examples on 119–22, 141–6. For the south, see Volpe 2016, 91–3.

[54] Arce 1999.

[55] Key papers for later Rome, its housing, population and sources are Guilhembet 1996; Guidobaldi 1999; Purcell 1999. Purcell notes that 'by the time of the Catalogues *insula* no longer refers to a free-standing block of many dwelling-units, but to the individual units' (151).

constructions on 'greenfield' sites, but reworkings of older structures, chiefly *insulae*, implying either a freeing-up of property or else an aggressive buying-up of such; in some cases they invade public spaces, such as above the vast 'Sette Sale' cistern serving the Baths of Trajan, or intrude on to roadways. Guidobaldi suggests we may see in all this a loss of imperial authority (once the court shifted to Milan – and equally to Constantinople) and greater power among the city prefects, who might have keenly allowed built expansions by fellow *clarissimi* and senators, jostling to display their worth and wealth.[56]

One of the best-investigated zones is the Caelian Hill: four major late Roman residences have been traced on the summit, three securely linked to Roman noble families (the Symmachi and the Valerii, plus Gaudentius, an early fifth-century senator), while on the western slopes additional *domus* include a converted apartment block under the church of SS Giovanni e Paolo and the claimed Domus Aniciorum encompassing the standing apsed hall known as the 'Library of Agapitus'.[57] Scale could be vast: the Symmachus *domus* comprised c.8,000 m² of audience/reception, dining and residential rooms plus courtyards, porticoes and c.2,000 m² of commercial and work space (including a dye-works); wealth, pedigree and culture were registered through statuary, inscriptions and extensive marble ornamentation, notably in *opus sectile*. Comparable-quality display has been revealed in a substantial fourth-century *domus* recently explored – and accessible to modern visitors – under Palazzo Valentini near Piazza Venezia. This late Roman complex involved a remodelling of two earlier houses, duly enhanced via fine mosaic (floor) and *opus sectile* (floor and wall) decoration over two storeys (Figs 11.6–8).

There is a sizeable unravelling of Rome's elite built landscape in the fifth century, caused first by the direct threat against and then sack of Rome under Alaric, and later by civil war and Vandal capture. Some high nobility took flight before 410 (some relocating permanently to Constantinople or to Ravenna) and others later. The Domus Pinciana, part-revealed under the Villa Medici, is associated with Anicia Faltonia Proba, who allegedly let Alaric's forces into Rome; when she subsequently fled to North Africa, her properties were taken over by the imperial fisc.[58] Some *domus* were damaged in the Gothic sack, such as that of the Valerii, while significant decay at the houses of Symmachus and Gaudentius can perhaps be connected to Geiseric's rampant Vandals in 455. Noticeably, activity persisted within parts of Gaudentius' *domus*, but not on any opulent level, being marked by stables, work zones and basic housing units.[59] Such archaeologies of destruction, decay, repurposing and/or robbing reveal the economic challenges (and opportunities) in fifth-century Rome, and also open up questions of site ownership.

---

[56] Guidobaldi 1999, esp. 56–9.
[57] Summaries in Carignani 2000; Spinola 2000; Pavolini 2000. On architectural forms and displays, Guidobaldi 2000.
[58] Broise et al. 2000. However, Procopius (*Bell*. 2.8.10, 9.5) relates that the eastern Roman *magister militum* Belisarius resided here in the later 530s, even though the Ostrogothic king Theoderic's agents had earlier removed marbles from here, perhaps following earthquake damage.
[59] At Palazzo Valentini, Napoli and Baldassarri 2015, 97 note use in the fifth century, but with fire in and collapse of Domus B by c. AD 500 (after likely decay and robbing), whereas longer activity, across the sixth century, was traced in Domus A.

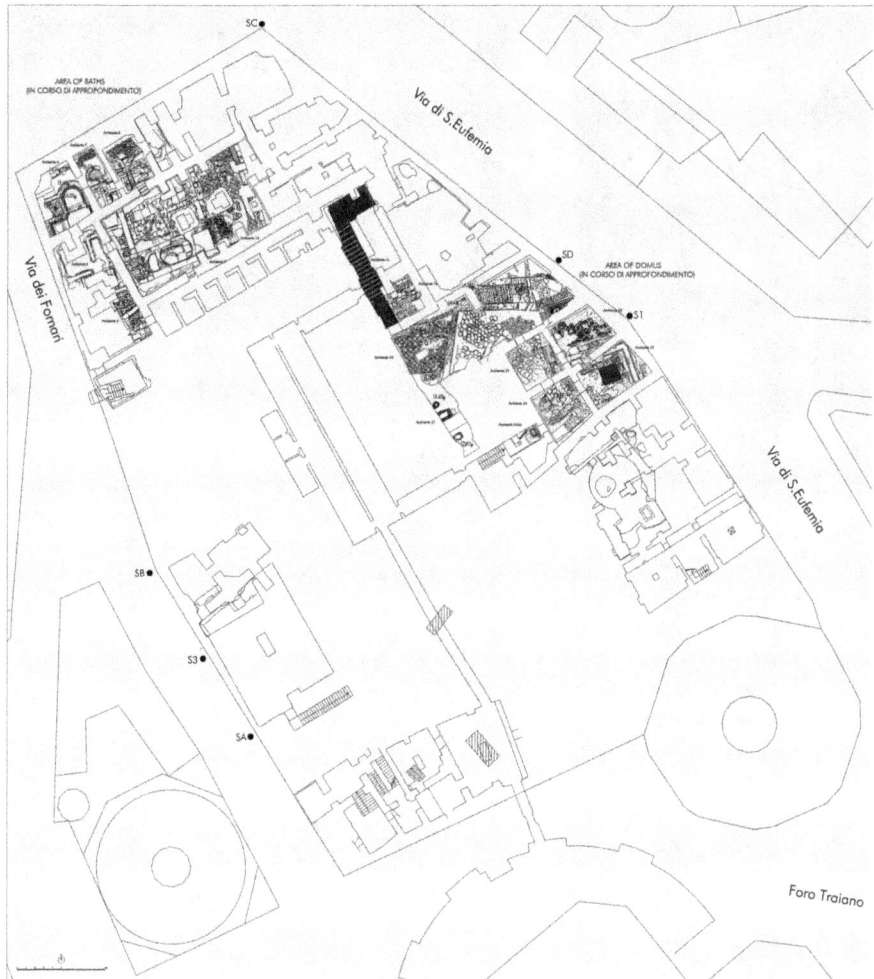

Figure 11.6 Location and site plan for the excavated *domus* complexes at the Palazzo Valentini, Rome. (Image courtesy of Luisa Napoli and Luisa Baldassarri; © Città Metropolitana di Roma Capitale)

The Church and the City

Sources such as the *Curiosum* and Ammianus Marcellinus' famous description of Constantius II's visit in the mid-350s record the mass of old imperial monuments – both symbolic and utilitarian – still dominating Rome's cityscape, and expanded under Constantine.[60] The noted elite *domus* express one new dynamic – namely a shift from

---

[60] Amm. Marc. 16.10. For classical to early Christian in fourth-century Rome: Curran 2000; fifth-century Rome summarised in Pani Ermini 1999; wider coverage in *Aurea Roma* 2000; Pani Ermini 2000a; Lançon 2000; Maskarinec 2018; also Salzman 1999.

Figure 11.7 Late Roman *domus*, Palazzo Valentini: area along via di S. Eufemia, Domus B, showing apsidal aula with *opus sectile* pavement. (Image courtesy of Luisa Napoli and Luisa Baldassarri; © Città Metropolitana di Roma Capitale)

Figure 11.8 Palazzo Valentini: view of the Domus A triclinium with its geometric mosaic floor. (Image courtesy of Luisa Napoli and Luisa Baldassarri; © Città Metropolitana di Roma Capitale)

civic euergetism to private display – but these came increasingly to be overshadowed by the new focus of state investment: the church.[61] By the 350s, even if they are ignored by Ammianus, Rome featured monumental church complexes within the city (notably in the Lateran zone) but chiefly in the suburbs, most prominent being St Peter's. The scale and quality of some of these earlier churches are evident in their structural endurance (albeit with restorations) for over 1,500 years.[62] At Rome, as elsewhere, the initial emphasis was on commemoration and veneration of martyr tombs and a concomitant investment in funerary churches; Pope Damasus (366–84) was hugely active in advertising Rome's saintly tombs and accommodating churches and catacombs to growing numbers of visitors.[63] All this signifies an injection of vitality to these burial suburbs, countering the image of towns hiding within walls.

---

[61] Note, however, that some *domus* likely hosted Christian groups already in the later third century; by the mid-fourth century the church clearly owned a number of (vacated or donated) residences and rented them out; some are documented into the fifth century as *iuxta* or *ad* specific basilicas; some might become replaced by churches – see discussion in Guidobaldi 1999, 60–1, 65–6.

[62] Prominent examples might be the fifth-century churches of Santa Maria Maggiore and Santa Sabina.

[63] For Rome, church placement and Pope Damasus: Pani Ermini 2000b; Fiocchi Nicolai 2003, 35–7; Yasin 2009, 157–61. A full eight substantial suburban churches belong to the reign of Constantine; many of these noticeably had funerary roles, and were designed to connect with but not directly overlie martyr tombs, as at Sant'Agnese and SS Pietro e Marcellino.

Yet bishops did not proliferate everywhere immediately from Constantine's reign, and while fourth-century church councils indicate a spread of bishoprics across the peninsula, for a high number of cities first documented attestations can be late – as in Liguria (sites like Albenga in 451 and Luni, 465) and the Picenum region, with a majority as late as AD 499 or 502.[64] Larger, politically charged centres were among the first equipped, with imperial funds to support construction of episcopal churches and to support later expansions, as at Aquileia (Figs 11.9 and 11.10). Elsewhere, ecclesiastical visibility may have been dependent on presence or absence of martyr remains, the strength of a pre-existing Christian community (and elites within these), and episcopal vitality. It is striking that few episcopal *ecclesiae* have been proven archaeologically to belong to the earlier fourth century; far more can be assigned to the late fourth century or the fifth.[65] These were predominantly intramural insertions, the earlier examples on city fringes, close to gates leading to key cemeteries. Later, fifth-century examples

Figure 11.9 Aquileia: reconstruction of the early fourth-century episcopal complex from above. (Image courtesy of Yuri Marano)

---

[64] Liguria: Marcenaro 2003, 183; Lusuardi Siena 2003, 197. Picenum: Marano 2019. For south-central Italy one comparable late example (AD 499) is Segni (southern Lazio), a relative backwater in the Late Roman period – see Cifarelli and Colaiacomo 2011, 97–105, noting no secure archaeological trace yet for the palaeochristian church (likely beneath the Duomo).

[65] Chavarría Arnau 2018, 559–60; even Milan's earliest cathedral dates to the latter fourth century – coinciding with the energetic bishop Ambrose (see papers in *La città e la sua memoria* 1997). For bishops and first churches, see Testini et al. 1989; Cuscito 1989; Christie 2006, 91–112; plus Marano 2007 for early episcopal residences, and for Aquileia. On bishops and episcopal authority, see Chapter 12 in this volume.

Figure 11.10 Exterior view of Aquileia's cathedral church and baptistery of the later fourth century. (Image courtesy of Yuri Marano)

can appear closer to city centres, sometimes within former *fora* (e.g. Aosta, probably Albenga), or in elevated spaces in former acropoleis (as for Fermo and Ancona in Picenum).[66] In all cases there is scope to debate location choice – whether granted by or negotiated with civic authorities or perhaps donated by elites (hence the occurrence of some churches over *domus*) and whether positioned in abandoned, redundant or else active space.[67] For each, building work required clearance operations and marshalling of resources that will have made a strong physical, economic and symbolic mark on the respective townscapes.[68] We might also anticipate that some ecclesiastical spaces then expanded in the next generation or two through additional donations and purchases of properties and space, hence the evolution evident archaeologically in church form, attendant structures (especially related to 'episcopal complexes') and also burials (intramural burial becoming a norm from the sixth century).[69]

---

[66] Chavarría Arnau 2018, 560 states that older claims of early bishop seats in suburbs over martyr tombs are inaccurate; this is neatly discussed by Marano 2019 for examples within Picenum, such as Fano: p. 62.

[67] Testini et al. 1989; more widely, Cantino Wataghin 2003. Examples of an episcopal church over a *domus*: Lusuardi Siena 2003 for Luni; imposed over a temple platform: Marano 2019, 76–8 for Ancona's San Lorenzo under the duomo of San Ciriaco; imposed on and adapting a temple: Bonacasa Carra 2003, 55 for Agrigento's cathedral in the Temple of Concordia.

[68] Pani Ermini 1999, 39–42. We rarely hear how long projects took, but for large-scale edifices at least a decade must have been required.

[69] Episcopal complexes/groups: Marano 2010. Some churches/roles may also have been relocated as town centres became more 'Christianised': hence the possibility of the fifth-century fringe/suburban baptismal (episcopal?) church identified over baths at San Clemente, Albenga, being superseded by the centrally sited cathedral and baptistery by the mid-fifth century – see Massabò 2003.

It is important thus to recognise the church as the major economic stimulus in fourth- and, especially, fifth-century Italian cities through its logistical needs for buildings (architects, masons, workers, materials), art (stone/marblework units such as altars and chancels, mosaics, as well as hangings, candelabra and liturgical vessels) and products (oil for lights, food and wine for clerics and workers) alongside stimulating local tourism (via shrines, blessings, relics). To a large degree, workforces would surely have been local, and likewise core building materials (including *spolia*); but we must assume some skills mobility, such as in terms of architects and marble- and mosaic-artisans, with the capitals (Rome, Milan, Ravenna – but also larger regional centres like Naples and Palermo) their likely prime bases.[70] Bishops will have been central in deciding on church and artistic designs, and episcopal connectivity (and competition) no doubt stimulated this market.[71]

However, not all bishops were urban-based: for southern Italy, there is relatively scant evidence for churches in towns (and in the countryside) in the fourth century; in fact, bishops are better attested only from the later fifth century and tend, in regions such as Apulia province, to be associated with imperial properties and rural seats (both villas and *vici*), the best known being San Giusto within the *saltus Carminianensis*.[72]

Defence and the Late Roman City

Despite the new 'glue' of the church, the late Roman centuries saw much damage to the Italian peninsula through conflict – both civil war and enemy incursions – whose scale and impact intensified especially in the late fourth and earlier fifth century. Cities were the inevitable focus of much of this conflict: in internecine warfare, control of seats of power was crucial, along with possession of ports, mints and arms factories; to barbarian assailants, towns were storehouses of wealth, to be extracted through capture, ransoms or bribes. Responses to this insecurity are fully evident in the urban fabric, most prominently in the construction of defensive curtains, whether the rebuilding and reinforcing of older circuits (as in the case of planned towns in the north, such as Aosta, Turin, Como) or the creation of a new defensive line, responding to growth beyond old confines (as at Milan, Verona and, of course, Rome).[73] Some centres were on the front line, and investments in defences are clear guides to strategic, political as well as economic value. The first investments were likely state-funded (whereas later

---

[70] Foletti 2019 on mosaic workshops; using comparanda with the design and iconography of mosaics in Milan's Sant'Aquilino chapel of c. AD 400, Foletti argues for a branch of a/the Rome workshop – presumably one 'owned' by the Rome church – coming to Milan.

[71] Bishop Ambrose of Milan in the latter fourth century did much in this regard: see papers in *La città e la sua memoria* 1997, notably those by Lusuardi Siena, pp. 34–67. Paulinus of Nola in the early fifth century is a strong example of episcopal involvement in commissioning and contributing to church and shrine building and ornamentation: Yasin 2009, 181–9. Archaeologically, albeit deriving from the second quarter of the sixth century, the building, industrial and artistic works stimulated by the programme of church and monastery construction under bishop Sabinus at Canosa stand out: see Volpe 2007; 2016.

[72] Volpe and Turchiano 2010, 546–9.

[73] On sequences, see Christie 2006, 284–99, 308–14. See also examples for fourth- and fifth-century north Italy in Haug 2003. Rome: Pani Ermino 1999, 37–9; Dey 2011.

works may well have required city-drawn resources) and centred on northern Italy: in part this reflected areas affected by raids by Iuthungi and Alamanni, and involved in Roman civil wars, but it also denoted the new politics of Italy, with emperors often present in the empire's northern territories, making Milan a principal tetrarchic court and occasional residence from 284; we see also cities in Italy's Padane region especially selected for the various *fabricae*/state arms factories.[74] The insertion of military units in some centres is likely, along with winter-quartering arrangements; little of this is understood, however, especially in terms of scale and its impact on urban demographics, and it is rarely recognisable archaeologically, but laws in the *Codex Theodosianus* do refer to soldiers, disputes, supplies and billeting as common in the late fourth and especially the fifth century.[75] In periods of heightened stress, when threats were immediate, such as in conflicts between Alaric's and Stilicho's forces in the 400s, garrisons were installed to guard defended cities, stockpile supplies and ensure citizenry loyalty.[76] And, following Stilicho's execution, 'barbarians' in Roman garrisons and bodyguards in a number of northern cities were massacred, or else managed to flee.[77]

Walls became essential components of the late imperial urban form, and new circuits or revisions are attested into the mid-fifth century (Fig. 11.11) – for example, the *magister militum* (and, later, brief emperor) Flavius Constantius renewed the defences of Albenga in Liguria (one of the few epigraphic attestations of such works)[78] – and with further attention given under the Ostrogothic regime from the 490s to sites like Verona, Pavia, Como and Tortona.[79] Few sites remained unfortified by the fifth century, although some southern and Sicilian centres may have delayed investment or, as evident from Procopius' account of the Gothic Wars of the 530s–40s, came to rely on citadels (earlier acropoleis) for military defence. But the possession of a strong wall circuit did not guarantee urban survival, as is evident in the loss of central Italian sites

---

[74] Christie 2006, 308–10; Roncaglia 2018, 119–27; Brogiolo 2018, 3; Chapter 2 in this volume. Rambaldi 2009, catalogue, pp. 207–18, shows investment in walls and repairs in northern centres in the 260s–70s. On the *fabrica* (for arrows) at Concordia, see Cresci Marrone 2001, noting good epigraphic evidence and traces of urban growth, although, oddly, the city walls seem not to have been restored. A few arms factories were based over the Apennines, including Lucca (for sword production), which revitalised a townscape that had struggled in the third century – see Abela 1998, 30.

[75] E.g. *CTh* 7.8.3–6.

[76] Zos. 5.26, 30–2. Cosentino 2020, 123 discusses 'barbarians' in Roman troops at the new fifth-century capital, Ravenna, with contingents attested fully to the time of Odoacer. On the army and Italy, see Chapter 7 in this volume.

[77] Zos. 5.35. See also Wijnendaele 2018, 269–73.

[78] *CIL* 5.7781 for AD 415–17, recording repairs in Constantius' name to counter the 'flood of evil people' (*et rabidos contra fluctus gentesque nefandas Constanti murum nominis opposuit*) – likely referring to the passage of Athaulf's Goths en route to Gaul after their brief occupation of Rome in 410. See Marcenaro 2003, 182–3. Contemporary is Rutilius Namatianus' *De reditu suo*, with the poet-senator seemingly an eyewitness to the city's rebuilding, with his verses noting the cutting of stones from the mountains, and the raising of the walls and *propagnacula* (towers/bastions) using cranes – see Lamboglia 1976–1978.

[79] Settia 1995; Pani Ermini 1995. Dating of the fortress-city (*castrum*) of Grado, seen as strategic replacement for Aquileia, and a site designed without any classical monumentality (i.e. lacking any theatre, forum, cult temples), has migrated from the mid-fifth century to eastern Roman to Ostrogothic occupations – see Brogiolo 2007.

Figure 11.11 The Porta Pinciana on the north-western flank of the Aurelianic Walls of Rome. (Image: Neil Christie)

like Falerii Novi and Rome's ports of Ostia and Portus; here, exposure to (regular) threats in particular damaged site sustainability (see below).[80]

A notable example of a battered but enduring, yet altered defended city is Aquileia at the head of the Adriatic. Long a notable trade focus for Rome looking north to the Danube and beyond, its location made it the first city reached via the north-east Alpine passage, which became the main land route for attacks on Italy. Unsurprisingly, Aquileia witnesses various defensive reinforcements across the third to sixth centuries in response to sieges or threats: first, a doubling of the Republican walls in the 230s; then an expanded, new curtain in the late third century, enclosing but also incorporating a tetrarchic palace and circus complex; U-shaped and pentagonal towers on the western flank (mostly not investigated) are likely fourth-century additions, while the canal-side eastern flanks saw different towers imposed. These expansions, remodellings and reinforcements reflect a need to maintain Aquileia, less as a trade city and more as an imperial bulwark, vital for military containment and supply; its imperial role is also reflected in the early implantation of a bishop and a monumental cathedral and other religious structures. Its fabric necessarily changed, and the city's

---

[80] For mapping of 'lost' Falerii Novi, see Keay et al. 2000, noting surface finds pointing to some activity into the fifth century at least. New work at this townscape is underway by teams from the British School at Rome and the universities of Toronto, Harvard and Ghent, in conjunction with the Soprintendenza Archeologia, Belle Arti e Paesaggio per la provincia di Viterbo e per l'Etruria meridionale.

physical spaces mutated, with structures quitted, demolished and/or repurposed; cutting ditches, erecting new wall lines or towers meant clearances of spaces, cemeteries, shops and even neglected public monuments, hence the reuse in the defences of vast quantities of stonework, bricks, columns, epitaphs and diverse architectural units.[81] We sadly lack information on how long such sizeable projects took, how messy they were, how disruptive for residents (merchants, clergy, workers, soldiers alike) and how they were viewed by these – certainly, however, they came to define a different-looking cityscape compared to earlier classical times.[82]

Damaged Towns and Failing/Failed Cities

In some cases, cities and their authorities were struggling against nature as well: for Forum Popili (modern Forlimpopoli, Emilia-Romagna) fourth-century evidence for floods and alluviation episodes (from the Ronco and Ausa torrents) shows a damaged townscape, with reduced ability to recover, leading to urban shrinkage.[83] Alluvial deposits are recognised in other late Roman centres such as Vercelli and Modena, indicating recovery, but without full clearance of the debris generated by the flooding; Rome likewise suffered from a number of floods, including one major episode in the early fifth century.[84] Discussion continues about climatic changes in the late Roman and early medieval periods and their impact, especially in terms of the potential blockage of harbours through silting (as at Luni) and damage to agricultural productivity.[85]

The Italian peninsula suffers from seismic activity, and various episodes are attested in the late Roman period, many either noted in inscriptions or recognisable from structural damage. At Luni, for example, an earthquake in the later fourth century caused destruction of houses (e.g. the Domus Settentrionale and Domus degli Affreschi), and we subsequently see some structural damage partially plugged, alongside the exploitation of materials from ruined/abandoned buildings, as evident at the Domus dei Mosaici, just north of the Capitolium, which was enlarged in the

---

[81] Buora 2016, 91–9, noting also temporary counter-siege earth-ditch defences in the 360s, and the later eastern Roman 'zig-zag' wall which sliced the city in half, rejecting the northern space. Interestingly, there are traces of whitewashing on the Late Roman wall exterior at least, perhaps to cover up the (unattractive?) miscellany of materials. See Marano 2012 on the nature of Aquileia after the AD 452 Hunnic sack. The archaeology of Late Roman Aquileia's monuments and houses is summarised in Haug 2003.

[82] Christie 2013 discusses the physical and mental impact of city-wall building; see also Dey 2011. For Rome in AD 402, note inscriptions referring to debris cleared during renewal work: 'The Senate and People of Rome to the Imperial Caesars, our lords, unconquered leaders, Arcadius and Honorius, victorious and triumphant, eternal emperors, for restoring the walls, gates and towers of the Eternal City, after removing masses of stone debris, at the behest of Stilicho, most distinguished, illustrious Count and Master of two commands, to the perpetuation of the Name, set up statues. Under the charge of Flavius Macrobius Longinianus, most distinguished, Prefect of the City, dedicated to their divine majesties', *CIL* 6.1188–90.

[83] See Morigi, in Coralini 2010.

[84] Meneghini 2018, 12.

[85] Brogiolo 2018, 6, noting how the archaeology for such environmental damage belongs more to the sixth and seventh centuries – either a sign of ongoing civic ability to fulfil 'clean-up operations' in the fifth century and less so later, especially after the economic and demographic collapse brought by the Gothic Wars and by the Justinianic plague, or an indication that the scale of environmental change grew later. See Schoolman, Chapter 10 in this volume, revealing how current data point more to general landscape and environmental continuity across the whole Roman period.

early fifth century.[86] Mid-fourth-century inscriptions show the governor or *corrector* of the central-south Italian province of Samnium busily involved in restoring theatres, baths and other structures as well as re-erecting statues in (perhaps selected) sites like Isernia, Saepinum and Allifae, with damage seemingly due to earthquakes.[87] It is noticeable that these public amenities were deemed salvageable (by governor or by popular/civic choice) and worthy of the governor's input; what we cannot say, though, is whether these structures had in fact been fully active until the calamity, nor can we be certain if they lay damaged (and even robbed for materials) for long before restorations occurred.[88] For fifth-century Rome, texts record a number of earthquakes, notably in 422, 429 and 443; inscriptions reveal efforts – sometimes rapid, sometimes delayed – to restore damaged monuments, but we might imagine a focus of resources on key showpieces, such as the Colosseum (Fig. 11.12).[89]

Figure 11.12 Colosseum, Rome: inscription recording repairs to the monumental complex at the end of the fifth century following earthquake damage.
(Image: Neil Christie)

---

[86] Durante 2003, 208–10.
[87] Ward-Perkins 1984, 25, with nn. 30 and 34; *CIL* 9.2338, 2639, 2956. For earthquakes and late Roman loss and repair in Catania, Sicily, see Bottari et al. 2015.
[88] See Thomas and Witschel 1992; and Ward-Perkins 1984 generally on governors' input.
[89] For the Colosseum and analyses of its fabric for the late Roman to medieval period, see Rea 2002a, notably pp. 153–9; Rea 2002b; Orlandi 1999. Earthquakes and Rome: Molin and Guidoboni 1989. Recent scientific analysis in the Apennines argues for tracing a fifth-century seismic event, suggested as AD 443 (but conceivably later, or else earlier): Galli et al. 2019.

While natural calamities might cause damage and force some level of relocation of structures and activities or even population transfer, these do not seem to have caused instances of full urban loss in late Roman Italy. Potentially, however, warfare and imperial strategy (political as well as economic) could, ultimately, result in some towns fading or failing. Piedmont in north-west Italy features a number of 'abandoned' classical sites, including Chieri[90] and Libarna;[91] and in central Italy examples include Amiternum (prov. Abruzzo), Aquinum (Lazio), and Potentia (Fig. 11.4) and Suasa (Le Marche).[92] It is easy to seek a blanket explanation of depopulation through barbarian assaults, and yet this claim of martial destruction is offered usually where no careful archaeology has occurred. In fact, new survey technologies have been applied at some of these 'failed' towns, undertaken across sectors of their buried/ploughed-out/part-explored spaces, in order to map their plans and structures; such non-intrusive projects offer much scope to question when urban decay began to set in – although only systematic excavation campaigns will guide on the types of people who may have hung on in these places.[93]

Factors for terminal decline are many – economic marginalisation, exposure to threats, failing (elite and civic) investments, demographic relocation – and it is evident that some decay might begin as early as the second or third century and is not simply synonymous with the latest Roman centuries.[94] Warfare, inevitably, had some impact, and it may be the case that the elevated insecurity affecting the peninsula in the fifth century – especially the north of the Italian peninsula, suffering incursions and movements by Goths and others – resulted in scarred towns, hit directly or debilitated through food shortages prompted by damage to the farming landscapes and by loss of people through conflict, enslavement or disease.[95] Where towns lacked walls (or ones in good repair) or sufficient manpower to support and supply, we might envisage a resultant depopulation (progressive or rapid) and migration to more secure centres, including upland rural sites. Some larger sites that suffered in conflict often did recover, such as Aquileia, albeit with a level of decay and a shrinkage in populated space.[96] However, throughout, caution is required, since we must avoid reading each

---

[90] Pantò 2010, 35 and 45.

[91] Cirnigliaro and De Vingo 2004, 23–31, who stress how limited the modern archaeological interventions have been, perhaps shrouding more in the way of activity at these fading sites.

[92] Meneghini 2018, 15–16, with n. 5, on site losses in central Italy from the fifth to tenth century, citing seventeen out of forty-six towns; he highlights especially plague/disease and famine provoked largely by warfare (with the sixth century the most severely affected – also in terms of recorded earthquakes), but also through the 'Little Ice Age' of c. AD 500–700.

[93] See respective papers in Vermeulen et al. 2012; for work at Potentia, see Vermeulen 2012.

[94] Christie 2012. For wider surveys of 'lost' cities, see papers in Christie and Augenti 2012.

[95] Brogiolo 2018, 5–6. Here landscape archaeology and excavations reveal for many parts of the north and centre of the peninsula a fractured or even 'shrunken' working and settled landscape, failing villas and a rise in defensive installations commencing in the fifth century and accelerating in the sixth: see, for example, Bertoldi 2019, 17–22 for the Siena (Tuscany) region. The south of the peninsula was, however, more resilient for 'classical' and intensive continuity, extending fully into the sixth century, having suffered far less damage than the north in the fourth and fifth centuries: Volpe 2016; Goffredo and Volpe 2018.

[96] Note also how the inscription recording a restored/new wall circuit and gates under Constantius at Albenga (n. 78 above) also refers to renewal of houses, market and port here: Marcenaro 2003, 182–3.

excavated burnt or demolition deposit as a 'destruction layer' and avoid associating such with historically attested conflict episodes and potential urban 'ends'.[97]

Conclusions

While for the late third century we can start to see a notable change for some of the cities of Italy in terms of substantial city walls being erected and exterior spaces being remodelled, the textual and archaeological evidence does point to a core continuity of civic activity, even if the defensive wall-building had meant sacrifices of public works in some cases (e.g. Susa: forum; Rimini: amphitheatre).[98] Imperial refocusing on the northern plains and highways meanwhile generated accelerated growth in key centres there (e.g. Como, Brescia, Cividale) and formulated new urban models (notably palace-circus complexes in the capitals). We struggle somewhat to visualise how towns/cities looked and felt in the fourth century: in theory this was a stable enough period, but it was one where Christianity was thrown into the mix and imperial patronage of this soon weakened the old religions. There is a sense almost of places 'ticking over' but without great strength – unless one was in one of the favoured centres such as Milan, Ravenna, Como and Rome – as the 'old order' slowly gave way to a new one. Nonetheless, as seen, expressions of renewal and commemoration endured in many places, and elite houses likewise are attested in some – but not all – cities.

Within this fourth-century time frame, the Church could, through strong bishops, as at Milan, Brescia and Turin, create notable new landmarks within and around cities and, en route, exploit past, redundant public monuments as quarries. Yet bishops were not inserted in all cities at once nor automatically given funds to create new monumental foci; there is a patchwork of growth whose mechanics are not always easily understood – we often cannot say, for instance, if a church is mid-fourth, late fourth or early fifth century in date,[99] since we rely often on fragmentary architectural components or partial archaeological guides beneath later, successor structures. In general, however, few would dispute that by the first decades of the fifth century, many cities had an (intramural) episcopal church and at least a pair of suburban funerary churches, by when the majority of classical public structures had fallen redundant.

The period also sees increasing use of *spolia* – reused materials, whether bricks, stone, marble, plus architectural elements – signifying exploitation of such ruins.[100] In theory these ruins will have been owned by the civic authorities, and such blatant reuse (such as within a church) speaks of logical redeployment for the public good (including in the

---

[97] For Rome, however, one can observe fairly consistent and clear traces of damage caused in the sacks of Alaric and Geiseric in the earlier and mid-fifth century – see Pani Ermini 1999, 50–1.

[98] The evidence provided in Haug 2003, arguably, points strongly to continuity in many key towns, albeit with material and organisational change. She traces a series of generally common transformations which affect towns in the north to different levels and at different times and rates.

[99] Chavarría Arnau 2018, 559–60, 564. See the archaeology of the first church under Florence's duomo: Scampoli 2010, 53–6.

[100] Pani Ermini 1999, 51–2.

removal of dangerous debris/eyesores). More work is required on understanding the interplay between old and new space, such as whether classical ruins became marginal areas and when/if churches drew new habitational districts to them. In addition, some old monuments were too big to remove/rob out, and here a different type of exploitation can be seen, namely the conversion of amphitheatres and theatres to defensive citadels.[101] And there are extant examples of these vast monuments being adapted for houses (although often such 'accretions' have since been removed to 'restore' these complexes to their Roman form), as at Lucca, Rome's Theatre of Marcellus, and the theatre of Catania (Sicily); such adaptation is documented by the Middle Ages,[102] but this 'colonisation' perhaps began already in the fifth/sixth century.[103] If so, we need to ask how was it sanctioned, what type of people occupied these houses, where they relocated from (e.g. refugees, residents displaced by church building works, workers drawn to church building) and their status. Such questioning is essential to help better understand the workings and populations of these late antique/post-classical towns. Here, again, archaeology holds the key to unpicking urban change and transformation.[104]

Bibliography

Abela, E. (1998) 'Lucca', in S. Gelichi (ed.) *Archeologia urbana in Toscana: la città altomedievale*, Documenti di Archeologia 17, Mantua, 23–34.

Angeli Bertinelli, M. G. and A. Donati (eds) (2010) *Città e territorio: la Liguria e il mondo antico. Atti del IV Incontro internazionale di storia antica (Genova, 19–20 febbraio 2009)*, Seria Antiqua et Mediaevalia 12, Rome.

Arce, J. (1999) 'El inventario de Roma: *Curiosum* y *Notitia*', in W. V. Harris (ed.) *The Transformations of* Vrbs Roma *in Late Antiquity*, *JRA* Suppl. 33, Portsmouth, RI, 15–22.

Arnold, J., S. Bjornlie and K. Sessa (eds) (2016) *A Companion to Ostrogothic Italy*, Leiden.

Augenti, A. (2016) *Archeologia dell'Italia medievale*, Rome.

Aurea Roma (2000) = *Aurea Roma: dalla città pagana alla città cristiana* (Exhibition catalogue, 22 December 2000–20 April 2001), ed. S. Ensoli and E. La Rocca, Rome.

Bertoldi, S. (2019) 'L'insediamento in Provincia di Siena (secoli I–X d.C.)', in S. Bertoldi, M. Putti and E. Vanni, *Archeologia e storia dei paesaggi senesi: territorio, risorse, commerci tra età romana e Medioevo*, Biblioteca del Dipartimento di Archeologia e Storia delle Arte – Sezione Archeologica, Università di Siena 21, Sesto Fiorentino, 15–30.

---

[101] For example, Lucca – Abela 1998, 34. Based on the narrative in Procopius, it is assumed that such defensive roles were first manifested in the ebbs and flows of the drawn-out Gothic Wars of the 530s–50s: Pagano 2004 discusses the example of Spoleto.

[102] As from the tenth century for Lucca – Ward-Perkins 1984, 211.

[103] One Gallic example is the circus and, potentially, the amphitheatre at Arles: Loseby 1996, 52–5; Christie and Kipling 2000, 28–30.

[104] Sincere thanks are extended to Charlotte Van Regenmortel for her very helpful and critical reading of the final draft of this paper; the editor, Jeroen Wijnendaele, for perceptive comments on a first draft of the text; the peer reviewers for their invaluable suggestions to strengthen the whole; Giulia Bison for information on and images for Grumentum; Paola Baldassarri and Luisa Napoli (Dipartimento di Servizio, Provincia di Roma and Città Metropolitana di Roma Capitale) for information on and images of the Palazzo Valentini *domus*; Yuri Marano for papers on Picenum, Aquileia and episcopal complexes, and images of Aquileia's cathedral; Alessandro Carabia for recent papers on Luni and Liguria; and Pilar Diarte Blasco for guidance on sequences in Late Roman Hispania.

Bison, G., L. Pozzan, S. Haghani and L. Anguilano (2017) 'Metalworking Evidence from a Late Antique Context in the Forum of Grumentum', *STAR: Science and Technology of Archaeological Research* 3 (2): 220–37.

Boin, D. (2013) *Ostia in Late Antiquity*, Cambridge.

Bonacasa Carra, R. M. (2003) 'I modelli di Roma cristiana in area siciliana; aspetti e problematiche', in M. Marcenaro (ed.) *Roma e la Liguria Maritima: Secoli IV–X. La capitale cristiana e una regione di confine. Atti del Corso e Catalogo della Mostra, Genova 14 febbraio–31 agosto 2003*, Istituto Internazionale di Studi Liguri, Atti dei Convegni 11, Genoa, 51–62.

Bonacasa Carra, R. M. and E. Vitale (eds) (2007) *La cristianizzazione in Italia tra Tardoantico ed Altomedioevo: Atti del IX Congresso nazionale di archeologia Cristiana (Agrigento, 20–25 novembre 2004)*, 2 vols, Palermo.

Bottari, C., M. Coltelli and C. Monaco (2015) 'Evidence of Late Roman Collapse at Catania (Sicily, Southern Italy): an Earthquake in the 4th Century AD?', *Quaternary International* 357: 336–43.

Bowden, W., A. Gutteridge and C. Machado (eds) (2006) *Social and Political Life in Late Antiquity*, Late Antique Archaeology 3.1, Leiden.

Brogiolo, G. P. (1993) *Brescia altomedievale: urbanistica ed edilizia dal IV al IX secolo*, Documenti di Archeologia 2, Mantua.

Brogiolo, G. P. (ed.) (1999) *S. Giulia di Brescia: gli scavi dal 1980 al 1992. Reperti preromani, romani e alto medievali*, Florence.

Brogiolo, G. P. (2007) 'Grado: da castello a città', in A. Augenti and C. Bertelli (eds) *Felix Ravenna. La croce, la spada, la vela: l'alto Adriatico fra V e VI secolo*, Milan, 71–2.

Brogiolo, G. P. (2011) *Le origini della città medievale*, Post Classical Archaeologies Studies 1, Mantua.

Brogiolo, G. P. (2018) 'Transformation in the Cities of Northern Italy between the Fifth and Seventh Centuries AD: Forms, Functions and Societies', in P. Diarte Blasco and N. Christie (eds) *Interpreting Transformations of People and Landscapes in Late Antiquity and the Early Middle Ages: Archaeological Approaches and Issues*, Oxford, 1–9.

Broise, H., M. Dewailly and V. Jolivet (2000) 'Horti Luculliani: un palazzo tardoantico a Villa Medici', in *Aurea Roma: dalla città pagana alla città cristiana* (Exhibition catalogue, 22 December 2000–20 April 2001), ed. S. Ensoli and E. La Rocca, Rome, 113–16.

Buora, M. (2016) 'Le difese di Aquileia e dell'Italia nordorientale dal tardoantico al medioevo', *Temporis Signa: archeologia della tarda antichità e del medioevo* 11: 89–108.

Cantino Wataghin, G. (2003) 'Christian Topography in the Late Antique Town: Recent Results and Open Questions', in L. Lavan and W. Bowden (eds) *Theory and Practice in Late Antique Archaeology*, Late Antique Archaeology 1, Leiden, 224–56.

Cantone, V. (ed.) (2019) *Studi sulla circolazione del mosaico in area nord-adriatica*, Studia Artium Mediaevalium Brunensia 9, Rome.

Carignani, A. (2000) 'La domus dei Simmachi', in *Aurea Roma: dalla città pagana alla città cristiana* (Exhibition catalogue, 22 December 2000–20 April 2001), ed. S. Ensoli and E. La Rocca, Rome, 149–51.

Carneiro, A., N. Christie and P. Diarte-Blasco (eds) (2020) *Urban Transformations in the Late Antique West: Materials, Agents, and Models*, Coimbra.

Cavalieri, M. (2015) 'Étude des complexes monumentaux en Italie du Nord entre le IIe et le IVe s.: rupture, continuité ou transformation?', in L. Brassous and A. Quevedo (eds) *Urbanisme civique en temps de crise: les espaces publics d'Hispanie et de l'Occident romain entre le IIe et le IVe siècle*, Collection de la Casa de Velázquez 149, Madrid, 83–102.

Cavalieri Manasse, G. (ed.) (2008) *L'area del Capitolium di Verona: ricerche storiche e archeologiche*, Verona.

Chavarría Arnau, A. (ed.) (2017) *Ricerche sul centro episcopale di Padova: scavi 2011–2012*, Mantua.
Chavarría Arnau, A. (2018) 'The Archaeology of Early Italian Churches in Context, 313–569 CE', in W. R. Caraher, T. W. Davis and D. K. Pettegrew (eds) *The Oxford Handbook of Early Christian Archaeology*, Oxford, 557–80.
Christie, N. (2006) *From Constantine to Charlemagne: an Archaeology of Italy, AD 300–800*, Aldershot.
Christie, N. (2009) 'No More Fun? The End of Amphitheatres and Games in the Late Roman West', in T. Wilmott (ed.) *Roman Amphitheatres and Spectacula: a 21st-Century Perspective. Papers from an International Conference Held at Chester, 16th–18th February, 2007*, British Archaeological Reports International Series 1946, Oxford, 221–32.
Christie, N. (2012) '*Vrbes extinctae*: Archaeologies of and Approaches to Abandoned Classical Cities', in N. Christie and A. Augenti (eds) *Vrbes extinctae: Archaeologies of Abandoned Classical Cities*, Farnham, 1–44.
Christie, N. (2013) 'Safe in Their Homes? Reflections on Defending Towns and Populations in Northern Italy, AD 350–450', in R. García-Gasco, S. González Sánchez and D. Hernández de la Fuente (eds) *The Theodosian Age (AD 379–455): Power, Place, Belief and Learning in the Last Century of the Western Empire*, British Archaeological Reports International Series 2493, Oxford, 123–31.
Christie, N. (2016) 'Late Roman and Late Antique Italy: from Constantine to Justinian', in A. E. Cooley (ed.) *A Companion to Roman Italy*, Oxford, 133–53.
Christie, N. and A. Augenti (eds) (2012) *Vrbes extinctae: Archaeologies of Abandoned Classical Cities*, Farnham.
Christie, N. and R. Kipling (2000) 'Structures of Power or Structures of Convenience? Exploiting the Material Past in Late Antiquity and the Early Middle Ages', in S. Pearce (ed.) *Researching Material Culture*, Leicester Archaeology Monographs 8, Leicester, 21–36.
Cifarelli, F. M. and F. Colaiacomo (2011) *Segni antica e medievale: una guida archeologica*, Segni.
Cirelli, E. (2008) *Ravenna: archeologia di una città*, Contributi di Archeologia Medievale 2, Florence.
Cirnigliaro, E. and P. De Vingo (2004) 'Note su Libarna e sul suo territorio fra tardoantico e altomedioevo', *Rivista di storia, arte, archeologica per le province di Alessandria e Asti* 113 (2): 5–44.
Coarelli, F. (1999) 'L'edilizia pubblica a Roma in età tetrachica', in W. V. Harris (ed.) *The Transformations of* Vrbs Roma *in Late Antiquity*, JRA Suppl. 33, Portsmouth, RI, 23–33.
Coralini, A. (2010) *Cultura abitativa nella Cisalpina Romana*, vol. 1: *Forum Popili, flos Italiae*, Documenti della Cisalpina Romana 9, Florence.
Cosentino, S. (2020) 'I barbari e Ravenna nel V secolo: organizzazione sociale, practica economica, identità di gruppo', in P. De Vingo and J. Pinar Gil (eds) *Romana Gothica IV. Barbares dans la ville de l'Antiquité tardive: présences et absences dans les espaces publics et privés. Actes du Congrès International, Museu d'Història de Catalunya (Barcelone, 12–13 novembre 2010)*, Sesto Fiorentino, 121–32.
Cresci Marrone, G. (2001) 'Lo stanziamento militare, la fabbrica di frecce e la comunità di commercianti orientali nella Concordia tardo antica', in P. Croce Da Villa and E. Di Filippo Balestrazzi (eds) *Concordia: tremila anni di storia*, Rubano, 245–9.
Croce Da Villa, P. (2001a) 'Evoluzione dell'impianto urbano dell'antica Concordia: la forma urbis dal I sec. a.C. al VII sec. d.C.', in P. Croce Da Villa and E. Di Filippo Balestrazzi (eds) *Concordia: tremila anni*, Rubano, 125–211.
Croce Da Villa, P. (2001b) 'Il complesso paleocristiano di Piazza Cardinal Costantini', in P. Croce Da Villa and E. Di Filippo Balestrazzi (eds) *Concordia: tremila anni*, Rubano, 253–61.
Croce Da Villa, P. and E. Di Filippo Balestrazzi (eds) *Concordia: tremila anni di storia*, Rubano, 2001.
Curran, J. (2000) *Pagan City and Christian Capital: Rome in the Fourth Century*, Oxford.

Cuscito, G. (1989) 'Vescovo e cattedrale nella documentazione epigrafica in Occidente: Italia e Dalmazia', in *Actes du XIe Congrès international d'archéologie chrétienne*, 735–76.
Dall'Aglio, P. L. and I. Di Cocco (eds) (2004) *Pesaro romana: archeologia e urbanistica*, Studi e Scavi n.s. 4, Bologna.
Deliyannis, D. M. (2016) 'Urban Life and Culture', in J. Arnold, S. Bjornlie and K. Sessa (eds) *A Companion to Ostrogothic Italy*, Leiden, 234–62.
Dey, H. (2011) *The Aurelian Wall and the Refashioning of Imperial Rome, AD 271–855*, Cambridge.
Diarte Blasco, P. (2012) *La configuración urbana de la Hispania tardoantigua: transformaciones y pervivencias de los espacios públicos romanos (s. III–VI d. C.)*, British Archaeological Reports International Series 2429, Oxford.
Durante, A. M. (2003) 'La città vescovile di Luna nell'alto medioevo', in M. Marcenaro (ed.) *Roma e la Liguria Maritima: Secoli IV–X. La capitale cristiana e una regione di confine. Atti del Corso e Catalogo della Mostra, Genova 14 febbraio–31 agosto 2003*, Istituto Internazionale di Studi Liguri, Atti dei Convegni 11, Genoa, 203–14.
Durante, A. M. (2010) *Città antica di Luni*, Lavori in corso 2, Genoa.
Esmonde Cleary, S. (2013) *The Roman West, AD 200–500: an Archaeological Study*, Cambridge.
Fiocchi Nicolai, V. (2003) 'Gli spazi delle sepolture cristiane a Roma tra III e VI secolo', in M. Marcenaro (ed.) *Roma e la Liguria Maritima: Secoli IV–X. La capitale cristiana e una regione di confine. Atti del Corso e Catalogo della Mostra, Genova 14 febbraio–31 agosto 2003*, Istituto Internazionale di Studi Liguri, Atti dei Convegni 11, Genoa, 31–40.
Flaminio, R. (2015) 'Il mosaico di via Perti a Como', in *Rivista archeologica dell'antica provincia e diocesi di Como, 197 (= Atti del Convegno 'Luoghi, funzioni, trasformazioni tra Tardoantico e Primo Medioevo nel territorio dell'antica diocesi e provincia di Como', Como 24–25 ottobre 2014)*, Como, 5–25.
Foletti, I. (2019) 'Milano capitale, tra Roma e Ravenna: circolazione di botteghe, di materiali e di idee', in V. Cantone (ed.) *Studi sulla circolazione del mosaico in area nord-adriatica*, Studia Artium Mediaevalium Brunensia 9, Rome, 103–24.
Galli, P., A. Galderisi, E. Peronace, B. Giaccio, I. Hajdas, P. Messina, D. Pileggi and F. Polpetta (2019) 'The Awakening of the Dormant Mount Vettore Fault (2016 Central Italy Earthquake, Mw 6.6): Paleoseismic Clues on its Millennial Silences', *Tectonics* 38: 687–705.
Goffredo, R. and G. Volpe (2018) '*Per omnium villas vicosque cunctos*: Rural Landscapes in Late Antique Southern Italy', in P. Diarte Blasco and N. Christie (eds) *Interpreting Transformations of People and Landscapes in Late Antiquity and the Early Middle Ages: Archaeological Approaches and Issues*, Oxford, 27–42.
Guidobaldi, F. (1999) 'Le domus tardoantiche di Roma come "sensori" delle trasformazioni culturali e sociali', in W. V. Harris (ed.) *The Transformations of* Vrbs Roma *in Late Antiquity*, *JRA* Suppl. 33, Portsmouth, RI, 53–68.
Guidobaldi, F. (2000) 'Distribuzione topografica, architettura e arredo delle domus tardoantiche', in *Aurea Roma: dalla città pagana alla città cristiana* (Exhibition catalogue, 22 December 2000–20 April 2001), ed. S. Ensoli and E. La Rocca, Rome, 134–6.
Guilhembet, J. P. (1996) 'La densité des domus et des insulae dans les XIV régions de Rome, selon les régionnaires: représentations cartographiques', *MEFRA* 108: 7–26.
Harris, W. V. (ed.) (1999) *The Transformations of* Vrbs Roma *in Late Antiquity*, *JRA* Suppl. 33, Portsmouth, RI.
Haug, A. (2003) *Die Stadt als Lebensraum: eine kulturhistorische Analyse zum spätantiken Stadtleben in Norditalien*, Internationale Archäologie 85, Rahden.
Honoré, T. (1998) *Law in the Crisis of Empire, 379–455 AD: the Theodosian Dynasty and its Quaestors*, Oxford.
Jacobs, I. (2013) *Aesthetic Maintenance of Civic Space: the 'Classical' City from the 4th to the 7th c. AD*, Orientalia Lovaniensia Analecta 193, Leuven.

Jacobs, I. (2014) 'Temples and Civic Representation in the Theodosian Period', in S. Birk, T. M. Kristensen and B. Poulsen (eds) *Using Images in Late Antiquity*, Oxford, 132–49.

Kalas, G. (2015) *The Restoration of the Roman Forum in Late Antiquity: Transforming Public Space*, Austin.

Keay, S., M. Millett, S. Poppy, J. Robinson, J. Taylor and N. Terrenato (2000) 'Falerii Novi: a New Survey of the Walled Area', *PBSR* 68: 1–93.

Kristensen, T. M. and L. Stirling (2016) 'Introduction: the Lives and Afterlives of Greek and Roman Sculpture, from Use to Refuse', in T. M. Kristensen and L. Stirling (eds) *The Afterlife of Greek and Roman Sculpture: Late Antique Responses and Practices*, Ann Arbor, 3–24.

La città e la sua memoria (1997) = *La città e la sua memoria: Milano e la tradizione di sant'Ambrogio* (Exhibition catalogue, 3 April–8 June 1997), Milan.

La Rocca, C. (2001) 'Un vescovo e la sua "città": le trasformazioni tardoantiche e altomedievali di Concordia (secoli IV–X)', in P. Croce Da Villa and E. Di Filippo Balestrazzi (eds) *Concordia: tremila anni*, Rubano, 287–99.

Lambert, C. (2008) *Studi di epigrafia tardoantica e medievale in Campania, vol. 1: Secoli IV–VII*, Florence.

Lamboglia, N. (1976–1978) 'Albenga e i nuovi frammenti di Rutilio Namaziano', *Rivista Ingauna e Intemelia* 31: 32–8.

Lançon, B. (2000) *Rome in Late Antiquity: Everyday Life and Urban Change, AD 312–609*, Edinburgh.

Lavan, L. (2012) 'Public Space in Late Antique Ostia: Excavation and Survey in 2008–2011', *AJA* 116: 649–91.

Lavan, L. and W. Bowden (eds) (2003) *Theory and Practice in Late Antique Archaeology*, Late Antique Archaeology 1, Leiden.

Lavan, L., L. Özgenel and A. Sarantis (eds) (2007a) *Housing in Late Antiquity: from Palaces to Shops*, Late Antique Archaeology 3.2, Leiden.

Lavan, L., E. Zanini and A. Sarantis (eds) (2007b) *Technology in Transition, A.D. 300–650*, Late Antique Archaeology 4, Leiden.

Lizzi, P. (1990) 'Ambrose's Contemporaries and the Christianization of Northern Italy', *JRS* 80: 156–73.

Loseby, S. T. (1996) 'Arles in Late Antiquity: *Gallula Roma Arelas* and *Urbs Genesii*', in N. Christie and S. T. Loseby (eds) *Towns in Transition: Urban Evolution in Late Antiquity and the Early Middle Ages*, Aldershot, 45–70.

Lusuardi Siena, S. (2003) 'Gli scavi nella cattedrale di Luni nel quadro della topografia cittadina tra Tarda Antichità e Medioevo', in M. Marcenaro (ed.) *Roma e la Liguria Maritima: Secoli IV–X. La capitale cristiana e una regione di confine. Atti del Corso e Catalogo della Mostra, Genova 14 febbraio–31 agosto 2003*, Istituto Internazionale di Studi Liguri, Atti dei Convegni 11, Genoa, 195–202.

Machado, C. (2016) 'Italy', in R. R. R. Smith and B. Ward-Perkins (eds) *The Last Statues of Antiquity*, Oxford, 43–55.

Machado, C. with J. Lenaghan (2016) 'Rome', in R. R. R. Smith and B. Ward-Perkins (eds) *The Last Statues of Antiquity*, Oxford, 121–35.

Marano, Y. A. (2007) '*Domus in qua manebat episcopus*: Episcopal Residences in Northern Italy during Late Antiquity (4th to 6th c. A.D.)', in L. Lavan, L. Özgenel and A. Sarantis (eds) *Housing in Late Antiquity: from Palaces to Shops*, Late Antique Archaeology 3.2, Leiden, 97–129.

Marano, Y. A. (2010) 'L'edilizia cristiana: la testimonianza dei complessi episcopali', in P. Delogu and S. Gasparri (eds) *Le trasformazioni del V secolo: l'Italia, i barbari e l'Occidente romano. Atti del Seminario di Poggibonsi, 18–20 ottobre 2007*, Turnhout, 331–57.

Marano, Y. A. (2012) 'Dopo Attila: urbanesimo e storia ad Aquileia tra V e VI secolo d.C.', in J. Bonetto and M. Salvadori (eds) *L'architettura privata ad Aquileia in età romana: Atti del Convegno di Studio (Padova, 21–22 febbraio 2011)*, Antenor Quaderni 24, Padua, 571–90.

Marano, Y. A. (2019) 'La cristianizzazione delle città delle Marche in età tardoantica (IV–VI sec. d.C.)', *Picus* 39: 51–114.

Marazzi, F. (2016) 'Ostrogothic Cities', in J. Arnold, S. Bjornlie and K. Sessa (eds) *A Companion to Ostrogothic Italy*, Leiden, 98–120.

Marcenaro, M. (2003) 'La diocese di Albenga e il suo centro episcopale', in M. Marcenaro (ed.) *Roma e la Liguria Maritima: Secoli IV–X. La capitale cristiana e una regione di confine. Atti del Corso e Catalogo della Mostra, Genova 14 febbraio–31 agosto 2003*, Istituto Internazionale di Studi Liguri, Atti dei Convegni 11, Genoa, 177–88.

Maréchal, S. (2020) *Public Baths and Bathing Habits in Late Antiquity: a Study of the Evidence from Italy, North Africa and Palestine A.D. 285–700*, Late Antique Archaeology Suppl. 6, Leiden.

Marin, E. (2001) 'The Temple of the Imperial Cult (Augusteum) at Narona and its Statues: Interim Report', *JRA* 4: 81–112.

Maskarinec, M. (2018) *City of Saints: Rebuilding Rome in the Early Middle Ages*, Philadelphia.

Massabò, B. (2003) 'Dalle terme romane ad un insediamento cristiano: gli scavi di San Clemente ad Albenga', in M. Marcenaro (ed.) *Roma e la Liguria Maritima: Secoli IV–X. La capitale cristiana e una regione di confine. Atti del Corso e Catalogo della Mostra, Genova 14 febbraio–31 agosto 2003*, Istituto Internazionale di Studi Liguri, Atti dei Convegni 11, Genoa, 189–94.

Meneghini, R. (2018) 'Rome: an Analysis of Changes in Topography and Population between Late Antiquity and the Early Middle Ages', in P. Diarte Blasco and N. Christie (eds) *Interpreting Transformations of People and Landscapes in Late Antiquity and the Early Middle Ages: Archaeological Approaches and Issues*, Oxford, 11–20.

Mennella, G. (2003) 'La cristianizzazione della Liguria nelle fonti epigrafiche: una premessa didattica', in M. Marcenaro (ed.) *Roma e la Liguria Maritima: Secoli IV–X. La capitale cristiana e una regione di confine. Atti del Corso e Catalogo della Mostra, Genova 14 febbraio–31 agosto 2003*, Istituto Internazionale di Studi Liguri, Atti dei Convegni 11, Genoa, 107–16.

Micheletto, E. (ed.) (2013) *La cattedrale di Alba: archeologia di un cantiere*, Archeologia Piemonte 1, Florence.

Molin, D. and F. Guidoboni (1989) 'Effetto fonti effetto monumenti a Roma: i terremoti dall'antichità ad oggi', in E. Guidoboni (ed.) *I terremoti prima del Mille in Italia e nell'area mediterranea*, Bologna, 199–202.

Montevecchi, G. (ed.) (2004) *Archeologia urbana a Ravenna. La 'Domus dei Tappeti di Pietra': il complesso archeologico di via D'Azeglio*, Ravenna.

Moreno, P. (2002) 'Iconografia e stile della Vittoria di Brescia', in F. Rossi (ed.) *Nuove ricerche sul Capitolium di Brescia: scavi, studi e restauri*, Brescia, 119–57.

Napoli, L. and P. Baldassarri (2015) 'Palazzo Valentini: Archaeological Discoveries and Redevelopment Projects', *Frontiers of Architectural Research* 4 (2): 91–9.

Negrelli, C. (2008) *Rimini capitale: strutture insediative, sociali ed economiche tra V e VIII secolo*, Florence.

Negri, P. (2010) 'The Late Antique Cathedral of Bergamo: the Ceramic Context and New Perspectives from the 2004–06 Excavations', in D. Sami and G. Speed (eds) *Debating Urbanism: Within and Beyond the Walls, A.D. 300–700. Proceedings of a Conference Held at the University of Leicester, 15th November 2008*, Leicester Archaeology Monograph 17, Leicester, 195–208.

Orlandi, S. (1999) 'Il Colosseo nel V secolo', in W. V. Harris (ed.) *The Transformations of* Vrbs Roma *in Late Antiquity*, *JRA* Suppl. 33, Portsmouth, RI, 249–63.

Pagano, F. (2004) 'Le trasformazioni dell'anfiteatro di Spoletium tra tardo antico ed altomedioevo alla luce delle recenti indagini archeologiche', in *Settimana di Studi sull'Alto Medioevo* 51: 1547–54.
Pani Ermini, L. (1995) '*Forma Urbis* e *renovatio murorum* in età teodericana', in *Teodorico il Grande e i Goti in Italia: Atti del XIII Congresso Internazionale del Centro Italiano di Studi sull'Alto Medioevo (Milan, 2–6 Novembre 1992)*, Ravenna, 171–225.
Pani Ermini, L. (1999) 'Roma da Alarico a Teoderico', in W. V. Harris (ed.) *The Transformations of* Vrbs Roma *in Late Antiquity*, JRA Suppl. 33, Portsmouth, RI, 35–52.
Pani Ermini, L. (ed.) (2000a) *Christiana loca: lo spazio cristiano nella Roma del primo millennio*, Rome.
Pani Ermini, L. (2000b) 'Lo "spazio cristiano" nella Roma del primo millennio', in *Christiana loca: lo spazio cristiano nella Roma del primo millennio*, ed. L. Pani Ermini, Rome, 15–37.
Pantò, G. (ed.) (2010) *Archeologia a Chieri: da Carreum Potentia al Comune bassomedievale*, Turin.
Parello, M. C. and M. S. Rizzo (2016) 'Agrigento tardoantica e bizantina: nuovi dati dal Quartiere residenziale e dalle aree pubbliche', in M. C. Parello and M. S. Rizzo (eds) *Paesaggi urbani tardoantiche: casi a confronto. Atti delle Giornate Gregoriane VIII Edizione (29–30 novembre 2014)*, Bari, 51–62.
Pavolini, C. (2000) 'Le domus del Celio', in *Aurea Roma: dalla città pagana alla città cristiana* (Exhibition catalogue, 22 December 2000–20 April 2001), ed. S. Ensoli and E. La Rocca, Rome, 147–8.
Purcell, N. (1999) 'The Populace of Rome in Late Antiquity: Problems of Classification and Historical Description', in W. V. Harris (ed.) *The Transformations of* Vrbs Roma *in Late Antiquity*, JRA Suppl. 33, Portsmouth, RI, 135–61.
Rambaldi, S. (2009) L'edilizia pubblica nell'impero romano all'epoca dell'anarchia militare (235–284 d.C.), *Studi e Scavi* 22, Bologna.
Rea, R. (ed.) (2002a) *Rota Colisei: la valle del Colosseo attraverso i secoli*, Milan.
Rea, R. (2002b) 'L'Anfiteatro dal 411 al 526: da Onorio e Teodosio II a Teoderico', in R. Rea (ed.) *Rota Colisei: la valle del Colosseo attraverso i secoli*, Milan, 126–39.
Rizzo, M. S. (2014) 'Agrigento ed il suo territorio in età tardoantica e bizantina: primi dati da recenti ricerche', *Sicilia Antiqua* 11 (Studi in onore di Graziella Fiorentini 2), Palermo, 399–418.
Roncaglia, C. E. (2018) *Northern Italy in the Roman World: from the Bronze Age to Late Antiquity*, Baltimore.
Salzman, M. (1999) 'The Christianization of Sacred Time and Sacred Space', in W. V. Harris (ed.) *The Transformations of* Vrbs Roma *in Late Antiquity*, JRA Suppl. 33, Portsmouth, RI, 123–34.
Sami, D. (2013) 'Sicilian Cities between the Fourth and Fifth Centuries AD', in R. García-Gasco, S. González Sánchez and D. Hernández de la Fuente (eds) *The Theodosian Age (AD 379–455): Power, Place, Belief and Learning in the Last Century of the Western Empire*, British Archaeological Reports International Series 2493, Oxford, 27–36.
Sannazaro, M. (2015) 'Ceti sociali a Como nella produzione epigrafica di V e VI secolo', in *Rivista archeologica dell'antica provincia e diocesi di Como* 197 (= *Atti del Convegno 'Luoghi, funzioni, trasformazioni tra Tardoantico e Primo Medioevo nel territorio dell'antica diocesi e provincia di Como', Como 24–25 ottobre 2014*), Como, 34–44.
Sansoni, G. and F. Docchio (2005) '3-D Optical Measurements in the Field of Cultural Heritage: the Case of the Vittoria Alata of Brescia', in *IEEE Transactions on Instrumentation and Measurement* 54:1: 359–68.
Scampoli, E. (2010) *Firenze: archeologia di una città (secoli I a.C.–XIII d.C.)*, Strumenti per la didattica e la ricerca 107, Florence.

Settia, A. (1995) 'Le fortificazioni dei Goti in Italia', in *Teodorico il Grande e i Goti in Italia: Atti del XIII Congresso Internazionale del Centro Italiano di Studi sull'Alto Medioevo (Milan, 2–6 Nov. 1992)*, Ravenna, 101–31.

Sfameni, C. (2004) 'Residential Villas in Late Antique Italy: Continuity and Change', in W. Bowden, L. Lavan and C. Machado (eds) *Recent Research on the Late Antique Countryside*, Late Antique Archaeology 2, Leiden, 335–75.

Smith, R. R. R. and B. Ward-Perkins (eds) (2016) *The Last Statues of Antiquity*, Oxford.

Spinola, G. (2000) 'La domus di Gaudentius', in *Aurea Roma: dalla città pagana alla città cristiana* (Exhibition catalogue, 22 December 2000–20 April 2001), ed. S. Ensoli and E. La Rocca, Rome, 152–5.

Testini, P., G. Cantino Wataghin and L. Pani Ermini (1989) 'La cattedrale in Italia', in *Actes du XIe Congrès international d'archéologie chrétienne (Lyon, Vienne, Grenoble, Genève, Aoste, 21–28 Sept. 1986)*, Collection de l'École française de Rome 123 – Studi di Antichità Cristiana 41, Rome, 5–229.

Thomas, E. and C. Witschel (1992) 'Constructing Reconstruction: Claim and Reality of Roman Rebuilding Inscriptions from the Latin West', *PBSR* 60: 135–77.

Vermeulen, F. (2012) 'Potentia: a Lost New Town', in N. Christie and A. Augenti (eds) *Vrbes extinctae: Archaeologies of Abandoned Classical Cities*, Farnham, 77–95.

Vermeulen, F., G.-J. Burgers, S. Keay and C. Corsi (eds) (2012) *Urban Landscape Survey in Italy and the Mediterranean*, Oxford.

Volpe, G. (2007) 'Il ruolo dei vescovi nei processi di trasformazione del paesaggio urban e rurale', in G. P. Brogiolo and A. Chavarría Arnau (eds) *Archeologia e società tra tardo antico e alto medioevo: XII Seminario sul Tardoantico e l'Altomedioevo*, Mantua, 85–106.

Volpe, G. (2016) 'Città e campagne nell'Apulia tardoantica: un processo dialettico di trasformazione', in M. C. Parello and M. S. Rizzo (eds) *Paesaggi urbani tardoantichi: casi a confronto. Atti delle Giornate Gregoriane VIII Edizione (29–30 novembre 2014)*, Bari, 87–98.

Volpe, G. and R. Turchiano (2010) 'The Last Enclave. Rural Settlement in the 5th Century in Southern Italy: the Case of Apulia', in P. Delogu and S. Gasparri (eds) *Le trasformazioni del V secolo: l'Italia, i barbari e l'Occidente romano. Atti del Seminario di Poggibonsi, 18–20 ottobre 2007*, Turnhout, 531–77.

Walsh, D. (2019) *The Cult of Mithras in Late Antiquity: Development, Decline and Demise, ca. A.D. 270–430*, Late Antique Archaeology Suppl. 2, Leiden.

Ward-Perkins, B. (1984) *From Classical Antiquity to the Middle Ages: Urban Public Building in Northern and Central Italy, A.D. 300–850*, Oxford.

Wijnendaele, J. (2018) 'Dagli altari alla polvere: Alaric, Constantine III, and the Downfall of Stilicho', *Journal of Ancient History* 6 (2): 260–77.

Yasin, A. M. (2009) *Saints and Church Spaces in the Late Antique Mediterranean: Architecture, Cult, and Community*, Cambridge.

Part IV

Religion

12

FROM LOCAL AUTHORITY TO EPISCOPAL POWER: THE CHANGING ROLES OF ROMAN AND ITALIAN BISHOPS

Bronwen Neil

POWER IS NOT A STATIC THING. Between c.250 and 490, the basis for the power of the bishop in late Roman Italy was continually evolving. Recent research on episcopal power in the capital of Rome but also in northern Italy, southern Italy and the islands of Corsica, Sardinia and Sicily has shown that this was the formative period for the late antique Italian episcopate. Yet certain related questions remain to be answered: What sorts of power did bishops hold in late Roman Italy, and how did they hold on to it? What resources allowed them to develop and hold on to power? Did they operate as a body or as separate concentrations in significant locales? Who were their main rivals for power? The use of such focus questions in the present study will allow us to see how the roles of Italian bishops evolved from the mid-third to the end of the fifth century.

First, I examine the activities of Italian bishops before Constantine I became the western Roman emperor, in 312. These activities centred on the bishop's role in liturgical leadership: preaching, ordination of priests, baptism and defining the confession of the faith. Phase 2 covers the period from Sylvester, the first bishop of Rome to serve under a self-professed Christian emperor, and ends with Leo I and the ecumenical Council of Chalcedon in 451. This was the period of *imperium* or imperial power for the Roman church. The Council of Chalcedon appeared to be a high point of success for Italian bishops who attended in the place of Leo of Rome, but it sowed the seeds for future schisms between the West and certain eastern bishops and the eastern Roman emperors who supported them. In this period, the cult of Rome and its saints began in earnest, and with it claims for papal primacy, which annoyed everybody but the city of Rome. Phase 3 covers the diminishing returns of Roman episcopal power after Chalcedon, from 452 to 490, ending just before the institution of the Ostrogothic *regnum* based in northern Italy. I conclude with some words on the lasting legacy of the later Roman bishops of Italy.

The lives and deaths of Roman and a few other Italian bishops were recorded in the *Liber pontificalis*.[1] Composed only in the early sixth century by an unknown Italian author, the *Liber pontificalis* is a sketchy source at best for the church of Rome before

---

[1] Duchesne and Vogel 1955, vol. 1 (henceforth *LP* 1). See McKitterick *2020, 16–19*.

the fifth century and should be treated as an aspirational narrative of the Roman bishops' gradual rise to power, rather than a factual account. Philippe Blaudeau argues that its original author aimed to limit the impact of the Acacian schism of 484–519.[2] It does, however, preserve valuable accounts of the donations and financial management of the Roman church and its properties, including slaves. These will be explored under the rubric of civic leadership, and their remit points to a growing socio-economic influence by Italian bishops over their cities and regions in the fourth and fifth centuries. Several detailed studies of the management of the Italian churches and their reliance on the patronage of elites have been made in the past twenty-five years.[3]

I have avoided the use of 'pope', a term which was originally not specific to bishops of Rome, but commonly applied to bishops of other major sees like Alexandria and those throughout Gaul. The Latin term for bishop (*papa*) came to be used as a title of office by bishops of Rome from around the time of John I (523–6) until the Carolingian period as an exclusive badge of Roman office in the West.[4]

Phase 1: *Imperium* and the Early Martyr-Bishops of Rome

The episcopacy of Cornelius of Rome (251–3) is a good point at which to start this overview of episcopal power and its rivals, because he was the first bishop of Rome to become involved in a documented dispute over clerical authority. In the early period and until 311, Christians in Rome, as elsewhere, were still a barely tolerated minority, who lacked legal status and were treated with the suspicion owed to a new religious movement. They did not enjoy the same status as the 'ancient race' of the Jews to protect them against imperial persecution, even if these persecutions were small scale and sporadic up till Cornelius' day. In this context, the sacraments of belonging, baptism and penitence took on strong significance as markers of ecclesial unity.

Martyrs for the Faith

It is rarely noted that of the twelve bishops of Rome from Cornelius to Miltiades (310–14), no less than eight were martyred, or at least are recorded as martyrs.[5] The first of two phases of Decian persecutions began in 250 with an edict that all books of Christian scriptures should be burnt; in the second phase, clergy and bishops were arrested if they refused to make sacrifices to the gods or hand over their holy books to be burnt.[6] One of the defining features of Roman civic identity was loyalty to the

---

[2] Blaudeau 2015, 127–40; compare Blair-Dixon 2007, who argued that the *LP* is primarily concerned with the local schisms caused by disputed episcopal elections in Rome.

[3] Sotinel 1998; Pietri 2002; Moreau 2006; Cooper and Hillner 2007; Neil 2011; Sessa 2012; Salzman et al. 2016.

[4] Moorhead 2015, 69. Moorhead's study starts with Leo I (440–61).

[5] The exceptions were Dionysius (260–7), Eusebius (309 or 310), who nevertheless was exiled, as was Marcellus in 306/7 under Maxentius, and Miltiades (311–14).

[6] It has elsewhere been noted that the targeting of Christians by Decius (249–51) and later Diocletian (284–305) were not the systematic and coordinated activities that the label 'universal persecutions' seems to imply.

emperor, which meant also loyalty to the government-approved religion. Such loyalty was demonstrated by making sacrifices to the emperor and the pagan gods in the presence of government officials. This was the easiest test for identifying Christians – those who refused to comply were seen as traitors. Many did comply and later repented and wished to return to the church. Even bishops were numbered among those who lapsed, which caused a problem for those with a more rigorist attitude.

The main rivals to episcopal power in these testing times were the confessors, those who had suffered for keeping their faith but not to the point of death. Confessors claimed superior authority to those who had lapsed in the face of persecution, especially to lapsed bishops. Those confessors who had passed the ultimate test of their faith were often appointed as bishops themselves, which did much to strengthen the office of *episcopus*.

After Cornelius, another six bishops were martyred in quick succession: Lucius, Stephen I, Xystus II, Felix I (269–74), Eutychian and Gaius, according to Christian tradition a Dalmatian and a relative of Emperor Diocletian. Felix I is credited with the important new liturgical tradition of celebrating Mass over the memorials of the martyrs, thus anchoring their cults to local places. Marcellinus (295–303) lapsed and offered sacrifices to the gods but was later martyred, according to the *Liber pontificalis*,[7] but he is not mentioned in most Roman martyrologies. Marcellus (c.305–c.307), who followed him, was imprisoned in the imperial stable (*Ca[n]tabulum*) for refusing to offer pagan sacrifices, rescued and rearrested, dying 'in servitude to the animals' who had been brought from the stable into his church.[8]

Only the last two bishops of Rome in this period avoided death in captivity or martyrdom: the Greek Eusebius and Miltiades, an African bishop of Rome from the reign of Maximian to that of Maximinus Daia. Eusebius' brief entry in the *Liber pontificalis* tells us that in his years as bishop of Rome under Constantius I Chlorus, the cross of Jesus Christ was discovered, that Christian fasting on Thursday and Saturdays was banned because pagans fasted on those days, and third, that Eusebius laid his hands on the heretics to reconcile them.

This record tells us much about the limited roles of the Roman bishop before the first Christian emperor, Constantine. They centred around three activities: (1) defining doctrine and confession of the faith, which included readmitting heretics to communion; (2) liturgical leadership, including setting the days for weekly fasts; and (3) practical pastoral care, including the building and furnishing of churches, whose status was enhanced by the presence of holy relics like fragments of the so-called True Cross. Pastoral care in this period also meant ensuring the survival of the people under the church's care by providing food, shelter, clothing and basic health services such as public baths and heating.[9] Inadequate performance in any one of these spheres detracted from the bishop's authority, as we shall see below.

---

[7] *LP* 1.162.
[8] *LP* 1.164.
[9] Izdebski 2012, 160–1, identifies these spiritual activities as contributing to the Roman bishops' social importance up to the outbreak of the Gothic wars of the 530s, when they started to engage more with local politics.

Liturgical Battles

From the late second century, the bishop of Rome tried to lead the western church in the area of setting the new Christian calendar. Here too his authority was constantly challenged by other western bishops, especially that of Carthage. The Roman church had since its foundation celebrated Easter on the weekend after 14 Nisan, the Jewish Passover.[10] Victor of Rome (189–99) tried to impose the Roman way upon the whole church but was forced to back down when the bishop of Ephesus, whose side was supported by Irenaeus of Lyon, quoted apostolic authority for the non-Roman rite. In the third century, this continued to be an issue that tested the bishop of Rome's authority, with bishops of Alexandria claiming the authority to set the date for the major sacrament of the liturgical calendar. The bishop of Rome was obliged to write to Alexandria every year for the date of the following Easter.

By the mid-third century, only bishops had the right to preach, to baptise candidates who could then take communion, and to ordain priests and deacons. Episcopal leaders at this stage still relied on charismatic power rather than institutional power. This is why the debates over the rebaptism of those who had been baptised by clergy who had failed their faith in the persecutions were so critical. Those clergy who had lapsed under imperial pressure to produce statements witnessed on oath (*libelli*) that they had sacrificed to the gods were of indeterminate status as far as their spiritual authority was concerned. Some rigorists feared that a tainted bishop would not be able to give valid sacraments, and this had serious repercussions for the eternal futures of those with whom they shared communion and those they baptised. Roman bishops Fabian and Cornelius advocated a more moderate treatment of the lapsed than the rigorist faction led by the Roman priest Novatian (d. 257/8).[11] This controversy went to the heart of the bishop's authority to dictate the limits of ordination on behalf of local clergy. The debate over rebaptism and readmission to communion had wider repercussions for the power of the bishop: did his authority to administer sacraments like baptism and communion come from the office, regardless of his fitness to hold that office? Were baptisms performed by lapsed or heretical bishops still valid? On this question, the bishops of Rome were at odds with Cyprian of Carthage, who believed that rebaptism was required.

Bishops Cornelius, Lucius and Stephen of Rome (254–7) got embroiled in the debate over rebaptism when consulted by Cyprian and his council of North African bishops.[12] Stephen ruled that baptised schismatics or heretics could be reintroduced after the church elders had simply laid hands upon them. Novatian, the charismatic leader of the rigorist sect in Rome, opposed allowing the lapsed back into communion. A recent study on letters exchanged between Roman and North African bishops

---

[10] The Quartodeciman controversy (c. AD 180) over the dating of Easter tested the self-assumed authority of the bishop of Rome. Polycarp of Smyrna followed the churches of Jerusalem and Asia Minor's tradition of celebrating Easter on the day of 14 Nisan, rather than the weekend following. See Eusebius of Caesarea's account in *Hist. eccl.* 5.23–5.

[11] Novatian was eventually martyred in 257/8.

[12] All three bishops of Rome were martyred in Decian's persecution.

during the Novatianist controversy[13] gives us a clearer picture of how the bishop of Rome's power expanded at an irregular pace in this early period. Bishops of other major sees like Carthage applied to Rome selectively when they needed support to strengthen their position at local episcopal councils.[14] When powerful bishops like Cyprian got advice from Rome that they did not like, they simply ignored it.

The second wide-scale persecution began when Diocletian, together with the zealous anti-Christian Caesar Galerius, hero of Rome's recovery against Persia in 298, issued an edict against Christianity. Diocletian first demanded that Christians surrender their holy books and that their churches be destroyed. Then Christian worship was banned. The clergy were arrested but, since there was no room to hold them all in prison, they were released if they agreed to make a sacrifice to the emperor. Many complied, including Marcellinus of Rome. As many as 17,000 people were said to have been martyred in Rome over thirty days during his episcopate, according to the *Liber pontificalis*, whose testimony in this instance is unreliable.[15]

In 304, while his co-emperor Diocletian was ill and out of action, Galerius ordered a general sacrifice. Up until this point, only the clergy had been menaced, but now every Christian was forced to make a public action renouncing the faith or face the consequences. The penalty for disobedience was death or the mines. The persecution ended in the West in 305 with the abdication of Diocletian and his co-emperor Maximian, and the proclamation of Constantius I and Galerius as Augusti. After the death of his father a year later, Constantine became emperor of the Roman West.

Practical Pastoral Care

There is no single definition of pastoral care, but the term covers both practical and spiritual components, the latter including preaching, spiritual direction and religious mentorship, as Peter Gemeinhardt has recently pointed out.[16] Here I focus on its more practical aspects: the sharing of resources through almsgiving and practical and financial care for the poor: the sick, widows and orphans in the local community.[17] In the first to mid-third centuries, early Christian lay communities were organised around house churches, but over the third century, bishops gradually assumed the sole right to preach, while the presbyters and deacons had important roles in pastoral care and administering the sacraments.[18] With this responsibility came more episcopal power over the running of church affairs, including appointments and discipline of the clergy. Gradually a hierarchy of ministry developed, with the bishops governing the descending ranks of priests, deacons, subdeacons and readers. Episcopal civic responsibilities fulfilled an important social function in Italian towns, where social welfare was at the discretion of the governor and resources were scarce. In the first recorded example

---

[13] Baumkamp 2014.
[14] E.g. synods of Carthage held in 252–6. See further Dunn 2007, 90–178.
[15] The number of deaths is obviously inflated.
[16] Gemeinhardt 2019, 119; Allen and Mayer 2000.
[17] See Esler 2003, 19–42.
[18] Volp 2003, 189–209.

of such activity by a Roman bishop, Dionysius, a former monk, gave churches to the priests and organised the cemeteries and parishes as dioceses.[19] Felix built a basilica on the Via Aurelia where he was later buried, and Marcellus organised the twenty-five *tituli* or privately endowed churches within the walls of Rome.[20]

During the Diocletianic persecutions, Eutychian of Rome, a native of Tuscia, allegedly buried 342 martyrs in Rome. Gaius of Rome was martyred even though he was said to have been from Diocletian's family. In 311 Galerius' Edict of Serdica, known as the 'Edict of Toleration', officially ended the persecution of Christians begun by Diocletian in 303. Galerius' edict was followed by the Edict of Milan issued by Constantine I and Licinius in 313, and the death of Maximinus Daia in the same year marked the end of the persecution of Christians. The cult of the Roman martyrs, and especially of Roman bishops who were victims of imperial persecution, lent strength and prestige to those who held the office of bishop after them. Without the persecutions, the new Christian movement in Rome might not have got the kick-start it needed to become the leading power in the western church.

Phase 2: Bishops of Italy in the Service of the Emperors

Constantine I's legitimisation of Christianity would initiate a radical reversal in the fortunes of the Italian church and the status of its bishops, especially in Rome. At the beginning of the period from 314 to 451 the church of Rome was still tightly incorporated into the broader episcopal networks of northern and southern Italy, including the islands of Corsica, Sardinia and Sicily. The see of Rome had risen to dominate the rest of Suburbicarian and northern Italy, thanks in large part to Constantine I's adoption of Christianity, after which bishops generally enjoyed considerably broader powers as well as clerical tax exemptions. Constantine stamped the periphery of the city with *basilicae* and other Christian foundations,[21] although these were kept away from the city's senatorial centre in what Bruno Bleckmann calls 'separate communicative spaces', that represented different facets of the newly Christian emperor's self-representation.[22]

Starting with Sylvester of Rome (313–35), Italian bishops expanded their means of establishing and holding on to power, even though the medieval memory of the donation of Constantine to Sylvester was a forgery from around the eighth century.[23] Their roles now included: (1) defender of doctrine, defined by meetings of episcopal councils and promulgated in the preaching of homilies and circulation of letters; (2) leader of the Roman liturgy, which entailed imposing the liturgical calendar in place of the civic calendar; (3) civic leader and crisis manager, especially focused on the city of Rome. Let us consider these episcopal roles, as well as the bishops' new rivals for power.

---

[19] *LP* 1.157.
[20] *LP* 1.158 (Felix I) and *LP* 1.164 (Marcellus).
[21] See Chapter 2 in this volume.
[22] Bleckmann 2014, 312–14.
[23] Sessa 2010, 77–94.

Of southern Italian provincial bishops, we know relatively little except their limited correspondence with the bishops of Rome. In his monumental survey of Roman bishops up to 440, Charles Pietri mentions only four southern Italian bishops: Paulinus of Nola, to whom we return below; Theodore, a prelate of Campania; John of Naples; and Exsuperantius of Lucania, one of the senatorial bishops who emerged at this time.[24] Julian of Eclanum is well known for the strong line he took on the value of marriage for both clerics and the laity, against Augustine of Hippo's emphasis on celibacy in his condemnation of concupiscence.[25]

Bishops of the north are somewhat better served in the records. Marcellus, called a *sacerdos* by Ambrose of Milan (374–97), was probably a bishop. Of Ambrose and Petronius, bishop of Bologna from 432, Zeno the former monk and bishop of Verona (c.362–c.371),[26] Gaudentius of Brescia (387–410), Peter Chrysologus (c.383–450) and Chromatius of Aquileia (c.387–c.407), we know much more, thanks to their homilies and other liturgical writings.

Chromatius rivalled the bishop of Rome in ecclesiastical seniority by the beginning of the fifth century,[27] and Aquileia's bishops held great prestige until the sack of the city by Attila in 452. Later in the fifth century, Maximus of Turin left behind over 100 sermons,[28] and Epiphanius of Ticinum (now Pavia) (471–98) was feted in the biography composed by Ennodius between 501 and 504.[29] North–south conflicts were sometimes conducted along the lines of heresy: Pelagian clergy were exiled from Aquileia and other northern sees by Emperor Honorius in 418, and the consequences continued to trouble bishops of Rome into the 440s, as early letters from the pontificate of Leo I reveal.[30] Italian bishops reached their decisions collectively through major councils, such as the various synods of Rome, and endorsed the synods' decisions by signing the council acts and informing congregations of its canons in their letters and their preaching. Such synods were used to define and refine the expression of orthodoxy – especially over the vexed question of rebaptism or readmission of clergy and others who had lapsed in the persecutions – and sought to impose their views on the western churches of Spain and Gaul.

The Earliest Papal Decretals

The only way that bishops of Rome could impose disciplinary measures was through the writing of letters, framed as legal documents in the manner of imperial rescripts. On the occasions when Roman views on disciplinary matters were judged to have

---

[24] Pietri 1976, 958 and nn. 1–4.
[25] Rapp 2005, 190–1.
[26] See 'Zeno', in Pietri and Pietri 1999–2000, 2376–7. On the episcopal mentorship of new converts to Christianity in Zeno's homilies, see Gemeinhardt 2019, 128–30.
[27] McEachnie 2017, 51–3.
[28] Not all of these are considered genuine: see Ramsey 1989.
[29] Izdebski 2012, 161–3. See Ennod. *Vit. Epiph.*, trans. DeFerrari 1952, 303–52.
[30] Leo, *Ep.* 1, to the bishops of Aquileia, and *Ep.* 2, to Septimus of Altinum. See 'Septimus 1', in Pietri and Pietri 1999–2000, 2027.

universal applicability, these letters were given the special status of 'decretals' by clerics outside of Rome, starting with the Scythian Dionysius Exiguus in the early fifth-century *Dionysian Collection*. The subsequent medieval canon law collections all drew from similar collections of papal letters and canons.[31] The great age of Roman decretals lasted from 380 to 451.

Siricius of Rome (384–99) issued the earliest decretal letters, and these concerned matters of clerical discipline, such as the need for celibacy for priests. Siricius' letter to Himerius of Tarragona was the first decree on clerical celibacy and has remained in force ever since;[32] it was repeated by Innocent and Leo I. His other decretals concerned the regulation of Christian life: baptism, consecration, ordination, penance and the need for sexual continence. Siricius insisted that no bishop should be consecrated without the permission of the see of Rome. He asserted his authority with threats of excommunication against those who contravened his advice.

Innocent of Rome (401–17) took up the self-assumed authority of Siricius by issuing decretals on qualifications for clerical office.[33] His letter to Vitricius (*Ep.* 2) discusses qualification for the clergy, the rights of metropolitan bishops, and the problem of marriage for the clergy. Innocent's letter to Exsuperius (*Ep.* 6) deals with the treatment of clerics who have lapsed in celibacy, and with the question of the compatibility of marriage and clerical office. In his letter to the bishops of Macedonia (*Ep.* 17), he deals with married clergy, and readmission to communion of those ordained during schism and whether they could hold clerical office.[34] He also addressed questions that affected laypeople, such as remarriage during times of war.

The close links between the secular and ecclesiastical establishments are reflected in the development of a clerical *cursus honorum*, which mirrored the senatorial career path.[35] Celestine's letter to the bishops of Vienne and Narbonne dealt with a related question, that of irregular ordinations. With Leo I, we find a new and strengthened statement of the prerogatives of the bishop of Rome over other western and even eastern bishops.[36] In an attempt to control the bishops of Gaul,[37] Leo I wrote a decretal letter to the bishops of Vienne.[38] Leo addressed other letters in a similar vein to the bishops of Sicily, southern Italy and northern Italy on matters of clerical discipline and episcopal management. The act of gathering certain letters of Siricius, Damasus, Innocent, Celestine, Boniface, Leo, Gelasius and Hormisdas into medieval law collections did much to cement their reputation after the fact as issuers of binding *dicta* to the whole western church. Their authority, however, evolved gradually, and much

---

[31] Jasper and Fuhrmann 2001, 81–7, trace the earliest collections of papal letters – the *Collectio Thessalonicensis*, *Collectio Avellana* and *Collectio Arelatensis* – and their circulation in Illyricum, Italy and Gaul.

[32] On Siricius' letter of 385 and its impact on the rise of the papacy see Ferreiro 2015, 83–5.

[33] See Dunn 2015, 186.

[34] Dunn 2015, 186. More on papal letter collections and their means of transmission can be found in Neil 2016.

[35] Two early papal decretals dealt with the clerical *cursus honorum*: Celestine's letter to the southern Italian bishops and a letter of Zosimus; see Dunn 2013.

[36] Wessel 2009, 345–76; Demacopoulos 2013, 39–162.

[37] Salzman 2015, 109–26, suggests that Leo found an ally in Prosper of Aquitaine in these efforts.

[38] *Divinae cultum*, JK 407 in Jaffé and Herbers 2016.

depended on their handling of individual cases of doctrine and discipline. Roman authority in our period was constantly contested by bishops of other provinces.

Liturgical Leadership

Studies by Pietri, Sotinel, Sessa and Moreau have shown from material evidence that the Roman bishop participated actively and cooperated with imperial building programmes, especially of churches and baptisteries, in the fourth and fifth centuries.[39] In this period of service to the newly established Christian *imperium*, the public acts of baptism and penitence took on a new significance for enterprising bishops as avenues for the exercise of power and social control. Penance was useful as a means of exclusion and control over other rivals to power, such as emperors. We see this in the famous case of Ambrose of Milan and Emperor Theodosius I, whom he forced to perform public penance after the Thessaloniki massacre. The debate over the significance to the empire of continuing pagan cults continued. Emperor Julian's revival of them in Antioch in the early 360s was a brief hiatus in the process of phasing them out, in Italy as everywhere else. The Saturnalia and festival of the New Light in December were replaced by the Feast of the Nativity on 25 December. In Rome, the Feast of Peter and Paul at the end of June (29 June) came to replace the eight days of the *Ludi Apollinares*.[40] And yet they continued in Rome, with the pagan fertility cult of the Lupercalia plaguing Gelasius of Rome even at the end of the fifth century.[41]

Liturgical leadership in this period included the building and furnishing of churches, monasteries and shrines. These donations of hard and soft furnishings such as gold and silver plate, lamps and oil were sustained by the property that accrued to the church through donations from wealthy patrons,[42] especially aristocratic virgins and widows, many of whom had adopted an ascetic way of life. Donations were also directed towards famine relief, the ransoming of prisoners of war, and paying tribute to external foes such as the Vandal leader Geiseric in the mid-450s.[43] Starting with Constantine I, imperial funds were poured into an impressive building campaign to make the Christian church reflect and reinforce the glory of its emperor. Many pagan temples were converted into basilicas for Christian worship. Constantine offered priests immunity from taxes and civic duties, which attracted many to the profession. Julian of

---

[39] See n. 3 above.

[40] Leo I, *Homily* 82B on the Feast of St Peter and Paul, Chavasse 1973, 508–18.

[41] McLynn 2008, 161–75, analysed the resistance of senatorial factions to Roman episcopal authority at the end of the fifth century, when bishop of Rome Gelasius (492–6) criticised the celebration of the ancient Roman festival. McLynn questions whether the festival was still current at this time, suggesting instead that it was revived as an occasion for public spectacle by senators resistant to Gelasius' brand of 'muscular Christianity' (my phrase).

[42] Salzman 1999, 133; Hillner 2007, 225–61. For a case study of benefactions under Sixtus III of Rome, which included a *monasterium* at the catacombs, see Neil 2011, 58–60. For the range of meanings of this term – side chapel, monastery or residence for monks, private chapel – in the *Liber pontificalis Ravennatis*, see Deliyannis 2004, 330–2.

[43] Neil 2011, 62–5.

Brundisium (modern Brindisi) was warned not to ordain any 'foreigners (*peregrini*) or unknown persons or former penitents because they are barred from reverend offices'.[44]

Fostering the Cult of Roman City-Saints

The revision of the civic calendar coincided with the rise of Italian saints, which added new feasts to be celebrated and new focal points for civic pride. The overlap between civic and episcopal roles can be seen clearly in the career of Paulinus of Nola. After being appointed suffect consul in Rome by Gratian in c.377, Paulinus was made governor of the southern Italian province of Campania c.380. Observing the local people's devotion to a local saint, Felix of Nola, a town near Naples, Paulinus built a road for pilgrims and a hospice for the poor near Felix's shrine. All this was before he became a Christian. After his conversion he became devoted to the saint, writing an annual poem for Felix. After he became bishop of Nola in c.410, he did much more to further the cult of the local saint.

The opportunity to increase the bishop of Rome's power through the cult of its saints was first recognised by its bishops Damasus (361–84) and Siricius at the end of the fourth century. The Spanish-born Damasus 'searched for and discovered the bodies of many saints, whom he also acclaimed in verses', according to the *Liber pontificalis*.[45] He also found the spot at the catacombs where the apostles and founders of Christian Rome, Peter and Paul, were buried, and commemorated them with verses on the table at their grave. This was the first recognition of St Peter, who was styled as Rome's first bishop and became its most famous saint, and the focus of its civic pride. An inscription from 390 shows that Siricius dedicated shrines to the Roman martyrs.[46] The composition of a martyrology or list of Roman martyrs attributed to Jerome ensured the recognition of martyrs whose names might otherwise have been lost.[47] By the 530s, the anonymous author of the *Liber pontificalis* had filled in the gaps in the first century, and had established an unbroken line of episcopal leaders of Rome: Peter, Linus, Cletus and Clement I.

Damasus also fostered the cult of previous Roman bishops, celebrating them in verse and with foundations in their honour. One of those commemorated was the martyr Felix, who was beheaded under the Homoian emperor Constantius II, according to legend, and who was later confused with the anti-pope Felix II (355–65). Julius (337–52) and Liberius (352–66) were exiled under the rule of Constantius II, also a Homoian. Constantius recalled from exile Liberius, who had the support of the Roman laity, to co-rule with Felix, but the latter was pushed out by a popular uprising. Liberius died a year later and is excluded from the Roman martyrology, making him the earliest pontiff not to be venerated as a saint in the Roman rite. He was,

---

[44] Gelasius, *Ep.* 16.1, trans. Neil and Allen 2014, 51 and n. 48.
[45] *LP* 1.212.7–8: *hic multa corpora sanctorum requisivit et invenit, quorum etiam versibus declaravit.*
[46] *ILCV* 971, Diehl et al. 1967, dated 390. See Rüpke and Glock 2005, 1291–2, no. 3105.
[47] The *Martyrologium Hieronymianum* was fabricated in 430–50 in northern Italy, probably within the patriarchate of Aquileia, based on a Roman calendar, an African calendar and a compilation of Greek material made in 362.

however, remembered as a saint in the East for his support of the patriarch Athanasius of Alexandria, who also fought against the Homoians.

New Forms of Episcopal Civic Leadership

One of the new civic roles of the bishop of Rome was to advance the civic building programme that had been begun by Constantine I. The types of resources that allowed Italian bishops to develop and hold on to power included physical resources such as land, revenue including bequests, portable wealth, roads, aqueducts and other infrastructure, especially public buildings such as baths. Gelasius recommended to the bishops of Sicily a fourfold division of church revenues. These were to be split between the clergy, the upkeep of the church, the poor and the bishops (*cathedraticum*).[48]

In the Exarchate of Ravenna, most of the fifty-seven churches mentioned in the *Liber pontificalis ecclesiae Ravennatis* (*LPR*) were built between 400 and 600, that is, after Ravenna became a main imperial residence from Honorius onwards.[49] Peter I of Ravenna (431–50), only the second bishop to be provided with dates in *LPR*, founded the Petriana church (*LPR* 24). Galla Placidia gave funds for a mosaic of his image adorning the apse in the church of blessed John the Baptist (*LPR* 27). The empress also offered many gifts to the church of Ravenna, including a golden lamp with her image in a medallion. Such imperial patronage offered considerable prestige to both the bishops of Ravenna and Rome in this period of formation.

The laity played a large part in funding the ecclesiastical development of the fifth century through their foundation of titular churches which retained the donor's names, indicating a desire to maintain at least some control over their endowments, as others have noted.[50] The material and epigraphic evidence concurs with the literary evidence provided by the *Liber pontificalis* that 'the Roman bishops were highly involved in the construction of church buildings, though much of this was funded by the local Christian aristocracy and not by the bishop's private funds'.[51] This had three positive effects for the Roman episcopacy: first, it increased the visibility of Christianity; second, it testified to a growing episcopal urban organisation, and third, it gave weight to Roman episcopal claims in the second half of the fourth century to the leadership of both urban and regional Christian communities,[52] with implications for the status of other Italian bishops in large cities like Milan and Aquileia.

We also have frequent and lengthy building and donation lists in the *Liber pontificalis* and *LPR*, although the latter does not provide exact records for this early period, having been composed two centuries later and depending heavily on the Roman

---

[48] On the fourfold division of income: Gelasius, *Ep.* 17, to the bishops of Sicily; *Ep.* 14.27 (the General Decretal); fr. 20, to Bishop Sabinus; *Ep.* 16, to Julian of Brundisium (JK 676); 'Iulianus 11', in Pietri and Pietri 1999–2000, 1187. On the period up to Gelasius' accession in 492, see Moreau 2006, 80–4, with literature.

[49] Deliyannis 2004, 66. The Latin text is found in Deliyannis 2006.

[50] E.g. Sessa 2012, 231–4; Humphries 2014, 182.

[51] Van Espelo 2015.

[52] Van Espelo 2015.

example.[53] Gifts of gold and silver plate to the church of Imola – the burial place of St Cassian – by Peter Chrysologus (433–50) are vaguely described and may have been invented.[54] Projectus of Imola was a contemporary of Peter Chrysologus, and both were ordained deacon by Cornelius of Imola.[55] Agnellus of Ravenna, writing in the ninth century, confused Peter II (494–520) with Peter Chrysologus, the contemporary of Leo I. Peter Chrysologus and the empress Galla Placidia together dedicated a shrine to St Barbatian near the Ovilian gate in Ravenna.[56] General Baduarius built the Church of Saints John and Barbatian, which Peter Chrysologus consecrated near the end of his episcopacy.[57]

As well as public buildings and their furnishings, fifth-century bishops provided water, food, bathing facilities and even clothing for the people of the city. They appointed deacons to distribute money for the poor, especially widows and orphans. The bishop heard and judged disputes – ecclesiastical and civil – in his court (*audientia episcopalis*). From the fourth century, both ecclesiastical and civil cases were heard in episcopal courts, both in Rome and beyond. The court of the Roman bishop functioned as a court of appeal for other bishops,[58] but participation in the court process remained voluntary. This restriction gave the *audientia* rulings less force than a court of law, but it was better than the long wait for dubious outcomes that characterised the secular justice system.[59]

The institution of the bishop's court resulted in a proliferation of bureaucratic documentation. The office of the head notary (*primicerius notariorum*) was established for managing and archiving church documents including bonds, deeds, donations, exchanges, transfers, wills, declarations and manumissions. The head notary is first mentioned in the pontificate of Julius (337–52), in the *Liber pontificalis*.[60] Other early mentions of the Roman episcopal archives occur in Innocent I's *Letter* 13,[61] and in the *LP* entry for Celestine (422–32).[62] The system of archiving correspondence was well established by the time of Leo I (440–61), perhaps the best-known Italian bishop of this second phase.

While bishops in Gaul and North Africa were the Roman bishops' main challengers to Roman power in phase 1, this circle expanded in phase 2 to include key bishops of Spain and the eastern patriarchs of Alexandria, Antioch and Constantinople. A few

---

[53] Deliyannis 2004, 26 and 82.
[54] Deliyannis 2004, 163, with introduction at 82.
[55] *LPR* 51, Deliyannis 2004, 163.
[56] *LPR* 51, Deliyannis, 2004, 163.
[57] *LPR* 51, Deliyannis 2004, 163.
[58] The practice of the right to appeal to the Roman pontiff reached its peak in the fifth century: Belda Iniesta 2019.
[59] See Uhalde 2007, 29–43; Allen and Neil 2013, 186–91 on Pelagius I of Rome (556–61).
[60] *Julius, LP* 1.205.
[61] Innocent, *Ep.* 13 to Rufus, bishop of Thessalonica, PL 20.516B–517A: *omnem sane instructionem chartarum in causa archivorum cum presbytero Senecione, viro admodum maturo, fieri jussimus. itaque et ex priore nostra epistola, et ex his chartulis, bene recensens quid agere debeas, recognosce.* Dated 17 June 412.
[62] *Celestine, LP* 1.230: *hic fecit constitutum de omnem ecclesiam, maxime et de religione, quae hodie archivo ecclesiae detenentur recondite*; '[Celestine] issued a decree about the whole church and especially (one) about religious life – these are preserved today, stored away in the church archive.'

charismatic ascetics, such as Pelagius, attracted their circles of aristocratic admirers in the city of Rome, and the bequests of these often wealthy disciples were sometimes diverted from the coffers of Roman bishops, who were vocal critics of Pelagius and those like him.

Ascetic teachers such as Jerome also exercised rival authority, in Rome and later Bethlehem, and had their aristocratic networks, especially with wealthy women – including Melania the Younger, Paula and Julia Anicia – who took some of their wealth with them when they went to join their spiritual guides in the Holy Land. Other Roman ascetics chose to sell up their property and leave Italy due to Alaric's sieges on the *urbs* in the first decade of the fifth century. In North Africa, Augustine complained that his church in Hippo had lost two of its wealthiest patrons when Melania the Younger and her husband Pinianus left North Africa on a permanent pilgrimage to the Holy Land. One of the most interesting letters of this time is the anonymous letter to Demetrias, a young member of the powerful Anician clan, persuading her to dedicate her wealth to the church rather than giving it away, as Pelagius had advised her to do.[63] At this time the papal patrimonies were established, as witnessed by the *Liber pontificalis*, although their management through agents becomes much clearer from the time of Gregory the Great, due to that bishop's copious correspondence with his agents in Sicily.

Phase 3: *Regnum* – Diminishing Returns for the Italian Bishops

With the death of Valentinian III in 455, who had teamed up with the bishops of Rome to reinforce their authority on doctrinal and disciplinary challenges like those posed by Manicheanism,[64] the extent of Rome bishops' power began to wane. In this third section in the second half of the fifth century, we make a brief assessment of the diminishing returns of Italian episcopal power as *regnum* approached.

Even the main sphere of influence left for bishops, doctrinal regulation, began to fade into the background after the Council of Chalcedon, although its resolutions were not acceptable to northern Italian bishops. The shadow emperors who succeeded Valentinian were not even slightly interested in Christological disputes. Heterodox, Homoian Christianity took hold with Theoderic and then the Lombards, and became an issue that even the bishop of Rome, Gelasius I, could not discuss with the court.[65] With the establishment of Ravenna as the Ostrogothic capital and the headquarters of the eastern Roman exarchate after Justinian's reconquest in the Gothic Wars of the following century, the bishop of Rome's bold bid for authority over the broader church had heard the death knell. The rise in prestige of the Ravennan bishops came

---

[63] *De vera humilitate* (*CPL* 529 in Dekkers 1993), composed c.440. This tract has been attributed with some probability to Leo I of Rome; cf. Pelagius, *Ep. ad Demetriadem* a. 413. On this exchange of letters as an ascetic form of pastoral care, see Jacobs 2000, 719–48.

[64] Humphries 2012, 161–82.

[65] Neil and Allen 2014: 31–2. Gelasius' authority over his clergy was challenged on at least three occasions, when renegade priests sought protection from Theoderic: see fr. 12, Thiel 1867, 489–90, and Neil and Allen 2014: 180–1.

at the direct expense of their southern confrères. Liturgical conformity had reached a point where the only matters left to discuss were what to read. There are no papal decretals from the period up to 490, and then only two under Gelasius, one an index of apocryphal books. The last decretals were issued by Hormisdas in the first two decades of the sixth century. In the sphere of civic leadership there was still plenty for bishops to do, but their power to do it was much reduced by war and the loss of papal patrimonies to the north and south in the sixth century.

The Legacy of the Later Roman Episcopate in Italy

Bishops in Italy gathered power to their sees in the third to fifth centuries in various ways. Perhaps most striking was their appropriation of the right to define doctrinal orthodoxy, which expanded from stressing the importance of baptism and penitence during Diocletian's persecutions to the persecution of heretics within the established imperial church in the fourth and fifth centuries. Second, bishops could choose to embrace or reject liturgical conformity, as defined by Rome, especially in relation to events of the pre-Christian civic calendar. By the end of the fifth century, the eclipse of the secular calendar by the Christian was all but complete. The feasts of local saints who had enhanced the prestige of their city or town, and thereby contributed to the prestige of its bishop, were given fixed days in that calendar. Martyred bishops attracted special cults in the centre and the periphery, promoted by Damasus and other Roman bishops in Rome and by Paulinus in Nola. A third method was episcopal pastoral care and civic governance. This area drew the largest increases in episcopal authority, with the bishops of larger cities like Rome and Aquileia coming to fill the vacuum left by the western emperors in Italy in the fifth century.

Fourth, the bishops of Italy sought to eliminate or neutralise their rivals, especially ascetic leaders like Pelagius, by using their social networks and mobilising popular support. Playing off their imperial overlords in Ravenna, Antioch and Constantinople against each other was another strategy for maintaining influence in the West. Important bishops in Gaul and Spain could be pitted against each other by strategic letter-writing, and those letters with universal application became the decretals of canon law.

The fifth avenue of investigation was the operation of Italian bishops as a body versus the separate concentrations of episcopal power in significant urban centres of northern and southern Italy. Starting with local synods and delegations to ecumenical synods, the bishops of Rome by the end of the fifth century were holding centralised Roman synods for all Italian bishops, including those of Sicily and Sardinia. Early rivals to episcopal power included confessors and the early Roman emperors, and later the Ostrogothic kings and eastern Roman emperors. Heterodox religious leaders such as the Novatianist, Manichean,[66] Pelagian and Julianist bishops[67] also served as detractors from attempts to impose authority based on doctrinal uniformity.

---

[66] Samuel Cohen's chapter on the persecutions of Manicheans by Vandals (Chapter 13 in this volume) will examine the latter in more detail.

[67] That is, the followers of Julian of Eclanum. See 'Iulianus 10', in Pietri and Pietri 1999–2000, 1175–86.

Bishops who stood up to emperors – like Ambrose of Milan against Theodosius I and Felix III against the eastern emperor Zeno – were celebrated in the West. Some of the lesser-known later Roman bishops, for example the North African Miltiades, were famous in their day, but few records of their pontificates survive. Hagiographic stories of Roman bishops before the sixth century were sometimes mediated to the West only through the Greek tradition; for example, two stories about Leo I, which endorsed his *Tome to Flavian*, are preserved in a seventh-century Greek collection of improving tales.[68] These tales supplement the scanty records of the *Liber pontificalis* and warrant further investigation. This brief survey of episcopal power, with its emphasis on Rome, could be extended further to consider the episcopal networks and rivalries of northern Italy, especially in Pavia, Altinum, Ravenna and Milan. Separate networks governed southern Italy and the islands of Corsica, Sardinia and Sicily, and these too deserve much more scholarly attention.

These focus questions have allowed us to see the gradual evolution in the roles of Italian bishops over time, from 250 to 490. If we focused solely on the bishop of Rome, we would see only a slow process of decline from the end of the fifth century onwards. However, the waning of Roman episcopal power under Ostrogothic and later eastern Roman rule allowed other bishops to flourish. This is evident from the simple fact that the see of Ravenna had its own *Liber pontificalis* from the early ninth century, which reached right back to the first century. Meanwhile, the Roman *Liber pontificalis*, composed in the early sixth century, suffered from major gaps in its record due to loss of documentation. The history of Italian episcopal power in this period has to be reconstructed carefully, considering the omissions and silences just as much as the rhetoric of Roman triumphalism, and without letting the eventual success of the medieval papacy persuade us that such success was inevitable. After the 250 years we have examined here, the triumph of Roman episcopal power in the Middle Ages was anything but assured.[69]

Bibliography

Allen, P. and W. Mayer (2000) 'Through a Bishop's Eyes: Towards a Definition of Pastoral Care in Late Antiquity', *Augustinianum* 40: 345–97.

Allen, P. and B. Neil (2013) *Crisis Management in Late Antiquity (410–590 CE): a Survey of the Evidence from Episcopal Letters*, Leiden.

Baumkamp, E. (2014) *Kommunikation in der Kirche des 3. Jahrhunderts: Bischöfe und Gemeinden zwischen Konflikt und Konsens im Imperium Romanum*, Tübingen.

Belda Iniesta, J. (2019) '*Vox Beati Petri*: los Procesos conciliares a obispos y la sacra regula como instancia de apelación en el *ius antiquum*', *Revista de la Inquisición: Intolerancia y derechos humanos* 23: 127–52.

Blair-Dixon, K. (2007) 'Memory and Authority in Sixth-Century Rome: the *Liber pontificalis* and the *Collectio Avellana*', in K. Cooper and J. Hillner (eds) *Religion, Dynasty and Patronage in Early Christian Rome, 300–900*, Cambridge, 59–76.

---

[68] John Moschus, *Pratum spirituale* 147 and 148, trans. Wortley 1992, 120–1.

[69] I am grateful to the Australian Research Council for Discovery Project DP200100334, which funded this research.

Blaudeau, P. (2015) 'Narrating Papal Authority (440–530): the Adaptation of *Liber pontificalis* to the Apostolic See's Developing Claims', in G. D. Dunn (ed.) *The Bishop of Rome in Late Antiquity*, Farnham, 127–40.

Bleckmann, B. (2014) 'Constantine, Rome, and the Christians', in J. Wienand (ed.) *Contested Monarchy: Integrating the Roman Empire in the Fourth Century AD*, Oxford, 309–29.

Chavasse, A. (ed.) (1973) *Sancti Leonis Magni romani pontificis tractatus septem et nonaginta*, Turnhout.

Cooper, K. and J. Hillner (eds) (2007) *Religion, Dynasty and Patronage in Early Christian Rome, 300–900*, Cambridge.

DeFerrari, R. J. (trans.) (1952) *Life of St Epiphanius*, Washington, DC.

Dekkers, E. (ed.) (1993) *Corpus Patrum Latinorum*, Turnhout.

Deliyannis, D. M. (trans.) (2004) *Agnellus of Ravenna: the Book of Pontiffs of the Church of Ravenna*, Washington, DC.

Deliyannis, D. M. (ed.) (2006) *Liber pontificalis ecclesiae Ravennatis*, Turnhout.

Demacopoulos, G. E. (2013) *The Invention of Peter: Apostolic Discourse and Papal Authority in Late Antiquity*, Philadelphia.

Diehl, L., J. Moreau and H. I. Marrou (eds) (1967) *Inscriptiones latinae christianae veteres*, 4 vols, Dublin.

Duchesne, L. and C. Vogel (eds) (1955) *Le Liber pontificalis*, 2nd ed., vols 1–3, Paris.

Dunn, G. D. (2007) *Cyprian and the Bishops of Rome: Questions of Papal Primacy in the Early Church*, Macquarie Park, NSW.

Dunn, G. D. (2013) 'The Clerical *cursus honorum* in the Late Antique Roman Church', *Scrinium* 9: 132–45.

Dunn, G. D. (2015) '*Collectio Corbeiensis, Collectio Pithouensis* and the Earliest Collections of Papal Letters', in B. Neil and P. Allen (eds) *Collecting Early Christian Letters: from the Apostle Paul to Late Antiquity*, Cambridge, 175–205.

Esler, P. F. (2003) 'The Character of Early Christianity in Rome', in B. Neil, G. D. Dunn and L. Cross (eds) *Liturgy and Life*, Strathfield, NSW, 19–42.

Espelo, D. B. van (2015) Review of G. D. Dunn (ed.) (2015) *The Bishop of Rome in Late Antiquity*, Farnham, in *Bryn Mawr Classical Review* 2015.08.36.

Ferreiro, A. (2015) 'Pope Siricius and Himerius of Tarragona (385): Provincial Papal Intervention in the Fourth Century', in G. D. Dunn (ed.) *The Bishop of Rome in Late Antiquity*, Farnham, 73–85.

Gemeinhardt, P. (2019) 'Bishops as Religious Mentors: Spiritual Education and Pastoral Care', in C. A. Cvetković and P. Gemeinhardt (eds) *Episcopal Networks in Late Antiquity: Connection and Communication across Boundaries*, Berlin, 117–47.

Hillner, J. (2007) 'Families, Patronage and the Titular Churches of Rome', in K. Cooper and J. Hillner (eds) *Religion, Dynasty and Patronage in Early Christian Rome, 300–900*, Cambridge, 225–61.

Humphries, M. (2012) 'Valentinian III and the City of Rome (425–455): Patronage, Politics, Power', in L. Grig and G. Kelly (eds) *Two Romes: Rome and Constantinople in Late Antiquity*, Oxford, 161–82.

Humphries, M. (2014) 'Liturgy and Laity in Late-Antique Rome: Problems, Sources and Social Dynamics', *Studia Patristica*, vol. 71, Leuven, 171–86.

Izdebski, A. (2012) 'Bishops in Late Antique Italy: Social Importance vs. Political Power', *Phoenix* 66: 158–75.

Jacobs, A. S. (2000) 'Writing Demetrias: Ascetic Logic in Late Antiquity', *Church History* 69: 719–48.

Jaffé, P. and K. Herbers (eds) (2016) *Regesta Pontificum Romanorum ab condita ecclesia ad annum post Christum natum MCXCVIII*, ed. M. Schütz, vol. 1: *A S. Petro usque ad a. DCIV*, 3rd ed., Göttingen.

Jasper, D. and H. Fuhrmann (2001) *Papal Letters in the Early Middle Ages*, Washington, DC.
McEachnie, R. (2017) *Chromatius of Aquileia and the Making of a Christian City*, London.
McKitterick, R. (2020) *Rome and the Invention of the Papacy: the Liber pontificalis*, Cambridge.
McLynn, N. (2008) 'Crying Wolf: the Pope and the Lupercalia', *JRS* 98: 161–75.
Moorhead, J. (2015) *The Popes and the Church of Rome in Late Antiquity*, London.
Moreau, D. (2006) 'Les patrimoines de l'église romaine jusqu'à la mort de Grégoire le Grand: dépouillement et réflexions préliminaires à une étude sur le rôle temporel des évêques de Rome durant l'Antiquité la plus tardive', *AntTard* 14: 79–93.
Neil, B. (2011) 'Imperial Benefactions to the Fifth-Century Roman Church', in G. Nathan and L. Garland (eds) *Basileia: Essays on Imperium and Culture in Honour of E. M. and M. J. Jeffreys*, Brisbane, 55–66.
Neil, B. (2016) 'Papal Letters and Letter Collections', in C. Sogno, B. Storin and E. Watts (eds) *Late Antique Letter Collections: an Introduction and Reference Guide*, Berkeley, 449–66.
Neil, B. and P. Allen (2014) *The Letters of Gelasius I (492–496): Pastor and Micro-manager of the Church of Rome*, Turnhout.
Pietri, C. (1976) *Roma Cristiana: recherches sur l'Église de Rome, son organisation, sa politique, son idéologie, de Miltiade à Sixte III (311–440)*, Rome.
Pietri, C. and L. Pietri (eds) (1999–2000) *Prosopographie chrétienne du Bas-Empire 2: prosopographie de l'Italie chrétienne (313–604)*, 2 vols, Rome.
Pietri, L. (2002) 'Evergétisme chrétien et fondations privées dans l'Italie de l'antiquité tardive', in R. Lizzi Testa and J.-M. Carrié (eds) *Humana sapit: études d'antiquité tardive offertes à Lellia Cracco Ruggini*, Turnhout, 253–63.
Ramsey, B. (trans.) (1989) *The Sermons of St Maximus of Turin*, Mahwah, NJ.
Rapp, C. (2005) *Holy Bishops of Late Antiquity: the Nature of Christian Leadership in an Age of Transition*, Los Angeles.
Rüpke, J. and A. Glock (2005) *Fasti sacerdotum: die Mitglieder der Priesterschaften und das sakrale Funktionspersonal römischer, griechischer, orientalischer und jüdisch-christlicher Kulte in der Stadt Rom vom 300 v. Chr. bis 499 n. Chr.*, Stuttgart.
Salzman, M. R. (1999) 'The Christianization of Sacred Time and Sacred Space', in W. V. Harris (ed.) *The Transformations of Vrbs Roma in Late Antiquity*, *JRA* Suppl. 33, Portsmouth, RI, 123–34.
Salzman, M. R. (2015) 'Reconsidering a Relationship: Pope Leo of Rome and Prosper of Aquitaine', in G. D. Dunn (ed.) *The Bishop of Rome in Late Antiquity*, Farnham, 109–26.
Salzman, M. R., M. Saghy and R. Lizzi Testa (eds) (2016) *Pagans and Christians in Late Antique Rome: Conflict, Competition, and Coexistence in the Fourth Century*, Cambridge.
Sessa, K. (2010) 'Exceptionality and Invention: Silvester and the Late Antique "Papacy" at Rome', *Studia Patristica*, vol. 46, Leuven, 77–94.
Sessa, K. (2012) *The Formation of Papal Authority in Late Antiquity: Roman Bishops and the Domestic Sphere*, Cambridge.
Sotinel, C. (1998) 'Le personnel épiscopal: enquête sur la puissance de l'évêque dans la cité', in E. Rebillard and C. Sotinel (eds) *L'évêque dans la cité du IVe au Ve siècle: image et autorité*, Rome, 105–26.
Thiel, A. (ed.) (1867) *Epistulae Romanae pontificum genuinae et quae ad eos scriptae sunt a s. Hilaro usque ad Pelagium II*, 2nd ed., Braunsberg; repr. Hildesheim, 2004.
Uhalde, K. (2007) *Expectations of Justice in the Age of Augustine*, Philadelphia.
Volp, U. (2003) 'Liturgical Authority Reconsidered: Remarks on the Bishop's Role in Pre-Constantinian Worship', in B. Neil, G. D. Dunn and L. Cross (eds) *Liturgy and Life*, Strathfield, NSW, 189–209.
Wessel, S. (2009) *Leo the Great and the Spiritual Rebuilding of Rome*, Leiden.
Wortley, J. (trans.) (1992) *John Moschus: The Spiritual Meadow*, Kalamazoo, MI.

13

VIOLENCE AND EPISCOPAL ELECTIONS IN LATE ANTIQUE ROME, AD 300–500

Samuel Cohen

THIS CHAPTER RECONSIDERS the violence associated with the contested elections of three Roman bishops: Damasus (366–84), Boniface (418–22) and Symmachus (498–514). My focus on the Roman church is a consequence of the availability of evidence, but I will also consider how contested episcopal elections elsewhere in Italy compare to those at Rome. As we shall see, personal ambition, the size and complexity of the Roman church, the lack of clear procedures for episcopal elections, and the diminution of the coercive power of the state in the city from the late third century onwards increased the potential for intra-Christian conflict following the death of a bishop. These conflicts focused especially on controlling (or attempting to control) specific buildings and areas of the city. The descriptions of the resulting violence, which featured club- and sword-wielding thugs, massacres in churches and attacks against rival candidates in the streets, still shock with their apparent callous brutality. This has occasionally led to the mischaracterising of these episodes as riots or examples of mob violence, expressions that implicitly lay the blame upon the faceless, fanatical multitude. However, as I will argue below, the violence associated with contested Roman episcopal elections was intentional, carefully coordinated and deployed from the top down as part of a deliberate strategy to gain control of the see of St Peter.

How (Not) to Choose a Bishop: Three Disputed Elections at Rome

Each of the three disputed episcopal elections, which occurred at Rome during the period under consideration in this volume, is complex and worthy of extended consideration. But a brief sketch of the important events and actors will be sufficient for the purposes of this chapter.[1] The first took place following the death of Liberius

---

[1] There are numerous insightful studies on these three episodes. On Damasus and Ursinus, see, for instance, Pietri 1976, 407–23; 1997; Curran 2000, 137–42; Lizzi Testa 2004, 129–70; Reutter 2009, 31–55; Trout 2015, 3–10; Diefenbach 2007, 224–41, and the extensive bibliography in Raimondi 2009, 169–70 n. 1. On Boniface and Eulalius, see Cristo 1977; Wirbelauer 1994, 410–15; Norton 2007, 65; Diefenbach 2007, 242–50; Dunn 2015a. See also Duchesne's *notes explicatives* on *Liber pontificalis* 44 (hereafter *LP*) (Duchesne 1886–1892, 1.228 n. 1). The two most complete studies of the so-called Symmachian/Laurentian schism are Wirbelauer 1993; Sardella 1996. But see also the discussions in Richards 1979, 70–99; Moorhead 1992, 114–45; Noble 1993, 405–12; Amory 1997, 203–6; Sessa 2012, 208–18; Cohen 2015, 198–200. An overview of the disputed elections at Rome is also given by Latham 2012, 307–17.

(352–66), who had been banished from Rome by Constantius II for refusing to agree to the condemnation of Athanasius at the Council of Milan in 355, only to capitulate several years later.² While Liberius was absent from Rome, a priest named Felix had acted as bishop in his place, and Felix was unwilling to relinquish power when Liberius returned. Liberius eventually managed to reassert his authority, and Felix, if we believe the account in the *Liber pontificalis*, withdrew from the city and retired to an estate on the Via Portuensis.³ But the schism continued to distort episcopal politics for a generation. According to the highly tendentious *Gesta inter Liberium et Felicem episcopos* (hereafter, *Gesta*), the deacon Damasus initially supported Liberius, only to betray him following his exile.⁴ When Liberius died in late September 366, a group of clergy hostile to Damasus gathered at the *basilica Iulii* and chose Ursinus as bishop,⁵ while Damasus was elected at the basilica *in Lucinis*.⁶ Upon learning that Ursinus had been consecrated by Paul, bishop of Tibur (Tivoli), Damasus – at least according to the *Gesta* – suborned charioteers and the ignorant rabble (*imperita multitudo*) with bribes. These men then forced their way into the *basilica Iulii* and perpetrated a great slaughter (*magna caedes*) of Ursinus' supporters, which lasted for three days.⁷ The following week, Damasus was ordained at the Lateran.⁸ The *praefectus urbi* Viventius (called *iudex urbis* in the *Gesta*), together with a second official, the *praefectus annonae* Julianus, responded by expelling Ursinus and two of his deacons from the city. According to the *Gesta*, Damasus had arranged this by bribery.⁹ Despite his apparent victory, seven Ursinian priests, presumably in addition to other partisans, still occupied the *basilica Liberii* on the Esquiline. Just before 8 a.m. on 26 October 366, a group of sword- and club-wielding *arenarii* (gladiators), *quadrigarii* (charioteers) and *fossores* (gravediggers) recruited by Damasus, supplemented by members of the clergy, broke down the doors of the locked church and swarmed into the building. Some ran to the roof and began to rain down a barrage of massive roof tiles, killing a number of those who had gathered in the church to pray.¹⁰ Then the real slaughter began. Wielding axes and swords, the intruders massacred 160 people, including women and children. Many more were wounded and later died from their injuries. Much of the church was

---

² See Liberius' letter written to Lucifer of Cagliari, Eusebius of Vercelli and Dionysius of Milan, *quamvis sub imagine* (JK 216 = CSEL 65.164–6); trans. Flower 2013, 238–9. Compare Sulp. Sev. *Chron.* 2.39. An overview of the schism can be found in Curran 2000, 129–37.
³ LP 37 (Duchesne 1886–1892, 1.207).
⁴ *Gesta* 2.
⁵ On the identity of this church, see below, n. 55. Rufinus (*Hist. eccl.* 11.10) and Socrates Scholasticus (*Hist. eccl.* 4.29) claim that Ursinus was ordained at the *basilica Sicinini*, not the *basilica Iulii*. Strangely, Socrates also asserts that Ursinus' ordination did not take place in a church (οὐκ ἐν ἐκκλησίᾳ). The 'basilica' in question, then, must be a public building. Of course, this may have been intended to delegitimise Ursinus' claim to the episcopacy. In this instance, the account in the *Gesta* appears to be more reliable.
⁶ On this church, see below, n. 41. It is possible that this was less a formal election and more akin to a nomination of a candidate. See Ghilardi 2010, 174 n. 195 and De Spirito, 1994, 266.
⁷ *Gesta* 5.
⁸ This took place surrounded by his gang of liars and gladiators, if we believe *Gesta* 6.
⁹ *Gesta* 6: *[Damasus] redimens iudicem urbis Viventium et praefectum annonae Iulianum* . . .
¹⁰ Roof tiles could be very effective weapons in urban conflicts. See Barry 1996.

left in ruins.[11] Ammianus, likely describing a separate incident, claims that 137 corpses were left strewn in the *basilica Sicinini* as a result of the fighting between the factions.[12] One more massacre of Ursinus' supporters followed, this time at St Agnes' on the Via Nomentana, outside the city walls.[13] With his opponents dead or in exile, Damasus was left in control of the church.

Half a century later, the city experienced a second contested election. In late December 418, Zosimus, who had been bishop of Rome for less than two years, died. Days later, two separate groups gathered to choose his successor: the archdeacon Eulalius was elected and ordained at the Constantinian Basilica (the Lateran), while Boniface (418–22) was elected at the church of Theodora (now unidentifiable) and later ordained at the church of Marcellus[14] or the *basilica Iuliae*.[15] When deacons, priests and a mob (*multitudo*) of Eulalius' supporters blockaded Boniface at the Lateran, violent conflict seemed inevitable. However, the *praefectus urbi* Aurelius Anicius Symmachus moved quickly to restore the *quies urbis*. Symmachus initially supported Eulalius and wrote to Honorius in Ravenna indicating this fact. Honorius agreed, and Boniface was exiled from Rome.[16] But when Boniface's partisans appealed to the emperor,[17] Honorius reconsidered his earlier position and decided that a synod should be held to adjudicate between the competing claims. In the interim, both Boniface and Eulalius were asked to leave the city.[18] In early spring 419 the schism remained unresolved. With Easter fast approaching and Rome still without a legitimate bishop, Honorius appointed Achilleus, bishop of Spoleto, to conduct the Paschal services.[19] But Eulalius, against the orders of the emperor and supported by an armed mob (*multitudo armata ferro*), returned to the city with the

---

[11] According to the *Gesta* 7.

[12] Amm. Marc. 27.3.11. The *basilica Sicinini* is often identified with the *basilica Liberii* in secondary literature. This would mean that Ammianus and the *Gesta* are reporting the same incident. However, this is far from clear. Not only are the buildings given different names, but Ammianus also reports a different number of deaths. As we saw above (n. 5), Socrates and Rufinus mentions a *basilica Sicinini* in connection to Ursinus' ordination, which appears to have been a violent affair. Jerome (*Chron.* s.a. 366) also claims that Ursinus' partisans attacked the *basilica Sicinini*, resulting in 'very cruel slaughters' (*crudelissimae interfectiones*). One wonders if Rufinus and Jerome are discussing the same event described by Ammianus. In any case, the violence at the *basilica Sicinini* should be read as a different episode than the massacre at the *basilica Liberii* described in the *Gesta*. On questions related to the identity of this building and the events associated with it, see Den Boeft et al. 2009, 69–71. On Rufinus and Jerome's characterisation of the violence, see below.

[13] *Gesta* 12: *unde cum ad sanctam Agnem multi fidelium convenissent, armatus cum satellitibus suis Damasus irruit et plurimos vastationis suae strage deiecit.*

[14] According to the report of Symmachus sent to Honorius, preserved as *CA* 14 (*CSEL* 35.59–60).

[15] *LP* 44 (Duchesne 1886–1892, 227–8). This was the *basilica Iuliae* in the city centre. On the location of Boniface's ordination, see Geertman 2004, 30–1. Dunn 2015a, 2 initially argued that Boniface was ordained at San Lorenzo. He later revised this position, and he now believes this church is in fact San Marcello al Corso. See Dunn 2015b, 148 and n. 40. On this church, see also Brandenburg 2005, 164–5. Compare with the comments in Duchesne's edition of the *Liber pontificalis* (p. 227 and n. 4, p. 228).

[16] Imperial *rescriptum*, *CA* 15 (*CSEL* 35.60–1): *Bonifatium interdicta confestim urbe prohiberi* . . .

[17] Preserved as *CA* 17 (*CSEL* 35.63–4).

[18] As the emperor instructed Symmachus in *CA* 18 (*CSEL* 35.65–6). See also *CA* 20 (*CSEL* 35.67–8), Honorius' letter to the synod at Ravenna.

[19] See Honorius' letter to Symmachus, Achilleus and the senate, preserved as *CA* 21–3 (*CSEL* 35.68–70). See also *CA* 24 (*CSEL* 35.70–1), an edict of Honorius to the Roman people.

intention of celebrating Easter at the Lateran. Spasms of street fighting soon erupted, spilling into the Forum itself.[20] This quickly prompted action from Ravenna. Eulalius was forcibly evicted from the Lateran by Symmachus,[21] and Boniface was permitted to return to the city.[22] The schism was over.

The final episode under consideration in this chapter occurred at the end of the fifth century. In November 498, two competing groups gathered to select a successor for Anastasius II: one elected the deacon Symmachus at the Lateran, while the other, which included the powerful senators Festus and Probinus, met at S. Maria Maggiore and elected Laurence, a presbyter of the *titulus* S. Praxedis.[23] Although the situation must have been incredibly tense, both parties agreed that the Ostrogothic king Theoderic should adjudicate the dispute. Theoderic decided in favour of Symmachus because he had been elected first and by a majority, at least according to the pro-Symmachian account preserved in the *Liber pontificalis*.[24] The *Laurentian Fragment*, a pro-Laurence response to the *Liber pontificalis*, claims that Symmachus engaged in a widespread campaign of bribery.[25] Whatever the case, Theoderic's decision was approved by a synod held in Rome on 1 March 499, which Laurence, along with various members of the Roman clergy and Italian bishops, attended. A grateful clergy acclaimed the Ostrogothic king thirty times, presumably for his role in preventing the contested election from descending into bloodshed.[26] But the controversy flared up again in 501 when Symmachus was accused by Laurentian partisans of various offences, which likely included celebrating Easter on the incorrect date, sexual misconduct and the mismanagement of church property.[27] Symmachus was summoned to Ravenna

---

[20] Symmachus reported this in *CA* 29 (*CSEL* 35.74–6), a letter to the *comes* Flavius Constantius, the future Constantius III, who in 419, having married Galla Placidia in 417, was Honorius' brother-in-law and *magister militum utriusque militiae* of the West. See *PLRE* 2a.221–5, 'Fl. Constantius 17'.

[21] Reported to by Symmachus Constantius in *CA* 32 (*CSEL* 35.78–9).

[22] *CA* 33 (*CSEL* 35.78–9), a rescript of Honorius to Symmachus.

[23] Symmachus' biography in *LP* 53 (Duchesne 1886–1892, 1.260): *hic sub intentione ordinatus est uno die cum Laurentio, Symmachus in basilica Constantiniana, Laurentius in basilica beatae Mariae.*

[24] Theodorus Lector's *Hist. eccl.* 2.17 (*GCS* 54.131) claims only that Symmachus was elected by the majority.

[25] The *Laurentian Fragment* is edited by Duchesne in his edition of the *Liber pontificalis* (Duchesne 1886–1892, 1.44–6). There is at least some truth to this accusation, and Ennodius, an active Symmachian, noted with some embarrassment that Symmachus had a debt of 400 solidi to the bishop of Milan, which he had not repaid.

[26] *Acta synhodorum habitarum Romae I* (*Acta Synhodi a. 499*) (*MGH AA* 12.399–415, quoted at 405: *exaudi Christe! Theoderico vitam! (Dictum XXX)*. When he visited Rome the following year, Theoderic even visited Symmachus at St Peter's, at least according to *Anon. Vales.* 64 (*MGH AA* 9.324).

[27] *LP* 53 (Duchesne 1886–1892, 1.260) vaguely states: *post annos vero IIII, zelo ducti aliqui ex clero et aliqui ex senatu, maxime Festus et Probinus, incriminaverunt Symmachum et subornaverunt testes falsos quos miserunt Ravennam ad regem Theodericum, accusantes beatum Symmachum*. Both the chronology and the exact nature of the accusations levelled against Symmachus are unclear. Sardella 1996, 26–9, argued that the accusations were likely made in the summer or fall of 501, initially stemming from the celebration of Easter. Wirbelauer 1993, 21, believes that the allegations were made to Theoderic in the winter of 500/1 – that is, before Easter was celebrated. The other charges against Symmachus can be reconstructed from the admittedly hostile *Vita* preserved in the *Laurentian Fragment* (discussed below), which claims that Symmachus, while waiting for an audience with Theoderic, met a group of women *cum quibus accusabatur in scelere*. Realising that the women had been summoned to testify against him, Symmachus fled back to Rome. The *Laurentian Fragment* contains the additional accusation that Symmachus had mismanaged church property, and thus this accusation must have been central, at least for Symmachus' opponents. On this question, see Sessa 2012, 212–46.

by Theoderic, but rather than face his accusers, he suspiciously fled back to Rome in the middle of the night and ensconced himself in the safety of St Peter's.[28] This left the rest of the city under the control of Laurence, who, having taken control of the Lateran, acted as de facto bishop. Unlike the relative calm that had prevailed following Theoderic's arbitration in 498, the half-decade after 501/2 was marked by episodes of widespread disorder as supporters of each candidate fought openly in the streets, leaving many clergy dead and injured.[29] Order was finally restored by Theoderic in 506 or possibly in 507, when he ruled once again in favour of Symmachus and instructed Laurence and his supporters to hand over their churches to the Symmachians.[30]

The Intentionality of Violence

Although many of the sources used to reconstruct contested episcopal elections at Rome are polemical and prone to exaggeration, there is no reason to doubt that the violent conflict they depict was real, even if its scale cannot be known with certainty. Scholars have sometimes characterised these episodes as 'riots' or examples of 'mob violence'.[31] Peripheral to the elections themselves and with little to no planning, riots pulled in bystanders who, protected by the anonymity of the crowd, were free to express their anger against the established order or to engage in looting for personal gain.[32] Another interpretation understands violence as a mechanism by which the people could make their voices heard in the election of a new bishop. In this view, 'the mob' can be equated with 'the congregation'.[33] And given the obviously religious implications of an episcopal election, it would be easy to imagine the 'rioters' as religious fanatics, although this is more commonly asserted in the context of disputes within and between North African and eastern churches.[34] There is another possibility, however, that has largely been overlooked. The narratives discussed in this chapter strongly suggest that the violence prompted by disputed episcopal elections was not random, fanatical or a result of the machinations of the masses. Rather, it was an instrumental top-down strategy used by rival candidates and their supporters to secure control of the Roman church.

---

[28] Symmachus was exonerated – or at least not condemned – by two rump synods in 501 and again in 502: *Acta Synhodi a. 502* (*MGH AA* 12.438–55) and *Acta Synhodi a. 501* [in fact, 502]: *Quarta Synodus habita Romae palmaris* (*MGH AA* 12.426–37). For the dating of the synods, see esp. Wirbelauer 1993, 21–6, and for a survey of the Roman synods of 499–502, see Sardella 1996, 70–111.

[29] *LP* 53 (Duchesne 1886–1892, 1.260–1).

[30] Moorhead 1992, 124–5 and Wirbelauer 1993, 39–40 argue that the schism ended in 507. Sardella 1996, 38 suggests 506.

[31] For instance, Richards 1979, 72, 75; Frend 1984, 626; Collins 2009, 48; Moorhead 2015, 53.

[32] On the interpretative and terminological problems with the study of 'riots', see, for instance, Thompson 1971, 76; Rudé 1981, 6–9; Erdkamp 2002, 94–8.

[33] Norton 2007, 52–70.

[34] Gaddis 2005, 71, remarked, late antique church history 'appears to the modern student as a tangled mess of doctrinal controversies, schisms, councils, disputed episcopal elections, and riots'. That student would be forgiven for inferring a causal connection between religious concerns – the doctrinal controversies, schisms, councils and disputed episcopal elections – and the riots.

This can be seen most clearly in the Damasus/Ursinus controversy. Pro-Damasean sources predictably place the blame on Ursinus. Jerome, for instance, asserts that the massacre at the *basilica Sicinini* took place only after Ursinus and his supporters invaded (*invadit*) the building, implying an organised attack.³⁵ Describing the same event, Rufinus is even more direct, claiming that Ursinus recruited a 'riotous and querulous mass (*collecta turbulentorum et seditiosorum*)'. The resulting violence was more like battles (*bella*) than a riot (*seditio*), and the 'places of prayer were filled with human blood'.³⁶ But it is in the *Gesta* that the intentionality of the violence is most obvious. In fact, Damasus' actions are portrayed as particularly negative precisely because of their premeditation.³⁷ At each phase of the narrative, Damasus is depicted actively directing events, organising a campaign of beatings and murder which targeted his opponents following the attack against the *basilica Iulii*,³⁸ and spending huge sums of money to secure the support of the charioteers, gladiators and gravediggers who acted as his personal army, as well as to bribe imperial officials. The emphasis on the hiring of gladiators and charioteers indicated to the reader the planned nature of the violence, which was perpetrated by men recruited specifically because of their reputation for brutality. It also suggested that Damasus' faction was comprised of socially inferior outsiders who, although having no legitimate stake in the outcome of events, were willing to commit acts of cruelty for money.³⁹ Of course, the partisan nature of this text, which demonised Damasus and lionised Ursinus, makes it difficult to determine its reliability. But there is circumstantial evidence that Damasus' connection to these men was not merely rhetorical. The *titulus Damasi* (now S. Lorenzo in Damaso), which Damasus built or possibly restored, was located on his family property near the Theatre of Pompey in the Campus Martius.⁴⁰ Damasus was put forward as a candidate for bishop (but not consecrated) at a church called *in Lucinis* by the *Gesta*, today S. Lorenzo in Lucina next to the Via Lata on the eastern edge of the Campus Martius.⁴¹ Given his ties to this part of Rome, it seems reasonable to assume that the zone around

---

³⁵ Jerome, *Chron.* s.a. 366: *et post non multum temporis intervallum Ursinus a quibusdam episcopus constitutes Sicininum cum suis invadit.*
³⁶ Ruf. *Hist. eccl.* 11.10.
³⁷ The targeted application of violence was not out of character for Damasus. According to the so-called *Libellus precum*, later in his pontificate Damasus' clergy together with a group of *officiales* – municipal magistrates charged with enforcing laws in the city – assaulted and arrested a priest named Marcarius, possibly a supporter of Lucifer of Caligari, who was conducting a night-time vigil in a *domus*, injuring him badly. See *Libellus precum* 80 (SC 504.183–4). This episode is discussed in Sessa 2012, 210. On the definition of *officiales*, see the comments in SC 504.184 n. 1.
³⁸ *Gesta* 6: *coepit Damasus Romanam plebem, quae sibi nolebat procedere, fustibus et caede varia perurguere.*
³⁹ The pattern of violence at Rome mirrors that which was occurring in North Africa at about this same time. See Shaw 2011, 146–59.
⁴⁰ On this church and Damasus' familial relation to the site, see Krautheimer 1959, 145–51; Löx 2013, 49–58; Mulryan 2014, 86–9; Trout 2015, 188–9. It should also be noted that modern authors have occasionally confused and conflated the *titulus Lucinae* and *titulus Damasi*, presumably because both were associated with Damasus and both were later dedicated to St Laurence.
⁴¹ On the phrase *in lucinis*, which almost certainly refers to the *titulus Lucinae* (later S. Lorenzo in Lucina), see De Spirito 1994, 265–6. On the identity and location of this church to the north and east of the *titulus Damasi*, see esp. Diefenbach 2007, 225 and n. 35, but also Brandt 2012, 148–9; Curran 2000, 144; Krautheimer 1959, 152–8. *Pace* Cracco Ruggini 2003, 373, who states that this church is in Trastevere.

the Campus Martius was a Damasean stronghold. To the immediate west and just beyond the Aurelianic Walls was the *Ager Vaticanus*, which was associated with *peregrini* – non-citizens of the city – as well as entertainments including two circuses and cemeteries.[42] The *fossores*, perhaps not a particularly belligerent group in the modern imagination, had a reputation for brutality in Late Antiquity. By the fifth century, gravediggers came to be understood as a (low) class of clergy,[43] although they maintained their independence from episcopal oversight well into the late sixth century.[44] At Alexandria, bishops employed *parabolani*, a group who cared for the sick and disposed of bodies, as their personal enforcers.[45] Likewise at Rome, ecclesiastical burial personnel and other members of the lower clergy were 'an episcopal militia in the urban setting that could be mobilized easily at any time', in the words of Johannes Hahn.[46] Damasus' *fossores* may have been associated with one or more of the martyrial sites outside the walls in this same north-eastern part of the city. Moreover, the *titulus Damasi* was also known in antiquity as *in prasino*, possibly because it had been constructed above or nearby the stables of the Green Circus faction.[47] It therefore seems likely that Damasus' family owned this property before it became a church and this suggests further that he had a relationship with the Green *factio*.[48] Moreover, both pagan and Christian patrons in Late Antiquity were increasingly forming links of clientship with those associated with the entertainment and funerary spaces beyond the walls.[49] Rival candidates in a contested episcopal election would have naturally sought to mobilise these clients to support their claims.[50] This may well have been the context of Damasus' relationship with the *fossores*, *arenarii* and *quadrigarii*. It is also worth noting that the *Gesta* claims that Damasus drew support not only from these men, but also from members of his extended household including slaves and clients (*familiares* and *satellites*), who would have presumably been concentrated in this same area of the city.

These topographical details are important. The accepted model of episcopal oversight in the fourth century meant that Roman bishops were expected to be able administrators, spiritual leaders and, importantly, a visible presence within the city. Moreover, buildings such as the Lateran represented the symbolic and administrative centre of the Roman church.[51] And for much of the period under consideration in this chapter and unlike the situation at Constantinople, the continued dominance of

---

[42] Cracco Ruggini 2003, 374–5. On the status of *peregrini* in Late Antiquity, see Mathisen 2006, 1021. On the location of the *stabula*, see Richardson 1992, 366.
[43] As evidenced by *CTh* 13.1.1.
[44] See, for instance, Costambeys 2001, 187; Guyon 1974.
[45] Bond 2013, 137–43. See also Bowersock 2010.
[46] Hahn 2014, 398.
[47] Krautheimer 1959, 145–51; Lizzi Testa 2004, 134–5; Reutter 2009, 100–1; Löx 2013, 49–58; Trout 2015, 188–9; *LTUR* 3.179–82. On the Green Circus faction stables (*stabulum factionis praesinae*), see *LTUR* 4.399–70; Mulryan 2014, 86–7, with n. 4 on the archaeology of this site. But see also Blair-Dixon 2002.
[48] Trout 2015, 189; Cracco Ruggini 2003, 373–4 and n. 44.
[49] Cracco Ruggini 2003, 376.
[50] As Whitby 2006, 553 has argued, seemingly 'clerical' violence generated by the supporters of this or that bishop may have been like the mechanics of 'secular' violence between aristocrats and their retainers, and the Circus factions.
[51] Diefenbach 2007, 231–2.

traditional aristocratic public rituals meant that rival claimants to the episcopacy at Rome could not as readily contest and control urban space through Christian religious processions. Instead, rival candidates were forced to rely on a static strategy, which emphasised the occupation of monumental Christian buildings.[52] Taken together, control of the city's intramural basilicas was crucial for any candidate who wished to be viewed as the legitimate bishop.

This can be seen especially in the *Gesta*, which gives the impression of a deliberate strategy carried out by Damasus and his supporters to forcibly seize specific intramural churches.[53] Recall that, according to this text, Damasus first targeted the *basilica Iulii*, presumably the same church in which Ursinus had been elected and ordained.[54] There are at least two churches with this name; the first was *iuxta Forum Traiani* near the city centre, while the second was in Trastevere.[55] Stefan Diefenbach has cogently argued that the *Gesta* was in fact referring to the *basilica iuxta Forum Traiani*.[56] If this is correct, during the earliest phase of the controversy Damasus' supporters were concentrated in the north-west periphery of Rome, and it was from here that they launched their assault against the principal Ursinian church in the centre.[57] Once this building had been secured, Damasus moved to displace the remaining Ursinians from the heart of

---

[52] Latham 2012, 310.
[53] In this and the other schisms, control of specific buildings and, by extension, specific areas of the city, was crucial. See McLynn 1992, 16–19; Latham 2012, 312.
[54] Although see above, n. 12.
[55] Both *basilicae Iulii*, as their names suggest, are attributed to Julius I (337–52). The Liberian Catalogue, part of the *Chronography of 354* (Duchesne, *LP* 1.9), states that Julius *fecit . . . basilicam Iuliam quae est regione VII iuxta forum divi Traiani, basilicam trans Tiberim regione XIIII iuxta Callistum*. Similarly, the *Vita* of Julius in the *Liber pontificalis* (Duchesne, *LP* 1.205) asserts, *fecit II basilicas, una in urbe Roma iuxta forum et altera trans Tiberim*. The location of the former church is not known, although it may have stood somewhere near today's church of SS Apostoli. The latter building was the precursor to today's S. Maria in Trastevere. See Brandenburg 2005, 122; *LTUR* 4.84–6. According to *Gesta* 5, Ursinus was consecrated at the *basilica Iulii*, and it was in this same church that the first massacre of Ursinus' supporters occurred. But which *basilica Iulii*? *Gesta* 3 mentions the <*basilica*> *Iuli trans Tiberim*, which had been occupied by Felix in opposition to Liberius upon the latter's return to Rome – a clear reference to S. Maria in Trastevere. But when it describes the building associated with Ursinus, the *Gesta* simply calls it the *basilica Iulii*. The lack of geographic descriptor for this second church suggests that the author is referring to a different building, and thus this must refer to the *basilica Iulii iuxta Forum Traiani*. On the other hand, the *Gesta* mentions the *basilica Iulii in Trastevere* ten lines before it discusses the church in which Ursinus was elected. It would thus be strangely obscure if the second, less precise, reference in fact referred to a different church, especially in a document in which precision regarding geographic locations was important. Needless to say, scholars disagree about which of the two churches was the location of Ursinus' election and the subsequent massacre. Pietri 1997, 51; Curran 2000, 138; and Trout 2015, 6, argue that the building in question was in Trastevere, while Künzle 1961; De Spirito 1994, 267; Cracco Ruggini 1997, 170 n. 42; Latham 2012, 310–11; and Diefenbach 2007, 224–6 suggest the city centre. An overview of the debate can be found in Ghilardi 2010, 183–5. I am largely convinced by Diefenbach's arguments (cited in the next note), but they cannot be taken as definitive.
[56] Diefenbach 2007, 225–6 and n. 36.
[57] I remain open to the possibility that the church in question was the basilica in Trastevere. This building was not, of course, as central as the *basilica iuxta Forum Traiani*, but it was close to Damasus' base of support in the neighbouring Regio X. Assuming he would eventually target churches in the centre and east of Rome, it would make sense that Damasus would have wished to remove this possible threat to his rear.

the city. He seized the Lateran, the administrative heart of the Roman church, and it was here that Damasus was ordained. From this newly secured position of strength, Damasus arranged for Ursinus to be exiled from the city. The attack against the *basilica Liberii* took place soon after, likely as a direct response to the failed expulsion of seven Ursinian priests who had taken refuge in this church, which remained an important intramural Ursinian power base. And as Neil McLynn observed, the violence took place in the second hour of the morning (likely around 8 a.m.) – almost certainly too early for the passions of a mob to be inflamed.[58] This, then, was a carefully planned and organised assault. Interestingly, the *Gesta* claims that this was the fifth battle (*quintum bellum*) Damasus had waged, which implies that there were at least several other church takeovers not described in the text.[59] It was only after he had secured the city's intramural churches and the Ursinians had been banished to the *suburbium* that Damasus and his supporters began to target the spaces beyond the walls. It was this that led to the final massacre at the tomb of St Agnes.

Damasus was not alone in his desire to control particular church buildings.[60] Indeed, religious violence across the empire was often directed against the meeting places and holy sites of rivals.[61] Importantly, the *Gesta* portrays the Damasus/Ursinus schism as a continuation of that between Liberius and Felix, with Ursinus in the role of the loyal supporter of Liberius. This is obviously a polemical claim, but it does appear to reflect Ursinus' self-presentation. It is noteworthy, for instance, that Ursinus and his supporters associated with churches closely tied to the memory of Liberius, most obviously the *basilica Liberii*, which was likely constructed by the bishop following his return from exile,[62] but also St Agnes', where the *Liber pontificalis* claims Liberius spent time in exile before his return to the city and which Liberius later decorated.[63] The attacks by Damasus' supporters against these buildings may have been motivated by the desire to prevent Ursinus from claiming legitimacy through his association with Liberius. Importantly, this conflict was not only physical. Once Damasus had secured the see of Rome, he embarked on an ambitious programme to monumentalise Christian burial sites across the city, including St Agnes'. These interventions were, at least in part, intended to extend Damasus' control over contested areas of the city.[64]

The strategic use of violence is less obvious in the Boniface/Eulalius schism. But it is possible to detect organisation. Eulalius had initially been supported by an armed *multitudo*, which he used to take control of the Lateran and was ordained.[65] Following

---

[58] McLynn 1992, 16–17.
[59] *Gesta* 9: *quintum iam bellum Damasus fecit*. Exactly what constitutes the *quintum bellum* is not clear.
[60] For North Africa, see esp. Lander 2017.
[61] Hahn 2014, 380.
[62] Curran 2000, 131.
[63] *Liber pontificalis* 36 (Duchesne, *LP* 1.208); discussed in Cohen 2018, 149.
[64] See Sághy 2000, 280–1; Trout 2003; 2015, 10–12, with notes. The *elogium* of Agnes can be found in Trout 2015, 150.
[65] *CA* 14 (*CSEL* 35.59–60). According to this letter, penned by *praefectus urbi* Symmachus, who supported Eulalius, this was a peaceful affair. However, the priests who were in favour of Boniface described it as a siege of the Lateran perpetrated by large gang of *plebs* (*Lateranensem ecclesiam . . . multitudine turbatae plebis obsederat*). See *CA* 17 (*CSEL* 35.63–5).

his ordination in the city centre, Boniface's supporters marched towards St Peter's, presumably with the intention of taking control of the church.[66] In an insightful analysis, Jacob Latham noticed the double valence of the verb *procedere* used by the *praefectus urbi* Symmachus in his letter to the emperor describing this event, which suggests both a military and religious procession.[67] Whether this was an armed band or a solemn procession (or some combination), both imply organisation – an attempt by Boniface to inscribe his authority on the eastern side of Rome and the church of St Peter, while Eulalius exerted his control in the west, principally at the Lateran. At this point, a confrontation between the two parties must have seemed inevitable. Violence was only averted by the timely intervention of the urban prefect, who, following the orders of the emperor, banished Boniface from the city.[68] But Boniface did not remain passive in his exile. As Symmachus subsequently complained in a letter to Honorius, Boniface organised another religio-military procession, this time from his base at St Paul's outside the walls to the city, perhaps hoping to rally more supporters as he went.[69] The march ended with a brawl at the city walls, and 'the people' (*populus*, here Boniface's supporters) even attacked an agent of the *praefectus urbi*, the tribune Serenianus.[70] Following this failed attempt to use force, Boniface and his partisans adopted a more diplomatic approach, writing their petition to the emperor described above, which resulted in Honorius' decision to exile both men from Rome. It was after this that Eulalius illicitly re-entered the city. Accompanied by an armed *multitudo*, perhaps drawn from amongst the same men who had backed him at the start of the schism, Eulalius violently retook control of the Lateran. This appears an odd decision, since his chances of becoming bishop were, up until this moment, very good, especially given that he had the support of the *praefectus urbi* Symmachus. Perhaps he had simply miscalculated. But Eulalius' decision to return to Rome against the orders of the emperor may have been motivated by his desire to quickly seize control of the city's churches. By celebrating Easter as the legitimate bishop would have done, he presumably hoped to make his seizure of the see a fait accompli. And it is likely that Eulalius would not have embarked on such a risky strategy without first securing support within the city beforehand.[71] Obviously, things did not work out for Eulalius. But the above sketch makes clear that he, like Boniface, attempted to use organised violence as part of a strategy to gain control of the church of Rome.

The deliberate mobilisation of violence also features in the account of the Symmachian/Laurentian schism preserved in the *Liber pontificalis*. It is worth citing in full:

> Festus, the leader of the senate and exconsul, and Probinus the exconsul, began to battle with other senators in Rome, particularly with Faustus the exconsul. Their

---

[66] *CA* 14 (*CSEL* 35.60): *nam etiam presbyterum Bonifatium in ecclesia Marcelli ordinandum esse duxerunt atque cum eo ad sancti apostoli Petri basilicam processerunt.*
[67] Latham 2012, 313–14.
[68] *CA* 15 (*CSEL* 35.60–1).
[69] Again, the verb used is *procedere*, as noted by Latham.
[70] *CA* 17 (*CSEL* 35.63–5). See also PLRE 2, 'Serenianus'.
[71] *CA* 29 (*CSEL* 35.74–6).

malice caused slaughter and murder among the clergy. Those who were rightly in communion with the blessed Symmachus and who chanced to be at large in the city were killed by the sword; they even displaced dedicated women and virgins from their monasteries or houses; they stripped women, injured them with cuts, and wounded them with blows. In the middle of the city, they fought battles every day against the church. He even killed many *sacerdotes*, including Dignissimus and Gordianus, the priests of St Peter *ad vincula* and Saints John and Paul with clubs and sword. They killed many Christians, so that it was unsafe for any of the clergy to travel in the city by day or night. On the church's side there fought only the exconsul Faustus.[72]

As was the case with the schisms discussed above, this passage does not describe spontaneous acts committed by unorganised gangs of religious fanatics. The violence is targeted and directed, in this case by members of the senatorial aristocracy. Admittedly, the Latin, which employs both passive and third-person constructions without clear subjects, makes a full reconstruction of events difficult: the partisans of Symmachus *were* murdered (*occidebantur*); the women *were* wounded (*vulnerabantur*); they (who?) fought battles (*pugnas . . . gerebant*); he (Festus?) killed many priests (*occidit*); they (who?) killed many Christians (*interfecerunt*). Despite the ambiguities, Festus and Probinus clearly stand at the centre of the account, and we can infer that, at least according to the *Liber pontificalis*, the two senators were either directly engaged in violence themselves along with another senator Faustus, or more likely, they were responsible for directing it from behind the scenes.

Like the *Gesta*, this account is polemical. The author(s) of the *Liber pontificalis* were partisans of Symmachus, and thus the account shifts blame on to Symmachus' opponents. Interestingly, however, the narrative does not appear to describe a fight *within* the church, but rather a fight between the church and its secular opponents exemplified by Festus and Probinus. The emphasis on the senators externalised responsibility for the controversy, which perhaps served to facilitate a rapprochement of the clerical supporters of Symmachus and Laurentius in the years following the conclusion of the schism. But whether or not we wish to accept the claim that the violence was both endemic and extreme enough to make the entire city even more dangerous than usual, interesting parallels can be found in the *Laurentian Fragment* – written by Laurentian supporters – which similarly reports that the city was riven by 'civil wars' (*bella civilia*) and 'murders' (*homicidia*), although here it is Symmachus who receives

---

[72] *LP* 53 (Duchesne 1886–1892, 1.260–1): *eodem tempore Festus caput senati excons. et Probinus excons. coeperunt intra urbem Romam pugnare cum aliis senatoribus et maxime cum Fausto excons. et caedes et homicidia in clero ex invidia. qui vero communicabant beato Symmacho iuste, publice qui inventi fuissent intra Vrbem gladio occidebantur; etiam et sanctimoniales mulieres et virgines deponentes de monasteria vel de habitaculis suis, denudantes sexum femineum, caedibus plagarum adflictas vulnerabantur; et omni die pugnas contra ecclesiam in media civitate gerebant. etiam et multos sacerdotes occidit, inter quos et Dignissimum et Gordianum, presbiteros a vincula sancti Petri apostoli et sanctos Iohannem et Paulum, quos fustibus et gladio interfecerunt; nam multos christianos, ut nulli esset securitas die vel nocte de clero in civitate ambulare. solus autem Faustus excons. pro ecclesia pugnabat;* trans. (with modifications) Davis 2010, 46.

the brunt of the blame.[73] With the exception of a short reference to Laurence's ally Festus at the end of the *Vita*, specific senators are not named, possibly in an attempt to minimise Laurence's support from Festus and Probinus.

The intentionality of the violence during the Symmachian/Laurentian schism is further suggested when we turn to the surviving *acta* of the Roman synod of 502, which met in several sessions over the course of summer and autumn of that year, as well as correspondence between the bishops who had gathered for the synod and Theoderic.[74] The first meeting took place at the *basilica Iulii* in Trastevere. This location was likely chosen because it was relatively close to the Symmachian stronghold at St Peter's. It also meant that Symmachus and his supporters could attend without having to pass through the city centre, which was under the control of Laurence's supporters – a dangerous proposition given the ongoing violence.[75] The result of the meeting was inconclusive.[76] Theoderic, who was growing increasingly impatient with the prevarications of the bishops, demanded that the allegations against Symmachus be adjudicated once and for all in order to restore the *quies* of the city. It was intolerable, fumed the king in a letter to the bishops, that amongst all the cities of the kingdom, only Rome was not at peace. Even the borders with the barbarians were secure and at peace, and yet *civilitas* was absent at the very heart of the state – the *urbs* and the *arx Latii*.[77]

In response, a second, larger meeting was organised, only this time it was to be held at the *basilica Sessoriana* (S. Croce in Gerusalemme) near the Lateran on the very eastern edge of the city. Knowing that more violence was likely, the king dispatched three officials from Ravenna – the *maiores domus regiae* Gudila and Bedeulphus, and the *comes* Arigernus.[78] These men were ordered to ensure calm, which would allow Symmachus to go *citra urbem* (St Peter's was outside the walls) to the synod's new location without fear of attack. In this they failed. According to the *acta* and mirroring the account preserved in the *Liber pontificalis* discussed above, when Symmachus attempted to appear at the synod, he was assaulted and many of the presbyters who had joined him were killed. Theoderic's representatives were themselves wounded in the melee, and it was only with great difficulty that Symmachus managed to

---

[73] *Laurentian Fragment* (Duchesne 1886–1892, 1.46): *per quae tempora quae bella civilia gesta sint vel quanta homicidia perpetrata, non est praesenti relatione pandendum*.

[74] The *acta* of *Quarta [sic] Synodus habita Romae palmaris*, which culminated in a meeting on 23 October, contains the reports of several earlier meetings, which will be discussed below. Despite meeting in various locations over several months, this should be considered a single synod. On this see Wirbelauer 1993, 28; Sardella 1996, 32; Sessa 2012, 214.

[75] This can be seen in the *Praeceptio regis III*, written to the assembled bishops, in which Theoderic complains about riots (*tumultus*) and seditious disturbances caused by the crowd (*turba*), and demands that the bishops remain at Rome and finally solve the issue.

[76] Symmachus refused to accept the authority of the synod unless the churches of the city and their patrimony were returned to his control. He also demanded the withdrawal of Peter of Altinum, the *visitator* who had been appointed by Theoderic to celebrate Easter earlier that year. The bishops, who were unsure if they could even judge a sitting bishop of Rome, generally agreed with this.

[77] *Praeceptio regis IIII missa ad Synhodum* (501 (sic)), *MGH AA* 12.420–2, at 422: *sola tranquillitatem Roma non habeat* . . .

[78] *PLRE* 2, 'Bedeulfus', 222; 'Guiila', 521; 'Arigernus', 141–2. Arigernus is also described as a *maior domus* in the *acta* of 502 (*MGH AA* 12.423).

escape back to the safety of St Peter's.[79] Symmachus subsequently refused all requests to attend meetings, stating to the bishops (which was then reported to Theoderic) that 'when I came [to the synod] with my clergy, I was savagely attacked (*crudeliter demactatus sum*)' – an attack which he barely escaped with his life.[80] Symmachus' lament and the other evidence from the *acta* help make some sense of the violence described in the *Liber pontificalis*. This was a premeditated assault intended to prevent Symmachus from defending himself against the charges levelled against him, and possibly to injure or kill the bishop and his supporters. The priests Dignissimus and Gordianus were presumably two of the 'many presbyters' killed. Although it cannot be definitively demonstrated from our surviving evidence, it seems probable that the shift from the *basilica Iulii* to the *basilica Sessoriana* was a deliberate ploy by Symmachus' enemies to force the embattled bishop to travel through hostile territory, exposing him to attack.[81] At a minimum, the violence made it difficult and dangerous for Symmachus to attend.[82]

Motivations, Supporters and Opportunities for Violence at Rome

The preceding discussion makes clear that the unrest associated with contested episcopal elections at Rome is best understood as a carefully coordinated deployment of violence intended to achieve specific objectives. But important questions remain: why were some elections so controversial, and who were the supporters of each candidate? The fragmentary nature of our evidence, which allows only episodic and highly polemical snapshots of events, makes answering these questions extremely difficult. This has not prevented scholars from proposing various reconstructions – too many to review here in detail. What unites many of these is the tendency to view Roman ecclesiastical factionalism as a manifestation of broader social or political issues, or else as resulting from longstanding divisions amongst defined parties within the church – that is to say, to look for reasons external to the schisms themselves. This approach ignores another, admittedly less satisfying, possibility: Roman schisms and the violence they engendered were locally focused *sui generis* events, with alliances coalescing into and falling out of existence based on innumerable factors related to the controversies themselves and the personalities involved.

Interestingly, amongst all the vitriol including accusations of murder, sexual misconduct and the misuse of church funds, our surviving sources scrupulously avoid the language of doctrinal deviance. With the partial exception of Symmachus' supposed celebration of Easter on the incorrect date, religious questions are entirely absent.[83]

---

[79] *Quarta [sic] Synodus habita Romae palmaris*, MGH AA 12.429: *multis presbyteris qui cum ipso ierant per caedem ipsa mortis fuisset*.
[80] *Relatio Episcoporum ad regem*, MGH AA 12.423.
[81] I would perhaps not go quite as far as Townsend 1937, 248, who states, 'No doubt, the purpose of his enemies was to kill the pope.'
[82] Wirbelauer 1993, 28.
[83] Referring to the Damasus/Ursinus schism, Socrates Scholasticus (*Hist. eccl.* 4.29) and Sozomen (*Hist. eccl.* 6.23.2) specifically state that the conflict was not about faith, only who would be bishop.

This is all the more surprising given that actual heresy was not a prerequisite for the deployment of heresiological rhetoric. It also appears to be in sharp contrast to contested elections elsewhere in the empire, especially in the East and in Africa, which are commonly associated with doctrinal disagreements such as the Donatist controversy, the so-called Arian controversy and, later, the various disputes over Christology and the Council of Chalcedon (451). Upon the death of a bishop, the parties in these debates would rally their supporters to ensure that the 'orthodox' candidate (from each of their perspectives – no one thought that they were the heretics) was elected.[84] But we should be wary of too sharply dividing 'religious' and 'secular' concerns, both at Rome and elsewhere. Indeed, recent scholarship has stressed the embedded nature of religion in ancient societies, which makes it very difficult to distinguish 'religious violence' from other social and economic conflict.[85] Religion is not reduceable to theology and doctrine, nor is the world of theological ideas completely distinct from the daily lived experience of believers.[86] Ramsay MacMullen, who is sometimes accused of overemphasising the specifically Christian nature of violent contestation in Late Antiquity, points out how quarrels amongst church leaders could spread rapidly, buoyed by letters, sermons preached to the congregation and word of mouth.[87] Despite relatively low levels of theological literacy amongst ordinary believers, Christian symbols, often related to the liturgy but also hymns, credal statements, sacred places and even particular individuals like episcopal candidates, could rally groups within the community who were willing to inflict violence against opponents for ostensibly religious reasons.[88] These and related considerations may lie behind at least some of the events described in this chapter.

At Rome, the potential for factionalism was exacerbated by the large size and complexity of the church.[89] By the fifth century, the bishop of Rome oversaw as many as 130 churches, monasteries and oratories in the city, staffed by about 75 priests, seven deacons, perhaps as many as 49 subdeacons and acolytes, as well as approximately 90 others in junior grades.[90] The church also employed many more individuals in various tasks, some of whom were clerics, others were lay.[91] The management of a large (and growing) patrimony required specialists, but also many thousands of peasant farmers and slaves.[92] The result was the evolution of labyrinthine relationships of patronage and dependency, which must have exerted considerable influence on ecclesiastical

---

[84] Liebeschuetz 2001, 257–60. According to Liebeschuetz (at 258), 'Violence in the service of religion was up to a point distinct from other kinds of urban violence. Doctrinal partisanship had objectives and opponents which were not directly linked to any secular grievances.'
[85] Hahn 2004, *passim*, but esp. 271–94; Mayer 2013, *passim*, but esp. 3, 18. Some scholars have gone so far as to question the very category of 'religious violence'. See the comments in Van Nuffelen and Engels 2014, 11–12.
[86] Stroumsa 1998, 360.
[87] MacMullen 2003, 485–6. McLynn 2012, 308 and n. 21, suggests that MacMullen interpreted Damasus' followers as 'impassioned followers devoted to his cause'.
[88] These and related issues are explored in Tannous 2018. See also Gregory 1979, 6–7.
[89] On the size of Christian communities and its relationship to potential conflict, see Duval et al. 1997, 1064–5.
[90] Llewellyn 1977, 247–78.
[91] Some officers, such as the *notarii* and *defensores*, could be lay or clerical. See Sotinel 1998.
[92] Sessa 2016, 238.

politics, especially when it came time to elect a new bishop. Successful candidates would play a central role in the life of the community, acting not only as spiritual leaders, but also as patrons and arbiters of intra- and inter-communal conflict.[93] The growing influence of the episcopal office and the wealth of the Roman church also increasingly made it an object of personal ambition.[94] Jerome's oft-cited quotation of the 'pagan' senator and *praefectus urbi* Praetextatus illustrates the point. Enviously eyeing the extravagance of the papal court, Praetextatus teased Damasus, saying *Facite me Romanae urbis episcopum, et ero protinus Christianus!* ('Make me the bishop of Rome and I will become a Christian immediately!').[95] And because bishops (typically) held their position for life, communities would have to live with 'bad' choices for years, if not decades, while failed candidates were unlikely to have a second chance. Thus, it is not surprising that episcopal elections could become nodes of contestation during which rivalries were at their most extreme.[96] And as we have seen, charismatic (potential) bishops and their adversaries could mobilise a pool of supporters willing to use violence in support of their cause.

Given the pressures on the unity of the church enumerated above, it is remarkable that Rome endured only three contested elections during the period covered by this volume. To state it slightly differently, and despite my focus on violent contestation in the preceding pages, the Roman church in Late Antiquity was a relatively stable institution, which was ordinarily able to navigate transitions of power without controversy. It is therefore significant that all three schisms discussed in this chapter occurred in the immediate aftermath of controversial pontificates. Liberius' capitulation to Constantius II was extremely contentious, and whether we believe that Damasus was in fact a partisan of Liberius' adversary Felix, the church was deeply divided following Liberius' death. The schism between Boniface and Eulalius took place following the pontificate of Zosimus, who had badly mismanaged the Pelagian controversy.[97] This, together with his general ineffectiveness, produced enough uncertainty and discord that shortly before he died, a group of Roman clerics made a formal complaint against Zosimus to the emperor Honorius at Ravenna.[98] And Symmachus' predecessor Anastasius II's brief pontificate was acrimonious enough that his death was celebrated as an act of God by the author of the *Liber pontificalis*.[99] Put simply, violent contested elections at Rome occurred following the death of bad or otherwise divisive bishops.[100]

---

[93] MacMullen 1990, 268, evocatively (but exaggeratedly) described bishops as 'little kings'.

[94] Hahn 2014, 384–5.

[95] Jer., *Jo. Hier.* 8. Of course, Jerome's ascetic agenda, as well as his humourlessness, complicates our interpretation of this passage, although it is generally understood as an acknowledgement of the power and wealth of the Roman church. See McLynn 2012, 307. On Praetextatus, see below, n. 122 and *passim*. On Damasus' reputation for luxury and his interactions with Praextetatus, see Cain 2009, 47–8, and Kahlos 1997.

[96] Leemans and Van Nuffelen 2011, 4–5.

[97] Marcos 2013, 159–60.

[98] Zos. *Ep.* 14 (PL 20, coll. 678–80), dated 3 October 418. He died in December of that year. The complaint was likely regarding Zosimus' handling of the Pelagian controversy.

[99] *LP* 52 (Duchesne 1886–1892, 1.258): *qui nutu divino percussus est*.

[100] At Constantinople, in contrast, 'religious violence' typically occurred during periods of political instability. See Hahn 2014, 387–8, and more broadly, Van Nuffelen 2010.

This brings me to a second point. Modern students of the Roman church, familiar with the ceremony and ritual of the conclave – sombre cardinals gathered in the Sistine Chapel, crowds waiting in St Peter's Square for the distinctive puff of white smoke that indicates that a new pope has been chosen – are often surprised to find out that there was no recognised procedure for episcopal elections at Rome or indeed the election of any bishop in the late antique and early medieval periods. Canons from early church councils, which describe roles for the clergy, other bishops and 'the people', were vague and open to manipulation (if indeed they were consulted at all in many smaller sees).[101] Indeed, canons were often more concerned to delineate the procedures and prerequisites for ordination, not the selection of a candidate. Ordination was both religiously significant and an important public demonstration of the consensus of the community, which conferred legitimacy on the new bishop.[102] At Rome, episcopal elections generally took place shortly after the death of the bishop, with ordinations occurring on the following Sunday, although, as we have seen, candidates often attempted to have themselves ordained as soon as possible in order to consolidate their hold on the episcopacy and undermine the position of potential rivals.[103] It is sometimes stated that having been elected and ordained first and having the support of a majority of the electors were two important factors in determining who ultimately emerged victorious in contested elections.[104] This is true to a point. As we have seen, this is precisely the claim made by the author of the *Liber pontificalis* to justify Theoderic's initial support for Symmachus. However, this is a retrospective statement written after Symmachus emerged victorious, intended to cement his legitimacy by harkening back to his election. But during the schism itself, the legitimacy of the election process was not at issue. Indeed, for most of the period between 501 and 506/7, it was Laurence who controlled the Roman church, and the fact that he was elected second and by a minority of the clergy (if this is even true) does not seem to have undermined his position. Moreover, as Kristina Sessa has argued, at least in the later fifth and sixth centuries, Roman bishops appear to have simply named their successor, thereby subverting the election process entirely.[105]

The magnitude of elections, the lack of clear procedures, and the contentious pontificates of Liberius, Zosimus and Anastasius II were all important factors for the public disorder considered in this chapter. But there was also growing scope for violence at Rome in Late Antiquity more generally. In the early empire, various military and quasi-military units had been stationed in or near the city, which were available to maintain public order.[106] These included the *vigiles*, but especially the praetorian and

---

[101] The role of 'the people' in episcopal elections has been the focus of debate amongst scholars. However, we should be wary of overly schematic analyses positing trends across centuries and throughout the Mediterranean. In reality, local circumstances were far more important, and generalisations are difficult. On this question, see Duval et al. 1997, 1060–1; Leemans and Van Nuffelen 2011, 6.

[102] Norton 2007, 20–9. On the importance of ordination as distinct from election, see esp. Norton 2007, 30–1; Leemans and Van Nuffelen 2011, 8–11.

[103] By the mid-fourth century, Roman bishops were ordained by the bishops of Ostia. See Dunn 2011, 146–7.

[104] Wirbelauer 1994, 413–15.

[105] Sessa 2012, 204–5.

[106] Nippel 1995, 85–100.

urban cohorts, together with the *equites singulares Augusti*, as well as a smaller number of marines (*clasiarii*) and *frumentarii*, a group of soldiers tasked with delicate operations such as domestic espionage, arrests and executions.[107] Despite these resources, emperors accepted (or were forced to accept) a surprisingly high level of ambient disorder – at least surprising to modern observers – in part because urban rivalries, within reason, could distract from larger issues, (mis)directing popular aggression away from government. The chief reason for unrest, as was the case for other urban centres across the empire, was food and wine shortages (real and imagined).[108] But Romans also endured innumerable riots and small acts of brutality associated with the games and the Circus factions and criminality of various sorts.[109] In the third century and after, it was less and less likely that the emperor himself was resident at Rome.[110] In his absence, the individual responsible for responding to (or preventing) disorder was the urban prefect, who nominally had the responsibility for preserving law and order within the city of Rome and up to 100 miles around. But importantly, as Noel Lenski discusses elsewhere in this volume, the Praetorians and the *equites singulares* were suppressed by Constantine I.[111] And over the course of the fourth century, the urban cohorts[112] and the *vigiles* were also dissolved.[113] With little in the way of coercive power, the late antique urban prefect had to rely on his diplomatic skill, charisma and timely intervention, if he wished to prevent violent episodes from spiralling out of control.[114]

Some were better at this task than others. The prefects at the end of Liberius' episcopate and during the schism between Damasus and Ursinus, Orfitus[115] and Lampadius,[116] are both harshly criticised by Ammianus – Orfitus as arrogant and unschooled,[117] Lampadius as vain and ineffectual. Indeed, Lampadius' time as prefect was, according to Ammianus, frequently troubled by outbreaks of violence. In one such episode the *plebs infima* would have burnt the Baths of Constantine to the ground had the prefect's friends not arrived in time and driven the mob away by pelting them with roof tiles, which, as Damasus' partisans had already demonstrated, made excellent weapons. Lampadius, however, fled to the Milvian Bridge to wait out the violence.[118] Lampadius' successor Viventius receives a slightly more positive appraisal from Ammianus, who calls him *integer*

---

[107] On the numbers and these different categories of soldiers, which could typically be found in Rome between Augustus and Constantine, see Fuhrmann 2012, 124–30, 151–8.

[108] Africa 1971, 19–20; Lançon 2000, 47; Matthews 2007, 406; Wijnendaele 2019, 299–302.

[109] For an overview, see Jones 1964, 694. See also Africa 1971, 13–19; Cameron 1976, 271.

[110] Many of the above-mentioned units had personal ties to the emperor and his household. If the emperor was not at Rome, then it made little sense to preserve these units, which could constitute a threat to an absentee emperor.

[111] See Chapter 2 in this volume.

[112] Chastagnol 1960, 255–6.

[113] Nippel 1995, 99. On the *vigiles*, Chastagnol 1960, 258–64.

[114] On this, see Chapter 2 in this volume. As Hahn (2004; 2001, 3–4) argued, the late antique Roman state was probably much weaker and less responsive than is generally imagined, especially in the complex ways it did or did not react to religious conflict.

[115] Memmius Vitrasius Orfitius, prefect in 353 and again in 357.

[116] C. Ceionius Rufius Volusianus Lampadius, prefect in 365.

[117] Amm. Marc. 14.6.1.

[118] Amm. Marc. 27.3.8–9.

et prudens Pannonius.[119] The *Gesta* claims that he, together with the *praefectus annonae* Julianus, were responsible for Ursinus' initial exile from the city following the attack against the *basilica Liberii*.[120] But Ammianus also reports that the violence became so extreme that Viventius, like Lampadius, withdrew from the city entirely. Although the timing of his flight is not clear, it may have taken place before the massacre at the *basilica Liberii*, in which case Viventius' absence may have been a contributing factor in the bloodshed. It is also possible that he left the city as a result of the massacre. In either case, his departure left Damasus and his armed followers in charge of the city.[121] Viventius' failure to maintain order resulted in the appointment of the capable Praetextatus as his replacement in August of 367.[122] Praetextatus, under orders from the emperor, oversaw the return of the *basilica Sicinini* – the scene of one of the bloodiest Damasean massacres of Ursinians – to Damasus, and it was ultimately Praetextatus who expelled Ursinus from Rome once and for all.[123] Thus, Praetextatus' intervention was decisive in securing the episcopacy for Damasus.[124] But the violence continued. The final slaughter of the Ursinians at the cemetery complex at St Agnes took place following their exile from the city, possibly as late as the end of 368 or early 369. Indeed, Praetextatus' successor Olybrius[125] and his *vicarius* Aginatius[126] were both still dealing with the fallout of the schism. Aginatius wrote to Valentinian I informing him about disorder resulting from (religious?) meetings beyond the walls (*extramurani conventi*), possibly a reference to the Ursinians and perhaps to the massacre at St Agnes'.[127] In response, the emperor wrote to both Olybrius and Aginatius commanding them to ban religious factions – presumably a reference to the Ursinians – from assembling anywhere within 20 miles of the city.[128]

The urban prefect Symmachus was initially more effective during the controversy between Eulalius and Boniface, and he, together with Honorius (and more likely, Constantius – the future emperor Constantius III), took concrete steps to prevent further violence. Having little in terms of military aid other than his own private retinue, the support of other members of the Roman aristocracy and powerbrokers within the city was crucial. After Zosimus' death, Symmachus, who must have sensed growing factionalism amongst his possible successors, made a public appeal for calm and directed the *corporati* and the *maiores regionum* – guild members and the leaders of

---

[119] Amm. Marc. 27.3.11. *PLRE* 1, 'Viventius', *praefectus urbi* from October 365 to May 367.
[120] *Gesta* 6.
[121] Amm. Marc. 27.3.11–13. On the timing of Viventius' departure from the city, see McLynn 1992, 18.
[122] *PLRE* 1, 'Vettius Agorius Praetextatus 1', *praefectus urbi* from August 367 to September 368. For the chronology of the times in office of Viventius, Praetextatus and his successor Olybrius, see also Den Boeft et al. 2009, xv–xvi.
[123] *CA* 6 and *CA* 8 (*CSEL* 35.49, 50). On the role of Valentinian in this schism, see Lenski 2002, 239–40.
[124] Kahlos 1997 suggests a longstanding alliance between Damasus and Praetextatus.
[125] *PLRE* 1, 'Quintus Clodius Hermogenianus Olybrius 3', *praefectus urbi* from September 368 until 370.
[126] *PLRE* 1, 'Aginatius', *vicarius urbis Romae* from 368 to 370.
[127] That Aginatius wrote to Valentinian is derived from the emperor's letter to Olybrius, *CA* 8: *sed quantum Aginatii clarissimi viii vicariae praefecturae scripta testata sunt, adhuc aliquantos placata miscere delectat extramuranisque conventibus frequens strepitus excitatur* . . .
[128] *CA* 8 (*CSEL* 35.50), to Olybrius, banning *populo dissentienti*, and *CA* 9 (*CSEL* 35.50–1), to Aginatius, directed against *factiosorum impios coetus*.

the city's districts – to keep the peace.[129] He was also clear that it was Eulalius who had been properly elected, an assessment subsequently confirmed by the emperor. Honorius further ordered that Boniface be immediately ejected from the city, which likely had the short-term effect of preventing widespread violence.[130] The fragile peace in the city – and Symmachus' own authority – was dramatically undermined when Honorius backtracked on his initial judgment in favour of Eulalius. When Symmachus later reported to Constantius that Eulalius had re-entered Rome in March 419, supported by an armed mob (*multitudo armata ferro*) which engaged in street fighting in the Forum itself,[131] the *magister militum* and emperor responded by reiterating their expulsion of Eulalius and demanding that the *primates regionum* – presumably the same *maiores* mentioned above – bring the populace under control or else face the death penalty. Symmachus' staff too are fined and likewise threatened with death.[132] Ravenna was clearly taking the situation very seriously. And Symmachus, once again with the aid of the *corporati* and *maiores regionum*, managed to expel Eulalius from the Lateran and, ultimately, from the city.[133]

During the Symmachus/Laurentius schism, ex-*praefecti urbi* played important roles, not in the suppression of violence, but as its protagonists. Senators were involved in other forms of violence at Rome in this period, and Theoderic depended on his political acumen to gain the support of city's elites to help prevent outbreaks of disorder.[134] In the early sixth century, the king appointed Albinus and Avienus, presumably brothers, to take up the *patrocinium* of the Green Circus faction at Rome, in part in the hopes that they would be able to rein in the violence – the 'disruptive outbursts' that transformed the 'state of public happiness' into a 'frenzied turmoil' in the words of Cassiodorus.[135] And as we have seen, Theoderic's unsuccessful intervention in 502 entailed sending members of his court to Rome to keep the peace. Despite Theoderic's initial failure, the intervention of secular power was crucial for eventually bringing the controversy to its conclusion. And throughout, both Symmachians and Laurentians looked to the king to impose order – or, as the *Laurentian Fragment* put it, the two factions (*partes*) 'repeatedly asked for royal protection'.[136]

Contested Episcopal Elections Elsewhere in Italy

Thus far, I have examined violence connected to episcopal elections in the city of Rome. But how representative was this violence across the rest of Italy? Answering this question is difficult because the evidence from other Italian sees is often patchier

---

[129] As Symmachus reported to Honorius, *CA* 14. On the *corporati* and *maiores regionum*, see Jones 1964, 2.694, and more recently, Ruciński 2004.
[130] *CA* 15 (*CSEL* 35.60–1).
[131] *CA* 29 (*CSEL* 35.74–6).
[132] Constantius to Symmachus, *CA* 30 (*CSEL* 35.76); Honorius to Symmachus, *CA* 31 (*CSEL* 35.76–8).
[133] *CA* 32 (*CSEL* 35.78–9).
[134] Cassiod. *Var.* 1.30–3.
[135] Cassiod. *Var.* 1.20. See now the trans. in Bjornlie 2019, 54–5. On this, see also Cameron 1976, 24.
[136] *Laurentian Fragment* (*LP* 1.46): *dumque partes mutua se dissentione collidunt ac pro suis studiis regale praesidium saepe deposcunt . . .*

than that from Rome, especially before the fifth century. One obvious exception is Ambrose's Milan. Rufinus reports that the city teetered on the edge of violent confrontation between 'Arian' and 'orthodox' factions following the death of the 'Arian' bishop Auxentius in 374. Riots were only averted when a miraculous voice in the crowd called out for Ambrose to be made bishop.[137] Ambrose, like Damasus, was willing to use organised violence against his opponents. As he ominously stated to Theodosius I, bishops are 'the controllers of the crowds (*turbarum moderatores*) and anxious for peace – unless, of course, they are moved by some offense against God or insult to the church'.[138] The doctrinal nature of the factionalism at Milan would, at first glance, seem to contrast with the situation at Rome. But as Michael Stuart Williams has argued, Rufinus' account, as well as that of Ambrose himself, rhetorically framed what was a much more complex situation as a conflict between two mutually exclusive and hostile communities: the Arians and the orthodox.[139]

Ravenna is another partial exception, thanks to the survival of Agnellus' *Liber pontificalis ecclesiae Ravennatis* (*LPR*). This work, which was composed in the 830s or 840s, contains serial biographies of the city's bishops modelled on the Roman *Liber pontificalis*.[140] Unsurprisingly, the earlier lives are less dependable than the later ones. Still, it is noteworthy that Agnellus does not explicitly mention any contested elections before the eighth century. Indeed, he emphasises the miraculous in several of the early, legendary, elections described in the *LPR*. For instance, Severus (c.340s) is said to have been chosen as bishop when a dove landed on his head.[141] More interesting is Agnellus' confused description of the election of Peter Chrysologus (died c.458). According to this account, upon the death of the sitting bishop, an assembly of the people and the priests of the church (*convenerunt universus coetus populi, una cum sacerdotibus*) elected a successor. The bishop elect, together with members of the Ravennate church, went to Rome so that he could be ordained by Sixtus III (432–40). However, the night before the ordination was to take place, saints Peter and Apollinaris, the legendary first bishop of Ravenna, appeared to Sixtus in a dream and identified Chrysologus as the man they had chosen as the city's next bishop. The following day, Sixtus refused to ordain the unnamed bishop elect and instead sought the man from his dream from amongst the priests who had journeyed to Rome. After some time, Chrysologus, who was a deacon, was presented to Sixtus, and he was duly proclaimed as bishop of Ravenna.[142] Not only is the chronology of this *Vita* clearly garbled – Agnellus confuses Peter Chrysologus with Peter II (494–520) – it was also written centuries after the events

---

[137] Ruf. *Hist. eccl.* 11.11. Rufinus calls Auxentius the 'bishop of the heretics' (*haereticorum episcopus*).

[138] Ambr. *Ep.* 40.6, quoted in Hahn 2014, 398: *sacerdotes enim turbarum moderatores sunt, studiosi pacis, nisi cum et ipsi moveantur iniuria dei, aut ecclesiae contumelia.*

[139] Williams 2017, *passim*, but esp. 22–39 on religious identities at Milan and 58–110 on the election of Ambrose.

[140] On the date of composition, structure and intent of the work, see Deliyannis 2004, 20–45 and 2010, 5–9. Unfortunately, Deliyannis' excellent *CCCM* edition of the *LPR* was not available to me due to limited library access thanks to COVID-19. The edition used here is that of O. Holder-Egger (1878) *MGH SRL*, Hanover, 265–391.

[141] Agnellus, *LPR* 17, 285–6.

[142] Agnellus, *LPR* 49, 311–12.

it describes.[143] However, Agnellus did have access to various written sources, and we should not reject his account outright.[144] The miraculous nature of Chrysologus' selection as bishop masks what must have been important divisions in the Ravennate church. In fact, Agnellus describes two distinct groups of people amongst those who had travelled to Rome from Ravenna. The first was hostile to Chrysologus, claiming that as a neophyte, he could not be bishop. They further stated that he was an outsider (he was likely born in Imola) who had invaded the see like a thief. Others appealed to canon law, stating that it was unlawful to transfer to a metropolitan see from a subordinate suffragan diocese.[145] The other faction supported Chrysologus, noting his piety and wisdom. The impasse was only overcome when Sixtus told the querulous Ravennate clergy of his vision. If they still needed convincing, the miracle was backed up by the threat of schism with Rome if they refused to accept Sixtus' choice. There is not enough information to understand the motives of the factions (or whether this story has any historical merit at all); however, Sixtus' vision conveniently justified his intervention and/or justified Chrysologus' appointment as bishop, thereby peaceably averting a potentially volatile situation.

Although the churches in Italia Annonaria were not technically subject to Rome's jurisdiction, controversies in these churches occasionally came to Rome's attention.[146] For instance, in 482, Simplicius (468–83) wrote to chastise John, bishop of Ravenna, who out of jealousy (*invidia*) had used violence to consecrate a certain Gregory bishop of Mutina (modern Modena) against his will as a way of getting a rival out of the city.[147] There is not enough information to understand the nature of the dispute between the two men, but at a minimum it illustrates that factional enmity continued at Ravenna after Chrysologus, perhaps also as a consequence of a disputed election. Agnellus' much later account of John's life, which garbles the chronology of Ravenna's early bishops, laconically notes that 'the aforementioned blessed John ascended the episcopal throne'.[148] Simplicius' involvement in the internal ecclesiastical politics at Ravenna hints at Rome's growing interventionalist attitude. Simplicius' predecessors Hilary (461–8) and Leo (440–1), for instance, engaged in a decades-long struggle with Hilary and his successors over the jurisdiction of the bishops of Arles

---

[143] See the notes in Deliyannis 2004, 159–61, but *pace* the dates of Sixtus III in n. 5. Chrysologus' episcopacy is dated variously in secondary sources, due in part to the errors in Agnellus' chronology. One will commonly read that he was bishop beginning in 430 or 431 until his death in 450. More convincingly, the *PCBE*, 'PETRVS 9', vaguely suggests 445?–448/9 to before October 458.

[144] On the sources used by Agnellus, see Deliyannis 2004, 46–56.

[145] Agnellus, *LPR* 49, 312: *alii dicebant, quia neophitum non recipimus. non ex nostro fuit ovile, sed subito invadit cathedram episcopalem quasi latro. tollite, tollite eum de medio! non recipimus, quia de subiecta ecclesia non licet in maiorem transferre.*

[146] Gaudemet 1958, 384, 445–6. We often know about these controversies only when they came to the attention of Rome's bishop, whose letters are far more likely to have been preserved than those of smaller sees. On the preservation and circulation of papal letters, which often survive as recipient copies and later polemical collections, see Neil 2016.

[147] Simplicius, *Ep.* 14 (Thiel 1974 [1868], 201–2).

[148] Agnellus, *LPR* 37. The context of this statement is the historically incorrect assertion that John was bishop when Attila invaded Italy in 450–1. This is incorrect, and as Deliyannis notes, Attila did not come anywhere Ravenna in any case. On the chronology see esp. Deliyannis 2004, 139 n. 11.

in Gaul.[149] But the majority of our evidence for involvement outside the boundaries of the city itself survives from sees under the ordinary episcopal jurisdiction of the Roman church, which by the fifth century included almost 200 dioceses scattered across Italia Suburbicaria.[150] The bishops of these churches were usually consecrated at Rome, and disputes, especially over episcopal elections but also internal disciplinary quarrels, were adjudicated by Rome's bishop.[151] Thus, several examples of violence related to contestation over control of southern Italian bishoprics are preserved in the surviving correspondence of Roman bishops in the period covered by this volume, particularly amongst the letters of Gelasius (492–6).[152] In 496, Gelasius wrote to John, possibly the bishop of Vibonensis (Vibo Valentia in Calabria), describing the curious case of an archdeacon named Asellus.[153] The bishop of Asellus' see had been murdered. Shortly afterwards, Asellus had permitted the man accused of the crime to be killed in a riot, a fact which conveniently left no loose ends. Asellus, who was almost certainly complicit in the bishop's murder and stood to gain financially as his heir, then attempted to have himself elected bishop before reporting the details to Rome, presumably to secure his position before Gelasius could intervene. Gelasius deposed Asellus from his office.[154] In another instance which may or may not be related to that of Asellus, Gelasius described the double murder of bishops in the church of Scyllacenorum (Squillace, also in Calabria). Gelasius was deeply troubled by the crime and was likely also worried that if he permitted a new bishop to be elevated from within the local church, the same divisions that prompted the murder in the first place would continue to fester. After some delay, Gelasius decided to strip this church of the right to elect a new bishop and instead appointed the outsiders John and Majoricus to administer the church.[155] In yet another letter, Gelasius ordered that a presbyter named Coelestinus, likely from the nearby church of Vibonensis, be deprived of his office and excommunicated for one year since he had been convicted of killing his bishop.[156] This Coelestinus might well refer to a presbyter of the same name who is likewise

---

[149] See, for instance, Heinzelmann 1992.

[150] Otranto 2010, 86–7. Italy was not divided into provinces, and thus Rome was technically not a metropolitan see. Nevertheless, the growing prestige of the Roman church meant that its bishops gradually came to exercise metropolitan authority over Suburbicarian churches.

[151] Gaudemet 1958, 445–6.

[152] The following examples are drawn from four Gelasian letters, *Ep.* 36–9 in Andreas Thiel's edition. Both Thiel (p. 42–3) and Paul Ewald, who also examined these letters as part of his study of the *Collectio Britannica* (1880, 522 n. 7) assumed that they were related. However, it is also possible that the disorder they describe represents separate incidents. It is true that letters 36, 37 and 39 are all addressed to a bishop named Iohannes, who may or may not be the same individual, John of Vibo (see next note). Even if they do represent the same person, this John may well have been tasked by Gelasius to deal with several independent problems in the churches of southern Italy. Note that the *PCBE* 2.1.1058–1140 contains entries for 145 'Iohannes'. For a different take on these letters, see esp. the detailed analysis in Allen and Neil 2013, 163–4.

[153] *PCBE* 2.1.1066–7, 'Iohannes 13'; 2.1.203, 'Asellus 7'.

[154] Gelasius, *Ep.* 36 (Thiel, 449–50).

[155] Gelasius, *Ep.* 37 (Thiel, 450–2): *caedes geminate pontificum . . .*

[156] Gelasius, *Ep.* 38 (Thiel, 452). The town in question is not named. The addressees are Phillip and Cassiodorus, likely clerics in this church. This is almost certainly not Cassiodorus Senator (*PLRE* 2.265), *pace* Thiel 1974 [1868], 42.

condemned by Gelasius for continuing to minister to the Dionysii, a family which had been excommunicated for inflicting damages on the church of Vibonensis.[157]

Conclusions

In the preceding pages, I have made several observations regarding the violence connected with episcopal elections. At Rome, the violence was not senseless or 'mob' violence, if by these terms we mean indiscriminate acts perpetrated by gangs of *plebs*. Rather, our evidence makes clear that the violence was intentional, motivated and strategically deployed. That there was factionalism within the late antique Roman church is clear; but the composition of the factions and their motivations are difficult to reconstruct with any degree of certainty. Interestingly, the texts associated with these controversies do not employ heresiological rhetoric to denigrate opponents. Instead, they repeatedly evoke the language of warfare: swords (*gladii*), battles (*pugnae*), civil wars (*bella civilia*), sieges (*obsidiones*) and massacres (*strages*, *caedes* and *homicidia*). As Latham aptly summarises in his discussion of these disputes, 'the spatial strategies and behaviors of the Christian church, as represented by its various officials, were best understood as occupation and war'.[158] Moreover, divisions created by a controversial predecessor and the lack of a clear successor, together with a total lack of protocols for choosing a bishop, were a recipe for a violent and contested episcopal election.

Outside Rome, the patchy nature of the evidence makes firm conclusions difficult, but several observations are nonetheless possible. Contested, controversial and even irregular episcopal elections in other major Italian sees, including that of Ambrose at the end of the fourth century and Peter Chrysologus and John of Ravenna in the middle and late fifth century, do not seem to have experienced outbreaks of widespread violence and disorder on the same scale as that which occurred between the supporters of Damasus and Ursinus, and Symmachus and Laurence. Circumstantial evidence suggests a possible reason why this might have been the case: Milan during Ambrose's episcopacy was the seat of imperial power in the West. By the fifth century, the centre of power had shifted to Ravenna, first as the home of Roman emperors, and then of Odoacer (and subsequently, Theoderic). We can assume that both cities would have contained a substantial military force, which likely mitigated against the outbreak of widespread violence or else was able to quickly suppress disorder if and when it occurred. Even so, it appears that many of the same factors that prompted violence at Rome, especially local rivalries and the lack of clear mechanisms for electing bishops, were also present elsewhere in Italy. The smaller populations of Italy's minor sees, whose churches were likewise staffed by far fewer clerical and lay administrators than was the case in Italy's major cities, may have also reduced the scope and scale for violent confrontation around episcopal elections. On the other hand, the intimacy of rivalries had the potential to produce spasms of intense brutality. Gelasius' letters reveal the often sordid motives for regional rivalries, including greed, personal animus and ambition, which could on occasion manifest as fights to control local churches.

---

[157] Gelasius, *Ep.* 39 (Thiel, 453).
[158] Latham 2012, 325.

Perhaps the most obvious and important difference between Rome and the rest of Italy – especially Suburbicarian Italy – is that conflict in these sees could be adjudicated at Rome. There was thus an avenue within the church for appeal open to aggrieved clergy or failed episcopal candidates. This acted as a safety valve, which may have served to minimise outright violence in these sees. At Rome, in contrast, this was not an option, and as we have seen, disorder associated with Roman elections was ended only with the utter destruction of one faction, as occurred in the conflict between Damasus and Ursinus, or else with the direct intervention of secular power, which ultimately decided the schisms between Boniface and Eulalius, and Symmachus and Laurence.[159]

Bibliography

Africa, T. W. (1971) 'Urban Violence in Imperial Rome', *Journal of Interdisciplinary History* 2 (1): 3–21.
Allen, P. and B. Neil (2013) *Crisis Management in Late Antiquity (410–590 CE): a Survey of the Evidence from Episcopal Letters*, Leiden.
Amory, P. (1997) *People and Identity in Ostrogothic Italy, 489–554*, Cambridge.
Barry, William D. (1996) 'Roof Tiles and Urban Violence in the Ancient World', *GRBS* 37 (1): 55–74.
Bjornlie, M. S. (2019) *The Variae: the Complete Translation*, Oakland, CA.
Blair-Dixon, K. (2002) 'Damasus and the Fiction of Unity: the Urban Shrine of Saint Laurence', in F. Guidobaldi and A. G. Guidobaldi (eds) *Ecclesiae Urbis: Atti del congresso internazionale di studi sulle chiese di Roma (IV–X secolo)*, Vatican City, 331–52.
Boeft, J. den, J. W. Drijvers, D. den Hengst and H. C. Teitler (2009) *Philological and Historical Commentary on Ammianus Marcellinus XXVII*, Leiden.
Bond, S. E. (2013) 'Mortuary Workers, the Church, and the Funeral Trade in Late Antiquity', *Journal of Late Antiquity* 6 (1): 135–51.
Bowersock, G. (2010) '*Parabalani*: a Terrorist Charity in Late Antiquity', *Anabases* 12: 45–54.
Brandenburg, H. (2005) *Ancient Churches of Rome from the Fourth to the Seventh Century: the Dawn of Christian Architecture in the West*, Turnhout.
Brandt, O. (2012) 'The Early Christian Basilica of San Lorenzo in Lucina', in O. Brandt (ed.) *San Lorenzo in Lucina: the Transformations of a Roman Quarter*, Stockholm, 123–54.
Cain, A. (2009) *The Letters of Jerome: Asceticism, Biblical Exegesis, and the Construction of Christian Authority in Late Antiquity*, Oxford.
Cameron, A. (1976) *Circus Factions: Blues and Greens at Rome and Byzantium*, Oxford.
Chastagnol, A. (1960) *La préfecture urbaine à Rome sous le Bas-Empire*, Paris.
Cohen, S. (2015) 'Schism and the Polemic of Heresy: Manichaeism and the Representation of Papal Authority in the *Liber pontificalis*', *Journal of Late Antiquity* 8 (1): 195–230.
Cohen, S. (2018) 'Liberius and the Cemetery as a Space of Exile in Late Antique Rome', in D. Rohmann, J. Ulrich, and M. V. Girvés (eds) *Mobility and Exile at the End of Antiquity*, Frankfurt, 141–60.
Cohen, S. (2019) '"You Have Made Common Cause with Their Persecutors": Gelasius, the Language of Persecution, and the Acacian Schism', in É. Fournier and W. Mayer (eds)

---

[159] I would like to thank Julie Anderson, Éric Fournier, Noel Lenski, Jeroen Wijnendaele and the anonymous reviewers for their comments and suggestions.

Heirs of Roman Persecution: Studies on a Christian and Para-Christian Discourse in Late Antiquity, New York, 164–83.

Collins, R. (2009) *Keepers of the Keys of Heaven: a History of the Papacy*, New York.

Costambeys, M. (2001) 'Burial Topography and the Power of the Church in Fifth- and Sixth-Century Rome', *PBSR* 69: 169–89.

Cracco Ruggini, L. (1997) 'Spazi urbani clientelari e caritativi', in *La Rome impériale: démographie et logistique*, Rome, 157–91.

Cracco Ruggini, L. (2003) 'Rome in Late Antiquity: Clientship, Urban Topography, and Prosopography', *CP* 98 (4): 366–82.

Cristo, S. (1977) 'Some Notes on the Bonifacian–Eulalian Schism', *Aevum* 51 (1–2): 163–7.

Curran, J. (2000) *Pagan City and Christian Capital: Rome in the Fourth Century*, Oxford.

Davis, R. (2010) (ed. and trans.) *The Book of Pontiffs (Liber pontificalis): the Ancient Biographies of the First Ninety Roman Bishops to AD 715*, Liverpool.

De Spirito, G. (1994) 'Ursino e Damas: una nota', in D. Van Damme, A. Kessler, T. Ricklin and G. Wurst (eds) *Peregrina curiositas: eine Reise durch den orbis antiquus*, Freiburg, 263–74.

Deliyannis, D. M. (2004) (ed. and trans.) *Agnellus of Ravenna: the Book of the Pontiffs of the Church of Ravenna*, Washington, DC.

Deliyannis, D. M. (2010) *Ravenna in Late Antiquity*, Cambridge.

Diefenbach, S. (2007) *Römische Erinnerungsräume: Heiligenmemoria und kollektive Identitäten im Rom des 3. bis 5. Jahrhunderts n. Chr.*, Berlin.

Duchesne, L. (1886–1892) *Le Liber pontificalis: texte, introduction et commentaire*, 2 vols, Paris.

Dunn, G. D. (2011) 'Canonical Legislation on the Ordination of Bishops: Innocent I's Letter to Victricius of Rouen', in J. Leemans, P. Van Nuffelen, S. W. J. Keough and C. Nicolaye (eds) *Episcopal Elections in Late Antiquity*, Berlin, 145–66.

Dunn, G. D. (2015a) 'Imperial Intervention in the Disputed Roman Episcopal Election of 418/419', *JRH* 39 (1): 1–13.

Dunn, G. D. (2015b) 'Life in the Cemetery: Boniface I and the Catacomb of Maximus', *Augustinianum* 55 (1): 137–57.

Duval, Y., C. Pietri and L. Pietri (1997) 'Peuple chrétien ou Plebs: le rôle des laïcs dans les élections ecclésiastiques en Occident', in *Christiana respublica: éléments d'une enquête sur le christianisme antique*, Rome, 1059–81.

Erdkamp, P. (2002) 'A Starving Mob Has No Respect: Urban Markets and Food Riots in the Roman World, 100 BC–400 AD', in J. Rich and L. De Blois (eds) *Transformation of Economic Life under the Roman Empire*, Leiden, 94–8.

Ewald, P. (1880) 'Die Papstbriefe der brittischen Sammlung', in *Neues Archiv der Gesellschaft für ältere deutsche Geschichtskunde* 5: 275–414, 503–96.

Flower, R. (2013) *Emperors and Bishops in Late Roman Invective*, Cambridge.

Frend, W. H. C. (1984) *The Rise of Christianity*, Philadelphia.

Fuhrmann, C. J. (2012) *Policing the Roman Empire: Soldiers, Administration, and Public Order*, Oxford.

Gaddis, M. (2005) *There Is No Crime for Those Who Have Christ: Religious Violence in the Christian Roman Empire*, Berkeley.

Gaudemet, J. (1958) *L'Église dans l'Empire romain (IVe–Ve siècles)*, Paris.

Geertman, H. (2004) 'Forze centrifughe e centripete nella Roma cristiana: il Laterano, la basilica Iulia e la basilica Liberiana', in S. de Blaaus (ed.) *Hic fecit basilicam: studi sul Liber pontificalis e gli edifici ecclesiastici di Roma da Silvestro a Silverio*, Leuven, 17–44.

Ghilardi, M. (2010) '*Tempore quo gladius secuit pia viscera matris*: Damaso, i primi martiri cristiani e la città di Roma', in M. Ghilardi and G. Pilara (eds) *La città di Roma nel pontificato di Damaso (366–384): vicende storiche e aspetti archeologici*, Rome, 97–186.

Gregory, T. E. (1979) *Vox populi: Popular Opinion and Violence in the Religious Controversies of the Fifth Century* A.D., Columbus.
Guyon, J. (1974) 'La vente des tombes à travers l'épigraphie de la Rome chrétienne (IIIe, VIIe siècles): le rôle des *fossores, mansionarii, praepositi* et prêtres', *MEFRA* 86: 549–96.
Hahn, J. (2004) *Gewalt und religiöser Konflikt: Studien zu den Auseinandersetzungen zwischen Christen, Heiden und Juden im Osten des römischen Reiches (von Konstantin bis Theodosius II)*, Berlin.
Hahn, J. (2011) 'Spätantiker Staat und religiöser Konflikt: einleitende Bemerkungen', in J. Hahn (ed.) *Spätantiker Staat und religiöser Konflikt: imperiale und lokale Verwaltung und die Gewalt gegen Heiligtümer*, Berlin, 1–5.
Hahn, J. (2014) 'The Challenge of Religious Violence: Imperial Ideology and Policy in the Fourth Century', in J. Wienand (ed.) *Contested Monarchy: Integrating the Roman Empire in the Fourth Century AD*, Oxford, 379–404.
Heinzelmann, M. (1992) 'The "Affair" of Hilary of Arles (445) and Gallo-Roman Identity in the Fifth Century', in J. Drinkwater and H. Elton (eds) *Fifth-Century Gaul: a Crisis of Identity?* Cambridge, 239–51.
Jones, A. H. M. (1964) *The Later Roman Empire, 284–602: a Social, Economic and Administrative Survey*, Oxford.
Kahlos, M. (1997) 'Vettius Agorius Praetextatus and the Rivalry between the Bishops in Rome in 366–367', *Arctos* 31: 41–54.
Krautheimer, R. (1959) *Corpus basilicarum christianarum Romae*, vol. 2, Vatican City.
Künzle, P. (1961) 'Zur basilica Liberiana: basilica Sicinini = basilica Liberii', *RQA* 56: 1–61.
Lançon, B. (2000) *Rome in Late Antiquity: Everyday Life and Urban Change, AD 312–609*, Edinburgh.
Lander, S. L. (2017) *Ritual Sites and Religious Rivalries in Late Roman North Africa*, Cambridge.
Latham, J. A. (2012) 'From Literal to Spiritual Soldiers of Christ: Disputed Episcopal Elections and the Advent of Christian Processions in Late Antique Rome', *ChHist* 81 (2): 298–327.
Leemans, J. and P. Van Nuffelen (2011) 'Episcopal Elections in Late Antiquity: Structures and Perspectives', in J. Leemans, P. Van Nuffelen, S. W. J. Keough and C. Nicolaye (eds) *Episcopal Elections in Late Antiquity*, Berlin, 1–22.
Lenski, Noel (2014) *Failure of Empire: Valens and the Roman State in the Fourth Century* A.D., Berkeley.
Liebeschuetz, J. H. W. G. (1979) *Continuity and Change in Roman Religion*, Oxford.
Liebeschuetz, J. H. W. G. (2001) *The Decline and Fall of the Roman City*, Oxford.
Lizzi Testa, R. (2004) *Senatori, popolo, papi: il governo di Roma al tempo dei Valentiniani*, Bari.
Llewellyn, P. A. B. (1977) 'The Roman Church during the Laurentian Schism: a Preliminary Analysis', *AncSoc* 8: 245–75.
Löx, M. (2013) *Monumenta sanctorum. Rom und Mailand als Zentren des frühen Christentums: Märtyrerkult und Kirchenbau unter den Bischöfen Damasus und Ambrosius*, Wiesbaden.
McLynn, N. (1992) 'Christian Controversy and Violence in the Fourth Century', *Kodai* 3: 15–44.
McLynn, N. (2012) 'Damasus of Rome', in T. Fuhrer (ed.) *Rom und Mailand in der Spätantike: Repräsentationen städtischer Räum in Literatur, Architektur, und Kunst*, Berlin, 305–25.
MacMullen, R. (1990) 'The Historical Role of the Masses in Late Antiquity', in *Changes in the Roman Empire: Essays in the Ordinary*, Princeton, 250–76.
MacMullen, R. (2003) 'Cultural and Political Changes in the 4th and 5th Centuries', *Historia: Zeitschrift für Alte Geschichte* 52 (4): 465–95.
Marcos, M. (2013) 'Papal Authority, Local Autonomy and Imperial Control: Pope Zosimus and the Western Churches (a. 417–18)', in A. Fear, J. F. Urbiña and M. Marcos (eds) *The Role of the Bishop in Late Antiquity: Conflict and Compromise*, London, 145–66.

Mathisen, R. W. '*Peregrini, barbari,* and *cives Romani*: Concepts of Citizenship and the Legal Identity of Barbarians in the Later Roman Empire', *American Historical Review* 111 (4): 1011–40.

Matthews, J. (2007) *The Roman Empire of Ammianus,* Ann Arbor.

Mayer, W. (2013) 'Religious Conflict: Definitions, Problems, and Theoretical Approaches', in W. Mayer and B. Neil (eds) *Religious Conflict from Early Christianity to the Rise of Islam,* Berlin, 1–20.

Moorhead, J. (1992) *Theoderic in Italy,* New York.

Moorhead, J. (2015) *The Popes and the Church of Rome in Late Antiquity,* London.

Mulryan, M. (2014) *Spatial 'Christianisation' in Context: Strategic Intramural Building in Rome from the 4th–7th c.* AD.

Neil, B. (2016) 'Papal Letters and Letter Collections', in C. Sogno, B. K. Storin and E. J. Watts (eds) *Late Antique Letter Collections: a Critical Introduction and Reference Guide,* Oakland, CA, 449–66.

Nippel, W. (1995) *Public Order in Ancient Rome,* Cambridge.

Noble, T. F. X. (1993) 'Theoderic and the Papacy', in O. Capitani (ed.) *Teodorico il Grande e i Goti d'Italia,* Spoleto, 395–423.

Norton, P. (2007) *Episcopal Elections, 250–600: Hierarchy and Popular Will in Late Antiquity,* Oxford.

Otranto, G. (2010) *Per una storia dell'Italia tardoantica Cristiana: approci regionali,* Bari.

Pietri, C. (1976) *Roma Christiana: recherches sur l'Église de Rome, son organisation, sa politique, son idéologie de Miltiade à Sixte III (311–440),* Rome.

Pietri, C. (1997) 'Damase évêque de Rome', in *Christiana respublica: éléments d'une enquête sur le christianisme antique,* Rome, 49–76.

Raimondi, M. (2009) 'Elezione "iudicio dei" e "turpe convicium": Damaso e Ursino tra storia ecclesiastica e amministrazione romana', *Aevum* 83: 169–208.

Reutter, U. (2009) *Damasus, Bischof von Rom (366–384): Leben und Werk,* Tübingen.

Richards, J. (1979) *The Popes and the Papacy in the Early Middle Ages, 476–752,* London.

Richardson, L. (1992) *A New Topographical Dictionary of Ancient Rome,* Baltimore.

Ruciński, S. (2004) 'Position des *curatores regionum* dans la hiérarchie administrative de la ville de Rome', *Eos* 91 (1): 108–19.

Rudé, G. F. E. (1981) *The Crowd in History: a Study of Popular Disturbances in France and England, 1730–1848,* London.

Sághy, M. '*Scinditur in partes populus*: Pope Damasus and the Martyrs of Rome', *Early Medieval Europe* 9 (3): 273–87.

Sardella, T. (1996) *Società chiesa e stato nell'età di Teoderico: Papa Simmaco e lo scisma laurenziano,* Soveria Mannelli.

Sessa, K. (2012) *The Formation of Papal Authority in Late Antique Italy: Roman Bishops and the Domestic Sphere,* New York.

Sessa, K. (2016) 'The Roman Church and Its Bishops', in J. J. Arnold, K. Sessa and M. S. Bjornlie (eds) *A Companion to Ostrogothic Italy,* Leiden, 425–50.

Shaw, B. D. (2011) *Sacred Violence: African Christians and Sectarian Hatred in the Age of Augustine,* Cambridge.

Sotinel, C. (1998) 'Le personnel épiscopal: enquête sur la puissance de l'évêque dans la cité', in E. Rebillard and C. Sotinel (eds) *L'évêque dans la cité du IVe au Ve siècle: image et autorité,* Rome, 105–26.

Stroumsa, G. G. (1998) 'The Future of Intolerance', in G. N. Stanton and G. G. Stroumsa (eds) *Tolerance and Intolerance in Early Judaism and Christianity,* Cambridge, 356–61.

Tannous, J. (2018) *The Making of the Medieval Middle East: Religion, Society, and Simple Believers,* Princeton.

Thiel, A. (ed.) (1974 [1868]) *Epistolae Romanorum pontificum genuinae et quae ad eos scriptae sunt a S. Hilaro usque ad Pelagium II*, Braunsberg.

Thompson, E. P. (1971) 'The Moral Economy of the English Crowd in the Eighteenth Century', *P&P* 50: 76–136.

Townsend, W. T. (1937) 'Councils Held under Pope Symmachus', *ChHist* 6 (3): 233–59.

Trout, D. E. (2003) 'Damasus and the Invention of Early Christian Rome', *Journal of Medieval and Early Modern Studies* 33 (3): 517–36.

Trout, D. E. (2015) *Damasus of Rome: the Epigraphic Poetry. Introduction, Texts, Translations, and Commentary*, Oxford.

Van Nuffelen, P. (2010) 'Episcopal Succession in Constantinople (381–450 CE): the Local Dynamics of Power', *JECS* 18 (3): 425–51.

Van Nuffelen, P. and D. Engels (2014) 'Religion and Competition in Antiquity: an Introduction', in P. Van Nuffelen and D. Engels (eds) *Religion and Competition in Antiquity*, Brussels, 9–44.

Whitby, M. (2006) 'Factions, Bishops, Violence and Urban Decline', in J.-U. Krause and C. Witschel (eds) *Die Stadt in der Spätantike: Niedergang oder Wandel?* Stuttgart, 441–61.

Wijnendaele, J. W. P. (2019) 'Late Roman Civil War and the African Grain Supply', *Journal of Late Antiquity* 12 (2): 298–328.

Williams, M. S. (2017) *The Politics of Heresy in Ambrose of Milan: Community and Consensus in Late-Antique Christianity*, Cambridge.

Wirbelauer, E. (1993) *Zwei Päpste in Rom: der Konflikt zwischen Laurentius und Symmachus (498–514)*, Munich.

Wirbelauer, E. (1994) 'Der Nachfolgerbestimmung im römischen Bistum (3–6. Jh.): Doppelwahlen und Absetzungen in ihrer herrschaftssoziologischen Bedeutung', *Klio* 76: 388–437.

14

Religious Minorities in Late Roman Italy: Jewish City-Dwellers and Their Non-Jewish Neighbours

Jessica van 't Westeinde

Introduction

Have you ever wondered what the Roman Empire or indeed today's world would look like had Constantine listened to his mother?[1] After all, Christianity's rapid rise to fame and power is largely due to, or was facilitated by, Constantine's 'conversion' to Christianity: the famous 'Constantinian Turn'. Or was it? Oftentimes, the 'rise of Christianity' over the course of the fourth and fifth centuries of the later Roman Empire evokes images of a sharp numerical decline of any other religiously denominated 'group' or 'community'. The powerful voices of Christian rhetoricians together with imperial favouritism certainly do contribute to this picture, not to mention the distorted transmission history of literary and material evidence. As a result, studies have tended to juxtapose Christianity with either 'paganism' or 'Judaism'. However, these other people,[2] the so-called 'religious minorities' of late Roman Italy, deserve to be addressed in a different framework, namely that of urban religion. When religious groups are studied in their socio-geographical urban context, where it is understood that urbanity and religion mutually influence one another and grow into

---

[1] Of course, this is hypothetical and rather unlikely: not quite that Constantine would (not) have listened to his mother, but the claim made by the *Actus Sylvestri* that Helena had been Jewish, or that she would have preferred her son to have converted to this 'purer' religion, Judaism. The text presents 'correspondence' between Helena and Constantine, but most scholars accept this as forgery made up by the author of the *Actus*. The text presents the letter in the context of an event where Helena (living in Bithynia) comes to Rome together with a group of rabbis with whom she corresponds, and she suggest that her son convert to the purer religion (Judaism). In the contest between rabbis (twelve!) and then-bishop of Rome Sylvester (representing Christianity), with two pagan arbitrators, of course Sylvester wins, and all others are baptised, including Helena and the rabbis. Considering that the 'High Priest' sends his apologies, and that he sends twelve rabbis to represent him instead, makes the account highly doubtful. An interesting thought play, nonetheless.

[2] Due to the highly idiosyncratic nature of labels such as 'groups' or 'communities', which contain too many presuppositions, I will try to refrain from using these categories as much as possible. Instead, I will speak of people, individuals, or 'clusters of individuals' at best. The latter allows for an inclusion of both families and households, as well as other sorts of (semi-)organised gatherings of individuals, without necessarily presupposing hierarchically organised establishments or institutions.

what one may call 'urban religion', the resonating voices of the victors may be toned down.³ In this contribution, I will attempt to demonstrate what such an approach might bring to our understanding of Jewish and non-Jewish people within their urban context, where space is diverse and multifunctional. This allows for an illustration of a complex society where various 'groups' influence one another, and the city.⁴ I will argue that (1) boundaries between these 'groups' were much more porous in late antique Italy than is usually recognised, and it is necessary to situate Jewish practices within the larger (local) context of cultural practices in ancient Italy, and that (2) the relative absence of evidence for Jews in Annonaria compared with that for Suburbicaria may be explained as the successful efforts of powerful Nicene bishops in the north, but not so much in the south.

The chapter is divided into two sections corresponding to the administrative divisions of Italia Annonaria and Italia Suburbicaria, in which I analyse a selection of case studies. Unfortunately, the material evidence is rather scarce for Annonaria. The gist of this material has already been analysed in excellent studies by Lellia Cracco Ruggini.⁵ The larger part of my study is dedicated to Suburbicaria. Here, I will focus on two regions: Venosa and its environment, and the island of Sicily, where areas and cities will be dealt with individually. One could argue that there is a certain divide between Annonaria and Suburbicaria, which may be explained by shifting centres of power (military, administrative), as elaborated in other chapters in this volume. The choice to go by the division of Italy into Annonaria and Suburbicaria, and therefore by the administrative division of the peninsula, is deliberate. It emphasises what I believe might be the crucial role of the administrative and military context to explain Jewish presence or absence, and their attitudes towards Jewish citizens compared to attitudes towards non-Jewish residents. However, one cannot just assume that from the absence of evidence in Annonaria (see below), it follows that there was an absence of Jews. Nevertheless, prudence in dealing with (absent) evidence is mandatory. One counterargument to the influence of administrative or military presence to explain Jewish absence is Italy's own modern history. On average, the north has seen a greater impact of urbanisation, industrialisation and 'modernisation' than the south. This may have contributed to the fact that archaeological remains have disappeared to make way for new developments. In the more rural south, historical sites may have had a better chance to stand the test of time.⁶

The evidence, although scarce and scattered, exists in the form of texts, inscriptions, artefacts and architectural remains. It is essential (and typical) for the urban religion approach to take into consideration these various pieces of evidence and put them in dialogue with one another wherever possible, although the spatial and temporal scatteredness of these traces makes this a tedious task. By scrutinising the evidence

---

³ Rubens Urciuoli and Rüpke 2018, 117–35.
⁴ Rubens Urciuoli and Rüpke 2018, 120.
⁵ For example, Cracco Ruggini 1977; 1980; 2009a; 2009b; 2011.
⁶ Here it might be helpful to add the example of Rome, although the city is not part of this study. The Jewish archaeological evidence that has survived stems from catacombs mostly on the outskirts of the city. The inscriptions refer to synagogues, of which, although they do not necessarily refer to physical buildings (more likely they indicate clusters of individuals or congregations), none have ever been excavated in the capital.

for indications of how clusters of individuals match together, the role of religious agents or leaders and the use of urban space, the analyses of the individual sites serve to emphasise that religious groups and their dynamic nature have a primarily local character.[7] For reasons of brevity, and in order to better emphasise local diversity, I will not include the *urbs* itself, that is, Rome and its hinterland (Ostia, Portus). This is one of the aspects where my approach differs from previous scholarship. The latter has mostly attempted to draw links between other Italian cities and Rome rather than to appreciate the particularity of a city as a single and unique entity.[8] It maybe suggested that for some cities, Jewish or polytheist presence may not have been that 'minor' after all, although it is very difficult to tell.

A survey of the geographical locations of archaeological findspots shows that most Jewish settlements or at least some form of Jewish presence can be situated along the Roman arterial roads such as the Via Appia, and coastal or rather harbour towns. Economic considerations relating to trade may have had a hand in this.[9] The textual evidence that exists for the north seems to support this hypothesis, as these pieces of evidence, for example, refer to Jews living in Genoa and Aquileia: important trade harbours. However, it is important that one remember findspots are no conclusive proof of Jewish residence, particularly when one considers that these places are often stations along main trade roads.[10] Yet, these findspots do invite an approach that highlights socio-economic aspects rather than force religious presumptions upon the evidence. I will therefore explore in which places we may consider Jews as members of local elites, and what their social profile may have been, had they not been among the well-off in society, if this is at all discernible. A comparison of Jewish sources with

---

[7] See also the work of Karen Stern, who has adopted this approach for her study on Jews in North Africa, Stern 2007.

[8] The local focus therefore tries to understand the various religious groups in their unique socio-geographical context yet, simultaneously, I try to resist temptation to compare these groups with 'their' counterparts in Rome and Israel. Rome has often been at the centre of attention, which is understandable because of the relative abundance of evidence for Jewish presence in the capital, and its status as the centre of the empire (which Rome continued to hold long after it had ceased to be the imperial capital). See for example Leon 1960; Williams 1994; Rutgers 1995; 1998; Olsson 2001; Cappelletti 2006; Goodman 2007; Dello Russo 2011; 2012; Simonsohn 2014. Of course, David Noy's collection of inscriptions is indicative of Rome's primacy when it comes to Jewish evidence: his two-volume collection of Jewish inscriptions of western Europe has one volume dedicated to Italy, Spain and Gaul, and the other one is dedicated exclusively to evidence from the city of Rome; see Noy 1993; 1995.

[9] Simonsohn 2014, 94–5.

[10] Simonsohn 2014, 95. Localities in Suburbicaria that have a degree of certainty of Jewish residence or at least presence are Bova Marina, Reggio Calabria, Otranto, Taranto, Ori (Hyria), Venosa, Potenza (Potentia), Bari, Nuceria Alfaterna, Pompeii, Herculaneum, Brusciano, Naples, Pozzuoli (Puteoli), Marano, Capua, Telese (Telesia), Fondi (Fundi), Venafro, Porto, Ostia and Castel Porziano (Simonsohn 2014, 95–102). Although Rome was part of Suburbicaria – see Chapter 2 in this volume – I find that, when it comes to Jewish history in Italy, the last three cities listed by Simonsohn ought to be considered as part of the 'metropolitan area' of Rome. This explains why I have not included these cities in my study of Suburbicaria. Also questionable is the claim for Otranto, since Simonsohn includes this city in his list based on *Sefer Yosifon*, a tenth-century adaptation of Josephus that claims Titus exiled 5,000 Jews to Apulia, including Otranto. Regardless of these minute observations, what remains striking is that almost all cities in this list are situated along the Via Appia.

evidence from non-Jewish fellow citizens, if and where available, could demonstrate commonality among local residents as opposed to societal segregation in favour of connectivity with Jews further afield.

However, our major problem is the lack of evidence to draw firm conclusions; it is difficult if not downright impossible *really* to look at the urban context or to draw connections with other cities.[11] Yet, some hypothetical linking and thinking may be pursued. One of these trains of thought is that in the transition from *imperium* to *regnum*, for local Jewish and polytheist populations in provincial towns not much changed regarding civic positions.[12] Other contributions to this volume invited me to think along these lines when it comes to southern Italy being – to some extent – demilitarised and somehow less under imperial 'supervision'.[13] This may have resulted in an approach of 'live and let live' towards these 'minority' groups. It follows that, for example, it may be possible to identify some finds in fourth- or fifth-century Venosa as references to Mithraists; perhaps these inscriptions might hint at some Jewish–Mithraist 'syncretism'. Naturally, one ought to be cautious with any hypothetical labelling, as I will demonstrate in the detailed analysis below. Furthermore, there is the given that Jews occupied municipal office both in the fifth and in the sixth century, which suggests little enforcement of top-down anti-Jewish measurements.[14] Perhaps even more striking, from the period between 450 and 476 we have virtually no imperial legislation issued regarding Jews or Judaism – despite their continued public profile.

In my quest for Jewish and non-Jewish social interaction in urban contexts I will offer a reassessment of the interpretation of material collected in studies of scholars such as Lellia Cracco Ruggini, Shlomo Simonsohn, David Noy and Leonard Rutgers.[15] Shlomo Simonsohn's monumental work on the history of Jews in Italy offers a rich source, but the author presumes too much influence of the Patriarch (the *nasi* in Tiberias) on the Diaspora, including Italy.[16] Despite the monumentality of Simonsohn's work, this is

---

[11] Kraemer 2020 argues that the evidence for contacts and communication between Jews in different locales is modest at best, and that claims for such contacts have ideological agendas that are not explicit.

[12] See for example two laws promulgated under Arcadius and Honorius in 397, where in *CTh* 16.8.12 it is stated that Jews should not be attacked or harassed, and provincial governors should protect synagogues; and in *CTh* 16.8.13 it is ordered that Jews (esp. their clergy) are allowed to keep to their own laws and rituals, and that they are exempt from service in municipal senates. This law grants them the same privileges as Christian clergy.

[13] See Chapters 2, 3 and 5 in this volume. Throughout the fifth century, and especially after the sack of Rome in 455, there were periods of increased military activity in the south, but it is overall less than in the north; see Chapter 4 in this volume.

[14] See the laws mentioned in n. 12 above, aimed at protection of Jews rather than repressing them. Note that the law exempting Jewish clergy from municipal office reveals at once that Jewish clergy were called to municipal office, and that it does not exclude the possibility for non-clergy Jewish individuals to serve on the municipal senate. When Venosa became the administrative centre of the Ostrogothic kingdom in this region in the sixth century, there still seem to have been Jews in municipal office. At the same time, serving on the municipal council is not necessarily good, and laws do exclude Jews from holding major offices; see Kraemer 2020. Interestingly, either none of the emperors between Theodosius II in 450 and the deposition of Romulus Augustulus in 476 issued any legislation regarding Jews or Judaism, or it was not transmitted.

[15] Rutgers 1992; 1997; Noy 1995; Simonsohn 2014.

[16] Simonsohn 2014, 63.

a pity, and it shows the necessity of a local focus on Jewish life in Italian cities of Late Antiquity. Already Martin Goodman demonstrated the need for a more nuanced view, and the limited authority of the patriarchate, particularly before the late fourth century.[17] This contribution will try to offer exactly this more nuanced view with a local focus, to demonstrate that the boundaries between Jews and non-Jews are more blurred, and mutual influence occurs and is stimulated by each particular urban context.

Italia Annonaria

Annonaria possesses evidence for Jewish presence chiefly in literary and in some epigraphic sources. Material evidence of archaeological structures (e.g. synagogues) is virtually absent. Even the epigraphic record for the north is relatively scarce, with roughly ten inscriptions altogether.[18] There exist literary references to synagogues and cemeteries, but the archaeological remains of these sites have not been found. I would add that the nature of these literary accounts affects the level of 'reliability'; that is to say, Christian accounts of conversion and retribution are ubiquitous, but they may relate to events that happened elsewhere that have been projected on a given place by the author for, say, rhetorical reasons. Evidence of Jewish petitions to the imperial administration maybe considered 'more reliable'. Consider, for example, a petition sent to Theoderic by 'the Jews of Genoa', dated to 509.[19] In this petition, they request permission from Theoderic to have their synagogue restored; the request is granted.[20] This piece of evidence suggests two premises: (1) Jewish presence in Genoa, and (2) a 'cluster' large enough that they had the means to have their synagogue seemingly in an identifiable building. It does not allow one to conclude anything about clashes in Genoa between Jewish and Christian citizens, because the reasons for the state of decay of the synagogue are not specified. What it does demonstrate is a continuation of Jewish life in Annonaria, at least in Genoa, in the early sixth century, and moreover, that the Jews were still considered somewhat favourably: enough to merit the permission renovate their synagogue (although they were not allowed to build back better).[21]

An example of a different nature is found in Ambrose of Milan's *Exhortatio virginitatis*, where the author recalls a legend of two Christians who had been buried at the Jewish cemetery in Bologna.[22] Ambrose then goes looking for their graves, assisted by

---

[17] Goodman 2007, 240–1.

[18] Noy 1993 (*JIWE* 1): one in Concordia, two in Pula, one in Aquileia, one in Grado, three in Milan, two in Brescia, maybe one in Ferrara. Rita Lizzi Testa says perhaps three Christian and two pagan inscriptions may be added; see Noy 2005, 123–42.

[19] Linder 1997, 203 n. 7.

[20] This is mentioned in Simonssohn 2014, 104–5, but he offers no reference to primary sources (this is a major problem throughout his book). However, see Kraemer 2020, 317–18. Kraemer states that earlier laws had prohibited certain restorations of synagogues.

[21] Kraemer 2020, 317–18.

[22] Cracco Ruggini 1959, 211, 224; Ambr. *Exh. virginit.* 1.7–8, PL 16.351–4: *sepulti autem erant in Judaeorum solo, inter ipsorum sepulcra. ambierunt Judaei cum servulis sepulturae habere consortium, quorum Dominum negaverunt. sic et aliquando Balaam dixit: moriatur anima mea in animis justorum (Num. XXIII, 10); tamen non communicavit eorum operibus, cum viveret, quorum in animis cupiebat mori. et istos quos viventes persecuti sunt, mortuos*

local Jews. One could argue that this account would suggest there was a burial ground that was claimed to be Jewish, but Christians could be buried there, too. It would support the material evidence from Suburbicaria, and offer a northern equivalent to the practice encountered in the south (see discussion below on Venosa). However, this is the only (extant) account of Jews, or a Jewish cemetery, in Bologna. As Michael Toch prompts, this source is likely unreliable.[23]

In what follows, I will highlight and consider evidence from a selection of three cities: Milan, Aquileia and Ravenna, with some references to other settlements in the region. What is particularly interesting for northern Italy, as Rita Lizzi Testa has pointed out, is that 'Judaism' evolved and expanded in this region concurrently with 'Christianity'.[24] The example from Genoa may support this hypothesis. Lizzi Testa's observation appears to agree with Daniel Boyarin's argument concerning the 'parting of the ways', namely, that the two 'religions' emerged publicly around the same time, and competed with one another in the public space.[25] It is this assertion which invites a fresh look at the dynamics and interaction between religious denominations that challenges the narrative of a swift and smooth rise to power of Christianity (at the cost of other 'religions')[26]) in the post-Constantinian period.

Milan

Milan, the largest and most populous city of Annonaria, must have attracted visitors and prospective residents from far and wide. Towards the end of the fourth century, the pull factor of the metropolis increased once it became the imperial residence of the western emperor, its development in the final two decennia of the fourth century not unlike that of its eastern counterpart Constantinople.[27] It must also be acknowledged that Milan was at that time still a very pluralist society, much like Rome.

Yet, we hardly have direct evidence for Jewish presence in Milan. David Noy collected a total of three inscriptions that could be interpreted as Jewish.[28] However,

---

honorabant. illic igitur martyris exuvias requirebamus, tamquam inter spinas rosam legentes. circumfundebamur a Judaeis, cum sacrae reliquiae eveherentur: aderat populus Ecclesiae cum plausu et laetitia. dicebant Judaei: flores visi sunt in terra (Cant. II, 12), cum viderent martyres. dicebant Christiani: tempus incisionis adest (Ibid.). iam et qui metit, mercedem accipit (Joan. IV, 36). alli seminaverunt, et nos metimus martyrum fructus. iterum audientes Judaei voces plaudentis Ecclesiae, dicebant inter se: vox turturis audita est in terra nostra (Cant. II, 12). unde bene lectum est: dies diei eructat verbum, et nox nocti indicat scientiam. dies diei (Psal. XVIII, 3), Christianus Christiano: nox nocti, Judaeus Judaeo. indicabant ergo Judaei quod haberent scientiam martyrum, sed non scientiam Verbi; id est, non secundum illam solius boni, et solius veri scientiam: ignorantes enim Dei justitiam, et volentes se justificare, justitiam Dei non receperunt (Rom. X, 3).

[23] Toch 2012, 274.
[24] Lizzi Testa 2018, 244. In her argument she follows Fox 1986, 272–6.
[25] Boyarin 2004a; 2004b.
[26] Prudence is of course also required when speaking of 'religions' in comparison to Christianity as 'religion', particularly since our own contemporary understanding of 'religion' is a modern concept, as scholarship over the past twenty years has tried to show. See for example Boyarin and Barton 2016; Rüpke 2012; 2016.
[27] Cracco Ruggini 2009a, 7. On the 'flexibility' of imperial residences, see Chapter 3 in this volume.
[28] *JIWE* 1.3; Noy 1993, 1–5.

their interpretation is subject to debate. One of the inscriptions which Noy suggests as Jewish is of an uncertain date, and it is not certain whether it originates from Milan at all. What survives of the inscription are parts of Greek words (possibly reading 'grandchildren' or 'ancestors', but that is subject to reconstruction), and a word in Hebrew (which seems to read just לעולם, that is, 'eternity', without indication that it would have contained more Hebrew). The two inscriptions that have been retrieved from the Atrium of St Ambrose's Basilica are both in Latin and date from the fifth century or later. They may be identified as 'Jewish' based on the symbolism depicted on the marble plaques: possibly an amphora, a shofar, menorah, possibly ethrog and lulab on the one, just a menorah in the middle of וֹם . . . שׁל (*shalom*) on the second epitaph. Whereas the first inscription carries more symbols that suggest a Jewish character, where ethrog and lulab refer to the holiday of Sukkot, it lacks a personal name. The second inscription is an epitaph for a man named Ioses Alexandinus; although Ioses is a reconstruction (I..es), if it is correct, it could likely be a Jewish name.[29] These two inscriptions – I find the third one too unconvincing to consider it a 'Jewish' inscription for Milan – do not offer us any insight into Jews and their lives in Milan. The question is: is there other evidence to complement the inscriptions to grant a glimpse into Milanese urban Jewish life? This potential 'other evidence' comes from Christian and imperial sources. The best known, yet most questionable source is Ambrose, the Nicene bishop of Milan. Ambrose's strong anti-Jewish sentiments are reflected in his attempts to scapegoat them, for example by claiming in his *Letter* 40 how in the days of Julian the Jews of Milan set fire to churches.[30] The governor-turned-bishop also tried to interfere with due process of law with regard to the 388 destruction of the synagogue in Callinicum: initially, Theodosius I reprimands the Christians who were responsible, which in turn evokes Ambrose's reaction, and upon Ambrose's lobbying, Theodosius drops the charges.[31] However, in spite of Ambrose's pressuring, the emperor insists and reiterates religious freedom for the Jews throughout the empire, and in a law of 393 he forbids the Christians to destroy and plunder synagogues.[32] The reference is strange and indirect, but Ambrose's use of *hic* might hint at some Jewish presence, with synagogue, in Milan.[33] That a similar law is repeated four years later in

---

[29] Ilan 2008. The inscription has 'Alexandinus'; what is likely meant is 'Alexandrinus' ('of Alexandria'), *JIWE* 1.2.
[30] Ambr. *Ep.* 40.18 (*CSEL* 82). Compare Cracco Ruggini 1959, 206.
[31] Ambr. *Ep.* 74 (*CSEL* 82.2). For Ambrose's letter to Theodosius see *Ep. extra coll.* 1 (*CSEL* 82.3). See also Simonsohn 2014, 67–9 and n. 53. In Callinicum, Mesopotamia, local Christians led by their bishop destroyed the synagogue. Theodosius I ordered that they recompense the Jews and finance the rebuilding of the Jewish place of worship.
[32] *CTh* 16.8.9. In a letter to the *comes* of the Orient, Theodosius writes that 'it is certain that the sect of the Jews is not prohibited by law. Therefore, we are much disturbed by the prohibition in some places of their assemblies. On receipt of this order your supreme magnitude shall repress with suitable severity the excess of those who in the name of Christianity presume to destroy and despoil synagogues.' Compare Magnus Maximus, who had Christians rebuild the synagogue they had destroyed in Rome (Ambr. *Ep.* 40.23).
[33] Ambr. *Ep.* 74.8: *proclamo quod ego synagogam incenderim, certe quod ego illis mandaverim: ne esset locus in quo Christus negaretur. si obiciatur mihi, cur hic non incederim? divino iam cremari coepit iudicio: meum cessavit opus. et si verum quaeritur, ideo segnior fui, quia non putabam hoc vindicandum.* For a detailed discussion on Ambrose's underlying motives see Lizzi Testa, 2018, 252–6.

397 under Arcadius and Honorius may imply an increase in attacks against Jews and their synagogues. At the same time, it demonstrates a continued concern and care of duty vis-à-vis Jewish citizens on the part of the emperors, even though Christianity had been elevated to the singularly tolerated religion of the empire in 381.[34] Yet, what neither source reveals is concrete information about actual Jews in Milan. It is impossible to deduce from the sources whether Ambrose's animosity vis-à-vis Jews had anything to do with lived reality in Milan.

Aquileia

The case for Aquileia is quite similar to that for Milan. Again, we are presented with a combination of frail evidence. Textual evidence is found in Chromatius, bishop of Aquileia, and must therefore be dealt with cautiously because of its rhetorical nature. References in a variety of his sermons likely deal with rhetorical Jews, not with historical Jews.[35] Even expressions such as *nunc Iudaei* and *Iudaeos hodieque* do not necessarily refer to historical Jews – and certainly they cannot be taken as firm evidence for a substantial Jewish community in Aquileia, yet they may have been interpreted by the audience as referring to Jewish fellow citizens, and these words may well have instigated violence against actual Jews.[36] Other indications that suggest a certain degree of (vocal) Jewish presence in Aquileia are again to be found in Ambrose of Milan, namely in the Acts of the Council of Aquileia 381. Here, Ambrose blames the Jews for siding with the 'heretics',[37] but since he tries to categorise all non-(Nicene) Christians in one group, this cannot simply be understood as evidence of publicly active Jews – especially since no individuals are identified, but the rhetorically loaded denominator 'Jews' (*Iudaeus*) is used.[38] A positivist reading of the text could interpret Ambrose's choice of words as evidence that Jews held high positions in Aquileia, but again, this is reading too much into a few lines and does not allow one to draw conclusions about Jewish urban life in this city. Whereas Cracco Ruggini and Lizzi Testa both seem convinced that Jewish presence in Milan and Aquileia is confirmed by these texts, and moreover, that these Jews were willing to support other religious minorities,[39] I would

---

[34] On Theodosius and his stance on Jews, and the lobbying of Ambrose, see Kraemer 2020, esp. 124–57.
[35] For an overview of references to Jews in the works of Chromatius see Cracco Ruggini 1977; Noce 2012. For a comprehensive study of 'rhetorical' vs 'historical' Jews in Christian literature, see Jacobs 2004.
[36] Chromatius, *Serm*. 13.1.14–32. Lizzi Testa argues in favour of the historicity of Chromatius' Jews, against Noce's scepticism; see Lizzi Testa 2018, 262–3; cf. Noce 2012, 18–30. I would argue that although the references do not per se refer to historical Jews, they certainly will have had historical impact.
[37] See Gryson 1980 for the Arian *scholia*.
[38] See for example Ambr. *Ep*. 75.13: *intimantibus ne forte etiam gentilis aliquis aut Iudaeus qui ab Auxentio esset electus*, where he expresses his concern about the appointment of pagan and Jewish judges to the public disputation in the conflict between the Nicene bishops against Palladius of Ratiaria and Auxentius.
[39] Cracco Ruggini 1977; Lizzi Testa 2018, 261. Similarly, Samuele Rocca claims that when Ambrose accuses his rival Ursicinus, the Arian bishop, of seeking support for his cause both in churches and in synagogues, one should interpret this as referring to a de facto synagogue. However, Rocca seems to fail to see that Ambrose here is using a common 'Judaising' trope to attack his (Christian) opponent. See Rocca 2016, 43, where he bases himself on an article published in 1902 without giving the reference to the passage in Ambrose.

be more hesitant to draw such conclusions. Any claim that is made where Jews, pagans and heretics are aligned should be interpreted with utmost caution, and likely refers to rhetorical Jews rather than historical Jews, destined to besmirch rival Christians rather than saying anything about actual Jews.

When it comes to material evidence, this is also very fragile. The identification of the Basilica of Monastero as an erstwhile synagogue has been convincingly disproven by scholars in recent years.[40] Although there might have been a synagogue, even if so, remains of it have not (yet) been found. There is only one inscription that has been found in Aquileia whose contents sound most promising, as the Latin text speaks of Lucius Aiacius Dama, who is identified as a Jew (*L(ucius) Aiacius P(ublii) l(ibertus) Dama Iudaeus portor v(ivus) s(ibi) f(ecit)*).[41] However, there are three reservations to be made: (1) this epitaph is dated to the first century BC, definitely not later than the first century AD,[42] which (2) makes it strange to say the least that the text is written in Latin – this is usually found in Jewish inscriptions of much later date – and (3) the use of *Iudaeus* might suggest geographical origin rather than religious or ethnic affiliation. The most solid claim one could make about this inscription is that L. Aiacius Dama may have been working at the port of Aquileia, as *portor* might suggest (for *portitor*),[43] but this does not allow one to make any collective claims for 'the Jews' of Aquileia.

Ravenna

Ravenna offers a similar blurry picture. There are no archaeological remains or inscriptions that indicate Jewish settlement in the city, save an amphora inscribed with unidentifiable figures or letters, and the word 'shalo[m]' in Hebrew letters.[44] The latter, however, as suggested by Michael Toch, may well have belonged to a merchant who was passing through the city.[45] Ravenna is worth mentioning, though, since after 402 it had become Honorius' preferred residence, and succeeding emperors had their seats at least partially in Ravenna. The city was to become the permanent governmental seat with the accession of Odoacer.[46] This status upgrade must have made the city more attractive, and the fact that it remained a more or less stable bubble in an otherwise swiftly changing Italy under the 'barbarian' invasions speaks for its appeal. Yet, other than some fifth-century laws and an indication of a burnt-down synagogue in the early sixth century, there is no solid proof for Jewish life in Ravenna. The two laws that have been issued in Ravenna by Honorius in 415 and 416 do not necessarily refer to the situation in Ravenna. The laws concern possession of Christian slaves by Jews, and the return of Jewish converts to Judaism. Although the laws do have a

---

[40] Summarised in Lizzi Testa 2018, 247–9.
[41] Noy 1993, 11.
[42] Lizzi Testa 2018, 246.
[43] Lizzi Testa 2018, 246.
[44] Noy 1993, 17.
[45] Toch 2012, 277.
[46] I thank Jeroen Wijnendaele for pointing me to the more gradual progression of Ravenna as imperial residence.

clear addressee, Annas the Didasculus and the *maiores* of the Jews, this does not reveal anything about Jewish life in Ravenna. Rather, it may demonstrate Jewish presence at the imperial court, probably in the form of lobbying embassies.[47] These laws, and those issued before, do allow one to sketch a picture of Jews and their interaction with their non-Jewish 'neighbours' in cities across Italy and perhaps the wider empire. If a law needs to be issued concerning Christian slaves owned by Jews, this is likely because this reflects an actual situation. From this, one may deduce that there certainly would have been Jews who were more affluent, and not that they themselves were slaves or belonged to lower strata of society. When the emperors issue seven laws between 383[48] and 438 in an attempt to ban Jewish 'proselytism', it may suggest that this was a common occurrence (or the repeated promulgation of these laws may have been the result of Christian lobbying). Moreover, it may imply that it was not that easy to restrict: conversion to Judaism continued to occur even after Christianity had been promoted to official religion of the empire. Most laws, however, concern intermarriage (rather than conversion), which was put on a par with adultery and thus would result in capital punishment.[49] Still, if these laws had to be repeated many times, it might reflect a common practice which was not banned that easily (although it might also reflect a formulaic repetition). Ultimately, it demonstrates vivid interaction between people of different ethnic or religious backgrounds.

A less peaceful interaction occurred in Ravenna under the reign of Theoderic, when sometime in the first quarter of the sixth century a conflict erupted between Jews and Christians, during which synagogues were burnt down. Interestingly, this conflict erupted while Theoderic was away from Ravenna, which may in fact suggest that 'imperial', or in this case 'royal presence' asserted power in such way that inhabitants refrained from public confrontation when they knew the king was present, but as soon as they knew he was travelling, they saw this as their chance to act. Ross Kraemer explains how Jews from Ravenna chose to travel to Verona to personally address this event with the ruler.[50] In response, Theoderic punished the Christian citizens of Ravenna, and ordered them to finance the rebuilding of the Jewish premises.[51] However, in a similar fashion to what I have argued above with regard to Genoa, Ross Kraemer suggests that this segment, in spite of its difficult nature, may demonstrate

> a rather complex social dynamic . . . [where] Jews felt sufficiently safe not only to resist Christian efforts to baptize them but also to mock Christians by throwing their holy water into the river. They were not safe enough to prevent Christians from retaliating by torching synagogues, but they were sufficiently empowered to seek and obtain legal redress from both secular and orthodox catholic church authorities.[52]

---

[47] Toch 2012, 277. The fact that such embassies were sent to petition can already be found in Philo.
[48] *CTh* 16.7.3 forbids Christian converts to Judaism, 'paganism' and Manicheanism to make a will.
[49] Lizzi Testa 2018, 263; Kraemer 2020, 3.
[50] Kraemer 2020, 323.
[51] Cassiod. *Var.* 4.33. Cassiodorus is the only source that mentions the conflict, and so caution is needed concerning the accuracy of the report.
[52] Kraemer 2020, 323.

It follows that in the early sixth century the Jews still enjoyed some protection under Theoderic, and more so, that Jewish presence in Ravenna at that time may not have been that 'minor', if indeed a multitude of synagogues were burnt down.[53] This, in turn, may demonstrate that Theoderic's Ravenna may indeed have had some pull factors that attracted (Jewish) citizens from elsewhere in Italy to relocate here, including, most likely, the presence of the king and his administration.

In sum, material evidence for Jewish life in Annonaria is incredibly meagre. There are no archaeological remains for synagogues – there only exist some textual references to synagogues, and these are not always reliable. There have been no catacombs excavated: the inscriptions found come from *spolia*, mostly reused in churches.[54] A variety of factors may have contributed to the loss of evidence for Jewish presence that seem to have particularly affected urban life in the north, extending from the fifth-century invasions and subsequent wars to the industrialisation in the eighteenth and nineteenth centuries. Ross Kraemer also points to an order of Pope Urban VIII (1568–1644), that existing Jewish grave markers should be destroyed.[55] Such orders from church institutions throughout the Middle Ages and the modern period may also have contributed to a loss of both material and literary evidence (e.g. burning of Jewish books, bans on publishing Jewish books). However, it may also be that archaeologists have not yet found evidence because no one has stumbled across it, either whilst doing targeted excavations or by chance.[56] Be that as it may, the most reliable evidence currently available comes from imperial legislation, although that is not restricted to northern Italy. This legislation seems to contradict Christian victory narratives at least to some extent, as they attest continued Jewish life in northern cities, where Jews retained a position in society strong enough to warrant protection from the emperors and the early kings of Italy, such as Theoderic. Thus, one may contend that the presence of an imperial or royal court may have attracted Jews to a city, just as much as it attracted non-Jews. The role of military presence in Jewish presence or absence may have been less favourable, considering the ban on Jews holding military office. What had the greatest effect on the decline of Jewish presence in the north, however, seems to have been Christian animosity, chiefly instigated by their bishops. The most powerful bishops of Italy were attached to episcopal sees in the north (e.g. Milan, Aquileia). Therefore, it may be better to suggest that it was powerful bishoprics that affected Jewish presence, and that were responsible for the removal of visibly Jewish cultural references from the public sphere.

Italia Suburbicaria

The situation of available evidence is rather different in the south. The evidence here shows that religious or cultic boundaries were much more porous than is usually recognised. Furthermore, as I have argued above, the relative absence of Jewish evidence

---

[53] Admittedly, the number of synagogues does not reveal anything about the size of the population.
[54] For a discussion on this type of Christian spoliation of Jewish material, see Kraemer 2020, 18.
[55] Kraemer 2020, 18.
[56] It must be noted that most discoveries happened by chance, as is the case for at least some of the Jewish catacombs in Rome. I thank Ross Kraemer for this suggestion.

in Annonaria may be explained by successful efforts of powerful Nicene bishops in the north. Now, I try to demonstrate that for Suburbicaria, there were either less powerful bishops, or their efforts to annihilate visible Jewish presence were less successful. In what follows, I will first analyse a selection of the material available from Venosa, before hopping over to the Italian islands. The evidence from Venosa is chiefly epigraphic, whereas for Sicily there is a variety of evidence at hand.

Venosa

As far as the available evidence suggests, Venosa appears to be the city that hosted the largest Jewish population of Suburbicaria.[57] Their traces have been preserved in inscriptions which, for the most part, were dipinti: red paint on stucco.[58] None of these inscriptions contain even a single reference to a synagogue, no remains of a synagogue have been excavated, yet several persons are commemorated seemingly with titles of synagogue offices (e.g. *archisynagogos*). The inscriptions for our period of interest come from catacombs, which were in use until well into the sixth century, perhaps even the seventh century, thereby outdating the ones of Rome, which seem to have gone out of use after the fourth century. Although suggestions have been made that Jewish inhabitants of Rome fled south in response to Alaric's sieges of Rome in 408 and 410 – as many of Rome's residents did if they had the means – it would go too far to argue that the Roman Jewish population relocated to Venosa. Inscriptions from the fourth century testify to Jewish presence in the city already before the sack of Rome.[59]

Catacombs and a hypogeum (named 'Lauridia') have been excavated on Maddalena hill just outside Venosa. Some seventy-four 'Jewish' inscriptions have been identified, most of them from the main catacomb.[60] Christian catacombs have been found nearby,[61] but by contrast, only ten 'Christian' inscriptions have been unearthed.[62] Furthermore, in the baths of Venosa a fragment of a pottery vase with a menorah inscribed on it was found.[63] Although such symbols on pottery do not necessarily mean it was Jewish or it belonged to Jews, taking into consideration the findspot as well as the evidence from the

---

[57] For recent studies on the Jews in Venosa see Noy 1994, 162–82; Williams 1999, 38–52; Rutgers (et al.)'s ongoing Venosa project (Reconfiguring Diaspora: 3D Venosa Project, https://diaspora.sites.uu.nl/projects/3d-pilot-project-in-venosa/); Laham Cohen 2020, 7–64; Kraemer 2020, 342–401.

[58] Leon 1954, 268.

[59] It has been pointed out that letters from the sixth century attest a thriving Jewish presence in Rome, which demonstrates that the 'community' survived, ergo any sieges of the city did not challenge Jewish presence. One may think of correspondence of Gregory the Great (*Registrum epistularum*, CCSL 140 and 140A) through which it becomes clear that Jews of Rome lobbied for fellow Jews from other cities in Italy; on this see especially Laham Cohen 2013, 214–46. Only 26 out of 866 letters deal with 'real Jews' (and their specific problems or complaints); Laham Cohen 2015, 11. However, this is not the point I am making here; rather, I propose that Jewish presence in Venosa existed independent of any floods of refugees that might have come from Rome.

[60] Considering the high number of epitaphs that have been unearthed – and this is only a fraction, as most have been lost – it may suggest a relatively high percentage of Jews among the Venusian population.

[61] Colafemmina 1973, 56.

[62] Laham Cohen 2020, 19.

[63] Colafemmina 1980, 212.

catacombs, the picture that emerges is that of a provincial hub hosting a mixed population where Christians did not form a majority.[64]

Taking a closer look at the inscriptions, the earliest ones in the main catacomb from Gallery D might not be earlier than the early fifth century, although David Noy admits that some 'isolated inscriptions . . . may go back to the fourth century'.[65] The languages used for the inscriptions are Greek, Latin and Hebrew: mostly a combination of Greek and Hebrew or Latin and Hebrew, and sometimes all three languages.[66] The Greek inscriptions are generally considered to be the older ones. At times, the Hebrew is written from left to right, or Greek is written in Hebrew characters (*JIWE* 1.75). In the main catacomb 'every arcosolium . . . has some Hebrew, but there is only one surviving inscription of any length which is in Hebrew alone (*JIWE* 1, 82)'.[67] Interestingly, the Hebrew inscription stems from a later date of the late fifth or early sixth century. I will now highlight two distinct tendencies that make some epitaphs stand out: one is the use of the Latin *PP* (*pater patrum*), which may suggest a Mithraic connection; and the other is the emphasis on ancestry, which we do not find elsewhere to such an extent.

'PP' and Mithras

The possible Mithras link can be found in the Lauridia hypogeum, located some 100 yards from the main catacomb. The separate entrance with its architrave has been decorated with a spear, snakes and arrowheads.[68] Some scholars have suggested this may hint at a Mithraic structure. In Mithraic art one often finds snakes, whilst Mithras himself is at times presented with bow and arrows.[69] The spear, however, does not seem to have any particular Mithraic association.[70] Only four inscriptions on marble plaques have been excavated from here. Their Jewishness is subject to debate: certainly, there are titles, formulae and names that appear in the hypogeum and the main catacombs alike. However, as Noy points out, no Hebrew and no symbols appear on the Lauridia inscriptions.[71] Yet one must admit that in the main catacomb not all inscriptions that have Hebrew have symbols, and not all that have symbols have Hebrew, and some

---

[64] Venosa had been the centre of the cult of Cybele, and followers of Mithras were present too (see below). By contrast, Christian evidence for Venosa is scarce: the earliest epigraphic evidence is from 503 (*ICI* 13.75–81), and in literary sources Venosa is mentioned first only at the end of the fifth century. They 'disappear' again after the sixth century, although archaeological remains of a local church would suggest some form of continuity; see Laham Cohen 2020, 18.

[65] Noy 1993, xxi.

[66] For a detailed study of the names in the Venusian inscriptions, see Laham Cohen 2020, 7–64.

[67] Noy 1993, xix.

[68] Levi 1962, Luzzatto's photograph of 1932.

[69] Campbell 1968.

[70] Noy 1993, xvii.

[71] Noy 1993, xvii. Frenkel first understood them as Jewish; Luzzatto disagreed. Some indications that they may be Jewish: *teuseues* may be 'godfearer'; *pater*, *pater pateron* appear in both sites; Marcellus and Faustina are common names in the main catacomb too; yet Noy objects: they reveal nothing intrinsically Jewish, except perhaps that Marcellus in *JIWE* 1.114 could be the same as the one mentioned in *JIWE* 1.90. Compare Williams 1999, 38–52; Kraemer 2014, 61–87.

of them have neither Hebrew nor symbols. However, there may be some other hints that could suggest Mithraic influences, such as the use of the formula *PP*. Admittedly, there is no coherence in use of *PP* and the site of burial: the *PP*s are not unique to the hypogeum, of which it has been suggested that it may belong to a Mithras group. One example (*JIWE* 1.68) comes from the main catacombs and commemorates Catella, daughter of the *pater patrum* Sebbetius.[72] There are several points of interest in this epitaph. First, the use of the verb *pauso* is common in Christian inscriptions. More interesting however, is the use of the abbreviation *PP* for Sebbetius. In the main catacomb we find three inscriptions with *PP*: the above, *JIWE* 1.68, where Sebbetius holds the title of *PP*; in *JIWE* 1.85 it is again Sebbetius presented as *PP*, this time on the epitaph of his grandchildren, as well as Vitus, the great-grandfather, who is also a *pater patrum*. From the inscription it is not clear whether Vitus is the father of Sebbetius, but if he is, the office may run in the family; in *JIWE* 1.90 Marcellus and Sarmata are both named *pater patrum*. Both men are named as the grandfathers of the married couple who are buried there (Marcellus, grandfather of Gesua; Sarmata, grandfather of Agnella) – demonstrating an emphasis on ancestry. These are reminiscent of pagan aristocratic commemoration practices. One may propose that rather than self-identifying solely on the base of religion, the commissioners wished to self-identify on the basis of status or social standing.

In the Lauridia hypogeum we find only the one inscription with *PP*, and remarkably, this one is in Greek: *JIWE* 1.114 names Marcellus as *pater pateron* and *patron tes poleios*. Not only is Marcellus a *pater patrum,* he also holds the title patron of the city. The inscription is dated earlier than the Latin equivalents (late fourth to early fifth century); nevertheless, I would be less inclined to follow David Noy's suggestion that this Marcellus is the same person as the one mentioned in the Latin inscription above. The latter also lacks Marcellus' second significant title of 'patron of the city'. There is only one other inscription, also from the hypogeum, where a person carries both the titles *pater patrum* and 'patron of the city', and this is that of Auxanius (*JIWE* 1.115). Auxanius' wife Faustina holds the honorific title 'mother' (μητηρ, *JIWE* 1.116). There may be a familial relation between these three Greek inscriptions from the hypogeum, suggesting that this was a prominent family. This being the case, the occurrence of *pater patrum* is even more interesting. It was the highest title in Mithraic cult, which in the past has been interpreted as evidence of Jewish–Mithraic syncretism at Venosa. Noy sees it, however, as unnecessary to think of this link, pointing at the *Letter of Severus* (*PL* 20.731–46) in which the leading (*praecipuus*) Jew of the town of Mago on Minorca in 418, Theodorus, was *legis doctor et ut ipsorum utar verbo, pater patrum*; he had also held the civic office of that town. Elsewhere in the letter, Severus describes him as *summus sacerdos*.[73] However, this is a Christian account of a Jewish community, and the details may not be precise (see above). Furthermore, the Minorcan context is not necessarily comparable to the situation in Venosa.[74] Another possibility would be that

---

[72] *JIWE* 1.68: *hic pausat Ca|tella ann(orum) VIIII(I) | filia p(atris) | p(atrum) Sebbetei.* | (menorah).

[73] Noy adds that the abbreviation *PP* was used for the title by Mithraists at Rome (*CIMRM* 1.401–3, 521, dated 358–404).

[74] On the reliability of Severus' letter, see Kraemer 2009, 635–65.

Marcellus might have been a Mithraic *pater patrum* and not a Jewish one. Nonetheless, no conclusive answer can be given, although these observations do leave open the chance that there may have been a close proximity of groups at Venosa: a speculation which may be given more weight when one considers that various clusters of individuals (or families) shared the same burial space. There is to my knowledge at least one more piece of evidence of Mithraic evidence from Venosa: a person making a dedication to Mithras in Greek and to Mercury in Latin. However, the dating would not match: Noy argues it is unlikely that it is later than the third century.[75]

Ancestry

Interestingly, it is chiefly in the inscriptions with the *PP* formula that we encounter the emphasis on ancestry, although not exclusively. To illustrate, I will compare a couple of inscriptions where I think there is a clear emphasis on ancestry.[76]

Inscription *JIWE* 1.607 commemorates the infants Andronicus and Rosa. In the epitaph, their father Bonus is mentioned – he holds no title. Sebbetius, *pater patrum*, is their grandfather, and their great-grandfather Vitus is mentioned also, who held the same office. It is not clear whether they deliberately list the patrilineal line, or whether the grandfather and great-grandfather are named for the sake of their office. I mentioned this one in relation to a possible connection to Mithras, yet this Latin inscription bears a hint of Jewishness: not the names per se, but the fact that a menorah has been drawn on the plaster of the vault of the arcosolium. However, (1) the menorah sits outside the frame in which the text appears and may thus be a later addition; (2) it is the only inscription in Gallery D2 of the main catacomb that has a menorah.[77]

Another fine example of the combined emphasis on ancestry and prestigious officeholding is found in Noy's no. 107 (Plate XVI).[78] It is the only inscription from the Venosa catacombs with an exact date: the year 521. This inscription deserves our attention because of the information it contains and the development it reveals. The inscription is typical of its age: Latin, with a slightly more elaborate Hebrew than we find in the earlier inscriptions of the fourth and fifth centuries (with no strange spelling mistakes). The Hebrew reads 'peace to the resting-place of Augusta. Amen' (שלום על משכה אגוסתה. אמן), which appears to be a generic formula found in other Venusian Latin–Hebrew inscriptions also. The inscription states the date according to the 'profane' calendar, not according to the Jewish one – this was to be an even later development (ninth century). If we look at the content, we learn that Bonus, the husband of Augusta, holds the title of *vir laudabilis* (abbreviated in the conventional way). Daniëlle Slootjes remarks that *vir laudabilis* is an honorific title for 'local elites' below

---

[75] Noy 1993, xix.
[76] For a detailed study of ancestry (and titles) among Venusian Jews, see Williams' case study of the family of Faustinus: Williams 1999, 38–52. For titles see also Rajak and Noy 1993, 75–93.
[77] Critical of the identification of the use of a menorah with Jewishness are Rutgers 1992, 110–11; Goodman 1994, 208–24.
[78] Noy 1993, 137–8.

the rank of the clarissimate.[79] Bonus must have held some municipal office. Augusta's grandfather Symonas held the title of *pater Lypiensium*. Lypia is probably modern-day Lecce, between Brindisi and Otranto; Symonas may have acted as some leading figure or patron of that city. Both Augusta's father and grandfather also held the honorific title of *pater*, but not *PP*.

Finally, there is the fascinating early sixth-century epitaph of 14-year-old Faustina, whose funeral was read by two rabbis (*rebbites*) and two apostles (*apostoli*).[80] Unlike the previous inscription, the current one does not offer an exact date. However, I include this one because it is the first and only mention of rabbis in Venosa. A lot has been speculated about this, the most popular opinion being that they were sent from the patriarch in Tiberias, but the dating is problematic, because the patriarchate ceases in the fifth century.[81] This is also the only epitaph that contains 'genuine' information about any action on the part of officeholders or agents: the apostles and the rabbis are active; they perform a ritual act: they read dirges.[82] Why, then, is it only in this inscription that the commissioners deemed it appropriate to mention the course of events and the actors, whereas in all other surviving epitaphs no mention of rituals is made? Either it was so common that nobody else thought of it but Faustina's relatives, or it was so extraordinary that it must be mentioned. Alternatively, following Williams, this signifies diversity and heterogeneity within the Jewish population of Venosa. We do notice another emphasis on office and ancestry: Faustina's grandparents Vitus and Asella were *maiores cibitates*. Although Noy translates this as 'leaders of the community', this is too restrictive; it is more likely that they were leaders of the city in some administrative function, which implies Vitus may have been a *decurion*.

These examples demonstrate that prestigious offices were held by Jews. This is fascinating, for already Theodosius II had decreed that no Jews or pagans were to serve in service of the empire or in jurisdiction.[83] Venusian reality proves that this law seems to have had little effect locally.

Italian Islands (Suburbicaria)

Hopping to the Italian islands, I have opted to single out Sicily. Although Sardinia – as well as Malta – boast some evidence of Jewish presence and settlement, it suffices to look at the most intriguing amalgam of evidence found in Sicily, which helps to

---

[79] Compare Chapter 5 in this volume.
[80] The genealogy is convincingly reconstructed by Williams 1999, 38–52. Based on the study of this family, Williams demonstrates that the choice of how people wished to be commemorated or to commemorate differed within 'the community', and that there exists no proof of a linear process of Hebraisation (language relates to personal choice).
[81] Compare Schwartz 1999, 208–22; 2002, 55–69; Kraemer 2020, 359–60; Lacerenza 2021, 291–321.
[82] Kraemer 2020, 375–7. Kraemer contends that the increased use of Hebrew may indicate that some Jews constructed tighter social boundaries by adopting certain forms of Jewish practice, and they might have found appealing the different practices brought in by travelling rabbis. Where female officeholders occur in the inscriptions, Kraemer suggests this may reflect a situation of distress, where women take on responsibilities otherwise reserved for men; compare Kraemer 1985, 431–8; 2015, 287–300.
[83] *Const. Sirm.* 6, Galla Placidia in the name of Valentinian, and Theodosius II, Summer 425.

illustrate the significant difference in the nature and number of sources or forms of evidence between Suburbicaria and Annonaria.

Sicily

The evidence for Jewish (urban) life on Sicily seems a bit stronger, yet not unproblematic.[84] Some (questionable) sources suggest Palermo had a flourishing Jewish population who had multiple synagogues, yet firm evidence is lacking.[85] Simonsohn argues on the basis of one fragmentary Jewish epitaph that there was a Jewish open-air cemetery in Agrigento, which is a bold statement that does not prove Jewish settlement. In Sofiana (between Catania and Agrigento) brief inscriptions have been found on stone slabs, as well as an amulet.[86] I will restrict myself to a few examples from three types of 'evidence' that hint at cultural and cultic interaction: epitaphs, legends (concerning sites of religious tourism, synagogue) and amulets.

Epitaphs

The most fascinating inscription from Sicily was found in Catania. An expensive tombstone, the inscription appears on a sizeable white marble plaque of 29 × 47 × 1.7 cm; the inscribed letters show traces of red paint.[87] It was found (May 1928) near the Church of St Teresa, close to the ancient western walls of Catania.[88] This epitaph for Aurelius Samuel (*JIWE* 1.145) – note the double name – and his wife Lassia Irene, is the most elaborate one found in Sicily.[89] It opens with a Hebrew phrase, 'peace to Israel amen, amen peace Samuel' (שלום לישראל אמן, אמן שלום אל שמואל), and the body of commemorative text is in Latin. The Hebrew on this tombstone appears formulaic. However, considering the relatively early dating (383), I would advocate for caution. It is quite extraordinary to find a full Hebrew phrase this early: at least in Italy, including Sicily, the use of more than one word of Hebrew usually does not appear until the (mid-)fifth century, and elaborate, intelligible Hebrew is not used until the mid-sixth century (sporadically) or later.[90] The phrase *conparabi mihi memoriam* is common in

---

[84] Colafemmina 1995, 304–29; Simonsohn 1997; Rutgers 1997, 245–56; Van der Horst 2006, 37–42; Rutgers and Bradbury 2006, 429–508.
[85] Noy 1993, xxi refers to Gregory the Great, *Ep.* 8.25 and 9.38 for 'evidence' of the existence of more than one synagogue and a 'substantial community'.
[86] Simonsohn 2014.
[87] Noy 1993, 406 (Plate XX).
[88] Noy 1993, 188.
[89] Noy translates 'Samohil' for Samuel, Noy 1993, 191; also Kraemer 2020, 155, with a brief discussion of the epitaph on p. 156–7.
[90] One of the earliest may be *JIWE* 1.81 and 82 (Venosa, late fifth to early sixth century), which are fully in Hebrew; *JIWE* 1.84 from the same place and time has a Hebrew text and a Latin translation. *JIWE* 1.21 records a seventh-century (or later) bronze lamp found in Nola with a full Hebrew sentence (a biblical citation, Prov. 7:23; see Noy 1993, 39). One can agree with Noy, however, that the appearance of the phrase in the epitaph of Aurelius Samuel does not necessarily imply specialist Hebrew knowledge (e.g. the name Samohil is simply a Latinised form of Samuel, as we see in the Hebrew).

Latin pagan inscriptions; the use of *memoria* for memorial is also used by Jews, Christians and pagans alike. One finds parallels to Aurelius Samuel's claim of tomb acquisition in Greek inscriptions throughout Sicily. Aurelius Samuel's inscription is also the only one to offer an exact date: 21 October 383. This is not usual for what have been identified as Jewish epitaphs (though we find a later parallel in Venosa; see above), but very common for 'pagan' inscriptions. The dating is, in fact, 'pagan' (*XII Kal(endas) Novebr|es, diae Veneris, luna octaba, Mero | |baudes iterum et Satornino con|sulibus*). The specification of the day of the week finds parallels in Christian inscriptions.[91] Another interesting aspect of the epitaph is the protection invoked upon it: it appears to be fashionable in Sicily.[92] Here we also find parallels with 'pagan' inscriptions, for example from Syracuse, *CIL* 10.2.7136: *quod si [quis . . .] inferat al[. . .] (HS) CC milia*. David Noy has suggested that the phrase *quem Dominus dedid Iudeis* may indicate that the commissioner expected his epitaph to be read by non-Jews, too (*adiuratio* is thus directed to Jews and non-Jews alike). Thus, Aurelius Samuel's tomb is protected by the invocation of the powers of the rulers (*per victorias qui inperant* – possibly a reference to the emperors, or divine powers/cosmic rulers), the patriarchs and the law of the Jewish God, and if that is not enough of a threat, any potential violator risks a heavy fine (*dit fisco argenti pondo*). These phrases could be an indication that, potentially, some burial places – in Catania and Syracuse, as probably elsewhere on Sicily – may have been used by citizens from all 'religious' groups.[93]

Another example of an attempt to protect the grave is found on Irene Nymphe's epitaph (*JIWE* 1.151), which has the peculiar invocation 'by this mystery, let no one open here' (κατὰ τοῦ μυστηρί[ου οὖν τούτου | μή τ]ὶς ὧδε ἀνύξῃ). Her epitaph on a limestone tablet was found close to another Jewish one, prompting the identification of Irene as Jewish. They both come from Hypogeum XI of the Capuchin catacombs in Syracuse, an area mainly used by Christians; in other predominantly Christian catacombs lamps with *menorot* were found. Although there may have been Jews buried in these hypogea predominantly used by Christians, one should stress that one does not exclude the other. We ought to push away from the wish to determine burial places as only possibly being used by a single religious denomination at any given time. At the same time, it may also be evidence of desecration or spoliation.

As I have shown, there is a tendency in Sicilian Jewish inscriptions to stress that a tomb was purchased lawfully: again, this is a claim added to epitaphs of Sicilian pagans,

---

[91] Noy refers to Diehl, *ICLV* 3.311, twenty-eight examples of Friday; twenty-four of Sunday, eighteen of Saturday; Sicilian Christian epitaphs in Greek mention Sunday and Friday (Agnello 1953, 63, 69, 106). Noy further states that the eighth month refers to the Jewish calendar; in 383 Heshwan would have begun on 14 October (Mahler 1916).

[92] We do not find it elsewhere in southern Italy, which may hint at regional differences within the 'same religion'. We do find similar protective spells in Greece and Asia Minor. E.g. *CIJ* 719 from Argos, in Greek: Aurelius Joses invokes the great and holy powers of God, the powers of the law, the honour of the patriarchs and ethnarchs and the wise, the honour of reverence that is paid each day to God. Elsewhere in northern Italy, we also find *legem* against tomb violation. As for tomb violation, Noy (1993, 190) adds that numerous Christian tombstones in Concordia carry a similar threat of a fine.

[93] Or, at least, that the one who commissioned this epitaph was aware of formulas used in non-Jewish inscriptions. I thank Ross Kraemer for this suggestion.

Jews and Christians alike. It is probably a local trend, since it is not found in (Jewish) inscriptions elsewhere in Italy. Perhaps this was in reaction to the inscriptions threatening with fines, divine and human punishment in case of tomb violation, although we have seen that Aurelius Samuel's epitaph contains both a claim of lawful purchase and a threat to potential violators of his tomb. Compare the epitaph in Greek of *presbyteros* Irenaeus (some sort of elder; his Jewishness is debated), who claims to have 'bought the place, in no way offending the law'.[94] Some scholars have hypothesised that if the identification of this inscription as Jewish is correct, then the legal reference must refer to Jewish burial law. However, this is not necessarily the case. Even if this inscription were Jewish, there is nothing conclusive to be said about the law to which it refers. Another epitaph from Catania bears a similar reference to the law, stating that Jason, also a *presbyteros*, did in no way infringe the law when buying the burial place for himself and his children.[95] The wording is slightly different: ζημιῶ, i.e. punish in commercial or moral sense, is used instead of βλάπτω in the example of Irenaeus above; and κοῦπαν is used for burial place instead of the more generic τόπον. Neither inscription sheds clear light on what law is implied, but since these assure the potential reader that the one who commissioned the inscription did not infringe upon the law, it may likely have been local property or burial law, possibly reflecting a situation of conflict between acquisitors of burial plots.

Legend

In addition to epitaphs, there may be further evidence of Jewish presence and interaction with non-Jews in Catania. In the *Acts of St Agatha* (*Acta Sanctorum*, 5 February) Jews are mentioned as having venerated St Agatha's burial place alongside pagans ('gentiles') and Christians. The *Acts* date from the sixth century, but appear to tell a tale of earlier days when Christians were still 'persecuted', perhaps the time of Decius. The legend has it that when the city of Catania was in peril of Mount Etna's volcanic eruption, all citizens – Jews, pagans and Christians – ran to St Agatha's burial place, where they took her veil, which they then held up against the sea of flames, whereupon the flames were miraculously extinguished. Thus, St Agatha's final place of rest had become – at least rhetorically – a place of (inter-)religious tourism.[96]

In Syracuse there are some dubious literary accounts that refer to a synagogue, namely the *Acts* of a third-century bishop Marcian of Syracuse, who found a place to live in caves in the high part of the city (Acradina), with the Jewish synagogue to the south (*Acta Sanctorum*, 2 June 789, composed seventh or eighth century). Bishop Zosimus of Syracuse (d. 660) in *Acta Sanctorum*, 3 March 842, refers to the destruction of the synagogue of Syracuse by the Vandals.[97] These two references to a synagogue in Syracuse

---

[94] *JIWE* 1.148. Found 1896, Catania, wall of a tomb in via A. di San Giuliano; see Noy 1993, 194.
[95] *JIWE* 1.149.
[96] 'Jews and Gentiles as well as Christians revered her grave', *et tam Iudaei quam etiam Gentiles unanimes cum Chrisitanis communiter coeperunt venerari sepulchrum eius*, Acta Sanctorum, 1 February 615–18. Naturally, one must be wary of the propagandistic nature of hagiographical literature that promotes the recognition of Christian power (of saints) by Jews and gentiles.
[97] Noy 1993, 200.

may suggest that the building was constructed in the fourth or fifth century, or at least that it may (still) have been there at the time of composition of these bishop's tales. Then again, as much caution is required as for such references addressed in Annonaria above; these alleged 'synagogues' may not have been historical at all, although one must admit the context is slightly different: here they seem to be included as navigation aids to locate the dwelling place of the bishop.

Amulets

The last pieces of evidence I wish to discuss for Sicily are some amulets.[98] These invoke both angels and pagan gods. Two of them have been discovered: one probably from Sofiana, and one from Cómiso; both are dated sometime between the third and fifth centuries. The one from Sofiana, on a bronze sheet, is in Greek and transliterated Hebrew,[99] whereas the one from Cómiso, on a gold sheet, is in Hebrew only.[100] These are not the only amulets found in Sicily that use Hebrew-based divine names (Iao, Adonai) in combination with pagan deities. Although it has been claimed that this does not necessarily imply Jewish influence, one must admit that it may very well be an indication of vivid (cultic) interaction between religious agents (and here I use 'agents' deliberately: one could argue they were providers of such amulets). The bronze amulet from Sofiana lists many Hebrew angelic names and heavenly powers; it also mentions the law, and Juda. What is particularly fascinating here, is that the angelic, heavenly and divine powers are invoked to frighten off Artemis – that she (her evil influences) may flee from Juda.[101]

The gold sheet from Cómiso contains, as noted, only Hebrew. The text is rather incomprehensible apart from a few divine names and a couple of phrases. The 'twins' may refer to the cult of the Dioscuri, which was popular in Sicily. Thus, again, we may have some evidence of cross-cultic interaction. This gold sheet was found on a site where another copper sheet has been found inscribed with a Greek magical text (φυλακτήριον μωσέως), carrying many references to Moses.[102] David Noy suggests that this Greek text may be from pagan, Christian or Jewish hands; if the former two, they may have thought of Moses as a magician.[103] This is but one of many magical inscriptions that have been found in Cómiso – including one that invokes Christ yet depicts a *hanukkia* (nine-branched menorah).[104] It is interesting to see how Cómiso seems a kind of 'hotbed' for magical texts and artefacts, apparently irrespective of any cordoned-off religious denomination but freely manoeuvring between pagan, Jewish and Christian traditions.

---

[98] Noy 1993, 212–15.
[99] Noy 1993, 212–15.
[100] Noy 1993, 207–8.
[101] For an overview on late ancient Jewish magic see Swartz 2007, 198–221.
[102] Noy 1993, 208.
[103] Compare Gager 1972.
[104] Noy 1993, 209.

Conclusion

A number of scholars have concluded from the above evidence that there was or were well-organised hierarchical communities whose offices were clearly defined, and that all these inscriptions can and must be compared with those of Rome and Beth Shearim, seemingly irrespective of dating and vast distance between places. I hope that I have made it clear that jumping to such conclusions is untenable. For example, in Venosa there is (1) no evidence of a synagogue, (2) no evidence of communal organisation apart from the titles that occur in the inscriptions, which are open to interpretation to say the least, and (3) since there are local differences in commemoration practices, as well as other differences (time, space, formulae, symbolism, language), one cannot simply draw parallels with Jews in Rome or further afield. It is already difficult to ascertain exact roles of title holders in Rome, so the assumption that the titles imply the same offices in Venosa is built on very thin ice indeed. They may not have referred to offices within a Jewish community in the first place. The *maiores* of the Jews, as we encountered in legislation issued in Ravenna, do not hold (necessarily) the same office as the *maiores cibitatis* we find in Venosa.[105] Likely, the latter was a public office. The variation in nature and composition of the evidence suggests that nuance is important, as is an eye for regional differences.[106] Such an approach offers a new perspective and a renewed understanding of relations between adherents to various 'religions' or 'ethnicities'. That regional differences exist has become evident from the comparison between Annonaria and Suburbicaria. However, where I started by stating that the concentration of imperial and military presence in Annonaria may have directly affected the demise of (evidence for) Jewish presence in the north, my analysis has indicated that at least the presence of the imperial administration may rather have had the opposite effect, at least up until the reign of Theoderic: imperial presence may have been a pull factor. It may be more plausible that the presence of powerful, anti-Jewish bishops led to the demise of visible, traceable Jewish presence in the north. Absence of such bishops in the south may at least partially explain the presence of a richer variety of material evidence of Jewish presence there.

Moreover, one could also notice differences in the evidence between various localities in the south. In each city, epitaphs show slightly different tendencies of perhaps cultural and/or religious influences, titles, use of language and artefacts found. Cómiso stood out for its number of magical texts and amulets (irrespective of denomination); Sicily on average has shown a tendency for invoking protective spells or powers against tomb violation, whilst also revealing the tendency to stress lawful purchase of burial space. In Venosa ancestry was emphasised, especially in the later Latin inscriptions. There is also many a reference to civic office held by Jewish citizens. These references may imply that in some cities at least the Jews were not that 'minor' after all. Jews, Christians and possibly pagans were buried in close proximity to one another. Although general conclusions may not be drawn from such random finds, the evidence does suggest that well beyond the 'Constantinian Turn', and even

---

[105] For a discussion on *maiores*: Kraemer 2020, 360–2.
[106] As Karen Stern has demonstrated for other regions; see Stern 2007; 2018.

beyond the promotion of Christianity to official religion of the empire, people kept borrowing from multiple religions or cults to satisfy their needs or to structure their daily goings-about.

It would be wrong to *a priori* exclude pagan or Christian influences when it comes to determining Jewishness, and vice versa. Dynamics or fluidity of cultic identity was dependent on locale and differed by city or region, as I have tried to demonstrate. It does not mean that if in Venosa people are commemorated using a different formula than in Rome or Syracuse, it makes a person more Jewish or less Jewish. It might be a different kind of Jewishness, or a different understanding of Jewish identity. It is our own limitations set upon these definitions by our narrow frameworks that are so desperate to fit these ancient people into our categories which make us end up with these dilemmas.

Not to end on a negative note, we could say that at least in Suburbicaria Jews remained visible in the fifth century and beyond, despite Christian dominance, Christian anti-Jewish propaganda and anti-Jewish legislation. The religious landscape thus remained relatively diverse.[107]

Bibliography

Adler, H. M. (1901) 'The Jews in Southern Italy', *Jewish Quarterly Review* 14: 111–15.
Agnello, S. L. (1953) *Silloge di iscrzioni paleocristiane della Sicilia*, Rome.
Bognetti, G. P. (1954) 'Les inscriptions juives de Venosa et le problème des rapports entre le Lombards et l'Orient', in *CRAI* 98 (2): 193–203.
Boyarin, D. (2004a) 'The Christian Invention of Judaism: the Theodosian Empire and the Rabbinic Refusal of Religion', *Representations* 85: 21–57.
Boyarin, D. (2004b) *Border Lines: the Partition of Judeo-Christianity*, Philadelphia.
Boyarin, D. and C. Barton (2016) *Imagine No Religion: How Modern Abstractions Hide Ancient Realities*, Fordham.
Campbell, L. A. (1968) *Mithraic Iconography and Ideology*, Leiden.
Canella, T. (2006) 'Gli *Actus Silvestri*: genesi di una leggenda su Costantino imperatore', *Uomini e mondi medievali* 7.
Cappelletti, S. (2006) *The Jewish Community of Rome: from the Second Century BC to the Third Century CE*, Leiden.
Colafemmina, C. (1973) *Apulia cristiana: Venosa*, Bari.
Colafemmina, C. (1978) 'Nuove scoperte nella catacomba ebraica di Venosa', *VetChr* 15: 369–81.
Colafemmina, C. (1980) 'Insediamenti e condizioni degli ebrei dell'Italia meridionale e insulare', *Gli ebrei nell'alto medioevo, Settimane di studio del Centro italiano di studi sull'Alto Medioevo* 26: 197–227.
Colafemmina, C. (1995) 'Ipogei ebraici in Sicilia', *Italia Judaica* 5: 304–29.
Colafemmina, C. (2000) 'Hebrew Inscriptions of the Early Medieval Period in Southern Italy', in B. Cooperman and B. Garvin (eds) *The Jews of Italy: Memory and Identity*, Potomac, 65–81.

---

[107] I would like to thank Jeroen Wijnendaele and the anonymous reviewers for their helpful feedback, and most of all I would like to thank Ross Kraemer for taking the time to go over drafts of this piece, for her constructive comments, and her many suggestions for improvement. Any flaws that remain are, of course, my own.

Colafemmina, C. (2003) 'Le catacombe ebraiche nell'Italia meridionale e nell'area Sicula: Venosa, Siracusa, Noto, Lipari e Malta', in M. Perani (ed.) *I beni culturali ebraici in Italia: situazione attuale, problemi, prospettive e progetti per il futuro*, Ravenna, 119–46.

Cracco Ruggini, L. (1959) 'Ebrei e orientali nell'Italia settentrionale fra il 4. e il 6. secolo d. Cr.', *SDHI* 25: 187–308.

Cracco Ruggini, L. (1977) 'Il vescovo Cromazio e gli ebrei di Aquileia', *Aquileia e l'Oriente mediterraneo*: 353–81.

Cracco Ruggini, L. (1980) 'Pagani, ebrei e cristiani: odio sociologico e odio teologico nel mondo antico', *Gli ebrei nell'alto medioevo, Settimane di studio del Centro italiano di studi sull'alto Medioevo* 26, 15–117.

Cracco Ruggini, L. (1985) 'Tolleranza e intolleranza nella società tardoantica: il caso degli Ebrei', *Dieci prolusioni accademiche* (1975–1985): 189–208.

Cracco Ruggini, L. (2009a) 'Milano capitale: gruppi religiosi e conflitti fra IV e V secolo', in M. Pesce (ed.) *Conflitti e pluralità religiosa nelle città*, Annali di Storia dell'Esegesi 26.1, Bologna, 7–22.

Cracco Ruggini, L. (2009b) 'Gli ebrei nell'Italia tardoantica e gli studi nell'ultimo cinquantennio', U. Criscuolo and L. De Giovanni (eds) *Trent'anni di studi sulla tarda antichità: bilanci e prospettive. Atti del convegno internazionale, Napoli, 21–23 novembre 2007*, Naples, 103–18.

Cracco Ruggini, L. (2011) *Gli Ebrei in età tardoantica: presenze, intolleranze, incontri*, Rome.

Dello Russo, J. (2011) 'The Discovery and Exploration of the Jewish Catacomb of the Vigna Randanini in Rome: Records, Research, and Excavations through 1895', *Roma Subterranea Judaica* 5: 1–24.

Dello Russo, J. (2012) 'An Archival and Historical Survey of the Jewish Catacombs of the Villa Torlonia in Rome', *Roma Subterranea Judaica* 7: 1–24.

Dönitz, S. (2012) 'Historiography among Byzantine Jews: the Case of *Sefer Yosippon*', in E. Bonfil, O. Irshai, G. G. Stroumsa and R. Talgam (eds) *Jews in Byzantium*, Leiden, 951–68.

Ehrhardt, A. A. T. (1960) 'Constantine, Rome, and the Rabbis: an Evaluation of the *Actus Sylvestri*', *Bulletin of the John Rylands Library* 42: 288–312.

Fox, R. L. (1986) *Pagans and Christians: in the Mediterranean World from the Second Century AD to the Conversion of Constantine*, London.

Gager, J. G. (1972) *Moses in Greco-Roman Paganism*, Nashville.

Goodman, M. (1994) 'Jews and Judaism in the Mediterranean Diaspora in the Late Roman Period: the Limitations of the Evidence', *Journal of Mediterranean Studies* 4: 208–24.

Goodman, M. (2007) 'Jews and Judaism in the Mediterranean Diaspora in the Late-Roman Period: the Limitations of Evidence', in M. Goodman (ed.) *Judaism in the Roman World: Collected Essays*, Leiden, 233–59.

Gryson, R. (1980) *Scolies ariennes sur le concile d'Aquilée*, SC 267, Paris.

Hachlili, R. (1998) *Ancient Jewish Art and Archaeology in the Diaspora*, Leiden.

Horst, P. W. van der (1991), *Ancient Jewish Epitaphs: an Introductory Survey of a Millennium of Jewish Funerary Epigraphy (300 BCE–700 CE)*, Kampen.

Horst, P. W. van der (2006), 'The Jews of Ancient Sicily', in P. W. van der Horst (ed.) *Jews and Christians in Their Graeco-Roman Context*, WUNT 196, Tübingen, 37–42.

Ilan, T. (2008) *Lexicon of Jewish Names in Late Antiquity*, part 3: *The Western Diaspora, 330 BCE–650 CE*, Texts and Studies in Ancient Judaism 126, Tübingen.

Jacobs, A. (2004) *Remains of the Jews: the Holy Land and Christian Empire in Late Antiquity*, Redwood City, CA.

Kraemer, R. S. (1985) 'A New Inscription from Malta and the Question of Women Elders in Diaspora Jewish Communities', *Harvard Theological Review* 78: 431–8.

Kraemer, R. S. (2009) 'Jewish Women's Resistance to Christianity in the Early 5th Century: the Account of Severus, Bishop of Minorca', *JECS* 17 (4): 635–65.

Kraemer, R. S. (2015) 'Rufina Refined: a Woman *archisynagogos* from Smyrna, Yet Again', in J. J. Collins, T. Lemos and S. Olyan (eds) *Worship, Women and War: Essays in Honor of Susan Niditch*, Providence, RI, 287–300.

Kraemer, R. S. (2020) *The Mediterranean Diaspora in Late Antiquity: What Christianity Cost the Jews*, Oxford.

Lacerenza, G. (1998) 'Antichità giudaiche di Venosa: stori e documenti', *Archivo storico per le province Napolitane* 96: 293–418.

Lacerenza, G. (2019) 'Painted Inscriptions and Graffiti in the Jewish Catacombs of Venosa: an Annotated Inventory', *Annali Sezione Orientale* 79: 275–305.

Lacerenza, G. (2021) 'Rabbis in Southern Italian Jewish Inscriptions from Late Antiquity to the Early Middle Ages', in G. McDowell, R. Naiweld and D. Stökl Ben Ezra (eds) *Diversity and Rabbinization: Jewish Texts and Societies between 400 and 1000 CE*, Cambridge, 291–321.

Laham Cohen, R. (2013) 'Los judíos en el *Registrum epistularum* de Gregorio Magno y la epigrafía judía de los siglos VI y VII', *Henoch: Historical and Textual Studies in Ancient and Medieval Judaism and Christianity*, Brescia, 214–46.

Laham Cohen, R. (2015) 'Theological Anti-Judaism in Gregory the Great', *Sefarad* 75: 225–52.

Laham Cohen, R. (2020) 'The Names of the Jews in Late Ancient Venosa: Latinization, Rejudaization, or Rabbinazation?', in *Sefer Yuḥasin* 8: 7–64.

Leon, H. J. (1954) 'The Jews of Venusia', *Jewish Quarterly Review* 44: 267–84.

Leon, H. J. (1960) *The Jews of Ancient Rome*, Leiden.

Levi, L. (1962) 'Richerche di epigrafia ebraica nell'Italia meridionale', *La Rassegna Mensile di Israel* 28 (3): 132–55.

Levi, L. (1965) 'Le iscrizione della catacomba nuova di Venosa', *Rassegna mensile di Israel* 31: 358–65.

Lifshitz, B. (1962) 'Les juifs à Venosa', *RFIC* 90: 367–71.

Linder, A. (1997) *The Jews in the Legal Sources of the Early Middle Ages*, Detroit.

Lizzi Testa, R. (2018) 'Jews and Christians in Northern Italy: Conflicts, Violences, Conversions, and Daily Coexistence in Late Antique Aquileia', in P. Lanfranchi and J. Verheyden (eds) *Jews and Christians in Antiquity: a Regional Perspective*, Leuven, 243–65.

Mahler, E. (1916) *Handbuch der jüdischen Chronologie*, Leipzig.

Meyers, E. (1983) 'Report on the Excavations at the Venosa Catacomb', *VChr* 20: 445–59.

Noce, E. (2012) 'Judaísmo e identidad cristiana en el *corpus* de Cromacio de Aquileya', *Sefarad* 72: 7–54.

Noy, David (1993) *Jewish Inscriptions of Western Europe*, vol. 1: *Italy (Excluding the City of Rome), Spain and Gaul*, Cambridge (= *JIWE* 1).

Noy, D. (1994) 'The Jewish Communities of Leontopolis and Venosa', in J. W. van Henten and P. W. van der Horst (eds) *Studies in Early Jewish Epigraphy*, Leiden, 162–82.

Noy, David (1995) *Jewish Inscriptions of Western Europe*, vol. 2: *Rome*, Cambridge (= *JIWE* 2).

Noy, D. (2005) 'Jewish Inscriptions of Western Europe: *addenda et corrigenda*', in G. Lacerenza (ed.) *Hebraica hereditas: studi in onore di Cesare Colafemmina*, Naples, 123–42.

Olsson, B. (2001) *The Synagogue of Ancient Ostia and the Jews of Rome: Interdisciplinary Studies*, Stockholm.

Rajak, T. and D. Noy (1993) 'Archisynagogoi: Office, Title, and Social Status in the Greco-Jewish Synagogue', *JRS* 83: 75–93.

Rocca, S. (2016) 'The Impact of the Barbarian Invasions on the Jews of Roman Italy: New Perspectives', *Scripta Iudaica Cracoviensia* 14: 41–56.

Rubens Urciuoli, E. and J. Rüpke (2018) 'Urban Religion in Mediterranean Antiquity: Relocating Religious Change', *Mythos* 12: 117–35.

Rüpke, J. (2012) 'Lived Ancient Religion: Questioning "Cults" and "Polis Religion"', *Mythos* 5: 191–204.
Rüpke, J. (2016) *On Roman Religion: Lived Religion and the Individual in Ancient Rome*, Ithaca, NY.
Rusu-Bolindet, V. and R. Varga (eds) (2017) *Official Power and Local Elites in the Roman Provinces*, London.
Rutgers, L. V. (1992) 'Archaeological Evidence for the Interaction of Jews and Non-Jews in Late Antiquity', *AJA* 96: 101–18.
Rutgers, L. V. (1995) *The Jews in Late Ancient Rome: Evidence of Cultural Interaction in the Roman Diaspora*, Leiden.
Rutgers, L. V. (1997) 'Interaction and Its Limits: Some Notes on the Jews of Sicily in Late Antiquity', *ZPE* 115: 245–56.
Rutgers, L. V. (1998) *The Hidden Heritage of Diaspora Judaism*, Leuven.
Rutgers, L. V. (2016) 'Next Year in Sardis: Reflections on Whether the Jewish Diaspora of the Roman Era Was Diasporic at All', in C. Cordoni de Gmeinbauer (ed.) *'Let the Wise Listen and Add to Their Learning' (Prov 1:5): Festschrift for Günter Stemberger on the Occasion of His 75th Birthday*, Berlin, 167–96.
Rutgers, L. V. and S. Bradbury (2006) 'The Diaspora, c.235–638 CE', in S. Katz (ed.) *The Cambridge History of Judaism*, vol. 4: *The Late Roman–Rabbinic Period*, Cambridge, 492–518.
Schwartz, S. (1999) 'The Patriarchs and the Diaspora', *Journal of Jewish Studies* 50: 208–22.
Schwartz, S. (2002) 'Rabbinization in the Sixth Century', in P. Schäfer (ed.) *The Talmud Yerushalmi and Graeco-Roman Culture*, vol. 3, Tübingen, 55–69.
Schwartz, S. (2004) *Imperialism and Jewish Society: 200 BCE to 640 CE*, Princeton.
Sicker, M. (2001) *Between Rome and Jerusalem: 300 Years of Roman–Judaean Relations*, London.
Simonsohn, S. (2014) *The Jews of Italy: Antiquity*, Leiden.
Sivan, H. (2018) *Jewish Childhood in the Roman World*, Cambridge.
Stern, K. (2007) *Inscribing Devotion and Death: Archaeologcial Evidence for Jewish Populations of North Africa*, Leiden.
Stern, K. (2018) *Writing on the Wall: Graffiti and the Forgotten Jews of Antiquity*, Princeton.
Swartz, M. (2006) 'Jewish Magic in Late Antiquity', in S. Katz (ed.) *The Cambridge History of Judaism*, vol. 4, Cambridge, 699–720.
Swartz, M. (2007) 'Jewish Visionary Tradition in Rabbinic Literature', C. E. Fonrobbert and M. S. Jaffee (eds) *The Cambridge Companion to the Talmud and Rabbinic Literature*, Cambridge, 198–221.
Toch, M. (2012) *The Economic History of European Jews: Late Antiquity and the Early Middle Ages*, Leiden.
Walsh, D. (2018) *The Cult of Mithras in Late Antiquity: Development, Decline and Demise ca. AD 270–430*, Leiden.
Williams, M. (1994) 'The Stucture of Roman Jewry Re-considered: Were the Synagogues of Ancient Rome Entirely Homogenous?', *ZPE* 104: 129–41.
Williams, M. (1999) 'The Jews of Early Byzantine Venusia: the Family of Faustinus I, the Father', *Journal of Jewish Studies* 50: 38–52.

Part V

Culture

15

CHRISTIAN SARCOPHAGI IN LATE ROMAN ITALY: CULTURE AND CONNECTION

Miriam A. Hay

FOURTH-CENTURY SARCOPHAGI IN ITALY beyond Rome have hardly been considered as a subject in their own right. Amongst other regions in the Roman Empire, this area remains understudied and its monuments overlooked within the corpus of Christian sarcophagi – itself still largely isolated within the wider fields of Roman sarcophagi and late antique art. This chapter will offer an overview of the types of exports and locally produced works used for Christian burials in fourth-century Italy outside the metropolis, at a time bridging the classical and late antique worlds when the centrality of Rome could no longer be taken for granted.

With initial archaeological foundations having been laid, the focus will be reconstructing how sarcophagi would have been viewed in antiquity. Early Christian sarcophagi have in the past been viewed in a fragmentary way, with biblical motifs compared across different examples and different media, so that the personal funerary context of each monument is sometimes obscured. Biblical imagery has also been treated differently to earlier Roman themes, as representing a communal religious identity rather than the traditional personal praise of the deceased. However, as will be argued, biblical scenes could be used in highly complex, interconnected and innovative ways within individual monuments, and should be appreciated as continuing participants in the visual games of elite Roman funerary culture.

Sarcophagi are compelling objects to study because as the final, costly memorials of ancient people, their decoration can reveal what the deceased (or their family) felt was most important to surround their earthly remains and characterise their memory in perpetuity. Moreover, this decoration did not only reflect culture and society, but actively participated in its formation and reformation, in ongoing negotiations of identity. Death studies have seen special impetus in recent decades, and it remains to be seen what impact a possible era of pandemics will have on attitudes to death, when funerary traditions have been disrupted and mortality has once again been brought into sharper relief.[1]

Marble sarcophagi came into significant use in the Roman Empire in the early second century AD, and were the main mode of burial for those who could afford them into the fourth century and beyond; previously cremation had been the norm

---

[1] See e.g. Davies 2018, esp. 247–9 on the 'death turn'.

and ashes stored in urns or altars.² Original display contexts very rarely survive, though since some are known to have been buried, the main opportunity for viewing a sarcophagus may have been at the funeral or 'lying in state'.³ Studies indicate that the purchasers of Christian sarcophagi may have been more likely to be from the upper classes than previously, while they were also very often from more middling groups, those who could afford the considerable expense and aspired to the funerary culture of the elite.⁴ The first Christian images appear on Roman sarcophagi from the late third century, and by the first half of the fourth century are found on most surviving examples.⁵ Since Christian art first emerged in the funerary sphere, sarcophagi are of crucial importance in the development of Christian iconography.

Rome was the main centre of production, with sarcophagi from its workshops commonly exported to other parts of Italy.⁶ There were many works which were evidently made locally, including at smaller centres in Campania for example. In the fourth century, while sarcophagi continued to be produced in large numbers in Rome, they survive around Italy in much lower figures, with no major local production sites.⁷ It is possible that they have a lower rate of survival due to the spread of material, and less concentrated rebuilding and excavation outside of Rome. The northern city of Ravenna took over as the main location for sarcophagus production after 402, when it became a new imperial residence under Honorius, with a rather different aesthetic.⁸ Production in Rome meanwhile came more or less to an abrupt end after the sack of the city in 410.⁹

While there have been studies of sarcophagi from locations around the Roman Empire, the Italian provinces (beyond Rome and its port at Ostia) have escaped such singular attention.¹⁰ There are no studies dedicated solely to sarcophagi in Italy as a whole.¹¹ Some scholarship exists on individual locations, such as Ravenna or Sicily, but the nature of export and local production across Italy is largely restricted to the

---

² For introductions to the discipline and history of sarcophagus studies, see Elsner 2011; Zanker and Ewald 2012, 1–55; Ewald 2015.
³ Dresken-Weiland 2003 and Meinecke 2014 on the burial context of sarcophagi. Meinecke 2013 and Borg 2013, 236–40 on the 'lying in state'.
⁴ Dresken-Weiland 2003, 41–7.
⁵ Couzin 2019 on the lower survival rate of non-Christian sarcophagi from the fourth century.
⁶ Koch 2000, 444.
⁷ Koch 2000, 465.
⁸ On sarcophagi from Ravenna: Gabelmann 1973; Rebecchi 1978; *ASR* 8.2; for the Christian period: Lawrence 1945; Koch 2000, 379–98; Dresken-Weiland 2003, 150–60; Schoolman 2013. See Chapter 3 in this volume.
⁹ Brandenburg 2004.
¹⁰ On Roman sarcophagi in other geographical locations: for Gaul, *RS* 3; Benoit 1954; Turcan 2003, 269–331; Gaggadis-Robin 2005; 2013; for Spain, *RS* 4; Claveria 1998; for Istria and Dalmatia, *RS* 2; Cambi 1977; 1998; 2004; for North Africa, *RS* 3 and 4; Birk 2012; Baratte 2013; Rodà 2013; for Aphrodisias, e.g. Smith 2012; for Constantinople, *RS* 5; Deckers 2004; for multiple provinces, Koch and Sichtermann 1982, 268–72; Koch 2000, 366–8, 371–8, 466–590; 2012b; and numerous authors in Koch and Baratte 2012.
¹¹ Aside from sarcophagi, on funerary practices and burials in Italy, see Graham and Hope 2016 for pre-Christian, and Christie 2006, 148–56 for late antique.

invaluable work of Guntram Koch.[12] The fourth century is particularly neglected, falling in between the more valued second- to third-century Roman works and the fifth-century production at Ravenna. It is nevertheless a particularly dynamic time bridging 'classical' and 'late' antiquity, seeing the transformation of society from 'pagan' to Christian, while Rome was still the centre of production but no longer the imperial capital.

The three main sections of this chapter will reflect three categories of sarcophagi used for inhumation around Italy in the fourth century: exports from Rome; works made locally; and finally a distinctive group exported exclusively to northern Italy at the end of the century, the 'city-gate' type.[13] An advantage of this smaller corpus is the ability to consider a large proportion of the intact examples with biblical scenes in one chapter. The case studies also indicate the range of current contexts for displaying early Christian sarcophagi around the world, from historical reuse as medieval church furniture to objects in modern archaeological museums.[14]

This will not be an archaeological analysis concerned with identifying workshops or sources of marble, though there is clearly more work to be done in this area.[15] Instead this will focus on the ancient viewers of these monuments, attempting to reconstruct the kinds of complex connections and meanings created by their arrangements of motifs.[16] There is reason to believe that locally made works could be especially likely to show evidence of client influence, so these sarcophagi could give a particular insight into choices made by the fourth-century people who commissioned them.

Sarcophagi with biblical imagery typically juxtapose multiple abbreviated scenes from different narratives. They have not been viewed sufficiently as whole monuments, with few complete reconstructions of individual viewings attempted in depth and in their cultural context, apart from the most spectacular example of the sarcophagus of Junius Bassus.[17] Scholarship has focused on Christian sarcophagi as sources of iconography, identifying and comparing individual scenes not only across different monuments but also with other art forms such as painting or mosaic.[18] While this has

---

[12] On sarcophagi in Italy: Koch and Sichtermann 1982, 267, 276–95. Koch 2012a proposes a methodology for distinguishing local works from exports. For other pre-Christian sarcophagi in Italy, see the chapters by Vatta, Ciliberto, Sapelli and Valbruzzi in Koch and Baratte 2012; for Sicily, Tusa 1995 and Sodini in Koch and Baratte 2012; for Sardinia, Pesce 1957 and Teatini 2011. On early Christian/late antique sarcophagi in Italy: Koch 2000, 363–6 and 368–71 on exports, and 444–65 on local production; Dresken-Weiland 2003, 147–9, 345–50; RS 2 is the main catalogue that includes early Christian sarcophagi around Italy (amongst other locations): 83–103 for local works.

[13] I rely to a large extent on Koch's judgement about whether a sarcophagus is likely to be a Roman export or a local work, though analysis of the reliefs can offer some additional thoughts.

[14] On the later reception of sarcophagi from Late Antiquity to the present day: Elsner 2009; Prado-Villar 2011; Huskinson 2011; 2015, 245–96; Zanker and Ewald 2012, 1–21; Couzin 2019.

[15] On the workshop issue for Roman sarcophagi in general: Russell 2011; 2013, 256–310; Galinier 2013; Koortbojian 2019.

[16] On viewing and viewers in Roman and late antique art, see for example Elsner 1995; 2007; Birk and Poulsen 2012.

[17] Malbon 1990; Elsner 2008.

[18] Recent works include Dresken-Weiland 2010 and Jensen 2011.

produced invaluable insights into representation across media and between art and text, there is more to be done to reconstruct how these motifs interacted on single sarcophagi, as three-dimensional monuments including their lids and short ends, and visually as well as in reference to scripture.[19]

Pre-Christian sarcophagi are understood as prestigious monuments that display the status, wealth and virtues of the deceased, and their cultural belonging. Christian sarcophagi, however, are seen as reflecting primarily the owner's religious faith, in a fundamental break with the past. For example, in the three monographs on sarcophagi published in English in the last twenty years (none of which focuses principally on Christian sarcophagi), the religious identity professed by Christian imagery is considered to exclude traditional culture and display.[20] This dichotomy is encouraged by their separate treatment in the catalogues, and the terms defined by the debates over eschatology versus 'classicism and culture' in the field of Roman funerary art – not to mention the very origins of the discipline of early Christian archaeology in the apologetic climate of the Counter-Reformation.[21]

Despite recognition that the aesthetics and ways of viewing biblical sarcophagi can already be seen developing in previous centuries, they tend to be described in less positive terms, and their potential for visual complexity can be undervalued.[22] Non-Christian third-century sarcophagi with increasingly 'highly concentrated' images are seen as providing extended opportunity for creating meaning through association, for viewers with a 'heightened receptivity to extranarrative meanings', while increasing numbers of figures signify a need for greater complexity.[23] While earlier sarcophagi therefore seem increasingly geared to provide rich material for a skilled observer to interpret, Christian sarcophagi from subsequent decades are described as 'crowded', whose dense decoration's primary purpose is to surround the deceased with as many salvific images as possible.[24] Individual biblical motifs are 'as easy as possible to read', with fixed meanings tied to the biblical text and therefore no room for ambiguity.[25] The meanings produced by juxtaposition are 'simple' and 'uncomplicated', though often lacking any clear programme in the choice of images.[26]

---

[19] See Hay 2019; Elsner 2012 on the form and function of sarcophagi; Huskinson 2015, 105–10 on viewing the isolated motifs of strigillated sarcophagi together. Grabar 1968, 8 on the 'image-signs' of early Christian art pointing to the biblical narratives.

[20] Zanker and Ewald 2012, 265–6; Birk 2013, 113; Huskinson 2015, e.g. 209.

[21] The *ASR* series largely covers the non-Christian, and *RS* the Christian. Cumont 1942 and Nock 1946 defined the religion vs culture divide. On the origins of early Christian archaeology, see Frend 1996 and Hirschfield 2008.

[22] See Elsner 2012, 192–3 and Huskinson 2015, 237 for hints that Christian imagery was dependent on earlier ways of reading sarcophagus reliefs. Brilliant 1984, 163 and Koortbojian 1995, ch. 8 on typology on pre-Christian sarcophagi.

[23] Brilliant 1984, 163–4; Zanker and Ewald 2012, 248–9.

[24] Though writing from different perspectives, Malbon 1990, 17 and Zanker and Ewald 2012, 265 both describe the Christian sarcophagi as 'crowded'. Zanker and Ewald 2012, 264 on the large number of scenes on Christian sarcophagi linked to hopes for salvation; also Huskinson 2015, 236.

[25] Zanker and Ewald 2012, 264–5; Huskinson 2015, 209.

[26] Huskinson 2015, 216–17; Zanker and Ewald 2012, 264: 'No coherent programme can be found in the choice of biblical scenes . . . despite many attempts to do so.'

Considering the continuous and pervasive culture of *paideia* in Late Antiquity, it is not self-evident that decoration created to engage with the viewer by testing their powers of interpretation, as for previous generations within a competitive culture of learning, would be any less desirable. *Paideia*, the Graeco-Roman intellectual culture of the elite, was increasingly important in Late Antiquity as a marker of status for Christians and non-Christians alike.[27] Other aspects of late antique art have been interpreted in terms of *paideia*, with visual games and jokes included for the knowledgeable viewer, which would ultimately testify to the erudition of the patron.[28] The *Imagines* of Philostratus provide a glimpse of the kind of education Romans could receive in artistic interpretation, but anyone acquainted with elite culture would be acculturated to follow visual prompts and notice references.[29] In Late Antiquity especially, readers and viewers were trained to see and read more than was there whether in art or text, a trend also observed in the development of sarcophagus reliefs immediately prior to the first Christian imagery, alongside increasing numbers of intellectual figures like philosophers and muses.[30]

Reordered and juxtaposed motifs from a wide variety of biblical sources could similarly offer a wealth of potential interconnections to contemplate, relying on viewers' cultural and literary knowledge.[31] This method of representation is certainly not the clearest way to simply illustrate the story of salvation, and the degree to which the meaning of biblical texts was fixed and not open to interpretation should be questioned.[32] There are very few identical arrangements, so the potential for different combinations seems limitless. Just as the study of the Bible was the highest point of Christian *paideia* for the Church Father Origen, perhaps biblical scenes on sarcophagi could also be interpreted through this lens.[33] Such imagery could signify not just religious identity, but through complex interactions could take part in displaying the cultural knowledge of the deceased. Social status could be expressed not just in the rich clothing and jewellery of the portraits, but in the specific application of the biblical reliefs that surround them.[34]

---

[27] On *paideia* in Late Antiquity, see for example Kaster 1988; Bowersock 1990; Averil Cameron 1991; Brown 1992; Cribiore 2001; Alan Cameron 2004; also Averil Cameron 1997; Watts 2012; and Ramelli 2015 for useful introductions. On Christians and *paideia*: Jaeger 1961; Young 2006; Chin 2008; Nasrallah 2010, e.g. 50; Schwartz 2013; Stefaniw 2019.

[28] On aspects of *paideia* and elite culture in late antique art: Bassett 1996; 2008; Thomas 2002; 2016; Leader-Newby 2004; Stirling 2005; Kiilerich 2016. On private statuary collections in late Roman Italy: Stirling 2005, 173–8.

[29] Brown 1980, 22: 'an art that assumed onlookers who could supply the associations "triggered off" by a few clear pointers'.

[30] Onians 1999, 261–7 on seeing more in late antique art; Pelttari 2014 on the distinctive new space for the reader in late antique poetry. Brilliant 1984, 164 on reading 'out' from later sarcophagus reliefs (but not in reference to Christian sarcophagi); Huskinson 1999 on intellectual figures on Christian sarcophagi.

[31] See Grabar 1968, 8 on image-signs appealing 'above all to the intellect'.

[32] For appreciation of the complexity of Christian visual typologies, see Grabar 1968, 128–46 and Tkacz 2002 (both later material) and Malbon 1990.

[33] Gregory Thaumaturgus, *Oratio panegyrica* 7–15; Laistner 1951, 60–1.

[34] Zanker and Ewald 2012, 264–5. Couzin 2014 on the expense of Christian sarcophagi.

This chapter will consider how the sculptors of Christian sarcophagi created complex layers of meaning using biblical motifs, using juxtaposition, symmetry and iconographic parallels, within the formal structure of the sarcophagus, to compare, contrast and prompt interpretations by the attentive viewer. Such sarcophagi have been assumed to be crowded yet ultimately simple objects; close analysis of their visual programmes and strategies will show them to be complex and coherent.[35] We will see Christian iconography interacting with pre-Christian artistic concerns in thoughtful ways, and still actively engaging in the same cultural world, as much across Italy as in the metropolis.[36]

The study of Late Antiquity has been especially defined by its art, with changes in style and divergence from classical standards in some spheres seen as symptomatic of more general cultural, economic and political deterioration. The distinctiveness of late antique art has furthermore helped to define the period as worthy of study in its own right.[37] Challenging the narrative of artistic decline therefore traditionally has wider implications for late antique historiography, which this chapter will attempt by setting aside the contentious (and frequently subjective) issues of style.

Case studies will be made of the most complete surviving sarcophagi with multiple biblical scenes (with reference to other examples), to give the most complete view possible of how monuments would have been viewed in their entirety, and of the potential interaction between motifs.[38] This chapter will take the opportunity to pursue depth over breadth, and argue for the intrinsic value of previously denigrated late antique, local and Christian artworks, as well as their utility for understanding cultures and societies.

Since it has historically been easier to appreciate the skill and complexity of earlier sarcophagi, especially those with mythological scenes, it will be helpful to begin with one such example to introduce some aspects of the visual strategies that would be developed on early Christian sarcophagi.

A Roman sarcophagus in the Musei Capitolini (Figs 15.1–3) dates from the late second century AD and is decorated with scenes of Meleager and the Calydonian boar hunt.[39] As with many sarcophagi, the main relief can largely be read from left to right, in the same direction as a text. It starts with discussions before the hunt,

---

[35] Recent scholarship on late Latin literature increasingly emphasises unity over fragmentation, which is comparable to the argument made here for the coherency of each sarcophagus over the multiplicity of scenes usually emphasised; e.g. Kauffman 2020.

[36] For more on this theme in relation to Christian sarcophagi from Rome and southern France, see Hay 2019.

[37] Riegl 1901; Marrou 1949, 693; Brown 1980, 17; Elsner 2002, 362–3.

[38] The focus on snapshots from biblical or apocryphal narratives, above the more static images of disciples (particularly popular standing in rows in the second half of the fourth century) is of course slightly artificial; shepherds could also evoke biblical imagery depending on the context or viewer. However, the focus here is on the interaction of scenes from clearly identifiable biblical narratives. As is most typical for fourth-century sarcophagi, none of the case studies features solely the Old Testament in isolation from the New; hence their identification as 'Christian' rather than potentially Jewish.

[39] *ASR* 12.6 cat. 12. See Brilliant 1984, 145–61 and Lorenz 2011 on Meleager sarcophagi.

Figure 15.1 Frieze sarcophagus with Meleager and the Calydonian boar hunt. c. AD 190, Rome. Musei Capitolini, Palazzo Nuovo, Sala del Fauno, inv. no. 822. Photo: D-DAI-ROM-72.694 (G. Singer).

Figure 15.2 Left short end with men carrying nets in preparation for the hunt. c. AD 190, Rome. Musei Capitolini, Palazzo Nuovo, Sala del Fauno, inv. no. 822. Photo: D-DAI-ROM-62.804 (H. Koppermann).

leading up to Meleager spearing the boar, surrounded by his companions; the short ends of the coffin illustrate additional scenes in shallower relief. On the lid there is a complementary yet subsidiary relief of putti hunting various animals, framed by mask acroteria.

Figure 15.3 Right short end with Atalanta and Meleager. c. AD 190, Rome. Musei Capitolini, Palazzo Nuovo, Sala del Fauno, inv. no. 822. Photo: D-DAI-ROM-62.805 (H. Koppermann).

The use of the lid (and short ends, if decorated) to form a level of commentary on the main relief has been noted as a feature of some Roman sarcophagi.[40] For example, on another Meleager sarcophagus in Istanbul, Brilliant points out the depiction of a cooking-fire on the lid, directly above Meleager's mother on the main relief, recalling the fire by which she will cut short her son's life.[41] On the Capitoline sarcophagus, the link between body and lid is signalled primarily by the figure of Meleager killing the boar; directly above, an identically posed putto strikes his own boar, highlighted against the densest patch of vegetation.[42]

This overt parallel prompts viewers to look for further connections. The natural balance of the monument suggests another link in the symmetrically opposed putto hunting a bear; in this case the hunted animal is above the first appearance of Meleager, while the hunter is above the goddess Artemis. Although the figures in the main frieze face in opposite directions and are divided between two scenes, the lid stretching over them seems to foretell the future fulfilment of Artemis' revenge and Meleager's tragic fate. The lid adds to the strong theme of the inevitability of fate that characterises Meleager's story, with the symbolic outcome of the myth already playing out in the upper sphere. This connection can only be understood after first noticing

---

[40] Brilliant 1984, 162–3; Elsner 2011, 2; Zanker and Ewald 2012, 50–1.
[41] *ASR* 12.6 cat. 81; Brilliant 1984, 157.
[42] The paralleled positions are noted in *ASR* 12.6 cat. 12, 90 and Elsner 2018a, 373.

the two boar scenes, and thus represents a rather typically Graeco-Roman undercutting of triumph with the anticipation of tragedy.

Another significant pair on the lid is the putto hunting the ostrich with bow and arrow, the only hunter not armed with a spear. The hunter famously characterised by such weapons (and wielding them in her other appearances on this sarcophagus) is Atalanta directly below. Like the ostrich, she is known for her speed in running, and the unique costume she wears in this depiction even includes feathers sprouting from her helmet.[43] As with the first Meleager, she stands below not the hunter but the prey; below the hunting putto is King Oeneus, who is gesturing to Atalanta and challenging her place as a woman in the hunt. The position of his gesture below the putto's arrow visualises the querying of her status as a wounding action, weaponising her sex and turning her distinctive 'feminine' weapons back on herself.[44] This is the only scene not framed by trees on both sides, which mirrors the setting of the discussion below outside the hunt in the 'forest thick with trees' (one damaged tree is visible at the far right), and underscores the framing of Atalanta as an outsider by the king.[45]

The central putto hunts above the figure identified as Orcus, the god of the Underworld, conjuring up the image of death which hunts after all living things.[46] Meanwhile in the final pair on the far right, the putto's spear broadly mimics the direction of the hunter's below but reversed, so that the fallen figure below inadvertently finds himself in the position of the hunted animal. Overall this upper frieze, acting as a commentary on the main relief, frequently aligns the hunters with the hunted and pictures them as potential prey. This corresponds with the theme of such tragic hunting myths as Meleager or Adonis that made them apparently so fitting for funerary decoration: the beautiful hero in his prime yet entirely at the mercy of the gods. All people are prey to the whims of fate.

The creation of meaning through juxtaposition and parataxis would become increasingly important on fourth-century sarcophagi as abbreviated scenes became favoured over long narratives, though their ensembles are not typically credited with as much sophistication.

Roman Exports

The first category of sarcophagi in use in fourth-century Italy is monuments completed in Roman workshops and exported to other parts of the peninsula and major islands.[47] Roman manufacture accounts for the vast majority of the surviving corpus of Christian sarcophagi, and in most areas of Italy, imports from Rome outnumber

---

[43] *ASR* 12.6 cat. 12, 89 notes the unique costume.
[44] In Ovid's rendition, after Atalanta succeeds in claiming the first blood from the boar, one of the male hunters explicitly attempts to denigrate her 'feminine' weapons (just before his grisly death): 'O warriors, learn how much better a man's weapons are than a girl's, and leave the work to me!' Ov. *Met.* 8.392–3.
[45] Ov. *Met.* 8.329.
[46] Lorenz 2011, 316 and n. 24.
[47] Sarcophagi thought to have been made in Rome are described with the term 'stadtrömische' in German scholarship.

local works at least two or three to one. Roman works are often recognisable from their style and quality of execution, as is the case for the two examples to be considered here. Without further work in this area, it can be difficult to distinguish between exported and local works for monuments that survive in poorer condition. As categorised by Koch, the largest numbers of Roman exports are found in central Italy to the west of the Apennines, especially in the area north of Rome.[48] In the last third of the fourth century, the main destination for exports moves to the northern cities, following the movement of the ruling elite.[49]

The dating of exported Roman sarcophagi follows that of the monuments that remained in the metropolis. The first additions of biblical imagery appeared in the late third century, amongst more 'secular' or 'neutral' figures such as shepherds or philosophers (the sarcophagus from Santa Maria Antiqua in the Roman Forum is probably the most famous example).[50] Then for approximately the first two thirds of the fourth century, biblical scenes appear in large numbers, often with several juxtaposed in close succession on frieze sarcophagi, or occupying panels between fluted decoration on strigillated types, or, from the mid-century, between the pillars of columnar sarcophagi.

Two of the larger and more complete monuments that survive are also two of the most geographically disparate: one to the east of the peninsula, and the other at the southern tip of Sicily. The transport costs presented by the obstacles of the Apennines and the Mediterranean suggest they were perhaps ordered by particularly wealthy clients, as do their comparatively large size and high quality of execution, which appear to have aided their preservation by rendering them attractive monuments for later reuse. The fact that both survive with lids means that we may attempt to reconstruct more complete viewings.

Osimo

The first example provides an entry point for considering the biblical motifs alongside secular imagery, in this case of hunting, a theme shared with the Meleager sarcophagus just discussed. The sarcophagus from Osimo (Fig. 15.4) is a probable Roman export, thought to have been made in Rome around 320.[51] This is one of the few metropolitan sarcophagi transported east of the Apennines.[52] It is now in the crypt of the cathedral of San Leopardo, reused as a tomb for local martyrs since 1513.

---

[48] Based on the list compiled by Koch 2000, 368–71, there are approximately thirty-three fourth-century Roman exported sarcophagi or fragments in central/western Italy excluding Ostia (as per modern regions: twenty in Lazio, five in Umbria, eight in Tuscany), twenty-one in the north including Ravenna, nine in the east, six in Sicily, two in Sardinia and two in Campania, south of which there are no others on the mainland. I have omitted the Boville Ernica and Capua examples that Koch includes with question marks, as I agree with his opinion expressed elsewhere that these are likely to be local works (discussed in the next section).

[49] Koch 2000, 363–6 for dating of individual sarcophagi.

[50] RS 1.747.

[51] RS 2.185; ASR 1.2 (1980) cat. 59 pl. 94, 1; Koch 2000, 279, 347–8, 365: all with further bibliography.

[52] Koch and Sichtermann 1982, 267.

Figure 15.4 Frieze sarcophagus with hunting scenes, and biblical scenes on the lid. c. AD 320, made in Rome. Osimo, Duomo di San Leopardo, crypt. Photo: D-DAI-ROM-75.998 (C. Rossa).

The later carving of two peacocks on the back was probably executed locally in the post-Justinian period.[53] This supports the proposed export of the piece in antiquity, providing a *terminus ante quem* for its departure from Rome. The fact that the lid is fractionally bigger than the casket does not mean that they do not belong together, as this is not unusual among pieces whose shared origin is not questioned.

Combinations of hunting and Christian imagery are known among Roman sarcophagi, usually with the hunting scenes on the lid; this is the only extant example with an entirely Christian lid and entirely hunting-themed body.[54] The juxtaposition permits the patron to commemorate their Christian culture alongside the aristocratic pastime of hunting, a particular status marker in Late Antiquity.[55] In the *RS* catalogue only the biblical motifs are illustrated in detail, in accordance with the volume's interest in 'Christian' images, but, as we shall see, they are best understood together.

The casket is made out of stripy marble with three darker veins running horizontally across (clearer in colour images); as with other late Roman examples, the stone's natural veining seems carefully aligned to the coffin's orientation and carved

---

[53] *RS* 2.185.
[54] E.g. *RS* 1.6 with hunting on half of the lid and biblical scenes on the body; also *RS* 3.220 with graphic hunt scenes on the short ends, and Jesus and the disciples on the front. See Birk 2013, 111–13, in comparison with a lion-hunt sarcophagus reused by Christians in Rome.
[55] Compare the later sarcophagus of Junius Bassus (dated 359), with Christian imagery and inscription on the main front, and a 'secular' inscription and scenes such as dining on the lid; *RS* 1.680; Malbon 1990, 149.

decoration, and was therefore likely a desirable visual effect.[56] Here the stripes run roughly at the level of the human heads, beneath the bodies of the horses, and along the very bottom where animals are set upon by dogs. They divide the front into different zones broadly marked by humans, then horses, and finally the dogs and prey, fittingly reinforcing societal hierarchies through an expensive and thus especially status-enhancing aesthetic effect.

The sarcophagus reflects the standard repertory of fourth-century hunting scenes: to the left, a boar is attacked, and to the right, deer are driven into a net.[57] Most of the hunters ride horses, as befits the elite connotations of their pastime; the central rider is distinguished by his flowing cape and portrait features and is probably the deceased in heroic guise. His depiction follows the type used previously for the hero Hippolytus (itself related to imperial art), which had been used to represent nobles since the early third century, when the popularity of mythological subjects waned.[58]

On some similar examples, it is the central rider that spears the boar as does Hippolytus, though other times, as here, it is a dismounted figure on the far left.[59] As an unusually brave way of hunting such a dangerous animal, this distinctive representation inevitably recalls the earlier sarcophagus depictions of Meleager, always notably on foot; his stance and the surrounding figures match numerous earlier monuments exactly. Meleager continued to be a popular figure in domestic art into Late Antiquity, so the resemblance could be expected to be recognised.[60]

In contrast to the hunt's single narrative, the lid comprises numerous biblical scenes, but placed one after another so that this is not immediately obvious to the untrained eye. Although closely juxtaposed and overlapping, they are carefully arranged. The left side is occupied by New Testament and apocryphal scenes of the Adoration of the Magi and the rock miracle of Peter, while the Old Testament tales of Noah and Jonah are confined to the right.[61] The innermost figures of Peter and Noah turn towards the centre, while the larger narratives move outwards, the magi's procession to the left and Jonah's journey to the right.[62]

Apart from the Nativity, the images all involve water. Noah's Ark and Jonah's boat occupy the same sea, which can be imagined extending beyond the tabula, merging

---

[56] E.g. *RS* 1.86 (horizontal to highlight two registers); La Rocca and Presicce 2010, no. 5 (horizontal on lid and diagonal on strigillated body); *RS* 1.239 (horizontal through strigillation). Van Keuren et al. 2011, 181 on stripy Proconnesian marble sarcophagi in Rome.

[57] *ASR* 1.2; compare cat. 3 and 112 with similar fourth-century compositions.

[58] Zanker and Ewald 2012, 222–3.

[59] Zanker and Ewald 2012, 222–3 and 344–8 on the Hippolytus hunter type.

[60] Simon 1970; see *RS* 3.220 for similar Meleager-type hunters on a Christian sarcophagus.

[61] Matt. 2:1–12; *Passio ss. Processi et Martinianii*; Gen. 6–9; Jonah 1–2 and 4:6. See *RS* 2.181 for a lid probably exported from Rome to Genoa with a similar layout including the Jonah scenes, but with twin Victories framing the tabula rather than Peter and Noah.

[62] Scenes of Jonah are quite common on the lids of sarcophagi exported from Rome (as they are on sarcophagi that remained there): two lid fragments from the turn of the fourth century each include the composite scene of Jonah cast out of the boat and under the gourd (*RS* 2.173, 187), while the lid of a columnar sarcophagus dating from around 360–80 has the same three scenes on the right of the Osimo lid, though in this case spread across both sides (*RS* 2.123).

with the water Peter elicits from the rock.[63] Thus, interestingly, Peter seems to produce the water that flows back through time, from the water-producing rock to the prophet's rocky shore — especially as the order of the Old Testament scenes follows this left-to-right flow. Through Rome's chief saint 'setting the scene' for his predecessors, the lid presents the Old Testament as subsidiary to Christianity. Noah even unusually cups his hand to receive the olive branch from the dove, as the soldiers cup their hands to receive water from the rock, positioning the patriarch as a supplicant like the soldiers, while Peter opposite is the active accomplisher of the miracle.

One starting point for possible connections between the lid and casket is the inscription panel, where patrons had the option of naming the deceased, and the rider below who has been given portrait features of the deceased.[64] Another link may be found with the next most prominent character, the Meleager figure who is especially dominant here. He appears on a slightly larger scale than the other humans, and the shorter tree compared to other examples emphasises his stature; the adjacent rider also looks back at him despite preparing to throw a rock in the opposite direction. The position of this tall figure permits comparison with the diminutive figure of Jesus above. Both are the heroes of their narratives, though they represent different if not contrasting aspects of virtue: a legendary model of physical strength, juxtaposed with the archetypal 'power . . . made perfect in weakness'.[65] Knowledgeable viewers might find other points of comparison; for example, both heroes were betrayed, resulting in their premature though preordained deaths.

There are other intriguing resonances between the very different iconographies of body and lid. On the main casket, the horses and mounted riders gallop to the right, while on the lid the camels and dismounted Magi move to the left. The inverted depictions draw attention to their contrasting actions: threatening violent death to their quarry, and paying peaceful homage to new life. Hunting had traditionally been an erotic allegory of man's pursuit of woman, so there must be a knowing irony in the inverse to the hunting riders being the dismounted search for the virgin birth. In the context of a high-status tomb, these apparent opposites perhaps represent the balanced virtues of the patron, pious and valiant, able to take part equally in different spheres of culture. The contrast between life and death is also particularly appropriate for funerary decoration.[66]

Turning our attention to the right end, we observe a similar visual parallel. On the lid, the *ketos* ejects Jonah on to a sloping rock beneath the gourd; below, a man traps a deer by driving it into a curving net beneath a tree; the hollows of Jonah's rock even subtly echo the holes in the net.[67] The two appearances of the *ketos* also correspond

---

[63] Against this it can be noted that there is a small but defined break between the right side of the tabula and the water in front of the Ark; however, the water from Peter's rock does flow down and to the right (as far as the bottom edge shown by the cupped hands of the lower soldier), so it does align with the level of the Old Testament water.

[64] The extant text was added in the eighteenth century.

[65] 2 Cor. 12:9.

[66] There is also a life/death contrast between the two elevated, spherical rocks on the left-hand side: the one on the casket about to wound the boar, the one on the lid bringing forth life-giving water.

[67] A contemporary hunting sarcophagus (*ASR* 1.2 cat. 112) has matching curved nets on the same side of the lid and body, providing a more straightforward parallel for the matching sweep of rock and net here.

closely to the positions of the two deer directly below, the first with its head turned back to the left, the second continuing to the right. Again, the corresponding motions highlight the differing ends of life and death, with the dynamic between man and beast also reversed. Together they evoke an idealised world where people have the upper hand over the natural world, whether by divine assistance or human ingenuity (or both).[68]

This theme continues around the sarcophagus. There are trees at three of the corners: at either side of the body and right of the lid. At the remaining corner, the prominent top left position, is Mary's chair, made of wicker. A chair woven from plants in place of more rudimentary trees, in the context of the Nativity, seems to visualise the transformation or taming of nature entailed in the Incarnation.[69] The woven material of the chair is echoed in the various ropes that lead the camels, restrain the wind-blown sails and ensnare the deer, all designed to control nature. The Incarnation could be seen as the hinge for the rest of the interaction between humans and nature already described: a world where the relationship of superiority between humankind and nature has been restored, following the intervention of God in the natural world. Though depictions of wild-animal hunts hardly constitute what many today might consider a strictly biblical exposition on the Incarnation, to a fourth-century Roman for whom hunting represented a noble leisure activity, this could be a logical way of understanding their world.[70]

Hunting had long been popular on Roman sarcophagi, yet while earlier imperial examples focus on the tragic stories of mythological hunters such as Actaeon, Adonis and Meleager, those from the fourth century most often depict the patron himself and his retinue engaged in hunting as a pastime. The pathos that characterised the earlier themes is exchanged for triumph. The Osimo sarcophagus suggests a way of contextualising this transformation of the genre within the redemption of creation proclaimed by Christianity in Late Antiquity (whether or not a particular patron would have described themselves as a Christian). Violence was often inherent in earlier Roman depictions of landscape, which warned of the dangerous powers that lay in nature.[71] In a restored Christian world, all nature is symbolically set in order and poses no threat to the humans who steward it. Clearly the hunt represents a very Roman vision of a new earth, involving rather more violence than the biblical images.[72] The intermingling of

---

[68] The angle of the boar-hunter's driving arm is especially acute when compared with other examples. This provides a counterpart to the upward sweeps of the right-hand edges. While not as pronounced, the gesture of the Magus to the star on the upper edge provides the corresponding diagonal on the left of the lid, especially as the Magus is in mirror image to Peter reaching up to strike the rock, in turn balancing Noah.

[69] The theme of woven and tamed nature might also extend to the first Magus's gift, since, although too damaged here to tell for sure, in other iterations he often carries a foliate wreath.

[70] Compare *RS* 1.6, where miracles of Jesus are illustrated below the hunting scene. The traditional understanding of non-mythological hunting as an allegory for male *virtus* helps us to see the hunting here as an allegory for the natural order more generally; Zanker and Ewald 2012, 222–3, 254–5. This makes it more ironic (and therefore intellectually satisfying to the viewer) that in this scheme the hunt's typically masculine subjugation of nature hinges on the sole woman and child depicted.

[71] Newby 2012.

[72] Isa. 11:6–7 and 65:25 imply an end to predation in the author's vision of Paradise.

worldly and eschatological meaning in hunting imagery demonstrates how unhelpful it can be to distinguish between cultural and religious concerns in Roman funerary imagery. While hunting and biblical imagery have typically been seen as belonging to completely different worlds, the Osimo sarcophagus shows how hunting could have potential eschatological significance, while biblical imagery could play a part in enhancing social status.[73]

It remains unknown whether the lid and body were planned together in the Roman workshop (whether by client request or the imagination of the sculptors) and imported as one piece; whether the body and lid were produced separately to stock (as individually they are quite typical in terms of iconography) and chosen to sit alongside each other to bring out the themes discussed; or whether one was produced to a standard repertory and the other designed to align with it. It has been demonstrated that production-to-stock was far from the norm, though whether this was the same for those who lived far from Rome is less clear.[74]

It seems inescapable that to whatever degree the parallels were planned in advance, the choice to pair these two pieces was carefully made. The fourth-century viewer would be encouraged by the visual pointers to interpret the imagery together, establishing a channel of elite communication between patron and viewer. The later carving on the back, of symmetrical peacocks drinking serenely from a cross-topped font, also seems to partake in the theme of nature set in order through Christ; though added some centuries later, it attests to continuing engagement with the decorative scheme.

Syracuse

While the biblical scenes on the Osimo sarcophagus were confined to the lid, there are numerous exported Roman sarcophagi that have multiple biblical scenes across the main casket, including friezes as well as strigillated and columnar types.[75] To reach the example that stands out in terms of sheer number of scenes and state of preservation, as the only one whose lid survives, we travel south across the sea to the city of Syracuse in Sicily.

The sarcophagus of Adelphia (Fig. 15.5), so-called from the inscription probably added with a subsequent fifth-century burial, is thought to be a mid-fourth-century import from Rome.[76] It is a rare example where the details of its findspot are known, having been discovered buried in the city catacombs in 1872, within a large wall niche that had columns and an architrave added in the late fourth century, contemporaneously

---

[73] E.g. Birk 2013, 113 on hunting as social status and Christian imagery as heavenly status. See below, p. 435 for examples of elision between 'secular' shepherds and biblical imagery.

[74] Russell 2011 and Koortbojian 2019.

[75] Friezes: *RS* 2.10, 12, 20, 59, 60, 62 (the latter possibly local), and fragments including 17, 21, 26, 29; strigillated: *RS* 2.91, 96, 101, 108 and fragment 99; columnar: *RS* 2.122, 123 (on the lid only), 124. Also *RS* 2.145, a Bethesda type, and 181, a lone lid with biblical scenes. The late fourth-century city-gate types will be treated later in the discussion.

[76] *RS* 2.20; Tusa 1995, 87–91; Greco et al. 1998, including 32 for full bibliography; Koch 2000, 273 and 357. There are two small but similar fragments in Sardinia and Viterbo: *RS* 2.23 and 25.

Figure 15.5 Double-register frieze sarcophagus 'of Adelphia' with biblical scenes. Mid-fourth century AD, made in Rome. Syracuse, Museo archeologico regionale Paolo Orsi, inv. no. 864. Photo: D-DAI-ROM-71.859 (G. Singer).

to the similar monumentalisation of the catacombs in Rome.[77] However, it is unclear whether the fourth-century burial was located in the same setting.

The format of the lid is similar to the Osimo sarcophagus, with another version of the Nativity with Magi on the opposite side, and traditional erotes framing the tabula rather than biblical figures. While having the main body filled with biblical scenes is more typical of surviving sarcophagi from the first two thirds of the fourth century, the less common two-register format shows the full potential of the biblical frieze type, for those who could afford the expense of figural decoration on this scale.

To the untrained eye, it may appear a visually overwhelming assortment, intermingling Old and New Testaments. However, there is method behind the medley. Scenes involving Mary fill the lid, and the motif under the portrait shell. The remaining four sections of frieze progress from Old to New Testament from left to right within each segment. Each quarter starts with the Old Testament: Adam and Eve put to work, the sacrifice of Isaac, the idol of Nebuchadnezzar, and Adam and Eve with the Tree of the Knowledge of Good and Evil.[78] Moving to the right, each then features at least one story from the life of Jesus: the prediction of Peter's betrayal and the healing of the bleeding woman; the healing of the blind man, the multiplication of loaves and fishes, and the raising of Jairus' daughter; the water-into-wine miracle at Cana; and the entry into Jerusalem.[79] The exception to this scheme is Moses receiving

---

[77] Sgarlata 2003; Trout 2015, 115.
[78] Gen. 3:17–23; Gen. 22:1–19; Dan. 3:1–18; Gen. 3:1–7.
[79] Betrayal: Matt. 26:33–5/Mark 14:29–31/Luke 22:33–4/John 13:36–8; bleeding woman: Matt. 9:20–2/Mark 5:25–34/Luke 8:43–8; blind man: Mark 8:22–6/John 9:1–12 (plus other stories of healed blind men); multiplication: Matt. 14:13–21/Mark 6:31–44/Luke 9:12–17/John 6:1–14; Jairus' daughter: Matt. 9:18–26/Mark 5:21–43/Luke 8:40–56; Cana: John 2:1–11; entry: Matt. 21:1–11/Mark 11:1–11/Luke 19:28–44/John 12:12–19.

the Law, at the right of the top left quarter.[80] This scene is frequently paired with the sacrifice of Isaac opposite, both reaching up over the portrait, which seems to take precedence over chronology.

Each quarter can be read as its own miniature commentary. In the top left segment, God in the Genesis scene uses the same downward gesture as Jesus healing the bleeding woman. As well as indicating the trinitarian nature of God, the segment's internal narrative could be interpreted as God's forgiveness, healing and guidance in the face of the failings, suffering and sin caused by the Fall. This suggests the completion of the Old Testament in the New, a theme seen on the Osimo lid which continues in the other sections here.

In the top right segment, the eye is drawn to the conspicuous lines of the two staffs and the knife. The halted stroke of Abraham's weapon to slaughter Isaac contrasts in particular with the downward gesture of Jesus to raise to life.[81] This is underscored by following the line of the knife out past the other side of the shell, into another downward staff of Jesus accomplishing another miracle (the only other staff, now lost). The narrative here shows that God's mercy in the Old Testament finds fulfilment in the compassion of Jesus' miracles in the New. Interestingly, the sheep in Abraham's scene, the divinely provided substitute for his son, is barely visible (partially hidden behind Abraham's arm and shallowly carved); meanwhile Jesus is positioned behind the altar, which is not always present. The inference is that Jesus is the substitute sacrifice, in line with patristic interpretations of Isaac's sacrifice as prefiguring the Crucifixion.[82]

In the lower left segment, there is further interaction between the Testaments. The three Hebrews turn away from the idol and gesture instead towards the figure of Jesus, and his first miracle of turning the water into wine. The Hebrews appear to turn from the worship of a false god to acknowledge the first miracle of Jesus – the first of John's Signs of Jesus' identity, and frequent symbol for the Eucharist.[83] This narrative even continues beyond this quarter into the miniature scene of the Adoration of the Magi below the portrait. The rear Magus's foot crosses over Jesus', encouraging a continuous reading, while Mary's chair forms a more abrupt division with the lower right segment. The three Hebrews and three Magi are always dressed identically on sarcophagi, forming their own extra-biblical narrative (found only in art) on the rejection of false idols and worship of the true God, and the progression from Old to New Testament.[84] Here too, their offering of gifts to Jesus shows the completion of their journey from false to true worship, in this version via the archetypal miracle and sacrament.

---

[80] Exod. 31:18.

[81] A similar comparison is made on, for example: the Roman export to Soriano nel Cimino near Viterbo (RS 2.60), where Abraham holding Isaac's head follows two scenes of Jesus healing small figures with downward arms; the lid of the sarcophagus of Marcus Claudianus in Rome (RS 1.771); and the possible local work in Capua (discussed below).

[82] Dresken-Weiland 2010, 294–5 on the patristic views.

[83] A similar idea appears on the Claudianus sarcophagus (RS 1.771), where the central orant turns towards the Cana miracle in prayer or praise, signalling their acceptance of Christ. On the sarcophagus from Soriano nel Cimino (RS 2.60), an orant turns towards Jesus multiplying the loaves, which is another scene that foreshadows the Eucharist.

[84] Hay forthcoming.

This does not follow the order in which these events occur chronologically, but visually they are shaped into a completely coherent narrative. Furthermore, the surprise addition to the lower left segment's story, incorporating a structurally separate element, could be a delightful detail for viewers to notice that plays on their expectations. It would be impressed upon them that the patron must be fully *au fait* with the visual and literary tropes of Christian Roman culture, to select a monument that could so confidently engage with and even innovate upon such traditions.

The lower right segment continues the game of visual connections between scenes, this time with Adam and Eve in a depiction of the Fall, followed by Jesus' entry into Jerusalem on the donkey. The only two trees on the sarcophagus form part of each motif: the Tree of the Knowledge of Good and Evil, and the tree which a spectator has climbed (also reminiscent of the story of Zacchaeus).[85] Prompted to interpret this striking repetition, the viewer might contemplate how one tree traps humanity in sin, while the other supports one in viewing the source of salvation (out of a place of sin, if the viewer recalls the Zacchaeus narrative).

While Adam and Eve's nakedness is emblematic of their transformation from innocence to shame, clothing is also important in Jesus' *adventus*, when people laid their cloaks as well as branches on the ground before him; this is made an important element of the depiction here. With the large leaves covering the first couple's nakedness, and the palm branch depicted under the donkey (when most often the donkey's colt is depicted in this space), the shared emphasis of these two scenes is on both nudity/clothing and the trees.

One scene prefigures an exit from Paradise, the other an entry to re-establish salvation. Jesus was described as the New Adam, redeeming humanity following the Fall; here both the Old and New Adams noticeably make the same gesture with their right hands.[86] There is another adjoining figure making this gesture: the portrait of the deceased man in the shell medallion.[87] The decoration thus involves the deceased in the eternal narrative of humanity redeemed and reborn, stretching from its first creation, through the Incarnation, to the fourth century.

These two biblical scenes are not especially constructed as parallel events in Christian commentary, so this could be evidence of a unique visual reflection through this monument. The event with which the Fall is associated in patristic commentary is the Crucifixion, both involving 'trees'; as the suffering of the Crucifixion was not yet considered an appropriate image for elite commemoration, events such as the Entry scene or the raising of Lazarus often stand in its place in the narrative of sarcophagi.[88] Therefore this pairing can also hint at the patristic connection to the undepicted Crucifixion; the tree in the background becomes a proleptic detail, supporting a man in its outstretched branches.

---

[85] Luke 19:1–10.
[86] 1 Cor. 15:45, also 15:22 and Rom. 5:12–21.
[87] The only other figure making this gesture (with the forefinger and middle finger, viewed side on) on the sarcophagus is Jesus healing the blind man directly above this segment. Nebuchadnezzar on the bottom left edge uses a different gesture, with only the forefinger pointing and with the thumb raised.
[88] Dresken-Weiland 2010, 276–8 on the patristic interpretations.

There are various links between different segments around the sarcophagus (some already mentioned): for example, Adam and Eve are repeated on the left in two diagonally opposite segments, unusually with an extra sheaf of wheat added at the feet of Adam in both to accentuate this. All four Old Testament scenes involve some degree of nudity, perhaps stressing the 'primitive' origins of the oldest stories, preceding the fully dressed New Testament fulfilment.[89] The themes of dress and nakedness had a long tradition on Roman sarcophagi as self-referential motifs, on a format designed to clothe a decomposing body.[90] On Christian sarcophagi, the repeating deeply carved folds of cloth create a unique and recognisable texture across the reliefs, so the few nude characters do stand out.

Moreover, the form of the tree at the start of the lower right section recalls the column at the beginning of the lower left scene. Like the tree, the column has a straight shaft, wider base and foliate top thanks to its composite capital (an unusual choice for a statue base); the serpent winding round the tree trunk follows the direction of the column's spiralling flutes.[91] Both carry sources of potential sin in the Old Testament, in the form of the idol and the forbidden fruit, and Nebuchadnezzar and Adam gesture towards them with a similar stance.[92] Such visual links help to keep the eye moving around the relief from one segment to another, creating an endless chain of interpretation that reflects the cultural erudition of the central couple.[93]

Though the lid possibly dates slightly later to the fifth century and was made locally, there was still effort made to create interplay between the different levels of decoration.[94] If the scene on the far left of the lid is the Annunciation, then metaphorically the personified source could be understood as God himself, from whom Mary draws the living water; it is therefore fitting that this is placed above the figures of God (with Adam and Eve), and Nebuchadnezzar's idol.[95] The man in the Annunciation scene even gestures to the source as does the Hebrew adjacent to the idol. Meanwhile on the right side of the lid, Elsner has noted that the woven manger recalls the strigillated sarcophagus in the tier below.[96] Further below, the association of the Entry with the Crucifixion could fit with the theme of death and rebirth conjured by manger and sarcophagus.

---

[89] Nebuchadnezzar is richly dressed, but his image is depicted with exposed chest.
[90] Elsner 2018b.
[91] Kristensen 2014, 275 on the column and capital as atypical for a statue base.
[92] While Nebuchadnezzar is indicating encouragement, Adam could be advising against indulging (since his gesture is closer to Jesus').
[93] The scheme of four segments is found elsewhere on double-register sarcophagi, including one now in Pisa (*RS* 2.12; Koch 2000, 449), probably only moved from Rome in the Middle Ages. It is divided into four quarters dedicated broadly to narratives from Exodus, Jesus' life and stories of Peter, and there are thematic connections between the registers: Peter's water miracle emerges directly below the water of the Red Sea, and the miracle of the quails is situated above miracles of Jesus including the multiplication of loaves, an event which in the Gospels consciously echoes the divine provision of manna and quails.
[94] The repetition of the Magi on both pieces has been one reason for the suggested later dating, but even if this is the case, the repetition of Adam and Eve elsewhere shows that this is not a careless or out-of-place choice, but may similarly be to encourage reading around the sarcophagus.
[95] The other identification of the scene is the deceased drinking from the waters of Wisdom, which would also be appropriate; *RS* 2.20; Greco et al. 1998, 25–8.
[96] Elsner 2012, 184.

While the focus of this analysis is on the biblical scenes, it is the portrait couple that are at the heart of the relief, who epitomise the intention of this rich visual tapestry. The woman wears intricate jewellery, including a wide jewelled necklace and fluted bracelet, and an elaborate hairstyle; her husband (in an ornate toga) gestures assuredly to the scroll in his hand. As in previous centuries, this sarcophagus would have shown off the wealth of the deceased and their confident mastery of visual and literary culture (which now included Christian texts alongside the traditional Roman canon). The culture of learning took on a new significance for Christians, since study of such texts could now assure not just a good earthly reputation, but their own heavenly salvation, again showing the futility of separating culture and religion. Exhibiting this range of biblical scenes in such a complex and interrelated manner assured the viewer of the deceased's comprehensive understanding of the story of salvation, and their complete integration in the culture and aesthetics of Graeco-Roman *paideia*, which had nurtured their fluency in visual interpretation and composition.

Local Works

The possible local creation of the Syracusan lid leads us appropriately to the other origin for fourth-century sarcophagi in Italy, the potential creation of works by local sculptors. While most sarcophagi around fourth-century Italy originated in Rome, some appear to be locally made. It can be difficult to determine with certainty, especially since provincial production largely follows the format of the metropolitan sarcophagi, to varying degrees. Identification relies on differences in execution, as well as some unparalleled variations in iconography or design.[97]

As with the exports, most local works seem to originate from the west of the Apennines, at least before the late fourth century.[98] However, in this earlier period, while the sarcophagi in the area directly north of Rome were by far mostly exports from the city, to the south the sarcophagi have been mainly described as locally produced, from the outskirts of Rome down to Capaccio near Paestum. These are perhaps remaining traces of the earlier history of local manufacture around Rome and in Campania, close enough to the city to take inspiration from the metropolitan models.[99]

The three most complete examples with biblical scenes from the earlier fourth century were found in this area south of Rome, squarely between the two main exports of the previous section. Here the first two from Lazio will be considered, followed by one from Campania. They bear similarities with Roman works, though they include interesting innovations that do not seem merely forced by technical restrictions but appear to create significant readings of their own.

---

[97] Koch 2012a proposes a methodology for identifying locally produced sarcophagi.

[98] Koch 2000, 444–65 describes around eleven locally made fourth-century Christian sarcophagi thought to be from central Italy (including three in Lazio, three in Umbria, three in Tuscany and two now outside Italy whose precise origin is unknown), six in Campania, one in Sicily, one in Corsica and two possible fragments in Sardinia. There are also eleven in northern Italy and another five possible fragments, though these date mostly from the late fourth century.

[99] Koch and Sichtermann 1982, 288–93 on pre-Christian sarcophagus production in Campania.

Indeed, it has been convincingly argued that production-to-stock (completion ahead of customer order) is not typical for sarcophagi, and is thought to have been even less likely in smaller workshops with less capital.[100] The small numbers of local works suggest the presence of only very minor workshops or individual stoneworkers in Italy beyond Rome (who may not even have specialised in sarcophagi), and it is hard to imagine monuments being made ahead of a definite order in these circumstances.[101] They therefore potentially offer some of the strongest evidence of patrons' influence on decoration.

While the case studies of the previous section were two of the most sizeable and impressive examples of exports with biblical scenes, the works considered here will reflect the scale and format of the more 'mid-range' Roman sarcophagi.[102]

Boville Ernica

The sarcophagus from Boville Ernica in Lazio (Fig. 15.6), about sixty miles south-east of Rome, dates from the mid-fourth century.[103] It was found in the early 1940s on the site of a Roman villa near to the ancient site of Boville Ernica, with the remains of a burial and a lamp inside. Soon after its discovery it was reused as an altar in the local church, but has now been moved to a side chapel to the right. Like the Syracuse example, it possibly integrates a body and lid from different sources, though in this case probably the lid was imported, and the main casket made locally. The Osimo sarcophagus provided the chance to consider how biblical motifs could relate to secular figural imagery; here we can see how they could interact with ornamental or non-narrative decoration.

Figure 15.6 Sarcophagus with latticework front, and lid with biblical scenes. Mid-fourth century AD, excavated in Sasso. Boville Ernica, San Pietro Ispano. Photo: D-DAI-ROM-60.1363 (J. Böhringer).

[100] Russell 2011, 127: 'the smaller the workshop . . . the less feasible production-to-stock became'. Koortbojian 2019 also argues for client choice over production-to-stock.
[101] Russell 2013, 359 on the scarcity of stoneworkers by the early fourth century.
[102] Other possible local works include *RS* 2.90, 241, 243.
[103] *RS* 2.63; Koch 1990, 69–70; 2000, 446–8; 2012a, 6–7.

Its design is unique among the surviving corpus, translating into marble a wooden latticework screen that is fastened in the centre and could be wheeled apart – perhaps one of the local craftsman's 'new and uninhibited' features seen as characteristic of late antique art.[104] The regularity of the spacing becomes visibly distorted to the top left of the centre join, implying a less experienced hand. Koch has highlighted the unique lack of upper moulding on the casket as another indication of a local origin, since it is difficult to imagine such a feature being requested by the customer, concluding that the sculptor was not a sarcophagus specialist.[105]

Meanwhile the lid is very typical of Roman workshops; the lack of upper border here too is unusual, but not unparalleled among the metropolitan lids.[106] Importing this element alone would have supplied the biblical narratives that the local stoneworker was not experienced in depicting, while being more economical than transporting an entire work. However, we cannot exclude the possibility that the client had other reasons for commissioning the casket locally, and in any case, economy does not mean that the decoration was not still chosen with care and attention.

On the right is the Nativity with Magi familiar from the same location on the Syracuse sarcophagus (and showing the kind of Roman model for the Syracuse lid if made locally later). Opposite is the narrative of the three Hebrews in the fiery furnace, following their refusal to worship Nebuchadnezzar's idol.[107] As on the lower register in Syracuse, this pairing represents the clear progression from Old to New Testament.[108] However, the Hebrews and Nativity stories are used in different ways on the two sarcophagi to make different points, showing how the meaning of biblical motifs was not completely static, but could be flexible depending on the context.

In this rendition, the solid structures of pillar and furnace on the left contrast with the (similarly rectangular) wicker manger on the right, suggesting a commentary on the unexpected nature of Christian power and divinity, where the pagan edifices constructed to compel worship are superseded by the fragility and poverty of the Nativity, articulated through the material contrast of stone and wood. Moreover, the furnace appears to be fuelled by wooden logs, visible within the arched openings; while the stone consumes the wood as it tries to do with the Hebrew youths, it is actually the wood that provides the power for the stone, just as it is the power behind the Nativity that is working for God's glory through the king's futile attempts to destroy the Hebrews.

It seems that the casket was made subsequently to complement the imported lid, since it displays the same contrast between wood and stone, in the moveable wooden trellis fixed at the right corner by a static carved column. The woodwork front recalls the wickerwork manger, cleverly picturing the sarcophagus itself as a potential place of rebirth, as does the surprising motility of a trellis that can be wheeled aside and

---

[104] Brown 1971, 38. The closest parallel is in San Marino, California, with latticework replacing strigillated panels in between three figures; *ASR* 5.4 cat. 182; Koch 1990. See also the partially preserved short ends of *RS* 3.43 in Arles.

[105] Koch 2012a, 6–7.

[106] Koch 2012a, 7.

[107] Dan. 3.

[108] For more on the significance of this pairing, Hay forthcoming.

folded up, undercutting the solidity of the tomb and finality of death.[109] This all befits the Christian hope for resurrection, following the renewal of the body in the 'death' of baptism, but it also ties into traditional themes of Roman funerary decoration. For example, the lattice on the Roman San Marino sarcophagus is echoed in adjacent openwork baskets; such visual and material interplay was a popular trope on Roman sarcophagi, particularly around the depiction of containers, since the coffin was the ultimate container for the body itself.[110]

The interaction between body and lid continues in the one-sided placement of the column on the right. On the left of the lid, the image of Nebuchadnezzar is set atop a vertically fluted pillar; on the right-hand side, Mary sits directly above the larger vertically fluted column. The unique lack of balancing column on the left only emphasises this.[111] As the mother of Jesus, she is afforded a higher place of honour than the pagan king. This reading fits with the supercession of pagan by Christian and Old Testament by New signified by the juxtaposition of these two scenes, and is intelligible solely from the lid; the body appears rather as a decorative extension of the lid themes. This peculiarity increases the likelihood that the body was made subsequently to complement the imported lid.

Just as the Roman exports to Osimo and Syracuse played with the interaction of materials and textures across their lids and caskets, another interpretation of this theme is executed on this more modest local work. This sarcophagus shows how local patrons and craftsmen could create their own take on the works of the city, extending the comparative strategies of a Roman lid with an original concept for the rest of the casket. Although the sculptor may not have specialised in sarcophagi, the scheme could have been ordered by a client seeking to take part in the creativity of late Roman funerary culture with a novel idea of their own. Sarcophagi with a lower quantity of figural decoration have typically received less scholarly attention, and can be seen as less interesting. However, as has been argued for the less figurative forms of strigillated sarcophagi, this can bring the essential ideas into sharper focus.[112]

Velletri

The front of a Christian sarcophagus in Velletri (Fig. 15.7), nearly twenty-five miles south-east of Rome, dates from the turn of the fourth century and can be found in the local archaeological museum, having previously been located in the cloister of San Lorenzo in the late eighteenth century. It is thought likely to be a local work due to its unique structure and versions of biblical motifs.[113] It could also be a loculus plaque, used to cover the entrance to burial niches in catacombs or mausoleums.

---

[109] The closest parallel in San Marino, California has none of this implicit movement, with thick borders on all four sides of each panel.

[110] Elsner 2012 on sarcophagus decoration and containment; also Hay 2019, 70–5.

[111] Even if we hypothesise that the lack of column could have been linked to the left side being somehow less visible in the original display context, the effect of the single visible column would still be left on the viewer.

[112] Huskinson 2015.

[113] *RS* 2.242; Koch 2000, 446.

Fig. 15.7 Front of a frieze sarcophagus (or loculus plaque) with biblical scenes. c. AD 300. Velletri, Museo civico archeologico Oreste Nardini, inv. no. 171. Photo: D-DAI-ROM-57.783R (photographer unknown).

The slab uses the structure of the metropolitan strigillated sarcophagi, a few of which were exported to this area; the three larger figures of shepherds and an orant (or praying figure with raised palms who might sometimes represent the soul of the deceased) fill the positions of the three figural panels.[114] Yet, instead of strigillated patterns, the intervening fields are filled with various biblical stories. To the left of the orant is Daniel between the lions, alongside a figure with a scroll; below them are two scenes from the Jonah cycle.[115] To the right are Adam and Eve (unusually in *dextrarum iunctio* pose), Noah's Ark, and Jesus multiplying the loaves. The atypical depictions of some of the figures have made valuable iconographical comparanda, but a more comprehensive interpretation of the sarcophagus has not been attempted.

Considering the casket as a whole, numerous connections come into view. There is a kind of circular chronology in a broadly anticlockwise direction from Genesis (Adam and Eve together with Noah), to the prophets Daniel and then Jonah, and finally to Jesus. This timeline, starting from right to left and crossing twice over the central orant, does not follow the most straightforward layout, but is intelligible to the knowledgeable viewer.

The prophet protagonist of the Jonah cycle is repeated three times progressing diagonally downwards along this anticlockwise path, which encourages this circular, mobile viewing. The orant turns their face slightly to their right, following this flow, to the small reader sitting level with their head, who in turn looks towards the biblical

---

[114] Huskinson 2015 on strigillated sarcophagi. *RS* 2.90, 91, 108 and 112 are the most intact strigillated exports from Rome to central Italy; *RS* 2.96 and 101 were exported to the east, and 113 to the north of Italy.

[115] Dan. 6. See *RS* 2.241 and 243 for two probable local Italian works with Jonah as the dominant figure on the main relief.

scenes. The orant could be listening to the reader speaking scripture into being around them. The circular chronology has the effect of enveloping the orant (perhaps representing the deceased) in this biblical narrative, much as the decoration of the casket envelops the corpse.

Links between each side contribute to the encouragement to read comparatively. The watery settings of Jonah and Noah are diagonally opposed and linked by the birds that perch on Noah's hand and Jonah's bower. Meanwhile Daniel is positioned across from Adam and Eve, all standing nudes; their nakedness bears contrasting significance, however, of athletic victory and salvific rebirth on the one hand, but shame, sin, and death on the other.[116] Daniel and Noah also have mirroring poses of prayer (echoed to a lesser extent in the open-armed gesture of Jesus below); thanks to the tiny tree incised between Daniel and the scroll box, one of the lions could almost be carrying a branch in a manner akin to the dove and olive branch.[117] We can think of this as creating a web of associations, encouraging the attentive viewer to seek complex links and contrasts in the decoration of the tomb.

The division of the chronological progression across different fields creates further ways of grouping the figures, and further opportunities for interpretative viewing. To the left are the two prophets (and a figure potentially reading the prophetic words of scripture), escaping from naturally dangerous but divinely tamed animals; to the right, three stories about creation and its restoration, all featuring the animal world (serpent, dove, fish). A uniting theme is the relationship between humanity and nature, to be expressed some years later on the Osimo sarcophagus.

This is a theme that crosses into the larger structural figures thanks to the groups of shepherds and sheep, and there are further connections between these elements and the intervening biblical characters. The central orant is framed by two biblical orants on the same level, Daniel and Noah, somewhat reinforcing the tripartite structure. Christ is dressed in the same manner as the sheep-bearing shepherd on the left, recalling his own role as metaphorical shepherd. Conversely, Jonah reclining under the bower echoes the shepherd on the right resting under a tree, with raised right legs and arms; in place of Jonah's *ketos* rearing out of the sea, comically a tiny sheep looks up at its keeper. As well as exulting in the kinds of visual games expected on Roman sarcophagi, this blurs the boundaries between different worlds and cultural heritages, given the secular origins of the shepherd imagery.[118]

The arrangement is far from a random collection of biblical stories for their own sake, but is constructed more as a web of associations, to entice the viewer to draw on their own cultural knowledge of reading both art and scripture to make interesting connections. As at Boville Ernica, the local sculptor has executed an original take on the sarcophagi produced in Roman workshops, combining the structures of strigillated and frieze types to produce a novel viewing experience.

---

[116] Jensen 2000, 174 on Daniel and Jonah's nudity.
[117] *RS* 2.242 describes the tree.
[118] A Roman sarcophagus in Pisa (*RS* 2.90) and a local work now in Berlin (*RS* 2.241) depict Jonah as closely associated with shepherds; see also *RS* 2.91 for Daniel and Jonah in between shepherds.

Capua

In Capua, this early fourth-century frieze sarcophagus (Fig. 15.8) was once stored in the courtyard of San Marcello, and has now been reused as the altar in the church of Santi Rufo e Carponio.[119] Again the lid is lacking, but the casket is filled with a continuous stream of recognisable biblical figures from the Old and New Testaments. Koch notes that stylistic peculiarities suggest it may be more likely to share an origin with pre-Christian sarcophagi from Campania than contemporary examples from Rome. Campania was known as a centre of sarcophagus production in the earlier Imperial period, so although the later surviving numbers are small, it is interesting that in the fourth century this is the only region where the six local works outnumber the two imports.[120]

This example mimics the form of the single-register frieze sarcophagi made in Rome in the first half of the fourth century, where the biblical figures almost blend together in the repeating folds of the clothing. Several of this type were exported to central Italy; in particular the Capua sarcophagus shares many scenes with the contemporary Roman export to Soriano nel Cimino, near Viterbo.[121] That example was exported nearly fifty miles to the other side of Rome, but evidently reflects similar arrangements upon which the Capua sarcophagus drew. On the Soriano nel Cimino sarcophagus, the three scenes on the far right are the blind man, the paralysed man and the sacrifice of Isaac; the Capua right end is almost identical, but interestingly, the sculptor seems to have reinterpreted the paralysed man as Isaac carrying wood for his sacrifice, which is much rarer (and possibly unique on sarcophagi). Whether this was

Figure 15.8 Frieze sarcophagus with biblical scenes. Early fourth century AD. Capua, Santi Rufo e Carponio; pictured in former location in courtyard of San Marcello. Photo: D-DAI-ROM-60.1365 (J. Böhringer).

[119] *RS* 2.11; Koch 2000, 365, 450.
[120] Koch 2000, 369 also tentatively includes in his count of exports the example from Capua under discussion here, though I follow his thoughts elsewhere (450) in counting this as a possible local work. Arguably the larger number of local works in Campania in this period compared to just one certain import makes it more likely that this one is also locally made. See Christie 2016, 136 on this area remaining a 'senatorial stronghold' in Late Antiquity.
[121] *RS* 2.60; this example similarly features the bleeding woman, an orant, the multiplication of loaves, the blind man and the sacrifice of Isaac. Others of this type imported from Rome include *RS* 2.10 and 59 in central Italy, and 62 in Campania, though this last one could possibly be a local work.

a misreading of the source imagery or a free reinterpretation to better suit the monument's specific programme, this is one of the unique features that mark this sarcophagus out as a probable local adaptation.

Many of the biblical frieze sarcophagi have central and often symmetrical elements such as an orant, which help to orientate the viewer and create an expectation of connections through the balance of the two halves.[122] However, here any structure seems elusive at first glance, with no strong central figure. The orant has been moved close to the left end and faces away from the centre, while the central symmetrical motif from Soriano nel Cimino, the multiplication of loaves, also appears unsatisfactorily off-centre in this version. However, if we set aside for a moment the two leftmost scenes of Peter and the orant, a balanced structure comes into focus: framed by the only Old Testament figures of Adam and Eve and Abraham with Isaac, who each lean outwards, the symmetrical multiplication scene is in the centre, with two other New Testament scenes intervening on each side.[123] Perhaps we could imagine that a local sculptor found it useful to adapt a pre-existing scheme, adding two figures on the left.[124]

While these characters could merely serve a practical purpose in filling out the space, there are reasons to see the ends as complementary, and therefore that the additional figures were incorporated carefully and deliberately. Peter and Abraham both have upward gestures, likely with now-missing staff and knife. Abraham looks to the centre, yet Adam and Eve do not do likewise; Peter's head is sadly now missing, but it is possible that he did look backwards to balance Abraham.[125] On the two ends are the diminutive kneeling figures of the soldiers and Isaac, all with faces in three-quarter profile seen from above.[126] While the New Testament scenes have no strong narrative thrust, turning in various directions, the scenes of the rock miracle, the orant, Adam and Eve and Abraham all turn outwards.

The choice between two overlapping frames creates a visual play with the location of the relief's boundaries and teases the viewer's expectations. Indeed, since the extra end with Peter and the orant are both chronologically last and the only non-canonical characters (one a scene from later Roman tradition and the other probably evoking the soul of the deceased), this visual play also effectively translates into a question of when the story of salvation ends. The scenes from canonical scripture form their own complete narrative by themselves, and the additional left end cleverly creates another completed story without detracting from the integrity of the canon. The message conveyed is that the later deeds of Peter in Rome, and the contemporary context of fourth-century Christians, are but a continuation of the scriptural story of salvation. This second act is integrated into the biblical narrative by the gaze of the first man and

---

[122] As would have originally been the case for *RS* 2.62; *RS* 2.10 has an enthroned Christ in the centre, while *RS* 2.60 has a symmetrical scene of the multiplication of loaves.

[123] The New Testament scenes are the arrest of Peter related in Acts, and three miracles of healing or resurrection by Jesus in the Gospels.

[124] Perhaps the imbalance was also partially informed by the display context, for example if the line of sight when approaching the coffin was off-centre.

[125] This is more likely given the close relationship with the orant behind him; compare *RS* 1.674 where Peter looks back at Jesus.

[126] *RS* 2.11.

woman, who unusually do not look at each other or the tree; instead they seem to queue up behind the universal personification of the deceased, to witness the miracle of the empire's patron saint.

The positioning of Adam and Eve as viewers of Peter's miracle is yet another example of the presentation of the Old Testament as visually dependent on the New. Again, it is noteworthy that the only characters that are less than fully clothed are those of the Old Testament and the corpse, picturing the Old Testament as more primitive and even comparatively spiritually 'dead', especially when represented by scenes of sin and violence. The importance of the clothing metaphor is indicated by the scene placed near the centre of the relief, highlighted by the gesture of Peter's guard, of the bleeding woman clutching at Jesus' clothing to receive his healing power. Clothing signifies life, while nudity is equated with death. This metaphor makes sense in the context of sarcophagus decoration, uniquely concerned with issues of dress and undress, as seen already on the Syracuse sarcophagus for example.[127]

Moreover, Abraham appears to be prevented from sacrificing his son by looking back at Jesus; the Roman sarcophagus of Marcus Claudianus also depicts Abraham halted solely by a miracle of Jesus.[128] While Isaac's hands are tied behind him in expectation of his brutal sacrifice, the soldiers reach forward to receive the merciful waters of baptism. This is strengthened by an implied elemental contrast of water and fire, since additional effort has been made to depict a second Isaac carrying wood to burn on the altar. Meanwhile this Isaac is juxtaposed back to back with the blind man, whose healing by Jesus further contrasts with Isaac's treatment by his father: Jesus rests his hand on the man's head, while Abraham grabs his kneeling son's hair. Again, this does not follow the emphasis of early Christian literature, which focuses positively on Abraham's faith in the resurrection as his motivation; on the sarcophagi, a visual contrast is made repeatedly (first with Jesus on the Syracuse example, and here with Peter as well) in a way that highlights the violence of the Abraham motif.[129]

Despite Koch's conclusion that local works based on metropolitan models tended to simplification, the Capua sarcophagus, along with the examples from Boville Ernica and Velletri, shows that this did not have to be the case.[130] The unusual structure, which could initially be explained as practical measures taken by a less experienced local sculptor, in fact strategically opens up new interpretative opportunities for cultured viewers; the fact that decorative decisions in these local works may be directed at least partly by economy does not fully explain how viewers would receive the finished product. The kinds of visual references on display, building on the traditions of sarcophagus decoration, would ultimately reflect favourably on the cultural erudition and prestige of the deceased.

---

[127] Elsner 2018b.
[128] The damage to the Capua relief makes it unclear whether the hand of God was originally present as elsewhere, but this would usually be found at terminal points in the relief and most often in a balancing pair with a hand providing the tablets to Moses. *RS* 1.771 = Claudianus sarcophagus.
[129] Dresken-Weiland 2010, 294–5 on the patristic interpretations.
[130] Koch 2000, 627.

The City-Gate Type

The later fourth century can be distinguished from the previous decades both in terms of the types of sarcophagi produced in both Rome and Italy, and their geographical origin and spread. Outside Rome, most sarcophagi could now be found in northern Italy rather than the central regions, seemingly reflecting the movement of the ruling elite to the northern cities.[131]

In this period, tastes seemed to turn to the more non-narrative or iconic imagery of Christ framed by his disciples, either in long rows on frieze or columnar types, or one on either side on strigillated sarcophagi. The *traditio legis* (a triumphant Christ passing on the Law to Peter and Paul) was a recurrent motif in the centre of such monuments.[132] From the fifth century, the aesthetic of a high volume of biblical scenes seems to have had less currency on sarcophagi, as production shifted from Rome to Ravenna. Yet there are still some final flourishings. In terms of local works, a unique double-register biblical frieze sarcophagus in red onyx unfortunately survives only fragmentarily, making a complete reading impossible, but its complex engagement with themes of materiality and embodiment has been highlighted in a recent discussion, together with another distinctive biblical frieze in Milan from the turn of the fifth century.[133]

One of this period's most distinctive innovations, to be considered in this section, is a type of Roman export. The city-gate type, so-called for the distinctive architecture that forms the backdrop to its reliefs, was produced specifically for clients in the north, but imported from Rome (though they might have been copied locally, as the fragment in Vicenza could suggest).[134] Five impressive examples survive almost intact in the north and east of Italy.[135] Most have rows of apostles on at least one long side, reserving biblical scenes for the short ends or lid.[136] No two are alike, and they were evidently made on commission; some examples also have portraits, personal scenes or strigillated panels.

However, the use of biblical motifs still bears similarities with the earlier sarcophagi. The creators of the sarcophagus in Tolentino, for example, placed the visually associated scenes of the three Hebrews and the Magi on the short sides, while in Milan these scenes fill each side of the tall lid; on this latter example the Hebrews even gesture to a star in their scene, conflating the stories to an even greater degree than seen previously.[137] There are some initial indications of clear links between multiple tiers of

---

[131] Twenty-one Roman exports, eleven local works plus five possible fragments in northern Italy, largely dating to the end of the fourth century; Koch 2000, 370 and 457–63. See Chapter 3 in this volume.

[132] Couzin 2015.

[133] *RS* 2.249 and 250; Crowley 2018. Most other local works are fragmentary or lack imagery of biblical narratives.

[134] *RS* 2.251; Koch 2000, 454.

[135] Lawrence 1927; Sansoni 1969; *RS* 2.148–51; and Koch 2000, 365, 453–5 for other city-gate types in Milan, Ancona, Tolentino and Mantua.

[136] Other Roman exports to Italy with friezes of apostles are *RS* 2.74 and 143, as well as 123 between columns, and 112 and 113 on strigillated types.

[137] *RS* 2.148 and 150; Hay forthcoming. See also Ancona (*RS* 2.149), where the Magi are on the left of the lid and the Hebrews on the right short end, parallel to the scenes of Moses on the right of the lid and left short end. The fragment in Vicenza (*RS* 2.251) only preserves the right short end with the Magi.

decoration: for example, on the back of the Milan sarcophagus, Christ and the twelve apostles stand directly above a small frieze of one large sheep and twelve smaller ones, which emerge from brick-built arches as the disciples stand in front of similar edifices. Grabar concluded that this duplication of 'realistic' and 'allegorical' layers was specifically Christian, but we have seen precisely this kind of layering on the second-century Meleager sarcophagus in Rome.[138]

The monument that provides the most scope to examine the continuing potential complexity in the use of biblical scenes, however, is the sarcophagus now in the crypt of the church of San Giovanni in Verona (Figs 15.9–11), which has biblical subjects across all the decorated surfaces.[139] It was latterly supposed to contain the remains of the apostles Simon the Zealot and Judas Thaddeus, and in 1395 a reclining sculpture of the saints was added above the original lid, with additional foliate trims.

Each pair of pillars loosely frames one of the four biblical scenes on the main front.[140] The reliefs have a broadly chronological flow from left to right (excepting the central trio of Christ with Peter and Paul in a potentially extemporal Paradise): on the lid are three Old Testament scenes followed by one with Peter; on the body, the last

Figure 15.9 City-gate sarcophagus with biblical scenes. Late fourth century AD, made in Rome. Verona, San Giovanni in Valle. Photo: D-DAI-ROM-59.943 (J. Böhringer).

---

[138] Grabar 1968, 135–7.
[139] *RS* 2.152; Koch 2000, 365, 453–4.
[140] Similarly to columnar sarcophagi found in Rome and elsewhere in the latter half of the fourth century.

Figure 15.10 Left short end, with Cain and Abel. Late fourth century AD, made in Rome. Verona, San Giovanni in Valle. Photo: D-DAI-ROM-59.945 (J. Böhringer).

Figure 15.11 Right short end, with Adam and Eve. Late fourth century AD, made in Rome. Verona, San Giovanni in Valle. Photo: D-DAI-ROM-59.944 (J.Böhringer).

of four scenes of Jesus is the last chronologically.[141] There is thus a division between scenes of Christ on the main body, and the preceding and subsequent narratives of the Old Testament and the apostles on the lid.

The figures mostly turn to the right, promoting this direction of reading.[142] The four bodies of the clean-shaven Jesuses start off facing and gesturing in the opposite direction (though the right foot of the second Jesus has started the turn to the right). On the second half of the front, the third Jesus turns to the right, but still looks back to the suffering woman, with his leg lingering behind as he pauses, and his hand gesturing away but held closely to him. Finally the fourth Jesus strides forward with bent knee and outstretched arm, now fully facing to the right with his face in profile. The thrust of this reading evokes Jesus continually pausing on his journey in order to interact with humankind, reluctantly leaving them, before (literally) embracing his fate with determination.

This reading depends on the viewer's ability to deconstruct the building blocks of the relief's structure, isolating the central trio of the bearded Christ and apostles as its own formulaic entity around which the gospel scenes flow. This is lent weight by the even more formulaic motif directly above, the tabula supported by cupids. The two motifs seem directly comparable: the space for an inscription framed by symmetrical figures, and the embodied Word framed by symmetrical apostles. Beyond lending unity to the design, it might help to figuratively tie the identity of the deceased to Christ.[143]

The symmetry of the architectural backdrop encourages the reading of comparanda across the front. The centre trio set the pattern for this: Peter and Paul stand beneath matching fortified arches with battlements, framed as parallel chief apostles. The next groups outwards are both scenes of Jesus' healing miracles for diminutive figures (with two other men in the background); both take place in front of matching architraves with composite columns. As well as the visual similarities between these miracles, in the Gospels the Roman centurion and bleeding woman are both commended for their faith, after seeking healing in unusual ways: the former for his servant in his absence, the latter by merely touching Jesus' cloak. The depiction of these characters as small kneeling figures is similar to that of the husband and wife patrons of late sarcophagi; the deceased can thus be pictured here too as paying homage to Jesus, receiving miraculous renewal and being praised for their faith.[144] This implies a greater interaction between those commemorated and the biblical narrative than normal, or at least than is usually allowed by scholars.[145]

---

[141] The first two scenes appear next to each other in this order in John 4; the third scene follows the second in Matthew and Luke. Samaritan woman: John 4:1–42; healing the centurion's servant: Matt. 8:5–13/Luke 7:1–10/John 4:46–54; healing of the bleeding woman: Matt. 9:20–2/Mark 5:25–34/Luke 8:43–8; the kiss of Judas: Matt. 26:47–50/Mark 14:43–5/Luke 22:47–8.

[142] With exceptions including Paul to be symmetrical to Peter, and Judas at the outer edge.

[143] On the Milan sarcophagus, the same parallel is strengthened by the very similar books held by Christ and the husband in the portrait tondo.

[144] E.g. on the Milan and Ancona city-gate sarcophagi.

[145] See Huskinson 2015, 231–2 on the more restricted level of association between portraits and biblical images. Another example of this can be seen on the side of the Mantua sarcophagus, where the couple's union appears to be blessed by Peter. The adjacent figure of Moses receiving the law also looks very much like the husband, perhaps picturing similar divine inspiration in his learning and privileged interaction.

The final pair of scenes on the sarcophagus front are Jesus' encounters with the Samaritan woman and Judas. Each takes place under a fortified archway, and shares the theme of Jesus meeting a potential enemy: on the one hand his betrayer, on the other, a Samaritan who questions him on salvation.[146] They provide heavily contrasting examples of discipleship: while Jesus' betrayer was a fellow Jew from his closest circle, the Samaritan woman came to believe in Jesus as the Messiah and caused many other Samaritans to believe. Discipleship seems an appropriate subject for a city-gate sarcophagus, since most other examples are filled with figures of apostles. The use of the same architecture as for the apostles Peter and Paul underscores this theme, particularly since Peter is depicted alongside the cockerel that represents his own betrayal of Jesus, and the forgiveness he receives nevertheless.[147] The specific fortification of the architecture might be especially appropriate for scenes invoking potential conflict; in Peter and Paul's case, the sense could be as 'defenders of the faith'.[148]

While the woman at the well is only found in John, whose gospel is recognised as a source for much sarcophagus imagery, the poignant detail of Judas' kiss is not found in this account, but originates from Mark's gospel.[149] The contrast between Judas and the woman recalls another drawn in Mark: between the unnamed woman who anoints Jesus with perfume, and Judas, whose story of betrayal frames the woman's narrative.[150] They too are contrasted as examples of discipleship, the worst being one of Jesus' closest friends, the best a woman whose name is not even remembered. This woman can be interpreted as the first believer, believing Jesus' predictions of resurrection which will give her no time to anoint his body after his death, while on the sarcophagus, the figure who contrasts with Judas is another unnamed woman who is the first evangelist of John's gospel.[151] Therefore, the sarcophagus builds on a biblical contrast by drawing its own new and comparable pairing, with similar themes of Jew and Gentile, and good and bad discipleship.

The other visual link between the two scenes is the rope held by the Samaritan, suspended from the top of the well. The balance in the sarcophagus design prompts

---

[146] See *RS* 3.83 and 86 for other sarcophagi in Arles with these two scenes.

[147] The Samaritan woman appears next to Peter's betrayal on a late fourth-century frieze sarcophagus in the crypt of San Pietro in Vincoli, Rome (*RS* 1.755): the well is in the centre, preceding two scenes to the right of Peter's betrayal and then Jesus handing Peter the keys to heaven, even more explicitly drawing attention to the reward and responsibility given to Peter in spite of his earlier betrayal. The Samaritan woman is drawn into this theme of discipleship through the repetitive pairing pattern of woman–Jesus, Peter–Jesus, Peter–Jesus from the centre to the right end of the monument, with Jesus in a similar pose each time, and the woman and Peter standing in parallel too. There are also two examples in Arles (*RS* 3.86 and 218) with the well scene above or on opposite short ends from Jesus calling Zacchaeus the tax collector (an unlikely potential disciple) to follow him.

[148] For military metaphors for believers, see Phil. 2:25; Phlm. 1:2; 2 Tim. 2:3–4; 1 Cor. 9:7; Eph. 6:10–17.

[149] Dulaey 2006 and Jensen 2014 on the prominence of John's gospel in early Christian art.

[150] Mark 14:1–11; see Shepherd 1995.

[151] Borg and Crossan 2007, 103–7 on the unnamed woman as the first believer. The significance of both women for the universal church is highlighted: as a result of the Samaritan, 'we know that this is truly the Saviour of the world (τοῦ κόσμου)' (John 4:42). Of Mark's unnamed woman, Jesus says 'wherever the good news is proclaimed in the whole world (τὸν κόσμον) what she has done will be told in remembrance of her' (Mark 14:9).

the viewer to see past the figures of Jesus and Judas to the undepicted but implicit rope from the story of Judas' suicide by hanging, which will shortly occur as a direct result of this act.[152] While the woman retrieves 'the water of life' as a result of her interaction with Jesus, Judas' story will end in death. The contrast between eternal life and death drawn out by this pointed pairing is especially fitting for a funerary monument; as each scene is comparatively rare on sarcophagi, their juxtaposition here is carefully made.

The link of potential challenges or enemies extends directly upwards into the scenes featuring brick-built buildings at either end of the lid: Daniel defeats the dragon, and Peter commands the dog of his rival Simon Magus.[153] Each of the four end scenes represents God's representative confronting a challenge of an expected or unexpected foe, strengthened by the similar poses of the main characters. Interestingly, like the woman at the well diagonally opposite, Simon Magus was a Samaritan, though in contrast could be called the 'Bad Samaritan'.[154] The element of water in the well scene contrasts with the fire of the dragon's altar, while elsewhere on the monument the only nude figure, Daniel, is positioned above the scene of the woman being healed through touching Jesus' clothing.[155] As before, the repetition of figures such as Daniel and Peter encourages such reading across divisions.

The trees on the lid break up the scenes similarly to the architecture below; they are positioned above the foliate forms of the composite capitals, providing a playful contrast between artifice and (an artistic depiction of) nature. One of these structural trees is actually the Burning Bush in the scene of Moses, skilfully eliding ornament and narrative. Such elision also occurs on the bottom edge of the sarcophagus. The four rivers of Paradise beneath Christ's feet flow downwards towards the wave-like scroll motif that adorns the lower edge; the rivers thus seem to be the source of the watery ornament that frames the casket. The Samaritan woman draws water from a well above these same waves. This cleverly represents the fulfilment of Jesus' metaphor of living water in this scene, where the water that is drawn does indeed flow from Christ himself. At every level, the lines are blurred between real and artificial, physical and metaphorical. Naturalistic trees can be mere ornamental divisions akin to columns, while ornamental water can mobilise a spiritual metaphor between earth and Paradise.[156]

---

[152] Matt. 27:5.

[153] The scenes of Simon Magus' dog and Daniel and the dragon are also found on the lid of the Mantua city-gate sarcophagus, *RS* 2.151.

[154] Edwards 1997, 69. See *RS* 2.225, a fragment with these two scenes.

[155] The fire implied in the scene of the Burning Bush adjacent to Daniel also contributes to this elemental contrast.

[156] See also the sarcophagi in Milan and Mantua (*RS* 2.150 and 151), where the lower border of a floral scroll originates in an acanthus motif below Christ and spreads out beneath the apostles, conveying the fruitfulness of Christ's mission among his disciples, and their direct inheritance from him. On the short sides too in Milan, chains of flowers beneath Old Testament scenes spring from vessels beneath the apostles, underscoring the visual dependence of the Old Testament on the New that was already indicated in the former's confinement to the sides and lid. Finally, on the back of the sarcophagus in Ancona (*RS* 2.149), a vine emerges from an acanthus leaf below the portrait couple in *dextrarum iunctio* pose, suggesting instead the fruitfulness of their marriage, accentuated by spandrels of fruit-filled baskets on the lid above.

By way of confirmation of the central place of architecture and trees in the visual structuring of the sarcophagus reliefs, we need only turn to the sides of the sarcophagus, where these elements take centre stage on the left and right respectively. None of the Christian case studies considered so far has had surviving left and right ends that are decorated, but for sarcophagi that do, they offer another dimension of commentary on the main relief. On this sarcophagus, the sides are decorated with the earliest biblical scenes on the casket (Adam and Eve, and their sons Cain and Abel), giving the sense of a prologue in its own distinct dimension.

The left side centres on the contrast between Cain's gift of grain and Abel's more substantial sacrifice of a lamb. Their differing approaches to devotion, and the implied violence of Cain's subsequent murder of Abel, are depicted once again under fortified arches, befitting the use of such architecture to highlight themes of good and bad discipleship and potential confrontation. The story of offerings to God is fittingly positioned around the corner from the scene of Christ asking for water and offering living water in return, as well as Daniel's false offering to the guardian of the false god.

While the architectural scheme continues on the left, the other structural device of the tree is repeated on the right. On the lid it was used to delineate separate scenes, but here it divides man and woman with the advent of sin into the natural world. The two baskets that unusually frame the tree here recall the two upturned baskets that occupy the spandrels either side of Christ on the front. Eden on the side is thus clearly linked to Paradise on the front, whether the meaning of the spandrels would be read as the fruits of Paradise now being distributed to all, or the fruits of sin being overturned. Furthermore, the juxtaposition of Adam and Eve around the corner from Jesus and Judas is quite suggestive.[157] They have in common the perversion of relationships, from the introduction of sin that brought enmity to human relationships and separated humans and God, to the betrayal of God's son accomplished through the most intimate sign of friendship; as Jesus and Judas lean in for the fatal embrace, Adam and Eve lean outwards away from each other, covering themselves in shame.

The importation of such sarcophagi to the newly important cities in northern Italy at the end of the fourth century indicates a continuing taste for richly decorated funerary monuments with a complex aesthetic of biblical interaction. In the following centuries, the north would become the most important production site for sarcophagi in Italy, especially Ravenna. However, the paratactic style of creating connections between large numbers of scenes seems to fall out of fashion, in favour of focusing on a smaller number of motifs; the numbers of biblical scenes can be seen already starting to reduce on many of the northern city-gate examples, in exchange for apostles standing independent of any specific narrative. The change in aesthetic was considered by Lawrence to reflect Greek influence, which corresponds to the increasing importance of the eastern empire, and testifies to the shrinking influence of the city of Rome, especially after the sack of 410.[158]

The later reuse of the Verona sarcophagus for the relics of Simon the Zealot and Judas Thaddeus perhaps testifies to continuing engagement with its imagery. The sarcophagus

---

[157] This juxtaposition is also possibly made on the fourth-century silver-gilt ewer from Traprain Law.
[158] Lawrence 1945, 1–3.

could be considered especially appropriate to house the relics of these saints, with its rare depictions of episodes involving their namesakes Simon Magus and Judas Iscariot on the culminating right edges of the front and lid. The disciples reportedly buried within, and later depicted above with their own pupil Saturninus between them, could represent the antithesis to these biblical villains, in a similar spirit to the contrast drawn between good and bad followers in the sarcophagus's own design.

Conclusion

The premise of this study has been on one level quite a simple one: to spend time looking closely at a group of sarcophagi that have been comparatively overlooked and undervalued since Late Antiquity. It has hopefully shown that this is time well spent, but moreover just how much more work there is to be done, on the region of Italy in Late Antiquity, and the potential of Christian sarcophagi in general.

On Christian sarcophagi, we can see patrons and artists interacting in thoughtful and innovative ways with traditional iconography and funerary themes (e.g. hunting, mythological types, ornament, gender, architecture, dress/undress, materiality), while making use of established ways of reading and structuring the reliefs: parataxis, chronology, narrative thrust, using the lid and sides as commentary or expansion, and so on. Viewers could follow visual prompts including juxtaposition, symmetry, repetition and deviations from the narrative order, typical depiction or source text.

Though the individual motifs are highly recognisable, few are identical, nudging the meaning in different directions. Similarly, certain themes recur, but with unique combinations of images. Biblical motifs did not merely point to their source text, but through visual prompts and resonances they point to each other as well, creating a web of associations for viewers to take satisfaction in interpreting. Viewing the totality of the sarcophagus rather than individual scenes reveals the complexity of these monuments, and how the visual expression of Christian typology was shaped by the surrounding late Roman culture of *paideia* and pre-Christian ways of viewing. If there was a break in the tradition of sarcophagus commemoration, it came with the disturbances of the fifth century, not with the earlier advent of Christian images.

Beyond variances in execution, the local works share key visual strategies with the metropolitan works, as well as making some intriguing innovations perfectly in keeping with the playfulness of Roman visual culture. Even if technical limitations could partially explain differences such as the structure of the Capua sarcophagus, this does not help us to understand how these were received by viewers. It is even possible that patrons took the opportunity of greater flexibility and supervision in using local, less specialised craftsmen to introduce desired variations.

Across several of the exports and local works in late Roman Italy, we can see the intention of patrons to unite disparate elements and reinforce or create meaning around biblical images: from a hunting body exported with a biblical lid, to a fifth-century lid designed for a fourth-century body, to a local ornamental body created for an exported biblical lid. Locally produced elements might offer a unique view into choices made by the commissioners of sarcophagi.

The influence of Rome on Italian sarcophagi is in keeping with general trends observed with funerary practices since the Republican era.[159] The common aesthetic attests to a shared and continuous mode of elite communication across the peninsula and beyond – the utility or means of execution of which (or both) appeared to diminish during the transition from Imperial to Ostrogothic Italy. The picture the monuments evoke of a vibrant intellectual culture flourishing right up to the end of the fourth century in Italy certainly fails to anticipate the fifth-century troubles of the western empire, reflecting Brown's argument of an unexpected crisis linked directly to elite revival.[160]

Can any differences be discerned in the choice of images in Italy? Unsurprisingly, scenes of Peter appear not quite as dominant as in Rome.[161] One motif that stands out is the story of Nebuchadnezzar's image, which does seem more popular in this region.[162] One hypothesis could be that its self-conscious and self-reflexive commentary on image-making was particularly relevant outside of Rome, a city where the tradition and ubiquity of visual culture in public and private ironically made images less conspicuous as a theological problem to a more 'urbane' Christian community. Alternatively, the potential reference to the imperial cult latent in the motif made it a less popular choice for clients in Rome, still surrounded by so many imperial images.[163]

Aside from this, the great degree of similarity between the Italian sarcophagi and those of the metropolis means that the potential ways of viewing Christian images on sarcophagi explored here could also be applied to Roman works more generally. It should not be forgotten that these are costly Roman monuments with a specific purpose in the funerary sphere, and that the presence of biblical imagery does not mean that the only identity being expressed is religious. Moreover, it is clear that paying more attention to Roman visual culture does not mean the neglect of the Christian meaning of the imagery; on the contrary, it has revealed new Christian significance. Just as putting a jewel back into its original setting can allow it to shine in new ways, viewing Christian imagery against its surrounding cultural context reveals further meanings encoded in and communicated though the contemporary language of images.[164]

---

[159] Graham and Hope 2016.
[160] Brown 1971, 118–19.
[161] Dresken-Weiland 2013, 249–52 on the popularity of Peter motifs on Roman sarcophagi.
[162] Despite the hugely increased numbers, in Rome there are only a handful of surviving fragments from sarcophagus lids with this scene (e.g. RS 1.324), compared to two sarcophagi exported to Italy with the scene on the main relief and one exported lid (RS 2.10, 20, 63), without even counting the three surviving city-gate types depicting this on the short ends or lid (RS 2.148, 149, 150). The scene also appears on the main relief of at least two sarcophagi in Arles (e.g. RS 3.41) and once on a lid (RS 3.38).
[163] Elsner 2014, 345. See Hay forthcoming for more on the three Hebrews scenes, including links to Roman images of barbarians that may have also made them increasingly relevant in late Roman Italy.
[164] I am most grateful to Zahra Newby and Jeroen Wijnendaele for their helpful comments on earlier drafts of this chapter; Daria Lanzuolo of the Deutsches Archäologisches Institut, Rome, and Sandro Lorenzatti for their assistance with images; the Institute of Classical Studies (ICS), University of London, for providing funds for the images; and the staff of the Combined Library of the ICS and the Hellenic and Roman Societies for their help with accessing resources during the COVID-19 pandemic, when this chapter was written.

Abbreviations

ASR 1.2 = Andreae 1980.
ASR 5.4 = Kranz 1984.
ASR 8.2 = Kollwitz and Herdejürgen 1979.
ASR 12.6 = Koch 1975.
RS 1 = Deichmann et al. 1967.
RS 2 = Dresken-Weiland et al. 1998.
RS 3 = Christern-Briesenick et al. 2003.
RS 4 = Büchsenschütz 2018.
RS 5 = Deckers and Koch 2018.

Bibliography

New Revised Standard Version Bible (Anglicised edition) (1989).
Andreae, B. (1980) *Die antiken Sarkophagreliefs*, vol. 1: *Die Sarkophage mit Dartellungen aus dem Menschenleben*, part 2: *Die römischen Jagdsarkophage*, Berlin.
Baratte, F. (2013) 'Les sarcophages dans l'Afrique antique: images romaines et provinciales', in M. Galinier and F. Baratte (eds) *Iconographie funéraire romaine et société*, Perpignan, 173–91.
Bassett, S. (1996) '*Historiae custos*: Sculpture and Tradition in the Baths of Zeuxippos', *AJA* 100 (3): 491–506.
Bassett, S. (2008) 'The Late Antique Image of Menander', *GRBS* 48: 201–25.
Benoit, F. (1954) *Sarcophages paléochrétiens d'Arles et de Marseille: fouilles et monuments archéologiques en France métropolitaine, Gallia* Suppl. 5, Paris.
Birk, S. (2012) 'Self-Representation and Patronage: Two Case Studies of Self-Display and Patronage on Sarcophagi in Tyre and Rome', in S. Birk and B. Poulsen (eds) *Patrons and Viewers in Late Antiquity*, Aarhus, 107–34.
Birk, S. (2013) *Depicting the Dead: Self-Representation and Commemoration on Roman Sarcophagi with Portraits*, Aarhus.
Birk, S. and B. Poulsen (eds) (2012) *Patrons and Viewers in Late Antiquity*, Aarhus.
Borg, B. (2013) *Crisis and Ambition: Tombs and Burial Customs in Third-Century CE Rome*, Oxford.
Borg, M. and J. D. Crossan (2007) *The Last Week: What the Gospels Really Teach about Jesus's Final Days in Jerusalem*, London.
Bowersock, G. W. (1990) *Hellenism in Late Antiquity*, Ann Arbor.
Brandenburg, H. (2004) 'Osservazioni sulla fine della produzione e dell'uso dei sarcofagi a rilievo nella tarda antichità nonché sulla loro decorazione', in F. Bisconti and H. Brandenburg (eds) *Sarcofagi tardoantichi, paleocristiani e altomedievali: Atti della giornata tematica dei Seminari di archeologia cristiana*, Vatican City, 3–34.
Brilliant, R. (1984) *Visual Narratives: Storytelling in Etruscan and Roman Art*, Ithaca, NY.
Brown, P. (1971) *The World of Late Antiquity*, London.
Brown, P. (1980) 'Art and Society in Late Antiquity', in K. Weitzmann (ed.) *Age of Spirituality: a Symposium*, New York, 17–27.
Brown, P. (1992) *Power and Persuasion in Late Antiquity: Towards a Christian Empire*, Madison, WI.
Büchsenschütz, N. (2018) *Repertorium der christlich-antiken Sarkophage*, vol. 4: *Iberische Halbinsel und Marokko*, Wiesbaden.
Cambi, N. (1977) 'Die stadtrömischen Sarkophage in Dalmatien', *AA*: 444–59.
Cambi, N. (1998) 'Sarkophage aus salonitanischen Werkstatten', in G. Koch (ed.) *Akten des Symposiums 125 Jahre Sarkophag-Corpus*, Sarkophag-Studien 1, Mainz, 169–81.

Cambi, N. (2004) 'I sarcofagi della tarda antichità in Istria e Dalmazia', in F. Bisconti and H. Brandenburg (eds) *Sarcofagi tardoantichi, paleocristiani e altomedievali: Atti della giornata tematica dei seminari di archeologia cristiana*, Vatican City, 75–96.
Cameron, Alan (2004) *Greek Mythography in the Roman World*, Oxford.
Cameron, Averil (1991) *Christianity and the Rhetoric of Empire*, Berkeley.
Cameron, Averil (1997) 'Education and Literary Culture', in A. Cameron and P. Garnsey (eds) *The Cambridge Ancient History*, vol. 13, *The Late Empire*, A.D. 337–425, Cambridge, 665–707.
Chin, C. M. (2008) *Grammar and Christianity in the Late Roman World*, Philadelphia, PA.
Christern-Briesenick, B., T. Ulbert, G. Bovini and H. Brandenburg (eds) (2003) *Repertorium der christlich-antiken Sarkophage*, vol. 3: *Frankreich, Algerien, Tunesien*, Mainz.
Christie, N. (2006) *From Constantine to Charlemagne: an Archaeology of Italy, AD 300–800*, Aldershot.
Christie, N. (2016) 'Late Roman and Late Antique Italy: from Constantine to Justinian', in A. E. Cooley (ed.) *A Companion to Roman Italy*, Malden, MA, 133–53.
Claveria, M. (1998) 'Roman Sarcophagi in Tarragona', in G. Koch (ed.) *Akten des Symposiums '125 Jahre Sarkophag-Corpus' Marburg, 4–7 Oktober 1995*, Sarkophag-Studien 1, Mainz, 138–49.
Couzin, R. (2014) 'The Christian Sarcophagus Population of Rome', *JRA* 27: 275–303.
Couzin, R. (2015) *The Traditio Legis: Anatomy of an Image*, Oxford.
Couzin, R. (2019) 'Where Did All the Pagans Go? The Non-Christian Sarcophagi of Fourth-Century Rome', *PBSR* 87: 145–75.
Cribiore, R. (2001) *Gymnastics of the Mind: Greek Education in Hellenistic and Roman Egypt*, Princeton.
Crowley, P. R. (2018) 'Doubting Thomas and the Matter of Embodiment on Early Christian Sarcophagi', in M. Gaifman, V. Platt and M. Squire (eds) *The Embodied Object in Classical Antiquity, Art History* 41 (3), Boston, 566–91.
Cumont, F. (1942) *Recherches sur le symbolisme funéraire des Romains*, Paris.
Davies, D. J. (2018) 'The Death Turn: Interdisciplinarity, Mourning and Material Culture', in Z. Newby and R. Toulsen (eds) *The Materiality of Mourning: Cross-Disciplinary Perspectives*, London, 245–59.
Deckers, J. G. (2004) 'Theodosianische Sepulkralplastik in Konstantinopel 380–450 n. Chr.', in F. Bisconti and H. Brandenburg (eds) *Sarcofagi tardoantichi, paleocristiani e altomedievali: Atti della giornata tematica dei Seminari di archeologia cristiana*, Vatican City, 35–52.
Deckers, J. G. and G. Koch (2018) *Repertorium der christlich-antiken Sarkophage*, vol. 5: *Konstantinopel, Kleinasien – Thracia, Syria, Palaestina – Arabia*, Wiesbaden.
Deichmann, F. W., G. Bovini and H. Brandenburg (eds) (1967) *Repertorium der christlich-antiken Sarkophage*, vol. 1: *Rom und Ostia*, Wiesbaden.
Dresken-Weiland, J. (2003) *Sarkophagbestattungen des 4.–6. Jahrhunderts im Westen des römischen Reiches*, Rome.
Dresken-Weiland, J. (2010) *Bild, Grab und Wort: Untersuchungen zu Jenseitsvorstellungen von Christen des 3. und 4. Jahrhunderts*, Regensburg.
Dresken-Weiland, J. (2013) 'Société et iconographie: le choix des images des sarcophages paléochrétiens au IVe siècle', in M. Galinier and F. Baratte (eds) *Iconographie funéraire romaine et société: corpus antique, approches nouvelles?* Perpignan, 247–58.
Dresken-Weiland, J., T. Ulbert, G. Bovini and H. Brandenburg (eds) (1998) *Repertorium der christlich-antiken Sarkophage*, vol. 2: *Italien mit einem Nachtrag Rom und Ostia, Dalmatien, Museen der Welt*, Mainz.
Dulaey, M. (2006) 'L'Évangile de Jean et l'iconographie: Lazare, la Samaritaine, et la pédagogie des Pères', in C. Badilita and C. Kannengiesser (eds) *Les Pères de l'Église dans le monde d'aujourd'hui*, Paris, 137–64.

Edwards, M. (1997) 'Simon Magus, the Bad Samaritan', in M. Edwards and S. Swain (eds) *Portraits: Biographical Representations in the Greek and Latin Literature of the Roman Empire*, Oxford, 69–91.

Elsner, J. (1995) *Art and the Roman Viewer: the Transformation of Art from the Pagan World to Christianity*, Cambridge.

Elsner, J. (2002) 'The Birth of Late Antiquity: Riegl and Strzygowski in 1901', *Art History* 25 (3): 358–79.

Elsner, J. (2007) *Roman Eyes: Visuality in Art and Text*, Princeton.

Elsner, J. (2008) 'Framing the Objects We Study: Three Boxes from Late Roman Italy', *JWI* 71: 21–38.

Elsner, J. (2009) 'The Christian Museum in Southern France: Antiquity, Display, and Liturgy from the Counter-Reformation to the Aftermath of Vatican II', *Oxford Art Journal* 32 (2): 181–204.

Elsner, J. (2011) 'Introduction', in J. Elsner and J. Huskinson (eds) *Life, Death and Representation: Some New Work on Roman Sarcophagi*, Berlin, 1–20.

Elsner, J. (2012) 'Decorative Imperatives between Concealment and Display: the Form of Sarcophagi', in J. Elsner and W. Hung (eds) *Sarcophagi, Res: Anthropology and Aesthetics* 61–2 (Spring/Autumn), Chicago, 179–95.

Elsner, J. (2014) 'Rational, Passionate and Appetitive: the Psychology of Rhetoric and the Transformation of Visual Culture from Non-Christian to Christian Sarcophagi in the Roman World', in B. Borg and J. Elsner (eds) *Art and Rhetoric in Roman Culture*, Oxford, 316–49.

Elsner, J. (2018a) 'Ornament, Figure, and Mise en abyme on Roman Sarcophagi', in N. Dietrich and M. Squire (eds) *Ornament and Figure in Greek and Roman Art*, Berlin, 353–91.

Elsner, J. (2018b) 'The Embodied Object: Recensions of the Dead on Roman Sarcophagi', in M. Gaifman, V. Platt and M. Squire (eds) *The Embodied Object in Classical Antiquity*, *Art History* 41 (3), Boston, 547–65.

Ewald, B. (2015) 'Funerary Monuments', in E. A. Friedland and M. G. Sobocinski (eds) *The Oxford Handbook of Roman Sculpture*, Oxford, 390–406.

Frend, W. H. C. (1996) *The Archaeology of Early Christianity: a History*, London.

Gabelmann, H. (1973) *Die Werkstattgruppen der oberitalischen Sarkophage*, Bonn.

Gaggadis-Robin, V. (2005) *Les sarcophages païens du Musée de l'Arles antique*, Arles.

Gaggadis-Robin, V. (2013) 'Méthodes, questions et hypothèses d'interprétation concernant l'iconographie des sarcophages en Gaule Narbonnaise', in M. Galinier and F. Baratte (eds) *Iconographie funéraire romaine et société: corpus antique, approches nouvelles?* Perpignan, 203–31.

Galinier, M. (2013) 'À vendre. Les sarcophages romains dans les ateliers: suggestions méthodologiques', in M. Galinier and F. Baratte (eds) *Iconographie funéraire romaine et société*, Perpignan, 81–115.

Grabar, A. (1968) *Christian Iconography: a Study of Its Origins*, trans. T. Grabar, Princeton.

Graham, E. and V. Hope (2016) 'Funerary Practices', in A. E. Cooley (ed.) *A Companion to Roman Italy*, Malden, MA, 159–80.

Greco, G., G. Voza, M. Sgarlata, G. Ancona and C. Calvano (1998) *Et lux fuit: le catacombe e il sarcofago di Adelfia*, Palermo.

Hay, M. A. (2019) 'Classical Remains and Christian Remembrance: Reviewing Late Roman Sarcophagi', PhD thesis, Warwick.

Hay, M. A. (forthcoming) 'Elision as Erasure: the Three Hebrews and the Magi on Fourth-Century Christian Sarcophagi', in K. Boers, B. Grose, R. Usherwood and G. Walker (eds) *Erasure in Late Antiquity*, Budapest.

Hirschfeld, A. K. (2008) 'An Overview of the Intellectual History of Catacomb Archaeology', in L. Brink and D. A. Green (eds) *Commemorating the Dead: Texts and Artifacts in Context*, Berlin, 11–38.
Huskinson, J. (1999) 'Women and Learning: Gender and Identity in Scenes of Intellectual Life on Late Roman Sarcophagi', in R. Miles (ed.) *Constructing Identities in Late Antiquity*, London, 190–213.
Huskinson, J. (2011) '*Habent sua fata*: Writing Life Histories of Roman Sarcophagi', in J. Elsner and J. Huskinson (eds) *Life, Death and Representation: Some New Work on Roman Sarcophagi*, Berlin, 55–82.
Huskinson, J. (2015) *Roman Strigillated Sarcophagi: Art and Social History*, Oxford.
Jaeger, W. (1961) *Early Christianity and Greek Paideia*, Cambridge, MA.
Jensen, R. M. (2000) *Understanding Early Christian Art*, Abingdon.
Jensen, R. M. (2011) *Living Water: Images, Symbols, and Settings of Early Christian Baptism*, Leiden.
Jensen, R. M. (2014) 'The Gospel of John in Early Christian Art', in S. Prickett (ed.) *The Edinburgh Companion to the Bible and the Arts*, Edinburgh, 131–48.
Kaster, R. A. (1988) *Guardians of Language: the Grammarian and Society in Late Antiquity*, Berkeley.
Kaufmann, H. (2020) 'Unity in Late Latin Poetry', in J. Hernández Lobato and O. Prieto Domínguez (eds) *Literature Squared: Self-Reflexivity in Late Antique Literature*, Turnhout, 175–202.
Keuren, F. van, D. Attanasio, J. J. Herrmann, N. Herz and L. P. Gromet (2011) 'Multimethod Analyses of Roman Sarcophagi at the Museo Nazionale Romano, Rome', in J. Elsner and J. Huskinson (eds) *Life, Death and Representation: Some New Work on Roman Sarcophagi*, Berlin, 149–87.
Kiilerich, B. (2016) 'Subtlety and Simulation in Late Antique *opus sectile*', in P. A. Andreuccetti (eds) *Il colore nel Medioevo: arte, simbolo, tecnica. Tra materiali costitutivi e colori aggiunti: mosaici, intarsi e plastica lapidea*, Lucca, 41–59.
Kline, A. S. (trans.) (2000) *Metamorphoses*, https://ovid.lib.virginia.edu/trans/Ovhome.htm.
Koch, G. (1975) *Die antiken Sarkophagreliefs*, vol. 12: *Die mythologischen Sarkophage*, part 6: *Meleager*, Berlin.
Koch, G. (1990) 'Ein dekorativer Sarkophag mit Scherengitter in der Henry E. Huntington Library and Art Gallery, San Marino', in M. True and G. Koch (eds) *Roman Funerary Monuments in the J. Paul Getty Museum*, vol. 1, Occasional Papers on Antiquity 6, Malibu, 59–70.
Koch, G. (2000) *Frühchristliche Sarkophage*, Munich.
Koch, G. (2012a) 'Einige allgemeine Überlegungen zur Problematik "Original-Kopie" bei den kaiserzeitlichen Sarkophagen', in G. Koch and F. Baratte (eds) *Akten des Symposiums 'Sarkophage der römischen Kaiserzeit: Produktion in den Zentren-Kopien in den Provinzen'. Les sarcophages romains: centres et périphéries*, Ruhpolding, 1–16.
Koch, G. (2012b) 'Zusammenfassung – Conclusions' (trans. C. Hallett), in G. Koch and F. Baratte (eds) *Akten des Symposiums 'Sarkophage der römischen Kaiserzeit: Produktion in den Zentren-Kopien in den Provinzen'. Les sarcophages romains: centres et périphéries*, Ruhpolding, 235–60.
Koch, G. and F. Baratte (eds) (2012) *Akten des Symposiums 'Sarkophage der römischen Kaiserzeit: Produktion in den Zentren-Kopien in den Provinzen'. Les sarcophages romains: centres et périphéries*, Ruhpolding.
Koch, G. and H. Sichtermann (1982) *Römische Sarkophage*, Munich.
Kollwitz, J. and H. Herdejürgen (1979) *Die antiken Sarkophagreliefs*, vol. 8: *Die Sarkophage der westlichen Gebiete des Imperium Romanum*, part 2: *Die ravennatischen Sarkophage*, Berlin.
Koortbojian, M. (1995) *Myth, Meaning, and Memory on Roman Sarcophagi*, Berkeley.

Koortbojian, M. (2019) 'Standardisation and Transformation: Some Observations on the Roman Sarcophagus Trade and Sarcophagus Production', in C. H. Hallett (ed.) *Flesheaters: an International Symposium on Roman Sarcophagi*, Wiesbaden.

Kranz, P. (1984) *Die antiken Sarkophagreliefs*, vol. 5: *Jahreszeiten-Sarkophage*, part 4, Berlin.

Kristensen, T. M. (2014) 'Using and Abusing Images in Late Antiquity (and Beyond): Column Monuments as Topoi of Idolatry', in S. Birk, T. M. Kristensen and B. Poulsen (eds) *Using Images in Late Antiquity*, Oxford, 268–82.

La Rocca, E. and C. P. Presicce (eds) (2010) *Musei Capitolini: le sculture del Palazzo Nuovo*, vol. 1, Rome.

Laistner, M. L. W. (1951) *Christianity and Pagan Culture in the Later Roman Empire*, Ithaca, NY.

Lawrence, M. (1927) 'City-Gate Sarcophagi', *ABull* 10 (1): 1–45.

Lawrence, M. (1945) *The Sarcophagi of Ravenna*, New York.

Leader-Newby, R. (2004) *Silver and Society in Late Antiquity: Functions and Meanings of Silver Plate in the Fourth to Seventh Centuries*, Aldershot.

Lorenz, K. (2011) 'Image in Distress? The Death of Meleager on Roman Sarcophagi', in J. Elsner and J. Huskinson (eds) *Life, Death and Representation: Some New Work on Roman Sarcophagi*, Berlin, 305–32.

Malbon, E. S. (1990) *The Iconography of the Sarcophagus of Junius Bassus*, Princeton.

Marrou, H. (1949) *Saint Augustin et la fin de la culture antique*, Paris.

Meinecke, K. (2013) 'Funerary Cult at Sarcophagi, Rome and Vicinity', in M. Galinier and F. Baratte (eds) *Iconographie funéraire romaine et société: corpus antique, approaches nouvelles?* Perpignan, 31–49.

Meinecke, K. (2014) *Sarcophagum posuit: römische Steinsarkophage im Kontext*, Ruhpolding.

Nasrallah, L. S. (2010) *Christian Responses to Roman Art and Architecture: the Second-Century Church amid the Spaces of Empire*, Cambridge.

Newby, Z. L. (2012) 'The Aesthetics of Violence: Myth and Danger in Roman Domestic Landscapes', *ClAnt* 31 (2): 349–89.

Nock, A. D. (1946) 'Sarcophagi and Symbolism', *AJA* 50: 140–70.

Onians, J. (1999) *Classical Art and the Cultures of Greece and Rome*, New Haven.

Pelttari, A. (2014) *The Space That Remains: Reading Latin Poetry in Late Antiquity*, Ithaca, NY.

Pesce, G. (1957) *Sarcofagi romani di Sardegna*, Rome.

Prado-Vilar, F. (2011) 'Tragedy's Forgotten Beauty: the Medieval Return of Orestes', in J. Elsner and J. Huskinson (eds) *Life, Death and Representation: Some New Work on Roman Sarcophagi*, Berlin, 83–118.

Ramelli, I. (2015) 'Late Antiquity and the Transmission of Educational Ideals and Methods: the Western Empire', in W. M. Bloomer (ed.) *A Companion to Ancient Education*, Chichester, 267–78.

Rebecchi, F. (1978) 'I sarcofagi romani dell'arco adriatico', *Aquileia e Ravenna*, *AAAD* 13, 201–57.

Riegl, A. (1901) *Spätrömische Kunstindustrie*, Vienna.

Rodà, I. (2013) 'Los sarcófagos cristianos importados de Cartago en Tarraco: un inventario de los manufacturados en "kadel"', in M. Galinier and F. Baratte (eds) *Iconographie funéraire romaine et société*, Perpignan, 193–202.

Russell, B. (2011) 'The Roman Sarcophagus "Industry": a Reconsideration', in J. Elsner and J. Huskinson (eds) *Life, Death and Representation: Some New Work on Roman Sarcophagi*, Berlin, 119–47.

Russell, B. (2013) *The Economics of the Roman Stone Trade*, Oxford.

Sansoni, R. (1969) *I sarcofagi paleocristiani a porte di città*, Bologna.

Schoolman, E. M. (2013) 'Reassessing the Sarcophagi of Ravenna', *DOP* 67: 49–74.

Schwartz, D. L. (2013) *Paideia and Cult: Christian Initiation in Theodore of Mopsuestia*, Washington, DC.
Sgarlata, M. (2003) 'Nuove luci sulla rotunda di Adelfia nella catacomba di S. Giovanni a Siracusa', *1983–1993: dieci anni di archeologia cristiana in Italia. Atti del VII Congresso nazionale di archeologia cristiana: Cassino, 20/24 settembre 1993*, vol. 2, Cassino, 845–68.
Shepherd, T. (1995) 'The Narrative Function of Markan Intercalation', *NTS* 41 (4): 522–40.
Simon, E. (1970) *Meleager und Atalante: ein spätantiker Wandbehang*, Monografien der Abegg-Stiftung 4, Bern.
Smith, R. R. R. (2012) 'Monuments for New Citizens in Rome and Aphrodisias', in F. de Angelis, J.-A. Dickmann, F. Pirson, R. von den Hoff (eds) *Kunst von unten? Stil und Gesellschaft in der antiken Welt der 'arte plebea' bis heute*, Wiesbaden, 171–84.
Stefaniw, B. (2019) *Christian Reading: Language, Ethics, and the Order of Things*, Berkeley.
Stirling, L. (2005) *The Learned Collector: Mythological Statuettes and Classical Taste in Late Antique Gaul*, Ann Arbor.
Teatini, A. (2011) *Repertorio dei sarcofagi decorati della Sardegna romana*, Rome.
Thomas, T. K. (2002) 'The Medium Matters: Reading the Remains of a Late Antique Textile', in E. Sears and T. K. Thomas (eds) *Reading Medieval Images: the Art Historian and the Object*, Ann Arbor, 39–49.
Thomas, T. K. (ed.) (2016) *Designing Identity: the Power of Textiles in Late Antiquity*, Princeton.
Tkacz, C. B. (2002) *The Key to the Brescia Casket: Typology and the Early Christian Imagination*, Paris.
Trout, D. (2015) *Damasus of Rome: the Epigraphic Poetry*, Oxford.
Turcan, R. (1999) *Message d'outre-tombe: l'iconographie des sarcophages romains*, Paris.
Turcan, R. (2003) *Études d'archéologie sépulcrale: sarcophages romains et gallo-romains*, Paris.
Tusa, V. (1995) *I sarcofagi romani in Sicilia*, 2nd ed., Rome.
Watts, E. (2012) 'Education: Speaking, Thinking, and Socializing', S. F. Johnson (ed.) *The Oxford Handbook of Late Antiquity*, Oxford, 467–86.
Young, F. M. (2006) 'Towards a Christian *paideia*', in M. M. Mitchell and F. M. Young (eds) *The Cambridge History of Christianity*, Cambridge, 484–500.
Zanker, P. and B. C. Ewald (2012) *Living with Myths: the Imagery of Roman Sarcophagi*, trans. J. Slater, Oxford.

16

LATE ROMAN ITALY IN LATIN PANEGYRIC: FROM THE *PANEGYRICI LATINI* TO ENNODIUS

Adrastos Omissi

IN THE 1980s FERGUS MILLAR wrote that 'Italy under the Empire has no history.'[1] When one explores the late antique panegyrics looking in them for reference to Italy, one is tempted to conclude that this assessment is a fair one. A student or researcher who trawls through the panegyrical corpus looking better to understand the history of the Italian peninsula during the late Roman period is likely to be disappointed; whole speeches pass with Italy barely mentioned, and great changes that would define any survey of this region during the fourth and fifth centuries merit no notice. And trawl one must, for the corpus is a large one: between the first of the late Roman *Panegyrici Latini*, *Pan. Lat.* 10, which was delivered in 289, and Ennodius' *Panegyricus dictus Theoderico*, delivered in 507, no fewer than seven individual authors or corpora of Latin panegyric may be identified (and, indeed, by some counts one could pick out more). Between them, these corpora total something on the order of thirty speeches.[2]

Among these speeches, mention of Italy is rare, and genuine engagement with it as a distinct geographic, economic or social entity is rarer. Tore Janson's *A Concordance to the Latin Panegyrics* (which, admittedly, omits the verse panegyrics of Claudian and Sidonius Apollinaris) cites a total of 29 occurrences of the word *Italia* across the Latin speeches, along with a handful of related nouns and adjectives, a not unimpressive roster.[3] Bar Gaul, which clocks in at 37 occurrences (for both *Gallia* and *Galliae*), and which is explicable thanks largely to the preponderance of the Gallocentric *Panegyrici Latini* within the sample, no other western region is named so regularly: compare the 20 occurrences of *Britannia*, 14 of *Hispania*, and 11 of *Illyricum*.[4] Behind these bald numbers, however, lies a sense that Italy is being overlooked. In the first place, a significant number of these

---

[1] Millar 1986, 295.
[2] Speeches considered in this chapter are as follows: the eleven late Roman *Panegyrici Latini*, the three imperial *Orationes* of Symmachus, the *Gratiarum actio* of Ausonius, the six consular addresses of Claudian, along with his *Laus Serenae*, *Fescennina* and *Epithalamium*, the two fragmentary verse panegyrics of Merobaudes, the three verse panegyrics of Sidonius Apollinaris and the *Panegyricus* of Ennodius of Pavia. For a summary of the material pre-423, see Omissi and Ross 2020, 279–88. On Merobaudes, see Clover 1971; Bruzzone 1999; Kennedy 2019. On Sidonius, see Watson 1998; Gillett 2012; Kennedy 2019. On Ennodius, see Haase 1991; Rohr 1995; 1997; Arnold 2014, 11–36.
[3] Janson 1979, 379.
[4] Janson 1979, 77 (*Britannia*), 275 (*Gallia/Galliae*), 296 (*Hispania*), 325 (*Illyricum*), 379 (*Italia*).

references are exceptionally terse, and Italy is less described than it is evoked for emotional effect: the panegyrist of 313 asks merely 'what do I have to compare Italy, Africa and Rome?'; the orator Pacatus in 389 muses that, under the usurper Maximus, neither Italy nor Spain really suffered in comparison to Gaul; and Claudian's *Epithalamium* names Stilicho 'the general who by his spear upholds Gaul and Italy'.[5] Such examples could be multiplied.[6] Genuine and extended engagement with the region in panegyrical discourse is uncommon.

Two reasons for this can be cited. The first concerns genre. Panegyric was not history, nor was it geography. Its theme was the praise of an individual person (in our extant material, usually the emperor), and material was included only so far as it served that broader purpose. Menander Rhetor, in his *Basilikos logos*, suggests that place should only be brought in insofar as it entwines with imperial biography: native land may be praised (if famous), geographies the emperor has fought in may be described (to enhance the glory of the victories), and cities that have received the emperor's bounty may be enumerated.[7] Place serves the person, and detailed exploration of landscapes, of collective history or of broad sociopolitical change had no place in panegyric. Accordingly, Italy largely features in the panegyrics in only two contexts: as a background to imperial military activity, or as a beleaguered region in need of or (more often) in receipt of imperial ministration.

The second reason that we see less of Italy than we might expect is that Italy is continually outshone by Rome. When a panegyrist's eye turns to the Roman heartlands, it is not Italy but Rome that they invoke, and though Rome is *in* Italy, in the Roman conceptual landscape it was not *of* Italy. Accordingly, in this chapter I have made sure to separate Rome and Italy as distinct entities and have broadly eschewed consideration of panegyrical engagement with 'the City'. Were I to do otherwise, Italy would be thrust from my account just as it is from the panegyrists'. What will be explored, however, is where and how Rome dominates a narrative that might reasonably be expected to have Italy at its centre.

This chapter is broken into a series of short sections that consider various aspects of Italy's presentation within the Latin panegyrics. Beginning with a historical survey, we then explore Italy as a geography within the speeches. This leads to consideration of the twinned themes of Italy as a backdrop to imperial campaigning and Italy as a region rejuvenated by imperial efforts. Following this, we explore briefly the use of historical *exempla* relating to Italy from speeches across the period. Finally, we examine the extent and significance of what the speeches fail to say about Italy, before giving a consideration of the overly bright light of Rome and how the city served to edge Italy from late Roman political consciousness.

The conclusions of the chapter are largely negative: Italy features very sparingly within Latin panegyric and seems at times to be being actively ignored. Any engagement with it is of a very limited kind. Nonetheless, by exploring this limited engagement and

---

[5] *Pan. Lat.* 12.25.3; *Pan. Lat.* 2.24.5; Claud. *Epith.* 119–20.
[6] For other examples, see *Pan. Lat.* 9.12.1, 7.10.3; Claud. *III cons. Hon.* 120–1, *Cons. Man. Theod.* 200–1, *VI cons. Hon.* 142.
[7] Men. Rhet. 2.1.7–8 (homeland), 22–5 (warfare), 29 and 37 (cities).

by likewise exploring the reasons behind it, we will see that we can draw some conclusions about the (modest) place of Italy in the late Roman political consciousness, and the way the geography was seen to serve the imperial edifice.

Historical Trends

Given the paucity of detailed engagement with Italy, it seems appropriate to begin this chapter by giving a brief overview of the ways in which the peninsula *does* crop up, working chronologically through the material in order to highlight general trends in Italy's presentation and characterisation within the speeches.

A clearly distinct period is that from the delivery of the first speech in 289 to the death of Theodosius, that is the period covered by the eleven late Roman *Panegyrici Latini* (289–389), the *Gratiarum actio* of Ausonius (379) and the orations of Symmachus (368–70). During this period, the majority of speeches either make no mention of Italy whatsoever or give it only the most passing notice. Of the three speeches that actually devote some space to the peninsula, it is perhaps reflective of the political landscape of the fourth century that all three concern a civil war waged either in Italy (Constantine's war against Maxentius in 312: *Pan. Lat.* 12 and 4) or against an emperor in possession of the peninsula (Theodosius' war against Magnus Maximus in 388: *Pan. Lat.* 2).[8] Beyond the recollection of these campaigns, it is not a great exaggeration to say that Italy (as distinct from Rome) passes almost unmentioned in speeches delivered before 395.

Following this, the retreat of Honorius and his successors behind the walls of Milan (and, after 402, Ravenna) and the emergence of military threats that directly impacted upon Italy change the nature of the discourse.[9] The orators of this period are Claudian (with a clutch of consular addresses spanning the period 395–404), Merobaudes, whose very fragmentary panegyrical poems date from the 440s, and Sidonius Apollinaris, who addressed speeches to three emperors between 456 and 468. This period provides perhaps the most varied engagement with the peninsula, as the court and imperial armies became increasingly confined to Italy and, to a lesser extent, the south of Gaul, and accordingly, though the emphasis is still firmly military, one sees the position of Italy shift from a stricken region to be liberated to a home territory on which imperial armies operate on the defensive. The protection of Italy from external enemies thus features heavily in these speeches, but likewise it is here that perhaps some of the strangest omissions of the peninsula can also be found.[10]

A final phase may be charted with the establishment of Theoderic's kingdom in Italy, during which the *Panegyricus dictus Theoderico* of Ennodius was composed.[11] Here one again learns most about Italy as the backdrop for a military campaign, in this case Theoderic's conquest of the peninsula following a nearly four-year war with Odoacer in the Po valley. Though one gains glimpses of the wider state of the region outside

---

[8] On this political landscape, and the engagement of the panegyrics with it, see in particular Humphries 2008; Lunn-Rockliffe 2010; Omissi 2018.
[9] For good summaries of this period, see in particular Halsall 2007 and Börm 2013.
[10] See below, p. 466–8.
[11] On which period, see Moorhead 1992; Arnold et al. 2016; Chapter 4 in this volume; and above, n. 2.

this narrow focus, Ennodius, like the majority of his predecessors, is notable more for what he doesn't say than for what he does, a feature of his speech made more surprising by the fact that he was himself deeply embedded in the society and politics of Italy.[12] In his speech, one feels hints of a wider Italy, but they remain little more than this, whispers of a connection to the peninsula that never truly manifest in an overt exploration of it.

What this – admittedly broad-brush – survey hopefully indicates is that the panegyrics are a very poor source indeed to build up anything like a meaningful history of Italy. Italy's footprint within the speeches is highly attenuated, and occurs mostly in a handful of very specific contexts. The rest of this chapter will explore these contexts, the themes that tend to dominate Italy's presentation, and the reasons for such limited treatment.[13]

Italy as a Geography

One question to explore is the representation of Italy as a geographical space within the panegyrics. It is important to understand, in line with comments made in the introduction about the way that the honorand of a panegyric shaped its content, that geography within panegyric is not the geography of a Strabo or even an Ammianus: it is not an attempt to comprehensively delineate space, but rather a window on how space is framed within a very specific political context. How then, in praising the emperors and (occasionally) their consuls and generals, did the orators of the late Roman period represent the physical space of Italy?

First and perhaps most notable is the way that the peninsula is accentuated at its northern end. Of the events recounted in any detail within the panegyrical corpus, all take place within the Po valley or between the Po and Rome (in the latter case, usually when an individual is travelling from the north to Rome). A number of Italian cities find mention in the corpus, but with virtually the sole exception of Rome, none of these lies south of the Po valley.[14] Indeed, of the regions south of Rome barely a single explicit mention is ever made across the whole span of our period, barring Sidonius' brief account of warfare between Majorian and the Vandals in Campania in 458.[15] The

---

[12] Ennodius was a priest and later bishop of Italy whose time was divided between Pavia, Milan and Rome: Kennell 2000, 4–42.

[13] *Caveat lector*: this historical survey will also be the only section in the chapter in which material is divided chronologically; for the rest, we will explore thematic unities. Some contextual specificity will be lost by this approach, but it seems much the best way to approach a topic which the corpus treats so sparingly. For more context on these individual periods, see also Chapters 1–4 in this volume.

[14] Italian cities mentioned within the speeches are (in alphabetical order): Aquileia (*Pan. Lat.* 7.6; *Pan. Lat.* 12.11.1; *Pan. Lat.* 6.27.1; *Pan. Lat.* 2.38.4–45.7); Asti (Claud. *VI cons. Hon.* 203); Brescia (*Pan. Lat.* 6.25.1); Emona (*Pan. Lat.* 2.37); Milan (*Pan. Lat.* 11.4, 11–12; 12.7.5); Mutina (*Pan. Lat.* 6.27.1); Narnia (Claud. *VI cons. Hon.* 515–19); Pollentia (Claud. *VI cons. Hon.* 127, 202, 281); Puteoli (Sid. Apoll. *Carm.* 2.59); Ravenna (Claud. *VI cons. Hon.* 494–5); Segusio (*Pan. Lat.* 17.3, 21); Turin (*Pan. Lat.* 12.7.3; *Pan. Lat.* 6.22.1–24.7); Verona (*Pan. Lat.* 12.8, 11.1; *Pan. Lat.* 12.25.1–26.5; Claud. *VI cons. Hon.* 201; Ennod. *Pan.* 8.39). Narnia is a more southern town, mentioned briefly by Claudian in his account of the journey of Honorius from Ravenna to Rome in 403.

[15] Sid. Apoll. *Carm.* 5.342–9, 387–440.

reasons for this are virtually self-explanatory: Roman Italy had always been a region that geographical reality anchored northwards, and in the late Roman period this was only accentuated. Emperors – as Claudian himself laments – now rarely travelled even as far south as Rome, and as far as the sphere of imperial action was concerned, Italy consisted solely of the Po valley, in which the imperial centres of Milan, Aquileia and (later) Ravenna were to be found.[16]

Though imperial preoccupations naturally drew panegyrists' attention to the north, it is worth noting that the northern concertinaing of the peninsula happens even under orators one might expect to think more broadly. One sees it in the speeches of Sidonius, delivered in the midst of the fifth century, when Geiseric and his Vandal kingdom were perhaps *the* terror of the Roman state. Geiseric looms large in Sidonius' speeches, particularly his panegyric to Majorian, in which he is painted as the most lurid tyrant in true classical colours, but nonetheless the preoccupation with a southern threat does not imprint a more southern focus on to consideration of Italy itself.[17] Again, Rome is in a great measure to blame for this. Geiseric was a threat because from Africa he threatened Rome, not because he threatened the south of Italy. Of the very real depredations that Vandal raiding caused in the region, we learn nothing.[18]

Secondly, and connected to this, the presence of the Alps as Italy's defining geographic feature is unmistakeable. Here again one can turn to Janson's *Concordance* and note that the Alps receive no fewer than 22 mentions.[19] The Alps therefore are mentioned nearly as frequently as is Italy itself, and throughout the panegyrics they are explicitly conceived of as Italy's gateway and boundary.[20] This connection was so axiomatic that often the Alps were used as a metonym for the approach to Italy: in 291, a panegyrist imagined Diocletian and Maximian lighting up the Julian and Cottian Alps respectively as they travelled to a meeting at Milan; in 313 Constantine's invasion of the peninsula could be encapsulated with the pithy 'you seized the Alps on foot and the ports of Italy by ship'; and in his 395 panegyric on the consulship of Probinus and Olybrius Claudian could likewise describe the advance of Theodosius upon Italy as when 'the Augustus had loosened the trembling Alps'.[21] Again, this view of Italy as a land ringed by mountains belies the military preoccupations of panegyric. The *Expositio*

---

[16] Claud. *VI cons. Hon.* 384–425 has Roma claim that she has only seen an emperor three times (*ter*) in the preceding century. The number was in fact higher than this, with imperial visits known for 303, 304, 312, 315, 324, 357 and 389, a long-term imperial residence from 306 to 312, and a handful of other visits being inferable (cf. Barnes 1975). Nonetheless, the point remains that, compared to previous centuries, emperors were rarely in Rome. On imperial presence in Italy in general, see Chapter 2 in this volume.

[17] Sid. Apoll. *Carm.* 5.327–49: in this passage Africa begs 'that Carthage might no more war against Italy', but it is notably to Roma that she is speaking, and Roma to whom she looks for aid; cf. *Carm.* 2.332–86, 7.441–57.

[18] For which, see Merrills and Miles 2010, 111–24 (esp 111–12); Halsall 2007, 242–56; Wijnendaele and Hanaghan 2021, 269–70.

[19] Janson 1979, 37.

[20] *Pan. Lat.* 11.2.4; *Pan. Lat.* 12.5.4; *Pan. Lat.* 2.45.4; *Pan. Lat.* 2.30.2; Claud. *Cons. Prob. Olyb.* 105, *III cons. Hon.* 87–101, *IV cons. Hon.* 104–9, 357, 390–3, *Cons. Man. Theod.* 308, *Cons. Stil.* 2.411; Sid. Apoll. *Carm.* 5.373–85; Ennod. *Pan.* 2.7–8.

[21] *Pan. Lat.* 11.9–10; *Pan. Lat.* 12.25.2; Claud. *Cons. Prob. Olyb.* 74.

totius mundi et gentium, a firmly unmilitary text of the mid-fourth century written in the East by an individual who viewed the empire very much from a Mediterranean perspective (Plato's 'frogs around a pond'), sees the region very differently.²² In the *Expositio*, Italy is a land of cities, Rome its chief; the Alps go unmentioned.²³

Finally, we can note a generalised sense in references to Italy that it is a land of plenty, a fertile landscape of farms and of gentle countryside as well as one teeming with cities.²⁴ At the assembly of western regions who come to beg Roma that Stilicho may be awarded the consulship in Claudian's *De consulatu Stilichonis*, Gaul and Britain are warlike and barbarous, Africa sunburnt and decorated with grain, whilst Italy (whom Claudian likes to call Oenotria) comes 'entwined with pliant vine and ivy and streaming wines from abundant grapes'.²⁵ Sidonius, perhaps consciously borrowing from Claudian's imagery, likewise has Oenotria girt with a beautiful robe, and 'instead of hair a multitude of laden vines, binding fast her many towns, flowed out across her brow'.²⁶ Elsewhere, Claudian has Eridanus laughing at Alaric's defeat in Italy in terms that evoke the peninsula's easy climate and fecundity: 'Why have you changed your plans? Why do you hasten back? Are you dissatisfied with the shores of Italy? Do you not feed your horse upon Tiber's grassy banks as you hoped? Do you not plough the hills of Tuscany?'²⁷ And to Ennodius Italy was a 'fruitful land' (*potens terra*) and one (in contrast to the Germanic north) 'that knows how to accept the hoe'.²⁸ Perhaps more than any other region, Italy was regarded as the West's land of plenty and abundance, not least, one would imagine, because it was here that many of the great commercial estates of the senatorial class were concentrated.²⁹

Battleground Italy

Since warfare dominates so much of panegyrical attention, and since it is broadly as a backdrop to imperial warfare that Italy features within panegyrical discourse, it seems appropriate to explore the notion of Italy as the setting for military campaigning. Some of the contours of this representation have already been touched upon in the summaries above, but here we may explore more of the specifics of the presentation.

It is first worthy of note that, in virtually every instance in which an Italian war is described within the panegyrics, these accounts provide some of our most detailed

---

[22] On the setting and date of authorship, see Rougé 1966, 27–38; Mittag 2006, 339. For Plato's quotation, see Pl. *Phd.* 109a–b.

[23] *Exp. tot. mund. gent.* 13.

[24] E.g. *Pan. Lat.* 12.25.4, 4.32.5, 8.10.3, 12.7.3–4; Claud. *III cons. Hon.* 66–7, 120–1, *Cons. Man. Theod.* 200–1. Here, unlike on the Alpine boundaries of Italy, the *Expositio* accords with the panegyrics (*Italia ergo omnibus habundans insuper*, *Exp. tot. mund. gent.* 13).

[25] Claud. *Cons. Stil.* 2.262–4; *Oenotria* ('wine-land') was in origin a Greek name for Italy's south (e.g. Hdt. 1.167), and was a favourite synonym of Claudian's for the more standard *Italia*.

[26] Sid. Apoll. *Carm.* 2.323–6.

[27] Claud. *VI cons. Hon.* 180–4.

[28] Ennod. *Pan.* 6.23 and 15.73.

[29] Matthews 1990, 23–31; the *Expositio* makes this point explicitly: *post iam Campania provincia non valde quidem magna, divites autem viros possidens; et ipsa sibi sufficiens est et cellarium regnanti Romae* (13).

evidence for the course of that war.[30] Six Italian wars are described within the Latin panegyrics: 312 (Constantine and Maxentius); 388 (Theodosius and Magnus Maximus); 402 (Alaric and Honorius/Stilicho); 455 (the Vandal campaign that sacked Rome); 458 (Majorian against Vandals in Campania); and 489–93 (Theoderic and Odovacer).[31] It would be tedious and unnecessary to examine each of these and the wealth of details the panegyrics provide, so a single example (the first will do as well as any) can stand for all. Of the war between Constantius and Maxentius, historical accounts provide only so much detail. Between Lactantius, the various epitomators, Zosimus, Socrates, Sozomen and Zonaras, a fairly bare story can be furnished that sees Constantine cross the Alps and march south on Rome.[32] These accounts are general and involve little detailed insight into the movement of forces, the strategies of the belligerents, the strategic geography or the timescale of the war, and of all these accounts only Aurelius Victor (surprisingly for an epitomator) provides the names of places or persons within his narrative. Compare this, however, to the considerable detail offered by just two contemporary panegyrics, *Pan. Lat.* 12 and 4, delivered to Constantine in 313 and 321, which together provide a wealth of specific topographic and strategic detail, allowing for a careful reconstruction of Constantine's crossing of the Alps at their western end, his progression through the Po valley subduing cities as he went, a major engagement with the core of Maxentius' forces at Turin and Verona under the praetorian prefect, Ruricius Pompeianus, and finally the march on Rome and the south.[33] Numerous details found nowhere else – such as the involvement of a corps of *clibanarii* at Turin or Constantine's combined terrestrial and naval assault upon Italy – can be derived only from these speeches.[34] Nonetheless, it may be noted that whilst the panegyrics provide insight into the events of wars within the peninsula, their window on to the region itself is far more circumscribed. Beyond occasional (and unremarkable) comments, like the fact that Segusio had city walls or that there were *flamines* in Emona, the character of Italy and its regions is left largely to the audience's imaginations.[35] The topographic and historic detail related to these campaigns can tell us something of military history, but little about Italy itself.

Though we learn little of cities within these campaigns, a little more can be said of landscape. As we have explored already, the Alps were considered the defining feature of Italy, and virtually every military campaign described in the panegyrics evokes the fortress provided to Italy by the Alps. Because of the nature of panegyric, in the fourth century the impregnability of Italy's mountain barrier is virtually always invoked to draw attention to the astounding genius of a given emperor's crossing of it:

---

[30] The one exception here is Geiseric's sack of Rome, described in only the most passing detail by Sidonius (see following note).

[31] 312: *Pan. Lat.* 12.2–21, 4.6–15, 19–38. 388: *Pan. Lat.* 2.23–45. 402: Claud. *VI cons. Hon.* 127–330. 455: Sid. Apoll. *Carm.* 7.441–57. 458: Sid. Apoll. *Carm.* 5.342–9, 387–440. 489–93: Ennod. *Pan.* 7.36–10.52.

[32] Lactant. *De mort. pers.* 44.1–9; Aur. Vict. *Caes.* 40.16–23; *Epit.* 40.7; Eutr. 10.4; Oros. 7.16; Zos. 2.15–16; Socrates, *Hist. eccl.* 1.2; Sozom. *Hist. eccl.* 1.3; Zon. 13.1.2–3.

[33] *Pan. Lat.* 12.5–17, 4.19–30; for perhaps the most detailed modern reconstruction of this war, built largely around the panegyrical accounts, see Odahl 2004, 100–8.

[34] *Clibanarii*: *Pan. Lat.* 4.22.4–24.7; naval assault: *Pan. Lat.* 12.25.2.

[35] *Pan. Lat.* 4.21 and 2.37.4.

in *Pan. Lat.* 12, Constantine surprises soldiers in Italy's north who cannot believe he has crossed the mountains so swiftly; Pacatus in 389 marvels that Theodosius' forces could have crossed the Alps from Illyricum to Italy in a single day (which they most certainly could not); and at the end of the period, in the sixth century, the benevolent conqueror Theoderic found Odovacar's forces enervated by the protection that they thought the Alps offered them.[36] In the fifth century, by contrast with the fourth and the sixth, Italy and its Alpine rampart become the foundation of the defence of an Italian heartland, with many a hubristic foreign adversary being undone by them, none more so than Alaric. In his 404 offering on Honorius' sixth consulship, Claudian enjoys the image of Alaric, confounded by defeat in Italy and at a loss where next to go. In an extendedly conjured scene which runs across more than two hundred lines, he describes the campaign, culminating in the desperate Alaric being given direct voice as 'with teary eyes he looked upon the well-known Alps and brooded upon his present retreat, borne of a thread of fate so different from that which fostered his advance.'[37] Trapped in the north, between the cunning of Stilicho and the mountains that prevented his escape into Gaul or Raetia, Alaric longs for death: 'what land shall I see where the names of Stilicho and powerful Italy will not always sound in my ears?'[38]

A notably recurrent feature in these accounts of battles within Italy's bounds is the theme of beneficent rivers working alongside the honorands of our speeches. Two rivers in particular receive attentions as serving alongside Roman interest. The first of these, it should be little surprise to note, is the Tiber. The Tiber protects, it fights, it stands as a metonym for plenty and for ease, it acts personified as a protector of the Roman people.[39] Since it is my intention to avoid discussing Rome as much as is possible, however, I will skirt the Tiber's place in panegyric. The other great warrior-river is the Adige (the Athesis in Latin), which flows from the vicinity of the Reschen Pass in the Alps through the Po valley past Verona and thence to the Adriatic roughly midway between Venice and Ravenna. The Adige appears as an active and personified participant in no fewer than three of the panegyrics: *Pan. Lat.* 12, Claudian's panegyric on Honorius' sixth consulship, and the *Panegyricus* of Ennodius.[40] The centrality it is given, like the bastion of the Alps, is suggestive of the widely articulated worldview that the natural order served Roman interests.[41] Thus in his panegyric on Honorius' sixth consulship, delivered at Rome, it is among the rivers of Liguria and Venetia that Claudian has the great river god Eridanus summon to mock Alaric and his flight from the peninsula in 402, naming them one after another: 'they raise their watery heads from the leafy banks: beautiful Ticino, Adda blue to the eye, swift Adige, Mincio slow

---

[36] *Pan. Lat.* 12.5.5; *Pan. Lat.* 2.39; Ennod. *Pan.* 2.7–8. On the utter implausibility of the journey Pacatus describes, see Nixon and Rodgers 1994, 506 n. 141.
[37] Claud. *VI cons. Hon.* 127–330 (quotation at 266–8).
[38] Claud. *VI cons. Hon.* 316–19.
[39] E.g. *Pan. Lat.* 12.17.2–18.3; *Pan. Lat.* 4.30.1–3, 32.7; Symm. *Or.* 3.9; Claud. *Cons. Prob. Olyb.* 209–65, *Laus Ser.* 15–16, *Cons. Stil.* 2.186–9, 3.170–3, *VI cons. Hon.* 422–5; Merob. *Pan.* 2.5–10; Sid. Apoll. *Carm.* 2.317–406, 5.25–32.
[40] *Pan. Lat.* 12.8.2–3; for Claudian and Ennodius, see below.
[41] Hardie 2019, 78–87.

in its course, and Timavo breaking in his nine mouths'.⁴² These rivers, all tributaries of the Po bar the Adige and all flowing through the Po valley in which Alaric was defeated, are thus not a random assemblage of watercourses but rather a roll call of rivers that 'witnessed' the defeat of the first major invasion of Italy by foreign soldiers since the Iuthungi in 271.⁴³ The Adige, which flows past Verona, at which Alaric was finally defeated in battle, is given pride of place: 'rolling round the enemy's corpses, Adige dyed the Ionian waters with blood'.⁴⁴ Here, geography, infrastructure and military strategy intersect, for Verona was a natural destination for an invader entering Italy from the Balkans along the Via Postumia.⁴⁵ Thus Theoderic and Odovacar likewise fought upon the Adige's bank in September 489, and of the river Ennodius says to Theoderic 'the waves of Adige . . . opulent with the dead . . . the water fought for you. Hail, best of rivers, who washed the filth from the greater part of Italy, drawing up the dregs of the world without loss of your purity.'⁴⁶

The tendency to notice Italy largely only when it has soldiers marching through it goes hand in hand with another feature of the way in which Italy is represented: the determination that Italy is a land restored. Reading through the whole panegyrical corpus, one sees this theme emerge again and again at key moments in Italian history, so that the panegyrics can read like a cyclical story of Italy's subjections and restorations. As one repeatedly encounters the promise that Italy has at last been set upon an even footing, however, this assertion comes to sound increasingly hollow, particularly with the contextual knowledge that the lot of Italy was, in general, a downward one across the period, with warfare touching with increased frequency and savagery a region that had enjoyed extended and often unbroken periods of peace since the establishment of the empire.

The earliest such promise of an Italy restored is perhaps to be found in *Pan. Lat.* 8, the panegyric delivered to Constantius after the suppression of the British usurpers Carausius and Allectus, in which, at his conclusion, the orator charts the new peace granted to the western provinces (Italy named among them) by the suppression of a usurpation characterised as a Frankish piracy.⁴⁷ At the retirement of Maximian in 305 – so tells us the panegyrist of 307 – the collapse of Rome and Italy was predicted, yet now their confidence is restored.⁴⁸ Unsurprisingly, the fall of the usurper Maxentius in 312 likewise engendered delight at the restoration of Italy. After Constantine crossed the Alps, the cities of the north received him joyfully, and there was a triumph at Milan.⁴⁹ His victory at Rome accomplished, the cities of Italy gave to him a crown and shield of

---

⁴² Claud. *VI cons. Hon.* 193–200; for the events of this war, see O'Flynn 1983, 37–41; Kulikowski 2006, 170–1.
⁴³ Saunders 1992.
⁴⁴ Claud. *VI cons. Hon.* 208–9.
⁴⁵ The Via Postumia was northern Italy's main east–west highway, running from Aquileia at the eastern end of the Po valley, through Verona and on through Cremona across the Apennines to Genoa; cf. Laurence 1999, 14.
⁴⁶ Ennod. *Pan.* 8.46; for the events of this war, see Moorhead 1992, 17–31.
⁴⁷ *Pan. Lat.* 8.18.5 with 10.3; on the usurpation see Casey 1994; Omissi 2018, 80–101.
⁴⁸ *Pan. Lat.* 7.10.3.
⁴⁹ *Pan. Lat.* 12.7.

gold, and their people poured forth (presumably in embassies that came to the capital to make a noisy show of their loyalty).[50] Claudian likewise invokes this theme in 395 when he has Theodosius appalled at the idea 'that it would tax me to remember Probus, beneath whose guardianship I have seen all of Hesperia [viz. Italy] and her downtrodden peoples rise again?'[51] For Ennodius, Theoderic's conquest of the peninsula saw 'the unhoped for beauty of cities risen from the ashes and beneath the fullness of your good government palatine roofs glow golden everywhere'.[52]

These examples show that the theme of Italy's restoration was a recurrent one, though as we will see, this comes with some important caveats. The first is that such statements on it as we do find tend to be exceptionally terse and generic to the point of being historically worthless. What are we to make of *Pan. Lat.* 8's *nunc Italia nunc Africa nunc omnes usque ad Maeotias paludes perpetuis curis vacant gentes* or Ennodius' sparse *video insperatum decorem urbium cineribus evenisse*? Certainly, we can tentatively connect them to known events within the peninsula; Ennodius, for instance, likely references the well-documented drive of Theoderic to patronise civic works in various of the cities of the north, including Ravenna, Verona and Pavia, something known about both from contemporary historical sources and modern archaeological work.[53] But the panegyrics give us precious little of substance. Had the people of the peninsula really suffered under Maxentius, or indeed under Odoacer?[54] Were Italians really kept in fear by the British usurpers of the 280s and 290s? The speeches give us no tools with which to explore these questions, but in neither case does this seem at all probable. The rejuvenation of Italy is certainly mentioned, but it is hard to draw anything of substance from what all too often appears to be little more than a rhetorical trope.

The second caveat, and one which will be dealt with in more detail in the final section of this chapter, is that the restoration of Italy is almost always eclipsed by that of Rome.[55] If these examples of Italy's restoration seem few and far between, that is because they are, and though one can find, throughout the panegyrics, a generalised sense that the emperor (or the consul or general) being praised is in some way responsible for an improvement in the general condition of the empire, explicit statements linking imperial or consular action to tangible changes in Italy are vanishingly rare. Where such connections are made, it is between the honorand and Rome, either as a physical and political space, or else as the home of (to a court orator) its most important demographic, the senatorial class.[56]

---

[50] *Pan. Lat.* 12.25.4, 4.32.4–5.
[51] Claud. *Cons. Prob. Olyb.* 167–8; Probus was the father of the consuls of 395 celebrated in this speech, Anicius Probinus and Anicius Hermogenianus Olybrius. Probus had been, amongst a host of other offices, praetorian prefect of Illyricum, Italy and Africa from 368–75 and was again in this same office when Magnus Maximus seized power in 383 (cf. *PLRE* 1, 'Sex. Claudius Petronius Probus 5', 736–40).
[52] Ennod. *Pan.* 11.56.
[53] *Anon. Vales.* 12.70–1; Johnson 1988; Arnold 2014, 198–200.
[54] On this latter question, see Chapter 4 in this volume.
[55] See also Chapter 17 in this volume.
[56] See below, p. 468–71.

Italy as *Exemplum*

Oratory in general, and panegyric in particular, was a genre that populated itself with *exempla*, historical and mythological vignettes and *bons mots* that drove home a particular point or argument.[57] Within Latin panegyric, these *exempla* were drawn largely from three common stocks. The first and by a considerable margin the most common was the canon of Roman history, stretching from the earliest days of the kings through both Republic and Empire and into the contemporary world (at which boundary commonplace *exempla* blur with what one might call contemporary history). Secondly, *exempla* could be mined from the nebulously bounded compendium of classical myth, which encompassed both the doings of the gods and the quasi-historical activities of Homeric heroes. Finally, they might be drawn from the more culturally distant realms of Greek, Hellenistic and Persian history.

Exempla involving Italy are rare enough that a relatively comprehensive list of them can be made here, not least because the range of examples is distinctly limited. The clear favourite of the orators was Hannibal and his ravaging of the Italian peninsula, summoned by a wide range of orators to make a variety of different points.[58] The next most favoured *exemplum* is Tiberius and his infamous excesses upon Capri, a spectre of imperial indolence and moral corruption conjured by Symmachus for Valentinian I, by Claudian for Honorius, and by Sidonius for Majorian and Avitus.[59] In addition to these, four further Italian *exempla* can be cited. Firstly, in his panegyric to Constantine of 312, Nazarius compares the heavenly soldiers that aided Constantine in his invasion of Italy to the divine aid of Castor and Pollux at the battle of Lake Regillus in c.499 BC, in which the fledgling Republic fought against the Latins under Rome's former king, Tarquinius Superbus.[60] Secondly, Symmachus compares the very close shave Valentinian experienced in 363 in Gaul with the near execution of Marius at Minturnae (a Roman colony on the boundary of Latium) in 88 BC.[61] Thirdly, in 389, Pacatus compared the usurpation of Magnus Maximus to the uprising of Spartacus, an example also used by Sidonius in relation to the Huns in 468.[62] Finally, in 458, Sidonius compared the slaughter of the Vandals in that year to the losses suffered by Pyrrhus at Asculum in 279 BC, an example he had likewise used two years previously to glorify Avitus (Sidonius can rarely bear to use an example just once).[63]

---

[57] Cf. Roller 2009.
[58] Favourable comparisons to the generals who defeated him: *Pan. Lat.* 10.8.1, *Pan. Lat.* 12.15.5, Claud. *Cons. Stil.* 2.381, 3.praef., 145–6, and Sid. Apoll. *Carm.* 2.530–1; favourable comparison to his crossing of the Alps: *Pan. Lat.* 11.9.4–10.3; unfavourable comparison to Geiseric, king of the Vandals: Sid. Apoll. *Carm.* 5.342–6 and 7.104; comparison to the grief felt at the losses of Cannae: *Pan. Lat.* 2.19.2; framing relations between Rome and Africa: Sid. Apoll. *Carm.* 5.85–7, 7.129–35.
[59] Symm. *Or.* 1.5; Claud. *IV cons. Hon.* 313–15; Sid. Apoll. *Carm.* 5.320–1, 7.104.
[60] *Pan. Lat.* 4.15.4. On the events of this *exemplum*, see: Dion. Hal. *Ant. Rom.* 6.13; Cic. *Nat. D.* 2.6.1–6, 3.11.10; Val. Max. 1.8; Plut. *Cor.* 3.5, *Aem.* 25.1–3; Frontin. *Str.* 1.11.8.
[61] Symm. *Or.* 1.5. On the episode, see Amm. Marc. 25.10.6–8 and Zos. 3.35.2. On the *exemplum*, see: Plut. *Mar.* 37–39; Carney 1961.
[62] *Pan. Lat.* 2.23.2; Sid. Apoll. *Carm.* 2.235–42. On Spartacus, see: Plut. *Crass.* 8–11 and App. *B. civ.* 1.116–20. Spartacus was sufficiently well known that he might also be employed by Greek orators: Them. *Or.* 7.86c–d.
[63] Sid. Apoll. *Carm.* 5.424–30, 7.226–7.

For the avoidance of doubt, it should firstly be made clear that these Italian *exempla* form a very small proportion of the totality of the *exempla* deployed by the panegyrists. From the days of the Republic, Brutus and Tarquin, the Fabricii, the Curii and the invading Gauls are favourites (though Hannibal is every bit as present as any of these).[64] From the late Republic, the cruelty of Sulla, the eloquence of Cicero and the victories of Caesar are perhaps the most commonly evoked.[65] Of emperors, Trajan is a favourite, either for his magnanimity or his conquests, and Alexander the Great likewise.[66] Homer and the canon of Greek myth are likewise great sources of *exempla* (Claudian at times seems determined to do little more for his audience than to beat them into submission with the sheer breadth of his poetic and mythological knowledge).[67] The Italian *exempla*, therefore, are a drop in a considerably broader ocean.

Perhaps more importantly, it should be understood that such Italian *exempla* as there are are included only because of the fact that Rome's history was so grounded in the peninsula. Those exempla that summon the history of Italy to mind are really, in fact, only those that summon to mind the interactions of Rome with its Italian hinterland. Of the examples quoted above, note that all are Republican, and most early Republican at that. They are chosen by their orators not because they reflected upon Italy or because the orators wanted to reflect upon Italy, but because, before a certain point in the past, Rome's relations with the outside world were largely confined to relations with Italy. Thus, Symmachus' evocation of Marius hiding himself at Minturnae or, indeed, the frequent evocations of Hannibal, encompassed an evocation of Italy only insofar as it related to Rome. Marius hid in Minturnae to escape events that had overtaken him in the city, and the depredations of Hannibal in Italy conjured such existential dread within the Roman imagination less because they had brought violence to Italy (per se) than because they had brought it near to Rome; as weeping Africa says at the court of Roma enthroned in Sidonius' panegyric to Majorian, 'you . . . crushed me after Trebia and Cannae, though my Hannibal saw Roman roofs before Scipio saw ours'.[68]

As with so much in this chapter, then, we certainly cannot deny that Italy featured within the imaginative space from which literate Romans drew their *exempla*. As elsewhere, however, Italy largely existed as an adjunct to its more famous cousin, the city of Rome. Of genuinely Italian heroes and history, we may assume that fourth- and fifth-century Romans knew as little as we do.

---

[64] Brutus and Tarquin: *Pan. Lat.* 3.30.3, 2.20.3–6; Claud. *IV cons. Hon.* 310–11, 613–15, *Cons. Stil.* 2.322–6, 3.192, *VI cons. Hon.* 11–12; Sid. Apoll. *Carm.* 5.66–8. Fabricii and Curii: *Pan. Lat.* 10.14.2, 2.9.4; Claud. *Cons. Stil.* 2.377–95; Sid. Apoll. *Carm.* 2.373, 7.69. Gauls: *Pan. Lat.* 2.46.3; Sid. Apoll. *Carm.* 5.80–4, 7.129, 560–4.

[65] Sulla: *Pan. Lat.* 12.20.3–21.1, 2.7.4, 46.1. Cicero: *Pan. Lat.* 2.46.2; Sid. Apoll. *Carm.* 2.185–6. Caesar: *Pan. Lat.* 5.3.3, 12.6.1–2, 15.3, 2.46.1; Claud. *IV cons. Hon.* 310–11, *VI cons. Hon.* 395–402; Sid. Apoll. *Carm.* 2.120, 5.505–8, 7.88–92.

[66] Trajan: *Pan. Lat.* 2.4.5, 11.6, 16.1; Claud. *IV cons. Hon.* 315–20, *Laus Ser.* 56, *VI cons. Hon.* 333–8; Sid. Apoll. 5.317–9, 560–1, 7.116–18. Alexander: *Pan. Lat.* 12.5.1, 2.8.4–5; Claud. *IV cons. Hon.* 374–7; Sid. Apoll. *Carm.* 2.121–6, 5.201–2; Ennod. *Pan.* 17.78.

[67] Across the 236 lines of his *Laus Serenae*, for instance, he makes no fewer than 33 individual mythological and (occasionally) historical references, a density of slightly less than one such reference every seven lines.

[68] Sid. Apoll. *Carm.* 5.85–7.

Italy Unnoticed

Again and again in this chapter I have returned to the theme of a very partial and incomplete consideration of Italy within the panegyrics. In general, my point has been that the exploration of Italy stays grounded within a few very closely delimited themes. In this section, we look at moments within the speeches where Italy seems a notable absence, unmentioned when one could reasonably expect to see its name.

As we have seen, bar three moments of civil war, Italy is virtually absent from the panegyrics of the fourth century. Ausonius and Symmachus never mention it, and eight of the eleven late Roman *Panegyrici Latini* are largely unconcerned with it.[69] Yet this is also hardly a surprise; during the fourth century, emperors were not frequently in Italy.[70] Far more interesting is that the movement to permanent imperial residence in the region after 395 does not seem to be combined with a refocusing on Italy and its interests. Claudian's speeches coincide exactly with the moment when the previously peripatetic court grounded itself, first at Milan and then later at Ravenna. One looks in vain, however, for any explicit engagement with this fact. Indeed, even at moments when one might expect the emperor and his Italian residence to come clearly to notice, they pass by unremarked. In the second book of Claudian's *De consulatu Stilichonis* there is a moment when the regions of the western empire come to the court to give thanks for their peaceful condition under Honorius.[71] That this must have taken place at Milan, the city in which Claudian delivered the first part of the oration (and the part in which these embassies fall) passes without any comment from the orator. Indeed, despite the fact that the vast majority of his speeches were delivered there, Milan is never once mentioned in Claudian's speeches, and various encounters in unnamed palaces that Claudian describes pass without ever being located in a specific place.[72] One could argue that this is simply a feature of scansion, *Mediolanum* being impossible to fit neatly into Claudian's hexameter, and of genre, with the epic poetic panegyric a poor place in which to obsess over set and setting, were it not for the fact that, when in Rome (and even when not), Claudian happily indulges in the evocation of the landscape of the ancient capital. Rome is evoked repeatedly throughout Claudian's corpus, and on the two occasions when he can link the emperor or Stilicho directly to the city he positively loses himself in the recounting of this fact.[73] Only once does he name the emperor's home (Ravenna by this point), and then only to illustrate Honorius' journey from that city down to Rome in 404.[74]

None of this is to suggest either that Claudian was blind to the place of Italy in the empire or even that he was intentionally hiding or maligning Italy. Indeed, one could easily fill this chapter with examples mined from Claudian of engagement with

---

[69] *Pan. Lat.* 10, 11, 9, 8, 7, 6, 5 and 3.
[70] Chapter 2 in this volume.
[71] Claud. *Cons. Stil.* 2.184–207.
[72] On the location of Claudian's panegyrics, see Cameron 1970, xv–xvi and Gillett 2012, 290. On scenes within palaces that are never located in space, see e.g. Claud. *III cons. Hon.* 142–62, *IV cons. Hon.* 214–420, *Cons. Stil.* 2.269–422, *VI cons. Hon.* 53–76.
[73] Claud. *Cons. Stil.* 3, *passim*, *VI cons. Hon.* 356–660.
[74] Claud. *VI cons. Hon.* 494–522.

Italy, either as a geography or an idea, and the peninsula is repeatedly evoked in his panegyrical poems; in addition to examples already quoted through speech, one might fasten on his evocative imagining of four reins that lead out from the chariot of the goddess Virgo, the first of which harnesses 'Po and Tiber and Italy gleaming with its many cities'.[75] To this one could add many other instances in his panegyrics in which the name or notion of Italy is summoned before his audience.[76] Nonetheless, one could likewise counter these with instances in which Claudian seems to be purposefully omitting Italy from his consideration, not least in his monumental three-book panegyric on Stilicho's consulship, from which the region is almost entirely absent.[77] Rome, it should go without saying, suffers from no such inattention.

Claudian's omissions are curious, but probably ultimately stem from a disinterest in any city or geography, other than Rome, that did not witness military action. Yet there are instances in the fifth century in which Italy's absence can seem more intentional. At Rome on 1 January 456, Sidonius delivered his first imperial panegyric, a triumphant offering delivered to his own father-in-law, Avitus, just a few months after the latter had taken power. Sidonius and Avitus were both native Gauls, whilst Avitus' military sponsors were Goths now long settled in Gaul, and the speech, delivered in a Rome recently subjected to a brutal Vandal sack, reads as bullishly pro-Gallic.[78] Gaul is overtly vaunted as the saviour and at times even master of Rome. 'We [the Gauls], guided by the words of our forebears cultivating worthless laws and, thinking it a sacred thing to follow the old order through disaster, bore the shadow of empire . . . [but] not long ago the perfect situation shone forth by which Gaul might show her strength.'[79] Rome herself appears in the speech downtrodden and broken: 'her neck bent and head bowed, her hair limply hanging and covered with dust, not a helm, her shield striking her with each weary step, and heaviness, not terror, in her spear'.[80] Above all, Italy passes utterly unmentioned.

Lastly, Ennodius. Ennodius' speech to Theoderic was delivered at an unknown location and occasion, almost certainly in the year 507.[81] Alone of our panegyrics, it was delivered in an Italy more or less explicitly defined as an independent kingdom, sundered from the rest of imperial territory. Yet if we look in Ennodius' panegyric for any overt consciousness of an Italian kingdom or of his own identity as an Italian, we look in vain.[82] Certainly he is happy to employ Italy as a *geographical* concept – the Alemanni are settled within the *Italiae termini*, and Sirmium is to be considered

---

[75] Claud. *Cons. Man. Theod.* 200–1.
[76] E.g. Claud. *Cons. Prob. Olyb.* 64, 139, 180, 270, *III cons. Hon.* 70, 129, *IV cons. Hon.* 360, 566, *Cons. Man. Theod.* 216, *Cons. Stil.* 2.281, 325, 3.praef.1, *VI cons. Hon.* 25, 152, 194, 217, 292, 310, 342, 366.
[77] Aside from the personification mentioned above, p. 459, the peninsula is virtually unmentioned in the speech. See also Claud. *IV cons. Hon.* 390–5, *Cons. Man. Theod.* 50–7, *Cons. Stil.* 1.137–47, *Laus Ser.* 60–5.
[78] On the context of its delivery, see Sivan 1989, esp 90–1.
[79] Sid. Apoll. *Carm.* 7.538–45; cf. 116–22, 585–98.
[80] Sid. Apoll. *Carm.* 7.46–59.
[81] Haase 1991, 4–8; Rohr 1995, 16–26.
[82] Even if we accept that Ennodius had been born in Gaul (as Kennell 2000, 6–7), he nonetheless lived his entire adult life in Italy.

both the *limes Italiae* and an *Italiae possessio* – but on Italy as a political concept he is far more close-lipped.[83] Theoderic, it is true, is declared *Italiae rector* ('the master of Italy') at the conclusion of the speech, but his statements within the panegyric about the nature of the polity that Theoderic ruled are ambivalent to say the least. The settling of the Alemanni just mentioned, for instance, might be 'within the borders of Italy', but this was praiseworthy to Ennodius because it did not damage *Romana possessio* ('the Roman possession'), and it ensured that Alemannic spears would now guard *Latiare imperium* ('the Latin Empire').[84] Likewise, the recapture of Sirmium served to grow an *imperium*, not a *regnum*.[85] Indeed, *regnum* is a word that Ennodius uses only once, at least in the singular.[86] He talks rather of *regna* ('kingdoms').[87] The plural here is usually interpreted to encompass the diverse sub-kingdoms of what had formerly been the western Roman Empire, or indeed the empire itself.[88] Thus, though modern scholarship tends to focus on Theoderic's rule as the establishment of an Italian kingdom, Ennodius never calls it this, and when he does qualify *regna* with an adjective, it is *Romana*: 'the Roman kingdoms'.[89] Indeed, it seems reasonable to say that though we tend to talk about the Kingdom of Italy in this period, both under Odoacer and Theoderic, what contemporaries conceived it as, at least as far as the evidence of Ennodius panegyric is concerned, is the 'Roman kingdom' or the 'Roman dominion', modelled very much upon the empire of the western emperors.[90] Italy was not its boundary nor its limit, and though Italy might occasionally be evoked as its core territory, Rome was its beating heart.

Rome, Not Italy

Throughout this chapter, we have skirted the city of Rome. In this final section, we turn our attention to the empire's ancestral capital and explore the way that Rome serves to define the role of Italy within panegyrical discourse. Italy is not a presence within the speeches, and indeed, as I have argued, it frequently seems determinedly underrepresented within the corpus. One can read the *Panegyrici Latini*, for instance, and learn at least *something* of the social and economic world of fourth-century Gauls.[91] Viewing these same worlds for fourth-, fifth- or sixth-century Italians is a virtual impossibility, and if there is a singly identifiable culprit (other than the constraints of genre), then that culprit is Rome. Rome dominates Italy, and when we might, on

---

[83] *limes*: 12.60; *possessio*: 12.61; *termini*: 15.72.
[84] Ennod. *Pan.* 15.72.
[85] Ennod. *Pan.* 12.61.
[86] He hopes for a *heres regni* at 21.93.
[87] Ennod. *Pan.* 10.51, 12.69.
[88] E.g. Fanning 1992, 294–5.
[89] Ennod. *Pan.* 12.69.
[90] Moorhead 1992, 39–51; Arnold 2014, 57–115. As Arnold 2014, 179–80 points out, this viewpoint certainly was not Ennodius' own, but was the expedient one to voice in a panegyric.
[91] Absent are any Italian insights that might rival Gallic miscellany such as the restorations of the school of rhetoric at Autun (*Pan. Lat.* 9, *passim*) or the remission of 7,000 *capita* and the cancellation of arrears from this same city's tax census under Constantine (*Pan. Lat.* 5.11–14).

geographic grounds, expect to find Italy within our speeches it is very often Rome that we find.

Rome, it must be stressed, was not Italy. The city was administered separately from the rest of the peninsula and, indeed, was accorded an organisational status afforded to no other city (bar, from the middle of the fourth century, Constantinople).[92] Indeed, at times the panegyrics even explicitly draw contrast between Rome and the regions that contained it, as did Nazarius in 321 when he viewed the recovery of Italy by Constantine in 312 merely as the first step through which 'the City' would be recovered, and in the enumeration of the evils of Maxentius' rule and the justification for the war that Constantine would embark on against him, it is not Maxentius' possession of Italy but of Rome that is routinely invoked.[93] At the other end of our period, the same can be said of Odoacer and Theoderic. Thus, while one can point to occasional references to Odoacer as scourge upon all of Italy, it is not Italy but Rome that calls Theoderic to lift Odoacer's tyranny – 'Rome, the mistress of the world demanded that you restore her to her station' (*te orbis domina ad status sui reparationem Roma poscebat*) – and it is Rome that Ennodius calls upon to witness the glory of Theoderic's victories in the north.[94] Likewise, although when Theoderic claims final victory over Odoacer there is a generalised sense of the restoration of Italy ('I see the unlooked-for beauty of cities risen from the ashes and, under the fullness of your government palatine roofs glow upon all sides'), nonetheless it is again Rome that merits the only specific and localised mention: the city grows young again, the senate is heaped with benefactions.[95]

Telling of this imaginative landscape is the last of Sidonius' imperial panegyrics, that delivered to Anthemius at Rome in 468. Anthemius was an eastern appointee to the western throne, a man who had made his career in the eastern military, and Sidonius chose, in the speech, to lean into this eastern angle, advancing the thesis that Anthemius was so remarkable that all the West chose to summon him from the East to be their emperor.[96] Precisely *how* Sidonius frames this conceit within his speech, however, reveals a great deal about Italy's place within the imaginative geopolitical configuration of western territory, and the perpetually junior status it was accorded in political rhetoric. After a little over three hundred lines exploring the career of Anthemius before his acclamation, Sidonius conjures the moment in which the emperor Libius Severus died and 'Oenotria [Italy], when she beheld this calamity from the cloud-bound summits of the Apennines, set out for the glassy halls of blue Tiber'.[97] We have already explored Italy's characterisation here, her hair heavy with grapevines that bind her many towns. Italy begs the god Tiber to intercede for her; Tiber is thus persuaded and goes to speak with Roma, and Roma likewise goes to the East and persuades Dawn to give up an

---

[92] Lançon 2000, 45–65; Grig and Kelly 2012.
[93] *Pan. Lat.* 4.27.5, *Pan. Lat.* 12.3, 4.6–13.
[94] Ennod. *Pan.* 7.30 and 9.48; on Odoacer and Italy, see 6.23 and 8.46.
[95] Ennod. *Pan.* 11.56–9; nearly fifty years ago, Sabine MacCormack noted the senatorial bent of Ennodius' rhetoric (MacCormack 1976, 73–5).
[96] On Anthemius' career before taking power, see Härtel 1982, 151–2; Roberto 2015.
[97] Sid. Apoll. *Carm.* 2.319–20.

easterner to rule the West.⁹⁸ Italy thus comes as junior and as supplicant. But she is not a provincial governor approaching the emperor. Dawn is the emperor, and it is Roma that comes to her as supplicant. Nor, however, is Italy a local delegation coming to the provincial governor, for Tiber is Rome's petitioner. In this analogy, rather, Italy is the poor farmer, the individual at the very bottom of the ladder of Roman political patronage.

Thus, there existed a clear ideological subordination of Italy to the city of Rome. That ideology has very meaningful consequences for the way in which one finds Italy represented in the speeches and for how it is perpetually eclipsed by its famous neighbour.⁹⁹ If we make direct comparison between the representation of Rome and of any other Italian city, this point comes through very clearly. Of the many passages one might choose to elucidate this point, perhaps none is better than Claudian's fulsome description of Stilicho's procession through Rome upon his appointment to the consulship, from the Flaminian Way strewn with flowers, to Stilicho's ascent of the Pincian Hill, to the crowds in the Theatre of Pompey and in the Circus Maximus between Palatine and Aventine.¹⁰⁰ This closing section to the second book is then complemented by the third book of the piece, delivered in Rome, which dwells entirely on Stilicho's relationship to the ancient capital.¹⁰¹

The richness and vividness of this description, alive not only to the city's history but to the specifics of its physical topography and to the ritual significance of its space and the uses to which that space is put, cannot be paralleled by any like evocation of *any* city, Italian or otherwise, within the Latin panegyrics. Claudian, as we have seen, has no interest in Milan.¹⁰² One can even compare Claudian's passage (or others like it, though there are none quite so rich) directly to the one detailed account occurring within the panegyrics of events that took place within an Italian city, the visit of the dyarchs Maximian and Diocletian to Milan in the winter of 290/1.¹⁰³ The descriptions of Milan – such as they are – that are to be found within this passage offer nothing like the richness or the specificity of Claudian's colourfully evoked Roman landscape. Of the city itself, we learn only that it had a palace (or at least a large audience chamber) and that it had people in it. Hardly a stirring evocation of place and space, and it would be fair to say that the Milan of the panegyrist could in fact be any major city within the empire. Though prefaced with remarks on Maximian's approach from the Alps (discussed above, and again fairly generic as they go), the city itself is a kind of blank imperial space, upon which no Milanese particularity is written.

The utter dominance of Rome in the imaginative space of Italy also explains the surprising absence of Italy from the speeches of authors for whom one might reasonably expect it to be a preoccupation. Symmachus is perhaps first among this number.

---

[98] Sid. Apoll. *Carm.* 2.319–438.
[99] On which see also Chapter 17 in this volume.
[100] Claud. *Cons. Stil.* 2.397–407; Claudian speaks of the *vallis Murcia*, a name for the Circus based upon the valley in which it was situated.
[101] Claud. *Cons. Stil.* 3, *passim.*
[102] Above, p. 466.
[103] *Pan. Lat.* 11.9–12; on the occasion of the speech and the visit, see Omissi 2018, 87–91.

Born into a noble Roman family (albeit one of perhaps relatively recent noble status), Symmachus was a man thoroughly grounded in Rome and Italy. Though his education appears to have been undertaken in Gaul, his early career was centred upon Rome, where he had held the quaestorship, praetorship and a role as *pontifex maior* by the year 365. In this same year he served as *corrector Lucaniae et Bruttiorum*, governor of Italy's toe.[104] His family owned at least three urban villas in Rome and more than a dozen estates in central and southern Italy, which his letters make clear were very dear to him.[105] Symmachus was, therefore, at least by modern thinking, a thoroughly Italian individual, his life, career and inherited wealth largely grounded in the peninsula. Yet one looks in vain for Italy amongst Symmachus' speeches. His three imperial speeches were delivered to emperors – Valentinian I and the young Gratian – based at Trier, and the events they communicate are largely Gallic. When we find the world of the south entering these speeches, it is Rome and not Italy that commands his attention. Across the three panegyrics that he delivered in Trier, on only two occasions does he turn his attention to the land south of the Alps, and on both occasions these references are to Rome, not Italy.[106] This first, in his second panegyric to Valentinian, is passing in the extreme, a promise to relate everything he has seen in Gaul and Germany 'through the peoples' (*per populos*) and to the senate and people of Rome.[107] His second comes in his panegyric to the young Gratian, in which he compares the bridge that Gratian's father has set up across the Rhine with that which he had built (or rather rebuilt) in Rome.[108]

Thus, even if only with the figurative hierarchy of panegyric, Italy stands perpetually subordinated to Rome. Ills that befall and benefits that accrue to the lands of Italy seem largely to be viewed by the panegyrists as ills and benefits for the city of Rome, with Italy merely its attendant geographical setting: less a place in its own right than the padded container in which Rome is cushioned. Of course, the tendency is by no means universal: we have explored, for instance, Sidonius' evocations of Italy, and we might quote here his determination to see Geiseric effectively countered, 'so that Carthage may cease to war against Italy', but the point remains that such energy and creativity as the panegyrists are willing to lavish in their speeches on the land south of the Alps is drawn almost entirely towards Rome.[109]

Conclusion

This survey of the panegyrics has led us to largely negative conclusions about the place of Italy within the imaginative landscape of Roman political oratory. Though the peninsula certainly does not pass unnoticed, mention of it is always tailored to the very specific goal of praising the honorand of the given speech. Because of the nature

---

[104] Salzman and Roberts 2011, xxiii–iv.
[105] Vera 1986; for various references to Symmachus' properties, see Symm. *Ep.* 6.11, 12, 66, 7.66, 9.32, 52.
[106] Barring of course the Italian *exemplum*, discussed above p. 464.
[107] Symm. *Or.* 2.31.
[108] Symm. *Or.* 3.9; cf. Chenault 2020, 201–5.
[109] Sid. Apoll. *Carm.* 5.348–9.

of the panegyrics we have (i.e. almost exclusively those delivered to emperors), Italy most frequently merits notice as the backdrop to major military campaigns. In this, we find a recurrent theme of a land of plenty laid low either by the depravity of a tyrant or the depredations of a foreign invader. Of the major social, political and economic changes wrought in the peninsula, we learn surprisingly little. Genre plays its part, for panegyrics were not concerned with charting complex change over time but with direct and unqualified praise of an individual. But the primary culprit for all of this is Rome, which draws and monopolises the attention of any orator whose gaze falls upon the Italian peninsula.

This does not mean that those who composed or delivered oratory were uninterested in Italy, or blind to its existence as an entity separate from Rome. What it points us to, however, is the high threshold of political importance required for any event, individual or region if it was to merit consideration within the relatively constricted limits of time and genre that dictated the content of panegyric. For the most part, Italy does not cross this threshold. When it does, it is as a backdrop to wider imperial action, and it is clear that to no author throughout our period is the fortune or condition or identity of wider Italy of any particular concern. Orators looked to Rome and to its senate far more easily as a barometer of the emperor's relation to his people than they did to any loose conceptions of a corporate Italy. To trace any meaningful history of Italy from the speeches is an impossibility.

What more can be said? It came as a surprise to me in drawing the material together for this chapter how difficult it was to draw any clear thematic structure to Italy's presentation in the panegyrics, and this may perhaps be a conclusion in itself. Imperial culture – that is the discourse, the ceremonial and the monumentality – was highly centralised. Viewed from the top, the empire existed to serve its emperor and the administrative and military apparatus that surrounded him. We see this in Italy's presentation. Viewed from the panegyrics, and from the point of view of the political class that made up their authors and audiences, it is broadly a geography: a place, but not an idea or an entity. Though this place might be evocatively and emotively referenced, its ideological significance was made subordinate to the two brighter lights to which it was subordinate: the city of Rome and the emperor.

Bibliography

Arnold, J. J. (2014) *Theoderic and the Roman Imperial Restoration*, New York.
Arnold, J. J., S. M. Bjornlie and K. Sessa (eds) (2016) *A Companion to Ostrogothic Italy*, Leiden.
Barnes, T. D. (1975) 'Constans and Gratian in Rome', *HSCP* 79: 325–33.
Börm, H. (2013) *Westrom: von Honorius bis Justinian*, Stuttgart.
Bruzzone, A. (ed.) (1999) *Flavio Merobaude: Panegirico in versi*, Rome.
Cameron, A. (1970) *Claudian: Poetry and Propaganda at the Court of Honorius*, Oxford.
Carney, T. F. (1961) 'The Flight and Exile of Marius', *G&R* 8: 98–121.
Casey, P. J. (1994) *Carausius and Allectus: the British Usurpers*, London.
Chenault, R. (2020) 'Roman and Gallic in the Latin Panegyrics of Symmachus and Ausonius', in A. Omissi and A. Ross (eds) *Imperial Panegyric from Diocletian to Honorius*, Liverpool, 189–208.
Clover, F. M. (1971) 'Flavius Merobaudes: a Translation and Historical Commentary', *TAPhS* n.s. 61: 1–78.

Fanning, S. (1992) 'Emperors and Empires in Fifth-Century Gaul', in J. Drinkwater and H. Elton (eds) *Fifth Century Gaul: a Crisis of Identity?* Cambridge, 288–97.
Gillett, A. (2012) 'Epic Panegyric and Political Communication in the Fifth-Century West', in L. Grig and G. Kelly (eds) *Two Romes: Rome and Constantinople in Late Antiquity*, Oxford.
Grig, L. and G. Kelly (2012) 'Introduction', in L. Grig and G. Kelly (eds) *Two Romes: Rome and Constantinople in Late Antiquity*, Oxford, 1–30.
Haase, B. S. (1991) 'Ennodius' *Panegyric of Theoderic the Great*: a Translation and Commentary', MA dissertation, University of Ottawa.
Halsall, G. (2007) *Barbarian Migrations and the Roman West 376–568*, Cambridge.
Hardie, P. (2019) *Classicism and Christianity in Late Antique Latin Poetry*, Oakland, CA.
Härtel, G. (1982) 'Die zeitgeschichtliche Relevanz der Novellen des Kaisers Anthemius', *Klio* 64: 151–9.
Humphries, M. (2008) 'From Usurper to Emperor: the Politics of Legitimation in the Age of Constantine', *Journal of Late Antiquity* 1: 82–100.
Janson, T. (1979) *A Concordance to the Latin Panegyric: a Concordance to the XII Panegyrici Latini and to the Panegyrical Texts and Fragments of Symmachus, Ausonius, Merobaudes, Ennodius, Cassiodorus*, Hildesheim.
Johnson, M. J. (1988) 'Toward a History of Theoderic's Building Program', *DOP* 42: 73–96.
Kennedy, S. (2019) 'Winter Is Coming: the Barbarization of Roman Leaders in Imperial Panegyric from AD 446–68', *CQ* 69: 422–34.
Kennell, S. A. H. (2000) *Magnus Felix Ennodius: a Gentleman of the Church*, Ann Arbor.
Kulikowski, M. (2006) *Rome's Gothic Wars: from the Third Century to Alaric*, Cambridge.
Lançon, B. (2000) *Rome in Late Antiquity: Everyday Life and Urban Change, AD 312–609*, trans. A. Nevill, Edinburgh.
Laurence, R. (1999) *The Roads of Roman Italy: Mobility and Cultural Change*, London.
Lunn-Rockliffe, S. (2010) 'Commemorating the Usurper Magnus Maximus: Ekphrasis, Poetry, and History in Pacatus' Panegyric of Theodosius', *Journal of Late Antiquity* 3: 316–36.
MacCormack, S. (1976) 'Latin Prose Panegyrics: Tradition and Discontinuity in the Later Roman Empire', *REAug* 22 (1–2): 29–77.
Matthews, J. (1990) *Western Aristocracies and Imperial Court, AD 364–425*, rev. ed., Oxford.
Merrills, A. and R. Miles (2010) *The Vandals*, Oxford.
Millar, F. (1986) 'Italy and the Roman Empire: Augustus to Constantine', *Phoenix* 40: 295–318.
Mittag, P. F. (2006) 'Zu den Quellen der *Expositio totius Mundi et Gentium*: ein neuer Periplus?', *Hermes* 134: 338–51.
Moorhead, J. (1992) *Theoderic in Italy*, Oxford.
Nixon, C. E. V. and B. S. Rodgers (ed. and trans.) (1994) *In Praise of Later Roman Emperors. The Panegyrici Latini: Introduction, Translation, and Historical Commentary, with the Latin Text of R. A. B. Mynors*, Berkeley.
O'Flynn, J. M. (1983) *Generalissimos of the Western Roman Empire*, Edmonton.
Odahl, C. M. (2004) *Constantine and the Christian Empire*, London.
Omissi, A. (2018) *Emperors and Usurpers in the Later Roman Empire: Civil War, Panegyric, and the Construction of Legitimacy*, Oxford.
Omissi, A. and A. Ross (eds) (2020) *Imperial Panegyric from Diocletian to Honorius*, Liverpool.
Porena, P. (2013) 'La riorganizzazione amministrativa dell'Italia: Costantino, Roma, il Senato e gli equilibri dell'Italia romana', in A. Melloni et al. (eds) *Costantino I: Enciclopedia costantiniana sulla figura e l'immagine dell'imperatore del cosiddetto Editto di Milano, 313–2013*, vol. 1, Rome, 329–49.
Roberto, U. (2015) 'Politica, tradizione e strategie familiari: Antemio e l'ultima difesa dell'unità dell'impero (467–472)', in U. Roberto and L. Mecella (ed.) *Governare e riformare l'impero al momento della sua divisione: Oriente, Occidente, Illirico*, Rome.

Rohr, C. (1995) *Der Theoderich-Panegyricus des Ennodius*, Hanover.
Rohr, C. (1997) 'Zum Theoderich-Panegyricus des Ennodius: textkritische Überlegungen im Rahmen einer Neuedition und Übersetzung', *Hermes* 125: 100–17.
Roller, M. B. (2009) 'The Exemplary Past in Roman Historiography and Culture', in A. Feldherr (ed.) *The Cambridge Companion to Roman Historiography*, Cambridge, 214–30.
Rougé, J. (1966) *Expositio totius mundi et gentium: introduction, texte critique, traduction, notes et commentaire*, Paris.
Salzman, R. and M. J. Roberts (2011) *The Letters of Symmachus: Book 1*, Atlanta.
Saunders, R. T. (1992) 'Aurelian's "Two" Iuthungian Wars', *Historia: Zeitschrift für Alte Geschichte* 41: 311–27.
Sivan, H. S. (1989) 'Sidonius Apollinaris, Theodoric II, and Gothic–Roman Politics from Avitus to Anthemius', *Hermes* 117: 85–94.
Vera, D. (1986) 'Simmaco e le sue proprietà: struttura e funzionamento di un patrimonio aristocratico del quarto secolo d.C.', in F. Pashoud (ed.) *Colloque genevois sur Symmaque: à l'occasion du mille six centième anniversaire du conflit de l'autel de la Victoire*, Paris, 231–76.
Watson, L. (1998) 'Representing the Past, Redefining the Future: Sidonius Apollinaris' Panegyrics of Avitus and Anthemius', in M. Whitby (ed.) *The Propaganda of Power: the Role of Panegyric in Late Antiquity*, Leiden, 177–98.
Wijnendaele, J. W. P. and M. P. Hanaghan (2021) 'Constantius *Heros* (*ILCV* 66) – an Elegiac Testimony on the Decline of the Late Roman West', *Chiron* 51: 257–76.

17

STEPPING OUT OF THE SHADOWS: ITALY IN LATE ANTIQUE HISTORIOGRAPHY

Peter Van Nuffelen

THE FIRST TERRITORY CONQUERED by Rome, Italy profited and suffered from its proximity to the *caput mundi*. Praised as a providential land, it nevertheless stood firmly in the shadow of Rome in the representations of Roman territory found in Latin literature. Late antique literature inherited such a view, which, in turn, has shaped the focus of modern scholarship on Rome, be it its material appearance or the ideological meaning it carried.[1] In the late antique drama, Italy is an extra, always present in the background, but rarely graced with a line to utter. Late ancient and modern writers wax dramatic on the sack of Rome by Alaric in 410, which caused little damage and was quite a 'genteel affair',[2] whilst Alaric's ruthless and thorough destruction of the smaller Italian cities between Ravenna and Rome needs to be gleaned from a few lines in Procopius' history.[3] If the traditional spatial representation of Italy persisted in much of late antique literature, in particular geography and panegyric,[4] I argue that signs of Italy's 'emancipation from Rome' can be noticed in historiography. This was a consequence of the institutional weakening of the central institutions of power in Rome,[5] and of the critical reflection initiated by Christian literature on the traditional way in which Roman history was told. Towards the end of the period surveyed here, Italia is depicted as the land of destiny for the Ostrogoths. The story, however, is not one of linear progression towards a spatial representation in which Italy has left the shadows. Rather, there were many experiments, often dead ends, which reflect the weakening of the traditional ideological discourse about Rome. Yet that discourse never fully collapsed: Italy will by and large remain a passive subject, even after the sixth century, whilst discourses that emancipate Italy do this on the basis of the traditional Romanocentric narratives.

This chapter is about the spatial representation of Italy in relation to Rome, in a specific genre, historiography. It is not about Italian identity. In a series of studies, Andrea Giardina has argued that an Italian identity never developed in Late Antiquity. Most cities were embedded in a Roman network through patron–client relations, wherein

---

[1] Paschoud 1967; Inglebert 1996; Brodka 1998; Curran 2000; Fuhrer 2011; Grig and Kelly 2012.
[2] Mathisen 2013 for the expression.
[3] Proc. *Bell.* 6.16.24.
[4] For geography, see below, p. 476–9; for poetry, see Chapter 16 in this volume.
[5] See Chapters 1 and 2 in this volume.

the patron would be based in Rome.⁶ When I argue that Italy as a geographical term acquires independent contours in historiography by 500, this does not mean that its inhabitants had a stronger sense of Italian identity. When terms such as 'Romans'⁷ and 'Italians' are used in the sources, I regard them as ascriptions that are related to the spatial representations I am interested in. How they might connect to the self-understanding of the individuals concerned is not our interest here. The representation of Italy in late antique panegyric is the subject of Chapter 16, by Adrastos Omissi. There Italy would continue to play its role as a foil for Rome, whilst in historiography we do notice a greater impact of the political and cultural changes of the later Roman Empire. Although historiography was also bound by generic expectations,⁸ its role of recording events rendered it more susceptible to reflecting the changed conditions.

Basking in the Shadows of Rome

In his *Chorography*, composed under the emperor Claudius (AD 41–54),⁹ Pomponius Mela makes the following comment when reaching Italy: 'On Italy a few things will be said, more because the order of the work demands it than because it would need to be explained. Everything is known.'¹⁰ The *praeteritio* of sorts underscores the central position of Italy in the work, also visible from the fact that it is described in the middle of the second out of three books. Rome itself receives a proper *praeteritio*: 'Rome, a long time ago founded by shepherds, would now need another work to do justice to the amount of material.'¹¹ Pomponius Mela's comment hints at the opportunities and drawbacks for Italy of being Rome's hinterland. On the one hand, Italy basks in the glory of Rome and is extolled over other regions of the empire. On the other, this can only happen when one does not speak of Rome, whose description would demand as much space as that of the entire world. In the conceptual geography of the Roman Empire, Italy is both central and peripheral.¹²

In geographical works from the fourth century, Italy keeps this privileged position in the shadows of Rome. Solinus opens his *Collectanea rerum memorabilium* with Rome followed by Italy, before following the order of the seas and oceans.¹³ He thus reorganises the material from Pliny the Elder, his main source, who had described Spain and Gaul before arriving in Italy,¹⁴ effectively disrupting the geographical order to start with the centre of the empire. When arriving at Italy, the anonymous

---

⁶ Giardina 1994, 67; 2010. On the Republic, see Carlà-Uhink 2017.
⁷ Maskarinec 2013 studies the changing meanings of that term.
⁸ Van Nuffelen and Van Hoof 2020, xxvii–lxxvii.
⁹ Cf. Silberman 1988, xiii for the date of 43–4.
¹⁰ Pompon. 2.58: *de Italia, magis quia ordo exigit quia monstrari eget, pauca dicentur; nota sunt omnia.*
¹¹ Pompon. 2.60: *et Roma, quondam a pastoribus condita, nunc si pro materia dicatur alterum opus.* Something similar in Pliny the Elder, *HN* 3.5.39.
¹² A distant consequence of such representations may be the fact that in the geographical digression that concludes his *Ecclesiastical History*, Pseudo-Zachariah (writing after 568) does not mention Italy.
¹³ Schmidt 1995 for a fourth-century date; Brodersen 2014, 8 argues for a date in the late third century.
¹⁴ Plin. *HN* 3.3–5.

author of the *Expositio totius mundi et gentium* praises its providential riches: 'And after it [Campania],[15] Italy, which, named, displays its glory alone by being mentioned or named, has many and different cities and is filled with all goods. It is ruled by providence.'[16] Besides great wines, this is evidenced in the location of Rome within Italy – Rome that then receives extensive attention (at least for the habits of the genre). In his *Cosmographia*, made up of lists of rivers, provinces etc., Julius Honorius does mention Italy, but not Rome. Maybe it was too well known, but it could also be an ideological choice: Honorius would locate it ideologically outside the *orbis terrarum*. *Italiam rerum dominam* Rutilius Namatianus would sing towards the end of his poem narrating his return from Rome to Gaul[17] – a work that is the most charming illustration of Italy basking in the shadows of Rome. Indeed, whilst praising Italy, the poem opens with the difficulty of leaving the centre behind, and when travelling along the coast of Italy, Rutilius encounters Roman history.

There is, however, another side to the story. History is a less gentle genre than geography. Roman history was conceptualised as a series of conquests, which started with the nearest neighbours, the Italians. With characteristic brevity and with a nod to the same trope as Pomponius Mela, Festus, writing under the emperor Valens, put it this way:

> Under seven kings through 243 years, Roman *imperium* did not advance beyond Portus and Ostia, within 18 miles from the gates of the city of Rome, seeing that she was as yet small and founded by shepherds, while neighbouring cities were hemming her in. At the same time, through 467 years under consuls, among whom there sometimes were dictators, too, Italy was occupied as far as beyond the Po, Africa was subjugated, the Spains added, and Gaul and Britain made tributaries.[18]

The tradition stretches back at least to Livy and is exemplified in Florus, Appian[19] and Cassius Dio, historians who narrated the providential rise of Rome to become the fourth empire in world history.[20] In the fourth century, Festus and his contemporary Eutropius develop that tradition. Being Rome's eldest conquest was, then, the flip side of the coin of enjoying the proximity of the *caput imperii*.

---

[15] *Exp. tot. mund. gent.* 53–6 has an idiosyncratic sequence of Italian provinces, which does not match any provincial catalogue: Calabria, Bruttium, Lucania, Campania, Italia and Tuscia. Yet in 57 all the preceding are called Italia. On this section, see Mittag 2006, 342–7.

[16] *Exp. tot. mund. gent.* 55: *et post eam Italia, quae et nominata verbo solum aut in nomine gloriam suam ostendit, multas et varias civitates habens et omnibus bonis plena, regitur a providentia.*

[17] Rut. Namat. 2.19. The work is dated to 416. Compare the expression *gentium domina* in *Pan. Lat.* 2(10) 2.2–4.

[18] Fest. 3.2: *utpote adhuc parvae et a pastoribus conditae, cum finitimae circum civitates premerent, Romanum processit imperium. sub consulibus, inter quos nonnumquam et dictatores fuerunt, per annos simul CCCCLXVII Italia usque trans Padum occupata est, Africa subacta est, Hispaniae accesserunt, Galliae et Brittaniae tributariae factae sunt* (trans. Banchich and Meka).

[19] His second book is called *italike* and narrated the conquest of Italy.

[20] Hose 1994.

The Imperial *Habitus*

Geography and historiography are genres closely linked to Roman imperial power. As analysed by C. Nicolet, the creation of an empire implied not just physical control of a territory but also the claim to knowledge about that territory and what lies beyond – an activity that was directed and perceived from the centre.[21] With the Roman dominance over the Mediterranean, historiography became closely linked to the empire: history was written *from* the centre – that is, Rome – and *for* that centre. Even histories composed from a provincial perspective, like that of Pompeius Trogus, were stories of the rise of the centre.[22] Such a perspective was perpetuated through elite education, and authors and officeholders (two overlapping categories in the ancient world) shared in, and continued, that culture. The correlation between officeholding, social position and literary activity was strong during the empire, and was especially visible in historiography. Tacitus and Cassius Dio are just the most obvious examples of this link. Thus, social status and career, education and literary tradition conspired to produce a culture which had its geographical centre in Rome. P. Gautier Dalché puts it aptly: 'This culture of an ideological nature was a vital condition of building a career in the bureaucracy and grounding administrators' actions in a perception of the unity of the empire.'[23] That culture presupposed a dominant centre, Rome, that not only historically but also geographically risked swallowing Italy.

The imperial *habitus* came, however, under pressure in Late Antiquity.[24] Three elements played a role. First, internal reorganisation. The tetrarchic regime of multiple travelling emperors meant at least a symbolic decline in Rome's importance. Diocletian was aware of the risk of centrifugal tendencies and sought to counteract it through an ideology of political and filial unity.[25] While the return to dynastic rule in 324 eliminated one challenge to unity and hence to the centrality of Rome, Constantine's decision to found Constantinople set in motion a process that would create a new centre for what moderns tend to see as a new empire, the Byzantine one. For a long time, Romans had, at least temporarily, been able to dissociate the ideological Rome from the physical one: as Pompeianus put it, when trying to dissuade Commodus from leaving the Danube frontier, 'Rome is where the emperor is.'[26] Yet the creation of new imperial residences since the Tetrarchy also meant the creation of new, physical Romes. A first victim of the reorganisation of the spatial imagination of the Roman Empire was Italy. In 293 it was, for the first time, divided into provinces by Diocletian, and thus reduced to an administrative status identical to that of the rest of the empire. In 312/13 Constantine

---

[21] Nicolet 1991. See further Clarke 1999; Hänger 2001; Talbert and Brodersen 2004; Woolf 2011, nuancing the relationship between empire and knowledge; Geus and Rathmann 2013; Rimell and Asper 2017.

[22] Yarrow 2006; Hofmann 2018.

[23] Gautier Dalché 2014, 182: 'Cette culture de nature idéologique était une condition indispensable pour faire carrière dans la bureaucratie et pour donner à l'action des admininistrateurs un sens fondé sur la perception de l'unité de l'empire.' See Lozovsky 2006 for a similar argument relating to the Carolingian period. Witakowski 2007, 221 explains the absence of geographical literature in Syriac by the fact that Syriac speakers did not have an empire to run.

[24] See further the introduction to Van Nuffelen 2019.

[25] Van Dam 2007, 35–78. See further Chapter 1 in this volume.

[26] Hdn. 1.6.5. See Roberto (Chapter 1) in this volume.

even divided the single diocese of Italy and assigned the North to a *vicarius Italiae* located in Milan and the southern half to a *vicarius urbis*.[27] This was also to have an impact on the ecclesiastical geography of Italy, rendering the authority of Rome strong in southern Italy and more contested in the north.

A second factor were the external threats to the Roman Empire, especially in the West. However one wishes to conceptualise the mechanisms that led to Roman military weakness and the loss of effective control over large swathes of territory from the battle of Adrianople (378) to the Vandal invasion of North Africa (429),[28] there is no dispute that contemporaries understood these events to betray imperial weakness. As we shall see, one could respond with optimism, as did Orosius, or by pinning hope on the bishop of Rome, like Prosper of Aquitaine, but none failed to see that the Roman Empire was not as strong as it used to be. The panegyrist Claudian repeatedly plays with the idea of a mortal threat to Rome, albeit always to show how Stilicho did save the empire.[29] The sack of Rome in 410 appeared to be such an ominous event not just because it seemed to belie the idea of an eternal Rome, but also because it rendered real fears that had been mere literary tropes so far.[30]

Third, Christianity developed in the Roman Empire and thus took fully part in its culture. At the same time, it harboured a degree of critical distance from that empire, which, in Augustinian language, represented the *saeculum*.[31] In this context, two of its manifestations are important. Whilst Christian authors were mostly trained in the Roman schools of rhetoric, they also expressed criticism and doubt about rhetoric, as a form of ostentation that risked distorting reality. The fishermen that were the Apostles did not need such a language.[32] If Christians could ideologically identify themselves with the Roman Empire,[33] they rarely forgot the distinction between the secular and the ecclesiastical, between this life and the true life to come. Unsurprisingly, then, one of the most stringent (and underappreciated) criticisms of the imperial *habitus* is found in the *Histories against the Pagans* by Orosius,[34] who, as we shall see, would also give a voice to Italy.

These factors did not quickly nor radically overturn the spatial representation inherited from the High Empire. As the papers in a recent volume on space and historiography in Late Antiquity show, it is only in the sixth century that Greek historiography puts Constantinople at its heart. In the West, the centrality of Rome is equally slowly dislodged: towards the end of the sixth century John of Biclar refocuses his narrative on Visigothic Spain, suggesting that the in his eyes heretical empire had forfeited God's favour.[35] We should, then, not expect the relationship between Italy

---

[27] These changes are detailed in Chapters 1 and 2 in this volume.
[28] For diferent views, cf. Goffart 2006; Heather 2006; Halsall 2007; Kulikowski 2007. See further Chapters 3 and 4 in this volume.
[29] E.g. Claud. *Gild*. 1.17–128, with Harich-Schwarzbauer 2013.
[30] Van Nuffelen 2015.
[31] Markus 1988.
[32] Gemeinhardt 2007; Gemeinhardt et al. 2016.
[33] This is in scholarship usually called Eusebianism (Inglebert 1996) and supposedly challenged by Augustine. Such a reconstruction is too easy: Van Nuffelen 2012, ch. 8 with further references.
[34] Van Nuffelen 2012, 63–82.
[35] Humphries 2019; Kaldellis 2019.

and Rome to be suddenly reconfigured. Rather, we encounter a series of innovations that show how the imperial *habitus* and the associated spatial representation were shaken without being completely dissolved.

'Reread the Ancient Books'

In our edition of the Latin fragmentary histories of Late Antiquity (AD 300–600), Lieve Van Hoof and I have edited the fragments of two local Latin histories. The grammarian Carminius, whom we can only date between the second and fourth centuries,[36] composed a treatise *De Italia*. The only extant fragment deals with Etruscan and Sabine customs.[37] Interest in Italian customs and history went back at least to Cato's *Origines*, which collected such material in its first three books,[38] but it had never (so it seems) received attention in a separate book. A work on early Roman history composed by a grammarian, Pseudo-Aurelius Victor, *Origins of the Roman People*, records an earlier work 'On the Origin of Padua'.[39] As much as its citing authority, the *Origo patavina* seems to have been built around a commentary on Vergil. We hypothesise that it was written by a local grammarian from Padua who in the first half of the fourth century summarised traditions regarding the early history of Padua.

Much is uncertain about these two works, not least their precise date. They nevertheless deserve some attention here because they represent – as far as I know – the only evidence for local histories in Latin historiography. Local historiography is a well-studied phenomenon in Greek historiography of the Hellenistic and Roman period and even in Late Antiquity. For example, the *patria* (a distinct type of usually poetic compositions on the history of a particular city) only exist in Greek. Latin historiography, by contrast, was Roman historiography.

Is it significant that such local works, focusing on Italy, were (probably) written in Late Antiquity? One swallow (or even two) does not a summer make, but there is a third example. Protadius, a Gaul, *praefectus urbi* in 401, was busy writing a history of Gaul in 396. We know very little about the work, except that it probably included Caesar's campaigns (58–50 BC) and those of Germanicus (AD 14–16) and that it relied heavily on extant literary sources.[40] Again it is the only work written in or about Gaul that seems to deviate from the imperial focus.[41] In all three cases, the authors were wedded to the imperial *habitus* by their social position as grammarian or senator. Yet they produce works that have a different focus from the one usual in Roman historiography. It is tempting to think that the fragilisation of the imperial spatial representation, under the influence of the three factors highlighted above, created the intellectual opportunity to compose such a work. Interestingly, such works

---

[36] See *FHistLA* 1. We are critical of the early date proposed by Schmidt 1989, although it is not impossible.
[37] Carminius, *De Italia*, *FHistLA* 1 F1 = Macrob. *Sat.* 5.19.12–14.
[38] *FRHist* 5.
[39] *FHistLA* 2 T1 = Pseudo-Aurelius Victor, *Origins of the Roman People* 1.5–6.
[40] Protadius, *FHistLA* 5 T1 = Symm. *Ep.* 4.18.5.
[41] Eigler 2013, 401. Notice, however, that the *Chronicon* of Sulpicius Severus starts to focus on almost exclusively Gallic events for the last decades of its account.

with a local focus could only be composed by relying on the standard accounts of Roman history (Vergil, Livy and Caesar) and by rearranging and rewriting what one found there. A local focus thus had to be retrieved from works propounding what I have called the imperial *habitus*. In a less gentle but not dissimilar way, the Christian historian Orosius would also use the tradition perpetuated by the centre to give flesh to a peripheral identity that was to be pitted against that centre.

'Let Italy Speak for Herself'

Orosius composed his histories about the same time as Rutilius Namatianus praised Italy as *rerum domina* in his *De reditu suo*. The *Histories* are basically an argument about the representation of the past and how it is coloured by education. The Roman elite, so he argues, is trained to think of their own history as a succession of greatness – great deeds, great individuals, great results – and they measure their current situation against that image. Yet it is but an image, the product of the imperial *habitus*. If one takes an objective look at the past, one sees that that history of greatness is one of suffering and misdeeds. Measure the present against this true measure and you will see that recent events are far from disastrous and even that the present is better than the past.[42] The argument is achieved by giving a voice to regions, like Italy, that common historical narrative reduced to a stage in the geographical expansion of Rome. In the preface to Book 5, Orosius argues against a rosy view of Roman conquest:

> Finally, let Italy herself speak. Why did she quarrel with, oppose, and fight back against the Romans, who are one of her own, for 400 years, unless good times for Rome signalled bad times for herself, and that the common good was harmed by Rome becoming the dominant power?[43]

Italy, then, the providential land, the cloak of Rome, is here turned against Rome. The violence and suffering of the conquest are not hidden as they were in Festus' brief note, but rhetorically imagined and turned against Rome. Indeed, Italy was, Orosius spells out, for a long time Rome's enemy: 'Or all of Italy, which for 400 years yearned, whenever it dared, for the destruction of Rome?'[44] The contemporary relevance of all this is then rendered explicit:

> From all this we can say that while at present she suffers vexations from foreigners, Italy can console herself by thinking of her past troubles, which were born of her, turned themselves on her, and which tore her to pieces with incomparable cruelty.[45]

---

[42] Van Nuffelen 2012, 63–73.

[43] Oros. 5.1.7: *ipsa postremo dicat Italia: cur per annos quadringentos Romanis utique suis contradixit obstitit repugnavit, si eorum felicitas sua infelicitas non erat Romanosque fieri rerum dominos bonis communibus non obstabat?* (trans. Fear 2010, 207).

[44] Oros. 6.1.14: *an tota Italia quae per quadringentos annos, dum audere potuit, excidio eius inhiavit?* (trans. Fear 2010, 265).

[45] Oros. 5.24.20: *ex quo admonemus ut ipsa se consoletur Italia de vexatione externorum praesentium per recordationem praeteritorum ex se atque in se et ipsam se inconparabiliter crudelius dilacerantum suorum* (trans. Fear 2010, 260).

The flip side of freeing Italy from the smothering embrace of Rome was to render it a region just like any other part of the empire. In the geographical description of the world with which he opens the work, Italy appears as one province among others. Interestingly, there is no mention of Rome.[46] This may be the result of his relying on a source that was shaped by the imperial spatial representation of the empire, for we have seen that Julius Honorius, a text used in rhetorical schools, also ignores Rome. Rome was too obvious to be mentioned. But its obliteration may also have received a new meaning in Orosius and reflect his desire to dislodge Rome from its ideological centre.

A Bishop and His Land

For the year 452, Prosper of Aquitaine composed a memorable vignette in his chronicle, when he depicted Leo of Rome heading an embassy to dissuade Attila from continuing his invasion of Italy:

> When Attila had recruited new troops for the ones he had lost in Gaul, he planned to enter Italy via Pannonia. Our commander Aëtius did not take any measures in line with the ones of the previous war, so that he even did not close off the Alps, by which he would have been able to forbid entrance to the enemy. He deemed that this alone was left as a hope, namely to leave Italy entirely with the emperor. Whilst this seemed to be very shameful and dangerous, shame held fear in bounds, and it was believed that the cruelty and greed of the enemy would be satisfied by the great destruction of so many important provinces. To the emperor and the senate and Roman people none of all the proposed plans to oppose the enemy seemed so practicable as to send legates to the most savage king and beg for peace. Our most blessed Pope Leo – trusting in the help of God, who never fails the righteous in their trials – undertook the task, accompanied by Avienus, a man of consular rank, and the prefect Trygetius. And the outcome was what his faith had foreseen; for when the king had received the embassy, he was so impressed by the presence of the high priest that he ordered his army to give up warfare and, after he had promised peace, he departed beyond the Danube.[47]

The episode imparts many of the views Prosper wished to convey in the later editions of his chronicle (433–55) composed in Rome: a disenchantment with secular

---

[46] Oros. 1.61–2.

[47] Prosper, *Chron.* 1367: *Attila redintegratis viribus, quas in Gallia amiserat, Italiam ingredi per Pannonias intendit nihil duce nostro Aetio secundum prioris belli opera prospiciente, ita ut ne clusuris quidem Alpium, quibus hostes prohiberi poterant, uteretur hoc solum spebus suis superesse existimans, si ab omni Italia cum imperatore discederet. sed cum hoc plenum dedecoris et periculi videretur, continuit verecundia metum et tot nobilium provinciarum latissima eversione credita est saevitia et cupiditas hostilis explendi nihilique inter omnia consilia principis ac senatus populique Romani salubrius visum est, quam ut per legatos pax truculentissimi regis expeteretur. suscepit hoc negotium cum viro consulari Avieno et viro praefectorio Trygetio beatissimus papa Leo auxilia dei fretus, quem sciret numquam piorum laboribus defuisse. nec aliud secutum est, quam praesumpserat fides. nam tota legatione dignanter accepta ita summi sacerdotis praesentia rex gavisus est, ut bello abstinere praeciperet et ultra Danuvium promissa pace discederet* (my translation). On the episode, see Deliyannis 2012; Becker and Kötter 2016.

commanders, an identification of Leo of Rome (440–61) as a figure of salvation, with his activity in this world as a sign that his path is to be followed for salvation in the next.[48] An almost identical episode is recorded for the last year of the chronicle, 455, when Leo is depicted as remaining in Rome and treating with the Vandal king Geiseric (428–77) to make sure that the sack of the city is executed without the customary violence.[49]

At first sight, the episode conforms to a traditional spatial representation: Italy is attacked and saved from the centre, that is, Rome. Leo appears as a substitute for the secular authorities, as he explicitly is in the episode of 455. Indeed, Leo helps to prevent the disgraceful separation of Italy and emperor by preventing Aëtius' plan from being executed. Thus, the papacy represents secular leadership in Italy. In this representation, one senses the reorientation of the chronicle after Prosper moved to Rome, for its first edition, in 433, did not have the same focus on Rome. Even if it is not visible in this episode, Leo is nevertheless a figure of identification who points towards what lies beyond history and events. Indeed, the chronicle concludes on a discussion of the quarrel about Easter dates of 455, thus hinting towards what really counts: the right celebration of the major Christian feast as a foreshadowing of our resurrection, a fact that is ensured by the care of Leo.[50]

Prosper reminds us of the fact that a traditional spatial representation could be adopted in an ecclesiastical source, albeit not without reminding its reader of what really mattered. Prosper's testimony is also of interest for another reason: we have relatively few histories written in Rome from an ecclesiastical perspective. In the East, we have histories written in Constantinople, Antioch, Alexandria and even Jerusalem. As analysed by P. Blaudeau, such works projected geo-ecclesiologies, that is, spatial representations that depicted the patriarchical sees as dominating a particular geographical region and as possessing symbolic centrality in the geography of orthodoxy.[51] There were not many ecclesiastical histories written in Latin, and none are interested in Italy. In 402/3 Rufinus translated and continued the ecclesiastical history of Eusebius in Italy (Aquileia), but did not provide an Italian, let alone western inflection of the work. Cassiodorus' *Historia tripartita* is an adaptation of three Greek church historians, Socrates, Sozomen and Theodoret, but the selection does not show up a particular Italian or Roman interest. In Bede's *Historia ecclesiastica gentis Anglorum*, of the early eighth century, the focus has shifted to England, just as Isidore of Seville had shifted it to Spain in his *History of the Goths*. The bishops of Rome, thus, did not spur the writing of ecclesiastical history. Rather, the papacy represented itself in the *Liber pontificalis*, composed from the 530s onwards, which as a series of biographies of bishops of Rome heavily focused on Rome itself with little attention for its hinterland.[52] Prosper's testimony may lead us to think that the bishops of Rome might have adopted his inflected form of the imperial representation focused on Rome, but how precisely the relationship with

---

[48] Muhlberger 1990, 127–35; Becker and Kötter 2016, 20–41.
[49] Prosper, *Chron.* 1375.
[50] Becker and Kötter 2016, 38.
[51] Blaudeau 2006.
[52] Blaudeau 2016 for reflection on the reasons why the papacy did not write ecclesiastical history.

Italy, and especially northern Italy where the grip of the bishop of Rome was always more contested, was represented, we cannot tell.

Regnum Italiae

In 476 the last western emperor appointed in Italy was forced to step down, and in 493 Theoderic the Amal started ruling Italy, albeit nominally for the eastern emperor Zeno (474–91). These changes made Italy more like another region of the empire, thus leading to a changed representation. Indeed, Italia becomes the geographical designation of Theoderic's realm. Indications are numerous. For the year 489 Cassiodorus marks the following event in his chronicle: 'Under these consuls, the most felicitous and strong lord king Theoderic entered Italy.'[53] For 504, the chronicle notes: 'Under this consul, through the valour of our lord king Theoderic, Italy received Sirmium when the Bulgars were defeated.'[54] In the *Variae*, the term *regnum Italiae* is used, in a letter of Theoderic to the Frankish king Luduin,[55] and in a letter to all provincial governors, Athalaric delineates his realm as *per universos fines Italiae*.[56] Such a representation had also political attraction, for it salvaged the interests of the eastern empire (Theoderic did not go to Italy to become the western emperor) and of the Goths (Italy is the land his Goths had been seeking for a long time). It survived the demise of the kingdom, as it is found in the *Anonymus Valesianus* 2, a (probably) sixth-century account of Theoderic's reign that was composed in Italy.[57]

Texts written in Constantinople use the same vocabulary. This is not very surprising for Jordanes (writing in 551),[58] whose debt to Cassiodorus in the *Getica* is acknowledged. Alaric's attacks on Italy are described as precisely that, attacks on Italy, possibly consciously so to establish a parallel with Theoderic's claim to the land.[59] The conquest of Italy by Theoderic is, again, a conquest of *Italy*, the term occurring in virtually every paragraph describing the event, whilst Rome is never named.[60] Interestingly, the western empire is also reduced to Italy: in 473–4, Theoderic's uncle, Vidimir, migrated to Italy, 'where Glycerius then ruled as an emperor'.[61] Jordanes did not merely copy the identification of Italy as the land of the Goths from his source, Cassiodorus, but also interiorised it. In the famous description of the 'fall of the western empire', where he notes for AD 476 that Romulus Augustulus was deposed, he adds the word 'Italy' to a phrase copied from his source Marcellinus Comes. Whilst the latter states that 'The kings of the Goths now held Rome', Jordanes has 'The kings

---

[53] Cassiod. *Chron.* 1319: *his conss. felicissimus atque fortissimus dn. rex Theodericus intravit Italiam.*
[54] Cassiod. *Chron.* 1344: *hoc cons. virtute dn. regis Theoderici victis Vulgaribus Sirmium recepit Italia.*
[55] Cassiod. *Var.* 2.41.3.
[56] Cassiod. *Var.* 9.20.3. See also *Var.* 1.1.3 (*ut cuncta membra Italiae componam*), a letter by Theoderic to the emperor Anastasius and the very first letter of the collection.
[57] *Anon. Vales.* 2.11.49, 2.12.73.
[58] For the date, see Van Hoof and Van Nuffelen 2020, 9–13.
[59] Jord. *Get.* 148–59.
[60] Jord. *Get.* 293–7.
[61] Jord. *Get.* 283: *ut ille in parte Italiae, ubi tunc Glycerius regnabat imperator.*

of the Goths now held Rome and Italy.'[62] Indeed, the identification of the Ostrogothic kingdom with Italy can be observed in Jordanes' *Romana* too.[63]

Significantly, the vocabulary also penetrates Greek sources of the later fifth and sixth centuries. Priscus of Panium, writing after 474 or 475,[64] names the Roman inhabitants of the remains of the western empire (that is, largely Italy) 'Italians' and thus has Attila fight against Goths, Franks and Italians.[65] Ambassadors are sent to Italy or militate in favour of Italy.[66] In one fragment, Attila is said to have shifted his attention from enslaving Italy to enslaving 'the Romans of the East' – the asymmetry in formulation is glaring.[67] Priscus regularly uses 'western' and 'eastern' Romans to designate the two parts of the empire,[68] but given the small size left to the western empire its territory came naturally to be identified with its main chunk, Italy. Some traces of such usage can be observed in later sources too. Procopius identifies the two groups in the Ostrogothic kingdom as 'Goths and Italians',[69] whilst for John Malalas 'the West' (*dysē*) and Italy can be interchangeable.[70] From an eastern perspective, such a vocabulary reflected the idea that the heart of the empire was in the East, and Priscus already imagined the empire in that way. It was a representation that Theoderic could adopt to his own advantage: by being ruler of Italy he did not make an ideological claim that could trouble the somewhat difficult relationship with the eastern emperor even more.[71]

Through this shift in vocabulary, Italy is allowed to step out of the shadows of Rome, even if one should note that the terms 'Rome' and 'Romans' remain predominantly used to designate the empire and its inhabitants. Such emancipation came, however, at a price. It was only possible by the loss of political status of the western empire: it had lost its emperor, and its territory had shrunk more or less to Italy. Theoderic occupied a territory whose status had been downgraded within the Roman Empire and resembled very much Gaul, Spain and Africa, even though its history as the imperial heartland and the remaining imperial institutions, such as the senate, granted it a particular aura. As we have seen, Rome had lost much of its symbolical capital. As a

---

[62] Jord. *Get.* 243: *Gothorum dehinc regibus Romam Italiamque tenentibus*; Marcell. Com. s.a. 476.2: *Gothorum dehinc regibus Romam tenentibus*.
[63] Jord. *Rom.* 367, 379.
[64] Blockley 1983, 2.50; for the later date, see Van Hoof and Van Nuffelen 2020, 84.
[65] Priscus of Panium, F15 l. 21 Müler = 20.1 l. 18 Blockley. See also Priscus, F24 l. 4 Müller = 31.1 l. 4 Blockley, 30 l. 29 Müller = F39.1 l. 22 Blockley. Priscus F8 l. 164 Müller = F11.2 l. 146 Blockley, calls the notary Constantius (*PLRE* 2, 319 (7)) an 'Italian', which may not mean more than that he hailed from western imperial territory.
[66] Priscus of Panium, F16 l. 11 Müller = 20.3 l. 9 Blockley, F29 l. 3, F31 l. 2, 28.
[67] Priscus of Panium, F19 Müller = 23.1 Blockley.
[68] E.g. Priscus of Panium, F15 Müller = 20.1 Blockley, F16 l. 18, 30 Müller = 39.1 Blockley, 35 l. 3 Müller = 45 l. 3 Blockley.
[69] E.g. Proc. *Bell.* 5.1.1: τὰ μὲν οὖν ἐν Λιβύῃ πράγματα τῇδε Ῥωμαίοις ἐχώρησεν. ἐγὼ δὲ ἐπὶ πόλεμον τὸν Γοτθικὸν εἶμι, ἐπειπὼν πρότερον ὅσα Γότθοις τε καὶ Ἰταλιώταις πρὸ τοῦδε τοῦ πολέμου γενέσθαι ξυνέβη; 5.1.29: ἔρως τε αὐτοῦ ἔν τε Γότθοις καὶ Ἰταλιώταις πολὺς ἤκμασε ... Cf. *Bell.* 5.4.29, 6.6.21–4. On the origin of the term *Italiōtai* in the second century BC, see Carlà-Uhink 2017, 288–9.
[70] John Malalas 1.10, 4.2, 7.5.
[71] On Theoderic's self-representation and perception, see Goltz 2008; Arnold 2014; Wiemer 2018.

consequence, Italy could now be invested with new meaning. The *Getica* of Jordanes traces the migration by the Goths from Scandza to a settled status in Italy. Possible allusions to the Exodus narrative suggest a Moses-like quality for Theoderic.[72] If this can be traced back to Cassiodorus' *History of the Goths*, it may be that he represented Italy as the promised land for the Goths, led by a providential leader, Theoderic. Rarely before had Italy held such significance in the spatial imagination of antiquity.

We should not be overenthusiastic: Italy never was fully emancipated. The year 489 is recorded as the year when Theoderic 'occupied' Italy. In Roman sources, the reconquest of Italy from 535 onwards was depicted as Italy's return to the empire, which we can see even in later western texts, such as the *Continuatio havniensis Prosperi*, an Italian text of 610. When mentioning the defeat of the Goths in 552, it notes: 'He [Narses] returned Italy to the Roman Empire and restored the destroyed cities. With the Goths driven away, he brought the former happiness back to the peoples of the whole of Italy.'[73] Few scholars would agree with the last assessment, given the economic destruction of Italy. Even so, the phrase implies that the region Italy, which had come to the fore under the Ostrogoths, was now part and parcel of the spatial imagination: it was not Rome anymore that was conquered, but Italy.[74] The Lombards too are usually depicted as entering Italy, for example in the *Origo gentis Langobardorum*.[75] In 580, Secundus of Trent even used the arrival of the Lombards as the beginning of an era, counting 12 years since they had taken up residence in Italy.[76] By now, Rome's power existed only in books and minds, allowing the greater geographical entity, that is, Italy, to come to the fore. Ironically, though, it performed at the end of antiquity the same role in the historiographical representation as the one in which it had entered the scene: a land of conquest.

Conclusion

In imperial spatial representation, Italy basked in the shadow of Rome, implying both a higher status than other regions and a risk of disappearance behind the city that was also the world. Its emancipation in Late Antiquity was the result of the weakness of the centre, that is, Rome. The erosion of traditional ways of imagining the empire allowed Italy a greater role to play in the spatial imagination in historiography, most strongly so in the description of Italy as the land of destiny for the Goths and its

---

[72] Jord. *Get.* 290. For such an interpretation, see Wilkinson 2018.

[73] *Continuatio havniensis Prosperi* (Hille 1866, 34): *Italiam Romano imperio reddidit urbesque dirutas restauravit, totiusque Italiae populos expulsis Gothis ad pristinum reducit gaudium.*

[74] Note that in Constantinople; Procopius defines Justinian's wars by the people they are fought against and not the region. Hence the 'Gothic War' (*Bell.* 5.1.1). In the eastern justification of the war against the Goths, Rome's location in Italy did matter: see, e.g., Continuation of Marcell. Com. s.a. 535.1: *de Roma Italiaque deliberat* (a Constantinopolitan source); the proliferation of allusions to Roman traditions in Proc. *Bell.* 8 (e.g. 8.22.7–16 8.29.4–5, 8.33.13).

[75] *Origo gentis Langobardorum* 5.

[76] Secundus of Trent, *FHistLA* 19 F1 = Scholion in Stuttgart, Landesbibliothek HB VI 113, f. 92r: *residentibus in Italia Langobardis anno XII* . . . Note that it is not entirely certain that the fragment derives from Secundus' history.

subsequent survival in the perception of it as an identifiable geographical entity. All forms of emancipation that we have surveyed were the result of appropriating and adapting texts, vocabulary and ideas that emanated from the centre, be it Rome or Constantinople. The rise of the periphery happened under the influence of the centre. But emancipation also meant a loss in status: as Rome had lost its central position, its hinterland did not stand out anymore above all other regions of the former empire. Indeed, from the sixth century onwards histories project different spatial organisations of the Mediterranean world. If around 468 the chronicler Hydatius, writing in Gallaecia, represented himself as living at the margins of the empire, a century later we see that histories being written in what used to be the periphery claim centrality. Isidore of Seville depicts Spain as the focus of God's action, and Mark Humphries has recently argued that we see this already announced in John of Biclaro's chronicle.[77] Merovingian histories slowly develop similar conceptions of centrality for Gaul and the Franks, even if a strong claim for centrality only occurs under the Carolingians.[78] It is telling of Italy's diminished status that the only major history of the Lombards, by Paul the Deacon, was composed at least a decade (c.787–96) after the kingdom had been defeated by Charlemagne in 774, and Italy thus was to be incorporated again into a larger entity.

Bibliography

Arnold, J. J. (2014) *Theoderic and the Roman Imperial Restoration*, New York.
Banchich, T. and J. A. Meka (2001) *Festus: Breviarium of the Accomplishments of the Roman People*. http://www.roman-emperors.org/festus.htm.
Becker, M. and J.-M. Kötter (2016) *Prosper Tiro, Chronik: Laterculus regum Vandalorum et Alanorum*, Paderborn.
Blaudeau, P. (2006) *Alexandrie et Constantinople, 451–491: de l'histoire à la géo-ecclésiologie*, Rome.
Blaudeau, P. (2016) 'Narrating Papal Authority (440–530): the Adaptation of *Liber pontificalis* to the Apostolic See's Developing Claims', in G. D. Dunn (ed.) *The Bishop of Rome in Late Antiquity*, London, 127–40.
Blockley, R. C. (ed.) (1983) *The Fragmentary Classicising Historians of the Later Roman Empire: Eunapius, Olympiodorus, Priscus and Malchus*, vol. 2: *Text, Translation and Historiographical Notes*, Leeds.
Brodersen, K. (2014) *Solinus. Wunder der Welt: lateinisch und deutsch*, Darmstadt.
Brodka, D. (1998) *Die Romideologie in der römischen Literatur der Spätantike*, Frankfurt am Main.
Carlà-Uhink, F. (2017) *The 'Birth' of Italy: the Institutionalization of Italy as a Region, 3rd–1st Century BCE*, Berlin.
Clarke, K. (1999) *Between Geography and History: Hellenistic Constructions of the Roman World*, Oxford.
Curran, J. R. (2000) *Pagan City and Christian Capital: Rome in the Fourth Century*, Oxford.
Deliyannis, D. (2012) 'The Holy Man and the Conqueror: the Legend of Attila and Pope Leo I', in M. Coumert (ed.) *Rerum gestarum scriptor: histoire et historiographie au Moyen Âge*, Paris, 239–48.

---

[77] Wood 2012; Humphries 2019.
[78] Reimitz 2015.

Eigler, U. (2013) 'Gallien als Literaturlandschaft: zur Dezentralisierung und Differenzierung lateinischer Literatur im 5. und 6. Jh.', in S. Diefenbach and M. Müller (eds) *Gallien in Spätantike und Frühmittelalter: Kulturgeschichte einer Region*, Berlin, 399–420.

Fear, A. (2010) *Orosius: Seven Books of History against the Pagans*, Liverpool.

Fuhrer, T. (ed.) (2011) *Rom und Mailand in der Spätantike: Repräsentationen städtischer Räume in Literatur, Architektur und Kunst*, Berlin.

Gautier Dalché, P. (2014) 'L'enseignement de la géographie dans l'Antiquité tardive', *Klio* 96: 144–82.

Gemeinhardt, P. (2007) *Das lateinische Christentum und die antike pagane Bildung*, Tübingen.

Gemeinhardt, P., L. Van Hoof and P. Van Nuffelen (eds) (2016) *Education and Religion in Late Antique Christianity: Reflections, Social Contexts and Genres*, London.

Geus, K. and M. Rathmann (eds) (2013) *Vermessung der Oikumene*, Berlin.

Giardina, A. (1994) 'L'identità incompiuta dell'Italia romana', in *L'Italie d'Auguste à Dioclétien: Actes du colloque international de Rome (25–28 mars 1992)*, Rome, 1–89.

Giardina, A. (2010) 'Italy and Italians during Late Antiquity', in P. Delogu and G. Gasparri (eds) *L'Italia, i barbari e l'Occidente romano*, Turnhout, 101–20.

Giardina, A., G. A. Cecconi and I. Tantillo (2014) *Cassiodoro: Varie*, Rome.

Goffart, W. A. (2006) *Barbarian Tides: the Migration Age and the Later Roman Empire*, Philadelphia.

Goltz, A. (2008) *Barbar, König, Tyrann: das Bild Theoderichs des Grossen in der Überlieferung des 5. bis 9. Jahrhunderts*, Berlin.

Grig, L. and G. Kelly (2012) *Two Romes*, Oxford.

Halsall, G. (2007) *Barbarian Migrations and the Roman West, 376–568*, Cambridge.

Hänger, C. (2001) *Die Welt im Kopf: Raumbilder und Strategie im Römischen Kaiserreich*, Göttingen.

Harich-Schwarzbauer, H. (2013) 'Die "Mauern" Roms in Claudians "De bello Gildonico" und "De bello Getico" – Diskurse der Angst in den Jahren 398–410', in H. Harich-Schwarzbauer and K. Pollmann (eds) *Der Fall Roms und seine Wiederauferstehungen in Antike und Mittelalter*, Berin, 37–52.

Heather, P. J. (2006) *The Fall of the Roman Empire*, London.

Hille, G. (1866) *Prosperi Aquitani chronici continuator havniensis*, Berlin.

Hofmann, D. (2018) *Griechische Weltgeschichte auf Latein: Iustins 'Epitoma historiarum Pompei Trogi' und die Geschichtskonzeption des Pompeius Trogus*, Stuttgart.

Hose, M. (1994) *Erneuerung der Vergangenheit: die Historiker im Imperium Romanum von Florus bis Cassius Dio*, Stuttgart.

Humphries, M. (2019) 'Narrative and Space in Christian Historiography: John of Biclaro on East, West and Orthodoxy', in P. Van Nuffelen (ed.) *Space and Historiography in Late Antiquity*, Cambridge, 86–112.

Inglebert, H. (1996) *Les romains chrétiens face à l'histoire de Rome: Histoire, christianisme et romanités en Occident dans l'Antiquité tardive (IIIe–Ve siècles)*, Paris.

Kaldellis, A. (2019) 'Constantinople's Belated Hegemony', in P. Van Nuffelen (ed.) *Space and Historiography in Late Antiquity*, Cambridge, 14–35.

Kulikowski, M. (2007) *Rome's Gothic Wars: from the Third Century to Alaric*, Cambridge.

Lozovsky, N. (2006) 'Roman Geography and Ethnography in the Carolingian Empire', *Speculum* 81: 325–64.

Markus, R. (1988) *Saeculum: History and Society in the Theology of St Augustine*, Cambridge.

Maskarinec, M. (2013) 'Who Were the Romans? Shifting Scripts of Romanness in Early Medieval Italy', in W. Pohl and G. Heydemann (eds) *Post-Roman Transitions: Christian and Barbarian Identities in the Early Medieval West*, Turnhout, 297–363.

Mathisen, R. W. (2013) '*Roma a Gothis Alarico duce capta est*: Ancient Accounts of the Sack of Rome in 410 CE', in J. Lipps, C. Machado and P. von Rummel (eds) *The Sack of Rome in 410 ad: the Event, Its Context and Its Impact*, Wiesbaden, 87–102.

Mittag, P. F. (2006) 'Zu den Quellen der *Expositio totius mundi et gentium*', *Hermes* 134: 338–51.
Muhlberger, S. (1990) *The Fifth-Century Chroniclers: Prosper, Hydatius, and the Gallic Chronicler of 452*, Leeds.
Nicolet, C. (1991) *Space, Geography, and Politics in the Early Roman Empire*, Ann Arbor.
Paschoud, F. (1967) *Roma aeterna: études sur le patriotisme romain dans l'Occident latin à l'époque des grandes invasions*, Rome.
Reimitz, H. (2015) *History, Frankish Identity and the Framing of Western Ethnicity, 550–850*, Cambridge.
Rimell, V. and M. Asper (eds) (2017) *Imagining Empire: Political Space in Hellenistic and Roman Literature*, Heidelberg.
Schmidt, P. L. (1989) 'Carminius', in R. Herzog (ed.) *Restauration und Erneuerung: die lateinische Literatur von 284 bis 374 n. Chr.*, Munich, 131–2.
Schmidt, P. L. (1995) 'Solinus Polyhistor in Wissenschaftsgeschichte und Geschichte', *Philologus* 139: 23–35.
Silberman, A. (1988) *Pomponius Mela: Chorographie*, Paris.
Talbert, R. and K. Brodersen (eds) (2004) *Space in the Roman World: Its Perception and Presentation*, Münster.
Van Dam, R. (2007) *The Roman Revolution of Constantine*, New York.
Van Hoof, L. and P. Van Nuffelen (2020) *Jordanes, Getica and Romana: Introduction, Translation and Commentary*, Liverpool.
Van Nuffelen, P. (2012) *Orosius and the Rhetoric of History*, Oxford.
Van Nuffelen, P. (2015) 'Not Much Happened: 410 and All That', *JRS* 105: 322–9.
Van Nuffelen, P. (ed.) (2019) *Space and Historiography in Late Antiquity*, Cambridge.
Van Nuffelen, P. and L. Van Hoof (eds) (2020) *Clavis historicorum antiquitatis posterioris*, Turnhout.
Wiemer, H.-U. (2018) *Theoderich der Grosse: König der Goten- Herrscher der Römer. Eine Biographie*, Munich.
Wilkinson, R. (2018) 'Theoderic Goes to the Promised Land: Accidental Propaganda in Jordanes's Gothic History?', *Early Medieval Europe* 26: 259–81.
Witakowski, W. (2007) 'Elias Barshenaya's Chronicle', in W. J. van Bekkum, J. W. Drijvers and A. C. Klugkist (eds) *Syriac Polemics: Studies in Honour of Gerrit Jan Reinink*, Leuven, 219–37.
Wood, J. P. (2012) *The Politics of Identity in Visigoth Spain: Religion and Power in the Histories of Isidor of Seville*, Leiden.
Woolf, G. (2011) *Tales of the Barbarians: Ethnography and Empire in the Roman West*, Malden, MA.
Yarrow, L. M. (2006) *Historiography at the End of the Republic: Provincial Perspectives on Roman Rule*, Oxford.

Epilogue:
Late Roman Italy – Paths Explored and Paths to Explore

Giusto Traina

Long ago, Andrea Giardina highlighted Italy's 'incomplete identity'.[1] The papers collected in this book cover several facets of this changing reality. One of the main issues concerns the relationship between Rome and Italy. According to the literary sources, Rome's authority seems to overshadow the rest of the peninsula; in one of the finest papers, Adrastos Omissi (Chapter 16) makes here a good point for the Latin panegyrical literature: 'though Rome is in Italy, in the Roman conceptual landscape it was not of Italy'.[2] No wonder the emperors considered the *Regio Annonaria* more favourably than the *Regio Suburbicaria*, which was under the control of the senatorial class;[3] Rome was where the *basileus* was as early as third century and, *a fortiori*, after 410.[4] On the other hand, the events of the fifth century implied a 'reorientation of imperial priorities towards Italy . . . effectively turning the Mediterranean into a frontier zone'.[5] As Jeroen Wijnendaele shows (Chapter 4), we need to revalue Odoacer's role for 'the recovery and resilience of the unified peninsula'.[6] Finally, as Peter Van Nuffelen argues (Chapter 17), Italy's 'emancipation in Late Antiquity was the result of the weakness of the centre, that is, Rome'.[7]

The historical narrative of this volume stops in AD 500, when 'Italy was finally ready to become the linchpin of Theoderic's western Roman commonwealth'.[8] This leaves aside the valuable evidence provided by sources like Cassiodorus and Procopius, and shows the editor's choice of field – a perspective more western than eastern.[9] In Averil Cameron's words, this would imply that 'the real heirs to Roman ideals are the

---

[1] Giardina 1986; 2010; Roberto (Chapter 1, p. 16).
[2] Omissi (Chapter 16, p. 455).
[3] Lenski (Chapter 2).
[4] Herodian, 1, 6, 4; see Roberto (Chapter 1, p. 17).
[5] Humphries (Chapter 3, p. 83).
[6] On Odoacer, see also Caliri 2017.
[7] Van Nuffelen (Chapter 17, p. 486).
[8] Wijnendaele (Chapter 4, p. 105).
[9] On the other hand, Stuart McCunn and Niels P. Arends (Chapters 6 and 9) consider the evolution of the West over a longer chronological range. We should also take note of the mammoth commentary on Cassiodorus' *Variae* edited by Andrea Giardina from 2014 onwards.

Goths, not the Romans who invaded Italy under Justinian, and for most the idea of a seriously intended reconquest is dead in the water, together with that of the sixth century as a hinge between antiquity and Byzantium'.[10]

As concerns the changes in the administrative system, Danielle Slootjes (Chapter 5) considers the gradual steps that may be traced back to Caracalla. One of the side effects of the *constitutio Antoniniana* was the subdivision of the imperial territory into *civitates*.[11] As a result, the empire intensified its control over individuals.[12] Another important factor was the composition of the army units; Philip Rance makes here a good point (Chapter 7, p. 159–78), and it is worth noting the decrease of the distinction between 'regular' and 'irregular' soldiers during the fifth century.[13] However, in some cases we also find barbarian farmers: Ammianus Marcellinus 28.5.15 provides evidence of captive Alamanni sent to the Po valley to settle in fertile lands with the status of *tributarii*. It goes without saying that a number of slaves in Roman Italy were war prisoners.

A decisive point is about the control of foreign communities; Jessica van 't Westeinde (Chapter 14) offers a state-of-the-art discussion about the Jews, but this could be also extended to the other Oriental communities.[14] In fact, Greek inscriptions from northern Italy give evidence on Syriac individuals, possibly traders (*Syrus* often designated an Oriental trader).[15] A particular case is offered by eunuchs: as Shaun Tougher has pointed out, despite the literary clichés, eunuchs, usually imported from beyond the eastern border of the empire, were not employed only in the East, but also in the West.[16]

Cityscapes and landscapes are relevant issues. Can we still speak of 'continuitists' and 'catastrophists' as Bryan Ward-Perkins wrote towards the end of last century, even drawing a diagram to show the position taken by various scholars?[17] Neil Christie (Chapter 11) asserts the importance of archaeology and, of course, of the process of Christianisation (to be read together with the valuable contributions by Bronwen Neil and Samuel Cohen, Chapters 12 and 13). In the future, it will be useful to recall the seminal contributions by the late Augusto Fraschetti on the 'conversion' of the city of Rome, marking the difference between the material reality and the ideological attitudes found in Christian authors (see, e.g., Saint Jerome's *Ep.* 107, welcoming the Christianisation of the *urbs*) and some hagiographic texts, which present the *lieux de mémoire* of ancient Rome, such as the Capitol, as strongholds of paganism haunted by dragons and demons.[18]

---

[10] Cameron 2016, 29.
[11] Mathisen 2006.
[12] Moatti 2011; 2014; Traina 2022.
[13] On the strategies of distinction of 'barbarians' within late Roman Italy see Rummel 2007; Moatti 2011; 2014; Traina 2022, 256; Traina forthcoming.
[14] See the seminal, massive study (almost unknown outside Italy) by [Cracco] Ruggini 1959; other references in Traina 2022.
[15] See the case of Concordia; Lettich 1983. For other cases, see Traina 2022.
[16] Tougher 2015. For a contribution in social history focusing on gender, see Vihervalli and Leonard (Chapter 8).
[17] Ward-Perkins 1997.
[18] Fraschetti 1999, 109–30.

As for landscapes, Edward M. Schoolman (Chapter 10) criticises the emphasis on the sixth century, prompted by the discussion on Kyle Harper's controversial book,[19] and suggests the need to explore 'stories of local resilience and continuity in the management and use of environmental resources in the face of multiple dramatic political, cultural and economic changes'. Schoolman wisely considers the paradigms of older historiography, especially the influence of Emilio Sereni's history of the agrarian Italian landscape;[20] producing three examples of resilience strategy, he advocates future collaborative research. In fact, Roman and medieval landscapes are still considered with simplistic formulas, linked to evocative images of the catastrophic progress of swamps and forests against the more disciplined Roman landscape, whereas we have no solid evidence of such a clear-cut 'end of the past'.[21] On the other hand, we do have evidence on swamps or forests registered as agrarian units, showing the evolution of cadastral systems as well as the recognition of realities formerly recorded as marginal lands.

The publication of such a volume is an opportunity not only to take stock of the picture as it is at present, but also how it might be developed in future. Late antique Italy awaited reconsideration, in response to the changes of paradigm related to the infamous 'explosion'[22] or 'elephantiasis'[23] of Late Antiquity. This is not merely a matter of periodisation: after the 'Long Late Antiquity',[24] we now need to cope with a 'Large Late Antiquity', expanded at least on a Eurasian scale.[25] As Kristina Sessa has argued, 'the vast geographic and cultural expanse of the late Roman empire and its manifold connectivity with regions to the north, south, and east mean that Late Antiquity generated an exceptionally heterogeneous, polyglot archive'.[26] For Italy, this presents a considerable challenge. In the future, it would be useful to revise also the historiographical traditions, as well as the reflections on the late antique period in the ideological construction of the unified Italy during and after the Risorgimento.

Bibliography

Bowersock, G. B. (2004) 'Riflessioni sulla periodizzazione dopo "Esplosione di tardoantico" di Andrea Giardina', *Studi storici* 45: 7–13.

Caliri, E. (2017) *Praecellentissimus Rex: Odoacre tra storia e storiografia*, Rome.

Cameron, A. (2002) 'The "Long" Late Antiquity: a Late-Twentieth Century Model?', in T. P. Wiseman (ed.) *Classics in Progress: Essays in Antique Greece and Rome*, Oxford, 165–91.

Cameron, A. (2016) 'Late Antiquity and Byzantium: an Identity Problem', *Byzantine and Modern Greek Studies* 40: 27–37.

---

[19] Haldon et al. 2018; in his reply, Harper 2018 is brilliant yet not convincing.

[20] Traina 2000. In fact, Sereni's work is a popular book, conceived as the synthesis of a five-volume encyclopedia that he never managed to complete.

[21] See my vintage observations in Traina 1989.

[22] Giardina 1999; Cameron 2002; Bowersock 2004; Cracco Ruggini 2004; Zecchini 2015; Lizzi Testa 2017: xi–xvi; Cosentino 2020.

[23] Fowden 2002.

[24] Marcone 2008.

[25] Giardina 1999.

[26] Sessa 2022, 213. See also Humphries 2017.

Cosentino, S. (2020) 'Tarda antichità, Bisanzio e periodizzazione', *Occidente/Oriente: Rivista internazionale di studi tardoantichi* 1: 51–61.
[Cracco] Ruggini, L. (1959) 'Ebrei e Orientali nell'Italia settentrionale fra il IV e il VI secolo d. Cr.', *SDHI* 25: 186–308.
Cracco Ruggini, L. (2004) 'Come e perché è "esploso" il tardoantico?', *Studi storici* 45: 15–23.
Fowden, G. (2002) 'Elefantiasi del tardoantico', *JRA* 15: 681–6.
Fraschetti, A. (1999) *La conversione: da Roma pagana a Roma cristiana*, Rome.
Giardina, A. (1986) 'Le due Italie nella forma tarda dell'impero', in A. Giardina (ed.) *Società romana e impero tardoantico*, vol. 1: *Istituzioni, ceti, economie*, Rome, 1–30 = A. Giardina (1997) *L'Italia romana: storie di un'identità incompiuta*, Rome, 265–321.
Giardina, A. (1999) 'Esplosione di tardoantico', *Studi storici* 40: 157–80. English translation: 'Explosion of Late Antiquity', in A. Cameron (ed.) (2016) *Late Antiquity on the Eve of Islam*, London, 1–23.
Giardina, A. (2010) 'Italy and Italians during Late Antiquity', in P. Delogu and S. Gasparri (eds) *Le trasformazioni del V secolo: l'Italia, i barbari e l'Occidente romano*, Turnhout, 101–20.
Haldon, J. et al. (2018) 'Plagues, Climate Change, and the End of an Empire: a Response to Kyle Harper's *The Fate of Rome*', 1–3, *History Compass* 16 (12), https://doi.org/10.1111/hic3.12505–12507.
Harper, K. (2018) 'Integrating the Natural Sciences and Roman History: Challenges and Prospects', *History Compass* 16 (12), https://doi.org/10.1111/hic3.12520.
Humphries, M. (2017) 'Late Antiquity and World History', *Studies in Late Antiquity* 1: 8–37.
Lettich, G. (1983) *Le iscrizioni sepolcrali tardoantiche di Concordia*, Trieste.
Lizzi Testa, R. (2017) 'Introduction', in R. Lizzi Testa (ed.) *Late Antiquity in Contemporary Debate*, Newcastle upon Tyne, vii–xlix.
Marcone, A. (2008) 'A Long Late Antiquity? Considerations on a Controversial Periodization', *Journal of Late Antiquity* 1: 4–19.
Mathisen, R. W. (2006) '*Peregrini, barbari*, and *cives Romani*: Concepts of Citizenship and the Legal Identity of Barbarians in the Later Roman Empire', *AHR* 111: 1011–40.
Moatti, C. (2011) 'La mobilité négociée dans l'Empire Romain tardif: le cas des marchands étrangers', *Settimane di Studio sull'Alto Medioevo* 58, Spoleto, 159–88.
Moatti, C. (2014) 'Mobility and Identity between the Second and the Fourth Centuries: the "Cosmopolizations" of the Roman Empire', in C. Rapp and H. A. Drake (eds) *The City in the Classical and Post-classical World: Changing Contexts of Power and Identity*, New York, 130–52.
Rummel, P. von (2007) *Habitus barbarus: Kleidung und Repräsentation spätantiker Eliten im 4. und 5. Jahrhundert*, Berlin.
Sessa, K. (2022), 'Keep Late Antiquity Weird', *Studies in Late Antiquity* 6: 213–16.
Tougher, S. (2015) 'Eunuchs in the East, Men in the West? Dis/unity, Gender and Orientalism in the Fourth Century', in R. Dijkstra, S. van Poppel and D. Slootjes (eds) *East and West in the Roman Empire of the Fourth Century: an End to Unity?* Leiden, 147–63.
Traina, G. (1989) 'Continuità e visibilità: premesse per una discussione sul paesaggio antico', *Archeologia Medievale* 16: 683–93.
Traina, G. (2000) 'Paradigmi per antichisti: la *Storia del paesaggio agrario italiano*', *Annali Istituto Alcide Cervi* 19: 175–82.
Traina, G. (2020) 'L'Impero d'Occidente e l'identità etnica dei *magistri militum*: brevi osservazioni', in F. Oppedisano (ed.) *Procopio Antemio imperatore di Roma*, Bari, 221–7.
Traina, G. (2022) 'Orientals in Late Antique Italy: Some Observations', *Electrum* 29: 249–60.

Traina, G. (forthcoming) 'Armenian Soldiers in the Gothic War: Some Clarifications', in H. Dey and F. Oppedisano (eds) *Justinian's Legacy: the Last War of Roman Italy / L'eredità di Giustiniano: l'ultima guerra dell'Italia romana.*

Ward-Perkins, B. (1997) 'Continuitists, Catastrophists, and the Towns of Post-Roman Northern Italy', *PBSR* 65: 157–76.

Zecchini, G. (2015) 'L'Antiquité tardive: périodisations d'un âge noir et heureux', in S. Ratti (ed.) *Une Antiquité tardive noire ou heureuse?* Besançon, 29–41.

INDEX

There has been no attempt to enforce a single format of place-names (i.e. Latin, Italian or Anglicised), given their continuity with many cities in present-day Italy. Instead freedom has been given to authors to decide for themselves, whilst maintaining consistency in respective chapters. Authors of literary sources are not listed, unless they appear as participants in the historical events discussed (e.g. Ambrose of Milan) or are part of extensive analysis (e.g. Claudian). Offices or other personalia are only listed in the case of homonymous individuals, exceedingly common names or where confusion might occur with similar established names (e.g. John, Maria or Augustus). Individuals with multiple names, especially senators, are categorised according to the conventions of the *Prosopography of the Later Roman Empire*.

abortion, 209–10, 217
actor, 224, 251
adaeratio, 56, 178, 180n
Adda river, 99, 461
Adige, river, 157, 461–2
Adrianople, Battle of, 55n, 70, 102, 479
Adriatic, 74, 83, 168n, 297, 310
Adventus, 2, 51, 72, 188n, 428
Aemilia, 40n, 116
Aemilia et Liguria, 16, 37, 39, 57–8, 115, 117–19
Aëtius, 72, 73, 78, 80n, 87, 88n, 104n, 167–8, 170–5, 188n, 205, 215, 482–3
Aetna, 79
Africa, 7n, 37, 46, 50, 54, 59, 73, 80, 83, 87–9, 92–3, 102n, 122, 133, 135, 147, 156, 159, 166, 168n, 175, 229, 239n, 271
    Bishops: 342, 351–3
    Jews: 386n
    Panegyrical representation: 458–9, 464n, 465
    Religious Violence: 361n
Aginatius, 52

Agnellus of Ravenna, 101n, 350, 375–6
agriculture, 183, 225–8, 234, 240, 265, 270, 289–92, 294–6
Agrigento, 306, 314, 320n, 400
Alamanni, 91, 100, 118, 155–7, 161, 183–4, 322, 491
Alans, 94, 157n, 159, 162–3, 184
Albanum, 38, 154, 160
Alaric, 5, 8, 55, 71–2, 74–5, 94n, 100, 125, 147–8, 158, 163–5, 170, 181, 212, 215, 316, 326n, 459–62, 475, 484
Alexander Severus, 44, 253
Alps, 42, 49, 70, 92, 97–8, 100, 119, 156–7, 161, 186, 297, 458–61, 471, 482
Altinum, 71, 345n, 353, 367n
Alypia, 96, 215–6
Ambrose of Milan, 53, 71, 74–5, 186, 210, 216, 227n, 239–42, 319, 321n, 345, 347, 375, 378, 388, 390–1
Ammianus Marcellinus, 46–7, 180, 208–9, 358, 372–3

Ampelius, 52
Anastasia, 47
annona civilis, 3, 39, 51, 54, 148, 311
annona militaris, 55, 79, 155, 171, 178–9, 241–4
Annonaria, Italia
  creation, 20, 38–40, 112, 115
  government, 58–9 116, 125, 135, 155
  imperial presence, 41–4, 47–9, 69, 72, 137, 490
  military, 49, 147, 167
  religious situation, 376, 385, 388–9, 404
  supply, 55, 178
Antioch, 4, 69, 142, 347, 350, 483
Apennines, 20, 38, 41, 148, 241n, 297, 322n, 325n, 420, 430, 462n, 469
Apronianus, 56n, 124n
Apulia, 56, 75, 82, 247, 321, 386n
Apulia et Calabria, 39–40, 58, 115, 117, 120, 183
aqueducts, 76–7, 146, 312, 349
Aquileia,
  church, 319–20, 345, 348n, 349, 352, 394
  imperial residence, 25, 48n, 69–72, 458
  military matters, 26, 68, 147, 155, 159, 161, 166n, 168, 183, 323–4
  mint, 49
  religious minorities, 386, 388n, 391–2
  routes, 42, 73, 83, 156, 462n
  urban infrastructure, 52, 312–3, 315n, 322n, 326
Aquitania, 58, 100, 173
Agri deserti, 182–3.
Anthemius, 81, 91, 95–8, 101, 103, 146, 176–7, 216, 469
Arbogast(es), 93, 162, 170, 187
Arcadius, 47, 80, 82, 125, 212, 387n, 391
Arenarii (gladiators), 52, 357, 362
'Arianism' *see* Homoians
Arles, 90, 164, 181, 376, 443n, 447n
Arno, 38
Asia Minor, 4, 57, 130, 342n, 401n
Aspar, 81
Athalaric, 135, 144, 249, 251, 484
Athaulf, 172, 212, 322n
Attila, 74, 80–1, 92, 100, 146–7, 157–8, 171n, 175, 190, 205, 212, 217, 345, 376n, 482, 485
Augsburg, 17, 42, 49, 117, 168n, 174n, 175n
Augustine of Hippo, 203, 345, 351, 479n
Augustus, definitely first Roman emperor, 1, 15n, 21–2, 35, 39, 41, 114
Aurelian, 18–19, 21, 30, 35, 45, 50, 53, 118, 157, 216, 308

Aurelianic Wall, 2, 312–13, 323, 362
Aurelius Victor, 21, 36, 460
Ausonius, 456, 466
Auxentius, bishop of Milan, 53, 375, 391n
auxilia palatina, 165–6, 168n, 174n, 175
aurum tironicum see recruitment, conscription
Avitus, 83, 89–91, 97, 103, 175, 464, 467

Balbinus, 44, 50, 68.
Balkans, 4, 70, 72, 81, 83, 100, 462
Barbaria, mother of Romulus Augustu[lus]?, 217
Basilica, in general, 306–7, 318n, 344, 347
  of Ambrose, 390
  of Felix, 344
  of Julius in Trastevere, 51, 357, 361–3, 368
  Lateran, 5, 187, 358
  of Liberius, 52, 357, 364, 373
  of Monastero, 392
  Sicinini, 358, 361
  Sessoriana, 367–8, 373
  Ursiana, 215
Basilicata, 306
Bassianus, 39, 47
baths, 27–8, 122, 124, 134, 209, 271, 311–12, 314, 315n, 316, 320n, 325, 341, 349–50, 372, 395
Bauto, 161–2, 170, 190
Beneventum(/o), 59n, 125, 135–6, 269, 312
Bergamo, 94, 157n, 314
bible, 227n, 400n, 415
billeting, 153, 179, 185, 314, 322
bishops, as a group, 145–7, 318–21, 327, 339–53, 356, 362, 367, 370–1, 375–8, 483
Bleda, 217
Bologna, 164, 179, 312, 388–9
Boniface, bishop of Rome, 346, 358–9, 364–5, 370, 373–4
Boniface, *comes Africae*, 73, 172–3, 187n, 205
Brescia, 70–71, 166n, 308–9, 314, 327, 388n, 457n
Britain, 4–5, 42n, 83, 163, 459
Brindisi (Brundisium), 42, 348
Bruttium, 53, 175, 241n, 249, 477n
buccellarii, 88, 163n, 170–3, 175–6, 189–90
burials, 73, 270–1, 304, 318, 320, 362, 364, 389, 397–8, 401–2, 411, 425–6, 431
Burgundians, 6, 97, 177

Caecilianus, *vicarius Italiae*, 39
C. Caelius Saturninus, 39

Caesar, Julius, 21, 132, 465
Calabria, 40, 53n, 82, 377, 386n, 477n
Campania
  economy, 53, 56, 147, 247–8, 269
  government, 37, 39, 57–9, 75, 115–17, 122, 124–5, 137, 348
  imperial presence, 45
  routes, 42
  military matters, 91, 153, 168n, 174, 186n, 457, 460
  towns, 308, 312
  sarcophagi, 412, 430, 436
Canusium, 59n, 135, 145n, 188n
capitatio, 40, 240
captives, 17, 74–5, 80, 213
Caracalla, 16n, 35, 120, 491
Carinus, 16, 27, 45, 308
Carminius, 480
Carus, 21, 27
Carthage, 73–6, 78–81, 96, 104, 157, 169, 213–14, 342–3, 458n, 471
Cassiodorus, 99, 137–40, 144, 148, 175, 249, 483–4
Cassius Dio, 35, 477–8
Castinus, 172–3
catacombs, 188n, 318, 347n, 348, 385n, 394–8, 401, 425–6, 433
Catania, 79, 325n, 328, 400–2
celibacy, 210, 345–6
cemeteries, 160, 305, 319, 324, 344, 362, 373, 388–9, 400
Christianity, 23, 186–7, 339–44, 346–7, 384, 389, 393, 423–4, 479
Chromatius, bishop of Aquileia, 53, 345, 391
Cicero, 291, 465
Claudian, 71n, 74, 166n, 206, 454, 456, 458–9, 461, 463–7, 470, 479
Claudius II Gothicus, 45, 308
claustra Alpium Juliarum, 69, 156, 161, 186
clergy, 74, 79, 133n, 233–4, 305, 324, 340–3, 345–6, 349, 351n, 357–60, 362, 371, 387
civil war, 46, 68, 72, 100, 190, 305, 316, 366, 378, 456
coemptio, 179, 240, 243
cohortes urbanae, 38, 154, 159–60, 372
coinage, 89n, 94n, 95n, 235–6
coloni, 21, 145, 184, 225, 235, 245–6
colonia (estate), 246
comitatenses, 157, 165, 167–8, 173, 175, 179, 183, 185
commodus, 17, 478

comes domesticorum, 89, 91, 102, 175
comes Italiae, 49, 157
Comiso, 403–4
Como, 19n, 123, 168, 315, 321–2, 327
Concordia, 49, 71, 183–5, 320n, 322n, 388n, 401n
confessors, 341, 352
Constans I, 46, 48n, 51, 119, 157n
Constans II, 144
Constantia, daughter of Constantius II, 205, 211
Constantina, daughter of Constantine I, 47
Constantine I
  accession, 29
  civil officials, 20, 38–40, 57, 99n, 133–4, 138
  church, 318–9, 344, 347
  'conversion', 384
  economic policies, 245, 254
  family and marriages, 47, 209
  military matters, 38, 100, 158–60, 183, 188n
  representation, 456, 458, 460–2, 464, 469
  Rome, 37, 46, 50–1, 72, 318
Constantinople, 4, 53, 61, 69, 72, 81, 162, 164, 213, 295, 316, 362, 469, 478–9, 483–4
Constantius I, 4, 43, 47, 73, 341, 343
Constantius II, 43, 46–8, 51, 82, 100, 133–4, 161, 208, 211, 308, 348, 357, 370
Constantius III, 71, 172, 359n, 373
Cornelius, bishop of Rome, 340–2
correctores, 36, 114–16, 120
correctores (totius/utriusque) Italiae, 16n, 19, 35–6
Corsica, 36, 39, 40, 42, 57–8, 69, 89, 94–5, 112, 116–17, 137, 147, 169, 182n, 344, 430n
consulares, 35, 57, 120
consulship, 57, 60, 82, 91, 98, 124
Cottian Alps, 97–8, 186, 458
council
  of Aquileia, 381
  of Chalcedon, 81, 339, 351, 369
  of Milan, 357
  of Serdica, 51
court, Imperial, 5, 20, 43n, 44, 67–72, 74–6, 78–81, 82n, 134–5, 213, 316, 351, 393, 456, 466
Crepereius Madalianus, 40
Crispus, 209
curiales, 75, 133–6, 138, 140–6, 148–9, 249n
Cyprian, Bishop of Carthage, 2, 342–3

Dalmatia, 6, 94, 96, 100–2, 104, 156, 164, 169, 174, 184n, 341, 412n

Damasus, Bishop of Rome, 51–2, 55, 318, 346, 348, 352, 356–8, 361–4, 370, 372–3, 378–9
Danube, 17, 40, 42, 83, 155, 159, 160–2, 177, 179, 241, 323, 478, 482
Dawn, goddess, 469–70
Decius, 17n, 45, 50, 216, 340n
decurions, 252–3, 399; *see also* Curiales
defensor, 138–41, 144–6, 148, 260, 369
Demetrias, 351
desertion, deserters, 77, 88, 163, 181–2, 186.
Diadumenianus, 50
dioeceses, 36, 69, 111–12, 115–16, 118–20, 158, 184, 344, 377
dioecesis Italiciana, 20, 30, 37, 41, 155
Diocletian, 20–1, 23–30, 36–8, 45, 49–50, 101, 115, 138, 155, 160, 178, 312, 315, 340n, 343–4, 458, 470, 478
Dionysius, bishop of Milan, 53, 357n
Dionysius, L. Aelius Helvius, 19n
Domitius Alexander, 37, 50
duumvir/duoviri, 131–4, 139, 141

earthquakes, 135, 307n, 310, 313, 315n, 316n, 324–5, 326n
Easter, 342, 359, 365, 367–8, 483
Edict of Milan, 344
Egypt, 42n, 51, 53, 61, 79n, 120n, 138, 182, 189n, 224n, 255n, 259
Emona (Ljubljana), 156, 457n, 460
Ennodius, 3, 99–102, 146, 215, 227, 241, 314, 345, 454, 456–7, 459, 462–3, 467–9
Epiphanius, Bishop of Pavia (Ticinum), 3, 96, 146, 255, 345
equites singulares augusti, 38, 154, 159–60, 372
Eridanus, 459, 461
Esino, river, 20, 38
Etna, volcano, 402
Etruria, 16, 75, 117
Eucherius, son of Stilicho and Serena, 207
Eudocia, daughter of Valentinian III and Eudoxia, 87, 212–13
Eudoxia, Licinia, 72, 81, 211, 213–14
Eugenius, emperor, 5, 46, 48, 71, 73, 93, 162,
Eulalius *see* Schism of Boniface/Eulalius
Euric, 97, 101n, 146, 157n
Eusebia, 208
Eusebius of Caesarea, 212, 483
Eutropia, wife of Maximian, 47
Eutropia, daughter of Constantius I and Theodora, 47, 207
exactor, 138–9

fabricae, fabricenses, 184–5, 322
Faesulae, 74
Fausta, empress, 47, 209
Faustina, Jewish girl, 399
Felix I, Bishop of Rome, 341, 344
Felix II, Antipope, 51, 357, 364, 370
Felix III, Bishop of Rome, 353
Felix, *magister militum*, 88n, 172, 187, 215
Festus, historian, 477, 481
Firmus, revolt in Africa, 54
Flaminia et Picenum, 37, 39, 58, 115–16, 120, 122
fleets, 46, 78, 81, 92–4, 99, 168–9
foederati, 78, 159, 162–4, 167, 170–1, 172n, 174–6, 179, 181n, 212, 184–5, 190
food supply *see* Annona Civilis
Formiae, 56, 135–6
forum, as an urban space, 306–12
fossores (gravediggers), 357, 362
Franks, 6, 485, 487
Frigidus, 46n, 99–100, 103.
fundus, 236–7, 257–8

Galerius, 29–30, 37, 158, 160, 215n, 308, 343–4
Galla, wife of Theodosius I, 208, 210–11
Galla Placidia, 47, 172, 349–50, 399n
Gallienus, 4, 17–18, 30, 45, 50, 118, 136, 155, 215
Gaudentius, son of Aëtius, 87, 205
Gaudentius, bishop of Brescia, 53, 227, 233n, 235, 345
Gaul
  church, 345–6, 350, 352
  cultural traits and representation, 21–2, 180, 454, 465, 467–8, 477
  government, 57, 70–3, 89, 104, 138
  imperial presence, 83, 92–3
  military conflicts, 96, 98, 146, 161, 169–71, 175–7, 186, 322n
  Regna, 102, 149, 214n, 487
  sarcophagi, 412n
  usurpations, 2, 5, 155, 161
Geiseric,
  Conquest of Carthage (439), 5, 78–80, 104
  conquest of remaining African provinces (455), 89
  raiding Sicily, 79
  Sack of Rome (455), 89, 213, 326n, 460n, 483
  conflict with Valentinian III's successors, 93–5, 458

Gelasius, bishop of Rome, 346–7, 349, 351–2, 377–8
generalissimo, 91, 98, 103n, 162, 170, 190
Gennadius Avienus, 74, 146n, 482
Genoa, 40, 42, 266, 268, 386, 388–9, 422n, 462n
Gildo, 54–5, 153, 163, 166, 186n, 180–1
Glycerius, 97–8, 103, 484
Gordian III, 1, 44, 50
Goths 45, 73–4, 104, 145, 159, 163n, 171n, 183, 212, 289, 322n, 484, 490
  Aquitanian Goths, 89, 97, 101–2, 173, 175–6, 467
  Visigoths, 100, 149, 483
Gratian, 43n, 47, 52n, 70–2, 82–3, 100–1, 161, 205, 253, 348, 471
Greece, 4, 45, 163, 180–1, 234, 401 (n. 92)
Gundobad, 97, 99, 146n, 177, 216

Hadrian, 35, 68, 308
Hannibal, 464–5
Hannibalianus, 47
Helena, mother of Constantine I, 47, 123, 384n
Helena, daughter of Constantine I and wife of Julian, 47, 208–9
Heraclianus, 73, 158
Herodian, 17, 22
Herennia Etruscilla, 216
Hispellum, 137n, 141, 142n
Homoians, 162, 186–7, 348–9, 351, 369, 375, 391
honorati, 57, 142–5, 149, 181–2
Honoria, Justa Grata, 210, 212
Honorius, emperor
  civil officials, 82, 142, 145
  church, 48, 345, 349, 358–9, 365, 370, 373–4
  court, 69, 71–2
  family and marriages, 47, 206–7, 212
  military matters, 74–5, 162, 164–7, 171–2, 187, 456
  representation, 461, 466
  Rome, 73
  taxation, 147
Hostilian, 45, 50
houses, 144, 265–6, 268, 273, 309–11, 313–14, 316, 325, 328
Huneric, 87, 212–13
Huns, 74, 81, 92, 159, 161–3, 165, 170–1, 173, 175, 464
hunting, 289, 312, 416–25
Hydatius, 487

Illyria, 18, 20–3, 30, 140
Illyricum, 4, 23, 40, 74–5, 92, 104, 140n, 155–7, 161n, 164, 241, 346n, 454, 461
Imola, 350, 376
Innocent, bishop of Rome, 75, 346, 350
Italia Annonaria see Annonaria
Italia Suburbicaria see Suburbicaria
iugatio, 40, 240
Iulianus, *Praefectus Annonae*, 51
Iulius Cassius, 39
Iunius Bassus, 39, 57n, 60n
Iunius Tertullus, 40
Iuthungi, 17–18, 157, 168, 174, 322, 462

Jerusalem, 213, 342n, 426, 428, 483
Jews, 82, 187n, 227n, 340, 385–95, 398–402, 404–5
Johannes, praetorian prefect, 75
John, emperor 423–5, 100n, 166, 170, 173, 190
John of Antioch, 88, 94, 208n, 211
Jordanes, 484–6
Julian, 43n, 47, 48n, 54, 56n, 73, 161, 208, 347, 390
Julian Alps, 70, 74, 98, 157n, 161
Julius I, Bishop of Rome, 51, 211n, 348, 350
Julius Nepos (last western Roman emperor), 86, 98, 102, 146, 177
Justina, 205, 208, 210
Justinian, 6, 144, 149, 178, 214, 351, 486n, 490
Justinianic Code, 146, 182

Kreka, 217

Lactantius, 24, 26, 29
Laeta, wife of Gratian, 47
laetus/i, 183–4
landholding, 56, 112, 182–4, 191, 223, 237–8, 251, 260
Laterculus Veronensis, 37
latifundia, 223
Lampadius, C. Ceionius Rufius Volusianus, 55, 160, 372
Late antique Little Ice Age, 294, 299, 326n
laudes Italiae, 21–2
Laurentius, 366, 374
law, Roman, 133, 149n, 205, 211, 233n, 245–7, 254
Lecce, 399
legio, legiones, 38, 154, 157, 159–60, 165–6, 168n 174n

Leo I, bishop of Rome, 203n, 339, 345–7, 350, 353
Leo I, emperor, 5, 90, 95, 125, 254
Libanius, 142, 257
Liberius, Bishop of Rome, 51, 348, 355–7, 364, 370, 372
Liberius, official of Odoacer and Theoderic, 101
Libius Severus, 83, 91, 93–5, 103, 184n, 469
libertas, 23–6
Liber Pontificalis, 339, 341, 343, 348–9, 353, 357, 359, 364–8, 370–1, 483
Licinius, 39–40, 155n, 158–9, 212, 215n, 344
Liguria, 3, 16, 97n, 99, 116–17, 120n, 146–7, 264–9, 310, 315n, 319, 322, 461
Lilybaeum, 59n, 79, 314
limitanei, 157, 163, 165, 167–8, 177, 183, 185, 190
liturgy, 82, 321, 339, 341–2, 344–5, 347, 352, 369
Lombards, 6, 244, 351, 486–7
Lucania, 19, 53, 83, 94, 241n, 248, 477n
Lucania et Bruttium, 117, 120, 123, 148, 179n, 180n, 183
ludi saeculares, 1–2

Macrinus, 50
magic, 403–4
magister militum (equitum, peditum, utriusque militiae), 38, 94, 97, 103–4, 169–173
magistrates, 15n, 77, 130–4, 136–7, 139–40, 145, 150, 256, 361n
Magnentius, 43n, 46, 48, 50, 158, 161, 207–8
Magnus Maximus, 46–8, 55n, 70, 73, 92, 102n, 153, 155n, 158, 161, 210, 216, 390n, 456, 464
Majorian, 83, 87–96, 102–4, 130, 140, 145–8, 169, 173, 175, 205, 457–8, 460, 465
Malta, 399
Mamertinus, 22–3
Manichaeism, 351–2, 393n
marble, 310, 316, 321, 327, 390, 396, 400, 411, 413, 421, 422n, 432
Marcellinus, 'of Dalmatia', 91, 93–6, 169, 173, 175, 184n
Marcian, 81, 175n
Marcus Aurelius, 17, 35, 134, 155
Marcus Simplicinus Genialis, 17
Maria, daughter of Stilicho, 206–7
markets, 54, 56, 61, 131, 179, 190, 226, 231n, 37, 232, 240–5, 247–9, 257, 267, 270–3, 304, 306, 321

marriage, as institution, 170, 172, 176, 187, 202, 204–9, 345–6, 393
Martin of Tours, 49, 179
martyrs, 318–20, 340, 348
massa, 236, 270
Maxentius, 4, 26n, 29–30, 37–9, 43, 45–6, 48–50, 100, 104n, 159–60, 212, 215, 340n, 460, 463, 469
Maximian, 22–5, 27–8, 43n, 45, 53, 72–3, 93, 159–60, 343, 458, 462, 470
Maximilla, Valeria, 215
Maximilianus, Attius Caecilius, 51
Maximinus, *Vicarius Vrbis Romae*, 52, 58
Maximinus Thrax, 17, 50, 68
Maximus, bishop of Turin, 53, 146, 227, 253, 310, 345
Memmius Vitrasius Orfitus, 48n, 372
Melania the Younger, 75, 351
Menander Rhetor, 455
merchants, 315, 324, 392
Merobaudes, panegyrist, 456
metal working, 306–7
Milan
  church, 53, 186, 319, 349, 353, 359n, 375
  economy, 49, 240, 248n
  imperial court, 5, 18, 245, 43n, 48, 52, 69–73, 104, 147, 155, 161, 205, 316
  military matters, 18, 20, 26, 29, 96–7, 100, 162, 176, 215
  religious minorities, 389–91
  representation, 458, 462, 466, 470
  sarcophagi, 439–42
  urban infrastructure, 18, 207, 306, 312–3, 315, 321
Mithraism, 310, 387, 396–8
Monica, mother of Augustine, 203
mosaics, 4, 187, 311, 313–16, 318, 321, 325, 349, 413
munus/munera, 133–5, 137, 142–3, 182, 185

Naples, 6, 56, 135, 217, 248, 269, 321, 386n
Nepotianus, commander, 91, 94
Nepotian(us), emperor, 46–7, 50, 161, 207
Nicetas, bishop of Aquileia, 80
Noricum, 45, 102, 104, 116–17, 156, 159, 164, 168, 174, 177
Notitia Dignitatum, 20n, 40, 49, 69, 115, 117, 119–20, 157–9, 162n, 67, 69, 165–8, 174, 183–4, 189
Novatianism, 342–3, 352

Odoacer, 86–7, 97–104, 177, 182–4, 215, 322n, 392, 456, 463, 468–9
Oenotria, 459, 469
Olybrius, emperor, 87n, 91, 94, 97, 205, 213
Olympiodorus, 56, 206
officiales, 140, 361n
Orestes, 104n, 177, 217
Orosius, 479, 481–2
Ostrogoths, 6, 100n, 135–40, 144, 149, 178–9, 184, 190, 214, 242–4, 249–54, 256, 272, 314, 322, 359, 485–6

Pacatianus, 50
Pacatus, 71, 102n, 455, 461, 464
Padua, 70, 480
'paganism', 187, 227n, 309–10, 341, 347, 362, 388n, 391n, 393n, 399, 401–5, 413, 432–3, 491
paideia, 415, 430, 446
palaces, 1, 24, 313, 466, 470
Palermo, 321, 400
Palladius, son of Petronius Maximus, 87, 213
Pannonia, 22–3, 45, 57, 98, 120n, 156, 159, 162n, 173, 175n, 211, 241, 482
pater patrum, 396–8
patriarch(ate), episcopal, 348n, 350, 423, 483
patriarch, Jewish, 82, 387–8, 399, 401n
patriarchate, male, 202–4, 210
patricius, dignity, 92, 170
patronage
 Ecclesiastical, 187, 309, 340, 369
 Imperial, 60, 93, 349
 Military, 161, 169, 170n, 190
 Political, 15, 470
 Urban, 123, 125–6, 131, 312
Paulinus of Nola, 58, 188, 225n, 227n, 228n, 247–8, 252, 321n, 348
Paul the Deacon, 487
Pavia (Ticinium), 3, 18, 26, 49, 69, 99, 102, 146, 163–4, 179, 184, 255, 314, 322, 353, 463
Pelagia, 172, 187n, 205
Pelagianism, 345, 352, 370
Petronius Maximus, 76, 78–9, 87–9, 97n, 103, 211, 213–14
Philip 'the Arab', 1, 17n, 44
Piazza Armerina, 4, 188n, 296
Picenum, 40n, 75, 117, 125n, 137, 172, 319–20
Pierius, 102
Placentia (Piacenza), 18, 42, 90, 175, 179
Placidia, daughter of Valentinian III, 87n, 205, 213

plague, 2, 288, 299, 324n, 326n
Pliny, the Elder, 476
Pliny, the Younger, 123, 136n
Pomarolo, 157
Pompeianus, Ruricius, 38n, 460
Pomponius Mela, 476–7
Po river
 as a boundary, 16, 20, 35, 41
 economy, 42n, 49, 178–9
 environmental situation, 290, 297–8
 military features, 17–18, 20, 26n, 82, 99, 100, 147, 155–6, 457–8
 Panegyrical representation, 460–2, 467
 settlement of war prisoners, 491
Ports, 135, 168 9n, 266, 269, 321, 323
Portus, 72, 323, 386, 477
possessores, 21n, 140n, 143–5, 149, 225, 249n
potiores, 233
praefectus annonae, 39, 51, 54, 58, 357, 373
praefectus vrbi Romae, 25n, 38, 40, 154, 160–1, 183n, 357–8, 365, 370, 480
Praetextatus, Vettius Agorius, 48n
praetorian guard, 26, 38, 154, 371–2
praetorian prefect, 25, 38, 40, 50, 59, 74–6, 78–9, 102, 124, 127, 140–1, 147, 155–6, 179
principales, 137, 141–2
Prisca, 215
Priscus of Panium, 81, 205, 217, 485
Proba, Anicia Falcona, 214n
Probus, emperor, 19, 21, 30, 35, 45, 118, 308
Probus, senator, 75
Procopius of Caesarea, 214, 322, 475, 485, 486n, 490
Prosper of Aquitaine, 346n, 479, 482–3
Protadius, 480
protectores, protectores domestici, 178
provincialisation of Italy, 3, 16, 20–1, 36, 41, 49, 112, 114, 155
Pulcheria, 210
Pupienus, 44, 50, 68
Puteoli, 56, 124–5, 142, 312n, 386n, 457n

quadrigarii (charioteers), 52, 357, 362
quinquennalis, 131, 133, 137, 141
Quirinal Hill, 28

Radagaisus, 55n, 73–4, 100, 157–8, 163–4, 170
Raetia, 20, 26, 36–9, 42–3, 45, 48, 161n, 163, 167–8, 174, 178, 183, 461
ransoms, 55, 74–5, 211, 321, 347
rape, 202–4, 209, 211–13

Rationalis Vinorum, 39
Ravenna,
  Exarchate, 6, 349
  imperial Court, 45, 53, 71–4, 78–80, 92, 358–9, 370, 466
  church, 234, 349–50, 353, 375–6
  civil bureaucracy, 40, 149
  court of Theoderic, 351, 367, 463
  military matters, 69, 90, 94n, 99, 101–4, 164–5, 168, 172, 185, 215, 322n
  papyri, 233–6, 247, 249
  production of sarcophagi, 412–13, 420n, 439, 445
  religious minorities, 392–4, 404
  urban infrastructure, 313, 315–16, 321
recruitment, military, 49, 77, 104, 155, 167–8, 171, 177–80, 189–90
refugees, 76, 328, 395n
regiones, 35–6, 38n, 112–19
regnum, 6, 87, 100, 102, 105, 468
rex, 94, 97–8
Rhegium (Reggio Calabria), 73, 386n
Rhine, 48n, 69, 160–3, 179, 471
Roman Forum, Rome, 27–8, 48, 359, 374, 420
Romulus 'Augustul[us]', so-called last western Roman emperor, 97, 101–3, 217, 484
Ricimer, 83, 89–97, 101, 103, 146, 157n, 158, 169, 173, 175–7, 184n, 187, 215–16
Rieti basin, 290–5, 297
Rimini, 42, 71–4, 172, 185n, 312, 315, 327
Rugians, 102, 104
Rufinus of Aquileia, 73, 358n, 361, 375, 483
rusticus/i, 225, 239n, 247, 248n, 249, 251n, 260n
Rutilius Namatianus, 322n, 477, 481
rye, 265, 294–6

sack of Rome (410), 8, 73–5, 203, 212, 214n, 289, 316, 387n, 395, 412, 475, 479
sack of Rome (455) *see* Geiseric
Salernum, 123, 135–6
Salona, 174, 184
Salonina, 215
saltus, 246, 289, 321
Samnium, 40n, 53, 56, 75, 115, 117, 121–2, 312, 325
Sardinia
  bishops, 352
  grain, 53–4, 56, 69
  Jews, 399
  military conflicts, 95–6, 147, 168–9

government, 20, 36–7, 39–42, 57–8, 112, 116–17, 137
sarcophagi, 420n, 425n, 430n
taxation, 182n
villa culture, 269
Sarmatians, 161, 183–4
Sarus, 163–4, 172, 186
Scandza, 486
Schism
  Acacian, 340
  Boniface/Eulalius, 358–9, 364–5, 370
  Damasus/Ursinus, 364, 372–3
  Laurentian, 359, 365–7, 371, 374
Scholae Palatinae, 38, 160, 165, 178–9, 185
Secundus of Trent, 486
Senate of Rome
  cursus honorum, 21, 57, 59–60
  estates, 56, 126
  food distribution, 55–6
  relationship with emperors, 17–19, 24–30, 48, 86
  religion, 308
  senatorial emperors, 45, 50
  membership, 133, 142
Septimius Bassus, 39, 48n
Septimius Severus, 22, 124, 154, 308
Serena, 206–7, 215–16, 454n, 465n
Severina, Ulpia, 216
Severus, Tetrarch, 27–8, 37, 104n
Sicily
  church, 236, 344, 346, 349, 351
  environment, 294–8
  estates, 4, 56, 269
  officials, 144
  grain, 53
  military matters, 76n, 79, 81, 89, 91, 93n, 94–6, 99, 101–2, 161, 168–9, 173–5
  religious minorities, 400–3
  routes, 42
  province, 20, 40
  taxation, 155
Sidonius Apollinaris, 83, 88, 91n, 95–6, 146, 215, 260, 454, 456–9, 464–5, 467, 469, 471
Sigisvult, 77–8
Siricius, bishop of Rome, 346, 348
slavery, 224n, 246, 248n, 261
Sirmium, 40, 45, 156, 467–8, 484
Sofiana, 400, 403
Solinus, 476
Soluntum, 79

Spain, 54, 83, 91–4, 134, 149, 166n, 169, 345, 352, 455, 476–7, 479, 483, 487
Spolia, 321, 327, 394, 401
St Peter's, Rome, 48, 72, 318, 360, 365, 367–8, 371
statues, 27, 86, 104n, 123–4, 188, 306–11, 324n, 325, 429
Stilicho, 54–5, 73–4, 81, 103, 162–7, 170–2, 180n, 183, 187, 188n, 190, 206–7, 322, 324n, 455, 459–61, 466–7, 470, 479
Suburbicaria, Italia
  church, 344, 377, 379
  creation, 20, 38, 69, 112
  government, 39–40, 52, 57–9, 116–17, 125, 155
  imperial presence, 490
  military matters, 49–50, 157, 174, 179–84, 186, 189
  religious minorities, 385, 389, 394–5, 404–5
  routes, 41–2
  supply, 51, 53–6, 61
  taxation, 147–8
Sueves, 100
Sulla, 131, 465
Sunigilda, 215
Sylvester, bishop of Rome, 339, 344, 384n
Symmachus, bishop of Rome, 356, 359–60, 366–8, 371
Symmachus, Aurelius Anicius, 358–9, 364n, 365, 373–4
Symmachus, L. Aurelius Vaienius, 48n, 55
Symmachus, Q. Aurelius, 49, 54–6, 59, 153, 181, 257, 260, 316, 456, 464–5, 470–1
Syracuse, 79, 188n, 314, 401–2, 405, 425–6, 431–3, 438

Tacitus, emperor, 45, 50
Tarentum, 133
Tarracius Bassus, 56
Tarsatica (Rijeka), 156
taxation, 5–6, 15, 20–1, 36, 77–9, 102, 112, 134, 138–9, 144–5, 147, 229, 240n, 252, 288–9
temples, 305–7, 309–11, 320n, 322n, 347
Tetrarchy, 16, 18, 27–30, 137, 158–9, 180, 478
Tetricus, 19, 35, 45
theatres, 124, 132, 309–10, 312–14, 322n, 325, 327–8, 361, 470
Theoderic the Amal
  Aventus, 2
  civic policies, 147, 253
  ethnicity, 5n
  'Kingship', 6, 468, 484–6
  land settlements, 184
  military matters, 98–103, 146, 178, 456, 461–3
  Rome, 3
  religious policies, 351, 359–60, 367–8, 371, 374, 388, 393–4, 404
Theodora, empress, 47
Theodorus, praetorian prefect, 74
Theodosian Code, 43, 49, 81, 137, 145, 235
Theodosius I, 4–5, 40, 43, 46–7, 92, 153, 162, 187, 208, 210, 347, 375, 390, 458, 460–3
Theodosius II, 78–9, 81, 158, 210, 399
Thermae, 27–9, 312
Thermantia, daughter of Stilicho, 206–7
Tiber, 17, 264n, 459, 461, 467, 469–70
Ticinum *see* Pavia
Titianus, T. Flavius Postumius, 19n, 48n, 60n
tombs, 72, 318, 320n, 400–2, 404 423, 433, 435
tractus Italiae circa Alpes, 157
traders, 76, 491
Trajan, 35, 114, 120, 136, 316, 465
transport, 39, 42, 53, 168, 185, 264, 267, 297, 420
Trebonianus Gallus, 50, 216
tribunus fori suarii, 38–9
Trier, 5, 43n, 69–70, 73, 161, 210, 471
Trinitapoli, 145
Trygetius, 74, 146n, 482
Tullius Menophilus, 44
Turin, 100, 297, 313, 457n, 460
Turranius Decentius Benignus, 56n
Tuscany, 73, 262–4, 293, 298, 326n, 420n, 430n, 459

urban prefect of Rome *see* Praefectus Vrbi Romae
Ursa, captive of the Goths, 75
Ursinus, Bishop of Rome, 51–2, 55, 357–8, 361, 363–4, 372–3, 378–9
Urso, 132–4
usurpation, 5, 18, 44, 83, 155n, 170

Valens, 70, 82, 180n, 246, 252, 477
Valentinian I, 43n, 47, 48n, 52, 82–3, 140, 168n, 205, 208, 373, 471
Valentinian II, 43n, 46, 70–1, 73, 93, 161–2
Valentinian III, 25, 46n, 47, 50n, 72, 75–81, 83, 87, 91, 101, 134, 147, 166, 170, 173, 182, 205, 211, 240n, 351
Valeria (province), 40n, 117, 137, 148

Valerian, 45
Valila (Theodobius), 187
Vandals
  battles with Imperial armies, 89, 93
  conquest of Africa, 80–1
  raids on Sicily c. 440, 78, 81, 402
  sack of Rome and raids c. 455–74
    see Geiseric
  in panegyric, 458, 460, 467
Vatican, 73
Vegetius, 188
Velitrae, 142
Venetia, 71, 461
Venetia et (H)istria, 39, 58, 115–16, 122
Venosa, 385–7, 395–401, 404–5
Verona, 26, 49, 69–71, 99–101, 179, 184, 306, 312, 321–2, 393, 440, 445, 460–3
Verona List, 20, 36, 40, 115
veterans, 49, 102, 104n, 132, 179–80, 182–3, 186
Vexillatio (comitatensis, palatina), 155, 159, 165–6, 174n
Via Appia, 42, 153, 386
Via Flaminia, 29–30, 42, 160, 470
Via Salaria, 291
vicarius Italiae, 20, 25–6, 37–9, 53, 116, 118, 155, 183n, 479
vicarius vrbis Romae, 20, 25n, 38–40, 117, 155, 179n, 180n, 373, 479
Victor, bishop of Rome, 342

Vicus, 265, 268, 270–1, 321
vir clarissimus, 121, 141, 258, 315–16, 399
vir illustris, 141, 251
vir spectabilis, 249, 253n, 315
Vienne (Gaul), 73, 346
Vidimir, 484
vigiles, 38, 371–2
Viminacium, 70
Viminal Hill, 28, 38
Vincentius, 97–8, 157n
virginity, 206, 210–11
Viventius, 51, 55, 357, 372–3
volcanoes, 290, 299, 402

walls, urban, 18, 37, 39, 156, 305, 310, 312–13, 318, 322–4, 326–7, 362, 456, 460
warlord, phenomenon, 88, 92, 98, 158, 176, 189
wetlands, 297
Witigis, 214
woodlands, 291–3, 295, 297
workshops, 262, 269, 307, 309, 315n, 321n, 412–13, 419, 431–2, 435

Zeno, emperor, 86, 91n, 98, 102, 353, 484
Zeno, bishop of Verona, 227, 239n, 248n, 345
Zenobia, 45
Zosimus, bishop of Rome, 358, 370–1, 373
Zosimus, bishop of Syracuse, 402
Zosimus, historiographer, 46, 71n, 206–7